ASPIRING TO GREATNESS

Learn more about the early years of West Virginia University in
West Virginia University: Symbol of Unity in a Sectionalized State
by William T. Doherty, Jr. and Festus P. Summers

ASPIRING
to
GREATNESS

———

WEST VIRGINIA
UNIVERSITY
SINCE
WORLD WAR II

———

RONALD L. LEWIS

FOREWORD BY CHARLES M. VEST

MORGANTOWN 2013

West Virginia University Press 26506
Copyright 2013 by West Virginia University Press
All rights reserved
First edition published 2013 by West Virginia University Press

Printed in Canada

20 19 18 17 16 15 14 13   1 2 3 4 5 6 7 8

Cloth   978-1-938228-42-1
EPUB   978-1-938228-40-7
PDF   978-1-938228-41-4

Library of Congress Cataloging-in-Publication Data
Lewis, Ronald L., 1940-
 Aspiring to greatness : West Virginia University since World War II / Ronald L. Lewis. -- First edition.
    pages cm
 Includes bibliographical references and index.
 ISBN-13: 978-1-938228-42-1 (cloth : alk. paper)
 ISBN-10: 1-938228-42-1 (cloth : alk. paper)
 ISBN-13: 978-1-938228-40-7 (epub)
 ISBN-10: 1-938228-40-5 (epub)
 [etc.]
1. West Virginia University--History. I. Title.
 LD5923.L49 2013
 378.754--dc23
 2013020169

Cover design by Galbreath Design
Art direction and book design by Than Saffel
Images provided by WVU News and Information Services and West Virginia and Regional History Collection. Image of WVU Institute of Technology courtesy of WVU Institute of Technology.

Front cover image: WVU's Evansdale campus from the air. Back cover image: Visitors at the Mountainlair Information Desk, ca. 1967 (WVRHC image no. 019085).

Many people from across West Virginia University helped bring this book to fruition.

West Virginia University Press gratefully acknowledges the help and support of Jay Cole, Chief of Staff, and the West Virginia University administration, along with Greg Ellis and West Virginia University News and Information Services.

Heartfelt thanks also to our friends and colleagues at the West Virginia and Regional History Collection, notably the ever-helpful Catherine Rakowski.

TABLE OF CONTENTS

—

PART III
THE CORPORATE UNIVERSITY:
COMMERCIALIZATION, 1990– 345

LIST OF TABLES

FOREWORD

BY CHARLES M. VEST

PROFESSOR RONALD L. LEWIS has given us a clear-eyed, multi-faceted, extensively researched, and eminently readable modern history of West Virginia University. Like most of us who graduated from WVU in the 1950s and 1960s, I remember the history of this period and my own undergraduate experience with gratitude and not a small amount of nostalgia. *Aspiring to Greatness* gives us a more objective and therefore far more valuable view of the period from 1945 to the present.

This account of modern WVU is told here largely through the stories of its presidents, their key visions, actions, and accomplishments as well as their fiscal and political woes and successes. Several presidents left major legacies in WVU as we find it today. Although focused sharply on WVU, its culture, presidents, finances, politics, athletics, hospitals, aspirations, struggles, accomplishments, and failures, Professor Lewis's book nicely maps the university's history onto the framework and broader trends of American higher education.

Before reading the book, I wondered about the significance of the title *Aspiring to Greatness*. Why is West Virginia University *aspiring* to greatness? Why has it not arrived at greatness? Or, why has it not chosen some different though compelling goal? It cannot be because it is an unimportant institution. Indeed, I cannot think or conceive of another university that is as critically important to the state in which it resides—to the state's economic and social progress and to the opportunities afforded its young men and women. It cannot be because its fundamental mission is unusual or misunderstood. WVU is a wonderful exemplar of a Land Grant University. The establishment of Land Grant schools was arguably the most important innovation in higher education this nation has ever made, and their basic missions are now well honed and broadly understood. It cannot be because the institution lacked visionary and capable leadership. It has had its share.

Could it be that WVU has not yet arrived at greatness because that has not been the goal of the institution or its leaders? I suppose that some observers tinged with cynicism and using a narrow definition of greatness might find some instances of this, but the history of the University surely has been one of steady upward progress in quality, size, and breadth. Especially in recent decades, the working definition of the greatness to which WVU aspires has largely been to become a world-class research university. The aspiration is not only to provide excellent and accessible education, but also to contribute substantially and at a high level to discovering new knowledge, creating new technologies, and advancing scholarship. WVU's extraordinary president during the immediate post World War II era, Irvin Stewart, pushed the institution and the people of the state to commit to making WVU "a university in fact as well as in name."

The fact is that West Virginia University faced three very strong headwinds in its quest for greatness and status as a major research university, and they are the three themes that weave much of this book together: (1) the university has never had sufficient financial resources, largely though not exclusively because of its state's perpetually weak economy; (2) the university suffered in untold ways because of a persistent and corrosive regionalism in West Virginia's public attitudes, politics, and media; and (3) the university was hampered because of constant and debilitating changes in its governance system and its relation to the state's governors and legislatures.

An astounding example of lost opportunity because of counterproductive state policies occurred in the immediate post World War II era. This is the period of time in which most leading public and private research universities began their climbs to become research intensive. The federal government, starting during the war, began to enter into research contracts with top universities. Soon after the end of the war, the government began providing competitive grants as well as contracts. WVU was basically unable to participate in this rapid growth of federal research support, primarily because West Virginia legal restrictions did not permit state institutions to accept federally funded projects unless they could finance the contract. The federal government reimbursed universities or other contractors for the research work once it was completed, so the university needed to have the cash to fund the work and be reimbursed later. The University was not able to accept such contracts under state law.

As President Irvin Stewart stated in 1950, "Unfortunately, we cannot participate to any extent in such a program because of the fiscal limitations within which we must operate." Thus, WVU was forced to lose the opportunity to climb quickly up the path to doing more research, upgrading its laboratories, and providing opportunities for graduate students. There is an irony in this matter, because the primary advocate and architect of federal support of university research and advanced education, both during and after the War, was Vannevar Bush. Bush's right hand man as he headed the U.S. Office of Scientific Research and Development (OSRD) throughout the war was WVU's future president, Irvin Stewart.

Throughout its modern history, WVU has been affected by a debilitating regionalism that is thoroughly documented in this book. The origin of this regionalism is quite understandable—WVU, although clearly developing into the state's flagship university, was located in the northern part of the state, but the population center was much farther south, in the Charleston-Huntington area. Over several decades, this regionalism seems to have permeated university budget battles and the far-too-frequent changes in governance structure of WVU and other state institutions.

The best-known manifestation of regional fights was probably the drive to locate WVU's medical school in Charleston. From the perspective of patient base, this would have made sense, but as modern medicine and medical education subsequently evolved, it has become clear that to have separated the School of Medicine from the rest of the campus would have been tragic. Today the continual interaction among the basic medical sciences, the traditional science and engineering programs, and the medical school and hospitals is absolutely essential for first-rate medical and health education, research, and practice. Fortunately for WVU and for the state (in my view), Governor Okey L. Patteson in 1952 made the courageous decision to do what he believed to be the right thing and locate the medical school and a new hospital complex in Morgantown.

In more recent decades, there have been many twists and turns in the high-level governance of the university, and they used up a great deal of the energy and political capital of several WVU presidents. Several governors have put their stamps on this system. There have been boards of regents, boards of trustees, and boards of governors. WVU and Marshall University have been treated differently in some periods and considered more on a common basis with other four-year colleges in others. The current governance structure, under which I have the honor of serving as a member of the WVU Board of Governors, dates only to President David Hardesty's tenure (1995–2007) when then-Governor Joe Manchin and the state legislature gave the WVU Board of Governors true oversight of its own resources and reduced multiple administrative layers. Indeed, in 2005 Governor Manchin said that he wanted "to remove the shackles from higher education."

Although I found the details of the continual institutional and political interplay of constrained financial resources, regionalism, and governance very enlightening, there is much more in this volume. Racial equity and diversity issues are here, Jerry West and Sam Huff are here, the party school image problem is here, Vietnam era activism is here, service to the state and region is here, the complexities of a major medical center are here, the rise of a modern athletic enterprise is here, the role of economic development is here, and the recent growth of major philanthropy is here, as is much more.

I admit to having a special interest in this history, because I grew up in Morgantown in the 1940s and 1950s as the son of a WVU professor, earned my undergraduate degree from the University's engineering school, and have known many of the people in the book, including all but one WVU president. The volume has given me important insights that will be valuable as a member of the board of governors. But this is a unique and important history of a state and its flagship university that holds interest and value for a much wider audience.

PREFACE

THE HISTORY OF HIGHER EDUCATION in the United States since World War II is divided into three overlapping periods. The first, 1945 to 1975, often called the "golden age" of higher education, was one of dramatic expansion as millions of veterans returning from World War II enrolled in American colleges with the aid of the GI Bill. Children of the veterans, the "baby boom" generation, continued to fuel the growth in college enrollments until the mid-1970s. Institutions also expanded in organizational complexity in order to serve their burgeoning student bodies, and to manage federally financed programs in student affairs and research. In the second period, 1975 to the early 1990s, expansion gave way to diversity as the prevailing force shaping American higher education. The student population represented by those in their late teens to early twenties stopped growing in 1975 after the predominantly white male baby boomers completed their studies. Taking their place were students from nontraditional backgrounds, whose enrollment led to an unprecedented gender, racial, and ethnic diversification of college campuses. The third period was the commercialization of higher education, a recognizable development by the 1980s that grew into a full-fledged movement from the 1990s into the twenty-first century. The globalization of markets, shifting demographic pressures, and the transition of a market economy into a market society all facilitated the penetration of business values and practices into university life. Public universities, called upon to generate more of their own revenues, hoped that commercializing their non-classroom activities would create new income streams.

In order to place the history of West Virginia University within the context of these national trends in higher education, this volume is divided into the same three thematic parts: expansion, diversification, and commercialization. While neither chronologically nor thematically discrete, these periods do represent the prevailing force molding higher education in the United States and at WVU. However, the experience of WVU does not precisely mirror national developments because the University has been shaped by unique local, state, and regional influences. One expectation shared by all members of the WVU community since World War II is that the university should take its rightful place among the pantheon of great universities. Hence the title, *Aspiring to Greatness: West Virginia University Since World War II.*

This history was intended neither as a repository of factual information pertaining to WVU nor a documentary of remarkable people and special events in the life of the University. Rather, the intention was to focus on historically significant developments that chronicle the evolution of WVU from a small provincial institution into one that stands at the threshold of national prominence. As the individuals responsible for formulating and implementing the policies that govern the development of their institutions, presidents are the single most important catalysts for change. But universities, including WVU, are institutions with shared governance responsibilities, and are composed of many constituencies that often hold competing perspectives on just what a university is and ought to be. Sports fans, legislators, faculty members, staff, students, alumni, and the public all have very different views concerning the University's successes and failures. These varying perspectives are represented in this study through a thematic organization of historical material into chapters focusing, for example, on governance, research, and student life, rather than a strictly chronological approach.

Originally, this book was initiated as an "update" to William T. Doherty Jr. and Festus P. Summers's study entitled *West Virginia University: Symbol of Unity in a Sectionalized State* (Morgantown: West Virginia University Press, 1982). It soon became apparent, however, that a modern history of the University was required that accessed documents that were unavailable when Doherty and Summers published their history thirty years ago. A word about the subject of this history: In an attempt to provide some relief from the overuse of *West Virginia University*, I have also used *WVU*, *University* (capitalized), and *campus* interchangeably. References to *the university* or *universities* in a general sense are lowercased. A word about the sources used in this study is also in order. All references cited are found in WVU's libraries, particularly the West Virginia and Regional History Collection

(WVRHC) in Wise Library, which houses the University's special collections. My extensive use of the state's newspapers was possible because they are available on microfilm in the WVRHC, as are many of the interviews conducted at an earlier date by Professor Barbara Howe, transcript copies of which she graciously provided to me. Also, the numerous interviews conducted with University officials, along with the other material generated for this study, have been deposited with the WVRHC in the Ronald L. Lewis Papers. Two former University presidents, Neil S. Bucklew and David C. Hardesty Jr., were very generous with their time and greatly advanced my understanding of the initiatives undertaken during their administrations. Former acting president and special assistant to four presidents, Harold Shamberger, also contributed significantly to this study.

The documents generated by the president's office are located in the WVRHC and provide the major primary sources for *Aspiring to Greatness*. Originally known as the University Archives and now called the President's Office Papers, this collection consists of well more than six hundred banker boxes of documents generated by the president's office. Although the finding aid provides descriptions by box and file, it does not describe the contents of each file. Therefore, it is not possible to search this vast resource by the name of the president. The finding aid was created after publication of the Doherty and Summers study; consequently, their occasional references to the "Presidents' Papers" do not provide the series or box numbers, thereby rendering sources nearly impossible to relocate. Unfortunately, documents were often mixed together as they were pulled from file cabinets in preparation for removal to the library, making it a daunting task to fully research a particular topic in the President's Office papers. Two exceptions are noteworthy. Most of Irvin Stewart's papers are in a collection under his name, as are many of the David Hardesty Papers. Therefore, all manuscript collections cited in this study are from the President's Office series, the Stewart Papers, or the Hardesty Papers. In fact, with the exception of secondary publications found in the library's general collection, this book was researched almost entirely in the WVRHC and supplemented by interviews, newspaper articles, and WVU publications and reports.

Two additional constraints hinder the historian of West Virginia University. When presidents leave office, they are not legally required to transfer all of their files to the President's Office papers in the WVRHC. While it may be difficult to locate particular documents in a president's papers, it is impossible to know what documents he or she regarded as private or too sensitive to become part of the public record. Moreover, meetings of the Board of Governors are often held behind closed doors, particularly when sensitive matters such as personnel issues are discussed. Understandably, members are obliged to maintain the confidentiality of those discussions. A full understanding of how some critical decisions and policies were reached will ever remain just beyond the researcher's grasp.

Finally, I want to acknowledge my indebtedness to the staff at the West Virginia and Regional History Collection, whose helpfulness cannot be overstated. Woefully underappreciated, the WVRHC is the best and largest collection of historical materials related to West Virginia in existence. Researching this vast collection would be nearly impossible without the assistance of a knowledgeable staff, and I want to express my gratitude most particularly to Kevin Fredette, Michael Ridderbusch, and Christy Venham. Also, the WVU Department of History has been very helpful even in my retirement, particularly administrative assistant Martha May, who managed the research expenses provided for the completion of this project. Similarly, the Eberly College of Arts and Sciences technology experts Tom Moran and Steve Geissler were instrumental in maintaining my computers; without their able assistance this project could not have been completed. I also benefitted at the initial stage from the reliable services of my research assistant, then-PhD candidate Charles D. Dusch Jr. Research expenses for this study were arranged by former Provost Gerald Lang, who saw the need for a modern history of the University and, to his credit, also recognized the importance of scholarly independence. The pages that follow are therefore the result of my own research and judgment, informed by the wise counsel of many University leaders. Finally, my wife Susan E. Lewis selflessly offered her critical judgment and editing skills during the preparation of the manuscript, which significantly improved the final result.

Ronald L. Lewis
Morgantown, West Virginia
May 2013

PART I

THE EMERGENT UNIVERSITY: EXPANSION, 1946–1967

DURING THE POST-WORLD WAR II ERA, WVU was transformed from a small school that attracted a few thousand in-state students into an institution three times as large and came to regard itself as a university on the rise. WVU's evolution mirrored national trends during the postwar period, when the number of undergraduates on the nation's campuses grew by nearly 500 percent and the number of graduate students by nearly 900 percent. During the sixties alone, undergraduate enrollment more than doubled from 3.5 million to nearly eight million, and the number of doctorates awarded each year tripled. Reflecting the expansion of PhDs awarded, the number of faculty hired was greater "than had been hired in the entire 325 years of American higher education prior to 1960," according to one scholar. At WVU, the Great Depression and World War II had decimated enrollments, but the postwar expansion was dramatic, nearly doubling enrollments between 1938 and 1948, from 3,500 to 6,735, and more than doubling them again during the sixties, to 14,888.[1]

The Servicemen's Readjustment Act of 1944, generally known as the "G.I. Bill of Rights," played a major role in the postwar expansion of college enrollment. In addition to helping servicemen readjust to civilian life by providing hospital benefits and special home loans, veterans could attend college or vocational school at government expense. Approximately 8 million veterans took advantage of the opportunity during the seven years that followed the war, making the GI Bill the most significant piece of education legislation ever implemented by the government. The impact of the influx of federal revenues on the public colleges and universities is indicated by the fact that, in the late forties, 67 percent of all student tuition and fee revenue came from the Veteran's Administration.[2] Moreover, a college education was no longer reserved for the elite, and new economic opportunities were opened to all. Likewise, WVU became the great engine for upward mobility for state residents.

While enrollments skyrocketed after the war, the institutions themselves also experienced a great separation between those that were primarily undergraduate colleges and the rising research universities. The emergence of these major research universities was greatly facilitated by the federal government. Scientists organized by the government during the war to produce technologies such as the atomic bomb, radar, radio-controlled fuses, ballistic missiles, penicillin, and other scientific breakthroughs were coordinated by Vannevar Bush, a former vice president and dean of engineering at the Massachusetts Institute of Technology who served as chairman of the National Defense Research Committee and then as director of the Office of Scientific Research and Development. Bush created the model for the organization and funding of basic science and technology that prevailed during and after the war. His ideas about national science policy, and about bringing scientists, academic leaders, high-ranking military officials, and industry leaders together to pursue a common goal, influenced how "big science" was conducted for a half-century after World War II.[3]

Prior to World War II, federal research was conducted independently in government or in industrial laboratories. Vannevar Bush shifted government research to private enterprise and channeled federal money to support basic science at universities and scientific institutes. Like most scientists, Bush believed that basic scientific research should be independent of government intervention. Therefore, he advocated a decentralized approach, in which government would pay for research and the facilities and scientists would be selected on the basis of their ability and the quality of their proposals, as determined by peer review. His underlying belief was that basic scientific knowledge would gather into a common reservoir to be drawn upon when needed to discover new technologies. This model had worked during the war, and he believed it should also be applied afterward.

America's rise as a world power carried a responsibility to produce new scientific knowledge. That goal was best achieved by providing funds to the nation's best scientists to pursue research without government interference, Bush argued. In this desire, he would be disappointed, because many political leaders were convinced that applied, mission-driven research was the appropriate way to spend the people's money.[4]

Bush's nemesis in Congress was Senator Harley M. Kilgore of West Virginia, a leading New Deal Democrat who held hearings during and after the war on national science and technology policy. Kilgore believed that Congress should set the government's research priorities, whereas Bush was convinced that scientific knowledge grew out of a free marketplace of ideas rather than government planning. Kilgore correctly believed that, under Bush's plan, most federal support for science would flow to the most distinguished universities. He therefore argued that some portion of public funds should be distributed geographically, and he also wanted to fund the social sciences. On both points, Bush balked; the first flew in the face of his notion of meritocracy, and the second was not science at all. Kilgore objected to the government giving away the rights to intellectual property it had paid for, and he also argued that the director of the new National Science Foundation should be appointed by the president. On these points, Bush argued for a semi-independent organization. When the NSF was created in 1947, it was a much different body than the one envisioned by Vannevar Bush. Support for the sciences was decentralized among a number of agencies, such as the Atomic Energy Commission, the National Institutes of Health, and the Office of Naval Research, instead of centralized in Bush's NSF. Federal funding for basic research, primarily in physical sciences and mathematics, was centered in the NSF.[5]

The fact that Senator Kilgore represented the state of West Virginia clearly influenced him to support a science policy that benefited citizens generally and funding policies that did not favor a few elite institutions. WVU, the state's leading institution, could benefit greatly from federal science funding. Unfortunately, that funding did not materialize. With the onslaught of the Cold War, which consumed American foreign policy from the late forties through the seventies, federal resources generally flowed to the most distinguished universities. WVU President Irvin Stewart, who had been a prominent administrator in government science circles and a close associate of Vannevar Bush, understood how the system worked and tried to position WVU to take advantage of the new research funds flowing out of Washington. Dependent as it was on the state for its support, however, WVU could not garner enough resources to pay for research and therefore could not claim reimbursement from federal agencies under the "contract overload" (contract plus indirect costs) system utilized for government-funded research. Notably, grants coming to WVU were routed through the state treasurer's office and hence became the state's property rather than the University's, a practice the federal government would not allow. Consequently, WVU was unable to partake of the federal dollars pumped into the science facilities at more affluent universities. The elite universities thus benefitted from the influx of scientific research dollars initiated during the Cold War, but poorly funded institutions like WVU did not. By the "accumulation of advantage," the elite institutions were able to attract stronger students, who achieved greater success as alumni and had more wealth to contribute to their alma maters, resulting in better research facilities and more prominent faculty.[6] The infusion of federal funds simply accelerated the process of the rich getting richer. Even with a president as sophisticated in the ways of Washington as Irvin Stewart, West Virginia University was unable to elevate its programs and facilities by competing for federal resources.

The state of West Virginia was in no position to increase its funding on the scale required for WVU to take advantage of the federal funding schemes. During each decade from 1950 to the end of the century, mining employment in the state was slashed by half, decimating the tax base. The number of miners employed in the state's leading occupation declined by two-thirds between 1950 and 1970, from 127,304 to 40,513. By the nineties, the ranks of miners would decrease to fewer than 10,000. Nearly half a million miners and their families, one-quarter of the state's population, suffered an economic depression as the coal industry lost market share to other fuels, forcing operators to increase efficiency by shifting from manpower to mechanization. From 1950 through the nineties, approximately one million residents migrated to other states to find employment. Because of the population loss, West Virginia's congressional delegation shrank from four to three. A story in the *Saturday Evening Post* focused on the state's chronic unemployment, poor roads, polluted streams, and lack of amenities, pondering the paradox of a state so rich in natural resources being mired in abject poverty. The author's depiction of West Virginia as "remote, backward and dangerously provincial" certainly did nothing to present the kind of image that would attract the investment necessary to revitalize and diversify the economy.[7]

During the 1960 presidential primary, candidate John F. Kennedy toured the decimated southern West Virginia coalfield towns, promising to wage a "war on poverty" if elected, a promise kept by him and by his successor, Lyndon B. Johnson. President Kennedy established what became the Appalachian Regional Commission (ARC) in 1963, but in the political wrangling over how the money should be distributed and by whom most ARC funds were invested in public works and infrastructure projects like roads, sewers, and waterlines. The War on Poverty launched by President Johnson channeled federal spending into agencies that sought to promote a fairer distribution of wealth by creating jobs for the unemployed on projects that were needed to improve community life. However, agencies such as the Equal Employment Opportunity Commission, established in 1965, directed federal funding to projects controlled by local political brokers who often opposed EEOC policies that circumvented their political power. The Appalachian Regional Commission and the War on Poverty did not direct the kind of federal resources to higher education that would have helped elevate more academic institutions into the ranks of the distinguished universities. WVU President Paul Miller reorganized the University in hopes that it would become a leading partner on federally funded projects in Appalachia. That strategy also failed to attract federal revenues to the University. Miller's successor, James Harlow, abandoned the Appalachian focus almost entirely.[8]

What the Cold War did accomplish for higher education in West Virginia, as well as nationally, was to establish federal policies that supported the expansion of student enrollment. These new students became an important source of revenues. In 1957 the Soviet Union launched a small satellite into space. Sputnik itself did not present a problem to the United States, but the rocket that propelled it into orbit caused a panic in the national defense community. Such a powerful rocket could be weaponized and aimed at the United States. In addition to focusing the nation's fear on falling behind the Soviet Union in science, Sputnik triggered passage of the National Defense Education Act of 1958, which targeted science and foreign languages for federal funds to support study in these fields. The rationale behind the act was that "the security of the Nation requires the fullest development of the mental resources and technical skills of its young men and women. . . . This requires programs that will give assurance that no students of ability will be denied an opportunity for higher education because of financial need." This rationale, representing a new concept called "human capital," justified federal support on the basis that an educated citizen was a "strategic resource" for the nation's security.[9]

The National Defense Education Act had just been enacted when the full wave of post-war "baby boomers" flooded college campuses. Between 1955 and 1970, the number of 18 to 24 year olds in the United States ballooned from 15 to 25 million. Magnifying the effect on campuses, the military draft provided a deferment for college students at least until 1970, when the lottery system was adopted. Consequently, by 1968, more than 63 percent of male high school graduates enrolled in college.[10]

Prior to their postwar expansion, even the largest state universities were small compared to their size after accommodating the new egalitarian philosophy promoted by the National Defense Education Act, which held that education should be available to the talented without regard to income. The new direction was pioneered by Clark Kerr, chancellor of the University of California, who developed the first "multiversity," a higher education system that integrated schools, colleges, and divisions in a way that allowed them to operate independently but with a complementary purpose. The California system he designed was accessible and excellent at the same time, allowing students who showed ability to matriculate from lower-tier colleges to the two pinnacle institutions at Berkeley and Los Angeles. The model was replicated around the country by individual state research universities, but critics charged that the multiversity placed a priority on research rather than on helping talented students who lacked adequate financing. They believed that this model threatened the core values of higher education by undervaluing teaching and overemphasizing research productivity. Moreover, critics warned that the multiversity would create an unwieldy bureaucracy that emphasized management over democratic faculty governance, a practice regarded by faculty as vital to fostering open discussion and tolerance of unpopular ideas.[11] The WVU presidents whose administrations serve as bookends to this history, Irvin Stewart and David Hardesty, were troubled by these same nagging concerns.

The "uni-versity" embraced by traditionalist academics idealized the medieval institution of masters and students who explored life's eternal questions as a unified, organic whole. Conversely, the American "multiversity" was cobbled together from many parts as universities adapted to a changing society. Kerr conceptualized it as a "city of infinite variety" that was constantly changing, somewhat unharmonious, even chaotic, and populated by an array of academic subcultures that identified more with their disciplinary colleagues across the nation than with the institution to which they belonged. Kerr traced its creation from the land-grant institutions spawned by the Morrill Act of 1862, which sought to bring academic knowledge to bear on practical problems of society, and the federal funding of science during World War II and the Cold War.[12] In the multiversity, Kerr observed, "many parts can be added and subtracted with little effect on the whole or even little notice taken or any blood spilled. It is more of a mechanism—a series of processes producing a series of results—a mechanism held together by administrative rules and powered by money." According to Kerr, John Maynard Hutchins, the influential president of the University of Chicago, and an arch-traditionalist, described the modern university as "a series of separate schools and departments held together by a central heating system. In an area [California] where heating is less important and the automobile more, I have sometimes thought of it as a series of individual faculty entrepreneurs held together by a common grievance over parking."[13]

Most students at WVU have no doubt experienced the confusion caused by the decentralized bureaucracy of the University and the bewildering range of choices they confront. WVU faculty and administrators have also been known to paraphrase Hutchins's remark by referring to the University as scattered buildings connected by plumbing and a common parking problem. However, WVU is also an institution that affords all West Virginia high school graduates the opportunity to acquire the education they need to succeed in life.

THE PAST AS PRELUDE: POLITICS OF GOVERNANCE BEFORE THE BOARD OF REGENTS

THE DECADES PRECEDING Irvin Stewart's administration, from 1946 to 1957, were periods of social, political, and economic upheaval: post–World War I, the Great Depression, the New Deal, and World War II. In West Virginia the localized effects of these national upheavals had their counterweights in a conservative political culture in which the "state house" faction resisted the political power of the state's federal delegation. The factional, sectionalized politics of West Virginia set the format of the politics that shaped higher education in the state. The struggles played a major role in hindering the development of West Virginia University as an institution and retarded its ability to achieve its mission as the state's land-grant university, or even fulfill its role as the state's only university. WVU's capacity to respond to the major changes that World War II brought to higher education was seriously compromised by the sectional politics practiced in West Virginia. The University consequently found itself unable to take advantage of federal resources being poured into American research universities to foster scientific discoveries and applications designed to keep the United States as the leading power in a hostile postwar world. The roots of WVU's weakness reached back to the nature of higher education governance before World War I.

SECTIONAL POLITICS AND HIGHER EDUCATION, 1909–1927

In 1907, Governor M. O. Dawson recommended that the nine boards of regents and the sixteen boards of directors governing each of the state institutions of higher learning be replaced by just two boards. In 1909, the legislature responded by passing legislation that reduced the system to a three-member, bipartisan Board of Control charged with administering the building and grounds as well as the financial affairs of state institutions, and a five-member Board of Regents appointed by the governor to administer the educational policy of the University and normal schools. Economy was the obvious motive, but professional educational administrators argued that a separate governing board for each institution was the more efficient way to administer higher education. Obviously, state officials disagreed because this structure remained until 1919 when the Board of Regents was replaced by a seven-member state Board of Education, which included the state superintendent of schools, who served at the behest of the governor. The Board of Control retained its charge set by the 1909 legislation until the system was reformed in 1947.[1]

From its earliest days, WVU believed that the University should neither be governed by the same rules as the state's normal schools nor treated by politicians as though it was just another state agency. Generally, this position was more a hope than a reality, though it did prevail on occasion. In 1911, for example, Senator Stephen B. Elkins, who regarded the University presidency as "proper spoils for the Republicans," wanted to appoint former governor A. B. White to the post. White declined, however, and Governor William E. Glasscock appointed his friend and business associate T. E. Hodges to the position. Glasscock reminded Elkins that Republicans should not ignore the "sentiment in the State," which favored Hodges, and that he, Glasscock, objected to action that looked like "injecting politics into our educational institutions." Nevertheless, Hodges's inauguration became a political event with President William Howard Taft delivering the keynote address in the presence of, according to historian Charles Ambler, "practically all the state elective officers."[2]

During the second decade of the twentieth century, there was a struggle between the "new" and "old" educators, the former being those who were followers of the "progressive" educational philosopher John Dewey, educators who believed that teachers should be professionally trained rather than called to the profession by aptitude and scholarship. The new educators favored substituting practical learning determined by community needs for the standard high school curriculum. They opposed the established practice of the "old" educators of requiring high schools and normal schools to submit complete and accurate data on curriculum and academic performance to the university for entering students. The boards of the state's normal schools were under the control of the "new" educators, and supported by the most influential of the "new" educators of the period, State Superintendent of Schools (1909–1921) Morris P. Shawkey. As state superintendent he sat *ex officio* as president of the Board of Regents and of the State Board of Education. Shawkey informed President Hodges that he was disappointed with his "old" ideas about university administration. Hodges responded that, fortunately for the University, its policies were established by the faculty. Between 1912 and 1914, Secretary of the Board of Regents J. F. Marsh and President Hodges discussed issues involving university administration and academic freedom. Marsh bluntly informed Hodges that the president must determine university policy, not the "Old Guard" faculty. Hodges emphatically rejected this demand, prompting Superintendent Shawkey to declare, in his 1914 biennial report, that Hodges's administration was a failure, and reserved the right for the board to devise new university policies that would best serve the state. President Hodges saw the handwriting on the wall and took the graceful exit offered by his political friends, who nominated him as the Republican candidate for congressman-at-large in the 1914 election.[3]

No university subject was too small to pass the notice of one political faction or another in a highly sectionalized state. Replacing Hodges prompted considerable political maneuvering and editorial comment framed by the "old" versus "new" education debate. The *State Journal* called for the next president to be an educator of "national" and, better still, "world-wide" caliber, whatever the cost. The *Wheeling News* similarly declared the need for "a big man for president of the university," indeed "a very big man." The *Morgantown Chronicle* announced that "a very big man" was not necessarily the best because the University was not that big, and a "big man could not create off-hand a great university in a state as lacking as was West Virginia" in high schools to prepare students for college.[4]

Even something as basic as the University's location was still a matter for serious political discussion from 1913 to 1915. Should the University remain in the city where it was founded in 1867? Someone from the Kanawha Valley complained to the *Morgantown Post Chronicle* that the citizens of Morgantown seemed intent on "bleeding to the last cent" students who attended WVU. He pointed out that there was no legal reason for the University to remain in Morgantown, which was so far out of the way for the "greater part of our people." The *Chronicle's* editors rebutted the charge of gouging the students and called for major defensive measures to save the University. The *Huntington Herald-Dispatch* heightened Morgantown's anxieties by pointing out that, while the "fine little city on the northern border" was inconvenient to most of the state's residents, southern West Virginia was much more directly interested in the development of Marshall College. Charleston boosters certainly saw their fair city as the more desirable location for the University, and real estate interests in that city sponsored a resolution, which was seriously considered in the state senate, to remove WVU from Morgantown to Charleston.[5] Morgantown supporters countered that "Character is Greater than Geography," and that Charleston, with its "relentless commercialism" and the "political chicanery of a state capital," would stunt the ethical development of students. Naturally, Charleston supporters saw Morgantown as "virtually a suburb of Pittsburgh."[6] True to the state's history of sectionalism, other cities came to the university's aid because they did not like the concentration of power in Charleston. The *Wheeling Intelligencer* regarded the idea of moving the university from Morgantown as "absolutely silly" and the declared the supposed inaccessibility of Morgantown as a bogus issue because railroads connected every section of the state. With Marshall College aspiring to be the state's second university, the *Huntington Herald-Dispatch* predictably did not want the relocated WVU next door, competing with Marshall. So the paper sided with WVU supporters and demanded that the University remain in its original location.[7]

Frank B. Trotter, dean of the College of Arts and Sciences, was appointed president by the Board of Regents in June 1916. With considerable support from the Republican politicians, President Trotter began a concerted building effort to anchor the University in Morgantown. Relocation was not the only threat for the University; it could also be decentralized and picked apart piece by piece. The College of Agriculture, for example, might be removed to the eastern Panhandle, which had been proposed in 1910. Other parts of the state regarded the School of Medicine and the College of Law as political plums, and on more than one occasion these units of the University became targets for possible relocation. Partially to deflect the talk of relocation or decentralization, President Trotter inaugurated a major building campaign. Monongalia County offered acreage for the expansion of the College of Agriculture, and the legislature provided funds for a new agriculture building. The legislature also authorized expansion of the engineering building and funds to construct a building for the School of Medicine. Oglebay Hall was completed in 1918, and Women's Hall was completed in 1919.[8] Physical expansion slammed the door on the agitation for removal, the "unseemly scramble among other West Virginia cities and towns to acquire the University." James S. Lakin, a member of the state Board of Control, informed the press in 1916 that the University was now "so well settled, there is little probability that the question of relocating it would be given any serious consideration." Following the fire that destroyed the state capitol building on January 3, 1921, WVU and Charleston interest groups supported each other to prevent removal of either the University or the state capital, which itself had previously been moved several times. The issue was now permanently settled.[9]

Following World War I, the University's major building campaign also provided facilities for the College of Law, Department of Chemistry, a gymnasium, a men's dormitory, a new physical education building for women, an armory, and a new commencement hall. The campaign probably helped President Trotter to retain the presidency, but Regent Morris P. Shawkey, who was just finishing his third term as state superintendent of free schools and had decided not to run again, was regarded by influential supporters as a better choice for president than Trotter. This possibility led to one of the stranger episodes of external political interference in the administration of WVU.[10]

PROMOTING PAROCHIALISM: SHAWKEY AND THE NORMAL SCHOOL BLOC

While Shawkey's friends on the state board of education and in the University alumni association promoted his cause, WVU faculty regarded him as a politician and challenged his academic credentials. Undaunted, board of education members secretly conspired to elevate him to the presidency of WVU. The plan was to be sealed at a special board meeting in November 1920, but Shawkey's supporters failed to anticipate the implacable objections of Governor Howard M. Gore. Shawkey was not prepared to fight for the post, and Trotter continued in office.[11]

Shawkey would not wait for elevation to the presidency of WVU indefinitely, however, and on June 28, 1923, the board of education chose him to become president of Marshall College. Marshall had been essentially a secondary school until 1920, when it was elevated to a four-year college. This episode was a pivotal moment in the history of higher education in the Mountain State. Upon becoming president of Marshall, the struggle against the University began in earnest. Supported by the "normal school bloc," Shawkey claimed that WVU was too distant and conservative in its approach to education to serve the educational needs of the entire state. This claim was especially true in southern West Virginia, and Shawkey's vision was for Marshall to become the leading collegiate institution for the southern part of the state.[12]

The die was cast for what became a century-long competition with WVU. "To friends of the University, as well as to those interested in state finances and in the future of education in general, this was an alarming turn of events," historian Charles Ambler wrote. "Among other things it meant that state support for higher education would be allocated among a number of institutions as determined largely by their political influence, and that none of them could become first rate." With the support of his personal friends on the state Board of Education, and supported by leaders of the other normal schools, Shawkey advocated for increased funding to alleviate Marshall's alleged overcrowding, its underfunding, and a change in its status from teachers training institution into a college of arts and sciences. A storm of protest emanated from all corners challenging the legality of such a course as well as the wisdom of this policy for higher education in West Virginia. Even though the state Board of Education clearly overstepped its authority, in 1924 it authorized Marshall to grant BA and BS degrees. Actually, Marshall had granted its first baccalaureate degrees in 1921 without opposition from either the state Board of Education or the governor. The other normal schools eventually followed without official constraint.[13] By ignoring state legislation and policy, West Virginia officials furthered parochialism in the state's educational system. Aggravated by political sectionalism, each local constituency was politically galvanized to protect its own local college. Thus was born a system with more colleges than the state could afford or made educational sense. Although much bemoaned ever since, the system is now politically impossible to reverse.

Opponents of an expanded role for Marshall and the normal schools pointed out that these schools were created to train teachers, but because teachers were in short supply the normals were "permitted to assume other obligations that were not imposed on them." This in effect turned Marshall into a liberal arts college without legal authorization. A written opinion by former Attorney General William G. Conley, published in a Morgantown paper, claimed that there was no "authority in the state board of education to enlarge that work at the normal schools." A few months later a Wheeling paper predicted a "knock-out contest between the 'normal school bloc' and the forces of the university," because the normal schools had a "thirst for power" that would adversely affect the University's appropriations.[14]

Having led the struggle against the university interests, Shawkey disqualified himself as a candidate when President Trotter offered his resignation in 1926. Consequently, the presidency was offered to native son J. W. Withers, a dean at New York University, with a beginning salary of $15,000. This was a nationally competitive salary, but he did not accept the offer immediately, giving Shawkey the opportunity to write a letter to the state superintendent, dated October 27, 1926, in opposition to paying such a high salary to the new president. He pointed out that paying so much to Withers would undermine the morale of those who had taught in the state for years with a low salary—a political hammer that would become a standard tool in West Virginia. The Marshall president then sent a copy of his letter to each of the Board of Education members. Inevitably, the letter went public, provoking the negative response that prompted Withers to decline the WVU offer.[15]

The Shawkey letter may have been a "tempest in a teapot," as Ambler characterized it, but the state press recognized the document for what it was, a self-serving political power play. Naturally, the *Morgantown New Dominion* was most outraged, demanding that Shawkey be disciplined by the Board of Education. He "clearly overstepped the bounds of propriety and executive sobriety . . . as the head of Marshall College," and the letter was "a serious reflection upon his temperamental fitness" for his position. The *Parkersburg News* editorialized that the letter came from "a man whose ambitions to be president of the university has led him into the incredibly narrow expression of jealousy that a little man has for a big man." The *Fairmont Times* asserted that the letter showed that "little school politicians will go to the mat to prevent the coming of a big man to Morgantown." Chiming in, the *Charleston Gazette* declared that Shawkey was "totally unfitted for the great position in Morgantown." Even the normally friendly *Charleston Daily-Mail* stated bluntly that the letter "creates in the minds of his former friends the very serious question whether they have not overestimated him." Only the hometown *Huntington Herald Dispatch* defended Shawkey, declaring that his only mistake was to address private thoughts to a Board of Education that he assumed might benefit from some sage advice.[16]

Shawkey's meddling certainly intensified the friction between WVU and the normal school bloc, and especially with Marshall, whose president seemed to be waging war against the University. This friction had consequences for the structure of higher education in the Mountain State. Shawkey's close and personal relations with members of the state Board of Education, their unwillingness to rein him in, and their determination to force the University to lighten its competition by participating in the West Virginia Athletic Conference, enshrined political provincialism in West Virginia higher education and set the framework for WVU-Marshall political hostilities for the century to come.

The "new educators" also interfered in the internal operations of WVU during the period immediately after World War I. This is illustrated in the establishment of graduate education, which the new educators advocated with far greater alacrity than they did the requisite academic standards. Influenced by the growing numbers of students who completed normal school and left for graduate work in other states, the new educators demanded that the University establish courses of study leading to master's and doctoral degrees, even correspondence courses. While the "old educators" at WVU admitted the need for graduate education within the state system, they worried about maintaining quality control in the programs, considering the totally inadequate library and laboratory facilities in place. Courses toward the MA degree might be offered, but WVU definitely was not equipped to offer the PhD. Following World War I, the "old guard" found itself under direct assault from the outside. Against the background of increasing numbers of students taking graduate-level courses, which grew from only 29 in 1921–1922 to 236 in 1926–1927, "new educators" on the state Board of Education ordered the faculty to establish a graduate school with courses leading to both masters' and doctoral degrees, and to find a suitable dean to administer the proposed school. The faculty responded by admitting only students holding the BA degree in the appropriate fields leading to the MA degree, which most of the normal schools and teachers' colleges did not offer.[17]

WVU alumni, many of whom were politically influential, were outraged by this overt attack on the University by the "new educators." At their behest, the legislature modified the system of governance in 1927 by removing authority over the University from the Board of Education and placing it in the hands of the University's own Board of Governors in order to protect it from the small school political faction. But this apparent independence was only illusory. Unlike earlier boards, which were dominated by professional educators, this Board of Governors was made up of political appointees, three lawyers, one newspaper editor, one stock broker, and one high school teacher. As state historian Charles Ambler observed, "professional educators had admittedly lost control of the University." He might have added that the Board of Control still made decisions about spending for buildings and grounds.[18]

The legislation creating the new arrangement took effect on July 1, 1927. It gave the University its own Board of Governors but left control over university finances and buildings with the Board of Control. It was hoped by University supporters that this reorganization might, as University historians have suggested, "rescue the University from being perceived as just another agency of state government under the direction of West Virginia governors."[19]

During the years after World War I, enrollment at the eleven state-sponsored institutions of higher education grew exponentially. By 1927 a total of 6,726 students were registered, 2,553 at the University and 1,247 at Marshall College. While nearly all of the students enrolled at the other institutions were drawn from the local and surrounding counties, the WVU student body represented all counties, twenty-six other states, and five foreign countries.[20]

GOVERNMENT INTERVENTION AND THE WVU BOARD OF GOVERNORS, 1929–1947

As a result of the Great Depression, New Deal, and World War II, West Virginia broke forty years of Republican rule between 1928 and 1935 and elected Democratic governors. During the two decades preceding the Irvin Stewart administration, structural controls also impeded the efficient operation of the state's university. It was hoped that political meddling would be stemmed by creating a board of governors in 1927 to oversee academic affairs at WVU. Unfortunately, the new system opened the door wider for political interference from state officials. Presumably, the Board of Governors was bipartisan, with seven members appointed by the governor serving four-year terms. The University's financial and business affairs were directed by the state Board of Control established in 1909. With a tight hand on the purse strings, the Board of Control often encroached upon the Board of Governors. Moreover, the plans and policies of both boards were limited by the budget-making capacity of the state Board of Public Works. In constructing a university budget, WVU administrators also found it necessary to consult the West Virginia attorney general, the state auditor, and the state budget director. Although the legislature was supreme, the governor also played a key role through the power of appointment and removal of members on the governing boards. This overlapping, often competing, but always politically complicated, system shackled presidents and others responsible for the financial and academic administration of the University. Presidents and professional consultants alike recommended a more efficient procedure to no avail until after World War II.[21]

Throughout this period the University's primary focus in the state appropriations process was in preparing the annual budget. Biennial budgets were compiled by the presidents from estimates of projected needs advanced from department chairs and deans. Prior to changes made in the process in 1947, the president consulted with the Board of Control, director of the budget, and the Board of Public Works, with the latter preparing the final form for submission to the legislature. In the legislature additional changes were made as political considerations were taken into account. In general, the success or failure of University presidents was determined by a procedure that was essentially beyond their control. Once the proposed budget was sent to Charleston, no one from the University, particularly the president, even frequented the capital. These expectations placed the presidents in an awkward position for, if they stayed away, they were charged with neglecting their responsibility; if they did appear at the capital, it was presumed they were lobbying. Only prior to the submission of the budget was it customary to lobby the decision-makers in Charleston. The University administration never knew what the final appropriation would look like, and the process was highly unpredictable. For example, in 1931 the senate approved a resolution containing a rider that denied state funds for any institution of higher learning belonging to the North Central Association of Colleges, because that organization supposedly discriminated against West Virginia in intercollegiate athletics. The rider was removed only after the University's athletic director convinced its sponsor that this was not the case.[22]

The problem of overlapping responsibilities and lines of authority in controlling the University were aggravated during the Great Depression, when "we can't afford it" became the state government's mantra in response to requests for financial assistance. Forced to defend his request for an increase in the 1931–1932 appropriation for the graduate school, President John R. Turner declared, "Don't tell me we can't afford it. We can't afford to do without it."[23] The graduate program, he said, "puts the well-being of the state above the interests of any locality," and "a vote against the graduate school is a vote against the state."[24] Educators might appreciate the sentiment, but legislators were not swayed and appropriated no funds at all. With some justification Turner complained, "We have a generous legislature in this state. They multiply institutions and then starve them."[25] The financial situation would only get worse as the nation sank deeper into the Great Depression.

The legislature controlled the state purse strings, but, as the chief executive, the governor inserted himself in higher education governance too. The newly elected Democratic Governor Herman G. Kump attended a meeting of the University Board of Governors in April 1934 to discuss the tenure of President Turner. At its July meeting, the board put Turner on notice when it only gave him a provisional appointment until the end of the year. In August, Governor Kump questioned why Democrats were not employed at the University, pointing to the fact that thirty-two of the thirty-eight top administrators were Republicans, including President Turner.[26]

Governor Kump appointed new members to the WVU Board of Governors in October 1934, and shortly thereafter the board announced that Turner's tenure as president would come to an end on December 31, 1934. Students called for a demonstration to protest Turner's firing, proclaiming that "our University has been a political football long enough." Gathering on October 16, students carried placards with messages such as "The University before Politics"; nearly 80 percent of the student body turned out.[27] Student enthusiasm did not save Turner, however, nor did it protect the University from its accustomed role as the state's "political football." During the years between the administrations of John R. Turner and Irvin Stewart, who assumed the presidency in 1946, the University's old desire for political independence continued to age without any hope of fulfillment. Historian Charles Ambler observed that, with the sacking of Turner through Kump's intervention, "University affairs were determined largely by the governor himself."[28] Turner's removal came about through Kump's inside men,

Professor John F. Sly, director of the Bureau of Government Research and head of WVU's Department of Political Science, and Professor Robert A. Armstrong, a former vice president who was appointed acting president by Kump's Board of Governors, effective January 1, 1935. Shortly thereafter, the governor's own "reform program" was announced. It included the establishment of a salary scale and a retirement system for faculty, perhaps in a bid to win their support for the third piece: to put more emphasis on the University's extension service, a favorite of the "new educators."[29]

Apparently the "Old Guard" faculty would not be bribed; they remained unenthusiastic about the governor's reform package. Consequently, in May 1935, the Board of Governors complied with the governor's request by appointing Professor John F. Sly as acting dean of faculties, who assumed for himself the title of "Dean of Deans" in order to oversee an enlarged reform program that included a reorganization of the University with the stated purpose of "improving faculty and administrative efficiency."[30]

On Sly's recommendation, the Board of Governors directed that professorial staff members would be automatically retired at age sixty-five, that the duties and contracts of faculty and staff could be changed at the convenience of the administration, and that other draconian measures could be taken as Sly deemed necessary. Such arbitrary measures created an atmosphere of deep mistrust and devastated morale. In mid-year, Sly resigned after the Board of Governors, apparently thinking he had gone too far, refused to accept his recommendations to further "streamline" the University's administration. According to Ambler, the period from 1935 through World War II was one noted for administrative efficiency under Presidents Chauncey S. Boucher (1935–1938) and Charles E. Lawell (1939–1945) but was also one in which "control of the University was left to the board of governors and the board of control." Both were dominated by the governor through his appointive power.[31]

The election of Governor Matthew M. Neely in 1940 brought a renewed effort to expand the governor's political influence over University administration. Neely was the state's first chief executive to have received the bachelor's and law degrees from WVU, and his personal interest in the University had positive potential. In his inaugural address on January 1,

1941, the governor announced an enlarged vision of WVU's role in the life of West Virginia. The University should be "so expanded and perfected that it would be unnecessary" for anyone to leave the state for an advanced education, he declared. At the dedication of the new Mineral Industries Building, Neely restated his intention to establish a four-year college of medicine to take the place of the two-year program, and to create a college of aeronautical engineering.[32] When the University failed to implement these projects in a timely fashion, Neely replaced five of the seven members of the Board of Governors. The governor then attended the Board of Governors meeting on June 16, 1944, and demanded that the president be replaced because the University was "making no appreciable progress" under the leadership of President Charles Lawall in numerous areas: the University failed to produce the professionals needed by the state; failed to attract students from southern West Virginia; failed to maintain an appropriate graduate extension program; lacked the faculty's confidence; failed to fight for increased appropriations; ended the fiscal year with unspent state appropriations, which reverted back to the state; and failed to maintain a university comparable to other major state universities.[33]

Within days, the Board of Governors complied and asked President Lawall to resign. The previous board had already approved Lawall's contract for the 1944–1945 academic year, so when the new board requested his resignation, Lawall refused on the grounds that it was not in the best interest of the University or the state. University faculty apparently regarded packing the Board of Governors as business as usual, but students and the state press voiced outrage at such a blatant demonstration of political manipulation of University affairs. On June 20, 1944, the students held a demonstration and expressed their disapproval of the "hand-picked board" and its demand for Lawall's resignation. On June 24, a committee from the student government sent an open letter to all West Virginians urging them to resist the governor's "dictatorial action." The letter denounced the University's once again being made "a greased pig in the field game of state politics" and demanded restoration of Lawall and the University to a position above "political greed and cunning." As the governor left the board meeting, he met with a chorus of boos from the students.[34]

The students first brought to light the issues involved in political interference, but the state press gave the story legs. The *Morgantown Post* declared that there was something seriously wrong with "a governmental structure that allows a Governor to take over the state university." Quite appropriately, the Post continued, "alumni all over the state are seething with righteous indignation," and "public spirited citizens are outraged" at such a reprehensible action.[35] Overt intrusion in University operations may have been bad policy, but it was legal. Legislation passed in 1921 established that anyone who held state office was under the jurisdiction of the governor. State employees or appointees, therefore, served at the governor's will and could be removed whenever the governor deemed it appropriate. On July 14, 1944, WVU Alumni Association President Charles Hodges delivered a one-hour address over statewide radio defending WVU against the governor's misleading statements. Governor Neely responded with his own radio address on the state of the University on July 6, 1944, in which he defended his actions and declared that, if the people of West Virginia wanted the University to be elevated "above the Dead Sea level of inferiority in which visionless greed has long kept it," they should support his efforts.[36]

The faculty refused to take part in the controversy on the grounds that they were not asked for advice on appointments and therefore would offer no opinion on administrative affairs. The *Morgantown Post* expressed regret that the faculty had, in effect, abdicated its responsibilities: "In our judgment the faculty has let the University down, let the alumni and the students down, and let the people of the State down."[37] In the end, it was a friend of the University who resorted to the courts to preserve the integrity of University governance from political manipulation. Charles Wise and his chapter of the WVU Alumni Association in Charleston filed a suit in the Kanawha County Circuit Court against Governor Neely's packed Board of Governors. The suit claimed that President Lawall's contract was valid, and that he could not be dismissed without threatening the academic tenure and freedom of all faculty. The plaintiffs also asked for an injunction to prevent the Board of Governors from carrying out its plans until a decision was rendered. The *Morgantown Post* explained to readers that the governor was acting within the letter of the law in making his appointments to the board; for WVU to be insulated from political interference, the legislature would have to amend the law and provide the Board of Governors with constitutional status in order to make it difficult to pack with political cronies. The *Post* editorialized: "The specter of political interference in higher education in West Virginia will not be banished until effective steps of some kind are taken to provide permanent protection against a repetition of Governor Neely's ripper tactics."[38]

The Neely Board of Governors asked the West Virginia Supreme Court of Appeals to intervene in the case, but the high court declined, and the case proceeded with President Lawall still in his Stewart Hall office. Meanwhile, during the 1944 general election, Clarence W. Meadows replaced Neely when the latter won election to the U.S. Senate. Meanwhile, in 1945 the state senate refused to approve the Neely-appointed Board of Governors. Governor Meadows appointed a new group and rescinded the order for President Lawall's resignation. Fed up with the political shenanigans, Lawall resigned in September 1945 and took a position with the Baltimore & Ohio Railway. The case was more than a tempest in a teapot; it struck at the very core of university values, illustrated how vulnerable the creative and discovery process is to those more interested in power than in truth, and encapsulated the weaknesses inherent in higher education governance.[39]

THE STRAYER REPORT AND LEGISLATIVE REFORM, 1945–1947

Matthew Neely's unsuccessful effort to administer the University from the governor's office brought about long-overdue reforms in University governance. On the order of Governor Meadows, a task force of experts led by George D. Strayer, distinguished professor emeritus of education at Columbia University, was organized to prepare a survey and report on the status of education in West Virginia. The survey was completed on December 10, 1945. It is worth pausing to examine this report because it provides a revealing picture of higher education in West Virginia near the midpoint of the twentieth century.

The report declared that the state of West Virginia had "created a number and variety of higher institutions beyond the apparent disposition of the State to provide adequate support and development" or coordination.[40] There was no broader, long-term plan of governance, Strayer reported, and until that happened "there is but little chance for the development of a system of higher education." Strayer reported that political leaders must decide how to deal with WVU "first and foremost," for "a state of the size and resources of West Virginia can maintain but one institution that will rank as an effective university." Moreover, when compared with other state universities, it was evident to Strayer that West Virginia should provide for "more liberal support of the institution." The history of WVU was one of "slow and groping development," he reported, and the University's ambitious plans over many decades were delayed or set aside for lack of adequate resources.[41]

WVU had the same form of organization as other land-grant institutions, but it lacked that characteristic spirit of a major university, Strayer concluded. The reasons were not difficult to discern. The University's location so far north, in relative isolation from the state's centers of population, presented a handicap because of the difficulties of transportation. Of course, the construction of railroads and the ever-improving highways of the post-World War II era lessened the difficulty. Secondly, WVU's location in downtown Morgantown left it little room to expand and ensnared it in constantly increasing traffic congestion.[42] This problem, already noticeable in 1947, was alleviated in the following decade with the acquisition of land for the Evansdale campus, the Medical Center, the College of Law, and the athletic facilities.

Strayer cited other problems that needed to be addressed, including more faculty involvement in the internal administration of the University, faculty salaries that needed to be raised at least by 25 percent, and a much greater effort to increase the state's college participation rate. The survey team was "completely convinced" that West Virginia should "maintain but one fully developed state university, that to West Virginia University should be assigned responsibility for all professional work, for all graduate work beyond the master's degree, and for all specialized areas of work leading to undergraduate degrees that can be satisfactorily and adequately provided for the entire state under the auspices of one institution."[43]

The most important criticisms in the Strayer Report centered on the dual controls over the University exercised by its Board of Control and Board of Governors. In March 1946, the legislature prepared an amendment to the state constitution to make members of the Board of Governors constitutional officials with overlapping terms of four years. Mountaineer Post 127 of the American Legion, organized by the University's veteran students, publicly supported the amendment, claiming that the higher education system was "incompetent" and "poorly administered."[44] Editors at the *Morgantown Post* reinforced the student veterans' assessment and declared that passage of the amendment would stop the outrageous practice of packing the Board of Governors with political appointees, which recently "outraged all the people of the state and did untold harm to the University." Unfortunately, the amendment was defeated at the polls by a small majority.[45]

A friendly legislature stepped into the breach, however, by crafting legislation that contained the same provisions as the amendment. Governor Clarence W. Meadows lent his voice to the effort in his State of the State Message on January 9, 1947, announcing that WVU should be "THE [sic] University both in theory and fact."[46] On February 25, 1947, the legislature enacted the new laws, which ensured that, henceforth, control and administration of the University were vested in a Board of Governors consisting of nine members serving overlapping nine-year terms. They were still appointed by the governor but could not be removed "except for official misconduct, incompetence, neglect of duty, or gross immorality and this only in the manner prescribed by law for the removal of the Governor or State elective officers."[47]

Finally, after eighty years of struggle, friends of the University believed they had achieved political independence. Supporters would be sorely disappointed, however, if they believed that politics would disappear from University governance.

A new president, Irvin Stewart, who began his tenure on July 1, 1946, arrived in Morgantown when these changes were initiated, and he lost no time in supporting them. Speaking in Charleston the month after his arrival, Stewart declared that, for the University to serve the entire state, "it must be accepted by all people of West Virginia as the State University and not merely a university which serves the northern part of the state," or one in which "other parts have only a passing interest." Repeating a frequently articulated refrain, he claimed that "an inferior university is a luxury which West Virginia is too poor to afford."[48]

TWO

IRVIN STEWART AND THE CREATION OF A UNIVERSITY "BOTH IN THEORY AND FACT"

IRVIN STEWART IS REGARDED as one of the most successful WVU presidents. The Board of Governors proceeded cautiously in appointing Stewart, "an outsider," but they ultimately were persuaded that he possessed sound political judgment and could be trusted with guiding the University. The state's press considered him a good choice because of his extensive contacts with national leaders in government, education, and science. Stewart was born on October 2, 1899, in Fort Worth, Texas, earned degrees from the University of Texas and received a PhD (1926) from Columbia University. Stewart was forty-seven years old when he assumed the presidency, and his administrative experience was primarily governmental rather than academic, but he had experience teaching law and government at several universities. The new president had served in the U.S. Department of State and later as a member of the Federal Communications Commission from 1934 to 1937. He assumed the post of executive secretary of the National Defense Research Committee from 1940 to 1945 and then took the same position at the Office of Scientific Research and Development from 1941 to 1945, before also serving as the latter's deputy director in 1946. He also held the position of director of the Committee on Scientific Aids to Learning from 1937 to 1946. During World War II, Stewart played a prominent role in the top-secret Manhattan Project, which led to the development of the atomic bomb, by negotiating 2,500 contracts for the project.[1]

The new president took office on July 1, 1946, with the strong support of a new Board of Governors, as well as Governor Clarence W.

Meadows. Governor Meadows had initiated the reforms recommended by the Strayer Report of 1945 and shifted the responsibility for governing WVU to its Board of Governors in 1947. The governor further gratified University supporters by proclaiming that WVU "should be THE University both in theory and fact." Stewart reiterated this theme in his inaugural address, delivered at the Field House on April 26, 1947, and repeated it thereafter. Unlike the few previous formal inaugurations, Stewart's was strictly an academic ceremony, free of politicians. The event was attended by 4,000 spectators and 153 delegates representing other institutions. Two featured guests were James B. Conant, president of Harvard University, and Vannevar Bush, president of the Carnegie Institution of Washington. Stewart had come to know Conant and Bush during his federal service in Washington, D.C. Both distinguished guests spoke highly of Stewart's administrative skills and also received honorary degrees during the exercise.[2] Stewart's prominence was reinforced when General Dwight D. Eisenhower addressed a convocation at Mountaineer Stadium on September 23, 1947. The crowd numbered more than 18,000 West Virginians, the largest ever assembled in the stadium for anything other than a football game. General Eisenhower had just stepped down as Army Chief of Staff but had not yet assumed the presidency of Columbia University. Of course, Eisenhower went on to head NATO and then became president of the United States. President Stewart presented the World War II hero with the honorary degree of doctor of laws.[3]

POSTWAR EXPANSION

Stewart came to a university that would be shaken from its sleepy days by the massive changes to American life in the era following World War II. WVU was transformed into a new institution, and Stewart's unique contribution was to anticipate and lead rather than react to those major changes in all areas. "It is my own view that a chief executive is sometimes most effective when he can help establish a desirable course of action, and yet act in such a way that few people are conscious of his participation," Stewart remarked at the end of his years in office. Stewart is rightfully viewed as one of the best presidents in WVU's history, and all the more so in light of his belief that "policies so made are likely to be more enduring than those adopted primarily because of the dictates of a single individual."[4]

The war interrupted the education of hundreds of thousands of young Americans. During the conflict, many thousands more came of age and decided to take advantage of the Servicemen's Readjustment Act of 1944, generally referred to as the G.I. Bill of Rights, which committed the federal government to underwriting the cost of a college education for veterans. On the job for a few weeks when he made his first address to the University faculty in July 1946, Stewart raised an issue troubling many higher education officials in the postwar era: the "abnormal increase" in enrollment of returning veterans. His solution reveals much about the new president's view of education. One position the University might take, he observed, was to limit the enrollment to a specified number that could be accommodated by existing facilities and staff. In his opinion, however, this would "betray the trust which our forefathers placed in us when they founded a state university dedicated to opening opportunities for higher education to the youth of West Virginia." Instead, the only "honorable" course was "to provide an opportunity for higher education to every West Virginia boy or girl capable of meeting University requirements. . . . We cannot fail them. Common decency dictates that we must do our job."[5]

Enrollment levels were difficult to predict during this period aggravated by the international tensions of the early Cold War years. The nation had to take precautionary steps to prepare itself for the actuality of war, as in Korea in 1950–1953, and continued threats of conflicts elsewhere. Americans took the Communist claims of world domination seriously, so preparedness was the byword. As a result, the number of men enrolled at any given time depended on the deferment policies and the military manpower needs of the U.S. government. Enrollment planning was also influenced by the postwar "baby boom," which was predicted to bring an increase of about 30 percent in the college-age population by 1970.[6]

In Stewart's view, the mission of the University was service, and the increase in enrollment represented an increase in the opportunity to serve. He thought each graduating class elevated the public's consciousness of

the University, so the larger the classes, the more pervasive that awareness. The rapid bulge in students challenged administrators to create conditions that made instruction possible, and professors were challenged
with maintaining quality instruction. Size was not in and of itself the
main factor. "The University will grow in greatness, not as it grows in size,
but as it grows in service," the new president asserted in his inaugural
address. The state of West Virginia established a "single University," he
declared, and charged it with the obligation of serving as many qualified
residents as presented themselves for admission, and that was the policy
of his administration.[7]

Education has ever been proclaimed as the only solution to the world's
ills. However, after two bloody world wars in a quarter century and the
emergence of the Communist threat after World War II, "serious doubt"
was cast upon "the efficacy of education alone as the salvation of a troubled world," Stewart stated in 1947. Something more was needed, and that
something might be providing a Christian education "designed to help the
student in the fulfillment of an active, intelligent citizenship in a democratic state." Before theocrats could jump to their feet, however, Stewart
denied the right of "those who would subject the moral or ethical content of
its teaching to a review for conformity to religious or other views." Stewart
was referring to a brand of open Christianity that carried with it the values
of Western civilization.[8]

The fullest development of students, Stewart believed, involved their
intellectual, physical, and spiritual growth. Although it was not the mission of public universities to promote any particular theology, spirituality
should be "strongly encouraged," Stewart informed a civic organization.
Churches surrounded the Morgantown campus and were located close
by for the convenience of the students. "We stress to the incoming freshmen that the educated man is developed spiritually as well as intellectually.
Rather than telling them how to get to the churches of their preference,
student guides on the Sunday and Freshman Week actually conduct the
freshmen to the churches of their choice," the president informed his audience. The University also gathered information on the religious preferences
of its students, so Stewart had the data at his fingertips. Of the first 4,200

students to register in the fall of 1952, more than 1,500, about 36 percent, were Methodists. Presbyterians and Catholics each comprised 14 percent, Baptists 12.6 percent, Episcopalians 4.2 percent, Lutherans 3 percent, and members of the Christian Church and the Jewish faith accounted for 1.8 percent respectively. The remainder represented seventeen other religious faiths, including one Muslim. Stewart also pointed out that there was a church and/or a student center for each of these faiths within easy walking distance of the campus.[9]

Even though University dormitories were reserved for residents of West Virginia, which undoubtedly limited the number of out-of-state students, the percentage of nonresident students during this period ranged from 10.1 percent to 13.5 percent. In 1957–1958, out-of-state students came from nineteen foreign countries and twenty-seven states. Following the common policy for state universities, tuition was higher for nonresidents. The tuition at WVU for nonresidents in 1955 was $434 to $700 per year, about $200 more than the rate paid by resident students. President Stewart recognized that this additional cost might dissuade out-of-state students from applying for admission, "but we do not feel that it is necessary to attract non-resident students on a price basis."[10]

Although West Virginia was a net exporter of college students and ranked far below the national average in the percentage of its high school graduates who attended college, resident students at WVU represented all counties in the state. Not surprisingly, Morgantown and vicinity provided the largest contingent. Consider this as a measure of the extraordinary expansion experienced by the University: between 1870 and 1945 WVU granted 12,516 undergraduate degrees, 1,973 master's degrees, and 52 doctorates; during the twelve years of Stewart's administration alone, WVU conferred 11,617 undergraduate degrees, 6,527 masters', and 131 doctoral degrees.[11]

STRAINED PHYSICAL FACILITIES

A doubling of the student population placed extreme pressure on classroom and laboratory facilities, as well as on faculty and staff. To alleviate the pressure, the legislature provided the University with extra resources by releasing a portion of the student fee accounts, thus increasing financial relief for each additional student. Classroom and laboratory pressures could not be alleviated immediately, so an emphasis was placed on using those facilities more efficiently by scheduling them from 8 a.m. to 11 p.m.[12]

Student housing was a much more intractable problem. Stewart resolved the University's immediate housing shortage by launching an appeal to local citizens for help. Just prior to the beginning of the fall semester in August 1946, the president announced that "the University is desperately in need of all living accommodations available in Morgantown or in outlying communities."[13] The *Morgantown Post* did not wait for the president. Several days earlier the paper editorialized that it was every citizen's patriotic duty to help with the housing of returning vets: "If they were good enough to fight for us, they are good enough to share the shelter of our roof if we can find a place for them."[14] Church, civic, service, labor, and veteran organizations were enlisted in the campaign. In addition, occupancy was doubled in dormitory rooms, lounges were turned into bunking areas, and the president set an example by providing half of the second floor of his home to five vets who paid to the University the regular dormitory rate for their accommodation.[15]

For decades the legislature and the University had been negligent in providing for the construction of women's dormitories, even though women were required to live in University facilities. The burden of that neglect fell on women in the postwar era. The problem for nonresident women was compounded because the demand for on-campus housing exceeded the supply, and available rooms were reserved for residents. This shortage "made it impossible for several hundred [resident] girls to attend the University during each of the postwar years," President Stewart lamented on West Virginia Day in 1952.[16] Housing was even tighter for nonresident women. Regetta Jones Parsons, who graduated in 1954, informed an interviewer: "I remember so well my outrage over the treatment of out-of-state students. At that time, we couldn't live in dorms but were placed in private homes under University rules and regulations. I wrote many papers and gave quite a few impromptu speeches on that subject."[17]

Many veterans had families, but adequate housing for married students was not available either. Some relief was secured in the form of 150 war surplus trailers, and one hundred apartments were carved out of war surplus army barracks. A substantial temporary building was acquired from the federal government's war surplus program for a student cafeteria in 1947, and another to serve as a student center in 1948. Formerly a recreation center at a Navy base, the student union building offered a bowling alley, ballroom, snack bar, theater, as well as game and meeting rooms. Students chose the name Mountainlair for the building in 1948, and in 1949 a student activity fee was initiated to support this and several new or reconstructed Mountainlairs in the future.[18]

The burgeoning student population also strained the classroom buildings, which, like the dormitories, had been woefully neglected. With a $2.7 million appropriation from the legislature in 1947, the University purchased several parcels of land between University and Beechurst Avenues across the street from the Field House, now Stansbury Hall. Armstrong Hall, which opened in 1950, was built first to be used as a general classroom building. A new biology building, Brooks Hall, opened in 1951; a physics building, now Hodges Hall, in 1952; and a music building, now Eiesland Hall, in 1954. During Stewart's administration, a new dormitory for women opened in 1956, and a new University bookstore in 1958. A superstructure built on top of Wise Library doubled its capacity. Numerous other minor buildings, renovations, and landscaping improvements added considerably to the University's physical plant and beautified the surroundings.[19]

The major construction projects necessary to accommodate the surging student body occasionally encountered obstacles because of the federal government's preparedness campaign during the Korean and Cold Wars. The War Planning Board sometimes controlled materials for construction. For example, in testimony before a subcommittee of the House Committee on Education and Labor in 1951, President Stewart pleaded with members to make it clear to the appropriate officials that "the drastic restrictions imposed upon the facilities for higher education may well have a serious adverse effect upon our national and local progress and security in the next few years." As an illustration, he cited the serious shortage of doctors, dentists, and nurses in West Virginia, and noted that WVU had undertaken to build a new four-year medical school to produce the professionals who would allay this shortage. Now that contracts had been let for construction, would the building materials be available, "or will the citizens of West Virginia continue to suffer unnecessary pain and to die untimely deaths because we cannot get the materials needed to train the doctors, dentists, and nurses who might have saved them?"[20]

The University also increased campus acreage under Stewart. In 1948 the state built Monongahela Boulevard, linking Morgantown and Star City. The new road stimulated the University to acquire the Krepps and Dille farms, totaling 260 acres of land on both sides of the right of way. The new road opened the way for a second campus, subsequently named the Evansdale Campus, one and a half miles from the main campus, and a master plan was commissioned to guide development. A large area on the west side of the road was reserved for athletic fields, and fifty acres was reserved for a University arboretum which would harbor native trees and shrubs and serve as an outdoor laboratory. The east side of the road space was set aside for new facilities for the College of Engineering, which had been homeless since its previous home on the downtown campus, Mechanical Hall, was destroyed by fire in 1956 (torched, it was rumored, by an engineering student disgruntled over a grade). Also, the College of Agriculture, which was then in the planning stages, would be located on the new campus. The consultant who drew up the master plan, Cincinnati architect C. F. Cellarius, thought that a new football stadium also would soon be needed, but that seemed too far off to contemplate in 1950 and was not on the list of construction priorities.[21]

Buildings for the Colleges of Engineering and Agriculture were financed by what was then an unusual method. Upon the request of Stewart and the Board of Governors, on June 2, 1956, the legislature authorized the issuance of $10 million in revenue bonds to construct and equip the two buildings. Appropriations from surplus revenues alone would not have been sufficient, so revenue-bond financing created a University capital improvements fund in the state treasury where student fees would be deposited to retire the bond. Student fees had not been used for academic facilities before, but the idea caught on, and other states followed suit.[22]

Several other major land acquisitions at no cost to the University came through the surplus property disposal program of the federal government during this period, including about 150 acres for an experimental farm in Mason County in 1948 and 495 acres from the Tygart Valley Subsistence Homestead Project in Randolph County in 1949 for an experimental forest.[23] While these acquisitions increased University resources in strategic areas of expertise, they did not alleviate the pressing need for space in Morgantown.

A second major land acquisition did alleviate the need, however, when 85 acres of the former county poor farm, a gift of the Monongalia County Court, was joined to 55 acres already owned by the University to create the space for a third campus for the new Medical Center.[24]

WVU FOUNDATION ESTABLISHED

In addressing the housing crisis that dominated this era of explosive growth, Stewart chose a strategy that emphasized private over either federal or state funding for dormitory construction. The University's first priority was to increase the funds for instructional facilities. Since the funds provided by the legislature were insufficient to fund both, he believed that public money should be devoted to instruction and private funds for living space. Stewart was the first WVU president to successfully embrace increasing University resources through private giving. Most presidents found it difficult to raise private money for a public institution because the potential donors thought tax-supported institutions were already financed through state appropriations. Many of Stewart's addresses were used to solicit money for the University. He encouraged members of the state Chamber of Commerce to regard money given to WVU as an investment in tomorrow. Speaking to the West Virginia Coal Mining Institute the following year, he urged members to contribute $100,000 per year for the next five years to initiate a program of coal research at WVU, research which would benefit the industry itself by attracting the best qualified students and faculty to prepare mining engineers.[25]

The lack of private support for the University was of long standing. Prior to President Stewart's tenure, the University suffered some ignominious debacles in fundraising. The local paper pointed to failed efforts at courting wealthy potential donors, none more fumbling than naming Oglebay Hall to curry favor with Wheeling tycoon Earl Oglebay in the vain hope that he would remember the University in his will. Similarly, numerous honorary degrees were awarded with the same vain hope in mind, even though, according to public opinion, WVU should better spend its time educating the legislature to University needs. Nevertheless, spirits were lifted by some notable exceptions, such as the gift of retired Beckley coal mine operator Fred G. Wood, whose bequest of 517 acres of coal land provided an estimated $200,000 in royalties each year.[26]

A gift of nearly $4,000 designated for scholarships demonstrated a major obstacle to increasing private giving to WVU. Six donors requested that their gifts be combined and invested in stock of American Telephone and Telegraph Company, but a problem arose because private gifts to the University were routed through the state treasurer's office, making them state funds. Moreover, the state attorney general's office advised Stewart that the West Virginia Constitution prohibited the state government or any of its agencies from becoming a stockholder in any company listed on the stock exchange.[27] For several years discussions had been underway regarding the creation of a private corporation that could operate outside this restriction, and whose sole function would be to raise money to support WVU. On December 3, 1954, the West Virginia University Foundation, Inc., was chartered as a nonprofit corporation, with the University president and members of its Board of Governors making six of the eleven-member board of directors. James M. Guiher, a former president of the alumni association, was appointed president. By the end of the year, contributors had donated $29,800. Stewart reported in 1958 that, "from a long-range standpoint, the creation of the West Virginia University Foundation may prove to be one of the most important steps in the history of the University."[28] Stewart once again proved to be a visionary.

The new attention given to increasing private giving did not mean that President Stewart paid any less attention to pleading the University's case for greater public funding from the legislature. In fact, state appropriations increased dramatically during Stewart's administration from a low of $2.95 million in 1946–1947 to a high of $6.3 million in 1957–1958. Income available to the University from all sources increased during these same years from almost $6 million to $21.7 million.[29]

ADMINISTRATIVE PROBLEMS AND THE BREWTON REPORT

Irvin Stewart left the president's office on June 30, 1958, after twelve years as one of the most successful chief executives who has ever served in that post. During Stewart's term, there were neither other vice presidents nor layers of associate vice presidents. The chain of command dropped from the president directly to the deans. Indeed, this might well be the origin of the long-held faculty view that the University was a "strong dean" institution. Stewart warned that with continued growth a new president less familiar with the institution "should undoubtedly have additional administrative assistance."[30]

In his final report to the WVU Board of Governors, Stewart found it noteworthy that during his tenure West Virginia had been served by four governors—three Democrats and one Republican—and they all "completely respected the position of the University. At no time has there been any suggestion of political interference with the institution." Stewart also claimed, "Only as statutes or the administrative regulations of the executive branch of state government restrict or interfere with the activities and policies of the Board of Governors has this body failed to govern the University in keeping with modern concepts of administration."[31]

While Stewart was generous in his assessment of state leaders, there were, nevertheless, ways in which "legislative or administrative action . . . made the efficient conduct of University operations more difficult." Most problematic was the budget process. For one thing, budget requests were reviewed by the Board of Public Works, which was composed of seven officers elected statewide. None of them were responsible for the University, and none were required to know anything about its operations. "In practice the Board of Public Works gives little support to University requests,"

Stewart explained, and "the University must then persuade legislative committees of its need for larger appropriations than those recommended in the Budget Document." Frequently, only the intervention of the legislature had "saved the University from being seriously handicapped in its operations."[32]

There were other annoyances, such as the state system of central purchasing. Also, requiring advance approval by the state Auditing Board for expenses while traveling outside of West Virginia was at best inconvenient and at worst "an arbitrary substitution of judgment" by a distant group with no particular expertise in making the decision. More serious was the provision that the University could belong to organizations only with prior approval of the Board of Public Works, which arbitrarily rejected association memberships that it had approved for years. "There seems to be no logical reason why the Board of Public Works, whose members are not chosen for their competence in the field of higher education . . . should be given the authority to substitute its judgment for that of the University."[33]

Irvin Stewart claimed that there had never been a hint of political interference in WVU's affairs during his twelve years as president. While it certainly would have been impolitic for him to speak too plainly, there were instances that must have perplexed a president with Stewart's sophistication. He regarded the "most frustrating controls over the University" as those exercised by the state auditor. In April 1950, the state auditor, Edgar B. Sims, attempted to extend his control over the University and precipitated a political struggle by refusing to pay the hospital and medical expenses for injured University athletes from a fund generated from ticket sales and athletic fees. He based his refusal on the argument that it was unconstitutional to use state funds to benefit individuals. The auditor had been overruled by the West Virginia Supreme Court of Appeals in a similar case in 1939, and the high court again ruled against the auditor in May 1950.[34] Yet once again the auditor arbitrarily interfered in University affairs in 1953, when he withheld the WVU's membership dues to the North Central Association of Colleges and Secondary Schools, an organization devoted to maintaining high accreditation standards for its member institutions. WVU had been a member since 1926 and appealed to the Supreme

Court for the right to continue. On June 8, 1954, the court once again ruled unanimously that the auditor had exceeded his authority.[35]

A survey headed by John E. Brewton of the George Peabody College of Teachers and commissioned by the West Virginia legislature was released in 1956. The Brewton Report echoed Stewart's assessment that the accounting system governing WVU violated the standards established by the National Committee on Financial Reports for Colleges and Universities. "No other state of the Union," the report asserted, "has so many agencies checking on the expenditure of so little money," and "no other state spends as large a proportion of the tax dollar to assure honesty and efficiency." While the legislation of 1947 removed the University from the administrative jurisdiction of the State Board of Education, "it has left it subject to the complicated machinery of state government" involving the state budget director, the Board of Public Works, and the state auditor.[36] These offices "should not, as they now do, concern themselves with the appropriateness of individual items of expenditure authorized by the proper officers in the institutions which compose the state system of higher education." These practices stemmed from "defects in the laws and administrative regulation rather than from the officiousness or malice of individuals." Nevertheless, the report concluded that the effect on the institutions of higher learning was to limit the effectiveness of governing boards and administrative officers.[37]

The Brewton Report had much to say about state agencies unrelated to education that nevertheless exerted so much influence over higher education. The 1947 legislature had removed fiscal responsibilities for education from the Board of Control, but the power was merely transferred to the Board of Public Works, which consisted of the governor, secretary of state, auditor, superintendent of schools, treasurer, attorney general, and commissioner of agriculture. Moreover, the Board of Public Works submitted all budgets to the legislature, which exerted line-item control over expenditures for higher education. The approval of the Board of Public Works was required for the legislature to increase higher education budgets, and the governor could not veto a budget approved by the board. "The Board of Public Works obviously tries to make discriminating and professional judgments in the field of education where it has no specific competence," the report concluded.[38]

The Brewton Report supported Stewart's claims by charging, like the earlier Strayer Report (1945), that higher education in the Mountain State was "not likely to conform to superior standards until its governing and administrative machinery is adequate and sufficiently permanent in character to plan continuously for the changing economic and social needs of the State." Brewton claimed in effect that the state wielded a heavy hand on control, but offered only a light touch on financing for higher education. "For at least a generation many citizens of the State have maintained that the Legislature does not provide adequate funds for the University and the state colleges," the report concluded.[39]

Brewton recommended that the Board of Public Works should abandon its practice of limiting the budgets to what it regarded as the University's "proper share of anticipated state revenue." Instead, it should evaluate budget requests according to the actual needs of the institution, and with revenues comparable with resources available to higher education in neighboring states.[40] Brewton found it a matter of concern that a large percentage of the state's youth moved to other states for higher education or employment and did not return. Exporting so much of the state's intellectual talent would inevitably have dire consequences for West Virginia. The consultants' analysis of per capita annual income suggested that West Virginia was not a particularly poor state, even though its income was "slightly below the national average."[41] Nor were the expenditures excessively heavy relative to West Virginia's ability to support higher education. The report concluded that the wisdom of investing in education was inescapable since its college-educated population could be expected to lead the state through its problems.[42]

The second important recommendation in the Brewton Report emphasized the need to rectify another weakness in the system of higher education in West Virginia. Because the system was governed by two separate boards, the inevitable result was a lack of coordination and centralized planning, as well as a competition among the institutions of higher learning that created "wasteful duplication or failure to provide needed educational services." State colleges might "fear domination by the University," the report acknowledged, but friends of the University might also "fear that the best interests of that institution will be submerged in the total state system of higher education. They may also feel that the limited financial resources available for higher education will be spread so thin that it will be impossible to support the program of the University which must necessarily be more expensive than that of the state colleges." Brewton was exactly right, and WVU supporters rejected any suggestion that these fears should be laid aside in the interests of a "common good" that was fractured by sectional and political factionalism. Brewton was also right to recognize that such a goal would require "political statesmanship of a high order," and friends of the University had no faith that this was something they could risk.[43] In fact, after a single board of regents serving all higher education was established in 1969, the University's great fear of homogenization into the larger system would be realized.

STEWART RESIGNS AND ELVIS STAHR IS HIRED

Irvin Stewart resigned the presidency effective June 30, 1957. Heralded as one of the University's greatest presidents, there is no question that his tenure marks the emergence of WVU as a significant state university. Since 1952, when the Board of Governors passed a resolution permitting an individual to hold an administrative and faculty post simultaneously, Stewart had also been a professor of political science. Upon retirement from the presidency, Stewart became a full-time faculty member in that department. In the following decades only two other presidents, Neil Bucklew and David Hardesty, remained at the University as faculty members.[44]

With the benefit of historical perspective, it is clear that Stewart's presidency was one of those watershed periods, a new plateau in the ascendency of WVU. But contemporaries also understood its importance. Commenting on Stewart's tenure as president, the *Morgantown Post* recognized that a unique period in the University's history had just come to a close and pointed out that the physical plant had doubled in size during Stewart's twelve-year tenure, even as other projects were still in progress. These developments were supplemented by a corresponding growth in student enrollment and in the number of faculty who taught them. Even more significant, the *Post* opined, was the elevation in attitude, confidence, and optimism about the future of the University that Stewart instilled in staff, the public, and legislators. Harold Shamberger admired Stewart as the man who turned WVU into a university, and made it "think like a university."[45]

In his customary way, Stewart deflected the praise to an "outstanding" Board of Governors, an able and dedicated faculty, responsive students, alumni, and the "mounting public realization" of the University's growing influence and importance in the development of the entire state. While the timing of Stewart's presidency was propitious, coming at the end of World War II and the postwar boom, Stewart himself must be credited with the University's "great leap forward." With the addition of the new campuses and the timetables set for construction of facilities for agriculture, engineering, and the Medical Center, Stewart believed that the time to step aside had arrived, leaving to his replacement the task of implementing the next stage in the University's growth.[46]

Elvis J. Stahr Jr. succeeded Irvin Stewart on February 1, 1959. In his early forties, Stahr was relatively young but nevertheless had extensive experience in university as well as federal government administration. Arriving in West Virginia just as the state was solidly entrenched in what became a long-term economic crisis, the time was not auspicious for a new president seeking to elevate the University to national recognition. The 1950s marked the beginning of a long decline in coal-mining employment, as the industry replaced manpower with machinery. The out-migration that had begun during World War II accelerated as unemployment rose, and West Virginia's population fell by almost one-quarter of a million during this period.[47]

The state's deepening economic recession and the negative national image of West Virginia were issues that the University's new president was forced to confront. The University's fate was affected by these circumstances, but Stahr was responsible for maintaining the forward progress initiated under Stewart. The financial resources to support a student population that had doubled under Stewart, and to pay the larger and higher caliber faculty necessary to staff the modern university envisioned by Stewart and Stahr, were in critically short supply. The emerging university in postwar America, often referred to by educators as the "multiversity," was, unlike the prewar university, very large, with many component schools and colleges. The "multiversity" was expected to perform widely diverse functions emphasizing not just teaching but also major research projects and the extension of its expertise in the service of society. The money required to elevate WVU to the level of its peer land-grant universities was unlikely to come from the legislature in Charleston, so, like its peers, WVU would try to take advantage of the opportunity presented by the change from the Republican administration of Dwight Eisenhower to the Democratic administration of John F. Kennedy, which emphasized using federal money to rebuild American prosperity.

Both Presidents Stewart and Stahr were consummate Washington insiders. Irvin Stewart returned to the faculty in 1957, but he had high-level administrative experience when he came to the University. Before he retired in 1967, he took a leave in 1962–1963 to serve as the first director of telecommunications management in the executive branch. Stahr, too, had valuable administrative experience and contacts in Washington. A native of Kentucky, he was a 1936 graduate of the University of Kentucky and attended Oxford University as a Rhodes Scholar, earning a law degree there. Returning to the United States, he attended Yale University and earned a certificate in the Chinese language. During World War II, he served with the U.S. Army in North Africa and China between 1942 and 1946, rising to the rank of lieutenant colonel. After the war, he lived in New York and practiced law on Wall Street before accepting a position as professor and dean at the University of Kentucky College of Law, while later serving as provost at the University of Pittsburgh. During the Korean War, Stahr served as a special assistant to the secretary of the Army, and in 1956 became executive director of the President's Committee on Education beyond the High School. In that capacity, he met extensively with college and university administrators, and from this position he was selected to become vice chancellor for professional education at the University of Pittsburgh. Stahr was serving in that capacity when he assumed the presidency of West Virginia University on February

1, 1959. A man of extraordinary talent, Stahr was tapped by President John F. Kennedy to serve as secretary of the Army in 1961–1962 during the Berlin Wall and Bay of Pigs crises. Subsequently, he returned to university life, serving as president of Indiana University from 1968 to 1981, and as president of the National Audubon Society from 1968 to 1981, where he played a major role in the growing field of environmental protection.[48]

Stewart's and Stahr's extensive experience and contacts in Washington, combined with an activist Democratic administration in Washington that was willing to stimulate growth and combat poverty in Appalachia, strategically positioned the University to take advantage of the funding opportunities provided by the federal government. Stewart regretted that the University was not able to participate in federal funding available for science research in the forties and fifties, and he fully supported Stahr's strategy to accelerate the development of research so WVU could compete for federal research funds.

A UNIVERSITY IN FACT AS WELL AS NAME

President Stahr was in full accord with his predecessor in believing that the perception of WVU's relevance to the lives of West Virginians must undergo a dramatic change if the University was ever to become "a university in fact" and not just in name. During his brief tenure, the new president seldom lost the opportunity to make the case. If the people of West Virginia did not want a university of which they were proud, Stahr asserted, then "they do not want me, because I shall devote all of my energies to continuing the upward momentum begun under Dr. Irvin Stewart's great leadership."[49] Elvis Stahr assumed full command of the University on February 2, 1959. Traveling throughout the state, introducing himself to various constituencies, he emphasized the same message everywhere he went. His assessment of the problems faced by West Virginia and its university were honestly and forcefully delivered, but always from a sympathetic and optimistic perspective. His message was clear: all West Virginians should support the University because the fates of the state and WVU were bound together.

In a WVU Day speech delivered before the Kanawha County Alumni Association in Charleston, President Stahr declared that there were "certain principles regarding the University" that, if adopted by West Virginians, would benefit them and the University but, if rejected, would cause both to suffer. The first principle was that "the future of West Virginia will depend very greatly upon the future of West Virginia University." Not only was WVU the state's sole university, but it was also a land-grant university. Therefore, it would greatly influence the quality of education in the state from primary school through graduate school. The University was the principal provider of opportunity for ambitious and talented youth, and the only institution in the state that trained people for the professions. WVU was dedicated to unbiased research into the agricultural, business, scientific, political, social, professional, cultural, educational, and technological problems confronting West Virginia.[50]

The second principle, according to President Stahr, was that WVU was largely supported by tax dollars; therefore, it was "responsible to all of the people of West Virginia," not to a single agency, political party, or interest group. Consequently, the University's programs must serve the best long-term interests of the entire state, and the use of state funds should be dictated by good educational decisions rather than political demands. "This principle has been violated many times in the 92-year history" of WVU, and was still not firmly observed, he informed the Kanawha County alumni. "It ought to be evident that bureaucratic regulation of higher education is the last form of government regulation which the United States of America or any American State should tolerate. Yet these simple propositions are apparently not yet accepted in West Virginia." Stahr emphasized that he was not referring to the amount of appropriations from tax revenues, which was obviously the province of lawmakers, but rather "government dictation of precisely what may or may not be done with other income of the University," and the "dictation from the executive branch of exactly how funds appropriated for University purposes shall be spent." Early in his term, Stahr dropped this emphasis, possibly because it did not play well among legislators who determined the University's annual appropriation. In its place, he focused on the strategic role of WVU as a land-grant in solving society's problems and stimulating economic development. This emphasis became a staple talking point for every subsequent president.[51]

Success in these aspirations required that the state create certain conditions, the most important being that "the University really must be a community of scholars, not a mere collection of 'employees with degrees.' The faculty is the heart of any university. If there is a great faculty, there will be a great university." Higher education had long anticipated a "tidal wave" of students in the 1960s when the post–World War II "baby-boom" generation reached college age. President Stahr pointed out that WVU would experience the same inundation, and there would not be "enough high-caliber teaching and research talent in this country to go around!" At a meeting with the Board of Public Works, he warned that West Virginia was at the crossroads now in the race for competent faculty. He claimed that WVU could "move up" in quality if it retained its most talented faculty and hired superior talent when replacements were required. But this moving up required an investment by the state, without which WVU not only would be unable to take this leap forward, but also would lose its best faculty to other institutions. WVU already possessed most of the attractions necessary for the University to retain and hire the best faculty, but it did not offer competitive salaries and benefits.[52]

It would be interesting to know what the political figures assembled to hear Stahr's presentation thought when he declared that WVU fell "seriously short" of its competitors in the area of "compensation of faculty, and the tools, services and facilities provided for them to work with." West Virginia's system of higher education was woefully underfunded for meeting the challenges of the "new era," as Stahr testified before the Board of Public Works in December 1958. Worse yet, West Virginia was losing ground: In 1951–1952, it ranked thirty-fourth among the forty-eight states in enrollment, and thirty-third in current income (from all sources) per student; four years later, in 1955–1956, the state ranked thirty-fourth in enrollment but had fallen to forty-fourth in current income per student available to its institutions of higher learning. During that same four-year period, the number of students in West Virginia attending college actually increased 35 percent, but current income per higher education student fell by 15 percent. Meanwhile, the average income per student for the United States grew by 8 percent.[53]

Comparing WVU with other universities revealed even more starkly the challenges facing the University. In 1955–1956, WVU's total current income per student was only $1,315, compared with the national average for universities of $1,570. Stahr focused on faculty salaries as the most critical way of measuring WVU's competitiveness among its peers. Although the salary increases appropriated between 1954 and 1958 helped WVU to improve its salary scale, the sad fact was that "even though we gained on ourselves, we lost ground nationally." That gap, furthermore, was between WVU and the national average, not the top of the scale. The University was locked in a perennial struggle to convince legislators that an increase in appropriations was necessary just to maintain its comparatively low ranking, while legislators were looking for ways to cut expenditures.[54]

President Stahr incorporated into nearly every speech before alumni and civic groups a plea for their help in educating West Virginians and their representatives about the special role of WVU, and in understanding what distinguished WVU from the state's four-year colleges. The public simply was not aware that education was "the goose that lays the golden eggs," a phrase he often employed. Therefore, in a time of declining revenues, cuts to higher education were counterproductive, akin to eating the "seed corn," he told a group of Fairmont businessmen.[55]

WVU's success rested on the University's ability to counter the politicians' impulse to treat every institution of higher education equally. The problem with this approach was that WVU was not just a "great big college" but rather seventeen colleges and major divisions, none of which were even remotely in competition with any other institution in the state. The University's competition was with other American universities, industry, government, and the professions for "top-notch human talent." In West Virginia only the University competes for "the kinds of physicists and chemists and mathematicians and physiologists and economists who can conduct doctoral programs." Supply and demand controls this competition, as it does throughout the marketplace, so "historians are not as well rewarded as atomic scientists." Therefore, a 5 percent across-the-board increase to all

English teachers might be progress, but all that would do for biochemists or research engineers is to make them "smile—and leave. It certainly won't attract anyone to replace him," President Stahr cautioned. And yet, in 1960, all of the seventeen divisions within the University combined received a smaller operating increase from state appropriations than the other ten state colleges.[56] Expanding on his predecessor's message, President Stahr articulated what would become the University's approach to relations with the state colleges and the sectional politics they channeled, emphasizing cooperation even when it was not reciprocated.

ADMINISTRATIVE CHANGES AND STAHR'S RESIGNATION

Stahr also attempted to modernize the University's administrative structure. He reorganized the president's office, appointing Harold J. Shamberger, former member of the WVU Bureau of Government Research, to the new post of assistant to the president. John F. Golay was recruited from Roosevelt University, where he was dean of faculties, to become the first dean of the graduate school. Stahr had begun to reorganize the president's office before his abrupt departure. He had appointed Golay dean of the graduate school and had suggested that he be given larger administrative duties. Stahr left before Golay arrived in Morgantown, however, and President Paul Miller determined Golay's duties.[57] On April 13, 1960, the Board of Governors redesignated this position "Provost of the University," and Golay was appointed to the post. Stahr had held such a position at the University of Kentucky, and he thought it was suited to his vision for WVU. Stahr told an interviewer that he was trying to bring in new blood to invigorate the University and jolt it out of its stodgy, old boys culture. Stahr also created the office of personnel and a student counseling service headed by James Carruth, associate professor of psychology, as its first director. A school of nursing was officially established in 1960, as was the new dental school. A new men's dormitory was also completed in the fall of 1959, and contracts were let for new apartments for young faculty and graduate students. Engineering and agriculture buildings were under construction during Stahr's tenure and completed shortly after his resignation in 1961.[58]

Speaking to the New York Alumni Chapter in February 1960, Stahr cited the important developments initiated at WVU during the previous year. One of the most important was laying the groundwork for a "modern development program," that would place a high priority on raising funds from sources other than state government. These included alumni, corporations, foundations, businesses, parents, and citizens friendly to the University. In the summer of 1959 Donovan Bond, associate professor of journalism, became the University's first full-time director of development, and in January 1960 a Joint Development Council was authorized with representatives from the Board of Governors, Alumni Association, the Loyalty Permanent Endowment Fund, and the WVU Foundation. The Council immediately began to plan for its first annual Greater University Drive, as well as a major campaign to be launched simultaneously with the University's centennial celebration in 1967.[59] It had been a long time since state universities could operate solely on state appropriations and student fees, and yet WVU was one of the last to establish a well-organized program. A development office to systematically encourage private giving would bear fruit in years to come, marking another of those initiatives that would eventually transform the University into a modern institution.

The University's new leader was off to a great start, but supporters were shocked to learn that President-elect John F. Kennedy had nominated Elvis Stahr to be Secretary of the Army under new Secretary of Defense Robert McNamara. The timing was inopportune. WVU was in a period of rapid transition with the new Medical Center becoming operational, the agriculture and engineering buildings on the Evansdale campus just about ready to open, a major construction program still underway, and the University's 1961–1962 budget proposal soon to come up for discussion in legislative committees. All of this prompted the local paper to declare, "West Virginia needs Elvis Stahr as president of the University more than the United States needs him as Secretary of the Army." Stahr explained that he had not sought the position but felt it was his duty to serve his country when called. He initially agreed to accept the Board of Governors' request to take a leave of absence rather than resign; however, on June 6, 1961, he submitted his resignation on the grounds that he did not know how long he would be gone, and it was not fair to either the University or the government for him to continue in a "lame duck" status.[60]

The Board of Governors turned to Clyde Colson to serve as acting president. Reluctantly, he consented, but at the same time continued to serve as dean of the College of Law. Colson disliked public speaking, and being on the road took a toll on his health. Also, he had suffered a heart attack in March 1958, just a few months prior to his previous term as acting president between the Stewart and Stahr administrations. With the state in a serious recession and the legislature short on money, Colson sacrificed his health by accepting the responsibility.[61]

MARSHALL BECOMES A UNIVERSITY

No sooner had Elvis Stahr left for Washington than he returned to West Virginia, in January 1961, to speak with legislative leaders against a surprise bid by Marshall College to become Marshall University. His advice was framed by the same principle that WVU had been struggling to maintain in one form or another for a very long time: West Virginia only needed one excellent university and would not benefit from two mediocre universities. In the end, however, the legislature once again splintered into sectional interest groups on a matter of higher education policy. Most of the state's newspapers came out against changing Marshall's status, according to the *Morgantown Post,* although the *Charleston Daily Mail* and the *Huntington Daily Dispatch* reliably supported Marshall's bid. As March 1, the moment of decision, neared, the *Morgantown Post* claimed that the legislators who supported the change had entered into an alliance with those who also wished to submit to voters a liquor-by-the-drink amendment to the constitution. According to the *Post,* an alliance of the "wets" and those in the southern section of the state who desired a university in Huntington gave credence to the charge that the decision confronting the legislators was: "Is it to be Bourbon University or Marshall by the Drink?"[62] Worse, the *Post* declared, if the "Marshall blitzers have misled any West Virginians into believing the name-changing maneuver is anything less than a well-organized scheme to scuttle the state's system of higher education for the interests of Huntington the evidence now shows the lengths to which the campaigners would go to achieve their ends."[63]

On March 1, 1961, the legislature once again gave good government a bad name by approving Marshall's bid to become a "university." While the president of Marshall claimed that he was not interested in a large institution, the Morgantown paper scoffed: "Despite repeated statements that Marshall wants to be only what it already is, but under the label of university rather than college, Marshallites will be most unhappy and most frustrated if this proves to be true."[64] If there was any question about whether the legislature knew the difference between a university and a college, it was thrown into doubt by this decision. But this was only the beginning. Over the ensuing decades many of the state colleges would be allowed to take the name "university," thereby denuding any specific meaning of the term. WVU would have to choose another avenue to defend its status as the state's land-grant public university.

SECTIONAL POLITICS AND THE WVU MEDICAL CENTER

The campaign of Presidents Stewart and Stahr to establish a statewide identity for WVU undoubtedly was achieved with the Medical Center. At the same time, the construction of the new Medical Center and the creation of a full medical school exemplify the difficulty WVU has experienced in efficiently managing the institution without political interference and inadequate state funding.

The first class to graduate from WVU's four-year degree program in medicine received their degrees at commencement ceremonies on June 4, 1962. These fifteen newly minted physicians entered the two-year basic sciences segment in 1958 and shared the grounds of the medical center with construction equipment and noise at the University hospital, where they would complete the two-year clinical program. With completion of the hospital in 1960, the new WVU Medical Center occupied more than one million square feet of space. A new era in health care for West Virginians began.

Historically, medical students in WVU's two-year program transferred to other medical schools that would accept them to complete their degrees.

Under an arrangement worked out in 1903, WVU students finished the last two years of training at the College of Physicians and Surgeons of Baltimore (subsequently the University of Maryland School of Medicine) and received MD degrees from both schools. They could, however, choose to take all four years of training in Baltimore, in which case their degrees were awarded from that institution. A similar program for women was arranged with the Woman's Medical College of Baltimore, but it appears that none participated. Phoebia Moore, of Marlinton, West Virginia, is acknowledged to be the first woman to obtain the MD through the WVU College of Medicine, but she transferred to Bennett Medical College in Chicago, rather than the Baltimore school, where she earned the MD in 1903.[65]

In 1912, the arrangement with the medical school in Baltimore was terminated, and WVU's two-year medical students transferred to the Medical College of Virginia at Richmond. The plan was amended in 1943 so that twenty to twenty-five seats were reserved in its junior class for WVU students. This arrangement prevailed until 1960. Many states without medical schools regarded the plan as a model for solving the problem of high costs for medical education. Approximately 1,600 students graduated from WVU's two-year program, and, although an accurate count is not available, it is estimated that a significant percentage of them went on to earn their MD degrees. Kenneta Shaffer was the first woman to graduate from WVU's four-year program in 1962. Before her, seventy women had completed the two-year program.[66]

It was a decades-long struggle, but the campaign by the state's medical professionals for a four-year medical school finally gained some traction in 1948 when the treasury showed a rare surplus. After extensive planning, the Stewart administration proposed a budget for 1949 that included $17 million, most of which was designated for the sciences, engineering, and medicine. The University's plan received a warm reception in the legislature but was stopped cold when the West Virginia Medical Association presented a proposal in October 1948 for the WVU School of Medicine to be upgraded from a two-year to a four-year program, and for the creation of a dental school. The proposal called for an immediate appropriation of $6.3 million to fund the schools and, more alarmingly, called for the new schools to be located in Charleston. President Stewart was skeptical of the proposal's premise that West Virginians were "entitled to receive a medical education in this state to the same extent as training is now given those seeking an education in other professions and businesses." He reminded members of the Board of Governors that applications to medical schools nationally outstripped acceptances. Attending medical school in West Virginia would not encourage students to remain in the state after completing the MD because the location of the internship was a more important factor in that decision.[67]

The idea of a state medical center caught the imagination of West Virginian legislators, however, and there was little the University could do to alter their enthusiasm. President Stewart asserted that state appropriations were already inadequate to fund the University's building program, and further investment in the medical college would endanger the quality of the engineering and agricultural programs. The president's warning fell on deaf ears. Failing to convince either the legislators or the powerful Medical Association, Stewart took a heroic public stand for financial solvency by declaring that the University could not assume the responsibility of a four-year program without assurances beforehand of a stable funding source.[68] With both political parties supporting the expanded medical school during the 1948 election year, Stewart publicly remonstrated that other established areas of expertise at the University, such as engineering and agriculture, were important to the state as well and should receive adequate financial support before WVU took on a new medical school. Of further importance for the history of the institution, on January 27, 1949, the Board of Governors issued a public statement supporting a unified campus, declaring that "all parts of the University should be located at the seat of the University in Morgantown."[69]

Driven by sectionalist politics rather than expert advice, the location of the new facility quickly drew the University into the quagmire of higher education politics. The state's newspapers were soon discoursing on the subject. The *Morgantown Post* editor, Brooks Cottle, steadfastly loyal to community interests, claimed that new state university medical schools were rarely established in a city other than the home of the university's main campus. Moreover, no city in West Virginia was large enough to provide sufficient clinical hospital facilities for a University medical school. Other local papers, of course, supported their perceived community interests. The *Raleigh Register* argued that the new school should be on the main campus in Morgantown, but otherwise Beckley had ample clinical facilities with two general hospitals, a veteran's hospital, and a tuberculosis sanitarium. The Huntington and Wheeling newspapers also proclaimed their cities much better choices than Charleston, and, naturally, Charleston found no reason to question the West Virginia Medical Association's choice of the capital city.[70]

Inevitably, Morgantown supporters were chagrined in January 1949 by the introduction of bills to construct the medical school in Charleston rather than on the main campus. The editor of Morgantown's paper editorialized that, when legislators regained their composure from seeing a budgetary surplus and calculated the long-term costs of selecting an off-campus site, the issue of locating the school in another city would evaporate.[71] Since the issue of location played directly into the sectional politics that dominated West Virginia, all the talk led to yet another political stalemate in the legislature. A joint public hearing convened on February 8, 1949, at the behest of the medical and health committees of the two legislative houses. All of the various factions were represented, as well as medical experts from out-of-state. Predictably, no clear consensus emerged, so an interim joint committee was established to report back in time to be included in Governor Okey Patteson's 1951 budget. President Stewart and representatives of the medical, dental, and nursing associations served on an advisory board.[72]

It was reported that the state medical association had dropped its insistence on Charleston, and the state dental association had made no comment on location, but the state nurses' association opposed separating the medical center from the main campus. Moreover, the state chamber of commerce called into question the wisdom of expenditures on a medical school when the current arrangement worked so well. Even the Charleston Chamber of Commerce announced that a medical school would not necessarily be a community asset, and that the decision about location should reflect the best interests of the state. WVU was disappointed when three of the five out-of-state experts in medical education consulted by the interim committee believed it preferable for medical schools to be located in metropolitan areas. A fourth expert was unable to participate, leaving only one who spoke in favor of location on the main campus. On the other hand, University proponents were heartened by the unanimous November 19, 1950 decision of the House of Delegates of the West Virginia Medical Association, made up of twenty-nine county and regional societies, to withhold a recommendation on the location.[73]

Governor Patteson addressed the legislature on January 16, 1951, urging approval of House Bill 477, which authorized the creation of a new medical school and a penny-per-bottle tax on soft drinks to finance it. The nation was rearming for the impending Korean War, and it was expected that a serious shortage of medical personnel would ensue. The governor pointed out the urgent need in West Virginia, citing statistics that revealed only one physician per 1,400 residents in the state, and reminded the legislators that, because of inadequate staffing, the Veterans Administration hospitals in Beckley and Clarksburg stood idle and an entire wing of the Huntington, VA hospital was closed. Patteson observed that the federal government would probably supply some of the funding to the states through grants as an incentive to construct new medical schools. In addition, the new "pop tax" would generate $3 million to fund the medical school. As an encouragement, bottlers were permitted to raise the price for a bottled drink from five to ten cents. The University reiterated its position that the funding must be assured, and the resulting legislation dictated that before the tax could be repealed a new source must first be made available to fund the school. This left only the issue of location to be resolved by the end of January 1951.[74]

The joint committee studying the measure decided on January 17, 1951, that a four-year medical school, a dental school, and a nursing school would be operated at the new medical center, but the committee split evenly over where it would be located; five favored Morgantown and five preferred Charleston. The split within the joint committee, reflecting a similar split in the legislature, where the house leaned toward Charleston and the senate favored Morgantown, made it impossible to render a recommendation. The division spurred the Morgantown proponents to even greater efforts. On January 29, 1951, State Senator Don J. Eddy of Monongalia County presented the report of Dr. Alan Gregg of the Rockefeller Foundation's medical division. Dr. Gregg was a member of the expert panel from out-of-state but had been unable to participate in the initial round of consulting. His report strongly supported locating medical schools on the main campus of their home universities, where they could interact with colleagues in related disciplines and administrative efficiencies were more likely to be achieved. He opposed locating medical schools in large cities because he believed that conflict with powerful professional city leaders was impossible to avoid and that doctors would be attracted to specializations that offered greater financial rewards. He brushed aside the reports of the other doctors consulted by the interim committee, asserting that doctors needed to be acclimated to and content with rural and small town life.[75]

By this time most newspapers had shifted their support to constructing the medical school on the main campus. There is little doubt, however, that the legislature avoided a potential deadlock between the house of delegates and the senate when, on March 9, 1951, it approved the new medical school and the funding mechanism but left it to Governor Patteson to decide the location by July 1. Some of the Morgantown contingent worried that the governor favored Charleston, but, even though he did not enjoy being "the goat," the governor accepted the responsibility. He wanted to ensure that something so important as the medical school would not go down to defeat due to sectional partisanship and political stalemate. Patteson had, in fact, not committed himself on the issue of location, and he promised that he would consult widely before making a decision, one which he promised would be in the best interest of the entire state. The Morgantown delegation met with the governor on May 7 and came away with the sense that sectional politics would not be a decisive factor. Because of the careful preparation that went into the task and the fact that he had placed himself in a "no win" political situation of disappointing at least one faction, most citizens believed that he would make his decision on objective grounds. Indeed, Patteson announced that he would not run for a second term as governor. The governor's closest advisers were convinced that the governor knew he was committing "political suicide" by choosing Morgantown, but that he believed he had made the right decision for the entire state.[76]

When Governor Patteson publicly announced his decision in favor of the Morgantown campus on June 30, 1951, he also released a lengthy report outlining eighteen reasons supporting his decision. He had been "working diligently on this problem for many weeks" before finally deciding that Morgantown was the most appropriate location for the new school. It had been public policy since WVU was established in 1867 to maintain a unified university on its main campus in Morgantown. When the College of Law and the School of Music were established, similar disputes occurred before political leaders resolved that they should be located on the main campus in order to integrate them with other departments. The governor observed that the same held true for the medical school: "Any dismemberment at this time would be a violation of almost a century old policy. We must bear in mind that the University, to be successfully and efficiently operated, must function as a unified institution." Like most politicians with a vision of a unified state, this perspective prompted Governor Patteson to see the tendency of West Virginia to fly apart by centrifugal force into its respective sections. The governor, therefore, was also aware of the danger of fragmenting WVU. He understood the argument that, if the medical school were established elsewhere, the state pharmaceutical association would soon lobby for removal of the Pharmacy School too. Next might come the suggestion that the College of Agriculture be relocated to the Eastern Panhandle, where the best farms were located. It was an issue that would reappear time and again.[77]

Written like a legal brief, the governor's report enumerated a long list of reasons why state university medical schools across the country were generally located on the main campuses, and how the evidence supported this arrangement as the most cost-effective organization. He was also impressed by the data, which demonstrated not only that medical schools were more expensive to operate in large cities than in small cities, but also that they were costlier when separated from their home campuses. Wherever medical schools were located, they required their own teaching hospitals to supplement basic science buildings and other facilities. It was most essential for a poor state like West Virginia to use its resources as economically as possible; therefore, Morgantown was the most logical place for the new medical school. There, basic science courses were already available, and an extensive library and laboratory space already existed. Moreover, located within a reasonable distance from Morgantown were Hopemont Sanitarium for tuberculosis patients in Terra Alta, a veterans hospital in Clarksburg, Weston State Hospital for the mentally ill, an emergency hospital in Fairmont, and a chronic disease hospital in Wheeling. All of these unique facilities were located much closer to Morgantown than Charleston.[78]

The newspapers quickly accommodated themselves to Governor Patteson's discussed decision in a statewide radio address broadcast on July 2, 1951. The University took immediate steps to create the new medical center. The Monongalia County Court transferred 85 acres, which, when added to an adjoining 55 acres already owned by the University next to the Evansdale campus, provided 140 acres for construction of the new facility. A building committee composed of medical school faculty consulted with a variety of experts in the health professions. An architectural consulting firm, Schmidt, Garden, and Eriksen of Chicago, was retained to draw up a preliminary plan for the site, and a hospital consulting firm from Minneapolis was contracted to conduct a survey of the state's health care needs.[79]

The plan that emerged called for a medical center that included a basic sciences building. It would house the first two years of the medical program, the dental school, the school of nursing, the college of pharmacy, a medical library, and an auditorium. The teaching hospital would sit next to the basic sciences building and provide 520 beds, with its outpatient clinics being designed to handle 45,000 visits a year. The Board of Governors declined an offer to use Monongalia General Hospital as part of the Medical Center. Construction of the basic sciences building began in the summer of 1954 and was completed in the summer of 1957. Construction of the hospital began that same summer and was completed in the spring of 1960.[80]

The project cost a total of $31 million, all but $5.6 million of which was covered by the "pop tax." The wisdom of President Stewart's stipulation that the cost of running a medical center should not diminish the University's general budget had been realized, since construction costs over the course of the nine-year project never exceeded the revenues generated by the soft-drink tax. The alternative, dissolving the costs of operating the medical school into the general budget of higher education, would have resulted in "a degraded system of higher education for generations to come." Stewart concluded that the people would not allow this to happen.[81]

Maintaining the tax became an ongoing struggle for WVU, as the bottling industry attempted to eliminate the tax from the state's annual budget. The West Virginia Bottlers Association's complaint that the tax was discriminatory and harmful to business was honed over the years to focus on reforming the tax system to make it "fair and equitable." WVU also refined a well-tempered defense of the tax, claiming that without the tax or an equivalent substitute the bottlers would destroy medical education in the state, and with it the opportunity for West Virginians to enjoy adequate health care services. Referring to a "war chest campaign" launched by the bottling industry to repeal the soft-drink tax in 1953, Stewart declared it to be nothing more than a "campaign to kill the medical education program." The tax generated $3 million annually, and the program cost $4.25 million per year. Stewart concluded, "Our efforts to get adequate support for regular University operations during these postwar years have not been completely successful. To throw upon the University the task of getting a 75 percent increase in its annual appropriations for its resident teaching operations in order to support the medical education program would be to do a vain thing."[82]

Although the four-year medical school and the new Medical Center complex was a truly transformative addition to the University, the method by which it was financed, and the political and economic environment in which it operated, handicapped the medical center from realizing its full potential from its inception. The tax on soft drinks, including the syrups and dry mixtures from which they were made, was set at one cent per sixteen-fluid-ounce bottle. The tax did not increase with inflation. Soft drinks were excluded from the sales tax until 1988, when the sales tax rose from 5 to 6 percent and soft drinks were included. The proceeds generated by the soft-drink portion of the sales tax, $1 million per year, were dedicated to the

WVU Mary Babb Randolph Cancer Center, and the remainder went to the higher education salary schedule. Meanwhile, the one cent per bottle "pop tax" remained in effect and did not increase with inflation in the decades following its inception in 1951. From that year until 1960, when the Medical Center was completed, the "pop tax" paid most of the construction and operating costs, including salaries for the Schools of Medicine, Dentistry, and Nursing. It became increasingly clear, however, that the tax would not be sufficient in the long term.[83]

The University hospital, in particular, was affected by funding restrictions imposed by the state. The annual budget provided by the legislature merely granted the authority to spend money that the hospital generated from patient billing for expenses such as salaries, fringe benefits, utilities, and maintenance; deficits were made up from the Medical Center's annual academic budget. The financial pressures were aggravated over the years by inflation, charity cases, and downturns in the economy, but still the "pop tax" did not increase. Moreover, in the early days, many people were under the impression that treatment at the University hospital was free. In 1961 neurosurgeon Dr. G. Robert Nugent stated, "Everyone worked very hard in the early days and we were strictly service oriented. By that I mean, we weren't concerned about making money or even, frankly, billing patients. Many patients were not billed and this led to the myth that was quite prevalent at that time that this was a hospital built for the citizens of West Virginia, offering them free care. Some people, when they did get a bill, were very upset because they understood that this was a free facility." The business office was not organized to bill patients effectively, but the staff looked beyond this shortcoming in order to get the hospital into operation. "Believe it or not," Dr. Nugent claimed, only one woman worked in the business office, and among her other duties she billed the patients. "She operated the whole billing process and she kept the funds that came in a shoe box in her bottom drawer. I remember seeing the box." By 1961, the medical center had become a $9–$10 million per year operation, but "it grew from the shoe box in Mrs. Martin's desk."[84]

Another obstacle to be overcome was the fact that the hospital, like the rest of the University, did not have the legal authority to set aside funds for future purposes such as expansion or new technology. Because the University did not have bonding authority, tax support for capital improvements was required, which seriously hampered the institution's ability to modernize. The only dependable aspect of state funding was that appropriations would be inadequate. After years of unfunded improvements, the University hospital began to decline and was on the verge of losing its accreditation in the early 1980s. Hospital renovations were estimated at $50 million in 1984, with long periods during which entire sections would be closed and generate no revenues. The hospital's board of directors was able to undertake the necessary upgrades only after the West Virginia legislature divested itself of the University hospital, the first such case of its kind.[85]

In an address before the West Virginia State Medical Association in August 1963, President Miller declared that the 1950s would likely be remembered as "the time of pyramiding obligations for American universities." He was convinced that "no state university in the land moved so far relatively and so fast as did West Virginia University in the past fifteen years. I say this realizing I had nothing to do with it." The 1960s saw the emergence of a "new kind of university," one capable of understanding itself within society. Realigning the University's mission with the new realities was, Miller declared, what his administration was trying to accomplish. In retrospect, it was clear that the construction of WVU Medical Center was "perhaps the act of greatest scope and fortitude in the history of West Virginia and the largest single commitment to serve West Virginians on the part of the State University." Completion of the center represented the capacity of West Virginians to push aside "the empty objectives of sectionalism" in order to advance the best interests of the people as a whole. Only six years earlier the basic science section had become operational; now it served 600 students who hailed from nearly every county in the state, twenty-three other states, and five other countries. Grants for research totaled nearly $1 million. The University hospital would not be fully operational until 1965, and it had already treated more than 25,000 patients, handled 25,000 emergency room patients, performed 6,000 surgical operations, and delivered 1,500 babies.[86]

There were problems that still needed to be addressed. One was the low number of in-state applications. More than one thousand out-of-state students had requested applications for admission to the School of Medicine, compared with only 122 West Virginians. Another issue confronting the Medical Center was that few people understood its commitment to education and research. The tendency to view the center as a public service facility blurred its primary responsibilities, and the heavy burden of absorbing the costs for medical indigents meant that WVU was subsidizing welfare services with funds allocated for educational purposes. The mission of the Medical Center was not just to train students, but also to improve the general level of medical and health care, community health institutions, and the opportunities for growth generated by the professions. In this capacity, the WVU Medical Center played a vital role in giving the University a truly statewide identity and outreach. In fact, Miller ventured on another occasion, "the Medical Center and the Evansdale developments are amongst the great achievements of higher education in this country since the close of World War II."[87]

THE LOST OPPORTUNITY TO BECOME A RESEARCH UNIVERSITY

To become a research university, WVU had to escape from some state-imposed controls and restrictions. It was unclear if this was politically feasible, but there was a strong incentive to try. During World War II and the postwar era, the federal government entered into research contracts with institutions of higher learning. In West Virginia, legal restrictions prohibited state institutions from participating in federally funded research projects unless they could finance the contract. These projects generally reimbursed money spent by the university on research, but federal funds reimbursed for expenses were deposited in the state treasury. WVU could obtain the money only by subsequent legislative appropriation, meaning that the University could not use revenue it generated from previous grants and contracts to finance new research.[88]

Moreover, WVU was unable to participate in government-sponsored research because the University followed the fiscal calendar beginning July

1 and ending June 30. It did not have the legal authority to make commitments beyond the funds in sight, or to carry over unspent balances into the next fiscal year; monies not spent reverted back to the state treasury. During World War II, federal government research contracts with universities helped them to develop laboratories and teams of scientists that could be ramped up in emergencies, and to maintain the nation's leadership in science. WVU boasted excellent chemical and biological laboratories, and there was an opportunity to improve scientific research laboratories and equipment at the University with federal funding. "Unfortunately, we cannot participate to any extent in such a program because of the fiscal limitations within which we must operate," President Stewart informed a group of alumni in 1950. "The federal government is like the state government: it operates upon the basis of reimbursement of expenses. Before one can be reimbursed, one must spend; before one may spend, he must have the money. We have no general balance or reserve funds from which expenditures can be made."[89] The inability to participate in this federal-university science network impeded WVU's scientific research capacity, while a number of state universities made giant leaps forward in building research laboratories and other facilities. The lost opportunity seems particularly poignant considering President Stewart's close relationship with Vannevar Bush, chief science advisor to President Franklin Roosevelt and principal founder of the federal initiative to boost scientific research at American universities.

This impediment to becoming a research university was modified somewhat during President Stewart's tenure when in 1951 the legislature authorized WVU to use $100,000 of excess collections as a revolving fund for contracts with the federal government. Since then, Stewart reported in 1958, WVU managed several of these so-called "reimbursable contracts" for scientific research, and received federal research grants for which funds were provided in advance and bypassed the state. "Collectively, they have served as a decided stimulus for research at the University and have contributed to the University's ability to obtain qualified personnel in the fields involved."[90]

Early in his career at WVU, Stewart promoted private funding for research projects at the University. Stewart realized that coal was the state's most powerful industry and a valuable economic resource, and so he culti-vated a closer relationship between the industry and WVU. In November 1946, he addressed delegates attending the West Virginia Coal Mining In-stitute in Bluefield, declaring his case directly: "The largest single factor in the economic life of West Virginia is coal. The largest factor in higher education in West Virginia is West Virginia University. The progress of coal should be benefited by the work at the University. This benefit, however, has not been as great as it should be from the standpoint both of the indus-try and the University."[91]

The economic health of the state depended on a thriving coal indus-try, and the University depended on the legislature for its funding. There-fore, it was of vital importance to the University that the industry should continue providing the state with funds. The University supported the coal industry primarily by training new mining engineers and providing skill training through Mining Extension. An expanded program of scholarships and fellowships subsidized by industry contributions and the promise of jobs after graduation was vigorously pursued by the University. Research was the other significant area in which WVU sought to enhance its rela-tionship with the state's coal industry. Together, the additional scholarships and fellowships for the most promising mining students, along with an ex-panded research program, would attract the best and brightest, who were then likely to be employed in the state. In one of his earliest speeches, Presi-dent Stewart proposed that the coal producers of West Virginia should pro-vide $100,000 each year for five years to bolster coal research at WVU. The funds had not yet materialized the following year when Stewart reaffirmed that the University was "eager to participate actively in a coal research pro-gram, but the path is not yet clear, for neither the state nor the industry has made the requisite funds available."[92]

Research was conducted by faculty, but the competitive faculty sala-ries necessary to attract and retain researchers has been a persistent issue for the University. The Strayer Report described the problem in 1946 just before Stewart became president: "As is well known, the present salary scale is far below that of institutions with which the University would choose to be compared." The report estimated that salaries should be raised "not less than 25 percent" in order to secure and retain those faculty who would help elevate the University to research institution status.[93]

In retirement, former President Stewart informed an interviewer that his "one big regret" about his years at WVU was his failure to raise faculty and staff salaries to competitive levels. "We tried everything we could think of," Stewart lamented, "but we never got salaries up to a satisfactory level where they were comparable to other peer universities."[94] President Stewart raised the issue of inadequate salaries at every opportunity, and he gave hundreds of speeches. WVU was a "good university, but one which has far to go before it becomes great," he told a group of alumni in 1950. "Its salaries have been too low and its physical plant inadequate. In my opinion both are the result of attitudes which go deep and which must be changed before the University will permanently attain that higher plateau on which it belongs." The University must shoulder at least some of the blame, he thought, "for we have not provided that aggressive leadership, that driving force, which the people have a right to expect from those to whom responsibility has been entrusted."[95]

Inflation and the inability to pay competitive salaries resulted in the loss of faculty, and Stewart often declared that faculty were the "heart of an institution." Comparative studies showed that WVU's salaries were substantially below those of comparable universities. "During the past two years we have lost an alarming number of faculty members to other institutions solely on the basis of salary differential." Stewart cited several specific examples to illustrate: "A professor to whom we paid $6,600 left for a position paying $9,000; one drawing $5,700 left for $9,000; two receiving $4,500 left for $7,000; one at $5,200 left for $9,600; one at $4,000 left for $8,400; one at $3,800 for $6,500; one at $4,300 for $8,000; one at $3,300 for $5,500 and so on." As enrollments increased, the situation would rapidly deteriorate, Stewart warned.[96]

Faculty and staff salaries became a top priority of the Stewart administration, and yet the independent Brewton Report, released in 1956, still pointed to instructional salaries that were substantially below comparable salaries at peer institutions. Professors were relatively mobile, according to the report, and WVU should not "expect to retain or to attract very many outstanding professors with its present salary policy."[97] One of the most truculent problems confronting the University administration was convincing legislators that higher faculty salaries were important. The University's Board of Governors reported to Governor Okey Patteson in February 1949 that WVU ranked in the lowest 8 percent of comparable institutions in its accrediting association, the North Central Association of Colleges and Secondary Schools. Governor William C. Marland was urged in 1955 to provide for an increase in faculty salaries, and the governor responded, while making no promises, that it was his "fondest hope" that the funding would be made available.[98]

Even though politicians often expressed an understanding of the consequences of uncompetitive salaries, any action taken was generally too little, too late. Civic-minded businessmen also offered sympathy and support. Walter Thurmond, secretary of the Southern Coal Producers' Association, wrote to President Stewart in 1956: "Certainly the West Virginia University professors and instructors are underpaid when compared with those of other Universities and with those in other occupations." He attached the SCPA's latest compilation of earnings in the mining industry for September 1956. The average annual earnings came to $4,923.24, for which the miner only worked 184 days of 6.5 actual work hours per day. Since September, the miners received a daily increase in wages of two dollars, which brought the average annual wage to about $5,400. "What I am trying to say is that a miner who can become proficient in his occupation in a very few months and who has no responsibility other than approximately 38 hours per week is doing better than a University Professor who has spent years in training for a job and who has great responsibilities almost every day in the week and with an indefinite number of hours. It is a sad comparison insofar as the university man is concerned," wrote Thurmond. "I want you to know any service I can render in helping to bring about a reasonable solution toward the salary situation at the University will be cheerfully given."[99]

There were improvements in faculty salaries during the Stewart years, however. As a professional manager, Stewart understood the importance of recognizing meritorious performance; a memorandum to all deans urged them to recognize and reward exceptional merit, and advised the deans not to consider across-the-board raises in their budget requests. The administration also made the case for higher salaries at each legislative session, and lawmakers responded. Between 1946–1947 and 1958–1959, nine-month faculty salaries nearly doubled: from $4,364 to $8,258 for professors; from $3,351 to $7,361 for associate professors; and from $2,845 to $5,611 for assistant professors. These salary increases exceeded those recommended by the Strayer Report. Yet salaries at other universities increased as well, so WVU did not close the salary gap with neighboring state universities with which it competed and compared itself.[100]

The State Teachers Retirement System provided coverage to the faculty during the Stewart years, but the benefits from the system were "substantially lower" compared with private companies serving professors and researchers, such as TIAA-CREF. Finally, in 1956, University faculty and staff fell under the coverage of the federal Social Security system, which improved the retirement plan, although it remained far from satisfactory. Also, in 1957, the legislature approved payroll deductions for group insurance. The legislature authorized sabbatical leaves in 1953, but by 1958, the year after Stewart's resignation, the legislature had not approved the funds, leaving the University still unable to adopt the program. Many faculty had chosen to remain at the University for non-monetary reasons. The state had benefited from their decision to stay, Stewart observed, but neither the state nor the University should "presume upon their affection" indefinitely.[101] Nevertheless, a half-century later, that tactful comment still resonated with WVU employees.

THREE

PAUL A. MILLER AND
"THE PEOPLE'S UNIVERSITY,"
1962–1967

PAUL A. MILLER WAS APPOINTED president of WVU on January 1, 1962. It was an inspiring story of a native son returning home and bringing with him years of experience as a top administrator at one of the great land-grant universities. Although he was born in East Liverpool, Ohio, his parents moved across the river to Hancock County, West Virginia when he was very young. There he attended elementary school, and graduated valedictorian of the thirty-three-member Wells High School class of 1933. Even though the country was in the depths of the Depression, Miller was a talented student who wanted to be a biologist. He attended Bethany College summer camps at Wheeling's Oglebay Park and attended Bethany for one year. But at age fifteen Miller visited WVU, and it was "love at first sight," he told an interviewer. He later hitchhiked to Morgantown, alone and without his parents' knowledge, to be sure he would be able to transfer to WVU. Assured of admission, he transferred as an agriculture major, entering in the fall of 1934 and sharing a basement room in Sunnyside. Miller worked his way through college as a busboy at the Sigma Nu fraternity and by earning money for setting up laboratories at the experiment station. Along the way he became a member of the WVU boxing team.[1]

Graduating with a BS in 1939, Miller took a position as county agricultural agent in Ritchie and then Nicholas Counties from 1939 to 1942, when he entered the Army Air Corps. After World War II he was admitted to graduate study at Michigan State University, where he earned MA and PhD degrees in anthropology and sociology. Joining the faculty at Michigan State, Miller rose through the ranks from professor of sociology to director of the Cooperative Extension Service to vice president of off-campus education and then university provost. He held this last position in 1961 when the chairman of the WVU Board of Governors, Forrest Kirkpatrick, contacted Miller to explore his interest in the University presidency. Miller expressed some reluctance at the offer because his wife was not in good health. Nevertheless, he met with the Board of Governors at the Pittsburgh airport and later met with them accompanied by his wife and two children. Affirmative action procedures did not yet exist, and, before he could get back to East Lansing, his acceptance had been publicly announced. Years later, Miller stated that he had been "appalled to see this could happen without search committees."[2]

Although Miller was only the third president of WVU to have received a portion of his education at the University, it was Miller's educational philosophy that truly distinguished him from all previous presidents. The state press and the politicians welcomed him as a hometown boy, and his views on the role of the University in the state ingratiated him even further. At his very first press conference he remarked that "we must find a way to help the patched-pants student," because the University had "an obligation both as faculty and citizens to help him get through college."[3] Many West Virginians took heart at Miller's admission that "no university with uplift ambitions should try to make itself a second Harvard. It should seek an individuality built upon the needs of the area it serves."[4] A Wheeling newspaper spoke for many when it declared that Stewart brought to WVU "an understanding of our people, our problems, and our potential denied a man with no West Virginia background."[5]

Miller arrived on campus just as a major restructuring of the coal industry reached full tide. Mechanization was displacing miners even as production soared. Unemployment rose to depression levels particularly in the southern coalfields. The legislature responded to the decline by slashing the budget. An atmosphere of despair settled over the state and all of higher education as tens of thousands left West Virginia to find jobs elsewhere. Miller thought West Virginia was "kind of Balkanized," and compared with Michigan State there simply was no "dynamism" at WVU. He saw a University that was accustomed to dealing with a "world that would never exist again," and he thought it imperative to get the University out in front of society to make it more "vibrant and vital." One of the main problems, as the new president saw it, was that the University had "no great power centers" beyond the walls, with state government and state businesses struggling to survive. Absentee coal owners had no interest in the state or the institution, and agricultural employment was in even greater decline than coal mining. The University found itself in the awkward position of arguing for more resources from the legislature at a time when graduates were leaving West Virginia. "I saw whole schools and divisions graduating people, not a single one stayed in West Virginia," with most of them heading for Washington, D.C., he observed. The problem was compounded when the number of out-of-state students began to increase. Supporters of the state colleges used this fact as leverage for arguing that state colleges were a better investment; their graduates stayed in state, whereas graduates of WVU did not. Moreover, Miller was abashed to hear people referring to WVU as the "University of Southwestern Pennsylvania" and claiming that it was aloof and far removed from the problems confronting the state. Something had to be done "to get advanced leadership" out into the state, Miller was convinced.[6]

Recalling those years, Harold Shamberger, then-assistant to the president, observed that Miller was "more of a force than many people on the campus and in the community would have bargained for. He firmly believed that foremost in any university was the technical authority of the faculty," but that authority must be expanded beyond the University to serve the state.[7] Paul Miller admired former president Irvin Stewart because the former president understood the University's leadership role, and that "the state is our campus."[8] Miller had an interesting perspective on the university presidency, believing that "college presidents are really not presidents" but rather more like "mayors of small cities" who have to deal with numerous, "small constituencies."[9]

Miller's inauguration dispensed with the pomp and ceremony in favor of a simple affair. His decision to wear his own black academic gown in place of the garish, and expensive, presidential robe of royal blue faille trimmed in heavy gold brocade projected the new president as a man-of-the-people. But Paul Miller was, as earlier University historians characterized him, "a sophisticated, dynamic, and benevolent conceptualizer" who came to WVU as a professional to "change its character."[10] The University faced difficulties, and he had the confidence (some thought arrogance) to believe he knew how to overcome them. "Over much of the last 96 years," he told a Morgantown audience, neither the state nor the community were "quite sure just what it means to have a great university, nor what a difference a great university may make to both the state and a given community." His assessment of the University's history was not flattering. In fact, for most of the history of WVU, he claimed, "students came and went without undue intellectual excitement, attended classes in a small number of relatively old buildings, in an institution operated on quite modest budgets with salaries paid in the mines and in industry throughout the community exceeding in many instances the salaries of the faculty. During those long years, few, if any state universities suffered more."[11]

Miller saw himself as a leader in the land-grant movement, which accepted all work as dignified and believed that the transforming influence of education should be open to every citizen according to talent rather than social or economic status. Instead of trying to be a liberal arts college, the University should be the catalyst for solving the problems that had shackled West Virginia's development. Miller's avowed purpose, therefore, was to transform the institution into an agent of change. Attaining this role required a radical reorganization of the University, and he saw several barriers impeding the road to success. There was a strong tendency to fragment into separate departments, schools, and colleges, which explained why faculty identity was stronger within their home units than within the larger institution. Weak networks of communications within the institution further fragmented the units, "Balkanizing" them so that WVU mirrored the state. Compounding its difficulties was a lack of dynamism. Miller employed "creative tension" to energize the institution and its organizational culture. The University "needs more tension, more fire, more conflict over ideals and ideas," he asserted, and the "price of peacefulness (as I have had to remind trustees from time to time) is mediocrity."[12]

The real issue facing WVU, therefore, was "how best to distinguish what we already have and to make it more useful," how to "nurture a distinctive university personality." Miller asserted that the University, "throughout its arduous yet proud history, has rendered undramatic and patient service." This was not a flattering picture. Objective supporters, however, suspected it was an accurate albeit discomforting assessment, so they gave Miller the lead in fostering a more stimulating intellectual climate as a way of generating the University's own unique identity.[13]

At a retreat with University administrators in April 1964, President Miller announced that he enjoyed the collegial atmosphere at WVU but that he had never worked in an environment "which seems so free of animosity or suspicion or the falsely clever." Indeed, "less politeness and more outspoken concern" would be welcomed. Miller expressed bewilderment that "after more than two years I can detect no momentous center of rancor."[14] The following year, 1964, his "bewilderment" had broadened: "There are no great centers of rancor within the University, within the legislative sector, or within the State as a whole." He must have equated the University's "sponginess in the intellectual climate" with his inability to identify "too few concentrations of scholarly brilliance."[15] By now friends of the University must have wondered what prompted Miller to take the presidency at all.

The University could not afford to hire outstanding scholars for every position, so Miller planned to create clusters of interdisciplinary faculty whose research would be mutually supportive. Nor could the University afford to reduce the teaching load as it ramped up research. Teaching, research, and service would be unevenly distributed, so some kind of balance was sought across the faculty as a whole.[16] Finding the right strategy for improving the "over-all scholarly competence of the faculty" was a major issue, according to Miller, because WVU did not "sponsor sharply prominent peaks of scholarly brilliance." In what must have been one of the first utterances of a strategic plan at WVU, Miller declared that the University must involve itself "in a continuous plan of manpower identification and recruitment, and (*and this is the catch*), according to a firm set of institutional objectives and needs."[17]

President Miller predicted in 1964 that a "brutal decade" in the history of higher education lay ahead. The University, for its part, would confront a dilemma: "namely, that support from the private and public sectors of the national level will follow those universities which are willing to accept some portion of these national and international challenges" for off-campus services. The university that ignored these pressures would not, he asserted, attract first-rate faculty and would be forced into the role of channeling superior talent to "the several great centers of academic activity." Miller believed that in the ensuing decade the number of "truly great" universities could double or even triple to thirty or forty powerful academic enterprises, rather than the current fifteen or twenty. These ascendant universities would be sifting through the faculties of weaker institutions to find replacements. Since WVU occupied a "muddled middle ground," not inconsequential but yet not among those institutions now "knocking on the door of greatness," competitors Penn State and Pittsburgh among them, the central issue facing WVU was how to position itself closer to that door of opportunity.[18]

Between 1957–1958 and 1967–1968, enrollment at WVU more than doubled from 6,184 to 14,888. To adapt to this massive increase in students, the University undertook a robust building campaign, yet salaries continued to be depressingly low. In 1964, faculty salaries for all ranks ranged from $4,200 to $15,000, with a mean of $8,036. Undoubtedly these salaries encouraged mobile faculty to leave for positions with higher compensation. There is little systematic evidence for this oft-repeated claim, but data gathered between 1960 and 1963 from 120 faculty who left the University indicate that "resignation" was the spur for 97 of them to move on; presumably they left the University to find employment elsewhere.[19]

Doubling student enrollments forced the University to recruit additional faculty in the national marketplace, where the University was uncompetitive. Like presidents before him, Paul Miller often addressed the problem. In presenting his 1964–1965 budget proposal to the state Board of Public Works, Miller argued that faculty already carried twice the teaching loads of their counterparts at other leading state universities, leaving them no time to actively seek external funding for research. WVU salaries at all ranks averaged 11 percent below all other land-grant institutions, and academic salaries nationally were rising at an average annual rate of 7 percent. While 1961–1962 salaries for WVU faculty jumped by 16.4 percent, raises declined precipitously in subsequent years, down to 8.1 percent in 1962–1963, 6.7 percent the year after, and only 5.4 percent in 1964–1965. These were historically high salary increases for West Virginia, especially considering the state's ailing economy and the ongoing rapid decline of coal industry employment. Legislators and WVU administrators alike tried to avoid answering the perennial question: was the cost of operating a major university more than the state could afford? How could WVU hope to compete in the national marketplace even in the best of times, let alone when the state's unemployment rate was increasing and tax revenues were decreasing? Meanwhile, the University's requests for increased appropriations so faculty with secure jobs could receive a pay raise seemed selfish and uncompassionate. The marketplace, however, was encumbered by neither compassion nor sectional politics, and the disparity continued to pinch the University's efforts to advance its research mission.[20] It was all relative, of course, and when West Virginians compared WVU with other state institutions of higher learning, the University and its faculty seemed well-off. The relevant comparison for WVU was not with in-state institutions but with the nation's other state land-grant institutions.

State subsidies for graduate education continued to be a problem because state legislators had never recognized the costs associated with research programs or graduate education. Consequently, both were undertaken at the expense of undergraduate programs. The only measure for appropriations was to consider full-time students, or cost per credit hour. Neither method accounted for the costs of research, community services, or professional schools, other than credit hours or headcount. A good measure of research activity depended on the amount of private and government money available for that purpose in West Virginia. During a period when research was receiving the greatest amount of federal funding it ever had, only two of the state's institutions received such funds. During the 1965–1966 college year, Marshall University received approximately $6,000 for contract research and services, while West Virginia University received $2,542,000. Most of this money came through the Medical Center and the College of Engineering.[21]

THE NEED FOR PUBLIC RELATIONS

One of Miller's first acts as president was to charge the administrative units to come up with ten-year planning reports. His next move, which surprised no one, was to launch a major reorganization of the University. Both administrative and academic structures would undergo consolidation and simplification. Some units would be discontinued, and others modified or expanded. According to the new strategic plan, the University would seize special opportunities to create centers of regional and national distinction in the biological and health sciences; in Appalachian social, economic, and cultural studies; and in the creative arts. In these and other designated fields the University would strive to assemble "a corps of eminent scholars, scientists, and artists." The University would also provide leadership in projects requiring inter-institutional cooperation among the other state colleges and universities in West Virginia in order to maximize the resources available for higher education.[22]

President Miller went before the state Board of Public Works in December 1963 to argue for an overall increase of 14 percent ($1.8 million more than the current budget of $11.5 million) in state allocations, highlighting the major organizational changes that had been implemented and the critical needs of the University. Miller asserted that the budget proposal he was submitting was not so much a budget as a program of University development. "We are not before you simply with our hands out for more money, but we came with a total program." Over the next decade, this program, he said, would lead the way to West Virginia's economic recovery.[23]

The request recognized certain basic facts about WVU. One was that it continued to grow "rapidly and persistently." Enrollments increased 26 percent over the past three years, 1961 to 1963, and graduate enrollment grew by 56 percent over the same period. Nevertheless, the average salary for all ranks was 11 percent below the average for all state land-grant institutions, and excessive teaching loads prevented faculty from pursuing external funding. With salaries down 11 percent and enrollment increasing 10 percent a year, the basic disciplines needed immediate assistance. Any amount less than a 14 percent increase in appropriations would be an example of "pathological timidity." If WVU was unable to compete for "first-rate academic talent," then it would become "a farm club for the big leagues."[24]

President Miller was keenly aware that state appropriations as a percentage of the University's operating budget were declining. Speaking on behalf of the University's budget proposal for 1965–1966, Miller claimed that WVU faced a crisis. "Good and able people" at the University were questioning whether West Virginia could "afford a first-rate university in all of its modern complexities." He was neither the first nor the last president to broach this topic. He laid the issue squarely before the board of public works: West Virginia University will not meet the severe competition for talent over the next decade as a "thinly-financed, struggling, medium-sized, and colorless state university." The organizational restructuring already underway at WVU was the result of reallocating internal resources. In fact, during the greatest enrollment growth in the University's history, its annual appropriations actually declined. In 1962–1963 the University was granted an increase of 8.1 percent; for 1963–1964 it received an increase of 6.7 percent; and for 1964–1965 a 5.4 percent increase. While this extra funding was appreciated and came during hard times for the state's economy, WVU was actually losing ground compared with other land-grant institutions. A 20 percent increase was necessary simply to keep pace.[25]

Like Presidents Stewart and Stahr, Paul Miller understood that the public and the state's legislators had to be persuaded that investing in a first-rate university was not an option they could afford to ignore. Therefore, he singled out public relations for urgent, immediate attention. The need was obvious from the lack of alumni enthusiasm, the low level of private giving to the University, and the preference of too many talented West Virginians to attend graduate and professional schools in other states.[26] WVU's image was created by a host of sources beyond the institution's control. To counter this, Miller created the Office of University Relations. "We feed our alumni and other patrons with too much warmed-over news about sports. Our fanciest bulletins say far too little about the academic heart of the University. We interpret progress too much in terms of construction projects," the president declared in 1964.[27]

How the public perceived WVU was simply too important to leave beyond the University's control. The imperative was heightened by "the lingering elements of sectional rivalry" in West Virginia that prevailed in state politics and between factions within the higher education system. These elements persistently hampered WVU's ability to fulfill its mission as the state's land-grant university. "West Virginia University carries a strange and heavy responsibility," Miller remarked to a group of WVU administrators, for it must be "concerned with its own welfare while it speaks out on behalf of all education at all levels within the State." The University's programs should be interpreted in a controlled fashion in order to develop "an increasingly strong foundation of legislative activity." Meanwhile, the president hoped the University would become more aggressive in pitching research projects to foundations and in securing grants and contracts from federal agencies.[28]

Perhaps some of this public relations effort paid off, because on July 11, 1966 the University received a donation of $500,000, the largest single gift in its history, from Mrs. C. S. May, who designated it for research in human reproduction and family planning. In its very first year (1965) the WVU Foundation received $750,000 in gifts to the endowment, and in 1966 donations passed the $1 million mark. Moreover, in August 1966 the University announced that the Benedum Foundation had provided a grant to improve "academic excellence" at the University, the only restriction being that the money could not be used for new physical facilities. The money used to create the Benedum Professorships required the University to raise an additional $200,000 over the next five years.[29]

CENTER FOR APPALACHIAN STUDIES AND DEVELOPMENT

The centerpiece of Paul Miller's reorganization of the University was the Center for Appalachian Studies and Development (CASD), established on February 5, 1963. It reflected his commitment to harness the University's assets in support of his conception of service and providing leadership in resolving the state's social, economic, and health problems. Miller, who still regarded himself as a professor rather than a career administrator, accepted the presidency with a private understanding that he would serve for five years and then would become a tenured faculty member in the Department of Sociology. He had big ideas about how to transform the University into an agent of change, and with the limited time he gave himself, he was impatient to initiate his plan.[30]

Dean of the College of Agriculture and Forestry Ernest J. Nesius was appointed vice president of the CASD. As director of the Agricultural Extension Service, which was at the heart of the reorganization, he was familiar with and supportive of the goals Miller had in mind. Moreover, Miller and Nesius became friends even before they came to WVU, and both held similar views about university outreach. Miller also respected Nesius's administrative abilities.[31]

According to the statement in the University's 1964 Self-Study Report, the Appalachian Center, as it became popularly known, was a "university-wide unit dedicated to the purpose of being a vital force in the destiny of West Virginia." It would focus on "developing people's attitudes, human and natural resources, private and public organizations and institutions, and state and international affairs," and coordinate those activities that tied West Virginia University to the state and region. Those University functions that were oriented toward public service were concentrated in the Appalachian Center, mobilizing into "one coordinated, flexible effort all special public service skills, extension, consulting, and research planning so as to bring them to bear on meeting the public needs." The center's activities would focus on both formal and informal education, on research that generated new knowledge, and on ways to disseminate that knowledge. Cooperative relationships would be sought with other government agencies, business-labor-agricultural groups, and educational institutions.[32]

A year-long national centennial celebration of the land-grant university system officially ended in January 1963, just as the centennial observance of West Virginia's statehood began. Miller used the publicity surrounding these celebrations to focus attention on the University's special role as the state's land-grant institution. In a report summarizing his plan for reorganization, which was approved by the Board of Governors in February 1963, President Miller described how the conditions under which the land-grant institutions operated had changed substantially. The old boundaries between rural and urban life had dissipated, and regional communities now formed around large central cities. Consequently, rural and urban problems, agricultural and industrial problems, and community and state problems had become increasingly interlocking. Technology had increased the rate of obsolescence for institutions, tools, and occupational skills. Knowledge was therefore increasingly more specialized, and the decision-making process increasingly more complex and uncertain. In this emerging world, continuing and life-long education was essential, and it was now more vital than ever that WVU help people "to make intelligent adjustments to the changing requirements of occupations, ideas, and institutions."[33]

Miller outlined the guiding principles that should govern plans for expanding the University's leadership role in West Virginia's social and economic development. First of all, it was essential that the academic disciplines be strengthened in order for teaching, research, and scholarship to flourish. Moreover, a consolidation of disciplines into broad interdisciplinary areas, such as biology and the medical fields, and the creative and performing arts, was overdue. Second, since the problems of West Virginia and Appalachia were complex and interlocking, comprehensive, university-wide planning was necessary to avoid wasteful duplication in addressing these problems. Third, inventing new ways for the University to coordinate its efforts with other state colleges as well as state and federal government agencies was also important. Higher education should be reconceptualized in order to more efficiently train the state's future leaders, with WVU in the leading role and the colleges serving as regional centers. The idea behind the Appalachian Center was that it would identify, realign, and coordinate major activities that were oriented toward direct public service. It mobilized into a single, coordinated effort "all special public service skills—extension, consulting, research, and planning—so as to more consciously and effectively bring them to bear on meeting public needs of the present and defining public goals for the future."[34]

Within a few years the Appalachian Center incorporated 250 full-time positions and seven part-time positions. The sweeping administrative and academic reorganization through the CASD incorporated numerous semi-autonomous units on and off campus, including: the Cooperative Extension Service, which provided the traditional educational service to agriculture and rural life; the Mining and Industrial Extension Service, which facilitated the flow of technical knowledge to that business and industry; and the University Extension Division, including the Labor Education Service, which provided credit and non-credit adult education programs and would be expanded to provide statewide educational conferences and planning activities. The CASD also administered broad research programs through an Office of Research and Development and facilitated collaborative research ventures across agency lines that were pertinent to West Virginian and Appalachian development. The University's several off-campus centers also fell under the aegis of the center, including the Kanawha Graduate Center, the Parkersburg branch of WVU, and the area development centers in Keyser, Weston, Beckley, Charleston, Parkersburg, and Morgantown. These centers conducted workshops, conferences, clinics, cultural activities, and short courses. Most of the informative programming centered on the state's extraction industries, such as coal, petroleum, farm and forest, the chemical industry, and human resources.[35]

Other newly organized centers sprang forth within the domain of the Center for Appalachian Studies and Development, like the Institute of Water Resources, the Institute for Labor Studies, and the National Youth Science Camp. Several of these centers, such as the Regional Research Institute (RRI), became nationally and internationally known within their fields. William Miernyk, a prominent economist newly recruited to serve as director, led the RRI to prominence in the emerging interdisciplinary field of regional science. Miernyk was one of the University's first Benedum Professors and, as Miller recalled, "a very real discovery." Most of these ventures were supported by funds from state and local government agencies like the Office of Economic Opportunity or from private sources like the Benedum, Ford, Kellogg, and Pew Foundations. The Creative Arts Center (CAC) was also set up as a result of Miller's campaign to reorganize the academic enterprise at WVU. Here art, music, and drama were merged to contribute to the state's cultural development. Approval for the CAC was a "difficult victory" because many legislators first wanted to build a new coliseum for basketball, Miller recalled years later. But the CAC was a neat conceptual fit into the president's reorganization plan. The legislature accepted his argument that the "highest standards in art, music, and performance should set the example for the whole state," Miller recalled. "I found counterbalance to the Appalachian Center in the Creative Arts Center, and we fought to get that building," he told an interviewer, emphasizing that he would have "fought through fire" for the CAC.[36]

Other major changes came during Miller's last two years. The Institute of Biological Sciences was created to link the research strengths of the biology faculty with the applied expertise of the medical school faculty. Miller believed that society could benefit more directly from pure scientific research through mechanisms such as this. Also, the combination maximized university resources and enhanced the prospects for external funding for medical research.

In 1965 a new College of Human Resources and Education replaced the College of Education as the administrative structure for the Division of Education; counseling and guidance, developmental reading, speech and audiology, rehabilitation counseling, and special education were placed under the Division of Clinical Studies; the Division of Home Economics was transferred in from the College of Agriculture and Forestry; and the Division of Social Work was moved into the new college from the College of Arts and Sciences.[37]

WVU was actively involved with five agricultural colleges in Tanganyika, Uganda, and Kenya. As of March 1964 there were two instructors in Tanganyika, four in Kenya, and eight in Uganda. WVU joined with the U.S. Agency for International Development (USAID) and the government of Tanganyika to plan, build, and staff a diploma-level agricultural college.[38] The Appalachian Center was also the administrative home for the Office of International Programs, which was responsible for projects such as the East African Program, a cooperative venture with USAID. The success of the East African program was noteworthy among the University's historical linkages with the region. Funded by USAID, the Ford Foundation, and the Rockefeller Foundation during the mid-1960s, WVU was the sole university engaged in agricultural development in the three East African nations. WVU representatives established an educational program much different from that left behind by the British. In Tanganyika (now Tanzania), a physical plant was constructed and a system of governance established. A two-year college was established in Morogoro, Tanzania, but in a few years it grew into a four-year institution. Instruction was in English. WVU also assisted the British in establishing schools in Uganda and Kenya and, under the auspices of USAID, helped to establish a vocational agriculture program in Kenya's secondary schools. WVU's involvement created a faculty and student exchange between Morgantown and East Africa, with University faculty teaching in East Africa and African students coming to WVU for training before returning to assume responsibility for the program. In the fall of 1962, the first fifteen Tanzanians arrived to study at WVU. Another fifteen followed in 1963, and thirty more the following year. In the fall semester of 1966, forty-three African students were studying agriculture at WVU. Under the plan, the students stayed for two years and received a diploma in agriculture before returning to their native lands to become the equivalent of county agents in the United States. Some returned to WVU for advanced degrees. Among the Tanzanians who did so, one became the minister of agriculture, another became the head of the nation's civil service, and a third became the first dean of the college at Morogoro.[39]

The arrival of African students in Morgantown in 1962 was cause for concern. Morgantown was still racially segregated to a significant degree, so WVU officials were anxious about the kind of reception the students would receive. James McCartney, an active business leader in Morgantown and in WVU alumni affairs, paid a call on downtown merchants to encourage them to welcome the Africans. Most readily agreed, but one restaurant did not cooperate. The African students also attended previously all-white 4-H camps, and generally received a warm reception everywhere they went in the state. In an interview, Earnest Nesius opined, "I always felt that . . . those first fifteen blacks did more good for opening up the race question in this state than anything that had happened [previously]." On the other hand, he observed, when Morgantown's African-American community attempted to welcome the students, it was rebuffed by the Africans, who "considered themselves above the black community here."[40]

Some distinguished African guests also visited WVU. Fergus Wilson, director of the Makerere University College of Agriculture in Uganda, and the chief of the Masai tribe visited Morgantown during the early sixties. Paul Bomani, Tanzania's minister of agriculture, visited in 1962. An unfortunate episode involved Tanzania's speaker of parliament, whose visit coincided with a WVU Board of Governors' meeting. President Miller attempted to schedule a dinner for him at Lakeview Country Club, where the speaker could be introduced to the Board of Governors, but the Lakeview management refused to serve him because he was black. To avoid an embarrassing situation, Miller instead arranged for a dinner at the Hotel Morgan.[41]

West Virginia University-Parkersburg was opened and registered 104 students in September 1961. Operating out of a renovated former Wood County high school building, the Parkersburg Center was initiated under the WVU Center for Appalachian Studies and Development. It offered introductory academic courses at first, and some WVU instructors, such as the well-known folklorist Patrick Gainer, drove to Parkersburg to offer courses that could be transferred to four-year institutions. In the fall of 1962, 170 students were enrolled; three years later, 410 students were being taught by 24 faculty. Students were admitted to the WVU College of Arts and Sciences under the same procedures as on the main campus. In 1966, the Parkersburg branch became the WVU Parkersburg Center. Financing the construction of a new college building was an issue because the West Virginia code prohibited state funds from being used to support branches and instead required them to be self-supporting. The problem was creatively resolved by civic leaders in Parkersburg. On March 26, 1966, a three-year $1.2 million bond issue was presented to the voters of Wood County, who approved the bond by a 70 percent margin. In 1971 the state Board of Regents converted the WVU Parkersburg Center into a comprehensive community college. Baccalaureate degrees in some fields, and master's degrees in education and business administration, could be earned on that campus.[42]

The Kanawha Valley Graduate Center was established in the fall of 1958 with encouragement from professional engineering and scientific societies in the Kanawha Valley, as well as the major industrial concerns in the area. Master's programs, overseen by a full-time resident director, were offered in chemistry and in chemical, civil, and mechanical engineering, as well as business administration. Students met the same admission and course requirements as those on the main campus. Two-thirds of instructors were resident members of the University graduate faculty. The remaining third were hired from other colleges in the Kanawha Valley. Chemistry laboratories were constructed and equipped by the University on the campus of the West Virginia State College at Institute, WV, and the University also rented classrooms from West Virginia State University for evening classes. Union Carbide provided research facilities and computer services. The graduate center was financed primarily from income generated by credit-hour fees and a substantial subsidy from leading Kanawha Valley corporations.[43]

President Miller's vision for the University made him receptive to the possibility of relocating some of its strategic parts in order to stretch the structure and location of the University to meet social needs. The Kanawha Valley held a major attraction for WVU's expansionary president. Nearly one-quarter of the state's population lived there, and it was home to the state capital as well as the research-based industries, particularly chemicals. A 1965 feasibility study contemplated relocating some or all of the College of Engineering to the Kanawha Valley, where it would form a research alliance with industry and government. The Board of Governors concluded, however, that such a plan was impractical and adopted instead a cooperative venture with other Kanawha Valley institutions. Because WVU faculty could not continue commuting from Morgantown, the Kanawha Valley Graduate Center developed its own faculty. Some of them taught at nearby colleges and were hired as part-time instructors to evade territorial conflicts with other institutions in the valley. Similarly, the Kanawha Valley Graduate Center advisory committee included college presidents and local civic leaders. The state legislature helped to fund the expansion by providing appropriations in 1966 and 1967. The new venture was renamed the WVU College of Graduate Studies and officially opened in the fall of 1969, in Institute, WV. The College of Graduate Studies remained under WVU's administration until July 1, 1972 when the state Board of Regents made it a separate institution.[44]

Although new centers and institutes sprouted like wildflowers under Miller's restructuring plan, not every proposal was welcomed. In 1966, planners for the Center for Appalachian Studies and Development prepared a study to establish the Law and Public Affairs Center in Charleston. This plan emerged out of a proposed new building for the College of Law at the same time that planners were contemplating ways to expand the University's presence into the Kanawha Valley, and it had Miller's enthusiastic support.[45]

Given Miller's vision that the University's mission was to take the lead in the state's development, the concept behind the proposed Law and Public Affairs Center was a sound one. With all levels of the trial and appellate courts located in Charleston, the capital was a service area with a constant need for such training programs. Also, as the seat of state government, it offered a host of regulatory agencies and a bureaucracy, which would provide opportunities for fieldwork and training. The center's faculty would, therefore, gain direct access to public affairs and link up expertise with those in need of it. The Kanawha Valley had the greatest concentration of business and industry in the state at the time, so the expertise found in WVU's College of Commerce would also be in demand. The location at the seat of state government was "especially appropriate for the state's development," Miller asserted. Over and against this need lay the handicap of Morgantown's location on the state's northern border, far removed from the political and industrial hub in the Kanawha Valley. The center would allow the University to extend its influence into that strategic area and improve its capacity to serve the entire state.[46]

Charleston had long craved to have at least some portion of the University relocated to its environs, so naturally the idea resonated in the Kanawha Valley. While the proposal grew out of the belief that the University should serve the Kanawha Valley, the idea was advanced at the very moment when a new facility was under consideration for the College of Law.

Its construction in Charleston would have provided the complete package for the proposed center.

In other quarters, however, the proposal posed a threat to WVU's evolution as a major university. As might be expected, there was serious opposition, both parochial and educational. The Morgantown newspaper, which always fought for a unified campus in Morgantown, sounded the alarm: "Surely there must be something wrong with the grotesque report that the University Board of Governors is giving serious thought to the dismemberment of the University on the eve of its 100th birthday."[47] More importantly, the law faculty was unalterably opposed to separating the law school from the main campus, arguing that the advantages for clinical training in the Kanawha Valley were overblown and questionable. To move "to such an environment would constitute regression to a trade school concept of legal education. . . . A college of law is a professional school, not a trade school, nor part of a university extension program," the faculty asserted.[48] One professor of law complained to the Board of Governors that the proposal was contrary to "the enlightened progress of legal education in this nation." Moreover, he wrote,

the faculty of the College of Law represents about six-tenths of one per cent of the licensed legal talent of the State. It is no waste of human resources to insist they be scholarly rather than service-oriented, and that their environment reflect such a choice. The law student spends twelve years in practice for every year in the College of Law. This ratio offers abundant opportunities for the development of practice skills. It is folly to substitute service for scholarship. It is even worse to substitute activity for learning. But such are the goals of the proposal.[49]

Another law professor publicly challenged the president on the notion that "the Legislature simply does not or will not support the University unless they have a toy to play with in Charleston, or that you are unable to get the funds needed from that admittedly simple body." Kanawha Center should not be involved with the Appalachian Center, for "this organism is threatening to swallow everything it touches," he asserted.[50]

Clearly, two dichotomous views of education collided on this issue. However, the really long knives in this struggle rested in the hands of the many lawyers throughout the state, and the West Virginia Law School Association vehemently denounced the proposal, charging that it would disrupt plans for constructing the new building and that combining the law school with other graduate programs in other disciplines was likely to prompt the American Bar Association to rescind WVU's accreditation. Moreover, the College of Law was already understaffed, and taking on additional part-time students in evening courses would only undermine the quality of training. Clinical opportunities were readily available in county courthouses and short-term field trips to Charleston if necessary. The West Virginia Bar Association supported this negative assessment. As a result, the Board of Governors had backed away from the proposal by the spring of 1966. Some of them already voiced strong reservations not only about "dismembering" the University but even about the plan's legality. In the end, Miller was forced to abandon his aspirations for the proposed center.[51]

Many years later, Miller informed an interviewer that the proposal to move the law school was the "big rhubarb" of his administration and admitted that he should have prepared the way more carefully before pushing such a major proposal forward. However, while the committee exploring the feasibility of creating the center still debated the issue, news of the proposal leaked to the press, and Miller had to take a public position before the concept had been fully vetted. Ultimately, the idea of relocating the law school was abandoned because it lacked support within the legal community, its primary constituency. Later, Miller claimed that he "did not expect to have his proposal to move the Law School approved," but the tensions it stirred led to support for expansion in the Kanawha Valley, and that was his primary goal.[52]

President Miller's vision of a reorganized, modernized land-grant university also encountered serious difficulty with the College of Arts and Sciences faculty. "I've always been troubled by Arts and Sciences," he said to an interviewer. For the most part, he believed, they just wanted to be left alone to teach and do their research and not be bothered about service. Nevertheless, Miller often stated his conviction that the College of Arts and Sciences was "the heart of the university," and that curriculum philosophy and academic leadership should emanate from the college. Unfortunately, no direct method existed for the college to communicate this kind of leadership to the rest of the University or to the public, so the professional schools filled the void. Connecting basic scientists with practitioners (biologists and medical doctors, for example) required establishing linkages between disciplines that the scientists found awkward. Even more daunting was bridging the gap between basic scientists and external corporations, and Miller believed this task led to the "unraveling" of the Appalachian Center.[53]

President Stewart had warned that his successors would be unable to manage the growing University with the simple administrative structure he utilized, and, judging from the administrative changes Miller initiated, he must have agreed. A new computer center, an office of admissions separate from the registrar, an office of university relations to coordinate public relations, the first educational television station in West Virginia, a ten-week summer session, and an office of physical planning were all among the organizational changes initiated by Paul Miller; many of them remain in place today. The president's office also required a more complex structure. Miller appointed John F. Golay to the position of provost, or second-in-command, as well as three vice presidents to head the Medical Center, the Appalachian Center, and Administration and Finance. In his own office, Miller hired three presidential assistants and a director of student educational services.[54]

President Miller requested College of Arts and Sciences administrators to "re-vision" their college, but major organizational changes had already taken place. Drama and parts of speech had gone to the Creative Arts Center, and social work was moved to the College of Human Resources and Education. Some of the basic sciences had been reoriented toward interdisciplinary institutes, and some social sciences seemed destined for the new Center for Public Affairs in Charleston, minus the College of Law. Other organizational changes great and small collectively transformed the structure of the University under Paul Miller. A separate philosophy department was created with support from the Benedum Foundation after it was separated from psychology; a program of religious studies was launched with funding from the Danforth Foundation; several departments were consolidated into one Department of Foreign Languages; a new Division of Statistics within the Department of Mathematics; a new core curriculum was inaugurated; and a modest Honors Program was launched. There were even rumors that the College of Arts and Sciences would be split into a new College of Humanities and Physical Sciences, on the one hand, and a College of Communications housing English, journalism, and what was left of the speech department, on the other.[55]

A larger issue that troubled many faculty had repercussions far beyond the structural changes initiated by Miller. Even though Miller's reorganizing fervor seemed like mere rearranging of the furniture, it signaled a fundamental redefinition of the University's mission. A "White Paper" presented by the Department of Philosophy in the spring of 1967 and signed by its chairman, Joseph F. Lambert, outlined the concerns many had about the reorientation of the University under Paul Miller. The immediate issue was the administration's refusal to approve a PhD degree in philosophy. The reasons given were that the department had few majors, that it had only two graduate students, and that additional faculty would have to be hired if the degree were approved. During the administrations of Miller and his interim successor, Harry Heflin, a consensus had emerged among faculty and administrators that the University should give priority to maintaining the strongest possible program of undergraduate instruction. Moreover, since the state was not likely to increase its allocations, the University should concentrate its resources for graduate education only on those programs of high academic quality and the most relevance to West Virginia. While a large majority of the faculty supported the administration's decision on the narrow issue of the philosophy Ph.D., the White Paper articulated the much broader faculty concern that WVU was being wrenched away from its traditional intellectual mooring and becoming more of a polytechnic institution. The "White Paper" argued that the drift toward polytechnic status was an inappropriate response to financial difficulties based on a misguided understanding of what constituted a "real university." The state needed well-educated people who were willing to make sacrifices in the present in order to secure a better future. Technicians were loyal to their trade but would leave the state for better opportunities. If West Virginia wanted technicians, it would be far cheaper to let other states train them and then recruit them later.[56] Without the support of the rest of the faculty, the philosophers' protest did not have the desired effect.

Rapid change, aggravated by the division into three campuses, outstripped continuity dramatically, and many feared that the once-unified University was in danger of fragmenting. Toward the end of his tenure, Miller recognized the signs of apprehension, declining morale, and a feeling of dislocation among faculty. His vision of linking University researchers with practitioners in the field required an overall upgrade in the quality of faculty, which many saw as a threat to their traditional role of teaching. The new emphasis on faculty research led to a new corollary emphasis on holding the terminal degree, usually the PhD, in relevant fields. The repercussions of this seismic shift were felt immediately in the general tightening of the promotion and tenure process, and a growing unevenness throughout the University between faculty who focused on teaching and those who also conducted research. Miller recalled later that this shift in emphasis created a "certain sensitivity" between "old timers" and the "new breed of people coming in who were more research oriented."[57]

Billy Coffindaffer, who spent most of his career as an agent in the University Extension Division and eventually became dean of the Appalachian Center, described another consequence of the inability to engage faculty in the traditional disciplines. He pointed out that the lack of support from WVU campus units put county extension agents "out on a limb." Miller and Ernest Nesius saw the land-grant university as a mechanism for helping citizens with almost any problem. The University's Extension Division had been very successful in agriculture and food production, but there were a host of other modern problems that need to be addressed, such as unemployment, illiteracy, teenage pregnancy, and economic development. The extension service and the research stations were established under specific legislation and funded specifically to address the older issues, while allowing no funds for work in non-agricultural fields such as medicine, sociology, or music. Nevertheless, WVU was the land-grant university with statewide obligations, and the Appalachian Center was an attempt to broaden the concept of the land-grant institution to include a new set of social conditions. Miller and Nesius sought federal money to expand by aligning the

Appalachian Center with the Appalachian Regional Commission, the federal agency that became instrumental in President Lyndon Johnson's War on Poverty by tackling social and economic problems in the region. Therefore, the name "Center for Appalachian Studies and Development" was intended as a tie-in to attract federal funding.[58]

Unfortunately, that federal funding never materialized, leading President Miller to expand the outreach projects through the Cooperative Extension Service system, which was already in place. The agents at the local level would identify the problems and the University would link them with the appropriate faculty to help them. The extension personnel had to accept this model, since they had their own local clientele and supporters, who were crucial to the agent's ability to perform his duties. A meeting of all the extension agents was held at Jackson's Mill, where Miller made the sales pitch with Nesius's support. The agents voted unanimously in favor of the plan, then returned to their counties to work on some new non-agricultural issues, such as planning and zoning for business development, health and medicine, music, training for local lawyers, and continuing education for public school teachers. After identifying local needs and developing a plan of work, the agents took the proposals to the main campus for assistance. Unfortunately, the academic support seldom materialized, for a variety of good reasons. According to Coffindaffer, these reasons included the facts that promotion and tenure required faculty to "publish or perish"; that faculty did not get paid to work overtime; that the travel distances involved could be substantial; that regular classroom work left too little time. The academics in the College of Arts and Sciences had the heaviest teaching loads on campus, Coffindaffer recalled. How could a professor of history or sociology teaching six classes and two hundred students realistically be expected to travel to the other end of the state to spend a few days working on local problems? In retrospect, Coffindaffer could readily understand that until there were rewards for service the focus would be on "publish, publish, publish." Publications equaled promotion, and tenure equaled security. It was "nobody's fault particularly, it just happened that way." On the other hand, the agents who were expected to deliver for their constituencies in the counties were let down. An agent's word became his bond, as good as a contract, so, when the University did not deliver, the repercussions were felt immediately at the county level. In Coffindaffer's words, the agents said, "Hey, if you guys are going to hang us out to dry, forget it." They began to retreat from making commitments because they feared not being able to deliver on them. In the short term, the agent lost some credibility in the county, and the University lost credibility with the agents, undermining the entire extension system. In the end, despite the best of intentions, the Appalachian Center failed to deliver, so its days were numbered.[59]

MILLER RESIGNS AND HARRY HEFLIN BECOMES INTERIM PRESIDENT

Rumors that Miller was preparing to leave WVU were circulating by 1966. In June the *Charleston Gazette* speculated that he was frustrated with the "provincialism" that dominated state politics, the constant struggle for state appropriations, and his loss in the battle to move the College of Law to the Kanawha Valley. Moreover, uncomplimentary rumors circulated about his involvement with Dr. Francena Nolan, chair of the Department of Home Economics, shortly after his wife's tragic death by suicide. Miller neither confirmed nor denied these sources of frustration, but he did say that "personal matters got in the way" of his duties. Provost John Golay also committed suicide during Miller's presidency, sharpening the edge on the rumors circulating about the president.[60] In July 1966 West Virginians read in the press that Miller had accepted a position as assistant secretary of education in the U.S. Department of Health, Education, and Welfare. In August the Board of Governors accepted his resignation with regret, and appointed Vice President for Administration and Finance Harry B. Heflin as acting president, effective August 15, 1966.[61]

In a statement regarding his resignation, Miller said he was convinced that "no other state needs a viable university more than West Virginia." He had not sought the new position, but, echoing Stahr's resignation statement when President Lyndon Johnson asked him to take the responsibility of "assisting a new worldwide emphasis of the United States in the field of international education," Miller said he could not refuse service to his country.[62] Miller provided the Board of Governors with a list of recommended priorities to assist his successor: First, a much higher level of state support for graduate and professional education was essential; second, a long-term method of funding for the Medical Center was vitally important to achieving financial stability; third, measures should be taken to enhance the Board of Governors' flexibility in budgeting state appropriations and to reduce administrative inefficiencies. Finally, Miller recommended that planning and cooperation between the University and the community should be emphasized in order to improve services that would make Morgantown as attractive as those normally found in university towns.[63] The priorities identified by Miller provide a snapshot of the issues the outgoing president regarded as most pressing at that point in time.

The announcement that Vice President for Finance and Administration Heflin would serve as acting president had a calming effect, but Miller's sudden departure caused a stir. Many wondered if this was further proof of West Virginia's inadequacy and inability to compete with other states. One alumnus wrote to the Board of Governors questioning why so many presidents came and went: "For a President to give up leadership of a great University to accept a junior cabinet position in one of the youngest and least important of cabinet secretaryships is clearly a reflection upon the university, its program, and its salary schedule." He noted that former president Elvis Stahr had left WVU to become secretary of the Army, a position he held for less than one year before accepting the presidency of Indiana University.[64]

Harry B. Heflin was an able and highly respected administrator with a long and distinguished career in higher education. He was educated at Glenville State College and George Peabody College (now part of Vanderbilt University), and he received his doctorate at the University of Pittsburgh. He taught in public schools, taught school teachers at the college level, and served in a training command during a stint in the U.S. Navy. He led the teacher education program at Marshall, served as president of Glenville State College for seventeen years, and in 1964 was appointed vice president of finance and administration in President Paul Miller's administration, the first to hold that new position.[65]

Heflin's mastery of higher-education finance was widely respected, and he proved his worth in the 1967–1968 budget battle. Following the formula honed to perfection by Stewart and Miller, Heflin emphasized the growth in enrollments, which reached an all-time high of 12,225 in 1967, WVU's centennial. In February President Heflin was accompanied before legislative committees by six student leaders, including student body president David Hardesty, to make his pitch for full funding of the $20 million request. Like his predecessors, Heflin emphasized that the basic disciplines needed "substantial upgrading" because all graduate and professional programs depended on the College of Arts and Sciences to provide pre-professional training. Once again, the University needed more faculty, eighty new positions in fact, to cover the increased enrollments, to begin to reduce heavy teaching loads, and to increase research productivity. In 1961 the faculty-student ratio was one to fourteen, but by 1967 it was one to twenty. Ever-growing enrollments were accommodated by increasing undergraduate class sizes. Consequently, per capita appropriations, which amounted to $859 in 1961, had decreased to $804 in 1967. Correspondingly, appropriations per student credit hour had decreased from $24.95 to $22.87 during the same period. None of the other state institutions had experienced such a decline, because graduate students brought the same amount of state support as undergraduates even though they cost considerably more to train and required a higher-paid graduate faculty. WVU continued to lag behind the marketplace, and mobile faculty continued to be lured to other institutions.[66]

DRAMATIC EXPANSION OF UNIVERSITY FACILITIES

The expansion of campus facilities that had begun under Heflin's predecessors continued on his watch. The Mountainlair was opened, and a major addition to the forestry building made room for the College of Human Resources and Education. Moreover, construction on an expansion of the Parkersburg Center began during Heflin's year in office, and the Federal Communications Commission approved the University's plan for the construction of a building to house an educational television station (assigned Channel 24 UHF) in Morgantown.[67]

The University's continued expansion exposed serious problems with the policy and method for property acquisition. Speaking to the American Right of Way Association in December 1966, Heflin explained that he had studied the University's program for property acquisition and found that "we have followed our usual West Virginia pattern." Instead of buying large blocks of property in anticipation of expanding institutions in the future, the state acquired property under the supposition that institutions would start and always remain small. Over the century between its founding and 1967, the University had been involved in 167 property transactions, with more than two-thirds of all property owned in 1966 having been acquired during the last twenty-year period. The largest blocks for the Morgantown campus were the acquisition of the Evansdale Campus in 1948, 85 acres given to the University for the Medical Center in 1951, and the 104 acres purchased from the Morgantown Golf and Country Club. These larger acquisitions necessitated the purchase of many small parcels to fill in between the Medical Center and the Evansdale Campus. The University purchased very few parcels of property by condemnation, believing that the negligible price of the parcel and the social cost in loss of goodwill were not worth the benefits.[68]

Construction of facilities posed a related problem. The construction programs at West Virginia institutions of higher learning were paid for entirely with money collected in one way or another from students. Until recently, Heflin declared in 1967, a special act of the legislature was required for each new project, and not more than $20 million in bonds could be outstanding at any one time for the state's entire higher education system. At WVU, an in-state student in the College of Arts and Sciences paid $254 per year, and an out-of-state student paid $884. WVU's construction program approved in 1967 was covered by a $20 million bond issue. Therefore, the construction projects at all of the state's schools were being paid for by WVU students without any appropriations from the state. "It seems to me that it is entirely unrealistic to expect the parents of WVU students presently enrolled to pay for all the construction taking place on the campuses of the entire State."[69]

Along with the radical changes in organization and mission during Paul Miller's administration, the University's physical facilities underwent a dramatic alteration as well. By June 1964, construction of two residence halls for nine hundred students, later known as Towers I and II, had begun on Evansdale Campus. In 1965, construction was completed on a new building for the Division of Forestry, named Percival Hall after W. Clement Percival, who headed the program from 1934 to 1966. A five-year plan for the general upgrading of Mountaineer Field was initiated, and an outdoor lighting system was installed on campus. The University began purchasing the land owned by the Morgantown Golf and Country Club, which, over the next five years, brought under University control the area between the Evansdale Campus and the Medical Center. The renovation of the chemistry building was also undertaken, and a new chemistry research addition was completed by 1968.[70]

A new student center was the only major construction project slated for the Downtown Campus during the Miller administration. Miller preferred to think of it as the "University Center," a sort of "Grand Central Station of our institution," because he envisioned it as the hub of activity for the entire university community.[71] To make way for the new Mountainlair and its attached parking garage, completed in 1967, Reynolds Hall, the Armory, and the Physical Plant shops were demolished, and the Health Center moved. The president and his family also moved out of the old stone house on the Downtown Campus to a more spacious residence out near Evansdale Campus, and the old president's residence was converted into Purinton Hall. The first of three phases of construction of the Creative Arts Center, which would house the music, drama, and art programs, was completed in 1968. That same year two more dormitories, Towers III and IV were added to the Evansdale Campus to accommodate the burgeoning number of students. The original plan calling for a dormitory complex of seven buildings was abandoned after the fourth of the Towers was completed. At that point, the administration decided to rely on the private market to supply further student housing, much to the delight of local real estate businesses. Planning was also underway for the Coliseum, an addition to Percival Hall, the educational television station, and a building for the College of Human Resources and Education, all on the Evansdale Campus.[72]

By inclination and experience Harry Heflin's approach to higher education was in accord with the philosophy of Paul Miller. When Heflin became acting president, therefore, he continued Miller's initiatives and attempted to resolve ongoing problems as well. One of the latter was the Kanawha Center. Governor Hulett Smith had opposed Miller's plan for the Law and Public Affairs Center, but the governor supported the concept of an expanding center for graduate education in the Kanahwa Valley. On July 18, 1966, leaders of Marshall and WVU met to see if they could collaborate on some "sensible arrangement" for providing graduate education in business, chemistry, and engineering in the Kanawha Center. Heflin supported the collaborative graduate center concept, and at its April 1967 meeting the Board of Governors approved expanding the courses it offered at the center. These developments raised cautionary flags in some quarters. Ever vigilant of fragmenting the University, the *Morgantown Post* editorialized that the state's financial support for higher education was so weak that diverting funds for a new facility was unwise. Also, in a message to the Board of Governors in April 1967, Heflin foresaw an increased competition for appropriations between WVU and other institutions, particularly Marshall, and Cabell and surrounding counties had more legislative representation than did Monongalia and surrounding counties.[73]

CELEBRATING A CENTURY OF CHANGE

In 1967 WVU celebrated its one hundredth anniversary with a year of festivities. Rep. Arch A. Moore Jr. of West Virginia's First Congressional District, who received his bachelor's and law degrees from WVU, launched the celebrations as principal speaker at the February 7 birthday dinner in Morgantown, followed by a series of events on and off campus. Prominent alumni speakers included Deputy Chief-of-Staff for the Marine Corps Brig. Gen. Earl E. Anderson (class of 1940) and Ambassador William K. Leonhart (class of 1939). But the year's major emphasis was meant to be a series of six symposia, leading off with "The Lessons of History," whose participants included eminent figures such as historians Arthur Schlesinger and Oscar Handlin, and regional novelist Jesse Stuart. Five other symposia followed: "The Frontiers of Science," "Man in His Community," "The Communication of Knowledge," "Man and His Regulation by Law," and "Man and His Religion." An international series brought famed CBS correspondent Richard C. Hottelet, and another series brought the Baroness Maria von Trapp.[74]

During the centennial year, Acting President Heflin frequently had occasion to muse on the University's past and the "great changes" that had occurred at WVU since its founding. In the early years progress had been slow but was overall "little short of amazing," he observed. And yet, "every major change the University has attempted has required a fight." The first major struggle was over location, with the city of Morgantown finally chosen because free land was offered. The struggle over whether to offer coeducation raged for fourteen years before the decision to admit women finally came 1889. Similarly, the system of governance for WVU affected the long history of the University, and it certainly did not cease to do so in 1967. Even then, discussions were underway to create a state Board of Regents in 1969. The establishment of a full-scale Medical School was one of the most far-reaching changes in the University's modern history, and that too came about only after a long political struggle. The face of WVU reflected in its buildings also marked major changes, but the building program was sporadic. During the major expansion of WVU's physical facilities between the fifties and the seventies, more construction was undertaken on the University campus than at any other period, but only after major campaigns for financing.[75]

The quest to become a respected academic institution among its perceived peers was another of those ongoing political struggles. Unfortunately, WVU had fallen short of its aspirations because inadequate state support left WVU "continuously spread too thin to do an outstanding job in any area." Becoming one the nation's largest universities was not a WVU ambition, Heflin proclaimed, and he doubted whether West Virginia University would ever have 30,000 students. Instead, "we would like to be one of the good universities with 12,000 students."[76] As the founders could not have imagined a WVU with 12,000 students, Heflin could not imagine in 1967 that in 2010 enrollment would nearly reach that unimaginable 30,000.

Former president Irvin Stewart retired from the Department of Political Science during the University's centennial year. In his departure speech at the Faculty Honors Convocation in March 1967, Stewart suggested that in future the University should redirect its perennial search for funding toward Washington rather than Charleston. In doing so, WVU would join a movement already well underway among the nation's research universities. However, Stewart cautioned, to be truly successful in this scramble for federal money, a constant presence and intimate knowledge of the inner workings of the federal agencies was the University's best chance.[77] In retirement, Stewart seemed to highlight Washington's rising allure for universities by moving there himself. University researchers and administrators thereafter followed close on his heels in their pursuit of federal dollars.

Heflin was a popular acting president, and many hoped that the Board of Governors would appoint him to the post permanently. The student legislature, the representative body of student government, made such a request to the Board of Governors in March 1967, but the board instead announced, on March 31, 1967, that James G. Harlow of the University of Oklahoma would become the sixteenth president of WVU. Like all decisions of the Board of Governors in executive session, the reason for choosing Harlow over Heflin was not disclosed to the public.[78]

FOUR

STUDENT AFFAIRS:
THE "SILENT GENERATION"

ENROLLMENT INCREASED during President Elvis Stahr's brief administration, from 6,278 in 1958–1959 to 7,514 in 1961–1962. Stahr favored encouraging out-of-state students to attend WVU. "Provincialism has definite limits and mixing students from different backgrounds is good for all of them, in particular the in-state students," Stahr informed an interviewer years later. There were some members of the legislature who questioned appropriating money to "educate somebody else's kids." Stahr countered that they came closer to paying their own way than in-state students did, but the main reason for encouraging out-of-state students was that it was "part of the education of West Virginia students." The increase in undergraduate enrollment was followed by a growing number of graduate students. By 1960, there were 1,300 graduate degree candidates, and the custom of handing a diploma to each graduate was abandoned. Thereafter, only PhD degrees would be formally awarded at commencement.[1]

The dramatic enrollment increases experienced during the postwar era of Irvin Stewart's administration continued as the first of the Baby Boom generation arrived on campus during the Miller administration. Student enrollment more than doubled from 6,184 to 14,888 between 1957–1958 and 1967–1968. Of the 8,655 students enrolled in 1963–1964, 74.4 percent were West Virginia residents, 23.4 percent were from other states, and 2.2 percent were foreign nationals. About one-quarter of the students lived in WVU housing, and almost 10 percent lived in fraternity and sorority houses. More than half lived off-campus. A number of factors attracted students to the University, including its moderate size, strong programs (especially in sciences, engineering, and music), modest cost, convenient location, and the fact that WVU was the only institution in the state that offered graduate and professional study.[2]

The aptitude of entering students, as judged by ACT scores, showed that WVU freshmen generally scored higher than students entering baccalaureate degree-granting institutions nationally, slightly higher than those entering the eight other schools belonging to the Southern Regional Education Board (SREB) that offered PhD degrees, and equivalent to the average for thirty-eight PhD institutions nationally. Most undergraduate students who applied were admitted; the average was an 89 percent acceptance rate for 1961, 1962, and 1963. The acceptance rate for graduate school during these years averaged even higher at 95 percent, although some programs, such as medicine, law, and engineering, were highly restricted. During this period, the nearly 12 percent improvement in the attrition rate, the measure of the percentage of the freshman class that remained for the senior year, indicated that the University was retaining a greater proportion of students.[3]

STUDENTS AND THE COMMUNITY

The main point made by the 1945 Strayer Report was that WVU could not advance until all sections of West Virginia accepted it as the state university. In accomplishing that goal, the report concluded, WVU faced two major obstacles. First was its location just a few miles south of the Pennsylvania state line, far from the center of population in the southern part of the state. The second referred to ambiguous "conditions surrounding the campus in the City of Morgantown"; the Strayer consultants failed to document any specific conditions. It is likely a reference to some of Morgantown's local color, which had chagrined older alumni attending University homecoming events in 1947. These alumni lamented that Morgantown was no longer a "quiet, picturesque community" as it used to be, and complained that the Morgantown Ordnance Works polluted the air with noxious smells.[4] The University city was "wide open," exposing students to slot machines, gambling dens, and liquor being sold openly, a Clarksburg editor complained.

Consequently, "racketeers of every kind" thrived in Morgantown, and he recommended that parents "withdraw their children" and send them "to some other school which is protected."[5]

Veterans returning after World War II made a profound impact on the campus and community. Vets made up half of the student body in the immediate postwar years, and they brought more maturity and a sense of responsibility to the student body because they were a little older in years and a lot older in experience. Their careers had been put on hold by the war; they were now ready to complete their education and get on with their lives. President Stewart alluded to this level of maturity among the vets in 1952 when he related a recent experience. Consuming a donut and coffee provided to donors at a Red Cross blood drive, the president initiated a conversation with a student donor. "I think I shall never forget his remark that he was two down, with two to go," observed Stewart. "I asked him what he meant. He replied that a transfusion of four pints of blood had saved his life in Korea. Since his return, he had given two pints of blood and he said that he owed two more to repay his debt before he could begin making his contribution on the plus side of the program. I think that the future of West Virginia will be secure with young people of that caliber."[6]

Veterans became a force on campus. The Veterans Association lobbied the legislature and could claim a measure of success for a liberal appropriation to meet their educational needs. The residents of "College Park," the makeshift housing made up of trailers and barracks converted to apartments for vets and their families, had already selected a "mayor" and "council" to represent their interests by the 1946–1947 academic year. Early in 1945 the vets organized Mountaineer Post 127, the first college American Legion post, and in 1946 the Women Veterans Organization came into being as an affiliate of Mountaineer Post 127. Returning vets were expected to transform undergraduate activities and traditions, but those concerns proved unfounded. Some vets were married, but many more were not. Single veterans joined fraternities and other student organizations and helped to revive less venerable traditions such as the honor court, which enforced customs like freshmen boys wearing beanies and striped ties and freshman girls observing regulated hours.[7]

President Stewart could hardly be blamed for failing to solve the traffic and parking problems exacerbated by the burgeoning student body. The student paper, the *Daily Athenaeum*, called on the city to protect students from drivers who "delighted in charging down upon groups of students, forcing them to sprint for safety." With the goal of reducing congestion, a campus parking permit system was implemented in 1950 costing $10 per semester, an amount that would stir envy in subsequent generations.[8] In years to follow, however, the entire University community experienced geometrical growth in parking and traffic congestion.

MOUNTAINEER TRADITIONS

Despite its long existence, WVU had few traditions with which students identified. Stewart initiated an effort to resuscitate some abandoned customs and to institutionalize new ones. Greater West Virginia Weekend was intended to restore traditions abandoned during World War II. The celebration of Mother's Day was revived in May 1946 as part of a weekend of festivities. Mother's Day, which originated in Grafton, West Virginia, and became a national holiday in 1914, was first celebrated by the University in 1930. It was fitting, therefore, that the final day of West Virginia Weekend festivities commemorated visiting mothers.[9]

The University's birthday, February 7, 1867, provided another occasion to recognize and celebrate the contributions of WVU to the people of the Mountain State. The very first University Day was celebrated in 1950 with a keynote address by Harold Stassen, the former governor of Minnesota and then president of the University of Pennsylvania. Significantly, more than two hundred alumni chapters and other organizations in all fifty-five of the state's counties also celebrated the observance.[10]

Mountaineer Week, inaugurated on November 8, 1947, provided another opportunity to highlight the quality and character of mountaineers for parents, alumni, and friends. Predictably, students seeking to poke fun at the supposed traits of mountaineers depicted them in less than flattering terms. Under the leadership of Arch A. Moore, the future governor, a sizable group of students attended the Kentucky-WVU football game adorned in overalls, plaid shirts, patched clothes, and other costumes caricaturing a "hillbilly." Everybody seemed to enjoy it, and the event was repeated in 1948 during Mountaineer Weekend, when hundreds of students, as well as the head football coach, Dudley DeGroot, attended a football game dressed as hillbillies.[11] Similarly, at halftime during the Mountaineer Week football game, the band formed itself into the shape of an outhouse to the tune of "When the Moon Comes over the Mountain."[12] When Stewart first came to WVU, he told an interviewer in 1990, "it seemed customary for West Virginians to make fun of themselves." A Morgantown reporter expressed his concern that the students misrepresented the Mountaineer by caricaturing him as "poor white trash" who spent a good part of his day "carrying a catalog to the outhouse."[13]

The students named their "hillbilly" mascot "Chop 'em Down." President Stewart was not amused, and he met with student leaders to consider changes. Led by All-American Leland Byrd, the basketball team was invited to the National Invitational Tournament held in Madison Square Garden, and the students were planning to take "Chop 'em Down" to help cheer on the team. Stewart argued that WVU would be a focus of national attention and thus needed to project a more positive image. He believed it was unfair for them to portray the people of West Virginia in such a degrading manner and convinced the students to leave "Chop 'em Down" at home.[14]

A few years later, a more dignified Mountaineer was created through the efforts of Mountain, the WVU men's honorary. The more dignified rendering of the Mountaineer in the Daniel Boone tradition is depicted in the Mountaineer statue that has stood vigil outside the Mountainlair since 1971. In November 1950, Mountain got behind the new image-building project by initiating a Mountaineer Statue Festival as a way to solicit funds to pay for the statue. The campaign was launched when Arch A. Moore Jr., then student body president, solicited the first $100 from the administration toward the eventual $15,000 cost.[15]

Stewart's efforts to elevate the students' consciousness and state pride met with further success on May 22, 1957, when student government leaders requested that the University Bookstore stop selling products displaying the hillbilly stereotype. Demijohn in hand, and decked out in felt hat, bare feet, and ragged clothes, the hillbilly caricature was "an unsavory and degrading" representation of the "Mountaineer spirit and tradition," in Stewart's opinion. A more accurate characterization would be displayed by the strong man of temperate demeanor clad in buckskin and a coonskin cap. In short, the Mountaineer looked like the rugged and independent Daniel Boone of legend rather than the comic caricature of Li'l Abner. Stewart agreed and informed the Bookstore manager to pull the items from the shelves and quit selling them. The manager complied but warned that pulling the hillbilly items would cost the Bookstore $300.[16]

Student leaders became engaged in two efforts that continue to play important roles as WVU traditions. Almost as important as the construction of the Mountaineer statue was the relocation of the mast from the USS *West Virginia*. It was a different kind of symbol than the Mountaineer, of course. The ship was sunk during the Japanese attack on Pearl Harbor in 1941, but was refitted and put back into service. At the end of the war, the Navy dismantled the battleship at the yard in Seattle. Assisted by the First National Bank of Morgantown and local citizens, student leaders began a successful campaign to salvage the ship's mast. On March 17, 1961, the mast was permanently erected before a crowd of well-wishers at its present location.[17] Although the mast arrived a few months after President Stahr left for a post in Washington, DC, much of the impetus for bringing the mast to Morgantown campus had been mounted during Stahr's tenure.

Throughout the Great Depression and World War II, the student newspaper continued to publish without interruption. It became a semi-weekly in 1943, but in 1946 the paper once again appeared every weekday. The *Daily Athenaeum* promoted policies that served the students' interests. It documented what became for historians a record of the day and provides us with a record of the constantly changing student conventions, interests, and values. For example, it supported freshmen initiation rites but opposed hazing; it opposed chewing gum by female students; it urged students not to smoke in the classroom buildings on Woodburn Circle because of the fire hazard; and it commented unfavorably on the growing inclination of men to use profanity. During the war, women dominated the newspaper staff. Men once again predominated after the war, but women remained henceforth a large percentage of the staff, which consisted of sixty reporters, twenty-six copyeditors, and a number of editors. A similar pattern characterized the life of *Monticola*, the long-serving student yearbook, where women dominated the staff during the war and continued in a prominent role after the war.[18]

WVU provided three major areas of cultural and educational programming for students and the university community generally: The Great Artist series presented eight major programs each year, including symphonies, plays, ballets, and solo artists. The Convocation series brought in six lecturers of national caliber, and the provost sponsored a series of specialized lectures in arts and sciences.[19]

It was a matter of policy during the Stewart administration that the intellectual development of its students was the University's primary concern. But WVU also made a conscious effort to create an institutional environment that fostered the "total individual" and "the student as a human being."[20] Not surprisingly, students were not always in accord with the administration on what constituted a proper environment. In 1949, for example, there was a flap over *Moonshine*, a campus humor magazine edited by students in the journalism school. Inevitably, some copies circulated in the community at large. The crude humor did not sit well with some community members, who complained to President Stewart. One "future student of the University" wrote to the president, to make him aware of the situation and to urge him to "look into this matter and see what you can do about improving the tone of this magazine." In a similar vein, sixteen students at Morgantown's St. Francis High School sent a letter stating that as future WVU students they objected to the content of *Moonshine*.[21]

This was not the kind of University image that Stewart wanted to convey. He wrote directly to the student editor, sending along copies of the letters from the St. Francis students. "It seems to me that some of the material which recently has appeared in *Moonshine* is in very poor taste," he remonstrated. "I am not sure just what justification there is for the publication of a magazine like *Moonshine*," he continued, "but it should stop somewhere short of smearing the good name of the institution."[22] Apparently the magazine's editors ignored Stewart's comments, and in November 1951

Moonshine created another public- relations problem for the president. In his letter of resignation that year, Patrick W. Gainer, the well-known professor of English and faculty sponsor for *Moonshine*, stated the reason for his resignation: "I accepted the position of faculty adviser . . . with the understanding that nothing would be printed in the magazine without my approval." The latest issue, however, contained some materials he had marked for deletion, and, "since my name appears in the magazine as faculty adviser, the harm done to me, as a respected member of the faculty of the West Virginia University, as a responsible member of my community, and as the head of a family, is so great that nothing short of a public apology could ever correct it." He concluded by demanding that his name "never again be connected in any way with this infamous project."[23]

Excessive noise and rowdiness among students has always been a source of complaints from city residents. In May 1953, President Stewart received a letter complaining about the men's dormitory, Boreman Hall. "For the past three nights we, and the entire neighborhood, have been unable to get any rest at all because of the noise, obscene words being screamed, bottles being thrown out the windows, fire crackers being set off, and just a general 'free-for-all' which continues until 3:00 a.m.," a disgruntled resident wrote. She had complained several weeks ago and the noise subsided for a week, but "Saturday night one of the fraternities serenaded a local sorority house around 12:00 midnight," and then "around 2:00 a.m. the same group . . . returned to the street and began cursing, screaming, and trying to sing obscene songs which sounded like a group of sailors home on a drunken shore leave" until 3:30 a.m. The students continued their antics Sunday and Monday nights. Only police intervention prevented a "Panty Raid" on the women's dormitories on Saturday night. The complainant declared that she would "gladly move from this neighborhood" had she not signed a one-year lease. She hoped the president could do something to "calm some of the very high-spirited young men," so residents could get some rest.[24]

Following an investigation of the episode by Director of Student Affairs Joseph C. Gluck, it was learned that Mrs. Ingram and her husband lived in a house next to Boreman Hall on Prospect Street. He noted that "since the house is very close to the dormitory the noise from the dormitory, even when fairly normal in volume, may be troublesome to the occupants of the house." Gluck asked the faculty resident of the dormitory and the proctors to make sure that "abnormal noises are held down," but advised Mrs. Ingram to call the city police to investigate any future disturbances.[25]

Panty raids were the fad on college campuses during the 1950s, and, as suggested in the above complaint, the overwrought enthusiasm did not escape WVU. Stewart's administration was in accord with the general off-campus opinion that such events fell into the category of pranks, rather than malicious or criminal acts. One of these episodes occurred on May 20, 1952, when, in Stewart's absence, the responsibility fell on Vice President Neff to request police assistance. He later provided President Stewart with a vivid account of the "arduous evening." The episode began with a gathering of students on North High Street who set off firecrackers and, with a bugle call, advanced on Terrace Hall: "At the south end of Terrace Hall, girls were hanging out the windows, encouraging the raiding party. The place by then was teeming with raiders," Neff reported. He pushed through the crowd into Terrace Hall and "drove out as many of the mobsters (stupid so-called students) as possible. However, they were swarming like bees at this time. It was suddenly realized that Terrace Hall was being vacated by the raiders, and I discovered that they were making a charge (if a charge includes stealing goods) on Woman's Hall."[26]

President Stewart issued a press release stating that both boys and girls were to blame: "From the facts presented to me it is clear that part of the blame rests with a few girls whose taunts encouraged the boys to enter the dormitories. The fact that the episode was conducted in a spirit of fun does not alter the fact that it was both unimaginative and incredibly stupid. The more mature and intelligent students share the administration's regret of this incident." The President reported to the Board of Governors that it was fortunate the police did not attempt to stop the raiders. Their exercise in "good judgment" prevented a raid from turning into a brawl.[27]

The spirit of fun accompanied most panty raids, but they could result in unexpected negative consequences. A panty raid in November 1955 apparently was the result of spontaneous combustion because of "the rising temperature in connection with the Pitt football game," according to

President Stewart. Around 11:30 p.m. on this night, a small group of students were spotted heading for Woman's Hall chanting "panty raid." Someone notified the local radio station, and a popular disc jockey announced on air that a panty raid was in progress. As a result, male students converged on Woman's Hall from all over town. The raiders gained entrance into the Kappa Delta and Chi Omega sororities and Woman's Hall, causing "considerable damage," President Stewart reported to the Board of Governors. Delta Gamma women had time to prepare for the raiders and had attached a hose to the water tap on the second floor. When the crowd gathered at the front door, they dampened the enthusiasm of the young men by turning the hose on them. Unfortunately this occurred just as President Stewart pushed his way to the front of the crowd, and his new hat was ruined. He warned the Board of Governors that this incident would undoubtedly be gleefully reported in the papers. Some of the raiders were identified and received "prompt disciplinary action," along with demands to pay restitution for damages.[28]

The Order of Vandalia award, a tradition of still another kind, was launched during Elvis Stahr's administration. The Board of Governors approved the new tradition to honor individuals who had rendered distinguished service to the University over a sustained period of time. The award was named after a tract of land roughly approximating the current state of West Virginia that eighteenth-century speculators hoped would become the fourteenth American colony of Vandalia. The American Revolution scuttled the plan, but the name continued to resurface.[29]

In 1960, foreshadowing the waves of protest that would sweep the nation's campuses later in the decade, thirteen students in the University's Army and Air Force Reserve Officer Training Corps sent a letter to the *Daily Athenaeum*. They objected to "militarism" and therefore regarded compulsory service in ROTC as an infringement upon their rights. They called on all students to join them in their protest. The next day, President Stahr reminded the cadets that the requirement was mandated by West Virginia law, and that they knew of the obligation when they enrolled. If they objected, he said, they should address the issue in a more "thoughtful way," rather than simply trying to evade their "own lawful obligations." President Stahr was not likely to be sympathetic considering his own military background, but he also reminded students that two years of ROTC training were compulsory as part of the University's land-grant contract with the federal government.[30] This student protest was one of the first against ROTC in the sixties, but protests later in the decade would prove much too disruptive to brush aside, as Stahr had done in this case, and would demonstrate how quickly change can come to college campuses.

STUDENT GOVERNMENT AND REPRESENTATION

University students were represented by a student government divided into an executive council, a student legislature, and a student court. All three branches worked closely with the administration. Other organizations represented students as well. Associated Women Students, which legislated and maintained rules for women, also was represented on University committees relating to women's issues. The Interfraternity Council and Panhellenic Council were self-governing bodies that determined policies governing Greek affairs for the eighteen national fraternities and ten national sororities represented on campus. The Mountainlair Governing Board, made up of five students and five faculty, made policy for the student center. It also coordinated the student program council and student committees working with the council, as well as eight class honor societies, about thirty-five academic and service honor societies, twenty-five professional honor societies, and six other interest groups. In 1964, about 4,000 students belonged to various student organizations, 4,600 participated in intramural athletics, and 355 participated in intercollegiate athletics. Also, 971 students participated in fraternities, and 600 in sororities.[31]

Even though the student body possessed higher-than-average admission test scores, students perplexed Miller with what he regarded as their overabundance of good nature. In matters of decorum, courtesy, and a lack of "intentional display in dress," WVU enjoyed some "fine examples of American college youth." Others might have seen this as cause for celebration, but it only puzzled President Miller. "Our students do not come through to me as lively scholars. I detect a kind of intellectual blandness, a sort of lock-step dutifulness about class attendance, a disinclination towards intellectual debate, and a shallow capacity for indignation. Needless to say, something is lacking in the overall campus environment," Miller lamented. He concluded that the students needed to be stimulated by more creative programming and teaching.[32]

The enthusiastic social life on WVU's campus was apparently well documented by the sixties. Thirty years later, after his presidency, Paul Miller recollected that, when he left Michigan State to take the presidency at WVU in 1962, his colleagues questioned why he would choose to move to a "low quality party school." Perhaps because of that perception, President Miller decided that change must come if WVU was to be seen as a "serious university." In his inaugural address, he announced that he would "insist that our campus life aim for a high level of decorum and taste." Considering the hard work and sacrifice of parents and citizens to provide for a college education, Miller thought it "intolerable for him to look aside from the loose and open practice of the minor vices" for which the student body was known. Part of the problem was that West Virginia was a dry state, forcing students to travel near and far to socialize with alcohol. Fraternity houses had their own bars, and wild parties on the weekends were standard fare. Moreover, student socializing focused undue attention on the alcohol they could not have, and this underground reveling was done in out-of-the-way havens that contributed nothing to the life of the University.[33]

President Miller's attempt to deal with student issues led him to establish the Office of Student Educational Services, with legendary student affairs' professionals Betty Boyd and Joe Gluck leading the effort. The administration also banned alcohol in fraternity and sorority houses. Speaking years later of this campaign to improve student behavior, Miller asserted that he was not "a bluenose teetotaler, but this had to be a serious place. The people of the state deserved better." If students were going to drink alcohol, they should do it on campus, where it was safer. The president called a meeting of parents one weekend and told them that they, like the administration, faced a choice; "Did they want their children staying on campus drinking in a public place in a reasonable ambience of decency, or in bars in basements of fraternity houses or spending weekends in

Pittsburgh?" The parents got the message, and eventually beer was served in the Mountainlair.[34]

DESEGREGATION

May 17, 1954, was a momentous day in the history of the United States. On that day the U.S. Supreme Court ruled in *Brown et al. v. Board of Education of Topeka, Kansas* that the doctrine of "separate but equal," which had been established in *Plessy v. Ferguson* in 1896, violated the Fourteenth Amendment guaranteeing citizens equal protection of the law and was therefore unconstitutional. The high court modified this ruling in the 1938 case *Missouri ex rel. Gaines v. Canada*, which declared that an African American could not be denied admission to a state law school because of his race; if a state provided whites with a law school then it must also provide blacks with equal facilities. In 1939, WVU quietly began accepting African American residents to the graduate and professional programs that were not available at either of the state's colleges for blacks, Bluefield State College and West Virginia State College. West Virginia University accepted African Americans in undergraduate programs that were not offered by the state's public black colleges. "In keeping with understandings among leaders of both races," a contemporary historian wrote, WVU's programs were opened to black students without publicity. That being the case, few enrolled.[35]

African American students encountered systemic obstacles as well as racist attitudes on campus and in the community. As "pioneers" they exposed themselves to life on the other side of the great American racial divide, and that act alone could produce intense personal anxiety. Still they came, and despite the difficulties they succeeded. In 1941, Kenneth James became the first African American to earn a master's degree from WVU when he completed the program in education. The first African American to enroll in graduate school at WVU, W. O. Armstrong, received the MEd degree in 1942 and then served as principal at Dunbar High School in Fairmont. Victorine Louistall's career was unique in more ways than one. The first known African American woman to attend graduate school at WVU, Louistall initially received a degree in business education from West Virginia State College in 1937 and began her teaching career at Roosevelt Wilson High School in Clarksburg. In 1942 she enrolled in the MEd program at the University and completed the degree in 1945. While still teaching at Kelly Miller High School in Clarksburg in 1943, she began study toward a master's degree in library science. After completing the degree, Louistall joined the WVU Library Science teaching staff in 1966, achieving another school record as the first African American faculty member to hold that position. She retired as associate professor of library science in 1978.[36]

John Reuben Sheeler posted another milestone in 1954 as the first African American to receive a PhD from WVU, taking a degree in history. Horace Belmear (MS '51), a coach at segregated Dunbar High School in Fairmont, enrolled in graduate classes in physical education prior to the 1954 *Brown* decision. While he encountered no overt hostility, white racial attitudes were a concern for Belmear. As the only African American in his first class, he recalled, "I felt very uncomfortable. The students would not sit by me or talk to me. When the professor realized what was happening he spent a good portion of the class extolling my virtues as a coach in Marion County, and he lectured against prejudice, segregation, and discrimination. My stead as a student increased after this."[37]

While African American students did not report any overt racism in the classroom, they did find their lives outside the classroom highly restricted. They could not eat in the University cafeteria, use the restrooms, or participate in extracurricular activities. Black students were not permitted to live on campus so they usually boarded with local black families. At least two racially motivated incidents were documented on campus, although other occurrences no doubt went undocumented. During World War II, the Young Women's Christian Association on campus invited the choir from the segregated Monongalia High School to sing at the Christmas program. The YWCA planned to serve refreshments following the program in E. Moore Hall, but the dean of women, Edna Arnold, refused to allow University students to take refreshments with the black high school students. In response, and to their credit, the YWCA refused to serve food to anyone. Dean Arnold also created a racial incident at a holiday dance when an ROTC cadet asked a young black woman who operated the elevator at the Hotel Morgan to dance the "jitterbug" with him. Both were good dancers, and delighted the students by their performance, yet Dean Arnold tried, unsuccessfully, to convince the ROTC commanding officer to dismiss the cadet. Instead, he was restricted to his quarters and lost two-thirds of his monthly pay for the remainder of the semester for behavior that brought "discredit upon the military services." Fortunately, wiser heads prevailed further up the chain of command, and the sentence was rescinded. The New York magazine *PM* denounced the episode as "the most blatant, unfair evidence of capricious, irresponsible Jim Crowism that has come out of the Army in a long, long time," the Morgantown paper reported. This atmosphere would have been part of the racial landscape navigated by Annette Chandler-Broome who, in 1957, became the first known African-American woman to earn a bachelor's degree from WVU.[38]

At least some compassionate individuals on campus tried to ease black students' anxiety. Blanche Price, the University cafeteria dietitian, was one such person. Arthur Garrison Phillips (BA '51), who worked as a cafeteria cashier during his senior year, said, "On the first full day of classes in the fall of 1950 . . . about five or six black students appeared to dine at the very last moment for their evening meal." Phillips believed this was their "first venture into a segregated dining room," and they had timed their entrance to be the very last because they did not know what kind of reception awaited them. Once served, the black students took a seat at the far end of the cafeteria.

Miss Price, observing this, got her meal and approached several of us student workers and said, 'won't some of you join me in helping make these folks welcome?' Several of us quickly picked up our trays and followed Miss Price to greet the black students. She paused when she reached their table and said, 'may we join you?' The blacks, somewhat taken aback at the request, invited us to their table. We pushed two of the long dining tables together and that was the end of segregation in the West Virginia University cafeteria. The very next day, to the best of my memory, at whatever meal and for the remainder of my senior year, the black students, who had made friends in their respective classes, dined with them and sat anywhere they chose in the dining room. The kind, Christian act of that gracious lady, Blanche Price, remains strongly in my memory.[39]

The story of Jack L. Hodge, the first African American to receive a bachelor's degree from WVU, indicates how contradictory the messages could be for the first individuals to cross over the racial divide in those days. Originally from Maybeury, in McDowell County, Hodge's application to study journalism at WVU was originally rejected because West Virginia State College offered a sophomore journalism course. "I was bitter, but determined," he recalled. After studying at Bluefield State and at West Virginia State, Hodge was finally admitted to WVU and arrived on campus in September 1950 because no further courses were available at the black schools. In contrast with the experiences of black students enrolling on white campuses in the South, Hodge recalled, "everything seemed to fit right into place." Like other black students, he boarded with a local black family. Hodge's first class at WVU was taught by Perley Isaac Reed, dean and founder of the journalism program. Reed's first lecture, Hodge remembered, began with an introduction: "Class, this is Mr. Hodge. He's going to like some of you. Some of you are going to like him. Some of you may dislike him, and he may dislike some of you. Hopefully not." Hodge was encouraged that "everything was going to be all right."[40]

Although there were a handful of African-American graduate students on campus in 1950, Hodge was, as far as he knew, the first to enter the undergraduate student body. His initial bitterness on being denied admission faded, however, "because of men like Dr. Reed and the many kind people who extended me a helping hand along the way." Stints of work at Bethlehem Steel in Baltimore, and at Republic Steel in Warren, Ohio, interrupted his studies when he needed more money to pay for his education. On another occasion, he informed Dr. Reed that he was unable to pay his student fees, and Reed approved a student loan on the spot, no cosigner required. In addition to his studies, Hodge joined the other journalism students working on the *Daily Athenaeum*. He was chosen sports editor, and that brought him into contact with football and basketball fans. Hodge acknowledged: "Just so I don't leave the impression that living in a white world on campus didn't have its moments, there were some incidents," such as the time when he was covering a football game and over the sound of 30,000 people came the voice of one man: "What's that nigger doing down there?" Social dilemmas also cropped up periodically. When a question arose about whether black students could attend campus dances, President Irvin Stewart reminded the student body that any student enrolled at WVU was entitled to attend. Stewart informed the downtown movie theater managers that he would place the theaters off-limits to all students if they denied admission to African Americans. The eighty-seventh annual graduation exercise was a proud day for Hodge, with his family and friends in attendance. But as he walked to the stage to receive his degree, someone in the audience exclaimed: "Oh, there's a little colored boy!"[41]

West Virginia's constitution, unlike the former Confederate states that developed a system of thorough segregation of the races sanctioned and codified in the law, contained only two specific racial restrictions pertaining to African Americans: a prohibition against intermarriage and a provision declaring that "white and colored persons shall not be taught in the same school." When WVU was established a few years later, in 1867, therefore, it was a segregated institution. The 1954 *Brown* decision advanced previous court rulings on civil rights for blacks in higher education by declaring that, even when equal facilities were provided for black and white students, segregated education imposed by law remained "inherently unequal." The U.S. Supreme Court further clarified its intent in the *Brown* decision by asserting that desegregation of the schools should proceed with "all deliberate speed." The vague phrasing, however, gave segregationists in the South an opportunity to slow down the process. West Virginia's far less strident commitment to segregation, primarily fixed in custom and local ordinances, allowed Governor William Marland to order state officials to comply fully and immediately.[42]

West Virginia Attorney General John G. Fox held that segregation as defined in the state constitution was rendered moot by the *Brown* decision, and the state board of education ruled that any qualified student, regardless of race, could enroll in any state institution under its control. Immediately following the *Brown* decision, President Stewart wrote to Attorney

General Fox for guidance on how to proceed. More specifically, the president asked whether WVU should admit African Americans to courses currently being offered at the state's black colleges, and whether the University was obligated to admit black transfer students and those from out-of-state. The attorney general replied that neither West Virginians nor out-of-state applicants should be denied admission because of race.[43]

With this clarification in hand, Stewart informed the president of the Board of Governors that he would institute the new policy immediately for the summer session. "It is probable that we shall have one or more Negroes in our classes in the elementary school and in the University High School. If this is the case, these will probably be the first Negro children to attend public schools on a non-segregated basis in West Virginia," the president observed. The following year, 1955, about fifty African Americans were enrolled at WVU.[44] Without ceremony, controversy, or public comment then, WVU began accepting African American students. Desegregation at WVU occurred without the "massive resistance" desegregation encountered at state flagship institutions in the Deep South. Nevertheless, the experience was a mixed blessing for African American students who enrolled at WVU in the immediate post-*Brown* era.

COLD WAR AND CIVIL LIBERTIES

President Stewart's tenure as president coincided with the start of the Cold War with the Soviet Union, the Korean War (1951–1953), and hysteria fanned by the investigations of Senator Joseph McCarthy (R-WI) and the U.S. House Committee on Un-American Activities. In a speech delivered before the Ohio County Republican Women's Club in Wheeling on February 10, 1950, Senator McCarthy infamously held up a sheet of paper containing a list of 205 high-ranking officials in the U.S. State Department. He claimed that they were members of the Communist Party and branded them "traitors from within." McCarthy's speech in Wheeling is generally thought to mark the beginning of his anti-Communist "witch hunt."[45] North Korea's invasion of South Korea on June 25, 1950, initiating America's involvement in the Korean War, exacerbated the ideological hysteria generated by the Cold War.

President Stewart seldom missed an opportunity to denounce Communism even before Senator McCarthy launched his witch hunt in February 1950. Intellectuals were favorite targets, and Stewart, an experienced Washington hand, understood which way the wind was blowing. As early as November 1947 Stewart informed the Board of Governors that "there is building up over the country an atmosphere conducive to witch hunting, and I assume that the University will be one of the places where some people will try to find witches." To build a defense before the storm, Stewart formed a committee of faculty whose integrity was "above suspicion." Its task was to investigate faculty suspected of Communist sympathies and to consider disciplinary action. "I would recommend the dismissal of any member of the faculty who is a Communist, because I believe that Communism requires intellectual dishonesty incompatible with serving on the University faculty."[46]

In many of the hundreds of speeches delivered by the president during his twelve-year term, Stewart reinforced over and over again his opposition to Communism, its incipient threat to democracy, and especially its potentially corrosive effect on young people. Nevertheless, he cautioned that the University would resist unreasonable requests, such as those coming from the House Committee on Un-American Activities, that violated the principle of academic freedom. In his speeches he frequently denounced Communism while also insisting that University students be exposed to disagreeable political ideologies through exchanges of factual information and open discussion in the classroom.[47] Stewart was a "Cold Warrior," but not a "witch hunter."

President Stewart's anti-Communism was a position taken by many university presidents during the early years of the Cold War, and it was based on both real and perceived threats from an aggressive Soviet Union and China. However, Stewart demonstrated in a speech before the state's school superintendents that he would not give in to the fear mongers. "As educators it is our job to help keep democracy strong," he proclaimed. At the same time, he anticipated that a frenzy could lead to McCarthyism. "We must fight those who would use the liberties which we cherish to deprive us of our liberties," he declared. "We must be on the alert against that small but vigilant minority who would play the Russian game—who would have us sacrifice the freedom which is ours for the promises which Russia has so often betrayed." At the same time, he insisted, the right to criticize and to advocate change must be defended: "We must avoid being swept up by a hysteria in which the advocates of the status quo could brand as communist every individual who questions the absolute correctness of any phase of our social and economic life."[48]

Stewart's defensive strategy was not long in being tested. In January 1948 the State Federation of Republican Women's Clubs and the *Jefferson Republican* of Ranson, West Virginia, requested an investigation of rumored Communist activities at WVU. If solid factual information could be presented, the president vowed that it would be taken into consideration. None was ever produced. Similarly, Rush D. Holt, a West Virginia politician who switched to the Republican Party in 1949, warned Stewart in 1951 that the names of two WVU faculty members were linked to suspicious organizations by the House Un-American Activities Committee. President Stewart permitted the two professors to answer the allegations; the Board of Governors found their explanation to be satisfactory, and the matter was dropped.[49] No member of the WVU faculty was ever discharged for being sympathetic to Communism during this fearful period of history.

Stewart's anti-communism was undoubtedly genuine, but he felt compelled to protect the University from demagogic politicians like Senator McCarthy who threatened cherished academic freedoms. To defend the University from potential claims that it harbored Communists, Stewart reiterated his conviction to all budget officers in September1950, the very height of the Cold War, that WVU had no place for Communist employees of any kind. He restated WVU's policy that required questioning all prospective faculty about their views on Communism, and advocated the additional step of screening out possible Communists among tenure-track faculty. Stewart thereby ordered that all future appointments be contingent on the candidate signing a loyalty oath similar to the one signed by appointees to major positions in the federal government, by which the oath-taker affirmed that "I do not advocate the overthrow of the Government of the United States by force or violence; that I am not a member of the communist party or any other political party or organization that advocates the overthrow of the Government of the United States by force or violence."[50]

Again President Stewart's defensive strategy was challenged and found durable in June 1949, when the House Committee on Un-American Activities requested that Stewart provide them with a list of textbooks used in the social sciences. Stewart complied with the request, even though he understood it to be a "fishing expedition." On the advice of the American Council on Education, when he informed the Board of Governors of the request, he revealed his awareness of the need to protect civil liberties and academic freedoms in crafting his approach to the threat posed by McCarthyism:

Strictly speaking, I assume that the separation of powers between the state and the national government is such that the House Committee has no proper jurisdiction over the University. In spite of that fact, my inclination would normally be to supply the desired information to any committee of Congress. The House Committee on Un-American Activities falls in a class by itself by the way in which it has used its official position to smear private individuals without giving them an opportunity to appear before the Committee. It is quite possible, for instance, that the Committee may have some private list of volumes with some points of which the chairman of the Committee may disagree. It would be in keeping with past performances of the Committee to publish a list of institutions in which one or more of those volumes were used as text, with a thinly veiled inference that the institutions using the volumes were hotbeds of communism.[51]

Stewart approved of faculty involvement in politics, particularly during elections. He did draw a distinction, however, between running for office and supporting someone else's candidacy, or working on behalf of a political party. Faculty members "have an obligation as citizens to participate in political campaigns" if they do not "adversely affect the University," he informed the Board of Governors in 1952, and faculty members ought not to be "political eunuchs." Later that year, the president informed Governor Okey Patteson that faculty and staff had the same political rights as other citizens, and that such activity occasionally created poor public relations for the University if the employee exercised poor judgment. Under no circumstances, however, should political partisanship extend into the classroom, nor should it affect a faculty member's obligation to meet classes.[52]

MODERNIZING THE GREEKS

The sixties brought tumultuous student protests and youthful rebellion against a host of other social issues. The antiwar protests of the latter part of the decade were larger and louder on white college campuses, but the civil rights movement produced far more positive and systemic change. On college campuses the attempt to root out racist practices reached into all quarters. For example, in the practice of racial discrimination the Greek system came under thorough scrutiny by the Miller administration. Sororities and fraternities on campus, like their white counterparts nationally, had always barred African Americans from membership. Consequently, membership was homogeneously white, Anglo-Saxon, and Protestant by policy and practice. The Greek system, Miller observed in October 1963, was "a vestige of an older and more immature day in university life." Greek organizations needed to choose which alternative they would embrace: establishing new ideals or getting in the way of the University's new priorities. Unless the Greeks found a new mission, he said, "the system must be gracefully led aside so that the main business of the University will not be delayed."[53] The message was unambiguous—and long overdue.

The student paper, the *Daily Athenaeum*, climbed aboard in 1964 by investigating the exclusion policies of the sororities and fraternities. The investigation revealed that no sorority on campus had ever actually pledged an African American, even though half of the presidents of the eleven sororities declared that they would accept a non-white woman if the right one applied. All of the fraternities, however, declared that desegregation should be on a voluntary basis, and that the ideals of their organizations would be undermined if they were "forced" to integrate. The University Senate passed a resolution on February 9, 1965, encouraging the University to withdraw all recognition and support from sororities or fraternities, or any other student association, whose constitution or bylaws denied membership on the basis of race, color, religion, or ethnic origin. Seeking a response from the sororities and fraternities, the *Daily Athenaeum* was generally referred to those organizations' respective national headquarters. A few months later, Forrest H. Kirkpatrick, the former president of the Board of Governors who had hired Paul Miller, challenged those attending a Greek leadership conference to break with the past and build a better society.[54]

One example of the need for change was the Kappa Alpha fraternity tradition of flying the Confederate flag from the chapter house on public occasions. A continuation of the practice was a symbolic affront to blacks at a time when the University was trying to recruit them, and the athletic department had requested that Kappa Alphas at least stop flying the flag on football game days. The fraternity refused, and the symbol that blacks regarded as the embodiment of America's racist past waved defiantly at the top of High Street when WVU played Syracuse on November 13, 1965. The Kappa Alphas, grudgingly, finally put away the flag only on demand from the Miller administration.[55]

There was some modest change afoot among Greeks on campus. As early as October 25, 1962, the Panhellenic Council asked students to boycott Pike's Restaurant downtown because it was allegedly the only such establishment that refused to serve African Americans. The Associated Women Students Executive Council followed suit several days later because a boycott would serve as a warning to other businesses that might be inclined to follow Pike's example. By 1967–1968 the fraternity presidents on campus were ready to meet with the Interfraternity Council to discuss major steps toward removing racially discriminatory practices. Thereafter, the revised rush system permitted blacks to sign up without restriction, and candidates were no longer required to furnish recommendations to receive an invitation. The first traditionally African American fraternity, Kappa Alpha Psi, was chartered at WVU in 1969, although it was not formally segregated by constitution or bylaws. The University had denied an African American sorority permission to establish a chapter at WVU in 1967, however, because it accepted only black women.[56]

Irvin Stewart's first year as president was a baptism of fire in which he fielded complaints from fans unhappy with the University's athletic program. One of the issues confronting Stewart was the funding and awarding of scholarships to WVU athletes. Critics believed that the scholarship money came from state appropriations and athletic gate receipts, and that state funds for general education were being diverted to athletics. A special committee to investigate the issue concluded that athletic scholarships were, and always had been, funded by private donors. The committee decided that there was nothing inappropriate with this manner of funding but recommended that a school official independent of intercollegiate athletics be responsible for controlling those funds. Also, a new University Athletic Council was established with the athletic director serving as its chief executive. The director set policy and supervised budgets, schedules, athletic awards, and employees. The council was also charged with resolving conflicts between the athletic director and the coaches, and served as the public spokesperson for the athletic program. The new University Athletic Council was formally approved by the Board of Governors on April 26, 1947, and assumed responsibility for the entire athletic program. With the athletic director now responsible only to the president and the Board of Governors, a clear line of authority established University control over athletics.[57]

Since the 1920s, when the state superintendent of schools attempted to force WVU to join the West Virginia Athletic Conference, the University has opposed the periodic efforts of politicians to dictate the scheduling of its athletic competitions. After World War II, politicians friendly to Marshall College repeatedly pressured WVU to play Marshall in football. In 1953, President Stewart objected to such a contest, and his reasoning would have a modern ring a half-century later:

The objection to athletic contests between Marshall and the University goes far deeper than the questionable wisdom of legislative action in matters of internal administration. One of the paramount needs in West Virginia is that of overcoming sectionalism. There are many forces working to fragment the State. There is little operating to unify it. One of the real services which the University should perform is that of providing an operation behind which the entire State can rally with pride. Athletic contests between Marshall and the University would operate in just the opposite direction. The University would become 'the enemy' in those sections of the State which for any reason would rally behind the Marshall athletic cause. If the University should win the athletic contests, it would be taken as evidence that additional support was needed for Marshall in order to enable it to compete on even terms with the University. If Marshall should win the contests, that fact would be adduced as evidence that Marshall was equal in stature with the University and should be supported comparably by the Legislature.[58]

Ardent fans applauded Stewart's stand against playing Marshall, but they must have found his perspective on the importance of collegiate athletics disquieting. "Every institution likes to see its athletic teams successful. Its friends hope that it will win more games than it loses." But, Stewart cautioned, "since a win for one team represents a defeat for its opponent, the total of victories and defeats will balance. For a properly scheduled institution over a period of years, the number of victories should approximate the number of defeats." West Virginia University desired to win athletic contests, he continued, but the University was not "unduly concerned over losses to teams representing comparable institutions. A well-played game, with good sportsmanship on the part of players, coaches, and spectators, is a credit to an institution. This philosophy is thoroughly consistent with the place of intercollegiate athletics as part of an educational program rather than a side show."[59]

President Stewart's perspective on the role of athletics offers no obvious explanation for why the "Golden Era" of both football and basketball was in full bloom at WVU in the fifties.

To be precise, the decade of the fifties was the second "Golden Era" of WVU football. The first "Golden Era" extended from the latter part of the first decade of the twentieth century and into the second decade. This was the era of Ira Everett Rodgers, the running back, who arrived in Morgantown in 1915 to begin a career that would eventually elevate him into the National Football Hall of Fame. In 1915 Coach Mont McIntire became head coach, and his innovative offensive formation and new emphasis on passing brought the Mountaineers to national notice. From 1921–1924, Clarence Spears led the program and continued the winning trajectory begun by McIntire. The rising popularity of the sport brought increased ticket sales and led to the construction of a new stadium in 1924 that would be the home of the Mountaineers until 1980. Ira Rodgers became an assistant coach, and in 1925 became head coach. Unfortunately, the Great Depression of the thirties brought a decline in students who could afford to go to college. The coal industry entered a depression as well and could not continue its support of Mountaineer football.[60]

World War II also had a major impact on Mountaineer sports, with so many young men entering military service instead of college. It took several years after the war for the Mountaineers to rebuild, even with so many returning veterans financially assisted by the GI Bill. Dudley DeGroot, who had extensive coaching experience at all levels, including professional teams, joined the squad as head coach in 1948. There were fans who favored hiring another candidate over DeGroot, and they made life miserable for the coach by constantly complaining about him. He finally took another job in frustration and left Morgantown. On leaving he was quoted as saying: "A person must coach professional football and then come to West Virginia to get a real education. In all my years of coaching I have never known so many wise guys who know all of the answers as I have met in West Virginia."[61]

The second "Golden Era" of WVU football came under Art "Pappy" Lewis, who replaced DeGroot as head football coach in 1950. Lewis loved his players and treated them like his own children, hence the nickname "Pappy." During the two decades prior to Stewart's presidency, football coaches came and went with regularity, but WVU became a consistent winner in football under Lewis's leadership. While an assistant coach at Mississippi State, Lewis learned of DeGroot's departure, and he put his name forward for the position. "I always will feel that they wanted me to take it for a year or two while they looked around for someone else," Lewis observed much later, "but I fooled them."[62]

From 1950 through 1959, Art "Pappy" Lewis compiled a 58–38–2 record, and won the Southern Conference championship five times, including four straight from 1953 through 1956. The 1953 season was a particularly eventful one for the Mountaineers. For the first time WVU entered the season ranked seventeenth in the nation, and they defeated Pitt in the season opener, the first of a seven-game winning streak. Also that year, Maryland and the Universities of North and South Carolina left the Southern Conference to form the Atlantic Coast Conference. WVU fervently hoped for an invitation, but in vain. However, with these formidable teams gone, the Mountaineers won the Southern Conference and ended the season ranked eleventh nationally in the Associated Press poll. That ranking earned the Mountaineers an invitation to the Sugar Bowl in New Orleans to face eighth-ranked Georgia Tech. The Engineers shellacked the Mountaineers 42–19, a loss that Hall of Fame linebacker Sam Huff remembered as the most disappointing of his brilliant career.[63]

Even though he had secured WVU's first major bowl appearance in the 1953 Sugar Bowl, Lewis was roundly criticized at home for embarrassing the state. Keeping his sense of humor during a sports banquet, Lewis went to his place at the head of the table and pulled out a toy pistol. People laughed when he quipped, in a barb aimed at Monday morning quarterbacks, "I went to New Orleans with four assistants [coaches], but I found almost two million [the state's population] when I came back to West Virginia." On another occasion, Lewis received a telephone call from an irate fan who demanded an explanation for the team's poor showing in the Sugar Bowl.

"Were you there?" Lewis asked.

"No, I couldn't get away."

"Did you hear it on the radio?" Lewis continued.

"No."

"Well, maybe you saw West Virginia on television," Lewis said, a thought suddenly popping into his head.

"Yes. I saw it on TV with my wife's folks."

"Well, tell me," Lewis interrupted, "how many other West Virginia coaches or teams have you ever seen on national television?"[64]

The 1954 team finished the season with an 8–1 record and ranked twelfth nationally. The following season, 1955, the WVU football team climbed the national rankings to the sixth spot, but was upset by Pitt, costing them a bid to play in the Sugar Bowl. It would be hard to imagine a team packed with more outstanding athletes than quarterback Fred Wyant, halfbacks Joe Marconi and Bob Moses, and the All-American linemen Bruce Bosley and Sam Huff, all of whom were drafted by the NFL in the first four rounds. Many die hard WVU sports fans argue that the 1955 team was the University's best team ever to play the game. The following two seasons dipped in the winning column, but in 1957 guard Chuck Howley received many post-season honors. Howley, who lettered in track, diving, gymnastics, and wrestling in addition to football, went on to a rewarding career in professional football, earning All-Pro honors six times.[65]

The Monday morning quarterbacks reemerged after the Mountaineers finished 1958 with a 4–5–1 record and sharpened their long knives when the team fell to a 3–7 record in 1959. As the criticism from disgruntled fans and boosters grew louder, the University Athletic Council voted unanimously against rehiring him. At this point, however, President Stahr stepped in to override the council's decision and extend a conditional contract to Lewis for another year. Stahr's seven-page letter of conditional appointment went to remarkable length to explain why he did not follow the council's recommendation. The president insisted that Lewis's firing was too hasty, that at the end of a losing season was not a good time to fire a coach, and Lewis deserved a second chance. Even though he had won more football games in his ten-year career (58–38) at the University than any other coach in WVU history, it was clear to "Pappy" Lewis that his days at WVU were numbered. Being in "cold storage," as Lewis phrased it, confused the players, so he resigned to accept a personnel position with the Pittsburgh Steelers. On April 21, President Stahr named Lewis's assistant, Gene Corum, the new head football coach.[66]

Art Lewis played a significant role in the history of WVU football. He led the Mountaineers out of the era of playing small college teams like Waynesburg College and West Virginia Wesleyan into what was then "the big time." The number of players he sent to professional teams remains unmatched: Sam Huff, Bruce Bosley, Chuck Howley, Joe Marconi, Fred Wyant, Gene Lamone, Bob Orders, Tommy Allman, and Bobby Moss remain among the University's most famous players. Several others were All-Americans who did not play professionally. There were many firsts too. During Lewis's tenure, the Mountaineers reached the national rankings in 1953, made their first national appearance on network television in 1954, and in 1959 played the first televised game from Mountaineer Field. Not until Don Nehlen began his coaching career at WVU twenty years later would anyone improve on the record of Art "Pappy" Lewis.[67]

Impressive as WVU football was on the gridiron during the fifties, those successes were eclipsed on the basketball court. Basketball coaches enjoyed somewhat longer tenures than their counterparts in football, and basketball was the first sport to lead WVU into its second "Golden Age" of sports history. The previous high point of the basketball program was back in the early forties. R. A. "Dyke" Raese's team capped WVU's most successful season by winning the National Invitation Tournament in Madison Square Garden on March 25, 1942, the equivalent of winning a national championship in that period. Lee Patton was in his second season as head coach, and on his way to compiling a spectacular record when Irvin Stewart assumed the presidency in 1946. Lee Patton's 1946 team also hinted of great things to come in the fifties, when it compiled a record of 22–2 and was ranked third in the National Invitation Tournament and fifth in the nation. The 1947–1948 team boasted a record of 18–1, and returned to the National Invitation Tournament. Their undisputed leader was All-American Leland "the Hammer" Byrd, the first player in WVU history to score one thousand points. Eddie Beach, Bobby Jackson, and All-American Fred Schaus led the 1948–1949 squad. The quality of these teams is indicated by the fact that, from 1944 through 1948, the Mountaineers did not lose a single game on their home court. Tragically, Coach Patton was in an automobile accident on the Pennsylvania Turnpike while driving to a game at Penn State and died from his injuries on March 7, 1950. During his five years as basketball coach, Patton compiled an impressive record of 91–26.[68]

WVU found Lee Patton's successor in Elkins, West Virginia. Robert N. "Red" Brown was athletic director and head basketball coach at Davis and Elkins College, his alma mater, when Athletic Director Roy M. "Legs" Hawley brought him back to Morgantown in 1950. Brown had coached the freshman team under Patton in 1946–1947, but he now returned as head coach. Brown continued the remarkable success begun under Patton. The Mountaineers won the Southern Conference championship in 1951 and were ranked in the Associated Press's top twenty for the first time ever. Much of the credit for this success went to Mark Workman who, at 6' 9", was WVU's first big man. A consensus All-American, he led the Mountaineers to the ninth spot in the national rankings. Workman was the first overall pick in the 1952 NBA draft, and Brown was elected Southern Conference Coach of the Year. Brown always regarded winning this honor when there were seventeen teams in the conference and then beating first-ranked New York University at Madison Square Garden in 1952 as the highlight of his magnificent coaching career.[69]

Athletic Director Roy Hawley passed away in March 1954, and "Red" Brown was quickly appointed to replace him, a position he held until his retirement in 1972. Chosen to fill Brown's shoes as head coach was Fred Schaus, an All-American in 1948 who went on to play professional basketball. Schaus's decision to return to WVU as head coach was not a difficult one, since Morgantown was his wife's home town, and WVU their alma mater. Expectations were high, but few could have anticipated that Coach Schaus would produce players who rank among the legends of basketball. His teams won six straight Southern Conference championships. Although the 1954–1955 team had some excellent players, it was sophomore Rodney Hundley who foreshadowed what was to come on the court. The following two seasons, 1955–1957, were led by consensus All-American Hundley and 6'11" sophomore sensation Lloyd Sharrar. This team not only won the conference championships each year but also the Orange Bowl championship in 1956 and the Birmingham Classic in 1957.[70]

As every serious basketball fan knows, Rod Hundley was one of a kind, a phenomenal basketball player who entertained the crowds with his on-court antics. Red Brown's recruit arrived on campus when Fred Schaus was a rookie coach. Hundley was a handful for Schaus, but the coach thought his antics entertained the fans at a time when the game needed some excitement. Fans turned into an audience when Hundley spun the ball on the tip of his index finger, passed behind his back, used a hook shot at the foul line, ran football plays on court, and generally pestered the opposing coaches. It was all in good fun, but Schaus permitted it only if the team was up by twenty points. A sports editor saw Rod play as a freshman and gave him the nickname "Hot Rod," a name that he has carried throughout his life. Another sports writer dubbed him the "clown prince of college basketball," another description that has endured. Hundley's heroics, rather than his clowning, however, made him a great player. His offensive skills were spectacular; he once scored 54 points against Furman in 1957. "Hot Rod" Hundley's career marked the opening of the pinnacle years of the second "Golden Age" of WVU basketball, 1955–1960. Hundley finished his college career in 1957, when there was a three-year limit playing varsity, with 2,180 points. He was the fourth player in NCAA history to surpass 2,000 points. He also had a career average of 24.5 points, 10.6 rebounds, and 4.2 assists per game. He made most All-American lists, and the Minneapolis Lakers selected him their number one pick in the draft.[71]

Mountaineer fans, who thought their team's greatest days were behind them when Hundley left for professional basketball, would be thrilled by the players who followed in the footsteps of the "clown prince." With a freshman class of recruits headed by Jerry West and Willie Akers, the Gold and Blue faithful allowed themselves to dream of a future national championship. Many Mountaineer fans believe that Fred Schaus's 1957–1958 team, including All-American Lloyd Sharrar, Jerry West, Willie Akers, Bobby Joe Smith, Joedy Gardner, and Don Vincent, was the best WVU basketball team ever to take the court. Heading into the Kentucky Invitational Tournament, the 1957 Mountaineers were ranked eighth in the nation. They proceeded to first defeat the fifth-ranked Kentucky Wildcats, then faced off against the top-ranked North Carolina Tarheels in the championship game, and upset them as well, to achieve the top ranking in the Associated Press poll for the first time. After watching Jerry West's performance, legendary University of Kentucky coach Adolph Rupp declared the sophomore to be one of the best guards of all time. WVU finished the season ranked first in both the Associated Press and the United Press International polls.

The next year, 1958–1959, the Mountaineers won the Southern Conference tournament, but two days later were upset by Manhattan in the first round of the NCAA tournament in New York. By achieving All-American status, West and Sharrar shone a positive light on an otherwise disappointing close to the season.[72]

The 1959–1960 season, led by consensus All-American Jerry West and Willie Akers, ended with the team having earned a regular season record of 22–4 and its sixth Southern Conference championship under Schaus. The tenth-ranked Mountaineers advanced through three rounds of the NCAA tournament and then handily defeated Louisville in the national semi-final game. In the championship game the Mountaineers played the University of California-Berkeley to a standstill but finally lost the national title in a 71–70 heartbreaker. As a senior during the 1960–1961 season, Jerry West was better than ever, averaging 29.3 points a game while leading the Mountaineers to twenty-six victories and a top-ten national ranking, despite his nose having been broken twice during the season. During his three years of varsity eligibility, West scored 2,309 career points and pulled in 1,240 rebounds, both all-time NCAA records, and he was twice selected All-American. His teams compiled a gaudy record of 146–37, a winning percentage of almost 80 percent, the best in the University's history. The numbers are dazzling: five twenty-win seasons, five nationally ranked teams, and six teams chosen to participate in what was then a much smaller NCAA tournament than the 64- and 68-team tournament it became years later.[73] As everyone now knows, Jerry West became a legendary professional player with the Los Angeles Lakers and later a respected manager in the NBA. The logo for the NBA, in fact, is fashioned from the image of "Mr. Basketball" Jerry West. There will never be another "44" at WVU; West's jersey was retired at a halftime ceremony in a game at the Coliseum against Louisiana State University on November 26, 2005. Rod Hundley's "33" joined West's jersey in retirement during halftime in a game against Ohio State on January 23, 2010.[74] Both honors were seriously belated.

With an aging Field House that seated only 6,500 and thousands who wanted to purchase tickets turned away, the University certainly needed better facilities. President Stahr agreed to begin planning for a new basketball arena with seating for 12,000, but he insisted that priority be given first to the construction of academic buildings that were even more desperately needed. During his six years at WVU, Fred Schaus turned down offers to coach at other universities, hoping that the promised arena would be built soon. With the decision to delay work on the arena, Schaus apparently decided that the wait would be too long, and he left for what became a brilliant coaching career in the NBA. His departure was a great disappointment, but in 1960 there was considerable opposition in the University administration, the state legislature, and the community, as evidenced by editorials in the local newspaper, to giving priority to the construction of a new basketball arena over academic facilities.[75]

PART II

THE CONSTRAINED
UNIVERSITY: DIVERSIFICATION,
1967–1995

WEST VIRGINIA UNIVERSITY EVOLVED into a mature institution
during this period not only in size but also in its mission as a comprehensive
land-grant university. While its mission became more complex, and its impact on the development of the state more widespread, the University's ability to meet its obligations was severely constrained by political controls imposed from the state capital. Sectionalism and the tension between whether
political power should rest with central or local authorities have always been
destabilizing forces in West Virginia politics. Confined within this context,
WVU has always fought for independence in administering its own internal
affairs. In retrospect, it would seem that WVU matured as an institution
despite the loss of self-governance to a centralized Board of Regents, which
controlled higher education during most of this period.

The political struggle for more autonomy under the Board of Regents
presented daily bureaucratic annoyances for WVU administrators and faculty, but the University also faced the more subtle demographic and philosophical shifts transforming higher education nationwide during this era.
It is noteworthy that the peak years of the "Golden Age," 1960 to 1968, began in a wave of youthful confidence in the power of American institutions
to change the world, a wave that carried John F. Kennedy to the presidency
in 1960. Unfortunately, the period ended with a collapse into pessimism
about the efficacy of those same institutions. Nowhere was this more apparent than on college campuses.

The sixties were years of profound transformation in American society. The fires of protest and reform were ignited by the civil rights move-

ment. That movement had accelerated during the forties and achieved a major breakthrough in 1954 with the U.S. Supreme Court decision in *Brown v. Board of Education of Topeka,* which declared the segregation of public schools unconstitutional. The most public period of the movement was the subsequent decade leading up to passage of the civil rights acts guaranteeing the right to vote and nondiscrimination in housing and employment. Civil rights activists challenged the status quo by leading massive demonstrations to force compliance with the new measures.

WVU opened its doors to African Americans immediately and almost without notice in 1954, although for the next two decades life was not easy for the relatively few blacks who enrolled. Black athletes played the most visible role in desegregating previously all-white campuses nationwide. The same was true at WVU, where the "pioneers" quickly became aware that the surrounding community was less progressive than the University. Like campuses all over the country, WVU also experienced its days of student demonstrations against the Vietnam War. Although they ended peacefully enough, the governor sent in the state police in 1970 to keep the demonstrations from getting out of hand. Most observers agreed that violence was avoided because the police were willing to negotiate with the demonstrators; unfortunately, this was not the case at Kent State University that same year, when a contingent of the National Guard fired on student demonstrators, killing four of them.

The burgeoning enrollment of Baby Boomers amplified the arrival of a new generation between 1955 and 1970, when the number of eighteen- to twenty-four-year olds in the country grew from fifteen to twenty-five million. Until 1970 college students were deferred from the draft, a policy which encouraged two-thirds of this age group to attend college.[1] Passage of the Twenty-sixth Amendment to the Constitution lowered the minimum voting age from twenty-one to eighteen, and many states subsequently lowered the drinking age to eighteen. Consequently, colleges and universities were relieved of their traditional responsibility of acting *"in loco parentis"* (in place of parents). Defined as legal adults, college students became responsible for their own behavior and actions. However, their newly achieved status brought protests against the continuance of older practices. They opposed the involuntary draft, now brought into sharp focus by an unpopular war in Vietnam. If they could be sent to war, students asked, why did they have to meet dormitory curfews? By what right did the administration tell them what to wear and how to behave? The campus mood reflected the national mood. African Americans had been protesting segregation for decades, and the civil rights movement had succeeded in sensitizing the nation to the destructiveness of racial discrimination. Then, too, there were the peace movement, the women's movement, the environmental movement, the gay rights movement, and multiple variants within each.

The end of the "Golden Age" was signaled when the college-age population ceased to grow in 1975. By then the Vietnam War was over, along with the draft deferment for college students. The economy slid into a recession, and the income differential between high school and college graduates fell from 68 percent to 48 percent. Higher education enrollments had quintupled in one generation, but the new dormitories and classrooms built to accommodate the growing student body were no longer filled. Universities also found that they employed too many staff and tenured faculty. The job crisis for those with PhDs in the humanities disciplines had begun because they were the most likely to seek employment as college professors.[2]

Higher education grew by about 1 percent per year after 1975. More importantly, it changed dramatically by diversifying demographically. In 1947, 71 percent of college students in the United States were male; by 2010 that figure had declined to about 42 percent. In 1965, 94 percent of college students were "white"; by 2010 non-Hispanic whites made up only 66 percent of the students enrolled in American colleges. Most of this change took place after 1975. Public intellectual Louis Menand observed that between 1984 and 1994 "the total enrollment in American colleges and universities increased by two million, but not one of those two million new students was a white American-born male. They were all non-whites, women, and foreign students." Faculty demographics reflected the shift in those who went on to graduate school after 1975. In 1998 only 28 percent of the full-time faculty who had been hired before 1985 were women, and 11 percent of those women were non-white or Hispanic; after 1985 women represented 40 percent of new hires, and 18 percent of those women were non-white.[3]

These demographic changes in the nation's student population affected WVU as well. After considerable effort, the University community became increasingly diverse according to race and gender, although the racial and ethnic increases still lagged behind national averages. The number of women enrolled at WVU began to rise dramatically each decade after 1960–1961, beginning with 1,823 women in a total student body of 6,816 in that academic year and reaching parity with men, 10,036 women in a total student body of 20,854, in 1990.[4]

The number of West Virginia high school graduates began to decline by the early eighties. Consequently, WVU enrollment reached a peak in 1978–1979 at 21,429 and began a decade-long slide to a low of 17,175 in 1986–1987 before resuming a climb toward the 30,000 mark. Like their colleagues nationwide, WVU presidents faced the problem of a diminishing pool of students after the Baby Boomers passed through the system, precipitating a decline in revenues and threatening a corresponding reduction in employees and offerings. It was politically unwise for WVU to be overly aggressive in recruiting more West Virginia high school graduates if, as a result, enrollments were siphoned away from the smaller state colleges. Therefore, the University further diversified by expanding its recruiting base to states in the region and the nation at large.

Diversity became the driving concept in higher education as a result of demographic and social change. These changes coincided with the "culture wars," a period beginning in the late eighties when higher education, art, the humanities, and intellectualism in general came under withering criticism from political conservatives who regarded these fields as bastions of left-wing elitism and radicalism. The penetration of federal money into postwar science at the major universities was based on a meritocratic rationale embodying the notion that there was a value-free, scientific model for university research.[5] The meritocratic model began unraveling as the Vietnam War laid bare the weakness of failing to challenge authority in exchange for generous funding. The war exposed the financial dependency of the major research universities on the federal government, and in particular the notion that it was possible to conduct value-free research for the "military-industrial complex." The war rekindled skepticism in the social science and humanities disciplines regarding the efficacy of value-neutral research. It also rekindled the desire to reinstate the historical role of universities as critics of society's values and policies, and as challengers of unchallenged beliefs.[6]

The meritocratic ethos was delivered a decisive blow when the new, more diverse students began showing up on campuses in large numbers in the seventies. Their arrival sharpened cultural distinctions between traditional and nontraditional students and made the differences seem more important than the similarities. Accustomed to entertaining multicultural points of view, the social sciences and humanities disciplines embraced the perspectives these students brought to campus and joined them in their criticism of the very idea of America as a "meritocracy." The coup de grace to the meritocratic ethos came when the U.S. Supreme Court handed down its 1978 verdict in *Regents of the University of California v. Bakke.* Allan Bakke had been rejected for admission to the medical school at the University of California at Davis even though his test scores were higher than some of the nonwhite applicants who were admitted. In the majority opinion written by Justice Lewis Powell, the court determined that Bakke had been denied equal protection of the law ruling that the use of racial quotas to address past discrimination was unconstitutional. Significantly, however, the high court also determined that institutions might legitimately consider race in admissions decisions. Justice Powell cited the common practice among the nation's elite colleges and universities of using criteria other than merit in admission decisions. Athletic and musical ability, for example, were often considered, as was alumni legacy. Some balance was also sought in entering classes to avoid overrepresentations of one high school, of a single sex, or of one discipline. The emphasis on "diversity," as Powell used that term, replaced quotas as a means of achieving well-rounded classes.[7]

As students and faculty became increasingly heterogeneous in the eighties, the humanities disciplines refocused the undergraduate curriculum to place greater emphasis on "multiculturalism" by exposing students to non-Western cultures. Awareness of cultures other than one's own was thought to be one of the pillars of a liberal education in the multiethnic, multiracial United States. Such an education should therefore expose students to redefined ideas of community and citizenship. Teaching became a collaborative inquiry. The emphasis on universal truths was replaced by context and contingency, and representations replaced objective realities.[8] The Core Curriculum and the General Education Curriculum, which have prescribed the cluster of courses that all WVU undergraduates must follow, have reinforced this multiculturalism project since the late sixties.

The literary critic Lionel Trilling claimed that university intellectuals constituted an "adversary culture" because "they tend to embrace antinomian attitudes and to oppose, if not scorn, aspects of the corporate world's ethic of functional rationality and bureaucratic efficiency, as opposed to creativity and originality." His remarks drew attention to a fissure in campus life that grew into a yawning chasm. As the humanities and social sciences became more receptive to non-Western influences, a huge rift opened up between scholars who had vested interests in maintaining the idea of an objective, value-free meritocracy and those who challenged the efficacy of that worldview. Traditionalists within the academy and political conservatives without thought they were witnessing an assault on the pillars of American civilization by a new and dangerous set of radicals. But the humanists and social scientists were simply resuming their historical role of challenging unquestioned beliefs and values, as former Columbia University provost Jonathan Cole notes, "to elevate the basis on which they are embraced or altered."[9] Between 1970 and 1990 the humanities and social sciences experienced an intellectual revolution. Although critics claimed that these disciplines had become irrelevant, they were in fact performing their traditional role, according to one scholar, by pushing the limits of inquiry and making "the rest of the academic world alive to issues surrounding objectivity and interpretation, and to the significance of racial and gender difference."[10]

Recognizing the idea that diversity is a positive value called for activities that enhanced the ability of people from different backgrounds to cooperate. WVU's Diversity Week was launched in 2008. Its theme, "One WVU," embodies the claim that we are all different but are also one. "Social justice" programs and activities also aimed to further this ethos. *The Strategic Plan for Achieving Social Justice at West Virginia University,* issued under President David C. Hardesty Jr., declared: "The principle of social justice encompasses the legal and moral obligations to promote opportunity, equality, civility, and respect for all people." The President's Office for Social Justice, established by President Neil Bucklew, was charged with promoting and maintaining these principles through teaching and communication. One of the core values behind the emphasis on diversity was ensuring "an absence of discrimination and harassment based on age, color, disability, ethnic origin, marital status, pregnancy, race, religious beliefs, sex, sexual orientation," as well as ensuring that "the rich diversity of people, their cultures, and the bonds that tie people together are appreciated and celebrated."[11]

In a 2001 press release entitled "Diversity: Tomorrow's Source of Organizational Strength," President Hardesty asserted that the University tried to incorporate the basic components of social justice into "all we do," that is, into the curriculum, activities, and mission. "The respect for diversity we strive to foster in students goes beyond a basic tolerance of each other. It broadens into truly valuing differences for their ability to make an organization stronger." Fostering diversity awareness was not just a moral issue; it made "good business sense" because WVU had "a duty to prepare students for life and work in the twenty-first century. Our world is more inclusive than it was even ten years ago, in large part because of the growth of the information superhighway." Since the workplace was quickly becoming an "interconnected global village," students should develop the skills preparing them to thrive in multicultural setting[s] that employers will expect their employees to have mastered. Consequently, minors were offered in Africana Studies, Women's Studies, and Native American Studies. A gay, bisexual, lesbian, and transgender course was offered, and more than a hundred exchange programs for study abroad were established so that students could experience foreign cultures. The President's Office for Social Justice, the Affirmative Action Officer, the Center for Black Culture and Research, frequent celebrations of ethnic cultures, and awards presented each year to faculty and staff who foster diversity and social justice only scratch the surface of WVU's campaign to further diversity.[12]

Despite the success in transcending the failures of Cold War constructions of reality, devaluation of the humanities both within and without academe became a long-term trend in the last decades of the twentieth century and the first decades of the next. As states and businesses demanded more accountability in university governance, funds for the humanities contracted, and no coherent unified resistance emerged. Undergraduate student interest in the humanities flagged, perhaps because the intellectual conflict became too abstract to be intelligible or too rarified to be useful. The slide in student interest led to a decline of undergraduate degrees in the humanities nationwide from a peak of 18 percent in 1968 to only 8 percent in 2004. The number of advanced degrees followed a similar pattern. By 2004 the number of master's degrees had dropped by 25 percent from the peak in the late sixties, and the number of doctoral degrees plummeted by 45 percent from the peak in the mid-seventies. One of the causes for this decline undoubtedly was a restructuring economy in which demand rose for graduates in technical fields, resulting in students simply taking courses they hoped would ensure future employment. One consequence, Jonathan Cole asserts, "is that the graduates of our great universities have weaker language and writing skills than earlier generations of graduates and limited experiences with literatures and cultures other than our own. Even worse, they have not confronted the kinds of moral and ethical questions critical for citizenship that are often debated in humanities courses."[13]

FIVE

POLITICS OF GOVERNANCE
UNDER THE BOARD
OF REGENTS

WORLD WAR I, THE GREAT DEPRESSION, and World War II brought
on an economic and political environment of excessive political interference that hindered the transformation of WVU into a "real university." But
for the twenty years following World War II, the University experienced
unequaled freedom to direct its own destiny and seized the opportunity to
create a first-class institution to serve an ever-growing student population,
expand the physical campus, and come much closer to fulfilling the public-
service function of a land-grant institution. The reestablishment of central
control in Charleston in the Board of Regents convinced WVU supporters
that once again the state was reconstructing old barriers to the University's
aspiration for greatness. Despite the perennial wish of WVU supporters
that the University be politically independent and self-governing, the idea
that all institutions of higher learning should fall under a single state governing board refused to die.[1]

BOARD OF REGENTS, 1969–1990

In 1964, during the presidency of Paul Miller, Governor Hulett Smith created the West Virginia Commission on Higher Education to administer the
Higher Education Facilities Act of 1963, and subsequently added responsibility for Titles I and VI of the Higher Education Act of 1965. Membership
on the commission included two representatives from the WVU Board of
Governors, two from the state Board of Education, two from the private
colleges, and three public members. Marshall desired to expand its gradu-

143

ate programs and, through friends in the legislature, requested that Governor Smith establish a committee to study the most desirable way to allocate fields of graduate study within the state's system of higher education.[2]

In June 1965, the governor appointed WVU President Paul Miller to chair a committee to examine this issue. The governor urged Miller to take a wider view that included higher education generally and to make recommendations for improvement. In the final report, released in October 1966, the committee recommended the establishment of a West Virginia Board of Regents to serve as a coordinating body for higher education. Under the Board of Regents would be a single Board of Governors for the state colleges, a Board of Governors for Marshall University, and retention of the Board of Governors of West Virginia University.[3]

Reminiscent of the Brewton Report commissioned by the legislature and released in 1956, the committee's report justified the recommendations on the grounds that the legislature could work with a single, system-wide budget for all of the institutions. Secondly, the reorganization would facilitate the coordination of academic programs and eliminate duplicate offerings. Even though President Miller chaired the committee, he opposed its plan because control of the University would pass into the hands of administrators in Charleston, which had not served the University well in the past.[4]

In the state Senate, the recommendations were incorporated into a single amended bill calling for the creation of a Board of Regents, a Board of Governors for the state colleges, and a Board of Governors for Marshall University. Although the bill was not taken up by the House of Delegates, the House Finance Committee's support for establishing a coordinating Board of Regents indicated the legislature's preoccupation with budgeting for higher education. House Finance Committee Chairman Ivor F. Boiarsky became speaker of the House of Delegates and played an instrumental role in the passage of the bill that created the Board of Regents in 1969. The strongest political opposition to a central coordinating board was the formidable phalanx of WVU supporters, including members of its Board of Governors who openly opposed changing the system. One board member, Dr. Thomas L. Harris, who also served on the governor's Committee on

Higher Education, wrote to new WVU President James G. Harlow that he was opposed to a Board of Regents concept because it would work to the disadvantage of WVU. An editorial in the *Charleston Gazette* noted that "once again a campaign against changing the higher education system has been mounted by the friends and employees of West Virginia University." The "childish rivalry between West Virginia University and Marshall, a competition in which Marshall has not been totally blameless," was also blamed for thwarting educational reform.[5]

The West Virginia concept of multiple boards in higher education bucked the rising trend in state governments toward centralizing agencies in the name of administrative efficiency. Economic necessity reinforced the trend toward centralization and motivated at least some legislators to support the Board of Regents measure, although it was expressed as "co-ordination," a term with more positive connotations. Certainly one could recognize the importance of coordination. In September 1967, Governor Smith declared, "The day has come when West Virginians must realize that a scattered, uncoordinated effort in higher education will not produce max-imum benefits to our students."[6] Smith continued to advocate for a Board of Regents even after the recommendations of his higher education com-mittee failed to pass in the legislature in 1967. "I am convinced that a better plan for coordinating the activities of our institutions of higher education is necessary," he declared in his 1968 State of the State message. He proposed that the legislature again take up the creation of a Board of Regents, and he maintained that the individual institutional boards at the same time would "assure that these institutions receive the attention they deserve."[7]

No doubt the editorial response of the *Morgantown Post* to the gover-nor's call for a Board of Regents reflected the attitude of the "W.V.U. Bloc" generally. The hometown paper proclaimed that the "most glaring draw-back" to the Board of Regents plan was its "total disruption of a governing system for the University that has been a model of efficiency, integrity, ef-fectiveness and economy" since it was established in 1947. The second fault was the cost of establishing and operating a "super-board." The editorial admitted that the current system did not always operate as well as it might, "but isn't West Virginia University the state university and doesn't its quest for excellence require that we provide for it the administrative tools" necessary to succeed in that quest? "The plain and simple fact of the matter is this: State colleges and Marshall do need a better administrative system. West Virginia University does not."[8]

As the governor requested, during the 1968 legislative session bills were introduced in both houses calling for the establishment of a single coordinating board for higher education. Both Senate Bill No. 102 and House Bill No. 313 would have abolished the WVU Board of Governors and reposed all of its responsibilities in the new Board of Regents. Both bills were killed in the finance committees of their respective houses, and once again the opposition to reorganization came from supporters of WVU, who brought considerable influence to bear on the legislature. An editorial in the *Fairmont Times* claimed that a letter from WVU President Irvin Stewart circulated among legislators expressing his objection to the Board of Regents concept, calling it an "administrative monstrosity which would constitute a continuing obstruction to the progress of education in the state" and the worst reorganizational proposal in the past two decades. In his opinion, Stewart declared, "the continuing autonomy of the University under its own Board of Governors who can devote their full attention to the University and who do not share responsibility with any other administrative body is the best way to advance higher education in West Virginia."[9]

The 1968 gubernatorial campaign between James Sprouse and Arch Moore Jr. kept the issue alive, as both candidates favored creating a Board of Governors for Marshall University. Most considered the issue an obvious ploy to attract votes in Cabell County and from Marshall University supporters. When Moore won, however, he spearheaded legislation to create a Board of Regents. Change in the governing structure of higher education was clearly at hand. On February 4, 1969, the finance and education committees of both houses of the legislature met in joint session to hear presentations from leading educators, including President Harlow of WVU. According to the *Charleston Gazette*, the president informed the legislators that professional administrators favored single boards with single executives because coordinating boards have not worked very well. Harlow argued that "a great deal of administrative machinery" was not necessary for

West Virginia's relatively small educational system, "and it seems to me that we should be holding for the principle of the least government necessary." He offered alternative approaches, one of which was the suggestion that the legislature create a single Board of Regents to govern all of public higher education.[10]

It is something of a mystery why President Harlow offered such choice bait to legislators who clearly intended to establish some form of coordinating board. Harlow was relatively new to state politics and may not have fully appreciated the significance of his comments, but he played directly into the hands of those who were working at cross purposes with WVU's well-established position on governance. His subsequent defense of the idea indicates, however, that he believed a Board of Regents was the most efficient plan of administration. The Board of Governors was divided over the merits of the bill, which, according to the WVU *Alumni Magazine*, left President Harlow "to stand alone at the Legislative hearings in opposition" to the multiple-board plan. At the urging of House Speaker Ivor Boiarsky, a bill creating a single Board of Regents reposed with financial and academic control for all higher education in West Virginia was immediately introduced. House Finance Committee Chairman Lewis N. McManus of Beckley requested that Harlow write a letter of support for the Board of Regents bill. President Harlow declined but reaffirmed his position that he regarded the Board of Regents concept as acceptable. Attempting to assuage the opposition among legislators favorable to WVU, McManus let it be known that Harlow "could live with" the proposed Board of Regents.[11]

According to the *Morgantown Post*, the college presidents all supported the concept of a single board because it enlarged the financial pie and gave them considerable political wiggle room for enlarging their own portions while controlling the University's share. The WVU *Alumni News* reported: "Ironically, the major casualty of the state's higher education reorganization will be the one facet of the old system which has been consistently praised, received high marks in the Strayer Report and other surveys, and seldom been subject to criticism—the University Board of Governors." It is likely that Harlow parted company with many members of the Board of Governors, as well as many alumni. Realizing that the faculty needed to be pacified, President Harlow informed them that passage of the Board of Regents bill was a milestone in the history of education in West Virginia, and there was no reason to be alarmed about the new system of governance.[12]

Following Harlow's testimony, WVU supporters were fragmented, and passage of HB 783 creating the Board of Regents was swift. The House of Delegates approved the bill on February 18, 1969, and after some slight revisions in the Senate the bill passed both houses on March 3, 1969. The Board of Regents consisted of nine members, appointed by the governor with the advice and consent of the Senate, and the state superintendent of free schools who served ex-officio. Members served overlapping terms of six years. No more than five could share the same political party affiliation, and there had to be at least one member from each congressional district. According to the statute, the Board of Regents was responsible for "the general determination, control, supervision, and management of the financial, business and educational policies and affairs of all state colleges and universities." Other duties of the board included making recommendations on higher education policy, the allocation of functions, and submitting budgets for all of the state colleges and universities. The statute also called for the colleges and universities to appoint their own advisory boards to give guidance to their presidents. Although the statutes did not permit board members to be removed without just cause, their six-year terms made it possible for a two-term governor to conceivably control the board's membership and gain a partisan advantage. In 1971 the Commission on Higher Education was abolished and its powers and responsibilities absorbed by the Board of Regents, thus completing the consolidation of all government agencies with responsibility for higher education in the board.[13]

From its inception, fractious, factional politics was the board's operational environment. Republican Governor Arch A. Moore Jr. was in the first year of his first term when the board was born. Senator Paul J. Kaufman, author of the Board of Regents bill, wrote a letter highly critical of Governor Moore's board appointments. Kaufman claimed that "without casting any reflections on the merit of individual members, the Board of Regents appointments, from start to finish, were politically inspired, of questionable legality and a rank miscarriage of much needed, sound legislation." The senator was particularly incensed by the appointment of John D. Hoblitzel Jr., a twenty-one-year-old WVU student, to the original board of nine members. Hoblitzel was from a prominent Republican family, and the Democratically controlled Senate refused to confirm the appointment.[14]

It would not take long for President Harlow and all University supporters to develop misgivings about the new governance structure. Before the Board of Regents, WVU experienced a major building boom with construction of the Creative Arts Center, Mountainlair, Allen Hall, the Chemistry Research Laboratory, two dormitories, and the new Coliseum. In addition, a proposed law building was in the works, as were an intensive care addition to University Hospital and the second phase of the Creative Arts Center. After the change in governance, construction at WVU slowed to a snail's pace, and Harlow saw scuttled his two favorite projects, the Grumbein Island tunnel and the computer-library complex. Harlow warned Morgantown civic groups that "the portion of city growth attributable to University construction" was about over, and hinted that the new Board of Regents might even cap the growth of the student body.[15]

The impact of the new system was sharp and immediate, not just in the decline in bricks and mortar projects but in all areas of funding. The Board of Regents developed a per-student funding formula, and so bringing the funding for institutions into line produced percentage increases for Marshall University, the state colleges, and the new community colleges; the percentage of state higher education general revenue expenditures allocated to WVU, on the other hand, began a decade of decline. In 1967–1968, the year prior to the creation of the Board of Regents, WVU received 50.75 percent of the state's total allocation to higher education. By 1975–1976 that percentage had fallen to 44.88 percent.[16]

In addition to the stifling control over University finances, other issues soon emanated from the new governing system. One of the most difficult for WVU was faculty performance evaluations. Regarding the three criteria for promotion and tenure (research, teaching, and service), WVU Provost for Instruction Jay Barton reported that the new procedures of the Board of Regents focused an "almost fanatical concern with teaching as the only professional effort worth rewarding" and were "heavily biased toward the conditions and situations in small colleges in the State rather than the University." The Board of Regents ignored the concern of faculty and administrators like Barton, and the resulting guidelines significantly diluted the criteria for promotion and tenure. The result was an unfavorable report from the North Central Association of Colleges and Schools accreditation team in 1974. WVU also lost control of its Parkersburg Center, which became Parkersburg Community College on June 30, 1971, and the Kanawha Valley Graduate Center, which became the College of Graduate Studies on July 1, 1972. WVU's financial investments in these institutions were lost during the process. Only Potomac State College in Keyser remained a University branch, and then only because the Board of Regents was forced to abandon its plan to convert it into a community college in the face of powerful local opposition.[17]

The University having suffered since implementation of the Board of Regents a loss of internal policy controls, a significant portion of state appropriations, control over its centers, and a dilution of promotion and tenure guidelines, President Harlow declared in his semiannual address to the Faculty Assembly in 1973 that the University had been transformed from "essentially a self-governing community of scholars to one very tightly controlled from outside." With the appointment of the first chancellor of the Board of Regents, Prince B. Woodward, WVU was "now merely one of 14 institutions operated under Chancellor Woodward's direction, and the WVU president now gets his orders directly from the chancellor." The chancellor gained his information about the campuses from faculty and student committees as well as administrators, and the president now performed "primarily ministerial functions," such as administering the budget.[18]

Not surprisingly, relations between President Harlow and Chancellor Woodward deteriorated into mutual disrespect. Harlow was joined by University faculty in resenting the changes ushered in with the Board of Regents. In December 1972, the Faculty Senate Executive Committee appointed a special committee to examine problems generated by University governance. An ad hoc Faculty Senate committee on university governance was established and spent the spring of 1973 interviewing primarily

Chapter Five

University administrators. The committee's report, which was completed in June 1973, reflected the sentiment of WVU officials. Understandably, the chancellor assumed that the report reflected the administration's views rather than those of the Faculty Senate. The committee revisited WVU's experience as a self-governing, semiautonomous institution and bemoaned the loss of this culture as a "traumatic experience." The decision by the Board of Regents to manage the institution's daily operations with little consultation led many at WVU to worry that all state institutions of higher learning would eventually be "cast . . . into a single uniform mold with a leveling and stultifying effect."[19]

The Faculty Senate's ad hoc committee went much further by enumerating multiple complaints about how the Board of Regents operated, including the volume of information it required from the institution; its rejection of University requests without explanation; policies and directives it issued without prior consultation; its excessive interference and control over academic affairs, such as faculty appointments and promotions; and its funding formula, which penalized the University by undervaluing graduate education. Clearly exasperated, Board of Regents President Frederick P. Stamp wrote to Harlow disputing each of these criticisms; Harlow merely passed along Stamp's response to the Faculty Senate Executive Committee on October 9, 1973, without comment. The executive committee claimed that it could not respond because it had not participated in the ad hoc committee's hearings. In the interim, the ad hoc committee had dissolved, and the Faculty Senate adopted none of the recommendations. The episode came to an inglorious end, but the issues poisoned relations between the Board of Regents and the University.[20]

Adequate salaries proved to be one of the most intractable issues confronting the Board of Regents as well as the University. The board compounded the problem by passing approved salary schedules for classified staff and faculty. Legislators, however, frequently did not appropriate sufficient money to cover even the minimum funding schedules. Of course, the legislature confronted its own funding problems, as revenues continued to decline because of the depressed state economy. Constitutionally mandated to restrict spending to projected revenues, the legislature during the 1970s and 1980s often found itself imposing budget cuts rather than injecting money into higher education.

Consequently, the era dominated by the Board of Regents was one of almost uniform discontent among University staff and faculty. By 1979, failure to resolve salary issues prompted the University's maintenance and crafts employees to protest in Charleston as they marched down Kanawha Boulevard. They were tired of the board's "take it or leave it" attitude regarding job classifications, equal pay for equal work, and grievance procedures. The employees' spokesman, David Walden, claimed that four years earlier there had been "equal pay for equal work," but then "the regents began giving different size wage increases depending upon when a worker was hired," with the result that some workers performing the same jobs were paid different wages. The new classification system, which was intended to bring wages into line by job, had not worked, and there were as many as "eight different pay scales for the same job." Chancellor Ben L. Morton refused to negotiate the workers' complaints even though the employees had challenged him on several occasions.[21]

Faculty salaries were a constant source of dissatisfaction during this era as well. West Virginia ranked forty-third among the fifty states in faculty compensation. In requesting increased funding for faculty salaries, Chancellor Morton stated in 1979 that the $18,000 average annual salary for a professor in West Virginia must be increased to $31,000 by 1986. Frequently, the legislature either could not or would not appropriate the additional funding requested by the Regents to address faculty discontent over low salaries. A survey of WVU faculty in 1979 revealed that "a majority of professors" at WVU blamed the Board of Regents for not responding to the needs of WVU faculty. "The average faculty salary at WVU, when computed in the normal fashion, is the lowest of any type of institution in the United States," according to John Harpell, chairman of the University Senate Committee on Faculty Welfare. Harpell saw a direct relationship between this lack of support and the faculty's negative opinion of the Board of Regents. To the statement, "I believe that the BOR is responsive to the needs of the WVU faculty," 512 of the 655 professors who participated in a survey indicated that they "disagreed" or "strongly disagreed." Harpell opined that the "typical faculty member" presumes the president is on their side, but believed that the Board of Regents' "interests are spread among all the universities in the state."[22]

WVU faculty not only held the Board of Regents responsible for their low pay but also for obstructing the University's progress. At a special work session at the Law School, faculty representatives informed the board that "financial constraints are 'stifling us' in efforts to make the University a national leader in education." In what was a recurrent theme, they declared that WVU should get "special consideration" because the University was not just one of the state's sixteen institutions, but an institution with a "special mission" in the state and the nation. One regent offered an explanation by declaring that "our hearts are with you," but emphasized their dependence upon allocations from the legislature. "We have never got what we have asked for and you have every right to be unhappy. We are trying and I get paranoid sitting up here listening to this. We do have your interests at heart."[23] No response to this plaint was recorded. Faculty of course recognized that the legislature controlled the purse strings, but they also understood that allocations among the institutions were distributed by the board in a manner detrimental to WVU.

Board of Regents Chancellor Ben Morton garnered special criticism for ignoring faculty interests. For example, a law passed in May 1979 required college and university presidents to notify untenured faculty members a year in advance that they would not be retained and set up an appeal procedure for those not renewed. Morton criticized the law, claiming that the new procedure was just the "first step toward collective bargaining," even though the previous system had allowed presidents to suspend faculty members, who could then appeal the decision after the fact. Referring to the old system, Robert Nelson, chairman of the Senate Education Committee, declared the "whole process a kangaroo court," causing education in West Virginia to suffer because "few young, intelligent faculty were willing to work under the system and most left the state." The new law, contrary to Morton's assertion, was not a "step toward collective bargaining," but a "small step toward guaranteeing due process rights of non tenured faculty which most people take for granted, but not the chancellor and university presidents."[24] Faculty took note that it was the legislature considering their rights rather than the Board of Regents.

By 1979 there was enough discontent with the board that a number of legislators openly discussed abolishing the system. Clyde Richey, a delegate from Monongalia County told the regents gathered for the board's April meeting that Chancellor Ben Morton should be replaced, but they cut him off without hearing his full statement. Outside the meeting Richey addressed reporters and listed his complaints. Richey, the vice chairperson of the House Committee on Education, stated that WVU professors had informed him that the University was on its way to becoming a "second- or third-rate institution," that he planned to join an effort during the next legislative session to "restructure" the Board of Regents, as well as to seek the removal of Chancellor Ben Morton.[25]

ACADEMY FOR EDUCATIONAL DEVELOPMENT CALLS FOR CHANGE

After a decade of operation and some serious disagreements regarding its management of critical issues, the Board of Regents, legislative leaders believed, was due to undergo a review. Consequently, in January 1979 the Joint Committee on Government and Finance retained the Academy for Educational Development (AED) of Washington, DC, to evaluate the board's performance. The final report, released in August 1979, provided the impetus for action among those legislators who favored replacing the board as the agency responsible for higher education in West Virginia.[26]

The AED study concluded that the Board of Regents had not been able to insulate the institutions from political intervention as hoped, nor had it been an effective advocate for higher education with the executive and legislative branches. Moreover, the board had failed to allocate funds as called for by its own formula and had failed to develop a comprehensive master plan for the state's system of higher education. Among the AED's recommendations were replacing the Board of Regents with a state coordinating board for higher education and creating three governing boards: a Board of Visitors for the state's universities and branches; a Board of

Governors for the eight four-year colleges; and a Board of Trustees for the three community colleges. These boards would be the "primary advocates" for the institutions for which they were responsible. Should the legislature choose not to restructure the Board of Regents, the study offered numerous revisions to the current system of governance, most of which devolved more authority to the institutions. Among the revisions was to "substantially expand the participatory process in its [the Board of Regents'] day-to-day management to reduce campus resentment for isolation from decisions."[27]

An editorial in the Morgantown newspaper, titled "Junking Regents Setup Is Right Thing to Do," undoubtedly articulated the general opinion of the WVU community. The legislative study, according to the editorial, demonstrated that separate boards were more desirable than one central board. The bureaucracy had proven ineffective and at times intolerable, and it was difficult to determine how higher education had benefited under the Board of Regents system. There were simply too many kinds of institutions for a single statewide board to administer. Like most, the editorial writer was not certain whether the alternative model suggested by the AED was the appropriate one, but the idea seemed sound. WVU and Marshall University should each have its own governing board. WVU President Gene Budig endorsed the AED's recommendations and publicly called for a meeting in Charleston of the Board of Regents, legislative leaders, and representatives from the governor's office to discuss the proposal. The West Virginia Education Association also endorsed the restructuring and added, for good measure, that Chancellor Morton should resign.[28]

After several months of public discussion and legislative maneuvering over the public policy implications of the AED study, Chancellor Morton launched his counteroffensive: Abandonment of the Board of Regents would create a "governance vacuum" that would last several years; result in a return to political and educational infighting; generate a duplication of programs; produce "competitive lobbying" of the several boards; and add $2 million in extra costs to maintain multiple boards. The Board of Regents already had incorporated many of the AED recommendations, and too much progress had been achieved to abandon the single statewide board now.[29] Morton was simply reiterating the reasons why legislators had overhauled the system in the first place.

The BOR adopted a new "road map" for higher education in the fall of 1979, *Profile of Progress: Higher Education in West Virginia*, which replaced the 1972 *Plan for Progress*. The new plan, later termed the "Master Plan," which had not been adopted yet, summarized the board's progress thus far and its prospects for the future. It noted that opportunities for education had been expanded geographically by "taking education to the people" through new programs and facilities, and that great strides had been taken toward a comprehensive system to replace the former "conglomerate of institutions competing for individual advantage." The agenda now called for cooperation rather than competition, and "fine tuning" rather than large-scale expansion.[30]

The board's supporters, however tepid some of them were, still outnumbered those who favored abolishing the system. Governor Rockefeller opposed abolition, believing that the the board had a "communications problem" that could be resolved. In the end, it was the complexities and costs of operating multiple boards that overcame the effort to abolish the Board of Regents in 1979. Three state senators on the subcommittee on higher education, including Robert Nelson, the "legislative father" of the Board of Regents who eventually became its harshest critic, came out against abolition. Senator William Moreland of Monongalia County stated that something needed to be done "to pull in the horns of the regents," but replacing one board with three was unlikely. Senator Si Galperin of Kanawha County agreed, declaring: "I honestly don't think the problems that exist today are going to be corrected by setting up three more boards." Many legislators also feared that a multiple-board system would force institutions to revert to competing with each other for operating funds from the legislature.[31]

Clyde Richey, the Monongalia County delegate who kicked off the debate, realized that he did not have enough votes to abolish the board. But he continued to argue that the current system did not operate in the best interests of WVU. The University fared better with its own Board of Governors, thereby bringing its "vast lobbying power" to bear on a generally friendly legislature. "There is a great difference between the needs of universities

Chapter Five

and colleges, and the regents haven't been able to address this under the present system." His concern (and he spoke for many WVU supporters) was that "something be created where WVU would have a more direct liaison with the legislature."[32]

Although the Board of Regents was not restructured as a result of the AED evaluation, changes were afoot. Early in January 1980 Chancellor Morton tendered his resignation. Board President Russell Isaacs said that the regents had not officially solicited Morton's resignation, but it was accepted by "mutual arrangement."[33] Appointment of the next chancellor, Dr. Robert R. Ramsey, became effective on June 15, 1980. His previous experience as secretary of education in Virginia had not equipped him with knowledge of higher education in West Virginia, and he recognized that his first priority was to become acquainted with the past and present politics of higher education in West Virginia.[34]

BOARD OF REGENTS RECEIVES BAD GRADES: THE BENEDUM REPORT, 1984

E. Gordon Gee assumed the presidency of WVU in November 1981, and, as part of his intention to modernize the institution and develop a long-range planning process, he launched a comprehensive external review of the University. Undertaking this review was the Academy for Educational Development, the same consulting firm used to evaluate the Board of Regents in 1979, headed by its president, Dr. Alvin C. Eurich. Fourteen review panels comprising a total of forty-two senior university administrators and educators were charged with evaluating and reporting on all facets of WVU. A general committee composed of such nationally known educators as Eurich, Clark Kerr, Frederick S. Lane, and John D. Wilson was empanelled to write the general report. In March 1982, the Benedum Foundation awarded the WVU Foundation a $400,000 grant to underwrite the evaluation, which, as President Gee stated, was necessary in light of the "significant changes and reorientation" that must to take place if the University was to continue to effectively deliver a high-quality education with declining resources.[35]

The general committee's cover letter to President Gee offered some "overall observations," including the problems associated with a "grossly underfunded" University, a phrase packed with multiple layers of meaning. Inadequate funding from the state meant that faculty salaries were "unduly low," therefore class size and teaching loads were "oppressively large," and library and scientific equipment were below acceptable standards. The Benedum Report was bound to anger BOR members by claiming that "the absence of a rational formula" for allocating state funds to WVU was a result of the board's "inadequate appreciation of the necessary costs related to West Virginia University's role as the land-grant, doctoral degree granting, research university in the state."[36]

The general committee "deliberated at great length" on the governing role of the Board of Regents because many of the policies that guided WVU were developed by the board rather than the institution. The committee concluded that governance would be enhanced by a delineation of the powers between the Board of Regents and the University Board of Advisors that declared that powers not specifically given to the board were delegated to the institution. When resources are limited, the Benedum committee reported, operational flexibility is essential.[37]

Acknowledging the deep recession that gripped the state, the committee nevertheless concluded that one of the major reasons for the University's underfunding rested with the Board of Regents because it did not recognize the need for University autonomy and tended to "share the wealth" among all of the state schools rather than establish "differential funding formulae." The failure to budget according to mission rather than institution, would "lead to a general leveling of higher education in West Virginia," the panel claimed, and in the end "mediocrity, not excellence, will prevail." The Benedum Report concluded, most importantly, that the incremental manner by which state funds were allocated to West Virginia's institutions of higher education was "irrational," and it recommended developing new resource allocation models that were equitable and recognized the differences among the state's institutions.[38] Even though WVU confronted serious financial difficulties and was hamstrung by tight external controls, the Report concluded that the University was "making the greatest effort of any research university in the United States to make the most effective use of its resources."[39]

WVU's problems addressed by the Benedum Report were shared with the nation's educators as a feature story in the nationally circulated *Chronicle of Higher Education.* "There is a dream here, on the banks of the Monongahela River, of a vibrant land-grant university—a richly financed 'flagship' institution—leading the state into a new era of prosperity. Both teaching and research at the university are first-rate. Its salaries are highly competitive, its facilities are outstanding, and its programs of extension and public service are among the best." That was the dream, the article declared, but the reality was something quite different. In fact, the *Chronicle* article continued, WVU was "widely acknowledged to be underfinanced, overextended, unable to hold onto many of its best people, saddled with old buildings and inadequate equipment, in danger of pricing itself beyond the reach of many students, and long frustrated in its desire for a truly preeminent role."[40]

President Gee responded publicly in the press that he was in complete agreement with both the Benedum Report and the *Chronicle* article. He indicated that one of the greatest "roadblocks" he had faced since becoming president three years earlier was the "burdensome bureaucratic regulation" imposed on the University by the Board of Regents. He cited as an example the desire to use $250,000 from football bowl and television receipts to purchase computers. "We had to get a special bill (passed by the state Legislature) to be able to spend it," which the president called "absolute silliness." Centralized purchasing provided many other examples: "Do you know how difficult it is to buy rhesus monkeys through state purchasing?" he asked rhetorically. Too often in West Virginia it is assumed that "university and college presidents are crooks and can't be trusted."[41]

West Virginians often shrug off legitimate criticism from within the state, but they are ever sensitive to criticism from outside sources. As might be imagined, therefore, the Benedum Report kicked off a lively controversy among West Virginia legislators, the Board of Regents, and leaders of the other university and state colleges, who feared that WVU might gain a disproportionate advantage. Legislative leaders sympathized with the complaint that WVU received inadequate support, but they were trapped in a "chicken and egg" dilemma. Economic development depended on allocating more money for education and research, they conceded, but without economic development to generate the revenues, there could be no money to spend on economic development.[42]

Other college presidents, particularly Marshall's Dale F. Nitzschke, bristled at the Benedum Report's suggestion that WVU's financial needs were unusual and deserving of a larger share of the state's appropriations to higher education. "We all suffer from a lack of funding and do not want to be forgotten. We are supportive of West Virginia University, but we want the legislature to understand that while the plight of WVU is significant, there are other institutions—particularly Marshall University—whose plight is even greater."[43] President Nitzschke's concern prompted him to appoint a panel to review the Benedum Report, and, not surprisingly, that panel found a number of factual errors and "possible distortions" possibly creating "misleading conclusions." Again, not surprisingly, one of the most significant "distortions" was the assertion that WVU was "grossly underfunded." Other institutions, such as Marshall, could make an even stronger case for underfunding, the panel said. Thus, in 1980–1981 WVU was underfunded by 44.1 percent when compared with Southern Regional Education Board (SREB) and national averages, but Marshall, using the same tables, was underfunded by 61.1 percent when compared with SREB schools and 80.3 percent compared with national averages.[44]

Leon H. Ginsberg, the former dean of social work at WVU and commissioner of human services in Governor Rockefeller's administration, assumed the post of chancellor on June 1, 1984. It fell upon him to counter the negative assertions of the Benedum Report. "There is no question in my mind that there needs to be more money put into West Virginia University," he told a reporter, but the real issue was "should all the money in this state go to that particular university, or should it be spread around? . . . If you don't have the money, how can you allocate it?"[45] Ginsberg claimed that the Benedum consultants failed to understand the issues because they didn't understand West Virginia. "I think it shows that 42 experts can be wrong," he declared.[46] Ginsberg claimed that the report was full of errors, but the errors cited by the chancellor were, in fact, provided by Marshall University President Dale Nitzschke. Ginsberg wrote to Alvin Eurich, who led the review, in January 1985 to complain about the report's supposed inaccuracies. Also, he insisted that the panel members misunderstood the funding formulas, and that the Board of Regents only allocated funds and did not have the power to increase an institution's resources. He chided Eurich for misleading the press, academics, government officials, and the general public.[47] Eurich's response to Ginsberg was polite but rejected the criticisms point by point. The AED had assembled forty-two of the most eminent and experienced higher education administrators in the country who arrived at a consensus, he asserted, and the report represented that consensus.[48]

Ginsberg resumed his complaints the following month, lecturing Eurich about inconsistencies and the need for clarification, and emphasizing that the Board of Regents had in fact made requests for increased funding that the legislature did not fulfill. In recent years, West Virginia had endured "the worst depression in the U.S. since the 1930s" and, over the past four years, the highest unemployment rate in the nation, Ginsberg wrote. The chancellor charged that it was "irresponsible to speak about funding and finances and the economy of the state without relating those items to the current economic context."[49]

Eurich acknowledged that West Virginia's economy was not robust but reminded Ginsberg that the study demonstrated that in 1981 West Virginia ranked fifteenth among the fifty states in "tax capacity," about 10 percent below the national average. However, West Virginia ranked forty-first among the fifty states in "tax effort." In short, compared with its neighbors, West Virginia taxed less than it could and spent less than it should on higher education. Moreover, in 1982 West Virginia allocated 29.5 percent of its state and local expenditures for elementary and secondary education, ranking it sixth in the nation. On the other hand, West Virginia allocated only 7.5 percent of its state and local funds on higher education, ranking it forty-fourth. In the final analysis, and "regardless of any particular details," Eurich wrote, "the Benedum Study Committee was certain that the future of the State of West Virginia is closely related to the teaching, research, and public service activities of West Virginia University. For this, we hope that the State would better recognize the needs of its only research, land-grant university."[50]

Upon learning of Chancellor Ginsberg's criticisms of the Benedum Report, President Gee publicly expressed that he was generally very pleased with the report. Julian W. Nash, a member of the WVU Board of Advisors, wrote directly to Ginsberg. Quoting the report's observation that "restrictions imposed by the Board of Regents and the Legislature prevent the University from becoming a first rate institution," Nash pushed his case: "Shocking, isn't it? The audacity, citing the Board of Regents! Leon, I know it hurts, but my advice would be to profit by the findings" of the distinguished educators who prepared the report. Adequately financing the University, "that's the bottom line, Leon."[51]

The state's newspapers generally gave the Benedum Report a favorable reception. One of the most influential editors, Don Marsh of the *Charleston Gazette*, opined: "I found the report instructive," even though Chancellor Ginsberg believed that the report's recommendations made "no sense at all." Marsh recognized that the basic message of the report was that WVU was "underfunded and over-regulated." Whatever statistics may be used, the editor wrote, "since the university ranks forty-ninth among the fifty similar land grant institutions in faculty pay, I will believe it is underfunded." And since Governor Moore's "freeze order on purchasing is being applied to WVU, as it is to the highway department's county garages, I believe it is over regulated." Marsh concluded that the report left Ginsberg with "unpalatable alternatives," since the legislature was not about to raise taxes and the idea of "doing away with any of the state's three medical schools or reducing the proliferation of community colleges obviously is anathema to the board."[52]

The politics of sectionalism, competition for resources between the state's colleges and universities, institutional self-determination, and the organizational structure of governance generated considerable conflict in higher education as well as in political circles. There were, of course, individual legislators who sought to use the system for both self-serving purposes, as well as individuals motivated by high-minded principles.

However, their particular maneuvers were subsumed within the collective decision-making process in the legislature. Add to this political mix the efforts of governors to extend the chief executive's power over education, and the difficulties of forming a consensus on higher education becomes apparent. Republican Governor Arch Moore injected another discordant element into higher education politics by trying to control the Board of Regents. Moore had signed the legislation creating the Board of Regents in 1969. Having been out of office during Governor Jay Rockefeller's two terms, Moore returned to a Board of Regents that confronted myriad problems. The governor's solution was legislation that would decentralize power in higher education by eliminating the thirteen-member Board of Regents and replacing it with a three-member Commission on Higher Education. This plan would concentrate wide-ranging power in the hands of just three political appointees chosen by the governor. Among the powers given to the proposed commission was the preparation of budget requests for each of the state's colleges and universities, as well as supervising their educational policies. The individual institutions, however, would be responsible for providing the legislature with analyses of their annual budgets. Under Moore's proposal, the sixteen state colleges and universities would have their own boards of trustees with more power to determine how to allocate their institutions' budgets. Some in the legislature, such as Moore's former aide Thomas Craig, supported the measure, as did most of the college presidents, who welcomed the increased autonomy offered. Twelve of the sixteen presidents met in Charleston during the first week of February 1985 to call for Ginsberg's resignation.[53]

Governor Moore informed a group of college presidents that under the Modern Budget Amendment, there was no "direct route" from the Board of Regents to the legislature. Instead, the presidents must channel their budgets through his office rather than the chancellor's. Several months later the governor surprised the college presidents by ordering them to bring their budgetary concerns to him rather than the Board of Regents. "I'm terribly sensitive as to whether or not the regents as such are meeting what we consider to be their general mission," Moore told them. He claimed that the governor's office was the "court of last resort for higher education" and that, since the presidents were "part of the political process," they should have the opportunity to discuss their concerns with him.[54]

Financial issues significantly aggravated the structural and political problems of the Board of Regents. Even as Governor Moore declared 1987 to be the "Year of Education," the legislature reduced Moore's budget by nearly $100 million to correspond with the shortfall in revenue estimates. When the governor then ordered the Board of Regents to reduce its budget proposal by almost $10.5 million, the board found itself between a rock and a hard place. To comply, it announced a plan to close the colleges and universities for one week, furlough those state employees for five days, and cancel the first session of summer school. This was an overreaction, Moore declared, and ordered the board to use money in its interest accounts to cover the cuts. Although this measure averted the regents' planned closings and furloughs, using the money in interest accounts also had undesirable consequences. The board earned interest from its own accounts, such as the $73 million bond issue for capital-building projects, and the institutions earned interest on their own accounts for student fees and auxiliary enterprises. WVU earned about $2.5 million per year from its accounts generated by self-operating units such as resident halls and the Mountainlair, but that money went to operations.[55]

The impact on students and employees at the state's colleges and universities was very demoralizing and confusing. A member of WVU's Student Board of Governors observed: "Right now we feel like we are a tennis ball in a huge tennis match," with the Board of Regents saying one thing, and the governor saying another. The student administration handed out black armbands for an April 10 rally in front of the Mountainlair. The theme was "mourning the death of higher education." A coffin filled with textbooks was placed in the Mountainlair, and students planned to encircle the student center hand in hand. The WVU student leaders had been in touch with student leaders on other campuses where similar demonstrations were planned. Emory Kemp, a longtime faculty member in the College of Engineering, informed a reporter that it was difficult to know what was going on in higher education. "It's a political football in this bizarre game Gov. Moore is playing. I'm angry, and I think a lot of people at the university are angry," he said, especially in this "year for education."[56] A Board of Regents member and a Governor Moore confidant laid the blame squarely on the legislature for picking apart board budget proposals for selfish sectional interests, complaining that "we don't have an integrated system of higher education. We've got a political football."[57]

WVU President Neil Bucklew commented at a Faculty Senate meeting on April 13, 1987, that the entire episode was "chaotic" and "embarrassing" for the state and the University. Everyone at the University was pleased that the furloughs and cancellation of classes were avoided, but Bucklew believed that the University was "harmed and hurt by the process." He did not blame the Board of Regents, however, since Governor Moore had ordered the $10.5 million reduction in the board's budget. Meanwhile, President Bucklew informed University employees that travel and equipment purchases would be "severely curtailed," and an "immediate freeze" placed on all hiring and overtime.[58]

With college presidents supporting Governor Moore's plan for abolition of the Board of Regents and the finger of blame pointed at the board, legislators now became vocal critics of the regents as well. Members of the Senate Finance Committee attacked the board in May for "panicking college students and employees" by threatening school closings and furloughs. The committee charged the the board chancellor with mishandling the entire affair. To make matters worse, Senate Education Chairman Keith Burdette presented a letter from State Auditor Glenn Gainer refusing the regents permission to transfer accumulated interest from special accounts to help pay for summer school. The auditor's letter, dated May 1, 1987, addressed to Senate Finance Chairman Earl Ray Tomblin, stated that the board had been informed that the interest must stay with the principal, and "we have prohibited them from transferring interest into a separate fund and then making the cuts from that account." The governor, on the other hand, had ordered the interest to be used to offset the cuts. Board of Regents President William Watson informed the press, and "if our checks bounce we'll know we're in trouble."[59]

The apparent lack of a coherent policy regarding the Board of Regents rendered planning nearly impossible for the state's college presidents.

There was plenty of blame to go around, but for the politicians the Board of Regents was a lightning rod, even though it was a creature of their own construction. The question of whether West Virginia could afford to maintain so many institutions of higher learning repeatedly bubbled to the surface. The resolution seemed obvious to knowledgeable people, but the inertia of self-interest and sectional politics quickly suffocated any discussion of the subject. In 1983, for example, House Education Committee Chairman Lyle Sattes declared that the higher education system was the outgrowth of teachers' colleges that were opened "when it took twenty hours to cross the state," and continuing to maintain them in modern times was highly questionable. However, "any attempt to consolidate institutions runs up against the problem that you can't get . . . a political body to close them."[60]

The question came up again three years later when former Chancellor Leon Ginsberg filed a report recommending that the state's sixteen colleges should be consolidated into four or five regional institutions. "The waste in higher education is the duplication of resources one finds in having 15 colleges and universities that all offer many of the same courses each semester, and many times not as well as those courses might be offered," Ginsberg declared. Each institution has its own foundation, alumni association, and "other costly structures designed, it has always appeared to me, to insure that the status quo is maintained."[61] No wonder the presidents turned on him.

BOARD OF REGENTS UNDER AN "OMINOUS SHADOW"

Chancellor Ginsberg finally resigned under pressure from all sides. Board members termed the cause of his resignation "friction" between him and Governor Moore. It was claimed that college and university presidents called for his resignation at a meeting in Charleston on February 4, 1986, because they believed that "the interests of higher education were being sacrificed as a result of an impasse between the executive branch and the Board of Regents," according to board President William Watson.[62] Cynics charged that the entire episode was orchestrated by Governor Moore, although he denied it.

In a wide-ranging interview with AP reporter Jill Wilson, former Chancellor Leon Ginsberg, a few months after his resignation, aired his frustrations with the regents system. Ginsberg claimed that faculty salaries were so low because the presidents placed too much emphasis on buildings. He further alleged that, even though the regents "catered" to the presidents' agendas, the presidents withdrew their support at a critical juncture. This tactic left Ginsberg standing alone to challenge the governor over higher education budget freezes and other "attempts to further politicize the system." The former chancellor regarded the system itself as a nineteenth-century relic ill conceived to meet the challenges of the twentieth century. He concluded that, "although all of my predecessors left under something of a cloud, my big mistake was probably in thinking the job could be done."[63]

In a special report released in July 1986, Ginsberg recommended replacing the higher education system. "The Board of Regents has virtually no real support. The Legislature has been itching to abolish it for years and has only sustained it because the alternative plan proposed by Governor Arch Moore was so much less palatable than the status quo." Moreover, the governor generally bypassed the Board of Regents, ignoring the education statutes by issuing orders directly to the presidents. Ginsberg recommended a commission, but, unlike that recommended by Moore, his proposal called for a commission composed of legislators. He suggested consolidating the state's sixteen colleges into four or five regional institutions to eliminate the waste and inefficiency that came from duplication, although such a measure was "guaranteed to gain their opposition."[64]

Ginsberg acknowledged that there was "some pettiness" born of resentment directed at WVU. In his report the former Board of Regents chancellor charged that WVU was partly to blame because it had a tendency to use "whatever means were necessary to achieve financial objectives." For example, Ginsberg claimed that, when WVU Hospitals and Charleston Area Medical Center affiliated, the negotiations were conducted in secret until the agreement was finalized. Moreover, WVU officials repeatedly denied they were lobbying the legislature when everybody at the capitol knew otherwise. Such actions harmed WVU, he insisted, and the best salaries and facilities "cannot save a university that has lost its fundamental commitment—to truth." The former chancellor claimed, "WVU has both resented being equated with the rest of the state's schools and also has been a victim of a few, often petty small college presidents who resent WVU's size and often special treatment." Declining to respond to Ginsberg's comments, newly appointed WVU President Neil Bucklew accepted the report as a "part of history" but preferred to "get on with the future." He claimed that the charges were "overstated" and noted that the regents had not acted upon any of Ginsberg's recommendations.[65]

Outgoing WVU President E. Gordon Gee had his own "very serious concerns" regarding higher education governance under the Board of Regents. Among members of the Board of Regents were some of his "greatest allies" who worked diligently on WVU's account, but their efforts were overshadowed by "a flawed system." The board governed community colleges, four-year colleges, and universities, resulting in "a natural tension which tends to drive wedges between those institutions." The board was established to eliminate inefficient competition between the institutions, but it simply did not function very well, in Gee's view. Consequently, schools within the system were "leveled" to the lowest common denominator. If the University had only maintained the same 18 percent of the state budget it had in 1969, when the Board of Regents was founded, the University's base budget would have been $45 million larger. Instead, since 1969, the percentage of state appropriations that WVU received dropped from 18 to 12 percent. Gee offered this budget analysis to demonstrate how funding for WVU had been formula driven, which "anyone with simple mathematics can understand is destructive."[66]

The state legislature also shared some of the blame for the problems confronting higher education in West Virginia. Gee dismissed former Chancellor Ginsberg's criticism that WVU sent representatives to lobby legislators despite its being unacceptable. Even though it was his job as a public university president to provide legislators with "appropriate information," so that "appropriate decisions will be made," Gee asserted that he did not lobby legislators. He insisted that legislators had not been willing "to make the tough kinds of decisions" about higher education and had treated WVU as a drain on the state rather than as a major investment. Unlike a highway department or a department of social services, the University is a catalyst for economic development, and legislative support for the institution was vital for the future of the state. When legislators imposed salary caps, developed centralized classification systems, opposed attempts to implement merit incentives, and imposed overly burdensome regulatory controls on the University, they were not acting in the best interests of the institution. Gee urged legislators to "stop or we are going to have a university only in name not in reality."[67]

In order to be successful, a university must push the "frontiers of knowledge" in all kinds of research. "We need to do a better job in explaining the value of research" to the legislature, Gee declared. This role distinguished it from all the other institutions of higher learning, not to mention the Department of Highways. "The research function of a university is very difficult to understand," but because of WVU's commitment to research in acid mine drainage, coal-liquefaction, any number of endeavors in medicine and business, and a bewildering array of other kinds of research, thousands of people were employed in West Virginia. As Gee recounted: "Several years ago we lost an engineering faculty member to Arizona State. That faculty member took a million dollars worth of research grants with him. If we had paid him another $10,000 in salary, we would have had that million dollars here in this state." Instead, he continued "we had to do two things. We had to spend $10,000 to recruit another individual, and we had to pay that individual a competitive salary which was the $10,000 or $15,000 and we lost the million dollars to boot. It is absolute insanity the way that we treat the university in terms of those kinds of issues."[68]

Both financial and cumulative difficulties confronted WVU. The University had been "substantially underfunded for a long time. This university is much better than the people of this state really deserve because of the kind of funding they have given to it," the outgoing president declared, and at least part of the blame he ascribed to the ineffectiveness of the Board of Regents. "I'm certain there will be key people who argue with that premise strenuously. I believe that the facts . . . are on my side, but whether or not the Legislature has the means or the will to do it whether or not the political will is out there I don't know."[69]

The legislature extended the Board of Regents for one year, from June 30, 1988, pending the release of a major study of the higher education system by the Carnegie Foundation. Clearly the board was under an "ominous shadow," observed one reporter, and the question on everyone's mind was whether it would be renewed when the legislation creating the board expired on June 30, 1989. WVU President Neil Bucklew voiced the opinion of most: "I think every president and every member of the higher education system is anxious to get this issue of governance resolved."[70]

CARNEGIE REPORT ENVISIONS A NEW SYSTEM FOR HIGHER EDUCATION IN WEST VIRGINIA

Since its founding in 1969, the Board of Regents had come under attack at various times from the governor, legislators, and the media, all of which called for its dissolution. In 1988, prior to the release of the Carnegie Report, the widely read *Chronicle of Higher Education* published a very negative story about the Board of Regents system. "By almost any measure," the article asserted, higher education in West Virginia was in "terrible shape." Most political leaders in the state reportedly had "little confidence" in their collegiate institutions, the article concluded, and the board was "plagued" by turnovers at the top, with the exit of three chancellors in the past two years. The state historically depended on the coal industry for tax revenues and well-paying jobs, the article explained, but education was deemphasized. Therefore, when coal employment went into a precipitous decline because of mine mechanization, the decline of the educational system followed closely behind. Now that state officials were clamoring for economic diversification, they were "confronted with colleges that never received enough money or attention." In time-worn fashion, officials reared up to defend the state from outside attack: Chancellor Simmons claimed the article was "very negatively biased," and Marshall President Nitzschke said it reflected a "lack of understanding."[71] Whether the article's charges were accurate or not, after more than five years of agitation over the governance issue, West Virginia educators and politicians were prepared to make some major changes when the Carnegie Report was issued in February 1989.

The Carnegie panelists were asked to envision a new system of governance, and they complied. To reduce unnecessary competition and duplication in graduate and professional education and research, the consultants recommended the formation of The University of West Virginia, a multi-campus structure incorporating WVU, Marshall, the West Virginia College of Graduate Studies, and the centers for medical education. The goal was to "build a network of high-quality, cost effective graduate research and medical institutions." Because of its location far in the north, WVU could not successfully serve all sections of the state. Therefore, Marshall would serve the southern part of the state as a comprehensive institution but would grow in a way that was compatible to, rather than competitive with, WVU. The College of Graduate Studies should serve as a nontraditional institution within the larger organizational structure. The new University of West Virginia would be directed by a chancellor, a vice chancellor for health affairs, and its own governing Board of Trustees, which would develop all basic policy decisions for the University. Unless the University possessed the "authority and respect" to establish policies and speak for the entire system before the legislature, then the new structure would also fail, the consultants warned. Consequently, the trustees should clarify the missions of the separate institutions within the multi-campus system. The Huntington campus would be a "strong undergraduate and master's level institution," while the Morgantown campus would provide advanced study, specialized institutes, and research.[72]

Unlike the earlier Benedum study, the Carnegie Report did not call for consolidating the four-year colleges but rather reaffirmed their "essential role" in promoting undergraduate education. The four-year colleges and community colleges would be governed by their own board and chancellor. The emphasis should be on strengthening the quality of the existing system, keeping all colleges intact but with improved quality control, and avoiding "unwarranted duplication." If the state was financially unable to improve the four-year institutions within three years, then the Board of Regents should "seriously consider campus mergers as well as changing the mission of one or more campuses from four-year to two-year status."[73]

Under the reorganization, the universities should take a leading role in the state's economic development by becoming more efficient and by being "vitally linked to the national and international community of scholars." As the flagship campus, WVU had the largest role to play in this mission by advancing research. WVU had been "exceptional in its ability to function within severely restricted resources," the report concluded, but the state was living on borrowed time. Like the other institutions, WVU had suffered from chronic underfunding. The Resource Allocation Model, the formula instituted in 1988 by the Board of Regents to provide for the equitable allocation of funds, demonstrated to the Carnegie team that WVU was "among the least successful institutions in receiving needed allocations. West Virginia University has been funded at 52.6 percent in peer-based comparisons—a shortfall of $61 million." Since WVU granted nearly all of the PhD and professional degrees in the state, "it would be tragic for WVU to be forced, by chronic shortages, to turn back from its essential missions."[74]

To counter this shortage of resources, the Carnegie team recommended that WVU become more selective, focus on excellence in graduate studies, and create endowed faculty chairs. Salaries should be averaged up to that of peer-group institutions and be based on merit. WVU administrators were gratified that the consultants recognized that "a great university needs flexibility to make day-to-day decisions about how resources will be used" and recommended that "responsibility be delegated to university officials in such areas as purchasing, salaries, and merit-pay adjustments."[75]

With a "sharply defined mission," Marshall University, recommended the consultants, "should take the lead in the economic, civic, and educational renewal of southern West Virginia" as a comprehensive university within the reorganized university system. If left to its own devices, the panel warned, Marshall was likely to develop in a way that duplicated WVU, and "it is unacceptable for two universities to compete for restricted funds in the high-cost area of graduate education and research." The College of Graduate Studies was considered a distinctive asset with a vital role to play in the state. It should be brought into the new university system to concentrate on nontraditional education, such as independent study under the direction of faculty mentors, rather than duplicate traditional classroom courses offered by Marshall and WVU. In this role, the College of Graduate Studies should expand beyond its current Kanawha Valley location to include the entire state.[76]

The Carnegie team was also convinced that medical education in West Virginia "must be overhauled" within the reorganized university system and the missions of the medical centers clearly defined with "an appropriate balance between research, specialties, rural, and allied health." WVU's School of Medicine should emphasize training specialties and high-level medical research. Because the state could not support two comprehensive medical centers, Marshall's School of Medicine should concentrate on preparing physicians for general practice focusing on rural health. The West Virginia School of Osteopathic Medicine "should become a private institution or be merged with the medical school at Marshall," the consultants recommended.[77]

A month after Gaston Caperton began his first term as governor in January 1989, the Carnegie Commission released its report. By early March, Governor Caperton and legislative leaders had endorsed the commission's recommendations. It was announced on March 2, 1989, therefore, that the Board of Regents would expire on June 30 as part of the higher education reorganization. The following week legislation was introduced in the Senate to abolish the board. Introduced at Governor Caperton's request, Senate Bill 420 called for replacing the board with a fifteen-member Board of Trustees to oversee the new University of West Virginia system, which included Marshall, WVU, and the College of Graduate Studies. The School of Osteopathic Medicine was to be removed from the public college system, although the president of the institution declared his intention to oppose the expulsion. The four-year and two-year colleges would be overseen by the fifteen-member Board of Directors. Both WVU President Neil Bucklew and Marshall President Paul Nitzschke supported the bill, as did a number of state leaders who attended committee hearings.[78]

Not every regent was sanguine about replacing the Board of Regents with a new system. Tom Craig observed that reorganization was the result of a changing state leadership rather than a fundamental change in approach. When the new trustees made difficult decisions, they would come under political fire as had the regents. Craig claimed that the Board of Regents was a "whipping boy" that got the blame "because politicians either don't want to or can't help us in fully funding a system that the politicians created." As an example, Craig pointed to the provision in Senate Bill 420 that would have phased out public funding for the School for Osteopathic Medicine. Responding to political pressure from osteopaths, employees, students, and local representatives, the legislature quickly abandoned the idea, and the school remained part of the new system.[79]

Governor Caperton appointed David Hardesty, former tax commissioner and a partner in the law firm of Bowles, Rice, McDavid, Graff, and Love, as the temporary head of the newly formed Board of Trustees. Among the other appointments to the new board were WVU graduates Kay Goodwin, John Hoblitzell, and A. Michael Perry. Five ex officio members included a faculty representative, WVU sociologist Joe Simoni, staff representative Martin Smelik of Potomac State College, and State Superintendent of Schools Hank Marockie. The Board of Trustees reported to Secretary of Arts and Education Stephen Haid, a former lobbyist for the West Virginia Education Association.[80]

SIX

THE ADMINISTRATIONS
OF JAMES G. HARLOW AND
GENE A. BUDIG

WHEN JAMES HARLOW RECEIVED his BS and MS degrees in mathematics and physics from the University of Oklahoma, the nation was in the grips of the Great Depression. Although he hoped to pursue a career in electronics, he found no demand for his services. Consequently, he accepted a high school teaching position and, from 1934 to 1941, also served as editor at Harlow Publishing Corporation, the family business that printed law books and high school textbooks. This experience enabled Harlow to write several teaching aids for high school science and math teachers. During World War II, Harlow entered the Navy and rose to the rank of lieutenant commander. With the surge in college enrollments following the war, Harlow was hired as an instructor of physics at the University of Oklahoma. When the postwar enrollment surge subsided in the early fifties, Harlow entered the University of Chicago. Upon completion of his doctorate in education, Harlow continued as a research associate and then associate professor of education. In 1957 he returned to the University of Oklahoma, where he served as dean of education for the next ten years.[1]

At the age of fifty-five, in August 1967 he became WVU's sixteenth president. Many observers nodded approvingly, confident that he would not follow the example of his immediate predecessors by using the office as a stepping-stone to a more prestigious position. Harlow's appointment thus promised greater stability at the University's helm. Unconfirmed reports indicated that about ninety candidates had applied for the job, but James Harlow was the unanimous choice of the Board of Governors.[2]

The new president demonstrated a sense of humor when he was interviewed by the press. The job came to him, Harlow avowed; "I would never look for a state university presidency. I never have. I think anybody who isn't afraid of one isn't safe with one." On town-gown relations, he claimed that "the university's relationship with the community is like a marriage. It is not friction free but is involved in a mutual activity from which neither can escape." He noted that the university president's average tenure was about four-and-a-half years, "not much longer than a football coach's—and perhaps for the same reasons." In response to those distressed because a West Virginian was not chosen, Harlow teased that the University's "last short-term president (Miller) was a native West Virginian and their last long-term one (Stewart) was a Texan."[3]

On the larger issues confronting university presidents of the day, Harlow's comments must have relieved some but disquieted others. He did not object to student activism and thought mature dissent should be encouraged. "Divergences of opinion are 'the blow-hole in the ice of our social system.'" He thought the funding at WVU was lower than it should be relative to comparable state institutions, although there was never enough money to go around. Also, he took a strong stand on faculty governance, declaring that "any good university has a strong faculty government." In fact, "the better the university, the better the faculty government will be." Harlow dismissed the notion that athletics were overemphasized at WVU. "Intercollegiate athletics and state universities are here to stay," Harlow told the press, and he saw no indication that athletics had distorted the academic mission of WVU. Sports were popular, large crowds filled the stadium, and "this is fine as far as I'm concerned. I think we ought to do whatever we do as well as we can. I would be embarrassed to have the least effective state university football team in this area. I would rather close it down than not have a good one."[4]

Although Harlow was an experienced administrator, he nonetheless received plenty of advice from the state press. Less than two weeks after he moved into the president's office, editor John W. Yago of the *Charleston Gazette* provided Harlow with "a civilian view of the University and your job." Yago's tongue-in-cheek open letter on the op-ed page warned Harlow that "few people in the academic world" would envy him his job. For one thing, most people in Morgantown were "suspicious of anything said or done south of Jane Lew, especially in Charleston, the evil big city that is trying to steal the university and move it piecemeal to Kanawha County." Second, managing WVU would be almost impossible, "especially since you won't be permitted to do it yourself without the help of nearly two million people who know more about running a university than you do." Third, even though WVU "can't by any stretch of the imagination be called a great institution," neither is it one to be "sneered at." Nevertheless, because of its size and complexity, it should be the "pre-eminent higher education institution in the state," but it has "never quite filled this role as it should." Instead, it has persisted in focusing on ever increasing undergraduate enrollments rather than developing smaller, higher quality undergraduate and graduate programs.[5]

Yago also informed the new president that for years WVU had been forced by politicians to "establish all kinds of questionable programs." As examples he cited the agriculture school, even though West Virginia was "as unlikely a farming state as you will find," and the Appalachian Center, a "curious amalgam" which had become "a new home for county agricultural agents." One of the most important political realities Harlow had to acknowledge as soon as possible was that "the main interest of most West Virginians is in the football and basketball teams." While there are thousands of citizens who will contribute to athletics, they would not "show the same willingness to endow a chair of history," and the president should think twice before suggesting that "a young English instructor should be paid as much as a young athletic press agent." The WVU president traditionally hosted "junkets to the [football] games for state legislators many of whom are lawyers with degrees from the state's only law school at WVU. Treat them well and you will have a friendly reception when financial pleas are made before statehouse committees." There was one more thing, Yago averred: the next time WVU constructed a new building on the Evansdale Campus, the new president should "have a long talk with your architect. Perhaps you can persuade him to abandon the Early Missile Site designs they have been using out there."[6] Just as Yago had warned,

President Harlow did discover at least two million people who seemed to think they knew more about running a university than its president. Fortunately, Harlow had a less jaundiced perspective on the state and its University than they did.

At his formal inauguration on September 14, 1968, President Harlow observed that, over the course of its first century, the University had evolved in complexity and was "entering maturity as a modern state university." He also noted that it had progressed beyond the critical stage of development, having reached 15,000 in enrollment on its four campuses in Morgantown, Keyser, Parkersburg, and Charleston. Moreover, the University was an aspiring center for graduate studies, having conferred a total of 225 doctoral degrees at the May 1968 commencement, and its growing recognition was earning WVU "a firm place among major universities." Harlow was encouraged by the acquisition of a new computer that would enable researchers to undertake major funded projects. The legislature's appropriation of the funds to appoint Centennial Professors, the first named professorships available at WVU, was also an encouraging sign. Harlow also regarded faculty involvement in the decision-making process and an active, engaged student government as further evidence of maturation. "Full maturity," however, required competitive faculty salaries, funding for graduate fellowships, and doubling the size of the library.[7]

REORGANIZATION AND ADMINISTRATION

Given the new president's background, it came as no surprise to the university community that Harlow intended to encourage "the application of programs, learning techniques, audio-visual, and computerized learning" at WVU. Apparently his enthusiasm infected the Board of Governors, which predicted in its 1969 report that, in WVU's second century, traditional group lectures would be eclipsed by electronic devices such as closed-circuit television, films, slides, tape recorders, and computers. Six years later, in 1974, President Harlow and members of the board must have been disappointed when the North Central Association of Colleges and Secondary Schools' accreditation team reported that the most complaints among students clustered around freshman English and the televised course in beginning biology.[8]

Still, there were applications for computer technology that would revolutionize universities just as they eventually would do for society at large, and Harlow was on the cutting edge of their use at WVU. One of his first acts as president was to order a new IBM 360–75 computer, which he informed the Board of Regents was the most dramatic advance made by the University in recent years. The impact of the new technology was as far reaching as it was invisible to the public. The professional staff was fully aware that a new day had dawned, however, when, in the fall of 1969, a new management information system was adopted. Immediate results, Harlow reported to the Faculty Assembly in 1969, were most rewarding: a computerized payroll system, saving countless boring clerical hours that could be spent more productively; a computerized master personnel file, replacing a confused and totally inadequate system of paperwork; a computerized budgeting system, giving the comptroller greater control over the University's finances and permitting an accurate account balance at the end of each month; and, finally, a manual of administrative policies and procedures for budget officers.[9]

Harlow also envisioned major changes for Paul Miller's Center for Appalachian Studies and Development. "The current name of the unit does not appropriately relate this unit to West Virginia University nor does it indicate that the unit performs a University function," Harlow informed Board of Regents Chancellor Ben Morton. He proposed that its name be changed to Center for Extension and Continuing Education, a title generally regarded "as being representative of the extended functions of land-grant universities." Moreover, since the center's establishment, the federal government had created the Appalachian Regional Commission to foster economic and social development within the region. Harlow believed that the similarity of names and functions caused confusion.[10]

President Harlow also had his own unique ideas about administrative structure. He created a "President's Office" to improve on the quality of leadership. Conceptually, the President's Office was to be a "team presidency," in which all major decisions were the product of the entire staff, rather than a one-person line organization. This reorganization called for the elimination of vice presidents, who were replaced by provosts. As early as December 1967, Harlow commented before a meeting of civil leaders in Charleston that "vice presidents are a disease of large organizations; they multiply endlessly, and are controlled only through the greatest effort. We already have five at WVU, and we'll shortly have a sixth." In his restructuring of the administration, Harlow implemented a presidential team headed by provosts, each of whom were responsible for specialized segments of the organization but none of whom had line responsibility; that was a collective responsibility of the President's Office. By the fall of 1971, Harlow had removed all but Vice President of Administration and Finance Harry Heflin. Harlow adopted quite literally Webster's definition of "Vice" as a prefix designating "one who takes the place of." Vice President Heflin assumed the duties of the president in his absence. A provost, on the other hand, was defined by Webster as "a high administrative officer in charge of strictly educational activities," and Harlow created six of them, each reporting directly to the president. In effect, Harlow had line responsibility for all phases of the University's operation.[11]

The North Central Association of Colleges and Secondary Schools accreditation team regarded the administrative organization adopted by President Harlow as "unusual, with six provosts serving as staff to the President, but with none having line responsibility." Although this horizontal structure provided ready access by deans to the University's leading officers, it also created confusion regarding which officers were empowered to make particular decisions.[12]

THE PERSONAL RAPID TRANSIT

With state financial support for the University lagged behind growth of the student body during the era of the Board of Regents, the Harlow administration redoubled efforts to attract ever larger resources from the federal government. In attracting federal support for the Personal Rapid Transit, or the PRT, as it became known, WVU landed the largest single expenditure of federal money in its history, about $128 million. The experimental, computer-controlled "people mover" attracted international attention. The PRT became perhaps the most distinctive physical feature on the WVU campus, but its construction also revealed the dark side of political intervention in university affairs.

Professor of Engineering Samy E. G. Elias was an Egyptian by birth who received his advanced degrees in the United States. Elias arrived in Morgantown in 1965, just as the growth of WVU and its expansion to the Evansdale Campus exacerbated already serious traffic congestion in a way that begged for a solution. After working out the best solution to these problems, Elias submitted a proposal to the U.S. Department of Transportation in June 1967 to fund a computer-controlled, electric, elevated transit system to replace the University's bus system, which linked the downtown, Evansdale, and medical campuses. Elias calculated that, by eliminating the wages of bus drivers and imposing a small student fee, the system would be self-sustaining at his estimated cost of $13.4 million.[13]

The University then applied for a federal grant. Hearing nothing from the government office regarding the proposal, Harlow contacted Congressman Harley O. Staggers, who represented the Morgantown district and chaired the influential House Interstate and Foreign Commerce Committee, to request that he intercede with U.S. Secretary of Transportation John Volpe. Harlow, Elias (now chairman of the Department of Industrial Engineering at WVU), and Staggers met with Volpe, who expressed interest in the project as an experiment for similar transit systems. Volpe charged the Urban Mass Transportation Administration (UMTA) to work with WVU to develop the PRT project, and on June 20, 1969, UMTA announced that it would finance a feasibility study.

The University study recommended a mass transit system consisting of six stations and one hundred computer-controlled vehicles to run on a 3.6 mile elevated guideway at speeds of up to thirty miles per hour. Alden Self-Transit Systems Corporation, a Massachusetts firm that already had a prototype available, was recommended as the producer. The estimated cost was $18 million, with the University paying $4.5 million for the land acquisition, and the UMTA picking up the remaining $13.5 million. The system could reduce the traffic congestion downtown by allowing drivers to park their cars at the periphery of campus and ride the PRT instead of driving between campuses.[14]

Shortly after the official announcement, UMTA also announced that it, rather than the University, would manage the experimental system. No explanation followed this decision, but since the PRT was the first such experimental project undertaken by the Department of Transportation, the agency probably thought it wise to retain control over its development. Whatever the reasoning, Elias became merely a consultant, and Alden Self-Transit was dropped as the systems manager in favor of Cal Tech's Jet Propulsion Laboratory (JPL). The Boeing Company would design the vehicles and also became systems manager when JPL left the project because of cost issues. In 1970, when Congress was informed of the project, the federal cost was estimated at $13.4 million, but by 1971 that figure had climbed to $37.4 million. Fearful of arousing congressional ire, the project was scaled back to $28 million for a two-mile link and three stations (Walnut Street, Beechurst Avenue, and the engineering building), known as Phase I. Construction of the rest of the original system, Phase II, would follow. Costs continued to spiral apparently out of control, and by 1974 they had rocketed to more than $115 million.[15]

Secretary Volpe became impatient and pushed everybody for a 1972 grand opening, according to the *New York Times*, so that President Nixon "could come here before the election and show it off." The White House chose October 25, 1972, for the official opening, only two weeks before the election. Nixon's daughter Tricia Nixon Cox represented the president on opening day, but the event was an embarrassment. According to Harlow, the system simply was not ready, but the University had been forced into a grand opening by political expediency beyond WVU's control. Everything had been "jerry-rigged" to accommodate the reporters and television cameras. Harlow and Elias joined Secretary Volpe and Tricia Nixon Cox in the three cars that had been prepared for the demonstration. Instead of traveling the 2.2 miles, the car carrying Elias and representatives of the press broke down and had to be towed off the track. Exacerbating the public relations fiasco was a confrontation between chanting antiwar protestors and the Young Republicans who tried to shout them down.[16]

Disenchantment replaced the initial excitement over the new project. In 1973, Transportation Under Secretary Robert Clement openly declared that "it was no secret" that the administration was frustrated with the PRT project in Morgantown. What went wrong? There were many reasons, but the spiral began when the original plan using an already existing prototype was scrapped. Consequently, a new system had to be designed from scratch. Second, the original proposal was based on cars carrying only eight passengers each, but the maximum was increased to twenty, causing the car weight to double, which then required an upward revision of the guideway's strength. Third, election-year politics prompted a rush to operation, costing additional millions. One Department of Transportation administrator reportedly commented that the best way to deal with the problem was to give up the on the computerized transit cars and supply every WVU student with a golf cart to travel the elevated guideway.[17]

Fully aware that the federal government wanted to abandon the project, University administrators began to prepare arguments supporting its completion. Primarily, they feared the costs of operating the system would fall on the University. Only 3.5 million passengers a year with the scaled-back system, compared with 14.5 million passengers for a completed system, would have a serious financial impact. And, because Phase I would serve relatively few students, the University could not charge a general student fee for the service. Moreover, the WVU bus system would have to be maintained because the Phase I system would reach neither the large University lots at the periphery nor the medical school complex. By legal agreement, the University had the right to accept or reject the system upon completion of Phase I, and President Harlow stated publicly that he was willing to let the government demolish the system if it did not intend to complete the project. If the University rejected it, the Department of Transportation would be required to remove the PRT and restore the landscape to its original condition. In this "war of nerves" the Department of Transportation blinked first. UMTA agreed to complete a system with five stations, expanding the line beyond engineering to stations at the Towers dormitories and the Medical School. The University agreed to abandon the Coliseum station.[18]

As everyone familiar with WVU or Morgantown knows, the PRT did not solve the traffic problems. The University bus service was eliminated in 1976, but the PRT never transported as many students as projected and proved to be far more expensive to operate than the bus system.[19] As student enrollments continued to rise, the WVU bus system was relaunched to operate alongside the PRT.

UNDERGRADUATE CURRICULUM REFORM

Changes in the curriculum begun under President Stahr continued under President Miller. A Faculty Senate committee studied the issue for two years and, after all of the colleges reviewed their curricula, developed a University core curriculum to replace the previous integrated studies program, which had permitted each college to develop its own general education requirements. Implemented in the fall of 1964, the University's new core curriculum was intended to provide students with a general education by requiring each student to take courses in three broad disciplinary areas: humanities, social and behavioral sciences, and mathematics and science. The core curriculum had its detractors, including some faculty who judged that, while the core might provide general education for engineering and technical students, the lack of science and technology courses for humanities or business students did not improve their general education. Others believed that general education should be linked to the discipline in which students were majoring, particularly for those in a preprofessional track.[20]

The core curriculum presented problems for some colleges, particularly engineering. In April 1979, the Department of Chemical Engineering presented the Faculty Senate with a proposal intended to address deficiencies in its program cited by accrediting teams. The department's response called for internal revisions in engineering course instruction but also required students to take two additional courses in chemistry. The first was easily accommodated, but the second required a reduction in credit hours from twenty-four to eighteen in the humanities and the social sciences groups within the core curriculum for engineering students.[21]

Although probably viewed as problem-solving by engineering Dean Bill Atchley, the Senate Core Curriculum Committee interpreted the proposal as an effort by one of the professional schools, which were considered most in need of more liberal arts, to skirt the general education requirements. After a hearing before the Faculty Senate, the Department of Chemical Engineering proposal was voted down. Because Dean of Arts and Sciences William Collins had collaborated with the Dean Atchley in trying to solve the accreditation problem, Collins was asked by his own faculty to explain his support for the proposal. He explained that if university-wide problems were not resolved cooperatively, each college would soon revert to its own general education requirements. If that happened, Dean Collins observed, the University itself was in danger of becoming "a loose confederation of colleges held together by the plumbing and the PRT."[22]

BRINGING THE UNIVERSITY TO THE PEOPLE

Outreach is defined as professional activities intended serve the state by bringing the University to the people. The Appalachian Center was President Paul Miller's principal vehicle for accomplishing this mission, but President Harlow expanded service outreach in other ways. Off-campus credit instruction attracted 2,700 participants each semester in the seventies, 90 percent of whom were public school teachers taking courses required for certificate renewal or to improve their salaries. The MBA program, added in 1972, offered courses for those already employed through televised lectures and weekend seminars. The School of Social Work also offered off-campus courses for employees in social work agencies. The University's outreach designed for undergraduates was located at three centers. The Greenbrier Valley Extension Center, where up to 48 hours of lower-level course credit could be accumulated and transferred to WVU, enrolled 125 students in 1972–1973. The Kennedy Youth Center, a federal reformatory near Morgantown, enrolled 30–40 in several courses offered each semester. The University also began offering some basic courses in the spring of 1973 at the Federal Institution for Women at Alderson.[23]

Off-campus credit instruction was hampered in several ways during the seventies. For one thing, until 1973 the WVU Graduate School distinguished between credits earned on and off campus by limiting the number of off-campus credit hours toward a master's degree to fifteen. A second problem was that the departments had no commitment to an outreach program. Demand rather than program design determined which courses were offered. As a result, requests for courses were submitted to the Appalachian Center's Extension Credit Office and forwarded to the departments. Historically underfunded for their mission, the departments could not give priority to extension courses when other needs closer to home were so pressing. Most University departments were, and still are, staffed according to requirements for on-campus instruction without regard for outreach. Third, until 1972, when the policy of paying instructors for off-campus teaching as though it was an overload was abandoned, there was no financial inducement for faculty to teach off campus. Fourth, the outreach credit courses were staffed primarily by part-time instructors from other institutions. Finally, state law prohibited the University from receiving fees for courses taught by television, and the educational radio available in West Virginia was not comparable to educational television.[24]

The greatest outreach provided by the University during the sixties and seventies was noncredit instruction. Defined as instruction or experiences designed for adult continuing education, most offerings were in the form of seminars, workshops, conferences, and short courses, which served 7,262 participants in 1971–1972. Most classes were offered through divisions of the Appalachian Center and the School of Nursing for practicing nurses. Training for teachers in the Head Start Program, in-service training for physicians, and workshops for businessmen also made up a sizable minority of the noncredit classes offered. The professional schools (Law, Medicine, Dentistry, Pharmacy, Agriculture, and Mines) also offered regular noncredit professional development courses. Extension specialists also engaged in a broad range of noncredit educational and developmental activities.[25]

Left unfinished at the end of Paul Miller's administration were plans for an educational television channel. James Harlow's administration continued the effort, winning federal approval to build a $1.1 million educational television station in Morgantown (Channel 24 UHF). Upon completion, the three West Virginia public television stations in Huntington, Beckley, and Morgantown would reach 97 percent of the state's population. By the winter of 1975 the equipment for WWVU-TV had been installed, and both the eastern and northern panhandles were within the thirty-nine county coverage of the University's signal in north central West Virginia. The Harlow administration regarded this development as one of the "most far reaching contributions to West Virginia adults." Together with the WVU Extension Center, the University now exerted a "total state-wide impact on adult education activity." The following year WWVU-TV was beaming credit courses to 850 students, many of them candidates for the Board of Regents Bachelor of Arts degree who were enrolled at state and private colleges throughout Channel 24's signal area.[26]

HOUSING IMPROVES, SUNNYSIDE DECLINES

All unmarried freshmen, with the exception of veterans and those who lived with their parents, were required to live in university-supervised housing so long as space was available. Dormitory rooms, primarily double occupancy, and approximately four hundred University apartments provided 4,060 students with University housing in the fall of 1973. Thousands of rooms were also available in private dorms and homes, as well as several thousand private apartments. Off-campus student housing has always been big business in Morgantown. Both WVU and Morgantown were challenged to find suitable housing accommodations for the increasing number of faculty and students after World War II, and the problem continued as enrollments grew in the sixties. The construction of new dormitories augmented the University's housing for students, but private housing was a serious problem. Faculty found very few houses for sale or rent in Morgantown, and students living off campus often found only substandard accommodations. Faculty often looked to outlying areas to find housing, like Point Marion, Preston County, and Fairmont. Conditions improved as new housing developments grew up around the city, and the University abandoned the effort to house students and faculty to the private sector.[27]

By 1975 President Harlow informed the Faculty Assembly that housing for students in the Morgantown area had improved significantly. "For two successive Septembers, my office has not been inundated with demands that the University police Morgantown landlords, with reports that students are threatening to pitch tents in Woodburn Circle and on the Library Mall, and that students are withdrawing in large numbers because of unavailability of housing. The private sector in housing has come through beautifully, and I believe that we can begin to look forward hopefully to remove all inadequate and dangerous student rental properties from the market."[28] Harlow's optimism proved premature.

In the fifties, Sunnyside was a different kind of neighborhood than the one Morgantown residents knew as of 2010. It was essentially a residential community where some families boarded students, as was also true in South Park and on Richwood Avenue. When student enrollments mushroomed in the sixties and seventies, the University began to build dormitories: Boreman Hall North, Arnold Hall, Daddisman Hall, and another set of twin towers on Evansdale Campus. The University's decision to drop the requirement that all students reside in University housing in the late sixties and early seventies put even more pressure on Morgantown's limited housing stock. Local developers sought to take advantage of the booming market and quickly constructed private residence halls. On the downtown campus, Knapp Hall, Summit Hall, Glenlock Hall, and Centennial Hall were also built as private residence halls, as was Pierpont Hall on the Evansdale Campus. But, as so often happens, the private developers overbuilt residence halls and could not keep them filled. Glenlock and Centennial were converted to other purposes. Most students preferred apartment living to the residence halls. By the seventies, a lot of families were leaving Sunnyside; as they vacated, their houses were converted into student apartments. With increased student occupancy, few were left who valued the neighborhood, and it began to degrade.[29]

Frank Scafella, an emeritus WVU professor and former Morgantown mayor, became involved in the Wiles Hill Neighborhood Association to prevent it from becoming a student ghetto like Sunnyside. From the late sixties to the mid-seventies, neighborhoods close to the university were "simply under siege," he remembered. According to Scafella, when a number of landlords and investors learned that the University was planning to expand student housing, "they went to Harlow . . . and said we would like to see your plans." As one of the local developers told the story, "they looked at Harlow's plans and we killed them right there." The president welcomed it as an opportunity to get out of the student housing business and the financial burdens it presented, and the developers began "to buy up housing as it came up for sale and that is what happened to Sunnyside. Up to the late fifties, early sixties, it was a desired faculty neighborhood . . . the city had no restrictions on occupancies, trash, parking, none of that." So it was that Sunnyside become a student ghetto.[30]

Safety became a major problem. Landlords allowed many of these rentals to become dilapidated and unsafe, and the constant rotation of students with no interest in their upkeep facilitated the decline. Fire was an ever-present danger, and the death of several girls in a house fire during the seventies made it paramount that the University step up its efforts to either improve the safety of student housing or remove the structures. From this point on, the University and the City of Morgantown fire inspectors increasingly worked together to remediate the problems presented by dilapidated, unsafe student housing and irresponsible landlords.[31]

HARLOW RETIRES, BUDIG IS HIRED

According to one of President Harlow's assistants, "nothing infuriated Dr. Harlow more than the policy of the Board of Regents requiring administrative officers to retire upon attaining the age of sixty-five." The mere mention of a search was enough to send the president into a rage. Consequently, Harlow did little to facilitate the selection of a new president or the interregnum. He reached retirement age in 1977, but the Board of Regents had set the replacement process in motion several months prior to that date. The procedures had changed substantially since Harlow's appointment. The Board of Governors no longer had much authority in the selection process as when Harlow was hired in 1967; that responsibility now resided with the Board of Regents, and now affirmative action procedures had to be followed. Relations between Harlow and Chancellor Ben L. Morton had deteriorated to outright dislike, so the regents probably regarded Harlow's departure with relief. The Board of Regents announced on January 1, 1977, that Dr. Gene A. Budig, then president of Illinois State University, would succeed Harlow on July 1, 1977. Chancellor Morton was familiar with Budig's work in Illinois, where Morton previously had served as executive officer of the Illinois Board of Regents.[32]

On the day after commencement, Harlow and the moving van left for his new home in Norman, Oklahoma without fanfare or farewell. Chancellor Morton appointed Harold Shamberger as interim president for the one and a half months between WVU's commencement and July 1, when Budig would take over. Shamberger was no stranger to the president's office, having served as presidential assistant and in other WVU administrative posts under three presidents, Stahr, Miller, and Harlow. A native of New Jersey, he enlisted in the Navy in 1939 and rose through the ranks to earn a commission by war's end. During the war he served with an officer from West Virginia, an alumnus of WVU, who urged him to attend the University. Shamberger entered WVU under the GI Bill, receiving a BA, MA, and PhD in political science. After six years working in the Political Science department's Bureau of Government Research, Shamberger accepted a position as lobbyist for the New Jersey Manufacturer's Association. He and his wife welcomed the opportunity to return to Morgantown in 1960 when Elvis Stahr became president and created the new position of assistant to the president. Shamberger accepted an appointment to this post and also became the University's chief lobbyist in Charleston for the next ten years.[33]

Shamberger continued to serve as assistant to the president, but without the lobbying duties, when Gene Budig assumed the presidency on July 1, 1977. At thirty-eight, he was the youngest president of WVU since Daniel Purinton in 1901. He was also a man on the move. After graduating from the University of Nebraska in 1962, he went on to earn a doctorate from the same institution. After serving as a member of the faculty at his alma mater, he successively served as an administrative assistant to the chancellor at Nebraska, was named assistant vice chancellor in 1970, and then assistant vice president and director of public affairs in 1972. The following year,

1973, Budig was appointed president of Illinois State University. Four years later, as president of WVU, he became the youngest executive officer in the nation to head a land-grant university.[34]

The new president informed reporters that he took a pay cut to accept the job because, as a land-grant institution with 182 program areas and an emphasis on graduate and professional education, WVU was a more complex university than Illinois State. He made it a priority to visit each school and college within the University. Budig also got right to work on his goal of building stronger ties of cooperation with the state by planning a visit to each of the counties, including a trip to Huntington to speak at a Marshall University luncheon. He also recreated the "Committee of 55," a group of loyal alumni representing each of the state's fifty-five counties. The committee had been initiated by Irvin Stewart thirty years earlier as a public relations vehicle to raise the WVU flag and to provide a direct line of communication with the president's office. It served Budig's vision of the land-grant university as a partnership between the University community and the people of the state.[35]

President Budig's constant theme, as every president's must be, was that "the future is with West Virginia and because of that, this will be the era in which West Virginia University comes into its own." WVU, he declared time and again, was the state's "principal asset," and the energy crisis of the mid-seventies, which refocused national attention on coal, would stimulate West Virginia's economy for the next quarter of a century. The robust economy he forecasted would be strong enough to turn WVU into a "first-class public university," a dream he shared with many WVU presidents before and since. In Illinois he had earned a reputation as an astute politician who could get support for his proposals, so it was a comforting sign when the Board of Regents agreed to start construction on a $4.5 million library on the Evansdale Campus and a $4.5 million shell building for recreation and athletics near the Coliseum. President Budig immediately attracted the attention of faculty and staff by his announcement, another message iterated by all presidents since World War II, that elevating their salaries above the bottom of WVU's thirteen Southern university counterparts was one of his top priorities.[36]

Budig preferred the more conventional hierarchical, chain-of-command administrative structure, perhaps because he was a colonel in the Air National Guard, to Harlow's central role in all decision making. Under Harlow, the provosts acted as advisors to the president and had no administrative authority of their own. Budig quickly replaced these multiple provosts with vice presidents, each with authority over their own divisions. With the exception of the health sciences, which had its own provost, college deans now reported to Provost for Instruction.[37]

Even before his arrival in Morgantown in the summer of 1977, Budig received a letter from the executive vice president of the Morgantown Area Chamber of Commerce, Joel M. Hannah, who expressed relief that a new president was assuming leadership of the University. The chamber's spokesman complained that under President Harlow the University had become a "ho-hum" institution, "because of the lack of foresight and courage by top administrators to make decisions affecting the future of the University, the future of the state, and the future of its people." He claimed that the chamber had attempted to work with WVU's administration in communicating the University's needs to the state legislature and alumni, but received little support for its efforts. "I personally feel that there are two medical colleges in the state of West Virginia because the University would not call upon us to help them fight the second in the Legislature. In fact, there are two Universities in the state because they did not call on us to help them fight the establishment of the second university in Huntington," Hannah declared. Consequently, the chamber had decided that it would not fight the University's political battles unless there was "concurrence, guidance, and direction of the administration at the University so that we are sure that we are going in the right direction and are united." On one occasion, the chamber had spoken in favor of a bill introduced in the legislature that would have established the West Virginia Research and Development Corporation, to be affiliated with WVU. Its members learned subsequently that President Harlow had spoken against the bill at a committee hearing.[38]

Hannah stressed that business and city leaders were vitally interested in the University because it employed more than 6,000 people, helping to maintain a vibrant and stable economy. However, large numbers of employees also required public services supplied by the city, services for which WVU did not pay taxes. Therefore, Hanna observed, "many City Council members have been prone to fight costly projects involving the University that will take city tax dollars to complete." He wanted Budig to understand the issue, but he also expressed "the sincere desire of the Chamber of Commerce to sit down with you and talk to you about your plans." A few months later, Budig and Hannah met in Morgantown to discuss Hannah's concerns.[39]

BUDIG RESIGNS, THE SEARCH FOR A SUCCESSOR BEGINS

A number of ominous external issues confronted the University during President Budig's administration. Budig placed great store in energy research to garner major research funding from the federal government. The energy crisis of the seventies stimulated the demand for coal, and that bode well for West Virginia's economy. He hoped that increased revenues from rising energy prices would enable the state to invest in developing WVU into a first-rate University. Congress passed the Strip Mine Reclamation Bill in the summer of 1977, and among its provisions was the establishment of ten national centers for coal and energy research. President Jimmy Carter created the Coal Industry Commission and appointed Governor Rockefeller as its chairman. Rockefeller then succeeded in designating WVU as a coal and energy research institute, making it eligible to apply for federal research funding. However, Ronald Reagan's defeat of Carter in the 1980 presidential election shifted the policy emphasis from coal to oil. Budig's dream of using coal money to finance the transformation of WVU into a major university seemed to disappear overnight as federal funding for coal research diminished and the proposed joint venture between the United States, Germany, and Japan to construct a synthetic fuel plant near Morgantown was abandoned. Budig correctly believed that federal support was not likely to return for some time to come.[40]

With the end of Budig's hopes for energy research funding, the Threshold to Greatness campaign to raise $20 million in private support, primarily for construction and renovation of University facilities, became all the more important. Launched in 1978, the campaign was the most ambitious fundraising effort undertaken by the WVU Foundation since its establishment in 1959. The drive ended in 1984 as the most successful ever, topping $21 million.[41]

Despite his successful fundraising efforts, President Budig confronted growing problems with the Board of Regents. One of Budig's closest assistants remembers that the president gradually became disenchanted with his prospects for success in dealing with the board. Like Harlow, Budig had very little contact with the board. He had forged a good working relationship with Chancellor Morton, but unfortunately Morton soon fell out of favor with the regents, who replaced him and left Budig without influence in Charleston. Moreover, as the Board of Regents expanded its control over the administrative functions of the University, Budig's frustrations mirrored those that confronted his predecessor. The president's growing marginalization magnified his frustration, prompting him to explore more promising opportunities elsewhere. His search ended in March 1980, when he was tapped by the University of Kansas to become its chancellor. At the end of June he bid West Virginia farewell.[42]

As he had on two previous occasions, Harry B. Heflin was called on to lead the University until a replacement could be found. This time around, Heflin assumed the title of president, rather than acting or interim president, on July 1, 1981. Heflin had already served two interim appointments in the presidency in 1966–1967 and again in 1973. A highly respected and trusted administrator, he was given full authority as the University's eighteenth president, and neither the University nor the Board of Regents regarded hiring a replacement for Gene Budig with much urgency. At sixty-seven, the oldest president replaced the youngest. Heflin was a unique individual in WVU's history. As detailed in an earlier chapter, he had served his entire career as an administrator in West Virginia higher education. On retirement he was given the honorary title of "President Emeritus," an official gesture of appreciation for his long and capable service.[43] The hiring of presidents at WVU and other universities generally takes place behind closed doors; therefore, it remains a mystery why Harry Heflin had never before been chosen to fill the office as a full-time president.

The Board of Regents established a special seventeen-member screening committee that included the seven members of the WVU Advisory Board, one student, one faculty member, and one staff representative. The president's position was advertised nationally, and an application deadline was set for June 15, 1981. Faculty, staff, and students expressed disappointment with their token representation on the screening committee. The National Association for the Advancement of Colored People President Herbert Henderson charged the Board of Regents with "total insensitivity" in selecting the membership of the screening committee. The NAACP was "shocked, dismayed and disappointed" with the board's selection of a "lily white" committee. The board should reconsider and place at least two African Americans on the committee, Henderson declared.[44]

During the search, WVU faculty were surveyed regarding the qualities they hoped for in an "ideal president." In addition to a president "less involved with PR and more involved with administration," a notion that was quickly becoming out of date for university presidents, faculty (predictably) expressed a preference for "someone with an extensive background as a teacher and scholar" who would leave "the fiscal problems to someone else." They preferred "someone who can bind the faculty, students and staff together into a community but who is aware that the university is not an oasis." Contradictorily, they cited the need for "a president who can relate with the legislators upon whom we depend for every penny."[45] The Morgantown paper editorialized about its own preferences in an open letter to the search and screening committee. Foremost among the many attributes to look for in a university president, the paper said, was attitude. Specifically, "how does a candidate really feel about West Virginia University and the Mountain State? Is there a deep sense of loyalty? A genuine affection for the University, the state, and its people?" Or, was this just a stepping stone to another job? "Is the candidate willing to pledge that he will stick with WVU, even with budget cuts and other problems?" In short, the *Dominion Post* expressed its belief that "the new president should be a native West Virginian."[46]

By July, the committee had received 115 applications and quickly cut the list to fourteen. Ninety percent of the applicants were eliminated in one fell swoop when the committee decided not to consider those candidates who had not been nominated by a third party. Only two self-nominated candidates advanced to the semifinal list. By mid-August, the list of candidates had been reduced to eight, all of whom had a strong academic background. Four candidates were either natives or current residents of West Virginia: WVU College of Law Dean E. Gordon Gee; Marshall University President Robert Hayes; WVU Vice President of Administration Ray Hass; and Richard R. Bond, the president of Northern Colorado University, a native of Lost Creek, and a graduate of Salem College with a master's degree from WVU. The four "in-staters" were regarded as the front-runners by the press, and the *Huntington Herald-Dispatch* called this "the year of 'let's choose one of our own.'"[47]

SEVEN

THE UNIVERSITY
AT ITS NADIR

E. GORDON GEE was not "one of our own," that is, a West Virginia native, but he was Dean of the WVU Law School. Therefore, it could be said the Board of Regents picked an "insider" when it was announced on November 16, 1981, that Gee would become WVU's nineteenth president. At thirty-seven, he was the youngest to hold that position since 1939 and one of the four youngest presidents in the institution's history. Gee received a BA in history from the University of Utah and went on to earn a law degree and a doctorate in education from Columbia University. After serving as a senior staff assistant to Chief Justice of the Supreme Court Warren Burger, he returned to his home state of Utah to become associate dean of the Brigham Young University School of Law, before coming to Morgantown in 1977 to take up the post of dean of the Law School at WVU. According to Harold Shamberger, who served as assistant to four University presidents, including Gene Budig, the hiring of Gee represented another example of the governor's interference in University business, albeit more subtly than on earlier occasions. "Gee was Governor Rockefeller's candidate for the presidency," Shamberger observed. "Normally the appointment of a president is announced by the chairman or a member of the governing board, but in this case, the Governor made the announcement." Shamberger surmised that the governor hoped to get better cooperation with his own president in office.[1]

One of President Gee's first major undertakings was to reorganize the University's administration. In the late fall of 1981, Gee appointed a Task Force on University Administrative Organization composed of ten members from a cross-section of the University to assess the "primary options available for the future structure of the Office of the President and central administration in the University." Under the structure proposed by the task force and submitted to the Board of Regents for approval in 1982, the President's Office would include a cabinet composed of the vice president for academic affairs and research, the vice president for institutional advancement, the vice president for health sciences, the vice president for student affairs, and the vice president for administration and finance. The cabinet would also include the executive officer and the associate vice president for administration and finance, who would also serve as the University's chief financial officer. The new structure would give the cabinet an advisory role in policy issues, give deans some flexibility within the budgets established for their units, and institute a new approach to University planning. Both President Gee and the Board of Regents approved the task force's report. Beyond achieving a more effective administrative structure, this reorganization was important for the goals it established for the University, many of which were intended to modernize university administration and bring WVU in line with an increasingly computer- and information-driven world.[2]

ENROLLMENT MANAGEMENT

Enrollment management became a serious issue during Gee's term as president. In West Virginia this was a multi-layered issue of historic proportions because it posed the question of how many institutions of higher education, and of what kind, the state could support financially. Earlier state historians have confirmed that a general consensus prevailed among West Virginians during the period before the mid twentieth century that the state could and should support only one self-governed university.[3] By the seventies, however, that consensus apparently was replaced by the idea that the state should support many institutions centrally-managed by the Board of Regents. Yet a decline in the college-age population during the eighties led educational planners to conclude that fewer students attending college in the future would mean not only smaller enrollments and, therefore, declining financial resources for higher education, but also that more institutions would have to recruit from a smaller pool of high school graduates.

The state's consistent underfunding of the University lay behind Gee's planning for a future with fewer students, although some higher education leaders apparently did not accept this vision of the future. In December 1983 the Board of Regents discussed the 1985–1990 Master Plan for Higher Education, which called for expanding access to academic programs, programs for adults, and continuing education. At the same time, one reporter observed, "I keep hearing about cutbacks at the university and other colleges. You can't have cutbacks and expand." President Gee agreed: "I would be happy to have 30,000 students in 1990 if the state is willing to pay for it. But we have too many students now compared with the number of faculty" to teach them. In the end, the Board of Regents approved a reduction in the student population at WVU, while expanding the University's off-campus graduate programs. "Selective reductions," such as teacher training and business, were proposed for undergraduate programs at WVU if those programs existed at other campuses. The idea of combining basic science programs at Marshall University and WVU failed to win approval, as did the idea of eliminating one of the three state medical schools.[4]

How to reduce enrollments when the institution depended on student revenue, and when state revenue was already inadequate to operate the University, presented a conundrum. Largely beyond the institution's control were a number of factors. The number of students on the Morgantown campus declined by 1,100 in the fall semester to a total of 17,400, a far cry from the record of 21,565 in 1977–1978. Demographic changes led to a 25 percent long-term decline in high school graduates from the region served by WVU. At the same time, an 84 percent increase in tuition and fees since 1981–1982 upset the tuition policy, which had previously made it less expensive for Pennsylvania students to attend WVU than to attend in-state institutions. Consequently, WVU became less attractive to Pennsylvania residents, who could now attend in-state institutions for 20 percent less than WVU. Freshman enrollment fell by another 400 students in the fall of 1984, three-quarters of them hailing from outside the state. Moreover, West Virginia's high unemployment rate forced students to attend lower-cost state colleges closer to home, especially in southern West Virginia. The decline in students was estimated to entail a loss of $500,000 in student fees, and the loss of another $600,000 in fees from student vacancies in WVU's residence halls. The only silver lining in this picture was an improved student-faculty ratio.[5]

Enrollment management was discussed in two of the president's cabinet meetings during the fall of 1984. Gee's special assistant, law professor John Fisher, argued that many political leaders attached great importance to the size of the University, and a decline in WVU's enrollment and a corresponding increase in Marshall's would likely result in Marshall being permitted to develop new programs, accompanied by a shift of appropriated resources. Family income levels in West Virginia played an important role in determining where a student attended college. In 1983–1984 tuition for an undergraduate resident at Marshall University was $423 per semester compared with $545 per semester at WVU. Room and board at Marshall was $552 per semester compared with $670 at WVU. If the student chose to attend a smaller state college, the difference was even greater. WVU was far more enrollment-driven than most people realized. A decline of 996 at the Morgantown campus would result in a loss of $519,708 per semester, or more than $1 million per year in direct loss of revenues. There would also be significant indirect losses because of overhead charges to units, such as housing, the Mountainlair, parking, and the book store. The notion that WVU could have fewer students with the same resources and consequently improve the quality of its programs simply was erroneous. Academic Affairs wrongly assumed that, if the existing WVU faculty taught fewer students, they would immediately become more productive researchers. The history of WVU suggested otherwise, for the faculty had not been research oriented to begin with so increased enrollments did not occur at the expense of research. "I challenge the basic premise that our current faculty would fill the void of fewer students by devoting their efforts to research, and thus generating external funds," Fisher reported to President Gee.[6]

Fisher argued for a strategy of "presenting our external constituencies with relevant demographic information and explaining that essentially all colleges and universities across the United States will be competing for students from a smaller applicant pool." For WVU to be competitive, the institution had to have resources comparable to those of its peer universities. This approach was more compatible with the "positive marketing of the University" and allowed the University "to speak in terms of the cost necessary for the science, engineering, and technology programs which represent the future, and are considerably more expensive to maintain than other 'traditional' academic areas."[7] This strategy was subsequently adopted by the University.

Unfortunately, the serious issue of enrollment losses and the consequent revenue losses that arose during the 1984–1985 academic year was set against the backdrop of major increases in the president's salary. In May 1984 the Board of Regents announced pay raises for the state's college and university presidents. Gee's increase was about 14 percent, from $60,108 to $68,808. At the same time, faculty received a 7.5 percent raise or $1,000, whichever was higher. State Senator Stephen Cook declared the presidential raises "incredibly insensitive" and said he had been contacted by faculty members who were "outraged." Two months later "outraged" faculty members learned with the rest of the public that the WVU Foundation would supplement President Gee's salary by another $21,000, bringing it to about $90,000 per year, a total increase of 49 percent. This action marked the first time in West Virginia that a college or university president's salary was supplemented by a private foundation. Although it created a stir, the arrangement was similar to that in which the WVU Foundation supplemented the salaries of the University football and basketball coaches.[8]

Faculty at WVU and other state colleges have historically been underpaid compared with their peers both regionally and nationwide. What was particularly irksome, however, was the fact that, while administrators and state officials often gave lip service to establishing competitive faculty salaries with their peers nationally (engineering faculty nationwide generally earned more money than English professors), over generations little effort, much less actual progress, was ever put forward in making salaries competitive within disciplinary peer groups. Faculty seemed perpetually to rank 20 percent or more behind their national peers, and they came to regard that situation as a result of the power brokers considering them as mere employees, no different than other public servants. Over the years the turnover of faculty at WVU had been comparatively high, as many sought better pay. Gee's large pay increase was a reminder of the inequalities in West Virginia and the fact that no one seemed to be protecting the interests of faculty. Gee, meanwhile, compared himself with other land-grant university presidents; even with his 49 percent pay raise, his $90,000 annual salary was still lower than the national median range among his peers of $95,000 to $125,000. In the end, WVU gave the new president on-the-job training at a bargain price and the opportunity to prepare for a better-paid position elsewhere.

Gee reportedly had "complained for months" that his salary was not equal to some of his peers, namely the presidents of the universities of Maryland and Kentucky. A random survey by the *Charleston Gazette* reportedly showed that Gee's salary was "now higher than many colleges with enrollments similar to WVU's, including the two mentioned above and North Carolina State, the University of Nebraska, and the University of Florida." The WVU Association of Concerned Employees, composed of both faculty and staff, accused Gee of using "administrative rhetoric" to quell the swell of dissatisfaction regarding employee salaries, claiming his lobbying efforts in the legislature on their behalf only gave the appearance of concern for low faculty salaries.[9]

The financial difficulties confronting the state during the late seventies and early eighties significantly impacted the University. For the first time in the past several budget years, there was no reversion of state funds for the 1984–1985 academic year. The legislature and the Board of Regents committed a little more than $82.5 million to WVU, of which personal services (primarily salary) represented 74 percent, leaving only about one-quarter of that amount to cover current expenses, repairs and alterations, and equipment. Although viewed by some as a "stand-still" budget, the numbers bore serious negative consequences for some essential programs. A decline in enrollment of one thousand students resulted in a loss of fees of about $1 million, and the lack of an offset for this loss meant that the University faced the necessity of either eliminating or reducing some important programs. During the ongoing recession, a kind of rolling recession from which the state never quite recovered, costs for utilities, fringe benefits, communications, and other vital services continued to rise, while the current expense budget did not. Once these necessities were covered, however, there was little left for providing up-to-date computers and maintenance agreements.[10]

The increase in external restrictions imposed on University operations by the Board of Regents magnified the problems. Even though the state did not require a reversion (give back) of state appropriated funds in 1984–1985, underfunding continued to have a negative impact on University financial planning. For example, the legislature mandated an across-the-board increase in personal services of 7.5 percent for faculty and professional salaries, but the raises caused a financial shortfall because the state funds for such mandated raises covered only those funded by state appropriations. The result was a decline of $2.6 million in operating revenues for the year; this was money that otherwise could have been devoted to enhancing instruction. The state intervened in other ways that were detrimental to the University. For example, a legislative resolution set the standard work week on all campuses at 37.5 hours. Implementation of this change resulted in a cost exceeding $2.3 million and represented a productivity loss equal to 164 employees. Also, the state impounded interest payments to University accounts in 1984–1985, causing a serious loss of income in 1985–1986. The money in these interest-bearing accounts generated by athletics, housing, the Mountainlair, and the University Book Store was primarily allocated to student support services. The Annual Report for 1984–1985 asserted that the University desperately needed "a strong advocate to guard against such impositions, particularly when the proponents are totally unaware of the costs or impacts of such programs."[11]

The reversion of funds was not the most serious fiscal constraint affecting the University; rather it was the persistently inadequate level of appropriations that the University received from the state, as well as the limitations imposed by that level of funding. The University had achieved remarkable success despite the historical underfunding which hindered its ability to carry out its mission as a land-grant institution. The list of other problems confronting the University was extensive: non-competitive faculty salaries and underpaid technical, clerical, and maintenance personnel; inadequate stipends for graduate students; high student/faculty ratios; lack of support for faculty development; inadequate library holdings; deteriorating facilities at the Medical Center; lack of computers for instruction; modern research equipment; underdeveloped University databases and information systems; inadequate current expense funding; inadequate and deteriorating physical facilities. The only explanation for the achievements of the University in the face of these financial constraints was the commitment of faculty and staff.[12]

UPGRADING LIBRARY AND COMPUTER SERVICES

These University services were increasingly being linked with each other and with the entire instructional process. The purpose of the library is to support teaching and research, and its ability to perform this function depends directly on acquisitions, staff, and space. For years the library had been inadequate on all three counts. Establishing the optimal size or expenditure levels for large academic libraries was more art than science, and there was no particular formula or model to guide University decisions regarding its library. The number of volumes the library should own, for example, was not easily determined. In the final analysis, the measure of a library's value was the degree to which its resources supported the University's instructional and research missions.[13]

In that regard, it is clear that by the mid-eighties the WVU libraries' ability to support the University's programs had improved significantly with the opening of the Colson and Evansdale Libraries in 1980. Previously, the lack of space in Wise and the Agriculture-Engineering Libraries had become critical. They had become "grossly over-crowded," seating was inadequate, and thousands of volumes had to be placed in dead storage. With the addition of Colson and Evansdale, these critical problems were resolved, and the University now had adequate library facilities "for the first time in several decades." The University library system contained more than one million volumes and additional pamphlets, maps, photographs, and microform materials housed in its nine libraries: Wise, Colson, Audio-

Visual, Evansdale, Medical, Physical Sciences, Law, Mathematics, and Music. They also housed special collections which were unique to the strengths of WVU. For example, the University had gathered one of the best collections in the country on the subject of coal, located in the Coal Room in Wise Library. Similarly, the West Virginia and Regional History Collection represented the largest accumulation of West Virginia materials in the nation. The installation of computer terminals in the Evansdale and Wise Libraries dramatically enhanced the ability to gain access to the library's resources.[14]

Even though there was no way to determine the optimal level of expenditure for library materials, it was clear for several decades that the University Library was not receiving adequate allocations to support its graduate and research programs. Every year brought small or no increases in revenues, on the one hand, and constant increases in the cost of library materials, on the other, placing the library in a double bind. Every administration since that of Irvin Stewart was painfully aware that the library continued to fall further behind, but there was never enough money available to arrest the slide. An attempt was made in 1980–1981 to arrest the decline by allocating $844,000 for the purchase of materials, and another infusion in 1983–1984 provided $1.6 million for materials. At this point it was believed that equilibrium had been achieved between collection development and academic and research needs, but without systematic investment the University libraries were always at risk from market forces beyond their control. By June 30, 1983, the library collection numbered 1,030,000 volumes, 62,000 reels of microfilm, and 775,000 other microforms.[15]

The strengths and weaknesses of the library staff mirrored the University at large. "A remarkable number" of staff members remained loyal to the University in spite of low salaries and "difficult working conditions." Nevertheless, younger professionals increasingly tended to identify with their discipline rather than with the University. Also, the impact of new library technologies would, it was accurately predicted, increasingly force greater changes on the libraries in the future. Centralized computer systems would make collections more accessible, and, while it was unknown at the time, the Internet would eventually link the University to resources around the world. At the time, however, the library catalog still needed to

e converted to a machine-readable form as soon as possible. The conver-
on of the library to the emerging measuring rod of "information technol-
;y" demonstrated that the transition would come with a high price tag.[16]

ENOVATING FACILITIES

en the University undertook its Self Study in 1984, the main campus
in Morgantown comprised 777 acres and 95 major structures with an estimated replacement value of $308.5 million. In the past ten years, significant
additions had come about as a result of renovations and new construction.
Outlined in its Self Study were "major concerns facing the University" regarding its facilities. The first was deferred major maintenance and code
compliance failure. Failure of the state government and the Board of Regents to provide funds for major maintenance and code compliance over the
years had resulted in "many of the structures" requiring structural repair
and replacement. "Most structures are both unsafe and inaccessible by any
standard, but are far below the minimum standards of today," said the study.
In fact, some of the building components, such as the chillers at the Medical
Center, were reported as "in imminent danger of complete collapse."[17]

The second major concern was capital equipment procurement and
replacement. Capital allocations over the past ten years for these purposes
had been limited. A modest estimate of $15 million for each of the next
three years was necessary to even begin such a program.[18]

Renovation and construction to meet program needs was a third major concern. Prior planning at the University resulted in upgraded and expansion of libraries, renovations on the downtown campus for the School
of Journalism and the College of Arts and Sciences, and major additions to
the athletic complex. Construction funds had been allocated and spent for
the renovation of Clark Hall, phase one of the Engineering Sciences Building, and phase one of the upgrading of the Medical Center.[19]

A number of capital improvements were completed between 1970
and 1984, dramatically modernizing the Morgantown campus. Among
them were renovations of Woodburn Circle, Clark Hall, and the Chemistry
Building; construction of the new Mountaineer Field, Natatorium, Shell

Building, Athletic Facilities Building, Law Center, Charleston Medical Education Building, Evansdale Library, the PRT, and the acquisition of Knapp Hall.[20]

OFF-CAMPUS AND COOPERATIVE PROGRAMS

Over the years the Center for Extension and Continuing Education has provided outreach to various public constituencies. From the 1890s into the 1960s the Extension Service was devoted to agriculture and farm families. In 1963 President Miller established the West Virginia Center for Appalachian Studies and Development to direct the University's many outreach programs and also broadened its mission to address problems such as poverty, unemployment, outmigration, and the state's economic and social development generally. The Appalachian Center's name was changed by President Harlow in 1974 to the Center for Extension and Continuing Education (CECE) to more accurately reflect its functions. Under Harlow's reorganization, its chief administrator became a dean rather than a vice president. The CECE was again reorganized under President Gee, and the dean's position was upgraded to associate vice president for university extension and public service. The center's primary mission was to reach out to the people and institutions of the state. It created a mechanism interaction which allowed the University to advance the state's social, economic, and human resource development by providing the knowledge to people, institutions, and policy-makers for solving practical problems.[21]

The CECE integrated the Cooperative Extension Service and Continuing Education, two of the University's primary outreach programs. On campus, the CECE was organized into three divisions with responsibility for cooperative extension: agriculture, forestry, and community development; 4-H youth development; and personal and family development. Two divisions had Continuing Education responsibility: off-campus credit and continuing education/non-credit. Off-campus included six area offices, fifty-five county extension offices, five graduate centers, and the Jackson's Mill State 4-H Camp.[22] The mission of the CECE was very broad, and so too were its programs.

Off-Campus Credit Programs. WVU was authorized to offer only graduate work off-campus, with most coursework available only at WVU graduate centers located in the northern part of the state; the southern part of the state was assigned to the College of Graduate Studies and to Marshall University. There were a few exceptions to this division: the Charleston Area Medical Center; the Charleston Center of the School of Social Work; and the joint doctorate in education offered by WVU, the College of Graduate Studies, and Marshall University. The largest off-campus program was in education, which accounted for more than one-half of off-campus registrations. In 1982–1983, approximately 180 graduate courses were offered each semester through WVU graduate centers located at Jackson's Mill, Parkersburg Community College, Potomac State College, Shepherd College, and West Liberty State College. The MEd was offered in a number of specialized areas, and a MBA was available at Parkersburg and West Liberty graduate centers. The doctorate in secondary and higher education was available in the southern part of the state in cooperation with the College of Graduate Studies and Marshall. A coordinator who served as local liaison staffed each of the four graduate centers (excluding Jackson's Mill). Department faculty from the main campus taught at the centers as part of their assignment, although the MBA courses were delivered almost entirely by television-lecture, electronic blackboard, and video tape delivered simultaneously to the off-campus locations.[23]

Continuing Education, Community Interest, and Service Activities Offered on a Non-Credit Basis. A total of 20,178 people enrolled in WVU non-credit courses, workshops, and conferences during 1983–1984. These activities covered the broad spectrum of the University, and the range suggests the University's involvement in outreach and service. WVU initiated an Elderhostel Program as part of an international network for lifelong learning for people sixty and above. A number of in-house training programs for individual firms were offered by Continuing Education, the College of Business and Economics, and the College of Human Resources and Education. All of the schools in the Health Sciences Center were also deeply involved in continuing professional education. Noteworthy was a unique program of continuing medical education that linked a professor with a local physician for one-on-one instruction. The Office of Institutional Advancement used the media in its service of outreach. EdTelCom produced television, featured its news service, and provided radio and television stations with various public service announcements, and its Office of Publications produced the WVU *Alumni Magazine.*[24]

Cooperative Doctoral Programs with Marshall. During the presidencies of Gene Budig and Gordon Gee, a genuine attempt to cooperate in promoting graduate education in West Virginia prompted WVU to join with Marshall University to offer doctoral programs. The state had been carved up by the Board of Regents (and southern West Virginia politicians), with Marshall assigned to serve the southern part of the state and WVU the northern. Since WVU was the only PhD-granting institution, there were political pressures to cooperate.

In 1976 preliminary discussions began between the two state universities to establish a cooperative doctoral program in educational administration. Informal discussions followed, and in November Marshall's dean of the Graduate School wrote to his counterpart at WVU asking whether his institution was interested in collaborating with Marshall University in developing formal programs for southern West Virginia that would lead to the EdD, "through courses and research supervision available at this institution under the auspices of West Virginia University."[25]

By the fall of 1979 both institutions had agreed upon the Cooperative Program in Educational Administration, but the academic mechanism had to be established. Participating Marshall professors needed to be approved for full graduate faculty status at WVU. Accordingly, faculty at Marshall submitted their credentials to WVU and had been granted full or associate graduate faculty status consistent with WVU guidelines. A list of names was submitted to the graduate faculty at WVU, and President Budig, who enthusiastically supported the program, wrote to Marshall President Robert B. Hayes to assure him that WVU was "very interested in making certain this program goes into operation at the earliest possible time, and that the collegial relationship thus far established continue and become stronger."[26]

Good intentions pushed the cooperative plan forward, but accumulated political hubris and the understandable reluctance of either administration to relinquish any authority inevitably undermined its success. In October 1981 agreements regarding the composition of doctoral committees were revised by the WVU Graduate School to require that three WVU members instead of two serve on the six-member doctoral candidate's committee. The requirement applied to all cooperative EdD committees, and previously approved committees would be amended accordingly.[27] Marshall President Hayes voiced his objection. He informed President Gee that, while he was pleased with the progress of the cooperative program, this new procedure required amendment if the collaboration were to continue. Considering the decision arbitrary because none of the Marshall faculty or administrators were involved, Hayes hoped the situation could be remedied immediately, and he sought a discussion with Gee to resolve the issue.[28]

Obviously WVU was reassessing the arrangement. Two months later Dean Stanley Wearden informed the coordinator of the off-campus EdD program that he was imposing a moratorium on admissions, explaining that the program's experimental status required a follow-up evaluation after several students had completed the program. Moreover, changes had occurred in the offices of president, vice president, and dean that might result in new priorities. Added to these changes was the fact that WVU would start the next fiscal year with a deficit; flexibility was therefore necessary. He emphasized that the moratorium was intended "to be a prudent rather than a punitive action."[29]

The decision to place a moratorium on admissions reflected ambivalence in the administration, but apparently not in the College of Human Resources and Education. Program Coordinator James A. Martin objected in writing for the record to Wearden's decision to honor the moratorium. As of May 1982, he wrote, eighty-six students had been admitted to the program, completion of which could take up to ten years. The Board of Regents, WVU, Marshall, and the College of Graduate Studies had already committed resources to the program through at least 1991, and Martin argued that WVU could not unilaterally terminate a program that had the blessing of the Board of Regents. All faculty involved had been fully vetted and approved, and they had taken on increased workloads at no extra pay. Marshall and the College of Graduate Studies had assumed increased expenses for facilities, teaching equipment, office space, maintenance, and others expenses; WVU had borne no more than several thousand dollars in costs, mostly in faculty travel expenses. Personnel come and go, Martin wrote, but the mission of the land-grant university remained. "Is the State our campus or isn't it?" Martin asked rhetorically. According to documents appended to Martin's memorandum to Dean Wearden, the Cooperative EdD in the Administrative Education Program had eighty-six students enrolled in various stages of progress. Marshall had obviously spent a lot of time and effort developing the guidelines for the cooperative doctoral program, with full support from the Board of Regents.[30]

President Hayes informed President Gee in the spring of 1982 that the first cooperative EdD students would complete the requirements and receive their degrees in May 1983, and he wanted to resolve the question of where the degrees would be granted. Since nearly all of the students had taken their entire course load on the Marshall campus, he deemed it appropriate to award the degrees at Marshall's commencement ceremonies. The diplomas should be worded along the line of "West Virginia University in cooperation with Marshall University." He added that he hoped Gee would join him in the ceremony.[31] Gee passed along the Hayes letter to Vice President for Academic Affairs William E. Collins for his comment. His blunt response to Gee concerning President Hayes's request to confer the EdD degrees at Marshall was to quote that famous commander of the 101st Airborne Division, General Anthony McAuliffe, who responded to a German demand for surrender during World War II: "Nuts!" In fact, Collins recommended that Gee "resist all efforts to award degrees jointly with Marshall and COGS, both EdD and the PhD in Medical Science." He probably voiced a common line of reasoning at WVU that "this is a degree given through the Graduate School of West Virginia University and therefore should be awarded, as all other degrees, at West Virginia University's Commencement exercise." In his letter Hayes also suggested that the registrar and other appropriate people confer about the appropriate procedures for issuing transcripts for those students, but Collins's response was again unequivocal: "A transcript is maintained by the institution responsible for the degree, WVU."[32] Collins also received a call from President Hayes inquiring whether Gee would attend the commencement ceremony when the joint-degree recipients received their doctorates. Collins observed: "It is obvious that he doesn't want us to be present, but it is equally obvious that perhaps one of the two of us should be present in order to assert our 'rights.'"[33]

Collins's attitude is reflected in the negative feelings of others about such cooperative doctoral programs with Marshall and the College of Graduate Studies. For example, when asked by Collins to review a Board of Regents draft of the Cooperative Doctoral Programs in Educational Administration, an engineering professor expressed his outrage to Collins and Gee. "If I were to make the comment in my mind right now, I would need to have it typed on asbestos paper. I feel that this memo is charting a path to disaster for the doctoral granting programs at WVU. . . . Let Marshall and COGS appeal to the BOR for authority to grant the doctorates." The professor apparently sat on the Graduate Faculty Executive Committee, for he was aware that many of the faculty from those institutions had submitted requests for appointment to WVU graduate faculty status. He noted that many of them "are people who have done little publishing in refereed journals and who show little evidence of previous experience in graduate research supervision." If the students who finished the cooperative doctoral programs under their guidance were poorly trained, then WVU would be blamed. "My feeling is that the decision to create cooperative doctoral programs was a political move to prevent Marshall and COGS from obtaining PhD and/or EdD authority. I say let them get the doctoral granting authority and then they will have to struggle to obtain accreditation. The way it is now, students at Marshall and COGS are being advised, supervised and effectively admitted to the Ed Ad program with WVU finding out about it after the fact." He was not unhappy that the program had been tried, but he believed the evidence was clear that the program existed because of "political pressure and not for valid educational reasons." To this letter he attached a note stating that, in the cooperative program in biomedical science, there was "a student ready to graduate with a WVU degree who has never taken a course at WVU. He doesn't even have a WVU transcript. . . . I can't see how we can allow such things to happen."[34] Gee confirmed that politics was indeed the explanation for how "such things"

Chapter Seven

happened: "There are many factors that come to bear on this particular problem, including the political issue that we want to preserve ourselves as the only doctoral-granting institution in the state. Unfortunately, when politics and quality clash the rightness or wrongness of an issue can sometimes become obscured." Nevertheless, these cooperative programs continued into the presidency of Neil Bucklew.[35]

PRESIDENT GEE RESIGNS

Gee's frustration with the legislature and the Board of Regents came to an end when he accepted a position as president of the University of Colorado. Among legislators, reactions were polarized. Senate President Dan Tonkovich and Senate Majority Leader Si Boettner both found good reason for Gee to leave. Boettner told reporters that some of Gee's complaints could be resolved in the upcoming review of the Board of Regents. "Frankly, I don't think the Legislature is that interested in higher education," so Gee's unhappiness was understandable, Boettner said. "I think he found the bureaucracy very frustrating." Senate Minority Leader Bud Harman, however, believed Gee created his own bureaucracy, which was the source of Gee's troubles. "Gee's leaving is the best thing that has happened to West Virginia in years," Harman said. "He overstaffed at a time when the student population was going down." Gee created a "top-heavy" administrative staff, Harman asserted, and when professors complained about their salaries "Gee kept blaming the Legislature." Senate Judiciary Chairman Truman Chafin observed that Gee assessed his own situation accurately in quoting former President Budig: "When your enemies begin to outnumber your friends, it's time to pack your bags."[36]

EIGHT

NEIL S. BUCKLEW
AND MODERNIZATION

DIANE L. REINHARD was the first and only woman to occupy the president's office at WVU. Appointed as interim president when E. Gordon Gee left for the University of Colorado, Dr. Reinhard assumed the post on July 1, 1985. At the time, she was serving as the dean of the College of Human Resources and Education, a position she had held since 1982. Prior to coming to WVU, she had served as assistant and then associate dean at the University of Oregon, and before that she taught at Ohio State and the University of Wisconsin at Milwaukee. Reinhard remembered that, as the first woman to hold the office at WVU, there was a sense that her appointment was a milestone event. "What happened is, the Board of Regents had a policy that if you wanted to be a candidate for the job, you couldn't serve as interim president. And all the vice presidents wanted to become candidates. The chancellor's office had to look for another person—one who wasn't interested in the position," Reinhard reflected to a reporter. The chancellor of the Board of Regents chaired the seventeen-member search committee for the next president (a majority of them being from WVU's Board of Advisors). When Neil Bucklew took over in April 1986, Reinhard returned to her position as dean of the College of Human Resources and Education until accepting the presidency of Clarion University in 1990. She retired temporarily in 2003 but six months later became president of Indiana University of Pennsylvania for a year while that institution searched for a president. Then she retired permanently to her home in Watertown, Wisconsin.[1]

A strong WVU connection characterized all three finalists for the position of president: Neil Bucklew, president of the University of Montana, was a native of Morgantown; Peter Kalis, a Pittsburgh attorney, was a WVU alumnus; and Herman Mertins Jr. was vice president for administration and finance at WVU. According to Board of Regents member and Morgantown attorney Clark Frame, "we need a little more continuity in our president and if at all possible this time we need to stay away from three-year presidents." Frame also claimed that a president with West Virginia connections would understand the political culture and the need for WVU to develop a research and service mission in harmony with the state's economic development goals. All three of the candidates met the criteria, and Frame considered not so much "a process of selecting the best man" as "selecting the right man for this particular time in our university's life."[2]

Neil Bucklew was revealed to the press as the search committee's candidate of choice in early January 1986, was appointed in February, and assumed the presidency in April. He grew up in the Jerome Park area of Morgantown, graduated from Morgantown High School, and attended WVU for two years before transferring to the University of Missouri. After graduating from Missouri, Bucklew received a MS degree in political science from the University of North Carolina while working in the personnel office at Duke's Medical Center. Finding personnel to his liking, he entered the doctoral program at the University of Wisconsin several years later. By the time he received his PhD in 1970, Bucklew was the director of employment relations for the University of Wisconsin system. He took over a similar position at Central Michigan, and, when he left six years later, he was also serving as acting provost. Bucklew held the position of provost at Ohio University before being named president of the University of Montana at the age of forty. The prospect of returning to Morgantown played a significant role in Bucklew's decision to accept the presidency of WVU. The University community welcomed Bucklew home, believing that he would bring some much needed stability to the presidency. He was formally installed as WVU's twentieth president on September 19, 1986, in a convocation ceremony on Woodburn Circle.[3]

Bucklew assumed the presidency in a period of serious difficulty for the West Virginia economy and, consequently, for the financial resources available to WVU. The Annual Report for 1988–1989 succinctly stated the University's plight: "Its financial resources continue to be insufficient to meet basic needs." In this year, as in preceding years during the eighties, a mid-year reversion of state appropriations resulted in the loss of nearly $3 million in operating funds. To make matters worse, the state transferred additional operating liabilities, such as the FICA costs and liability insurance premiums, to the University. Compounding the problem was the volatile nature of state funding, which forced the University to implement an internal deficit management program.[4]

Serious underfunding resulted. The Board of Regents' own Resource Allocation Model indicated that WVU needed an additional $61 million annually to effectively continue its operation. The model also revealed that it was one of the most seriously underfunded institutions in the state, in part because all budget increases over the past ten years had been used to support unfunded, but mandated, salary increases, leaving no money for non-personnel-related needs. Even so, WVU's most pressing problem continued to be an uncompetitive level of compensation for faculty and staff. The Board of Regents salary schedule for WVU was never funded at the established level, creating further stress because additional state funding was earmarked for those employees eligible for the salary schedule. This excluded most librarians and extension staff, while faculty continued to be paid much less than their peers at other major universities.[5]

WVU faculty salaries averaged 17.3 percent below those of faculty at peer institutions belonging to the Southern Regional Education Board. The direct result was the departure of more than 150 faculty members in 1988–1989, which also caused collateral damage to morale among those who remained. Most of these positions were lost, but a significant expense was incurred when a portion were refilled. The University tried to minimize the impact of inadequate funding on academic programs and services by increasingly relying on student fees, special revenue accounts, and interest earnings, all of which were non-state-appropriated resources. Unfortunately, these sources did not offset the lack of state funding, and inflationary pressures eroded the value of those dollars. Moreover, poor investment decisions in 1987–1988 by the state treasurer's office, which held such accounts for the University, resulted in a loss of $1.5 million in interest earnings that the University had relied on to augment operating revenues. Long-term chronic underfunding inflicted widespread damage on WVU, resulting in non-competitive salaries, outdated teaching and research equipment, inadequate library holdings, lack of faculty in high-demand disciplines, and deteriorating facilities.[6]

WVU's funding crisis was exacerbated by the University's expanding commitment to research and record increases in student enrollment. Research was, and still is, important not just for the educational value of training students but also for the direct economic benefits and improvements in the quality of life it generates. The emphasis on research presented WVU with a Catch-22. In order for the University to generate research dollars, it needed resources to invest in expanding capacity, but with inadequate funding those resources were not available. In addition to start-up funds for research projects, investments in proposal preparation and infrastructure such as laboratory equipment and computers were necessary to attract major external grant support from industry and the federal government. The only solution was to redeploy resources from other programs to invest in research, which meant sacrificing something of value to gain something deemed of greater value. The problem of determining what to sacrifice to enhance investment in research was rendered even more daunting by burgeoning student enrollments. A first-time freshman enrollment of 3,518 in the fall of 1988 represented a 17 percent increase in students from the previous fall. Enrollment totaled 18,746, an increase of 8.5 percent. This headcount increase was the largest for one year since the early seventies and reflected growth at all levels. The stress was felt most immediately in the Colleges of Engineering and Business and Economics, where it became nearly impossible to accommodate non-majors in basic courses.[7]

Excluding the University hospital, state appropriations represented about 45 percent of WVU's funding in 1988–1989, making the University responsible for generating a significant portion of its operating funds. State funds were the most critical component in the base budget, however, because most faculty-staff salaries and basic operating expenditures originated from that source. In 1988–1989, the University was forced to cover Social Security payments for employees, usually paid out of the state's general revenue fund, thus necessitating another increase in tuition. In addition, the higher education budget in West Virginia was reduced by more than $8.4 million during the year, and WVU's portion was about 45 percent of that figure. Tuition adjustments did not begin to offset budget reductions of this magnitude. Some West Virginians believed that instead of spending more money on education the University should cut back. This was shortsighted, Bucklew told a reporter, for the question was not "can we cut" but rather "will we invest." The consequences of not doing so would be disastrous even if measured only in economic terms. "When I first came to WVU, we faced a bad budget situation, and we eliminated more than ninety positions. Cuts can be made but what would be lost? The health of the University, and of the state's economic development, requires that we invest in WVU."[8]

Tradition militated against tuition increases being used to fund salary raises, but there was little choice. State funding for salaries was important because faculty research attracted major grants, which were economically beneficial, and also leveraged federal funds. A base research program funded by the state enabled the University to bring in an equal or greater amount of funding from competitive grants each year. In this way WVU landed federal projects such as the National Research Center for Coal and Energy and federal support for the Mary Babb Randolph Cancer Center. Major construction projects often perplexed West Virginia citizens. With all of those millions going into constructing buildings, why was WVU always deploring their low faculty and staff salaries? The University had entered one of those extraordinary periods of construction under Bucklew, with more than $200 million committed to physical plant, as embodied in such projects as the new hospitals, the cancer center, and the ambulatory care center. The Health Sciences Center campus alone was the site of some $150 million in new construction. "Out of that $200 million, however, less than $1 million came from state tax dollars. Every other penny came from student fees, client income, federal investment, the work of faculty physicians, and bonding that we took on at the hospital," President Bucklew informed a reporter. But these funding sources differed from those funds used to operate the institution. While only a small fraction came from state funds, the state benefited in "countless ways," not only in improved health care, and the education and training of health care professionals, but also in thousands of jobs and economic stimulus to other West Virginia businesses. This kind of construction came from one-time-only funds, which means "you get them, you build, you pay, and it's done." Salaries, on the other hand, are a continuous commitment, year in, year out, with no funding from the federal government. Certainly neither patients at the hospital nor benevolent donors wanted to fund salaries. First-rate research facilities were necessary to attract major external funding for research. That meant building new facilities, but also spending millions to refurbish older buildings after years of inadequate maintenance.[9]

President Bucklew's first item of business was changing the political equation in Charleston to address the chronic short-funding problem. To this end, he called to active duty all friends and supporters of the University. When the legislature met in the fall of 1987, he asked faculty and staff members to take it upon themselves to educate state lawmakers about the priorities of the University. At a joint meeting of the University Advising Board and the College Visiting Committee, he sought their help in presenting information to legislators and in providing them an "enhanced sense of the state of the University."[10] The following year, the student body president, vice president, and another twenty or so students joined the lobbying effort when they marched around the capitol entrance chanting "Save Higher Ed" and "Let's Vote Mountaineers." In case the lawmakers were unaware, the delegation reiterated the well-known if underappreciated facts that WVU ranked below all multi-campus universities bordering West Virginia in terms of increases in state appropriations over ten years, or less than one-half the national average. They also emphasized that WVU ranked near the bottom in every level of faculty salaries within this comparison group.[11]

In June 1988, when Governor Arch Moore proposed to double the taxes on beer, wine, soft drinks, and tobacco to raise nearly $18 million per year for higher education, the legislature voted to excerpt the proposal. Everybody involved in higher education agreed with a member of the Board of Regents, James McCartney, who called the act "disastrous" for higher education. President Bucklew repeated the sentiment at a press conference. "The consequences of inaction are serious and real," he declared and predicted major layoffs, increases in student fees, program reductions, and difficulties with reaccreditations for some programs if the legislature did not increase the University's appropriation. To help offset further losses, the Board of Regents decided to redistribute the Higher Education Resource Fee (HERF) to WVU. Typically, 80 percent of the HERF money was retained by the institution, and 20 percent was retained by the Board of Regents. The BOR decided to redistribute its 20 percent back to the institutions based on how much it collected from the individual schools. This amounted to slightly less than a $1 million, one-time increase in the regular distribution and did not even come close to addressing the financial difficulties at WVU.[12] In the evolving 1989–1990 budget, the legislature proposed to address faculty salary disparities by paying members based on the importance of their disciplines. Provost Frank Franz told reporters that this proposal was patently unfair: "I don't know of any university in the country that would operate or could operate under a scheme like that." Instead, he suggested, the legislature should bring the salaries of faculty members at the two universities up to the average of comparable disciplines at peer institutions in the Southern Regional Education Board. The legislature had established a minimum faculty salary schedule but did not fund it. Therefore, appropriations for salaries should first go to funding the schedule. Only then should merit, market, and equity adjustments be considered. The salaries of many faculty, almost 90 percent of those in the College of Human Resources and Education, for example, did not meet the minimum salary level on the schedule.[13]

During this intensive effort to halt the constant cuts in legislative appropriations, an issue arose over WVU personnel lobbying legislators. After its creation in 1969, the Board of Regents required state colleges and universities to refrain from lobbying legislators. The legislature's intent in creating the Board of Regents was to have a single body that spoke for higher education with a unified voice. Moreover, lobbying by University employees, whose salaries were paid by the state, created an ethical problem. Perhaps it is a gauge of the desperate times that President Bucklew and Marshall University President Dale Nitzschke worked closely together to represent the interests of the two universities. They even became friends. In March 1988 Nitzschke wrote to Bucklew to reaffirm what he had stated "over and over again," that he had "no problem whatsoever" with WVU lobbying the legislature. There were occasions when Marshall benefitted from the advice and counsel provided by WVU lobbyists, and Nitzschke assumed that they would not advance an agenda counter to the interests of Marshall. However, he informed Bucklew that among the Cabell legislative delegates "there is a lot of anxiousness, a lot of anxiety that prevails in the hearts and minds of some that as long as WVU and Marshall are working together, they stand to lose. On the other hand, you must protect your university and I must protect mine! I continue to believe that together we can accomplish an enormous amount for each of our institutions and for all of higher education. If our two institutions fall back into a pattern of confrontation rather than cooperation, the whole state will lose."[14]

With Bucklew in attendance, the Board of Regents called a closed-door meeting in early April to consider WVU's use of legislative lobbyists because some of the legislators objected to the practice. In the end, the board approved of WVU sending representatives to the legislature to represent interests vital to its development as an institution. Vice President for Institutional Advancement Ed Flowers, the University's chief lobbyist, spent only twenty-two days at the capitol that year, so the "impression that he is this high-paid lobbyist hanging around the Legislature" was simply not true, Bucklew told reporters.[15] President Nitzschke wrote to Bucklew again shortly thereafter to deny the insinuations of several reporters who had characterized the board meeting as the result of complaints from him. He said his position has consistently been that if the board instituted a policy permitting individual institutions to lobby the legislature, and if Marshall had the resources, he would see to it that Marshall would have such a person on staff. Nitzschke also observed that he had "numerous phone calls" from Marshall University supporters who volunteered to contribute a "substantial amount" for that purpose. They felt that "it was absolutely essential that Marshall University not be disadvantaged if other institutions were going to have lobbyists." Nitzschke reiterated still again that he did not want to compete with WVU except in athletics. "We each in our own way are very different institutions, institutions which ought to complement one another rather than compete with one another."[16] The presidents may have favored cooperation for mutual benefit, but Marshall supporters were suspicious of that strategy.

HIRING FREEZE OF 1990

Despite the years of cuts and reversions of state appropriated funds during the 1980s, the governor imposed a hiring freeze in 1990. President Bucklew attempted to forestall the freeze by demonstrating its harmfulness to WVU. In February 1990, he presented his case to Secretary of Education and the Arts Stephen Haid. WVU was enjoying rising popularity among prospective students. During the three years since he became president in 1986, he wrote, the student body had increased by 2,800 students, and applications for the freshman class doubled to nearly sixteen thousand for the class of 1990. Even with "our best efforts," however, the president still worried about the rising "close-outs" of students from classes, resulting in placement on a "wait list" for admission if spaces became available. The reason for this bottleneck was the growing number of students at the same time that the number of faculty to teach them had been declining because of lack of financial support. In the fall of 1989, there were 787 full-time non-health sciences faculty to teach an enrollment of 17,178 students. Southern Regional Education Board peer institution averages set the appropriate figure at 939, indicating that WVU was short 152 faculty members given the enrollment. If the the Board of Regents' own Resource Allocation Model was used, that shortage rose to 225 faculty.[17]

Research and development, on the other hand, presented an "exciting" picture. For the first time in the University's history, it was ranked in the top one hundred research universities in the nation, with funding reaching $50 million, double the figure of five years earlier. Most areas of strength were directly related to traditional areas of economic advancement for the state of West Virginia, such as energy and forestry. WVU was also becoming a major regional center for health care and medical research. A result of this "explosion" in enrollment and research was the "physical transformation" of the campus by means of construction of new buildings and refurbishment of older facilities. Approximately $240 million in new facilities were under construction, the president noted. "An amazing fact is that not one dollar of this has been from the state tax base," he said; it was funded by bonds, patient revenues, faculty grants, and other non-state sources. However, WVU would still require state help with maintenance and utilities. Finally, Bucklew observed, WVU was initiating a major capital campaign for private support. The key to its success was the "good news" about WVU and, because donors would not invest in a troubled enterprise, any disruption in state support might jeopardize the campaign's success. WVU needed to be seen as "a place of special value and priority." Even though times were tough, "our stable critical mass" of state funding must be protected.[18]

The hiring freeze, President Bucklew argued, did not create a positive image. The governor's proposed budget was to hold the higher education budget steady when other areas were recommended for a decrease. But why not fill positions when the budget is being held steady? Why penalize WVU when enrollments (and fee income), funded research, and income from auxiliary funds were all increasing, the president asked? The proper course, he reasoned, was to exempt WVU from the hiring freeze for the good of the University and the state of West Virginia.[19] The president advanced a compelling case, but the freeze remained in place for the time being.

Diminishing WVU's budget also posed a direct negative impact to the state's economy. This was verified in a 1990 report issued by the WVU Bureau of Business Research, which analyzed the direct economic impact of WVU and its affiliated off-campus organizations on the state's economy in 1988–1989. These points of contact included payroll, annual operating purchases, annualized capital expenditures, and purchases by University students and visitors. Along with the indirect effects of economic multipliers, the total dollar amount of the University's economic impact exceeded $1 billion dollars.[20] For the first time, hard quantitative measures were employed to persuade West Virginia politicians that cutting WVU's appropriations to save money would actually cost the state money.

The hiring freeze redoubled the importance of private giving to the University's success. The Campaign for West Virginia University, launched by President Bucklew and the WVU Foundation in 1988, set a goal of $102 million by 1993. Even in a depressed economy, however, the donations surpassed the goal by attracting $130 million dollars. Most of the funds raised during the campaign were dedicated to academic programs to insulate them from being adversely affected by the hiring freeze and to the creation of thirty-three endowed chairs, professorships, and lectureships, as well as 230 new scholarships. WVU libraries also were enhanced, and classrooms and laboratories modernized. About one-third of the donated money was given to the WVU Foundation's permanent endowment for investment, with the annual earnings devoted to the purpose designated by the donors. The Eberly Foundation contributed the largest single gift of $7.5 million for the College of Arts and Sciences, which was named in the family's honor. Carolyn Eberly Blaney, a 1946 WVU graduate and a director of the foundation, had contributed $1 million prior to the campaign, bringing the family's total contribution to $8.5 million.[21]

CONTRIBUTIONS OF OUT-OF-STATE STUDENTS

The Carnegie Report, issued in 1989, recommended that WVU initiate a more selective undergraduate program, since it could not garner the resources needed to support the size of the student body and programs offered. President Gee had adopted what administrators called the "Minnesota Plan," which was to get smaller and better. Gee had reduced enrollment by more than three thousand students, but the loss of fee revenues generated a financial shortfall for the University and created political problems for the University with legislators and the Board of Regents. President Bucklew reversed this course. He believed that if the University received the same revenues it might be possible to invest in Gee's plan, but almost no public university could succeed in such a plan. WVU, which was losing state support and becoming ever more dependent on student fees,

Left: President James Harlow and Governor Arch A. Moore Jr. at the presentation ceremony of the Mountaineer statue in 1971.

Below: Jack Hodge was the first African American to receive a bachelor's degree from WVU, in 1954 (Journalism).

Irvin Stewart, WVU president from 1946 to 1958, is regarded as one of the most successful WVU presidents. At a fundraiser for foreign students in 1954, President Stewart polishes student (and basketball star) Mark Workman's shoes.

Coach Fred Schaus diagrams a play while star player Jerry West looks on. Schaus led the WVU basketball team to five consecutive NCAA berths as head coach from 1954-1960. He returned to WVU in 1981 as athletic director.

The pylons located in front of the Health Sciences North building were designed in 1954 by the sculptor Milton Horn. On the sides of these pylons are 8 panels depicting important developments and individuals in the history of the healing arts.

A5

A6

Opposite: WVU's College of Engineering was housed in Mechanical Hall before it was destroyed by fire in 1956. After being homeless for a few years, the College was located on the new Evansdale Campus.

Left: Commencement, 1954.

Below: Faculty enter the old Field House for Commencement ceremony (1961).

A7

Top: The 1963 Southern Conference champion WVU baseball team with coach Steve Harrick. A 1924 graduate of WVU, Harrick was head coach of both baseball and wrestling at WVU. He was named to the Association of College Baseball Coaches Hall of Fame and the West Virginia Sports Hall of Fame; Bottom: WVU Basketball coach Bucky Waters instructs the team (1966).

Basketball great Ron Williams, one of WVU's first African American players, in a game against Richmond in 1966.

Mannon Gallegly, Professor of Plant Pathology, and his disease resistant "West Virginia '63 tomato."

Top: WVU President Elvis Stahr (1959-1962) cutting a cake model of the WVU Health Sciences Center (1959); Bottom: WVU President Paul Miller, who served from 1962-1966, with Board of Governors (ca. 1964).

Opposite: The lobby and access services desk in the Wise Library (1965).

Left: Victorine Louistall-Monroe, WVU's first African American professional librarian (ca. 1966).

Below: Acting WVU President Heflin with Senator Jennings Randolph, Vice President Hubert H. Humphrey, Congressman Harley Staggers, and student body President David Hardesty, among others (ca. 1966). Heflin served twice as interim president and retired with the honorary title of President Emeritus.

Opposite (top): Travel board in the Mountainlair (ca. 1967).

Right: *Daily Athenaeum* staff Dave Burke, Joanne Bachner, and Jim McCauley (1966). The popular student paper celebrated its 125th anniversary in 2012.

Below: Swahili language class (1965-1966). WVU was actively involved with five agricultural colleges in Tanganyika (now Tanzania), Uganda, and Kenya. Faculty and student exchanges between Morgantown and East Africa flourished during this period.

Architectural model for the Creative Arts Center. The first three phases of the Creative Arts Center, homes for the music, drama, and art programs, were completed in 1968.

A16

A24

Students Walking Across Grumbein Island, 1965

Samy Elias, professor of industrial engineering and father of the Personal Rapid Transit (PRT). Opposite: Early renderings of the Beechurst Avenue station (top), and the Engineering Sciences station (bottom), two of five total stations on the WVU campus.

Above: Clyde L. Colson served as dean and professor at the College of Law and twice served as acting president of the university during his 30 years at WVU. Colson Hall, which at one time housed the College of Law, was named in his honor in 1977.

Left: James Harlow, WVU's sixteenth president, served from 1967-1977.

Right: Judith Stitzel joined the English Department faculty in the 1960s. Stitzel and Sophia Blaydes were the first two women with PhDs in the field hired by the department. Stitzel was founding director of the WVU Center for Women's and Gender Studies.

Below: William H. Miernyk founded the WVU Regional Research Institute in 1965. His pioneering research brought WVU international prominence in regional economics and the new multidisciplinary field of regional science.

PRELIMINARY INTERINDUSTRY PROJ
WEST VIRGINIA, 1965-1975 (THOUSAN

	SECTOR TITLE	1965			1975		
		INTERMEDIATE DEMAND	FINAL DEMAND	TOTAL GROSS OUTPUT	INTERMEDIATE DEMAND	FINAL DEMAND	TOTAL GROSS OUTPUT
1	AGRICULTURE	43,256	84,198	127,454	61,032	80,809	141
2	COAL	102,492	656,808	759,300	158,531	991,094	1,149
3	PETRO, GAS, & OTHER MIN.	107,455	26,903	134,358	203,816	37,952	24
4	CONTRACTORS	134,835	355,112	489,947	231,217	510,685	74
5	FOOD & KINDRED PRODUCTS	27,633	180,408	208,041	61,234	242,454	3
6	MISC. NON-DURABLES	73,139	100,204	173,343	169,542	161,491	
7	CHEMICALS	213,661	1,083,430	1,297,091	232,322	1,995,876	2
8	STONE, CLAY, & GLASS	90,932	379,564	470,486	225,891	559,437	
9	STEEL	66,276	903,0	969,281	109,656	1,594,405	1
10	MISC. DURABLES	92,917	57,60	665,177	230,594	931,743	
11	TRADE	137,918	768	977,586	216,046	1,303,900	
12	FINANCE	159,26	081	539,343	245,838	634,101	
13	SERVICES	157,	20,307	877,756	263,399	1,177,35	
14	TRANSPORTATION	1	300,662	440,264	217,382	458,05	
15	UTILITIES	3	479,081	686,424	392,698	826,12	
	HOUSE HOLDS				3,317,310		
					76,194		
					166,455		
					349,690		
					714,370		

Joseph Gluck speaks at December 7, 1967 dedication ceremonies for the bell from the U.S.S. West Virginia. Gluck came to WVU in 1946 and served for over 35 years, working with five different presidents and forty-seven deans.

Visitors at the Mountainlair Information Desk (ca. 1967).

certainly could not succeed. Bucklew therefore did everything in his power to increase enrollment and terminated only a few programs.[22]

Strategies for growth were incorporated within the general goal of increasing student enrollments, and hence fee revenues. An example of what was to come involved the College of Engineering, one of the traditional areas of excellence in the University that had the potential to dramatically improve external funding for research. A critical mass of faculty was necessary to do that, and that called for a larger number of students. Bucklew proposed to the Board of Regents that computer science, engineering, and mining and engineering resources should lower the minimum ACT (or equivalent SAT) mathematics score from a very high 28 to 24 for admission of out-of-state students. The president said that 24 was a defensible standard. To support his case, he pointed to Ohio State, Ohio University, the University of Pittsburgh, and the University of Tennessee, all of which required a minimum of 25. Also, now that more space would be available with the construction of a new engineering research center, the previous out-of-state enrollment limit was no longer needed. Those standards were still very high, Bucklew observed. Nationally, fewer than 10 percent of students had ACT scores in mathematics of 28, and only 25 percent had scores of 24. At that time, out-of-state students accounted for 17 percent of the computer science program, 23 percent of the engineering program, and 31 percent of mining and engineering resources. Bucklew's arguments convinced the Board of Regents, and they approved his proposal.[23]

Increasing the number of out-of-state students generally appealed to a financially strapped WVU, and Bucklew adopted the strategy for several reasons. In 1985–1986, enrollment had declined from 21,600 early in Gee's administration to 17,200, and the school's image and morale were very low. As a result of Bucklew's decision to increase enrollments across the board, in 1989 enrollment jumped immediately to 19,997, the number of applications had more than doubled from five thousand to 10,600, and rejections mushroomed by tenfold to 2,600. The student body at the Morgantown campus totaled 19,680 (excluding medical students) in the fall of 1989, comprising 10,948 West Virginia residents and 8,732 non-residents

(44.4 percent). WVU continued to give highest priority to qualified West Virginia students, but a "critical minimum size" for the University enabled it to support faculty, staff, and programs. "Critical minimum size" represented a fixed set of costs which were independent of the actual number of students served. Non-resident students, therefore, helped provide the resources to support higher education on a scale necessary to maintain meaningful programs.[24]

The number of college-age students was declining in the state's primary and secondary schools, and the changing demographics predicted that the resident pool of college-bound students would decline significantly. Therefore, out-of-state students played a critical role in the continued vitality of higher education in West Virginia. Because higher education received no state subsidy for non-residents, they paid the full cost of their education. In fact, non-resident students were an asset for the state. Each paid an amount greater than resident tuition and fees plus the average state appropriation per student for instruction. In total, non-resident students contributed an estimated $29 million toward the operation of higher education in West Virginia in 1989, and a total economic benefit of more than $100 million to West Virginia. The academic tuition and fees paid by each resident per semester in 1989 was $1,692, to which was added the state appropriation per student for instruction of $2,333 ($4,024 total). However, the non-resident student, who received no subsidy, paid $4,222, an amount greater than that generated by the resident student.[25]

Out-of-state students also tended to elevate the academic level of the student body. In 1989, WVU accepted 88.6 percent of the 3,673 West Virginians who applied. Since the University received 10,600 applications and rejected a total of 2,600, the vast majority of rejections were non-residents. Out-of-state students enhanced the social and cultural diversity of the University, brought new ideas and experiences to West Virginia, and helped to foster national and international perspectives among resident students, who also benefited from the opportunities to interact, compete, and succeed in the world beyond their home state.[26]

Chapter Eight

INITIATING STRATEGIC PLANNING

One of the major changes brought to WVU by President Bucklew was in strategic planning. Even though someone on former President Budig's staff used the phrase "strategic planning," it was more of "a think tank at the central office" and did not attempt to incorporate campus-wide decision making, recalled Bucklew. He believed that universities in particular needed to think more strategically, paraphrasing noted higher education authority Clark Kerr's observation that universities were made up of a highly diverse collection of separate units tied together by a common parking problem. This certainly seemed applicable to WVU, especially since those units were also divided into separate campuses, and many streets resembled vertical parking lots. Bucklew was convinced by his own experience of the wisdom of strategic planning for university administrators. "If there was any major theme that was on my mind that involved change it was to start thinking in a systematic way, involving people, and actually making decisions" about the direction of the university, Bucklew told an interviewer.[27]

WVU inaugurated a planning process in 1986 "to guide the development of a strategic vision for the future." The process encouraged university-wide activities and initiatives that focused on themes selected as priorities for the institution. The University Planning Council was established that year and outlined the ways the relationship between planning activities and basic budget planning would be articulated at WVU. Formal strategic and budget planning processes were initiated in 1987 to guide University decision making and control the impact of a series of budget constraints. The budget-planning process provided the mechanism for measuring and evaluating the extent to which resources were being used efficiently toward achieving the priorities established for the University. Strategic priorities that required specific support focused the allocation of resources on the following priorities: economic development; student success; education reform and the public schools; international programs and activities; and faculty and staff development. Each unit developed its own strategic objectives within the planning categories. Each unit submitted its completed planning report to the University Planning Council, which then passed along its recommendations to the president for action.[28]

The comprehensive strategic and budget planning process inaugurated by President Bucklew was a major step in the modernization of the University, although it attracted little public attention. Nevertheless, WVU's fiscal problems placed a great constraint on what could be done to advance the University. The annual report for 1988–1989 stated the problem: "When the majority of our academic and administrative units have only basic operating funds for items such as telephones, utilities, fringe benefits, etc., it is extremely difficult to undertake planning activities. . . . The funding problems this institution faces continue to be astronomical, hindering the quality and growth of the University."[29]

According to the 1994 Self-Study Report, the fiscal problems facing the University at the time were "not simply that West Virginia is a poor state, but that there is disinterest in education as an agent of change." The report quoted the chancellor of the Board of Regents, who succinctly observed a few years earlier that "there are problems beyond money." Higher education was not perceived very favorably among West Virginians; therefore it was not given a priority in funding. Higher education made up only 18.4 percent of the state's overall budget in 1969–1970, fell to 12 percent in 1983–1984, and represented only 13.5 percent in the governor's 1991–1992 budget even though many costs had been shifted to the institutions during the 1980s.[30] The lack of financial resources was regarded far and away as the University's central problem during Bucklew's tenure as president, and the ramifications affected every segment of the institution. As one dean observed, "We're so busy bailing, we haven't the time to row."[31] Catch-22.

CAMPUS COMPUTING AND NETWORKING

Computing changed the operation of the University fundamentally. When Bucklew arrived on campus, the world was already rushing headlong toward the age of the personal computer, and WVU had to join other universities to get out in front of that wave, particularly since WVU's engineering and computer science departments were both strong units. The very essence of the university—teaching, research, and service—was rapidly becoming dependent on computing to remain competitive, not just in the technical fields but university-wide. For example, it was unacceptable to send new teachers out into the schools without the technological skills necessary to succeed, so their training had to incorporate those new skills. When the University assumed responsibility for its own computing, it put a lot of money into developing its own telecommunications and computing networks. The state's telecommunications center, WVNet, was developed under the Board of Regents to handle the computing responsibilities of all sixteen of the state's colleges and universities, but "they just couldn't move fast enough for us," Bucklew recalled.[32]

The consequences of developing the University's computer capacity were enormous. On January 21, 1987, Governor Arch Moore announced that the electronics giant Siemens had awarded a $2.1 million contract to WVU to develop a series of computer-based training courses in cooperation with the electrical engineering, computer science, and extension faculty. This contract was the largest ever signed by WVU with private industry up to that time. Three weeks later Bell Atlantic disclosed at a news conference in Morgantown that it had established a subsidiary, Bell Atlantic Technical Ventures Corporation, to pursue joint venture activities with WVU in the development of high-technology computer software systems. The arrangement came with support from the state Office of Community and Industrial Development, the Software Valley Corporation, which had been established at WVU with the backing of Senator Robert C. Byrd, and C&P Telephone Company. The potential was alluded to by President Bucklew, who noted that the Siemens contract was "an example of how the state's comprehensive research institution can apply its expertise in response to an economic development need."[33] It was also an example of how much WVU could fall behind if it did not get ahead of the computer technology curve.

Building-to-building connectivity did not exist in 1990, so the University's information and data services consisted of "multiple islands of information" that could not communicate. Even if connectivity did exist, interaction between existing local area networks (LANS) on campus would be difficult because there was "a crazy quilt of operating systems and hardware." Moreover, access to information outside WVU was strictly on a unit-by-unit basis, and the lack of a central policy and guidance over program standards meant that departments were "LAN-locked." The University was urged to adopt a central campus networking strategy, which would allow for connectivity both within the University and without. It concluded that "in the current high technology world, it is almost impossible to remain viable, much less competitive, as a major research university without the use of information technology, supported by highly sophisticated communications and a campus network."[34]

WVU administrators were indeed trying to stay abreast of the latest developments. They recognized that to facilitate WVU's mission to provide high quality programs of instruction at all levels and to foster basic and applied research and scholarship would require a "technologically rich campus environment." A "Blue Ribbon Team" formally launched a campus-wide study of computing needs on March 19, 1990. It developed an implementation plan, drafted a full report, and presented the final plan to President Bucklew on May 7, 1990. A number of LANS had been established on campus, but without a campus-wide network, including connectivity to that desktop, the classroom, and the laboratory, those capabilities could not be utilized by the faculty, staff, and students, the report concluded.[35]

According to the networking study, "there is no doubt that the computing environment of the future will consist of workstations on individual desks, linked to a campus network that provides resources to meet most of the computing and information needs of the scholar. The campus network will also be the gateway to more specialized resources around the country and even across the world."[36] Another expert proclaimed that "some experts envision a worldwide academic network offering every scholar fast and convenient access to colleagues, libraries, other information resources, experimental devices, and supercomputers. We can expect in the not-too-distant future, to access data from many resources."[37]

One of the most dramatic advances at WVU in the decade between 1984 and 1994 was in computer networking. In 1984, computing was in its infancy at WVU. By 1994 there were more than four thousand personal computers and thirty departmental mini-computers, most of them networked. In 1989 a new administrative position was created, assistant vice president for computing and information resources, to support WVU's expansion in computing and telecommunications. In 1991 the Office of Academic Computing was created within the Office of Computing and Information Resources to administer two campus public computing sites, one at Evansdale and another on the downtown campus in the Mountainlair. In 1992 users signed in to the Lair site 23,000 times during the sixteen-semester week.[38]

INTERNATIONALIZING THE CURRICULUM

Preparing students for a more complex, technologically integrated world was also placed on the front burner by President Bucklew. Although it did not directly affect economic development, upgrading education for this new world required not simply a mastery of a discipline, but also familiarity with new methods of delivery. Outreach became the means as well as the message, enabling reciprocal relationships far beyond the University walls. In the sixties and seventies WVU faculty helped the East African nations of Kenya, Uganda, and Tanzania to lay the foundations of a higher education system. When President Bucklew visited three of these nations in 1989, higher education had progressed considerably. Traveling with Dean of the College of Agriculture and Forestry Robert Maxwell, who had been involved in the African initiative in the early sixties, Bucklew's primary goal was "to rekindle that involvement, reintroduce WVU to these countries and identify joint programs that would enhance and develop our international activities" and to reestablish a "mutual sharing of expertise." In the early years, the East African higher education system had focused on subjects related to agriculture, but over time its universities had begun to incorporate other sciences, medicine, law, engineering, arts, and the social sciences. Areas identified during the visit as mutually beneficial to WVU and the East African universities included forestry and agriculture, medicine, computer utilization, environmental planning, and library development. Naturally, the implementation of these ventures hinged on major funding from foundations and governments.[39]

The internationalization of the curriculum followed many avenues. One of the most visible programs devoted to improving international education at WVU and in West Virginia was the West Virginia Consortium for Faculty and Course Development in International Studies, or FACDIS. Founded in 1981 as a way to further professional development among faculty involved in international studies and foreign languages in West Virginia, FACDIS offices were located at WVU, but twenty of the state's colleges and universities were members of the consortium. Limited funds among the schools prevented them from participating in professional exchange, so FACDIS served the professional development needs of some 250 faculty who taught courses in foreign languages and other international subjects to more than six thousand students each year. FACDIS sponsored annual workshops, summer institutes, a travel grant program, symposia, and supported the development and revision of international courses. The annual workshop in International Studies, the most important program offered by FACDIS, was funded by grants raised by the consortium, and participants attended at no cost to themselves. Internationally prominent experts were invited to make presentations and to interact with the participants.[40]

The internationalization of the curriculum also found its way into music and the arts. A unique example was the WVU World Music Center, founded in 1992 by Dean of the College of Creative Arts Phil Faini. "There's no better way to bring people together than the arts," according to Faini; "there are no divisions, no barriers and walls—it's all bridges." That characterization captures the essential ingredient of the postmodern world that was reshaping WVU. Bucklew understood and strategically focused the University's efforts at remaking itself for the new world. At the time, WVU was the only university in the nation that offered a PhD in music with a concentration in world percussion music, for which a large amount of credit belonged to Dean Faini. The Creative Arts Center was chock-full of gamelans from Indonesia and drums from Africa, China, and other nations. Perhaps the most distinctive feature of the program was its emphasis on the steel drum. The creator of the modern steel drum, Ellie Mannette of Trinidad joined the WVU faculty in 1992 to teach steel drum construction and tuning methods. The World Music Center premiered in the fall of

1992 with the annual WVU Percussion Ensemble Concert, which featured Djimo Kouyate of Senegal and the ensemble playing traditional African instruments. True to the spirit of "building bridges," Faini exposed University students to other cultures through music, but he also invited in musicians from other cultures to Morgantown.[41]

ADVICE TO THE NEW PRESIDENT

During his last weeks in office, President Bucklew prepared a Transition Report for incoming President David Hardesty, who assumed the post on July 1, 1995.

I. Major Pending Issues. Topping the list was state Senate Bill No. 547 (SB 547), which, in Bucklew's estimation, was "the most important public policy guidance that has been established in some time." Passed by the legislature during the spring session of 1995, SB 547 required substantial strategic planning from WVU by November 1. This plan was expected to provide a "road map" for actions that would be taken to create a more streamlined and consolidated university. It also was to include a financial plan showing how WVU would generate its portion of the funds required for the faculty and staff salary increases over the next five years—that is, funds originating internally.[42] The process would be difficult, Bucklew wrote, because "there is nothing in the bill that unravels the complicated policies and statutes currently in place regarding personnel changes. The layoff and bumping provisions required by statute make it difficult if not nearly impossible to accomplish rapid program change." Moreover, Bucklew expected that the federal government's effort to balance the budget would have a major negative impact on federally sponsored research and development. Several health care issues at the Health Sciences Center also would confront Hardesty because WVU Hospitals was "undergoing substantial changes" as a result of health care reform. A new state-wide HMO was being created, but new questions about the competitiveness of WVU Hospitals, and University Health Associates would arise as the new system was established. The Health Sciences Center was faced with "a difficult liability insurance expense in a longstanding and complicated disagreement with the State Board of Risk Management. This is adding a large and, we think, unfair expense on the shoulders of the University Health Sciences Center."[43]

II. Strategic Issues of Special Importance. Enrollments had stabilized at approximately 23,000 students and would require diligent management and attention to strategic marketing. Planning was the framework for developing the budget for the last decade, but it would be Hardesty's task to establish what form the planning and decision-making process would take. Bucklew noted, however, that it would be difficult to pursue a normal planning process in the face of the comprehensive "almost crisis planning" imposed by SB 547.[44] Also, he pointed out that one of the "areas of slow development" was the student information systems especially as it concerned computer-based registration. There had been progress, but the computer systems still did not perform as well as those used by WVU's peer institutions. Another issue that Hardesty would face immediately was the Grant Avenue Block Party. Even though it occurred on a city street, "it was viewed as a University problem." Construction of a new multi-purpose facility to be located on the Evansdale Campus had been under review by a special committee, and their report was expected soon. This would become the Recreation Center.

III. Chronic Issues Confronting the University. Tight budgets and frequent rescissions of funds back to the state were chronic problems. By any comparison WVU was "a tightly funded organization." When Bucklew came to WVU, he wrote that "we had drifted into a pattern of 'deficit budgeting.' Each year meant we began with more expenditures than income, and constantly pulled in dollars from vacancies and other sources to balance the budget." Bucklew insisted that the University begin the year with a balanced budget.[45] The tight budgets were further aggravated when the state government declared mid-year cuts, reversions, and freezes based on declining revenue predictions, all of which were "accompanied by explicit bureaucratic directions on how to handle the reduction." Bucklew's position was that "the state should tell us the figure that they have to cut and then give us maximum freedom in accomplishing that result." Moreover, the State of West Virginia was "very control oriented." Statutes and administrative requirements hamstrung the University, preventing it from operating efficiently. "I am still amazed that the state's largest employer and one of its largest enterprises is unable to write its own checks." Instead, the University had to "transmit extraordinary information to offices in Charleston where there are two or three 'pre approvals' before something as simple as a reimbursement check can be issued. . . . I believe we can stretch our tight dollars much further if we are not faced with so many bureaucratic controls."[46] Resources for the university library were also a chronic problem. The library, essentially a state-funded operation, had suffered erosion over the past decade from lack of resources. No new state dollars had been targeted toward the library for at least a decade other than incremental salary raises. "Thank goodness for our Athletic Department's success or we would not have been able to undertake the expensive yet overdue computerization project at the Library."[47]

IV. Other Priorities for Attention. Several items would require Hardesty's immediate attention. Implementing SB 547 was "undoubtedly the most important and demanding" issue the new president would confront. The WVU Hospitals and Medicaid payments, the block party, enrollment, and the University's method of using an airplane were other major issues that would demand immediate attention from incoming President Hardesty.[48]

NINE

FACULTY, RESEARCH, AND ECONOMIC DEVELOPMENT

TEACHING, RESEARCH, AND SERVICE represent the three legs to the academic stool. Of these three, research is by its nature the least understood and appreciated by the public. Most people, including some faculty, think of these three functions as separate and distinct activities when in fact they are inseparable. Discovering new knowledge and disseminating it through teaching, service, or publication is at the heart of the university enterprise. Faculty carry out research, but supporting them are graduate students, typically doctoral students who teach lower-level classes and serve as research assistants while learning the skills of the profession. Strong graduate programs, therefore, generally serve as a gauge to the status of an institution in the world of university research. Successful emerging research institutions identify what they can do best and then concentrate their resources in those areas. They are able to recruit and then retain research-oriented faculty who can initiate graduate programs that will attract advanced students to study with the researchers. Considering its historical lack of resources, WVU devoted considerable attention to the other intangibles involved in creating a culture of research in order to fulfill its aspirations of becoming a research university. During President Harlow's administration, University officials believed they had reached that elusive plateau.

IMPORTANCE OF GRADUATE EDUCATION

At his annual report to the Faculty Assembly in the fall of 1975, President Harlow reported with pride that the decennial accreditation review of the

North Central Association of Secondary Schools and Colleges (NCASSC) awarded the University full accreditation for the next ten years. The best news, however, was that for the first time the University's PhD programs had received unqualified accreditation until the next review ten years hence. "Our peers among the great state institutions of the 19-state North Central accreditation area finally have voted us into the club," signaling that WVU was "on the same level." Because WVU also belonged to more than fifty technical and professional accrediting associations as well, it was a matter of pride and a significant moment in the life of the institution that all the University's programs were fully accredited.[1]

Twenty-five to fifty years were required to build a competent graduate program at a four-year college, and the decision to establish a graduate school at WVU was made in 1930. In the late sixties, the legislature authorized the appointment of Centennial Professorships, supplemented by another endowed group of Claude Worthington Benedum Foundation Distinguished Professorships, to attract highly productive senior scholars to lead the thrust toward national recognition. In 1968–1969 the Board of Governors approved creation of a computer facility and staff. These and other strategic decisions required the unflagging support of nearly a dozen governors, hundreds of legislators, more than fifty board members, fifteen university presidents, and upward of two thousand faculty members. By the 1970 significant growth had occurred in graduate programs and enrollments. Seventy-four graduate programs conferred more than 1,300 master's degrees at the 1973 convocation, a significant increase over the 880 conferred in 1969. Professional doctoral programs were offered in law, dentistry, and medicine, and in 1973 a total of 221 first professional degrees were conferred, an increase over the 155 granted in 1969. Doctoral degrees in philosophy, education, and musical arts were also offered in 25 fields, and 131 doctorates were awarded in 1973, as compared with 76 in 1969.[2]

The rapid growth of graduate enrollment created unique problems, prompting concern among administrators by the mid-sixties. Robert F. Munn, who served as dean of libraries and in other central administrative posts including provost and dean of the Graduate School, filed reports with the graduate faculty in 1966 identifying some of the consequences of this growth. During the decade between 1955–1956 and 1965–1966 the number of graduate students ballooned from 550 to 1,900, and their percentage of the total student population swelled from 9 percent to 16.6 percent— and these figures did not include the growing numbers of law, medical, and dental students.[3]

While the growth represented success in moving the University toward its goal of national recognition as a research institution, Munn voiced concern about the wisdom of continuing this steep trajectory, considering that the costs of graduate education far exceeded those for undergraduates. Part of the load of this difference was born by departments and individual faculty, who offered graduate work and directed doctoral candidates without any reduction in teaching loads. This solution was undesirable and unfair to everybody involved; it was also impossible to maintain if the number of graduate students doubled again. Munn also believed that the rapid growth might diminish the quality of the program, and perhaps the integrity of the University itself. One of WVU's early presidents, William L. Wilson, observed that West Virginians had a strong tendency to call small things by great names, but usually were only successful in deceiving themselves. Paraphrasing Wilson, Munn cautioned that with the skyrocketing graduate enrollment administrators might be deluding themselves again. As evidence he cited the 1964 report from the American Council on Education, which evaluated the University's PhD programs as "marginal." They looked good enough in the catalog, but on closer examination they obviously had been developed "on the cheap." Smaller and higher quality PhD programs could be achieved by establishing higher admission standards for the Graduate School, Munn believed, while limiting the number of PhD programs and concentrating resources in the strongest.[4] "We simply do not have the faculty strength to offer an honest program" in some fields, such as classics. The vast majority of the eighty-two master's degree programs produced fewer than five graduates per year, and, Munn observed, there was pressure to build PhD programs onto them. "Certainly a few more thinly financed doctoral programs built on thinly financed and sparsely populated Masters programs would bring us nothing we care to have." Instead, he advised that WVU concentrate on quality undergraduate education and "a limited number of graduate programs which can achieve a national reputation."[5] The Graduate School embraced Munn's recommendations, and his emphases became University policy for years to come.

Until the 1970s, one of the great weaknesses of graduate studies at WVU was the lack of student financial support, which placed the University at a disadvantage in competing for the best graduate students. WVU made major strides toward addressing this problem during the Harlow years. An "outstanding milestone" in the maturation of the Graduate School was reached in 1969 when the WVU Foundation decided to provide graduate fellowships to outstanding students. Of the two thousand graduate students on the main campus, 1,448 (72 percent) received some form of support through WVU. Although WVU had taken a major step forward, "we still must be classed as an emerging Graduate School," the dean reminded faculty. By 1974, graduate students held fifty WVU Foundation fellowships and six National Science Foundation fellowships among some seventy other awards from various funding agencies, in addition to the institutional support provided.[6]

"For much of its history the University had no library worthy of the name," Dean Munn declared in his 1969 strategic plan for library development. If WVU hoped to realize its aspiration of becoming a major research university, an investment of resources would be required. During its first eighty years, the University library had collected only 200,000 volumes. It was only during the administration of President Irvin Stewart (1946–1958) that significant and sustained strides were taken to improve the library. A major addition to the main library, the hiring of a professional staff, and a steady increase in the book budget slowly lifted the library above the level of inadequacy. Nevertheless, the library's ability to support the University's teaching and growing research programs might have actually declined on a relative scale between 1950 and 1960 because of what Munn called the "undisciplined proliferation" of new graduate courses and programs. No review process existed for new offerings, and little thought was given to the library or other University-wide implications. Consequently, the gap increased between the University's objectives and the library's ability to support them.[7]

President Stahr took a significant step toward establishing University priorities when he initiated the University Planning Committee in 1962. The committee identified academic areas of particular relevance to the University and at the same time attempted to limit the development of weak doctoral programs. In addition to an increased book budget, these policies enabled the library to identify strategic areas of emphasis for developing strong research collections. With graduate enrollments expected to double and possibly triple by 1980, planning to expand the library to handle this growth was no small matter. The costs for developing research collections to support a doctoral degree program were the same whether there were four or forty students involved. With the new planning approach, resources would be limited to the strongest areas of concentration.[8]

As of May 1969, the University Libraries, which included the main, agriculture/engineering, law, mathematics, the medical center, music, and physical sciences, contained a total of 629,086 physical volumes, 29,200 total microfilm reels, and 286,565 total microforms, for a grand total of 944,851 items. The most serious problem facing the main library was space; there simply was no room to expand collections or to increase seating. The construction of the new Evansdale Library relieved the pressure, but all of the libraries were at or near capacity.[9]

In 1984 WVU offered seventy-four master's programs, thirty-one doctoral fields, and graduate professional degrees in law, medicine, and dentistry. With few exceptions all units offering a bachelor's degree also offered a master's degree, and by the same token all non-professional doctoral fields offered master's programs. About one-quarter of the total student body was enrolled in graduate programs.[10]

President Gee asked the Academic Planning Committee to establish priorities and develop plans to make the most effective and appropriate use of its resources. In its preliminary report released in November 1982 the committee offered several recommendations. First, doctoral programs should be authorized only when adequate faculty and support were available. Ordinarily no fewer than three faculty in the PhD-granting field should be offering the doctorate, and the number of doctoral students assigned to a single faculty member must be limited to the amount that could be guided effectively. Second, only faculty members with a strong record of research and publication during the previous five years should be authorized to direct doctoral dissertations. Third, examiners from outside the University should be involved in the dissertation defense to provide outside expert opinion and to monitor standards. Doctoral program units should average no fewer than three completed doctoral degrees per year.

Exceptions to that number were provided, however, in programs deemed central to the University's mission, for example. The Department of History doctoral program averaged 2.25 PhD degrees from 1978 through 1982 and had little national visibility, but it was recommended for retention. "The only compelling reason for retaining the doctorate [in History] lies in the fact that, as the state university, WVU had long been expected to have a strong program in state and regional history," the committee determined. Moreover, the resources were in place to support the doctoral program in the Library's West Virginia and Regional History Collection, which was by far the largest collection of such materials in existence. The Committee recommended, therefore, that the Department of History retain the PhD program but that it should focus on West Virginia and regional history.[11]

The University was "clearly over-extended." Maintaining a balance between resources and programs should be a priority in order to maintain the University's academic integrity, although the problem would be resolved best by increasing resources rather than cutting programs. Too many graduate programs had no chance to excel, and most of them had no "national visibility." Therefore, programs central to the University's mission should be strengthened; those that did not meet the criteria should be suspended and no new students admitted without the associate vice president's approval.[12]

FACULTY MORALE IN RECRUITMENT AND RETENTION

Significant faculty participation in university governance is one of the distinguishing features of research universities. It is viewed as essential to the academic culture that fosters research. Therefore, in the recruitment and retention of research faculty governance emerged as one of the important indicators of the University's commitment to developing a research university. Unlike a corporation or other large organizational structure, a university is an academic community with shared administrative and academic responsibilities. At WVU, all full-time members of the University faculty holding academic ranks, as well as the president, provost, and academic deans, are members of the University Faculty Assembly in accordance with the West Virginia University Faculty Constitution. Each faculty member is also a member of a college or school that elects senators, as determined by the size of the constituency. The elected senators plus the president, provost, academic deans, and five administrative officers appointed by the president constitute the University Faculty Senate. The Faculty Assembly constitutionally delegates its legislative power to the University Faculty Senate, which has the authority to recommend policies to the president within the academic concerns outlined in the faculty constitution. The senate normally meets once each month. Most of the business that comes before the senate originates from standing committees that report to the executive committee. Most academic departments within the schools and colleges also maintain committee structures like those of the college and the University senate.[13]

In 1973–1974, the University employed 1,351 full-time and 266 part-time faculty. They held degrees from more than four hundred American universities and 75 foreign institutions in 19 different countries. Two-thirds of them held a doctorate. The annual turnover rate was about 10 percent, most of which occurred at the lower ranks.[14]

Teaching was the primary function of faculty members. According to Faculty Activity Reports, about 22 percent of faculty effort was devoted to research, but there was great variation, from 50 percent to nil, in programs where the teaching loads or subject matter precluded research. The volume of faculty research between 1960 and 1969 was cataloged in a bibliography nearly 350 pages in length. The first research professorates were made with the appointment of four Centennial Professors (biology, chemistry, mathematics, and psychology) in 1967. In addition, a major grant from the Benedum Foundation provided funds for Benedum professorships in anatomy, economics, education, journalism, and public administration.

Most faculty service was performed through the Appalachian Center and varied greatly, with some faculty assigned to public service full time and others hardly at all.[15]

Academic practices varied by unit, but as a maturing university some recurring issues began to trouble WVU. For example, higher-ranked faculty commonly taught advanced students and the lower-division courses were taught by the junior faculty. The standard practice was to assign new faculty a heavier teaching load than senior faculty, with the latter given "release time" for research. The Harlow administration offered the novel notion that newer assistant professors might have more "research momentum" carried over from working on their recent dissertations. The question at issue was whether research activity became dormant as faculty aged in place; this would not be a good sign for an institution that aspired to become a research university. But if this assumption were correct, faculty would reach their peak upon receiving the PhD and over time fall behind the profession. In fact, close to the opposite was true: the leaders of the profession were active senior faculty. Faculty members have always been evaluated during their sixth year of employment, when the University decided whether they should be tenured, or when faculty were being considered for promotion to full professor. Otherwise, faculty assessment was casual at WVU, and President Harlow insisted that the University adapt a systematic annual assessment for faculty at all ranks. Mandatory student evaluations would not come for more than two decades into the future. Faculty generally questioned whether students were qualified to evaluate faculty performance. On the other hand, peer evaluation might be more reliable, but faculty members typically were reluctant to sit in judgment of their close associates.[16]

Research, or its equivalent scholarly activity, has ever been the easiest faculty effort to measure and evaluate. Typically, research culminates in a publication or some other scholarly or creative product that receives considerable evaluation by peers as well as national or even international experts in the field. On the other hand, faculty service, particularly off-campus, has always been the most difficult to assess because the unit's mission generally dictates the role of service, each having different priorities.[17]

Faculty morale is generally tied to the reward system, work assignments, respect as scholars and teachers, and perceptions of whether university governance is participatory or autocratic. Using these criteria, the Harlow administration regarded faculty morale at WVU to be good, although there were areas of discontent. Many were justified in thinking that their work space was inadequate, for example, but most of the blame was ascribed to the state or the Board of Regents, which controlled the University. Seemingly minor aggravations weighed heavily on faculty discontent. The requirement that faculty seek permission to spend travel funds was one of them, but the "most serious and most justified complaints relate to the purchase of necessary materials for the prosecution of research and scholarly activities," Harlow reported to the North Central Accreditation team in 1973. The problems were "traced to the rigidity and across-the-board enforcement of State purchasing requirements," which were designed for state agencies and were thus inappropriate for a state university. Unfortunately, President Harlow saw no likelihood that these constraints on the University would be alleviated in the immediate future.[18]

Harlow reported in 1973 that over the previous decade graduate enrollment increased at a higher rate than undergraduate enrollment. During the same period, non-instructional activities of the faculty, particularly research, had increased rapidly as well. In response, the University met the increased obligations by appointing graduate students as part-time instructors or teaching and research assistants. At that time, teaching assistants provided slightly more than 7 percent of the University's instructional effort. Even though this was a relatively modest proportion of the University's total instructional effort, it was "critically important" because of its concentration in the lower-division courses. Most were PhD students who were qualified to be teaching the introductory courses, a trend found at most public universities, where enrollments were burgeoning during the sixties and seventies. At WVU, where the supply of financial resources did not keep pace with demand, the use of graduate instructors allowed the senior faculty to shift more attention to research and upper-division and graduate courses that could only be taught by faculty. Looking back over the previous decade, the WVU Annual Report for 1983–1984 declared that, despite the obstacles it confronted, "it was during this time that the University came of age, achieving maturity as a comprehensive, land-grant, doctoral-degree granting research university."[19]

A faculty satisfaction survey was undertaken in 1982–1983 to gauge the level of job satisfaction among University faculty. Of the 516 faculty who responded, 25 percent declared that they were either displeased or very displeased in having accepted a position at WVU, but 41 percent were either pleased or very pleased with their decision. Also, 51 percent responded that they would encourage a friend to accept a position at WVU. The survey revealed that satisfied faculty outnumbered those dissatisfied without the encouragement of a pay raise in the previous two years.[20] It was certainly not a ringing endorsement, but neither was it a portrait of misery.

Faculty considered salary, security, and autonomy (faculty involvement in department and University governance, and control over their work assignments) as important in their assessment of their level of satisfaction. Asked to evaluate on a scale of one to five each of these rewards according to its importance and then its adequacy, between 70 and 80 percent of faculty respondents rated all three at the upper end of the scale, at either four or five. However, responses to the question of the adequacy of these three factors were not reassuring: 59 percent thought autonomy inadequate, 50 percent thought the same about security, and 72 percent regarded salaries as "totally inadequate." Almost three-quarters of all faculty gave salaries the lowest adequacy rating, and the vast majority of them were dissatisfied with the across-the-board approach to salary allocation; nearly 90 percent of them preferred merit pay over across-the-board raises. In assessing the relative emphasis their departments placed on teaching, research, and service, two-thirds indicated that research was given the highest priority, and 40 percent thought instruction was undervalued in their respective units.[21]

The survey invited faculty to write about their perceptions of WVU and their opinions on the future of the University. Written comments filled about seventy single-spaced pages, and the prevailing tone was characterized as "a melding of malaise and constructive criticism." A few recurrent themes were identified in the comments.[22] By a "wide margin" the most frequent issue mentioned was the inadequate financial support provided by the state to the University, its programs, and its faculty. For a third consecutive year, no salary increases were forthcoming, and the general salary level ranked at the bottom of the Southern Regional Education Board and other peer institutions. Some of these institutions paid professors 50 percent more, a condition one respondent aptly decried as "deplorable." A related issue was salary compression, which occurred when newly minted PhDs were brought in at a salary that reflected market increases while salaries of those already at WVU remained static. The difference was significant when inflation was high, as it was during the seventies and eighties, or when a hot new field, such as finance, found too few faculty to teach it. In fact, there were examples of long-serving senior faculty who were earning less than newly hired PhDs. There was also frequent mention of salary inequalities among the disciplines. For example, one person observed that failing to protect the liberal arts and privileging the technical and scientific fields would result in "well-paid engineers dependent upon core education supplied by underpaid, embittered historians and philosophers—an outcome which would disadvantage everyone, the students most of all." Some complained about the lack of adequate financial support for equipment and the poor maintenance of classroom and laboratory facilities. Generally, faculty blamed the state legislature for its failure to support higher education at a level that would keep WVU competitive with its peer flagship state universities.[23]

A second set of comments related to the internal reorganization undertaken by President Gee. The most persistent complaint referred to the growing number of administrators. One respondent's exaggeration captures the flavor of these comments in noting that the administration obviously is "top heavy" when six hundred administrators are required to oversee 1,200 faculty. Faculty were well aware of the Academic Planning Committee's role in Gee's plan to downsize the number of graduate degree-granting programs to only those that were nationally recognized or played a critical role in the University's mission. Science faculty often viewed the graduate programs in humanities and social science as unnecessary or misguided because the job prospects were so dismal after graduation. Faculty in the humanities had their own view voiced by one respondent, who asserted that "because of slavish adherence to mammon and the market place, feudal segmentation will be consolidated with schools such as Business, Engineering, Medicine, etc. receiving the lion's share of the budget. The center (humanities) will not hold, the periphery (vocationalism) will triumph." Nevertheless, the overall tenor of the comments on the theme of program consolidation and contraction was acceptance and the belief that ultimately the University would benefit from the restructuring.[24]

A third general theme in the survey responses related to the quality of the faculty and the student body. The perceived "exodus of faculty" and consequent "loss of faculty quality" was noted repeatedly and blamed on the financial shortfalls that plagued the University year after year. The implication that the "best" faculty left if they could was based on the notion that "self-respect" required one to at least make the attempt. These circumstances, and the "top down" approach that excluded faculty from the decision-making process, also bore direct responsibility for low faculty morale.[25]

A strong commitment to developing high-quality faculty and staff was imperative to meet the University's mission of providing high-quality instruction, research, and scholarship. In the fall of 1993, 82.9 percent of the 1,387 full-time instructional faculty held terminal degrees in their disciplines, which was by then a minimum requirement in recruiting faculty. The candidate's potential as a researcher increasingly became a key criterion in hiring decisions as well. One of the major difficulties in hiring quality faculty was the low level of salaries at WVU, which was consistently dead last among Southern Regional Education Board peer institutions.[26] In nearly all categories of comparison, in fact, WVU was not truly a peer of these institutions or of the flagship state schools in surrounding states with which it compared itself.

Despite the low salaries, which were set by state appropriations, faculty committees and administrators made earnest efforts to hire the most promising faculty by offering non-salary incentives, which, unlike state money, they could control. Start up funds for laboratory equipment, computers, and the opportunity for summer teaching as a salary supplement were added enticements for new faculty. WVU also accepted the Carnegie

Foundation's recommendation that the University "demonstrate its capacity to compete for scholars, both nationally and internationally," by creating five endowed chairs by the year 2000. By 1993, the College of Arts and Sciences alone had established ten endowed chairs, and there would be eight more by 1997 thanks to a major donation from the Eberly Family Foundation. Sabbatical leave was available to productive faculty after completing six years of employment at the University, and in 1992 the Professional Development Program provided faculty leave for professional development in teaching, research, and service. Additional financial support for faculty development was available through various University programs for travel, professional development, research, and public service projects. Seminars and workshops also were conducted each year. The Office of Sponsored Programs provided assistance with obtaining and managing external funding, and there were specialized projects, such as those at the National Research Center for Coal and Energy, Regional Research Institute, Office of International Programs, and the Office of Computing and Information Resources.[27]

In addition to the standard professional rewards of tenure and promotion, the University was increasingly active in recognizing outstanding achievements by faculty. Each year the Foundation Awards for Outstanding Teaching, the Benedum Distinguished Scholar Awards, and the Ethel and Gerry Heebink Award for Distinguished State Service recognized outstanding faculty performance with cash awards. Individual colleges also presented faculty awards for teaching, research, and service. In their survey comments, faculty recognized and appreciated the support for research, valued the high level of academic freedom, and perceived the University as a "collegial" place to work.[28]

The College of Arts and Sciences hired fifty-six tenure-track faculty during the two-year period between 1989 and 1990, and a short survey requested that they share their impressions and concerns at the time they accepted their positions at WVU. The survey also revealed the concern involved in attracting quality faculty to an institution with chronically low salaries.

Judging from the survey responses, the non-salary attractions of WVU were all qualitative. Among them were WVU's location in a small city surrounded by beautiful scenery and its proximity to Pittsburgh and Washington, DC. Recent hires frequently used adjectives such as "friendly," "collegial," and "enthusiastic" to describe their new colleagues. Others noted a good balance between teaching and research, and some noted the central administration's commitment to "building a first rate institution." Most found Morgantown attractive and affordable, while offering a high quality of life and a good place to raise children.[29]

The newly hired faculty did harbor concerns, however. One of the most commonly cited was the outdated library, which was not computerized and had major gaps in its collections. Also, singled out were the high teaching loads relative to the research expectations, the large class sizes, and low faculty morale. By and large, newly hired faculty recognized that lack of funding was WVU's fundamental problem, accounting for most of the other problems, particularly the low salaries. One person observed that "the low salary was pretty sobering." Others wondered how long the University would be committed to research when resources were so tight. They seemed to recognize that the University was trying to lift itself up by its own bootstraps and, even this early in their tenure at WVU, seemed to blame the state for the University's financial difficulties. Still others referenced the "dependence of the university on a legislature that isn't known for statesmanship," a "behind the times bureaucracy," and the "budget shocks from poor state planning and support." Some found the area around the downtown campus to be "quite run down" and the classroom buildings "shabby." Almost every respondent expressed concern about the lack of career opportunities for their spouses in Morgantown.[30] And these were the views of successful candidates.

RESEARCH AND ECONOMIC DEVELOPMENT

Progress toward becoming a research university is most easily measured by faculty productivity, and the evidence is quantifiable by the number and quality of faculty publications and grants. According to the Self-Study Report, 1984, research was "central to the intellectual life of any university. Not only is new knowledge itself enriching, the process of creating it helps to keep the researcher at the forefront of his or her discipline. Research is both a free-standing mission of the University and integrated with the two other broad missions of instruction and public service." About three-quarters of the faculty devoted 10 percent or more of their effort to research.[31]

While scientists generally publish their research results in journal articles and reports, the humanities fields are likely to publish lengthy studies best presented in the form of books. During the academic year 1982–1983, WVU faculty published a total of 54 authored books, 31 edited books, and 116 chapters published in volumes of scholarly essays. The faculty also published a total of 622 journal articles during the 1982–1983 academic year and presented 964 papers at conferences.[32]

The University had not established objective publication norms for research and publication, but it reported two steps to improve its research record. First, it now gave special weight to research in faculty evaluations, especially when considering faculty members for promotion and tenure. Second, in 1982–1983 graduate education was reorganized. The University strengthened the administrative leadership by creating the new position of associate vice president for research to replace the dean of the Graduate School. In order to give greater emphasis to graduate education and research, the new associate vice president reported to the vice president of academic affairs and research. The colleges and schools assumed a more active role in graduate education as well, and students were classified as majors in their respective colleges and schools rather than being enrolled in the Graduate School. The associate vice president also chaired the Graduate Council, which formulated and recommended policy for graduate education.[33]

The Gee administration reported some specific initiatives in the area of research during 1983–1984, including returning a larger percentage of indirect costs to the college deans, a portion of which was then returned to chairs and the principal investigators. Also, University-wide competition for equipment funds was initiated with money made available on a matching basis, and faculty travel was added to Faculty Senate grants for research. The Office of Sponsored Programs was organized to provide more effective assistance to those seeking research support. Success can be measured by the outcome. Support for research projects increased from $7.2 million in 1982–1983 to $9.7 million in 1983–1984. The total number of new research projects funded increased from 208 to 244 during that same period. Research funding from external sources rose 34 percent, during 1982–1983. The number of research proposals submitted in 1983–1984 was up 30 percent from the previous year, and the return on a National Science Foundation program to stimulate competitive research surpassed the $1 million mark.[34]

WVU's commitment to research grew by leaps and bounds beginning in the 1970s and vaulted to previously unknown levels by the mid-1990s. This feat was accomplished in the face of severe financial constraints and was, therefore, all the more remarkable. A 1992 report to the Board of Trustees summarizing the sponsored research activity at WVU highlighted the breadth of externally funded research activity undertaken at WVU. These areas were as diverse as clean fuels, mine reclamation, cancer research, smoking cessation, development of computer-based technologies, wooden and composite materials for bridges, poultry, economic and population growth patterns in West Virginia, low cost sheet metal coating, and improvement of social services in the state's southern counties. Sponsored research increased significantly after 1986, but so had the commitment of faculty to unsponsored (that is unfunded) research. The Eberly College of Arts and Sciences, for example, where unsponsored research in the humanities is the norm, reported an annual productivity for its 308 faculty of more than three hundred journal publications, twenty books, and more than four hundred professional presentations. Previously, the college's English and mathematics departments were both cited by the 1984 North Central reaccreditation team as producing "little or no faculty research." Between 1974 and 1983, Department of English faculty had published only seven scholarly books; between 1984 and 1993 that number jumped to twenty-four. The Department of Mathematics also improved its research productivity. Between 1988 and 1993, its faculty published more than 150 papers in refereed journals. This very substantial elevation in unsponsored faculty research occurred at a time when student enrollment was particularly high in both departments. Faculty commitment to service and outreach was equally impressive. In 1993, the WVU Office of Institutional Advancement published *WVU Services to West Virginia*, an exhaustive inventory of current university faculty service projects that filled 345 pages.[35]

With the dramatic expansion of the University, absent a corresponding increase in state funding, concerns abounded that the University was substituting temporary faculty to fill the faculty lines. The Advisory Council of Faculty was prompted to review the use of temporary faculty system-wide. Its analysis of faculty at WVU between 1985 and 1987 showed a significant increase in research faculty from twenty to thirty-four, reflecting the growth in sponsored research, but the number of non-tenure-track instructional faculty (which included part-timers) actually declined slightly from sixty-three to sixty-one.[36]

WVU celebrated its one hundred and twenty-fifth birthday in 1993. On West Virginia Day, June 20, 1993, four former WVU presidents joined Neil Bucklew to offer their perspectives on the University's history. Paul A. Miller, Elvis Stahr, Harry Heflin, and Diane Reinhard helped President Bucklew cut the birthday cake and praised the University's commitment to serving the state. "When historians 125 years from now look back on this period in the life of WVU," Bucklew declared, "I hope they will be able to say that this University was bringing a new era of prosperity to the state of West Virginia and that our faculty and staff created a catalyst and magnet for economic development that led the state into the twenty-first century."[37]

Early in his tenure, President Bucklew made a commitment to positioning the University as a leader in West Virginia's economic development. It was a commitment welcomed by a state suffering from a serious recession and high unemployment resulting from technological and structural changes in the coal and manufacturing economy. West Virginia needed to restructure its economy, and the University should play a key role in that process. Bucklew frequently spoke to community groups about how the University could accomplish that task. In June 1988, a Wheeling correspondent wrote to Bucklew to say he was "elated" to read an article from the local newspaper quoting the president's speech to the West Virginia Bar Association at Olgebay Park highlighting WVU's goals:

Chapter Nine

"I have long believed that the state university has a responsibility to tax-payers to do research concerning the economic development of the state. . . . But you must hurry. Our young people are leaving. Soon there will be nothing left but senior citizens and welfare recipients."[38] In that presentation, Bucklew emphasized that the University had a responsibility to be a leader in the effort to stimulate the state's economic resuscitation. The University's mission as a land-grant institution was to provide expert service and applied research, and to remain at the "cutting edge of research that can positively impact the state's businesses and industries." It would take a partnership of state and local government, of private business and labor, and of WVU to succeed in the task of revitalizing the state's economy, Bucklew asserted. And because of the ever more global economy, it was vital that the University strive for "a curriculum touched deeply by international understanding" and a much more diversified student body on campus.[39]

Far more than any previous president, Bucklew focused on educating the public about the University's role as an engine for economic development. A key component in this aspect of WVU's land-grant mission was research. By 1990, the growth of externally funded research at WVU had propelled the University into the ranks of the top one hundred research institutions in the United States. An Economic Development Council (composed of eleven deans and directors of key programs and chaired by an associate provost) was established during Bucklew's administration and given responsibility for developing the University's strategic plan for economic development. Its report in 1990 outlined some of the University's engagement, both directly and indirectly, in this kind of activity. Research performed by University faculty that directly affected the state's economy included energy, health sciences, software and artificial intelligence, and materials. These were the strategic areas selected for increased investment. A major emphasis for all such research was to build strong collaborative relationships with the state's industrial leaders. WVU also provided economic and policy analyses to assist in developing solutions to economic problems. For example, the West Virginia Input-Output Model, invented by Benedum Professor of Economics William Miernyk, enabled faculty to produce sophisticated projections and analyses of problems critical to health care policy, such as medical malpractice and health care costs.[40]

WVU also provided analytical tools, relevant research data, and training to West Virginia businesses and government agencies. The mechanisms existed already through the University's Center for Economic Research, the Office of Health Systems Research, the Extension Service, the Small Business Development Center, the Center for Entrepreneurial Studies and Development, and the Survey Research Center. A number of units provided hands-on assistance to start-ups and businesses in identifying and solving problems, applying technology, and improving labor/management relations. Bucklew also created a research corporation, which allowed for more financial and personnel flexibility in handling grants and contracts. A new position, the associate provost for research and director of the WVU Research Corporation, provided leadership for "the continued evolution of the infrastructure necessary to support a modern research enterprise." Soon added to the Research Corporation's portfolio was providing assistance to faculty in registering patents and licensing products.[41]

The mechanism and the expertise were already in place at WVU; the problem was making it accessible to practitioners. Reaching out was of vital importance for the success of any strategic economic development plan, and WVU's plan formalized that goal by calling for improved collaboration with local, state, and regional development agencies such as the Business Roundtable, the state Chamber of Commerce, the state Labor Federation, and a myriad of similar organizations. Of course, WVU's Division of Continuing Education still delivered credit and noncredit courses throughout the state by methods old and new. More emphasis was placed on opportunities for community service, and WVU concentrated more on improving the health status of all West Virginians. Finally, the University's plan for economic development declared that WVU should be a catalyst and leader in improving educational policy and the quality of public education from primary school through professional development. Since "a major stumbling block to further economic growth in the state" was the relatively low level of education and workforce skills, elevating the workforce was regarded as critical to success. In 1991 the WVU Economic Development Council created a Clearinghouse for Economic Development, a "user-friendly resource guide to university expertise, research projects and data bases" available both in print and electronic formats.[42]

WVU's research capacity increasingly attracted private and government research dollars, which generated an infrastructure for the new economy. Two new centers for energy research placed the University in the forefront of the development of alternative transportation fuels. The National Research Center for Coal and Energy (NRCCE) and the National Center for Alternative Transportation Fuels represented the University's newfound niche among the nation's research universities. The mission was to develop alternative fuels that were economically and environmentally acceptable, such as compressed and liquefied natural gas, and methanol. The centers administered research, but the testing and development was conducted in the College of Engineering and other WVU units. There were many such centers at WVU by the nineties, and they had a direct economic impact on the community and state, in addition to cutting-edge research that carried the potential for major scientific and technological advances. In 1988, $15 million was allocated for the construction of a new facility for the NRCCE, and it was expected that $3.5 million would be needed annually to pay for NRCCE research programs. New fuels seemed all the rage in 1990. That year the University converted fifteen of its gasoline-engine vehicles to operate on compressed natural gas. If Physical Plant's fleet was converted, the estimated fuel savings would be 60 percent, pollution would be reduced, and engines would last much longer. The alternative fuels research, therefore, held the potential for massive reductions in transportation cost and pollution on a national scale.[43]

The impact of WVU's research reaches deep into the state's economy and far into the future. The variety of benefits is bewildering. For example, orchard agriculture is of major significance in the eastern panhandle. In Kearneysville, at the University's Agricultural and Forestry Experiment Station, fruit growers from all over the nation gathered in the summer of 1989 to learn about the most extensive collection of apple and peach trellis systems in the world. Anticipating a future when the large parcels of land required for growing traditional peach trees or the tall, expansive apple trees became scarce, the experimental farm had developed dwarf trees. These smaller, more compact trees were trained on a wire trellis and assumed odd shapes with all the fruit-bearing branches on the same level. These trees could be planted densely, making it possible to mechanize many of the tasks involved in growing fruit.[44]

In a totally different arena, in 1988 the W. K. Kellogg Foundation awarded a $1.5 million grant to fund a four-year demonstration project that would link the resources of rural communities, the WVU Health Sciences Center, the University Extension Service, and the state government in an innovative project to improve the health of low-income children in fifteen West Virginia counties. They would work together in addressing problems such as inadequate prenatal care and nutrition, infant mortality rate, and teen pregnancy. West Virginia's economic woes exacerbated these health issues, accelerating a downward spiral in family health, financial condition, and general quality of the workforce.[45]

TEN

IN PURSUIT OF
FAIRNESS
AND DIVERSITY

WEST VIRGINIA UNIVERSITY'S social justice policy evolved out of the Civil Rights Act of 1964, particularly Title VI, which specifically prohibited discrimination in employment in any federally assisted program, and Title VII, which prohibited employers from discriminating against individuals because of their race, color, religion, sex, or national origin. Clarifying executive orders soon followed, including Executive Order 11357, which addressed equal opportunity for women and would have a dramatic impact on opening new avenues for them. The University adopted its own policy of nondiscrimination with regard to race, sex, religion, nationality, and marital status in 1965, which it incorporated into the WVU *Personnel Policy and Procedure Manual and the Handbook for Employees*. Administrators, faculty, and staff reportedly found some of the new federal requirements tiresome, but clearly there was a lot of ground to make up on social justice issues. It was obvious even then that the operational landscape of higher education had been transformed by the civil rights legislation.[1]

EQUAL EMPLOYMENT OPPORTUNITY
AND AFFIRMATIVE ACTION

Although WVU, like other public institutions across the nation, was compelled by federal legislation to adapt to the new legal realities in order to provide equal opportunity for minorities and women, it announced that it was more than willing to comply. According to the University's own proclamation in 1970: "We recognize the passage of laws asserting equality for all does not remove personal prejudices, nor ensure Equal Employment Opportunity.

However, the laws with an equally strong thrust of sincere and voluntary efforts on the part of all faculty, administrative, and management staff of the University can advance our total employment posture aggressively toward full and equal participation of all employees in opportunities available at West Virginia University." In fact, the proclamation continued, the ongoing success of WVU "as an educational enterprise will depend largely on whether we can practice an unyielding obligation to recruit and employ the best academic and staff personnel available and base our selection judgments on realistic job-related qualifications."[2]

An analysis of the 5,801-member WVU workforce that was made available in 1970 demonstrated some progress toward this goal. African Americans employed at the University had increased from seventy-six in 1968 to 184 in December 1970. WVU's minority workforce in April 1970, when the statistical analysis was conducted, stood at 5.15 percent of the total. Women made up 18.39 percent. African Americans made up 1.93 percent of the University's full-time labor force, marginally better than the total black population in Monongalia County of 1.5 percent. Among full-time faculty and extension staff, almost 2 percent were African American, slightly more than 5 percent were representative of all racial minorities, and 18 percent were women. Of the 3,184 full-time regular non-instructional staff, 2 percent were black; slightly more than 3 percent represented all minorities; and 66 percent were women.[3]

Although the University had a "fair representation" of African Americans and women among the faculty, they were underrepresented in the higher ranks of the professorate. Special efforts to increase the number of both groups included removing salary inequalities, implementing extra measures to improve recruitment, and providing more administrative oversight to ensure compliance with the plan of action. Recruitment literature, letters, and position announcements, all carrying the notice that WVU was an equal opportunity employer, were distributed widely. Those conducting recruitment searches visited predominately black and women's colleges, attended professional meetings and conferences to identify potential African American and women candidates, and sought assistance from other blacks and females already on staff to increase the pool of minority and women candidates for faculty and professional positions. When qualified members of a "protected class" were passed over in the hiring process, the individual responsible for the final decision was required to submit written justification for the decision to the respective dean or director.[4]

The University's analysis recognized that some progress had been achieved in the employment of African Americans in non-faculty positions since 1967, but deficiencies still existed in certain areas such as the junior and senior administrative and technical ranks. Remedial or immediate action called for more strategically targeted recruitment literature and announcements, requests for the assistance of members of those ranks in recruiting potential candidates, and weekly postings of all jobs. In some cases, in which the candidate was capable of doing quality work but lacked, for example, a high school diploma, the requirement could be waived. Otherwise, selection and promotion decisions were to be based solely on the qualifications of candidates, except that minority members and women were to be given preference if their qualifications were judged equal to all others. Major effort went into establishing objective criteria for hiring, performance evaluation, and salary equality in order to remove personal bias in these critical areas of judgment. Job classifications were rewritten to be strictly job-related. A manual including a grievance procedure, the *Handbook for Employees*, was prepared for all non-faculty employees. Some well-intentioned efforts created confusion, such as this opaque statement: "To the extent possible, redesign positions to more nearly fit the underutilized employees. . . . To the extent possible, shift lower skills from various positions, regroup and tailor positions to the needs and competencies assigned to those positions."[5]

The language might have been muddled at times, but the primary purpose was clear: "If any applicant or employee feels he has been discriminated against because of his race, color, sex, religion, age, or national origin," that person was encouraged to file a complaint with the president's office. The president forwarded the complaint to the chairman of the Committee on Interracial Policies and Practices for review. The committee then made a recommendation to the president, who decided on the appropriate action. Non-teaching employees who believed that they had been discriminated against could use the University grievance procedure specified in the *Handbook for Employees*, or, alternatively, they could file complaints with the West Virginia Human Rights Commission in Charleston, under provisions of the West Virginia Human Rights Act, Article 5-11-10.[6]

In December 1967, two African American student employees filed a complaint with the Human Rights Commission charging discrimination by administrators of the Mountainlair, the University's student center. Both male students claimed that they had not been called to work at the same time that white student employees had worked regularly. They charged that WVU and the Mountainlair had violated the state's Human Rights Act. Furthermore, they claimed that there was a "systematic pattern of racial discrimination in job hiring and employment at the Mountainlair of West Virginia University."[7] The assistant director of the Mountainlair, H. D. Jones, responded in a formal affidavit, declaring that the Mountainlair had "employed people of mixed races, religions, creeds and national origin since 1962. Being an employee of the Mountainlair since 1961, I can remember specific people who are of the colored race or of a darker color than white" who had been employed there. Jones said that one of the claimants had not been able to work because of his class schedule, but nevertheless he, Jones, had kept him on the payroll and asked him several times to come to work. The other student claimant had not applied for a job at the Mountainlair. The director of the Mountainlair, Robert F. McWhorter, also filed an affidavit refuting charges of a pattern of discrimination, as did, finally, President James G. Harlow.[8]

That two African American part-time student workers could have stirred so many University administrators to focus so much time on their complaints demonstrated the University's sense of insecurity during this period of sweeping national change. Not only were the director and assistant director of the Mountainlair required to reconstruct the employment history of the plaintiffs and to justify their own responses, but Director of Student Educational Services Joseph C. Gluck was engaged, as was the expertise of Londo H. Brown, professor of law and special assistant to the president, and, of course, President Harlow himself.[9]

What seemed an innocuous question from the Human Rights Commission, "how many Negroes were employed at the Mountainlair?" revealed how mystifyingly complex simply defining the term "Negro" could be, particularly to those unfamiliar with such rugged intellectual terrain. In the end, McWhorter and Jones decided to survey the 287 employees of the Mountainlair regarding how they identified themselves racially. Only 186 returned the forms, suggesting that many refused to answer the question at all. Of those who did, three said they were "Black" while none identified themselves as "Negro." Also, only 32 answered that they were Caucasian, but 149 said they were "White." In relaying the results of the survey, President Harlow echoed the concerns expressed by Professor of Law Londo Brown, who questioned whether the University should even be responding to the request of the Human Rights Commission. Writing to Carl W. Glatt, executive director of the West Virginia Human Rights Commission, Harlow observed that Professor Brown "was of the personal opinion that our compiling such information was in violation with the spirit of the Human Rights legislation if not in violation of the letter of that law." Brown had discussed the issue with the assistant attorney general, who apparently could provide no definitive answer. Moreover, "your request for the information concerning the race of University employees has troubled us considerably," Harlow wrote. "While you are apparently convinced that it is legal for us to furnish the information, and we have done it on that basis, we are yet of the opinion that the Attorney General should be asked to give an official opinion on the matter."[10]

That same spring, in April 1968, a circular was distributed across campus entitled "Statements of Discrimination Charges in Student Handbill." It proclaimed that the "students of West Virginia University, can no longer tolerate conditions of discrimination against some of our number or indeed against any man." In addition to demanding an end to the "system of bigotry," the students demanded an "open housing" policy, an end to "discriminatory hiring practices" by the University, the resignation of University officials who belonged to "segregated country clubs," and an "official stand" against all discrimination.[11] Harlow told the press that the handbill was "well written, but I don't agree with what it says." WVU "abhors discrimination of any kind," he said, and the University was an equal opportunity employer with a clear statement of its policy in the *Personnel Policy and Procedure Manual*. Because the handbill had been widely distributed on campus, however, Harlow believed that steps should be taken to determine with certainty whether there was merit to the charges of discrimination.[12]

President Harlow was quick to address the issue by assigning Director of Personnel S. Thomas Serpento to conduct a full-scale study in order to determine the validity of the accusations. The investigation itself was assigned to Richard D. Randolph, assistant director of personnel and employment manager, and involved conducting inquiries among students, individuals mentioned by students as affected by discrimination, selected minority employees, who provided "attitudinal comments" concerning employment practices, and individual conferences with administrators.[13]

The results of the investigation reveal how the lack of communication and the history of race relations affect perspective. The student distributing the handout was asked to provide information regarding the charges, but he could offer none. Neither did the fellow students who were queried. The secretary of the Black Unity Association on campus was aware of the two students who filed complaints against the Mountainlair, but she reported no knowledge of any other charges by minority students or employees and said that the organization had not endorsed the charges in the handbill. An African American graduate student who served as a resident counselor at Twin Towers expressed "deep concern over the conspicuous absence of Negro employees in the Department of Housing and felt the investigation should probe into the reasons for this situation." Personnel files showed that referents to that department demonstrated that "no Negro applicants have been rejected for employment consideration in the Department of Housing." The counselor suggested a person who might have been the victim of University discrimination. When the investigator questioned the woman, she said that she "assumed racial discrimination after not being called for employment at Summit Hall and another private operator of a student dormitory." She has assumed that these dorms were "part of the University," she replied, when informed that they were not. She also expressed her resentment toward the Mountainlair because the application sent to her requested a personal photograph, which she interpreted as an attempt to learn her race. She had been employed as a cook at the Mountainlair during the 1965–1966 school year, but the work terminated at the end of the spring semester. She was again offered a job as cook, but refused because it involved evening hours. In the meantime, however, the Mountainlair food operation came under new management, and she expressed the belief that they "would probably not want a colored face in such a new, modern luxurious building; consequently, she felt no real hope for reemployment at the Mountainlair despite previous offers of employment." When asked to explain her reasoning in light of the job offers, she responded: "We Negroes just think this way. I am not saying anyone outright discriminated against me, I just said they shouldn't have asked for that photograph." The investigator concluded that no actual discrimination occurred in her case. Following up on this matter, the investigator informed the Mountainlair directors that the practice of asking for personal photographs to accompany pre-employment applications was against University policy.[14]

The final report on the investigation into the charges of racial discrimination concluded that there was no evidence to substantiate the allegations. The investigator determined that the charges grew out of several contributing factors: the assumption that rumors and complaints were fact; an absence of communication among the University's various constituencies; deviation from University policy; general lack of knowledge of the law and procedures required for filing charges of discrimination; and a valid concern by students for equal opportunity regardless of race, color, creed, sex, or national origin. More concretely, he recommended that the University direct the Office of Personnel to serve as the central clearinghouse for posting all job announcements, applications, interviews, referrals, and the selection process. Also, the University should highlight its commitment to equal employment opportunity in all of its public postings and require the same from its contractors. In addition, a University ombudsman should play a critical role in improving communications among the diverse constituencies serving and being served by the University.[15]

This was not a newfound cause for new president Gene Budig. Female educators at his previous institution, Illinois State University, had applauded Budig in 1975 for aggressively promoting the welfare of women in education. Less than a week after he assumed the duties of president on July 1, 1977, Gene Budig met with the Affirmative Action Committee to explain and discuss his proposals for affirmative action at WVU. The kind of change that was required would be difficult but important. Everybody involved in the process must be convinced of its importance, and the president's office must take the lead. Therefore, he announced that the search for an affirmative action officer would begin immediately, and that that person would report directly to the president. The Affirmative Action Committee would consist of faculty, staff, and student representatives and would function as an advisory body to the president.[16]

Table 1. Non-Faculty Recruitment, 1977–1978

	1977	1978
Total Number of Positions	2,330	2,572
Number of Females Hired	1,274	1,517
Number of Females Promoted	303	334
Number of Blacks Hired	76	72
Number of Blacks Promoted	13	6
Number of Handicapped Persons Hired	17	6
Number of Vietnam Era Veterans Hired	76	74

Source: Non-Faculty Recruitment Analysis Covering Period March 1, 1977 to February 28, 1978, F5, Box 1, A&M 5009, WVRHC.

Budig's commitment to affirmative action at WVU provided it with support from the highest level. Institution-wide analyses of recruitment, hiring, distribution, and promotion patterns among non-faculty and faculty of the "protected classes" (women, minorities, the handicapped, and Vietnam Era veterans) began immediately. The great disparities in representation were readily visible in the statistical summary for 1977 and 1978, covering all non-instructional occupational categories:

Table 2. Non-Faculty Recruitment by Gender and Race, 1977–1978

	Total Applications Received	New Appointments
White Males	3,192	84
White Females	695	48
African American Males	22	2
African American Females	6	1
Hispanic Males	21	2
Hispanic Females	5	5
Asian / Pacific Isles Males	194	3
Asian / Pacific Isles Females	16	1
American Indian / Alaskan Males	15	1
American Indian / Alaskan Females	0	0

Source: 1978 Recruitment Activity Reports, June 19, 1978, F5, Box 1, A&M 5009, WVRHC.

The recruitment activity reports for faculty were considerably more complicated because of the special requirements of so many different academic departments and professions. Recruiting minorities and women was made significantly more difficult by historical patterns of representation in those professional fields. Consequently, the College of Engineering reported that there were so few black and female engineers with the appropriate academic credentials that their efforts were seriously handicapped. The School of Dentistry noted that the availability of qualified minority and female applicants for faculty positions was still "extremely limited." An "extreme shortage" of qualified candidates also prevailed in Agriculture and Forestry. Many academic professions had no minority organizations, further complicating recruitment. Faculty recruitment during the period from March 1, 1977, to February 28, 1978, reflected the level of the University's success in recruiting minorities and women—and how difficult was the task ahead:

Although there was a long way to go to achieve gender equality in hiring, promotion, and salary for female faculty at WVU, President Budig saw positive signs in 1978 that major changes were underway:

West Virginia University today is offering significantly more opportunity for women in many academic fields which historically attracted very few of them. Women comprise a third of our first-year law class and almost a fourth of our entering medical class this academic year. In the College of Business and Economics, 25 percent of the undergraduate majors are women—a 240 percent increase during the past five years. In the College of Engineering, the number of women enrolled has increased from 11 to 134 during the past five years—an increase higher than the national average. During the past decade, the number of women under 35 enrolled on the Morgantown campuses has more than doubled from 3,766 to 9,503. Female enrollment now is 44 percent of the student body compared to 32 percent in 1966.[17]

The first full-year report of Marion F. Dearnley, appointed to the newly created position of special assistant to the president and coordinator of affirmative action and equal employment opportunity, covered the 1978–1979 academic year. The most troubling statistic was the lack of women and minorities in administrative positions, and while administrators were "genuinely" concerned with affirmative action procedures, the level of committed faculty serving on search committees was an open question. Surprisingly to some, the median salary of faculty women ranged from 93 percent to 97 percent of what men received in comparable positions. Nationwide, the figure was 70 percent. Minority salaries ranged from 93 percent to 103 percent of white males. Although recruitment of black faculty was "disappointing," programming for African American students reported measurable progress. For example, the administration's Black Student Office worked closely with the students' Black Unity Organization to present the first Black Awareness Week at WVU.[18]

Some units reported successful efforts to recruit a more diverse body of students and faculty. Journalism and engineering, for example, initiated special programs for minority students, and both launched a concerted effort to recruit women and minority students into those fields. Consultants were brought to campus to conduct seminars and workshops for staff and academic advisors on race relations issues. Campus ministry hired an outreach counselor for African American students. The appointment of Horace E. Belmear as assistant dean of admissions charged with increasing black student enrollments was also a hopeful sign. He and his wife, Geraldine Belmear, a Black Student Affairs advisor who would work alongside her husband for many years to improve the diversity of the WVU community, became University legends in their own time. Judith Stitzel was appointed acting coordinator of women's studies. The Council for Women's Concerns also remained an active group in developing meaningful programs. The Affirmative Action Committee recommended a plan for the recruitment of faculty and another for training faculty in multicultural awareness, while continuous training for supervisors was declared essential for further improvement.[19]

Under federal civil rights legislation, universities filed plans to address inequalities and then were routinely evaluated for compliance with the law. Following a review of the University's Equal Employment Opportunity policies and practices in 1980–1981, the Department of Labor's Office of Federal Contract Compliance Programs outlined several areas of noncompliance and ordered remedies. These plans demonstrate how thoroughly these compliance procedures altered the structure and culture of the University. For example, the federal review found that female service workers and minority professional employees applied for promotion or transfer at a much lower rate than males and nonminorities, and required the University to survey these workers regarding the reasons for their lower rate of application. Based on the results of this survey, WVU was required to "devise and implement measures designed to increase the number of female and minority applicants for promotion/transfer in these categories, and to monitor promotions to ensure that the selection rates of female and minority applicants were consistent with male and non-minority selection rates."[20]

Similarly, the Office of Federal Contract Compliance noted that the percentage of minority and female applicants for faculty positions during the 1979–1980 academic year was "significantly below" the estimated availability of faculty positions in a number of departments. The University was instructed to implement specific outreach and recruitment programs in order to remedy the situation. Units targeted for increasing minority applications were law, pharmacy, social work, mineral and energy resources, and the Center for Extension and Continuing Education. Several nonacademic areas were also singled out, such as the custodians, health technology, and the non-farm-workers job group, in which the University was tasked to make a special effort to hire women and minority applicants "at least equal to their estimated availability."[21]

The civil rights and equal opportunity legislation of the sixties and seventies also necessitated major financial investments by the University to make its buildings handicapped accessible. Nearly all of them required at least some alteration. After inspecting all of the academic buildings, a review by the Department of Health, Education, and Welfare's Office for Civil Rights in 1980 found WVU noncompliant with the 1973 Rehabilitation Act. The department cited nearly every building for having some or all of the following problems: restrooms inaccessible to wheelchair-bound persons, water fountains too high, no raised lettering for sight-impaired individuals, no curb cuts from parking lots to sidewalks, and a lack of designated parking spaces. Consequently, the department instructed the University to develop a "corrective action plan" to achieve compliance.[22]

Some progress was realized as the issue of social justice became an integral part of the hiring process, and the University community understood the legal mandates established by the various civil rights bills of the era. Those conducting recruitment searches could expect some assistance, and a mechanism was established to resolve complaints and develop plans that would meet federal guidelines. In 1981, a more decentralized system was implemented by transferring the role of special assistant to the president to the position of assistant vice president for human resources, thus placing responsibility for social justice on the desk of a vice president, as well as the desks of each dean and director. Some successes stand out during this period. For example, a sexual harassment policy was developed, and in each administrative unit individuals were trained as liaisons. The Health Sciences Seminar was launched to introduce disadvantaged adolescents to health sciences careers. The Center for Women's Studies was established, a PASSKey Program was initiated to assist with the orientation of new African American students, and the Dial-a-Bus system was established to transport mobility-impaired students to and from classes.[23]

The Black Community Concerns Committee was established at WVU around the same time that a full-time affirmative action and equal employment opportunity officer was appointed by President Budig. The committee reported in January 1982 that, in cooperation with the University Affirmative Action Committee, a proposal was developed for a program to improve the recruitment of black faculty and graduate students. It proposed "recruiting field trips" to various predominantly black colleges and universities in order to establish formal and informal communication networks, but at this point its work had just begun.[24]

WVU's first Black Alumni Day was held on October 7, 1984, in conjunction with a Mountaineer football game. Approximately one hundred black alumni attended activities, which included a black alumni advisory board meeting, lunch at the home of President Gee, a pre-game tailgate party, a Mountaineer scoreboard salute, a musical tribute by the WVU Marching Band, and an athletic department salute to Mountaineer alumni who have played professional sports. The subcommittee on student life for the Black Community Concerns Committee examined the concerns of black students and their apparent lack of interest and involvement in student government in order to determine how to improve their participation. A directory of all African American alumni was being compiled, and another event for the fall of 1985 was planned. "It is hoped that the organization of Black Alumni will result in assistance from that group in the recruitment of minority students, the implementation of outreach efforts, and improvement in the quality of life for minority students at WVU."[25]

The results of these initial efforts under President Gee were decidedly mixed, and the University did not attain five-year numerical goals set by agreement with the Office for Civil Rights. WVU sought to increase black student enrollment to 4.6 percent of the student body, and to increase African American faculty to 3.6 percent. Unfortunately, black student enrollment reached only 2.6 percent, and black faculty represented only 1.4 percent of total faculty. It was believed by some senior administrative officials that the goals were either not understood or not fully accepted in every quarter of the University. Thus, when Neil Bucklew assumed the presidency in 1986, he developed plans for infusing social justice principles throughout the University organization, so that employees would become pro-active in the implementation of policies.[26]

SOCIAL JUSTICE INSTITUTIONALIZED

Affirmative action as a way to achieve racial and gender fairness received strong support during President Budig's four-year term, but when Neil Bucklew became president in 1986, social justice became a primary goal of his administration. At that time no unified effort existed but rather "disjointed concerns" among affected groups, and primarily women, African Americans, gays and lesbians, and the handicapped. The term "social justice" was not even in use on campus, he recalled. In retrospect, Bucklew regarded his efforts at bringing together people who shared common social justice goals as one of his most important contributions to the University community. Bucklew reinforced the importance of making social justice a priority in his agenda by delivering annual speeches to the campus on the status of the issue and by providing analytical progress reports. He expected others to be proactive as well. For example, he said, "We made rifle-shot appointments. I would simply say to units, if you are underrepresented in relation to women or minorities, and you could identify a high-quality person you would like, then you don't have to search. Just bring the person in and we will give you the money to hire for the position. We did that for four or five years. That would be patently illegal now. It would now be considered reverse discrimination."[27]

The University's mission statement proclaimed: "West Virginia University's role as the doctoral-degree granting, research, land-grant university in the State of West Virginia gives the institution a special responsibil-

Table 3. African American Enrollment, 1981–1982

	Enrollment	Percent
Potomac State	53	4.86
WVU undergrad	351	2.4
WVU graduate	91	1.6
MD	2	1.0
JD	15	3.6
DDS	1	0.4

Source: Judith DeStefano to Marion F. Dearnley, "Title VI: Utilization and Goals," January 5, 1982, Black Community Concerns Committee Folder, Box 338, A&M 690.

Table 4. Total Full-Time Students (for Affirmative Action) Enrolled as of October 15, 1982

	Men	Women
Non-Resident Alien	487	151
Black Non-Hispanic	211	146
American Indian / Alaskan	4	2
Asian / Pacific Islander	54	34
Hispanic	24	23
White Non-Hispanic	8,535	6,269

Source: Judith DeStefano to Marion F. Dearnley, "Title VI: Utilization and Goals," January 5, 1982, Black Community Concerns Committee Folder, Box 338, A&M 690.

ity as a leader in the area of social justice. The pursuit of truth underlying the University's mission focuses attention on issues of diversity, power and perspective, so that students, faculty and staff may study and work in a climate of academic freedom and social responsibility, developing the skills, knowledge and self-esteem necessary for participation as world citizens."[28]

President Bucklew's first move was to convene a social justice forum, which met on October 15, 1986, to announce his plans for a major initiative. The first step was to reinstitute the position of special assistant to the president for social justice as the person responsible for coordinating and overseeing social justice University wide. The system would remain decentralized. Deans and directors would continue to be responsible for their units, but initiatives would be implemented and administered more vigorously by the special assistant. The president also created a social justice council, a "confederation" representing groups concerned about women, African Americans, and the handicapped. The council would provide coordination of their efforts and place the responsibilities of the University's Affirmative Action Committee under the aegis of the council's broader concept of social justice. The idea was to build a coalition that would facilitate planning and development of larger issues that affected all of these groups. The council developed long-range goals: raise awareness of the importance of social justice; build alliances to enhance the climate for social justice; provide leadership for multiculturalism in the curriculum; enhance the evaluation process for addressing social justice; and provide social justice leadership development opportunities.[29]

Special Assistant to the President for Social Justice Dianne Brown-Wright defined social justice as "working out some system of fairness for everybody." This blanket statement covered a lot of ground, but considering the lack of equality of opportunity for women, African Americans, gays and lesbians, and the handicapped, "equality" logically could mean "fairness."[30]

The Center for Black Culture and Research (CBCR), which had been under development by a steering committee for two years, submitted its plan to President Bucklew on July 9, 1986. The idea emanated out of a WVU Counseling Center report released in the early eighties entitled "Black, White and Blue." The report emphasized the difficulties confronting African American students at WVU and discussed how they should be addressed.[31]

The CBCR moved from its temporary quarters in E. Moore Hall when an attractive brick house at 590 Spruce Street was renovated in 1987. More than one hundred members of the University community attended a formal dedication of the CBCR's new permanent home in February 1990. The highly respected African American professor of law, Franklin B. Cleckley, who had chaired the president's Task Force on the Center for Black Culture, declared this "the single most important event that's happened to black students and faculty in this university's history." When he first arrived at WVU, Cleckley said, "all the black students and faculty could meet in my office. Today, WVU's black population has grown to 15 faculty, 6 administrators, approximately 500 students and 100 classified staff."[32]

The CBCR was intended "to help alleviate the alienation found by Blacks on a predominantly white campus and will support the long-term success of Black students," Bucklew declared. Also, the CBCR would provide "an avenue for people to broaden their perspectives of the Black experience," said Charles C. Blue Jr., university coordinator for minority affairs. Blue predicted it would become a "home away from home" for black students on a predominantly white campus. The center offered a certificate program in African and African American studies, housed a library and research assistants, and published a quarterly newsletter. The African American campus community could also take advantage of counseling services, workshops, lectures, receptions, art exhibits, films, alumni activities, career events, tutorial services, and a busy schedule of related activities.[33]

African American recruitment and retention became a top priority under Bucklew's administration. By 1992–1993, more than five hundred individuals were involved in the University's project of incorporating social justice into the culture of WVU. Horace Belmear, assistant director of marketing and recruiting, assumed leadership of the effort to increase black student enrollment. A comprehensive recruitment and admission plan was developed, focusing on early identification of prospective students though print and electronic media, as well as visitations to homes, churches, and schools. The most informative part of the recruiting process was home visitation, followed by pre-enrollment seminars at high schools, which included students' parents. During recruitment, high school juniors were asked to indicate their interest in WVU on a search card; then Mr. Belmear sent their names to their respective high school counselors and offered to visit those schools. Although this plan was used with predominantly black high schools in Pittsburgh, Baltimore, and Philadelphia, a number of recruitment areas were targeted. In addition to many of the West Virginia counties, recruiters focused attention on Baltimore, Philadelphia, Pittsburgh, and Washington, DC; northern and southern areas of Virginia; Cleveland, Ohio; Manhattan, Brooklyn, and the Bronx; and "various areas" of New Jersey.[34]

Even with all of the reforms and initiatives, however, the number of students who enrolled was very disappointing. In 1992–1993 African Americans represented only 2.7 percent of the student body and 1.3 percent of the faculty. The big question then was why so few chose WVU. Clearly the relatively small African American population in Morgantown specifically and in West Virginia generally was the answer. In 1989–1990, 78 black students at WVU were in-state residents, with Pennsylvania (62), New York (54), Maryland (42), New Jersey (30), and Virginia (24) sending the most out-of-state African American students to WVU.[35]

A subcommittee considering University-wide issues related to black student retention was established following a student affairs retreat in 1990. Its report suggested that barriers to retention existed within the institution and recommended training programs and workshops for faculty and staff who worked closely with black students. The report recommended that pilot projects to carry out the programs should be initiated in units with experience in work-study, such as the University Advising Center. The best established techniques would facilitate expansion into other parts of the University. The Center for Black Culture and Research should be given more responsibility for promoting the success of African American students with recognitions such as the Social Justice Award. Initiatives designed to integrate African American history and culture into the curriculum, such as the African and African American Studies Certificate Program and the minority culture requirement in the Liberal Studies Program, emphasized greater sensitivity for diversity. Finally, the subcommittee recommended that the University establish scholarships for black students who demonstrated a high level of academic performance during their first year at WVU but had not received other awards from the Scholars Program.[36]

A MEASURE OF EQUALITY FOR WOMEN

Title IX of the Education Amendments enacted on June 23, 1972, generally referred to simply as "Title IX," made its most obvious impact on intercollegiate athletics. But the legislation also had a significant effect on academic programs. Prior to Title IX, males traditionally dominated majors such as engineering, business, law, and medicine, while women were concentrated in "helping professions" such as nursing, elementary education, and home economics. Title IX was intended to achieve a more equal distribution of the sexes in the professions by opening up the segregated fields to the opposite sex and offering a more "hospitable environment." After 1972, the departments that had openly discouraged women from entering their associated professions were required to show progress toward a more equal distribution of the sexes. One example illustrates the kind of ingrained male resistance to women in some disciplines. Judith Smith Wilkinson had earned a doctorate, and was a licensed professional counselor when she was interviewed for a newspaper article in 2008. She related that she had received the bachelor's degree in 1965 and a master's degree in 1967 in elementary education. Later she received two more master's degrees at WVU. In 1972 Wilkinson was exploring what would be required to pursue the doctorate in counseling. On learning that she was married and had children, an advisor told her, "Mrs. Wilkinson, go home and take care of your children." Later, in 1973, after Title IX had been passed, she had a followup interview with the same person about her plans to pursue a doctorate in counseling. As she described it, "within a year he had gone through a transformation—from suit and tie to flowered shirt and love beads—and was now receptive to her going back to school." Her assessment: Title IX had obviously helped to "level the playing field for women."[37]

Similar stories are easily duplicated for other academic fields at WVU, and these stories reflected what happened in higher education nationally. In 1976, a self-evaluation committee found very few programs out of compliance with the requirements of Title IX but recommended that women be given more encouragement to study business, dentistry, education administration, engineering, law, and medicine. The committee also advised the

University to withdraw support from student organizations that admitted only one sex as members unless they abolished the restriction.[38]

The reforms of the sixties and seventies were generated by a dramatic shift in the nation's temperament toward many social issues, including the traditional roles of women. But even before Title IX major changes were afoot in the lives of women at WVU. One of the first dramatic changes occurred during the late sixties when President Harlow gave the order to abandon curfew hours for women. He was reacting to a demand by the Associated Women Students, supported by other campus organizations, to achieve this milestone in the struggle for equality. The local newspaper headline trumpeted, "U Coeds Turned Free." It was announced toward the end of the spring semester of 1969 that, beginning in the fall, curfew hours would be lifted for sophomore, junior, and senior women, a privilege long enjoyed by male students. Harlow was receptive to the federal and state laws attempting to abolish discrimination, believing that WVU students were "mature and intelligent enough to accept this freedom responsibly."[39]

It was 1969, the same year Neil Armstrong became the first human being to set foot on the moon, that WVU women finally escaped the pettiness of curfew hours. Although the curfew was intended to protect young women, it also gave rise to numerous inequities that became indefensible in modern times. The exact time when women were required to be in the dormitories depended on rank and grade-point average. Even fifteen minutes past the deadline could result in restricting the offender to the dorm on the weekends. Still stricter curfews prevailed in the fifties, with female freshmen required to be in by 7:30 p.m. on weeknights. If students signed out to go to the library but did not report to the library proctor within ten minutes, they received a restriction. Parental permission was also required to leave the campus. At no time did the University ever impose curfews on men. Dean of Women Alice Elizabeth (Betty) Boyd reportedly "used to walk around the women's dorms before curfew with a flashlight, searching for couples kissing in the bushes."[40] Student affairs administrator Gordon Thorn believed it was the lifting of restrictions on residence hall life for women "that began the change in the campus culture and community which started an entirely different lifestyle."[41]

Margaret Workman, a successful lawyer elected to a seat on the West Virginia Supreme Court of Appeals in 1988 and the first woman elected to a statewide office, attended WVU in the mid-sixties. She lived in Towers when it was new, but vividly remembered "very strict curfews" as well as the dress code. Girls were not allowed to wear slacks on campus, so they wore trench coats to conceal them. "Do you know that when they first let women into WVU, they had to make the beds for the guys?" she commented. Those days were gone, but plenty of irritating restrictions on women remained during the sixties. Restrictions were relaxed further in 1973 when women were permitted to visit men's residences, wear shorts to class, and drink beer at the Mountainlair. A new era for women had indeed arrived.[42]

In a major sign that the times were indeed changing, in 1976 Lea Anderson became the first woman to be elected student body president and went on to earn an undergraduate degree in psychology, followed by a law degree. The only other woman to serve as president did so during World War II, when Betty Head, vice president of the student body, assumed the office when the male president-elect joined the Navy.[43] Lea Anderson had no recollection of hostility toward her campaign for the presidency in 1976, and her sex never became an issue. Nor did her running mate, Michael Burke, object to the role of "second fiddle" to a woman president. "I felt Lea was the most able candidate in the race," he declared after the election. "I didn't feel that running with her was taking a back seat to anyone. The fact that she is a woman didn't make any difference to me at all. As a matter of fact, I was very honored when she asked me to run." Anderson did not recall any direct hostility against her, even though someone did deface some of her campaign posters, and she did receive "threateningly obscene" phone calls nearly every night. Paraphrasing John F. Kennedy during his West Virginia 1960 presidential primary campaign, Anderson's campaign mantra was "Don't vote for me because I am a woman, but don't vote against me because I am a woman."[44]

Other memorable benchmarks on the road to equality for women during this period are worth noting. In 1962 Kenneta Shaffer became the first woman to graduate from WVU's four-year medical program. In 1966 Victorine Louistall-Monroe began teaching library science, thereby becoming the University's first black faculty member. On September 9, 1972, the Mountaineer Marching Band performed for the first time with female musicians at a football game between WVU and Villanova. In 1976 Donna Gaston and Sandra Onellion, became the first coeds to graduate from Army ROTC at WVU and commissioned as second lieutenants. The following year Carolyn E. Belton became the first African American woman at WVU to receive a commission in the Air Force through the ROTC program. That same year, 1977, Jill Gerwig Buchanan became WVU's first female graduate in mining engineering, joining her father and husband, who were both WVU alumni in mining engineering. Other traditionally male-dominated professions were opening up as well. By 1980, WVU expected to graduate more women dentists in the next four years than it had in the two decades since the School of Dentistry opened its doors. The dental school limited the size of its classes but imposed no restrictions on the proportion of women. The twenty-eight women students represented about 12 percent of the 243 students enrolled in the School of Dentistry. This was a significant step forward, considering that only thirteen women dentists were practicing in the entire state of West Virginia. One of the more visible signs that the times and culture were changing was the 1990 election of Natalie Tennant as WVU's first female Mountaineer mascot. The Fairview, West Virginia native drew some negative, not to mention very crude, comments from fans in the beginning but soon earned respect for her maturity in handling the highly visible role. Her experience undoubtedly helped prepare her for a political career; she was elected West Virginia secretary of state in 2008.[45]

Some of the female members of the faculty were true pioneers and remarkable individuals. Two illustrations suffice. Helen Margaret Lester Plants was the first woman appointed to the faculty in the College of Engineering (1947), the first woman to hold the rank of full professor of engineering, and the first woman in West Virginia to become a registered professional engineer. Born in 1925, Helen Lester graduated from the University of Missouri in 1945 with a BS in civil engineering. As a registered engineer, she worked for a construction company in Texas between 1945 and 1947. When she was hired as a professor at WVU, she wanted to be registered in West Virginia too, but was told "no, we don't register women." Plants told contacts in Texas of her dilemma, and they informed West Virginia authorities that, unless Plants was registered immediately, Texas would deny all registrations from West Virginia. The threat worked, and she got her registration, but there were other slights during her career. In 1974 she was ignored by British colleagues hosting a reception for foreign visitors attending a professional conference. When the American delegation heard of this indignity, a colleague called to ask why Plants, who at the time was serving as chairperson of Engineering Research Management and was also vice president of the American Society of Engineering Educators, had not been invited. "Well, old boy, it's not done. There aren't any female engineering professionals in our organization," the American was told. After a "quick caucus" Plant's colleague responded that if Plants was not invited then none of the other Americans would attend. An invitation was hand delivered to Helen Plants in short order. "Score one for the Yanks. I was proud of us," he said. Another colleague suggested that the reason she overcame so many obstacles was because she worked harder than everyone else. Helen Plants retired from WVU in 1985 and died September 6, 1999.[46]

Another female faculty member whose career at WVU illuminates the difficult road the pioneer women traveled during this era of transition was Betty Miller. She graduated from WVU with a bachelor's degree in chemical engineering in 1947, one of the first women to receive a degree in this field. It was difficult for her to find a job during the postwar period, but she was finally hired at Celanese, a synthetic fiber manufacturer. In December 1955 she decided to return to WVU to pursue an MS degree in mathematics. She switched fields because "I was sick and tired of hearing people say, 'that's a man's job,'" Miller informed a reporter years later. Ironically, she was hired to teach in the mathematics department in 1952, where most of her calculus students were engineering majors. According to Miller, the only criticism of her work was that she was too young and that she was a woman, although there was less discrimination against women in math than in engineering at the time. "Let me assure you, the faculty [in Engineering] did not like having women in their classes," she said. After Title IX she observed only modest, superficial differences, like the changing of

Table 5. Women Enrolled at WVU

	Men	Women	Total
1945–1946	1,394	1,092 (43.92%)	2,486
1950–1951	men: 4,045	women: 1,260 (23.75%)	5,305
1960–1961	men: 4,993	women: 1,823 (26.74%)	6,816
1970–1971	men: 11,283	women: 6,471 (36.45%)	17,754
1980–1981	men: 11,379	women: 9,841 (46.37%)	21,220

Source: "Enrollment by Gender at WVU," *Dominion Post*, March 31, 2008.

pronouns in textbooks. She retired in 1992 and was hired by the provost's office "temporarily," but that ninety-day stint grew to fifteen years.[47]

For many departments this was a transition period between outright opposition to women in graduate programs like engineering and efforts to actively recruiting them. The English department experienced dramatic change in the sixties and seventies. Sophia Blades and Judith Stitzel joined the faculty in the 1960s, the first two women with PhD degrees in the discipline to be hired by the department, and perhaps by the University. Both arrived at WVU as faculty spouses. Before them, women who might otherwise have been employed teaching in high school or normal school were teaching English composition. They were regarded as "second class citizens" compared with those who held PhDs. Nearly all of the men held PhDs or were finishing their degrees. The percentage of women in the English department increased dramatically in the seventies.[48]

Another indicator of the changing status of women at WVU is found in the increasing number (both absolute and as a percentage) of women attending the University.

The WVU Women's Centenary was celebrated during the 1989–1991 academic year, one hundred years after the first ten women students enrolled in 1889, twenty-two years after the founding of the University. One of them, Harriet E. Lyon, was awarded the BA degree, becoming the first female graduate in the University's history. One of President Bucklew's first speeches upon arriving at WVU announced that the centenary of women's education at WVU would be the focus of a two-year celebration. Planning for the event had already commenced, however, with a committee of twenty-six graduate students, faculty, and staff led by Director of Women's Studies Judith Stitzel and Dean of the College of Creative Arts Margaret Lucas. President Bucklew asked that the occasion be used to celebrate "the importance of women in the history and life of this University and state" but also to complement the broad goals established by his administration, emphasizing economic development and social justice.[49]

The "Women's Centenary, Excellence through Equity" celebration officially began on September 20, 1989, in a convocation assembled at the Creative Arts Center Concert Theatre. The keynote speaker, honorary Women's Centenary Chairperson Dee Caperton, Governor Caperton's wife, was among a number of speakers to honor the memory and purpose of the ten pioneers who initiated the women's experience at WVU a century earlier. A variety of lectures, concerts and other performances, and publications would follow over the next two years, culminating in the spring 1991 commencement.[50]

A women's centenary publication, described as a "historical digest," observed that the University was "gradually, and slowly, working toward equality for women and men." Enrollments were about equally divided among men and women, as were the number receiving bachelor's degrees. And yet there were still significant differences between men and women in the disciplines they chose to study, and in faculty expertise. In 1987–1989, women received a majority of the bachelor's degrees in only nineteen of the sixty-two degree-granting programs, most of them in the fields traditionally chosen by women, such as education, social work, communication studies, psychology, music and theatre, journalism, medical technology, and physical therapy. Although the traditional gendering of disciplines was beginning to break down in some areas, others were still "grossly overbalanced toward men or women," the historical digest noted. There was a near absence of men in fields such as elementary education, speech pathology, dental hygiene, and nursing, while in other fields such as finance, physics, and engineering, there was a near absence of women.[51]

The historical pattern persisted at the graduate level. Men received only 394 master's degrees in 1987–1988, while women received 681 of the master's degrees, nearly all of them in the traditional female fields of education, social work, and communication studies. On the other hand, the reverse was true for doctoral degrees, with men receiving ninety degrees and women forty-eight. A similar imbalance held true for the professional degrees of dental surgery and medicine, while law degrees were roughly balanced between men and women. Instructional faculty ranks still displayed the disparities of the past and were just beginning to show the signs of change, which were most visible in the tenure-track positions. The ranks of assistant professors showed a growing pool of women entering this previously male domain with 113 women and 204 men; among associate professors were 80 women and 275 men; among full professors were 34 women and 434 men. The imbalances continued in the colleges: 56 women and 227 men in the College of Arts and Sciences, 5 women and 47 men in the College of Business and Economics, and one woman and 79 men in the College of Engineering. Some of the discrepancy in the number of female administrators was addressed when President Bucklew hired Jane H. Applegate as dean of the College of Human Resources and Education in 1991, who initiated the five-year master's degree. In 1994 Teree Foster was appointed dean of College of Law, the first female dean to head the University's law school.[52]

Historical patterns of discrimination were well entrenched in American society, including the universities. Eliminating discrimination, a project initiated by the Baby Boomers, would require a long-term commitment, one that WVU has embraced.

ELEVEN

STUDENT CULTURE
TAKES A LEFT TURN

THE "BABY BOOMERS" ARRIVE

JOSEPH C. GLUCK, a popular and respected member of the campus community for decades, came to WVU in 1946 as veterans' coordinator. Having served as a Navy chaplain during World War II, Gluck was prepared to counsel returning vets turned students. Thirty-five years later, after stints as dean of students and university vice president under five presidents and forty-seven deans, he was asked to compare postwar students with those of 1980. "Generally speaking," he informed a reporter, "today's students are more thoughtful towards the needs and problems of others than they were 30 years ago." He did not claim to have an accurate way to measure this assertion, but he regarded the Baby Boomers as "more humane with each other than other generations. The vets were a good crowd. They were all business and not much trouble." Counseling veterans was simpler, he believed, because they were more mature, sophisticated, and serious about their studies. They were also highly critical of professors who were not doing their jobs properly. On the other hand, "more young people today are less interested in only earning money than they are in training for a field they feel is important to their lives."[1]

Gluck was responding to a question that was in the air. Older people knew the climate was changing on campus, but they were not so strategically positioned to understand where this new generation, in a phrase of the day, was "coming from." The World War II generation (the "silent

283

generation") often thought of the change in student mentality as a breakdown of personal discipline, which manifested itself in the questioning of constituted authority and institutions, and in the confusion of libertinism and irresponsibility with individual freedom. The winds of youthful rebellion characterized the sixties and seventies, but WVU's student body was fairly conservative when compared with its counterparts on many major university campuses. In fact, a fall 1967 editorial in the *Daily Athenaeum* that asked, "How long are we going to allow leftist infiltration to mock 'This Is My Own, My Native Land?'" was read into the *Congressional Record* by West Virginia Senator Jennings Randolph as evidence that college students in his state were still respectable citizens. The Morgantown evening paper editorialized that Senator Randolph's observation on WVU students did apply to "at least a part of them."[2]

ANTI-VIETNAM WAR DEMONSTRATIONS

The year 1968 was one of unparalleled events that not only traumatized Americans but also opened up a fissure in national life separating the present from everything that had come before. The Cold War continued unabated, the war in Vietnam continued to expand, civil rights leader Martin Luther King Jr. was assassinated, as was presidential candidate Senator Robert Kennedy, and black ghettoes burned as riots erupted in cities across the land. President Lyndon Johnson announced to a stunned nation that he would not seek a second term, and the very liberal U.S. Senator Hubert Humphrey was nominated by the Democratic Convention in Chicago while police bludgeoned antiwar protesters in the streets outside of the hall. Richard Nixon was elected president after a bitter campaign. By the late sixties college campuses were flooded by turmoil as the antiwar, women's liberation, and civil rights movements reached high tide.

For the most part, students at WVU remained quiet during these tumultuous years. The fall 1968 WVU *Alumni News* reported that, although higher education had braced itself for the worst, "there was a reassuring atmosphere here as the University" began another academic year. "The protesters and malcontents seem fewer and less spirited: a brief flurry or two in depleted numbers, then back to the woodwork." The *Alumni News* observed, with obvious relief, that "extra-curricular student energy seems directed to such old-fashioned pursuits as homecoming, football, and the social regime . . . and the barbers and beauticians have got to be doing a land office business for the boys look like boys and the girls look like girls again." With more resignation than relief, it also observed that "traffic and parking are still what can only be described as a mess, a condition which has existed for so long that the faculty and staff are used to it and the students accept it as a problem which won't be solved during their stay anyway."[3]

Students of the fifties have been characterized as quiescent. But Gordon Thorn, who attended WVU from 1949 to 1955 and spent a career in student affairs at his alma mater, rejected the notion that his was a "silent generation." The students were not so much "silent" as they were "cautious." And for good reason: "Most of us were born during the depression years. Then the Second World War started and our lives changed a good bit in our hometowns. Our models disappeared and a lot of them didn't come back. Then when we got into the late forties, the Korean War started and that was going on when we were in school. We didn't know what stable was." Quiescence ruled among WVU students during the sixties, when other campuses were coming under pressure from the "new breed" of students, who challenged the legitimacy of traditional institutions. Thorn recalled that "for those of us that were on the firing line it was a trying time."[4] In Dean of Students Joseph Gluck's view, WVU students diverged from this national norm because many of them "were first generation out of the hills and hollows, and couldn't afford to get caught up in the demonstrations."[5] The Vietnam War probably was much less abstract for many WVU students than it was for their national peers because more of their fathers and brothers were involved. Seven hundred and eleven West Virginians were killed in that Southeast Asian war, eighty-five for every 100,000 males in the state, a higher rate per capita than any other state in the union.[6]

But student attitudes began to change in 1969. On what student organizers called "Vietnam Day," set for October 15, 1969, students were planning to call for a moratorium on the war as part of a nationwide project. The month before, President Harlow had refused to take a position on the moratorium, claiming that the public would view his personal position as that of the University. He also turned down demands from the local chapter of the National Vietnam Moratorium Committee that the University not penalize students who observed the moratorium by not attending classes, and he did not agree to fly University flags at half-mast to note the occasion. In response, the student newspaper released a scathing editorial captioned "James G. Harlow—When the Name on the Door Should Mean More," declaring it a moral imperative that the University community take a stand in opposition to the war and the needless deaths it caused. The student paper rejected Harlow's position of neutrality and praised WVU students for at last taking a stand against the Vietnam War.[7]

The Morgantown newspaper was certain that "radicals" had established a foothold on the WVU campus, and it warned readers about four groups in particular. The most important of them was the Mountaineer Freedom Party (MFP), which supported the antiwar moratorium. Still relatively new, the MFP was recognized by the University. Its platform, written during the previous school year, called for a complete revision of the educational program at WVU, including the abolition of grades and a guarantee of "black rights." The new Student Activist League (SAL) had no elected officers and did not necessarily want University recognition. Not to be confused with the more radical national organization, the Students for a Democratic Society (SDS), SAL existed only briefly on campus, folding in 1968 for lack of interest. SAL's politics were socialist, and the organization was founded to raise consciousness on political and social issues. It never had more than ten or fifteen active members, according to FBI assessments.[8] Scott Bills, a senior history major, was one of the organizers. A member of Phi Beta Kappa, a former SDS member, and one of the founders of SAL, he played a key role in the moratorium. The WVU chapter of the American Civil Liberties Union (ACLU) was also a new organization. The ACLU fought civil liberties abuses through the courts, although the local paper characterized it as the "legal arm of the radical movement." The Young Americans for Freedom (YAF) had only recently held its first organizational meeting, so it was hard to say what its approach would be, but its politics would almost certainly be radical. The History Society, which had no connection to the Department of History, was a right-wing group whose members announced that they were prepared "to crush the hippies and their communistic takeover." None of these organizations had been called into action yet, but the *Morgantown Post* opined: "What will happen when they become functional? Will WVU suffer the agonies of a Columbia or a San Francisco State? Will there be riots and student takeovers?" Scott Bills did not think so. "Our purpose is to radicalize the campus, but, though I don't eliminate the possibility, I sincerely doubt that there will be a confrontation here." The *Post* expressed its belief that, unless something changed dramatically, WVU would remain "quiet."[9]

Despite the apprehension expressed in the hometown newspaper, the WVU antiwar moratorium was conducted without serious incident. A film, "teach-in" lectures at a "Freedom School," a fast and vigil on Memorial Plaza in front of the Mountainlair followed by a memorial service and placement of a wreath honoring the war dead on the courthouse square, a concert for peace, and a candlelight service completed the first peaceful day of the moratorium.[10]

While many locals regarded these events with deep suspicion, some observers with a broader perspective were not overly impressed. Nicholas von Hoffman, a columnist for the *Washington Post*, arrived on campus a few days before the moratorium with a CBS crew "to do a piece showing that the great unhappiness even had gotten to this campus of obedient children." The short clip shown on television gave the impression that a "small but respectable percentage" of people "on this football and fraternity campus" made their opposition to the war known. Von Hoffman wrote that six hundred or seven hundred members of the University community observed the moratorium. What it demonstrated, von Hoffman wrote, was that "even here you can see changes which are far more advanced on other campuses. You'll find oodles of pretty young girls in their Villager jumpers, and find straight boys in stapress pants." He described WVU as a campus where "Greeks dominate, a campus of the '40s and '50s," but "long hair has come" and "there is a large number of girls who've broken away from sorority standards and now wear the jeans and discarded army jackets that girls wear at big name schools." Before the moratorium, von Hoffman wrote, sponsors "feared the frat crowd would beat up on them. That didn't happen." Still, he continued, "this place strikes you as still essentially authoritarian," although the growing consciousness and questioning analysis of life and society had reached WVU too. "You can't get by on authority anymore, not even at West Virginia University. . . . Ever since Horace Mann advocated free public schools, it's been said that from education would come the questioning, skeptical, self-motivated, autonomous thinking citizen of perfected democracy. Well, he's here now and the managers of the dream factory are going to have to learn to talk to him."[11]

President Harlow's approach would not have been regarded as unreasonable several years earlier, but to the "new breed" of students it was an example of the authoritarianism they wanted to change. Presumably to nip the rising radicalism in the bud, Harlow issued a stern warning on January 26, 1970, declaring that the University administration was willing to work with dissident groups, but, as a branch of state government, WVU would not "tolerate disruptions of its activities, deliberate violations of its regulations, seizure of its properties, interference with the rights of the members of the total university community, or coercion of its officers by any means whatever." Furthermore, any attempt to do so would "call into question a student's right to continue his enrollment." The Faculty Senate approved the president's statement shortly thereafter, and the Board of Regents followed suit.[12]

Compared with many college campuses, WVU seemed calm, but there were several juvenile acts of destruction that went unnoticed beyond the campus. A former graduate student and resident assistant in Boreman Hall South during the months leading up to the demonstrations of May 1970 recalled that unsettled period as one of constant turmoil. Every night students threw soft drink bottles from the dorm windows. Some hit a sorority house behind Boreman, and some narrowly missed pedestrians walking through the parking lot. Fire extinguishers occasionally came flying through glass doors. "It was tough for anyone to get a good night's sleep," he recollected. At Towers, "students pulled fire alarms three and four times a night. Each time residents evacuated, and firemen and police responded. It got so bad that if a fire alarm rang, students were told not to evacuate unless they also heard air horns sounded in the elevator shafts." At Boreman Hall, the fire alarms were activated so often that the University proposed shutting them off, but the fire marshal would not give his permission. One night, Boreman students clogged the sinks, toilets, and urinals in a second-floor bathroom and turned on the water. The resulting flood ruined the cafeteria on the floor below, and food had to be brought in by truck until the damage was repaired. Afterward, the water supply was shut off during the night to prevent serious damage.[13] Finally, the approach of final exams promised to bring an end to what was a very ugly semester for the staff. Before students left for summer break, however, national events pulled the campus into the student rebellion. Although not officially called an invasion by the Nixon administration, the expansion of hostilities into Cambodia on May 1, 1970, reenergized the antiwar movement. On the nation's college campuses, antiwar protests turned violent with firebombings, gunshots, bricks, and bats. Policemen and National Guardsmen seemed much more ready to quell disturbances with violence. On Monday, May 4, 1970, on the campus of Kent State University, the Ohio National Guard confronted thousands of demonstrators, opened fire, and left four students dead and eleven people injured. For several days following the shooting, many of the nation's college campuses experienced unprecedented turmoil, and 760 of them either closed down or came to a grinding halt. A few days later, two students at traditionally black Jackson State University in Mississippi were shot by police.[14] Like the civil rights movement, which televised live into everybody's living room the treatment of African Americans, the nation witnessed police and National Guardsmen confronting "militant" white students. The difference between the previous generation of students, known more for pranks and "panty raids," and the "new breed" of students, who challenged authority and demanded political reforms, was shocking to the previous generations and especially to social conservatives.

The student demonstrations at WVU following the bombing of Cambodia and the shootings at Kent State have been interpreted either as a spontaneous outburst of anger over these events or as the result of a conspiracy of a few radicals to provoke a confrontation with the authorities.

Students and faculty believed the former, but state and University officials tended to believe the latter explanation. The evidence (and there is a lot of it) supports the conclusion that no such plot existed. Even the University's own news release claimed that most of the demonstrators were motivated by peaceful intentions.[15]

The demonstrations began on Tuesday, May 5, with an early morning vigil around four crosses erected on Oglebay Plaza in remembrance of the four Kent State students. About seventy students gathered for a midday rally on the plaza. From there they marched to the ROTC offices in Woodburn Hall, proceeded to the administrative offices at Stewart Hall, and then on to the selective service office at the county courthouse. Students carried a mock casket through the streets as they marched. As one student told a local reporter, they were just concerned about the events at Kent State, and the demonstration "grew out of this concern in a spontaneous manner." There were no reported incidents, and words like "somber" rather than "angry" characterized the mood at the end of the day.[16] For the next two days, however, the campus was in turmoil.

The following day, Wednesday, May 6, a larger crowd of about one thousand people gathered on the plaza at the center of the downtown campus, forcing the city police to divert traffic around both University and College Avenues. "Taking the streets" was intended to pressure President Harlow into signing a petition that had been delivered to his office demanding that he condemn the bombing of Cambodia and the killings at Kent State. Having received no response from Harlow, about one hundred students gathered for a rally at Oglebay Plaza around an effigy of the president in a mock coffin. The speeches were impassioned or inflammatory, depending on one's point of view, with references to the police and National Guard as "pigs" and to the Black Panther Party as an example of the only way to fight the system. Outraging nearly everybody other than the demonstrators was Professor William S. Haymond, chairman of the philosophy department, who denounced to the crowd the Cambodian intervention and the Kent State shootings. He declared that such actions were enough to make a "decent human being sick." He claimed that "we've got to protect ourselves against repression" because dissidents were "fair game" for the "bootlicking pigs." Hammond also cancelled his finals and announced that he would give everybody an "A" to demonstrate his opposition to the administration.[17]

In the afternoon, Mike Weber, a former student suspended for academic deficiencies, took the microphone and informed the crowd that President Harlow had refused to sign the petition condemning the Cambodia and Kent State actions because it was signed by "the people" rather than by individuals. A crowd of 150 students surged toward Stewart Hall chanting for the president to make an appearance. Security police blocked students from entering the building, but, when three representatives were permitted to enter, they found Harlow's office door closed. The president's assistant, Harold Shamberger, informed them that the president was at lunch and would return later that day. In a 2008 interview, and also in his reminiscences, Harold Shamberger claimed that Harlow was actually attending a meeting in Richmond, Virginia, that day. Even if he had been on campus, it is doubtful that Harlow would have signed such a petition, for he repeatedly stated his view that his personal opinion would inevitably be regarded as synonymous with the University's official position. He had also stated many times that college presidents could not function if they responded to ultimatums. Several students later claimed that if Harlow had met with them, they would have gone home, and that was the opinion of former radical student leader Scott Bills.[18]

From the administration building the students carried the mock coffin painted like the American flag and containing the effigy of Harlow to the center of University Avenue and burned them. Shouting antiwar slogans, some of the demonstrators marched to the ROTC office in Woodburn Hall. Leaderless, they milled about and then decided to return to the center of campus and block traffic. Soon city police took position and diverted traffic away from the plaza. Conservative students, mostly fraternity members and ROTC cadets, heckled the protesters and threw water balloons and rolls of toilet paper at them. One of the counter-demonstrators told a reporter that 95 percent of the campus opposed the demonstration and declared that the protesters were "a bunch of left wing radicals who want cheap publicity." The entire crowd gathered in the plaza in front of the Mountainlair, protesters and observers, totaling about one thousand people. Slowly the crowd thinned out, and at about five p.m. demonstrators began picking up trash. By 7:30 p.m. the day's demonstration was over. Local law enforcement was never far away at any point during the day. The city police directed traffic and patrolled with the campus police. The Monongalia County sheriff had nine deputies on standby, as the local detachment of the state police was in constant communication with the governor's office in Charleston. Neither law enforcement nor University officials believed violence was likely.[19]

Following a peace rally at the courthouse by local community organizations (Morgantown Citizens Concerned about Vietnam, WVU Campus Ministries, and the Women's International League for Peace and Freedom), on Thursday morning, May 7, students gathered once again on the plaza. They decided that the ROTC offices should receive another visit, and thirty or forty students descended into the basement of Woodburn and destroyed two bulletin boards, a door sign, some ROTC literature, and broke a door window; this was the only violence resulting from the demonstrations. The students then surged to the administration building to again demand that President Harlow issue a statement, but he again refused. Rebuffed and frustrated, about one hundred demonstrators withdrew to University Avenue to block traffic. A large group of counter-demonstrators had gathered in the afternoon on the other side of University Avenue to confront the hundred or so protesters, and a riot seemed about to erupt. The confrontation ended when the state police were ordered to intervene by Governor Arch Moore. Neither the University, city, nor county had requested the detachment. President Harlow claimed that he was not informed of the governor's decision even though he had been in constant contact with the state and city police and averred that "the University is state property." For his part, Governor Moore declared that if Harlow could not maintain order at the University, then he would use the state police to do so.[20] A police detachment arrived at the center of campus around 4:40 p.m. and gave the demonstrators ten minutes to clear the streets. Instead, they covered their faces with handkerchiefs in anticipation of tear gas. Several faculty and onlookers gained more time from the police to convince the demonstrators to clear the street. They agreed to cooperate if Harlow addressed them; when he refused, the demonstrators stood fast. Once again Professor

William Haymond addressed the crowd: "We will not leave the street until the pigs leave this campus," and declared that "ten pigs" should die to avenge the deaths of the students at Kent State.[21]

After nearly an hour more of discussion and inflammatory speeches, the police determined to disperse the demonstrators. About forty state and city police, armed with pistols, riot batons, shotguns, and tear gas, quick-stepped up University Avenue in a flying wedge formation to clear Grumbein's Island and University Avenue. They made two sweeps during which the crowd parted to let them through, only to regroup after each pass. A large crowd of bystanders surrounded the demonstrators, many of them hostile and shouting for the police to "bash their heads in." While the spectators shouted "Sock 'em, bust 'em, that's our custom, West, by God, Virginia!" the police again ordered the crowd to disperse and released the tear gas when they did not comply. The bystanders' cheers turned to screams when the gas drifted toward them, and a mad scramble ensued to evacuate the area. One observer concluded that the spectators were present because "to them, this is living theatre, not a possibly dangerous situation."[22]

One canister of tear gas dispersed the crowd of spectators as well as the demonstrators and prompted the protesters to parlay with the police. A truce was called and an agreement reached whereby the police would leave the campus and the students would finally clear the streets. All parties praised the police for their handling of a volatile episode that easily could have spiraled out of control. There were no injuries and no arrests, and property damage amounted to less than $100. President Harlow issued a statement summarizing the events of May 8: "Unpleasant events like today come and go in the lives of universities. We are fortunate that no one was injured and property damage was minimal. I believe that the cleavages among University groups revealed by the circumstances of the last few days are shallow enough and narrow enough that the university community will be able to heal them."[23]

Friday, May 8, was the last day of final examinations, and the campus was quiet. The state police were confined to their Evansdale barracks, and there were no demonstrations. Both groups soon returned to their homes, and the normal academic cycle appeared to have been restored. At the 101st commencement on May 17, WVU awarded more than three thousand degrees. The ceremony concluded without incident, but President Harlow was not sanguine. He informed a gathering of alumni: "I can tell you bluntly and explicitly that West Virginia University will face for a minimum of ten years trouble of the type that has befallen colleges and university campuses across the nation. We will need the support of our alumni more than ever before in the history of the school."[24]

As the protest fervor declined President Harlow's effort to remove the "radicals" intensified. The first to be disciplined was Professor William Haymond. Harlow was under serious pressure from Governor Arch Moore and the public to fire Haymond because of his "inflammatory statements" during the demonstrations, and Dean of Arts and Sciences Harold Gibbard informed Haymond that his ouster was under consideration. Gibbard reported to President Harlow that Hammond was well liked in his department and that his scholarship and teaching credentials were excellent. Dean Gibbard recommended that Haymond only be removed as department chairman, emphasizing that "poor professional judgment and poor social judgment" were insufficient reasons to fire a tenured professor.[25] Unlike those outside the academic community, Harlow understood the legal limitations imposed on his actions by tenure and freedom of speech. Harlow, therefore, removed Haymond as chair of the department, citing the professor's "display of emotional incompatibility with administrative assignment." After close investigation of Professor Haymond's actions, Harlow informed one writer, no violation of University regulations had been found, and he reported to Governor Moore that Haymond's academic abilities precluded any formal judgment against him on charges of professional incompetence as a way to sack him. President Harlow did, however, write a formal letter of reprimand to Haymond, and the professor was also required to write a formal letter of apology for making "intemperate, imprudent, and unwise" statements. This letter was subsequently published in the local paper.[26]

President Harlow took much more aggressive action against student leaders involved in the demonstrations. On June 5, the University disclosed that six students would be given a hearing before a disciplinary committee on June 24 on charges that they had destroyed University property and interfered with its operation. The students became known as the "Morgantown Six." Although they knew one another, they could not be described as friends, undermining the suggestion that they were leaders of the events that had transpired in early May 1970. Londo H. Brown, a professor of law and university attorney, informed President Harlow that denying the students readmission was indefensible unless it could be proven that they were guilty of conduct justifying their expulsion. Dean of Students Joseph Gluck reported to Harlow that no evidence existed for a criminal case linking the students with destruction of the ROTC bulletin boards, literature, or door window, and there were also insufficient grounds to bring charges against the students for breaking University regulations. Nevertheless, President Harlow chose not to heed this advice and charged the six students with violating University regulations.[27]

Meanwhile, several of the students retained Wheeling attorney H. John Rogers, joined by the noted civil liberties advocate William Kunstler, to represent them. On June 30, however, Harlow announced that the hearings would be postponed indefinitely, undoubtedly because to do otherwise would violate state and federal laws, since a few of the protesters were not enrolled as students at the time of the demonstrations. Instead, Harlow decided to turn over the files and evidence to the prosecuting attorney for Monongalia County and to the U.S. district attorney in Wheeling to determine if the students had violated state or federal laws. Both prosecutors responded immediately that they had already investigated the episode and found insufficient evidence to bring charges against the Morgantown Six.[28]

President Harlow was still determined that the students should not be reenrolled, if for no other reason than that their absence would help restore campus peace. Scott King had graduated in May; Peter Cowan was readmitted on probationary status; Mike Weber and Dan Bucca, dismissed for academic deficiencies, were to be refused readmission; Scott Bills and Stephen Stepto, permitted to take courses during the summer of 1970 in order to graduate, were to be denied admission to graduate school at WVU. Responding to Harlow's order, the Graduate School denied the admission of both Bills and Stepto on the grounds that in the past they had not abided by University regulations.[29]

Bills and Stepto's appeal of this decision to Acting President Harry Heflin was denied. Their only recourse was to take the case to court, and neither student was inclined to back down at this point. Weber and Bucca joined Bills and Stepto in taking their case to the U.S. District Court in Charleston, where the four brought suit against James Harlow, Joseph Gluck, Reginald Kraus (chair of the Committee for Student Discipline), Board of Regents Chancellor Prince B. Woodard, and Board of Regents President Early T. Andrews, seeking an injunction to block the University from denying them admission. Judge Sydney L. Christie ruled that the students were entitled to an appeals hearing at the University. Consequently, the Graduate School Admission Appeals Committee, a standing committee composed of three faculty and two graduate students, heard the students' appeal on October 6. At the conclusion of the ten-hour hearing, the committee found insufficient evidence to justify denying the admission of Bills and Stepto to graduate school and recommended that the decision of the director of admissions be reversed. Both were admitted in the spring of 1971 as graduate students. Mike Weber was readmitted in the spring of 1972 on a probationary basis; Bucca did not return.[30]

Even though the May 1970 demonstrations proved to be a relatively brief anomaly, Harlow's view of the future turned morose. In October 1970 he appealed to the faculty to be stalwart in the face of any further campus disruptions. He believed that the University was "under attack from within and without," that the "lines of distrust" between faculty and students were "more serious than terrorism." His fears proved to be unfounded, for the campus observed the rest of the politically tumultuous seventies without serious disruption. The *Daily Athenaeum* echoed the general consensus that had emerged by the early seventies that the "new breed" of students on the nation's campuses, including WVU, was concerned with the social, political, and economic changes that were transforming post-World War II America. With the abandonment of *in loco parentis*, students became adults who demanded respect for their individual freedoms. Like other college presidents, Harlow was forced to accept these much belated changes.[31]

By the winter of 1975, a very disillusioned President James G. Harlow communicated with alumni a similar message to the one delivered to the

Faculty Assembly during the previous fall semester. Even though it seemed "huge, impersonal, and impervious," the University was less about bricks and mortar than "a thing of the human spirit"; therefore, it was "as fragile as a blown egg." Great care must be taken or the University would be seriously damaged, and the best students and faculty would go elsewhere. Harlow identified the institution's greatest threats as inadequate funding, salaries, and space, all of which were the result of the stranglehold of the Board of Regents on University operations.[32]

Even though the University was strained under Board of Regents controls, it nonetheless grew exponentially during Harlow's presidency. During his tenure, Harlow facilitated the establishment of the Board of Regents but then became disillusioned with the system. He fell out with its first chancellor, Prince B. Woodard, and his relationship with the second chancellor, Ben Morton, did not improve. Harlow also supported the Kanawha Valley Graduate Center, but in the end the Board of Regents stripped it from WVU's control. He presided during the embarrassment of the construction of the Personal Rapid Transit (PRT), although he exerted little control over the project. He courageously argued for civil liberties, race, and gender equality, particularly in athletics and among faculty and staff, and he fought for his vision of the University as a self-governing community of scholars. Finally, James Harlow often proclaimed his aversion to physical exercise, and yet he oversaw the greatest physical expansion of athletic facilities ever undertaken at WVU with the construction of the Coliseum, new Mountaineer field (Milan Puskar Stadium), and the Natatorium, along with the Law Center and the Mountainlair.[33]

Yet his refusal to negotiate with radical students during campus protests in 1972 linked him with the state police breakup of the antiwar demonstrations. In his reminiscence on the years he served as an assistant to the president, Harold Shamberger claimed that Harlow's unresponsiveness to the protesters adversely affected how the various constituencies viewed the president. "The deference with which he had been treated in the past turned to ridicule by some, scorn by others, and lack of confidence by many, including a few members of the governing board. While hard-liners demanded a crackdown on protesters, Harlow knew that the consequences would be dire for squelching free speech and dissent in the one place that encouraged students to do just that."[34] A pessimistic tone permeated his final state of the University address before the Faculty Assembly on April 27, 1977. He predicted that, despite his best efforts, faculty salaries at WVU would continue to lag behind their counterparts nationally, and that the negative image created by student unrest and poor relations with the Board of Regents would continue into the foreseeable future. Although the outgoing president believed that the high demand for coal, a result of the energy shortage of the late seventies, would continue to stimulate the state's economy, he also worried that construction of the new football stadium might create serious financial difficulties for the University in the future. The new stadium had been thrust upon him, but Harlow responded to the politicians' initiative because "the legislature giveth, the legislature taketh away, and those of us who work in the state listen carefully to it."[35] The *Charleston Gazette-Mail* had selected James G. Harlow as "West Virginian of the Year" for 1975; it was the first time in the award's twenty-five-year history that a college president was named. The newspaper cited the progress made by WVU during Harlow's eight-year tenure, noting specifically the building program, which hoisted the University into "the ranks of quality institutions around the nation."[36]

The spring edition of the *Alumni News* commented on the absence of a "long, laudatory article" on the president, who was to retire on June 30, 1977. "This was certainly not an oversight on our part," the column read, "but in the quiet, unassuming manner in which he has always acted, Dr. Harlow has let it be known that he wishes to leave quietly." In accordance with Harlow's wishes, the *Alumni News* simply thanked the president for his long, dedicated service to the University.[37] When he died the following year, the *Dominion-Post* declared that James Harlow would probably "best be remembered because he presided over a growth of 75 percent in the University enrollment and the completion of more than $100 million in construction and expansion of facilities." Similarly, the chairman of the WVU Advisory Board, Charles C. Wise Jr., observed: "Under his quiet command, the University has taken one of the greatest leaps forward intellectually in its history."[38] Harry Ernst, who served on Harlow's staff, said of the former president, "He offended more people than I'm sure he could count. . . . Yet, I could not think of a more competent University president nor one who took greater pride to base his decisions on principle."[39]

STUDENT BODY PROFILE

The student body totaled 17,000 in 1972–1973, about one-quarter of them graduate or professional students. According to the University's own 1973 Self Study, the academic ability of entering freshmen, as measured by ACT scores, was equal to most PhD-granting institutions generally and in recent years was above the average for such institutions. The student body, therefore, "exceeds the national norms for all institutions of higher learning." A majority probably were first-generation college students. In a May 1973 sample of 950 graduating seniors, 45 percent reported that their fathers had attended college and 33 percent that their mothers had.[40]

A *Barron's* capsule profile of the student body in 1973 provides an excellent snapshot. WVU was classified as "competitive" in its selection of students who averaged ACT scores of 21.9. Of 6,188 who applied in 1972, 3,702 were admitted, and 2,900 actually enrolled. Approximately 25 percent of the students commuted to campus from the surrounding area; 68 percent were West Virginia residents; 20 percent came from the Northeast; 5 percent the South; and 5 percent the Central and West regions. Out-of-state students represented all forty-nine other states. Foreign students accounted for only 2 percent of the total but hailed from fifty foreign countries. The publishers found it significant that the University had sent seventeen Rhodes Scholars to Oxford, had produced thirty-four Fulbright Scholars, and ranked among the top five state universities in the percentage of graduates listed in *Who's Who in America*.[41]

In describing the "typical WVU student" to Barron's, University administrators characterized the student body as "mildly conservative, not extremist, not rebellious, not given to demonstrations or destructive actions. They're easy to work with, polite, diplomatic, from small communities generally." Moreover, "only a small minority have become involved in the struggles for social action. They are generally seeking upward mobility in choosing their professions. Most of them choose WVU because it is the state school, because it has the reputation as the finest university in West Virginia." According to one student, "you get to know your fellow students and profs here; teachers are glad to give you the extra help you may need." What the students found frustrating were the scattered campuses and heavy traffic.[42]

Barron's regarded the extracurricular programs at WVU to be the most important part of the educational opportunities outside of the classroom. They counted nearly two hundred recognized student organizations, including academic, athletic, honorary, religious, special interest groups, and service clubs. Among the most popular was the student newspaper, the *Daily Athenaeum*, which was established in the nineteenth century and had won several All-American awards. The report noted that "Women's Lib" was "becoming active," and "Gay Lib" was "beginning to make a showing." Among the new student organizations was the Black Unity Organization for the slowly growing number of African American students on campus, and Student Action for Appalachian Progress (SAAP), which sponsored big-brother and big-sister efforts, visitation of the elderly, home repairs, tutoring, and day-care centers. Between four hundred and five hundred students participated in these organizations. "WVU has an active participating student body," *Barron's* concluded.[43]

The University provided a lively cultural environment as well. The *Barron's* survey reported that WVU was a cultural center for the entire state. Students did not need to travel to other cities or other campuses for cultural stimulation. Thousands attended WVU programs, which brought in famous performers, such as Grand Funk, Chicago, Blood/Sweat/Tears, the Bob Hope Show, the Harlem Globe Trotters, and the Royal Philharmonic to the Morgantown area. Several lecture, film, and pop art series flourished, along with some eighty dramatic and two hundred musical productions and concerts per year. As one student reportedly observed, "The problem here is to decide what to skip—there's a tremendous lot going on culturally, and nearly all of it is right here on the campus."[44]

A decade later the number of students had grown, but the student body profile had not changed markedly. Enrollment for the fall of 1982 on the main campus was 19,177. Another 1,105 were enrolled at Potomac State, and 2,160 "off campus," mostly part-time graduate students in education were enrolled at one of the graduate centers. Undergraduates in Morgantown numbered roughly 15,000. Every county in West Virginia was represented in the student body, and all forty-nine of the other fifty states. Because of its close proximity and tuition that was comparatively low even for out-of-state students, the University drew most heavily from Pennsylvania (16 percent of the total). WVU also enrolled students from eighty-three foreign countries.[45]

Out-of-state students, including international students, accounted for 38 percent of the total enrollment, more than 40 percent of undergraduate enrollment, 28 percent of graduate enrollment, and 13 percent of the Schools of Dentistry, Medicine, and Law together. The student body was 96 percent Caucasian. Only 477 (about 2.5 percent) were African American. Asians or Pacific Islanders totaled 139, Hispanics 71, and Native Americans just 12. There were students from a variety of other countries, but only a light sprinkling. The student body mirrored the state, with most coming from rural areas or small towns. Well more than half came from places with fewer than 25,000 residents. A high percentage were first-generation college students, less likely to contemplate graduate school early in their student careers, and less receptive to disciplines with no apparent marketplace value, such as the humanities. The student body was relatively strong scholastically. The entering class for 1982–1983 had an average ACT composite score of 20.1, and a high-school grade-point average of 3.1. This compared favorably with the national averages of 18.7 and 3.0, respectively, and on par with the cross-section of doctoral degree granting institutions that used the ACT for admissions.[46]

WVU continued its relatively open undergraduate admissions policy for in-state students, while out-of-state students were admitted selectively. A special recruitment initiative to attract African American students was underway in major metropolitan areas out of state and in West Virginia communities, which, if successful, would help to diversify the student body.

Universities have always been more than institutions where students attend classes. Therefore, their attitudes are important and frequently sought out. WVU's graduating seniors in 1984 expressed satisfaction with their decision to attend WVU. In the fifth such survey since 1973, WVU sociologists Ann L. Paterson and Harold A. Gibbard polled the 441 members of the class of 1984 to obtain student opinions of WVU and its educational programs.[47] Student assessments were a major focus of the 1984 Self-Study Report prepared for the University's ten-year reaccreditation appraisal by the North Central Association of Colleges and Schools. The results of the survey revealed that WVU students were attracted by practical considerations such as cost and the quality of the program in their major field of study. Ranked from first through third were cost, in-state residence, and, tied in third place, nearness to home and quality of program. Athletic programs seem to have counted for little in terms of attracting students. As might be expected with undergraduates, family was the most important source of funding, with 81 percent ranking it as the primary or secondary source. Nearly one-half of the students took out loans, while government grants helped another one-quarter. Well more than one-half of the students earned some of the funds to pay for their education with full or part-time jobs. The student financial aid office estimated that the total cost of attending WVU for a nine-month academic year was $4,350 for single in-state students living either on or off campus, and $2,800 for those living at home. For nonresidents, the respective costs were $5,400 and $3,900.[48]

Students were asked to rate the importance of five traditionally accepted undergraduate objectives on a scale of one (low) to five (high). As expected, students attached high importance to career preparation, with 87 percent rating it four or five. Good grades also were important, with 85 percent rating it four or five. Counterintuitively, students regarded intellectual development as even more important than career preparation, with 95 percent rating it four or five, prompting the surveyors to speculate that students might not be as vocationally oriented as they seemed. Gaining an understanding of political, social, economic, and international issues was also important, with 74 percent rating this goal of education at four or five. "While the old myth of West Virginia University as a party school will not die, the reality is that perhaps one-fifth or one-quarter of the students place high store in these events," the report declared. This determination was based on questionnaire data revealing that the number of students rating the importance of social events at four or five was much lower than might be expected.[49]

Morgantown residents and WVU staff liked to believe that local people were "friendly," and student surveys supported that perception. Students found other students and faculty "friendly" by a significant majority as well. In the community, city churches were rated very highly, but merchants were less favorably viewed. Interestingly, landlords were regarded as "cordial." The students were generally "happy" that they decided to attend WVU. More than two-thirds of them would make the same choice again, and nearly three-quarters of the students replied that they would advise a close friend or relative to attend WVU. Notably, there were no significant gender differences.[50]

CAMPUS LIFE

The use of alcohol among students is a perennial concern of college administrators. "Beer! The blood of students," was a graffito scrawled on the wall of a fifteenth-century tavern in Cambridge, England, according to former newspaperman James F. Dent, an anecdote which reminds us that the link between students and alcohol is an ancient one. The popular columnist and editorial cartoonist for the *Charleston Gazette* (WVU '52) was happy to fulfill the request of the WVU *Alumni Magazine* in 1983 to find out "where today's students seek relief from the rigors of scholarship." In fact, feeling that he had earned some legitimate credentials during his student days to undertake the assignment, he declared it "an offer I could not refuse." Even though he was "familiar with the territory," in three decades "many of the landmarks had disappeared or changed." Reflecting his keen sense of humor, Dent observed that he would need a student guide because "if anyone my age wandered into a student bierstube, he would be mistaken either for a cop or a parent."[51] Two students volunteered to lead Dent on a one-night tour of Morgantown's student "watering holes." Much had changed, but the bars were still plentiful, and "basically the kids are still doing the same thing we were doing," he observed. However, as he got older, he had come to prefer to drink his beer in places with some "creature comforts," such as padded chairs, pleasant servers, muted music, and a "complete absence" of video game distractions. The places he visited with his student guides lacked "all such amenities." His advice for alumni of his age who wanted to quench their thirst in bars frequented by students was to possess "an amazing tolerance for noise and crowds of people jammed together."[52]

Relaxing with friends over some cold brews had a darker side for some students. Excessive use of alcohol was a persistent problem, and WVU tried to curb abuse with education and counseling, or with clinical help for those who would accept it. By the 1980s, studies to determine the extent of the problem were commonplace. Educating students about the dangers of excessive drinking was undertaken primarily by resident directors and assistants in the dormitories. There was no way to determine the scope of the problem among students who lived off campus unless they asked the counseling service for help, but alcohol abuse was definitely a problem in the dorms where beer was allowed. In 1983, one of the counselors reported, "there were more than 100 persons disciplined for rowdy, disruptive behavior, destruction of property, and vandalism. Almost all of the incidents were directly related to alcohol abuse."[53]

Alcohol abuse was prevalent enough that the administration began to take a more proactive position. In the fall of 1984, guidelines were drafted for the president's cabinet on "Marketing Alcoholic Beverages on Campus." These were intended to update rather than supersede previous guidelines. The prefatory comment to the document stated: "Alcohol abuse poses a serious threat to the health and welfare of a large segment of the college student population through acts of vandalism and property damage, automobile and other types of accidents, lessening of academic performance, estrangement of social relations, creation of mental health and physiological problems, and, in some cases bodily injury, illness, and death. . . . Inappropriate and irresponsible marketing and promotion of beverage alcohol on campus" can contribute to the problems of alcohol abuse. Therefore, the guidelines were intended to control the promotion and marketing of alcoholic beverages on campus by banning images that glorified drinking, the offering of free samples, the sponsoring of drinking contests, and other promotional devices that targeted the student population.[54]

In loco parentis had been abandoned, and the new relationship between students and the University presumed students were adults and, therefore, responsible for their own behavior. A WVU football player arrested for public intoxication might be suspended from the team, but a student participating in an off-campus street riot could not be disciplined by the University. The jurisdictional issue was a legal gray area because WVU had no authority to discipline students for off-campus activities unless they resulted in arrest or conviction. Although the University could initiate a disciplinary action within the state's legal system, it had never opted to do so. WVU could suspend a student only for offenses occurring on the campus. Students might be barred from extracurricular activities if their actions were damaging to the institution, but the institution could not assume jurisdiction for the off-campus actions of students. "Things have changed," Dean Henry Collins of the WVU College of Law informed a reporter in 1979. "We have an adult student body today, and the school doesn't stand in the place of parents."[55]

On-campus discipline was aggravated by the presence of alcohol. With the addition of beer sold at the Blue Tick Tavern in the Mountainlair, the increase in incidents at the Lair prompted administrators at the student union to request a full-time guard to be posted at the student union in the fall of 1980. Security provided a list of sixty-two separate incidents that occurred in the Mountainlair between August 24 and October 14, 1984. Underage drinking in the tavern was common, as were fighting, throwing beer, damaging property, vandalism, and theft, with some occurring "on a more or less continuing basis."[56]

A support system centered on residence directors and assistants existed for students living in University residence halls, but off-campus students could easily fly under the radar of counseling services. Only 3,500 students, 20 percent of the student body, lived in University housing. Personal problems undetected by counseling services could be brought to the University's attention dramatically, without either warning or an opportunity to help. For example, after several previous attempts one student committed suicide by self-inflicted gunshot while alone in his apartment. Another student suffering from depression left campus without notifying the University or her parents. One student became despondent over poor academic performance and began drinking excessively. To help detect these problems among the vast majority of the student body who lived off campus, the Student Neighbor Project was developed in 1981, one of the first of its kind in the nation. The city was divided into sixty neighborhoods and seven regions, each region under a student regional coordinator who was responsible for finding the home locations of his or her students. The role of the student neighbors, as they were called, was to relate information to students, listen to their concerns, make monthly contacts, and assist students who seemed to need help by calling the Off-Campus Housing Office.[57]

The Task Force on Quality of Life in University-Owned Residence Halls surveyed approximately one thousand freshmen students during the spring semester of 1986. The purpose was to provide the University with information regarding the students' experiences in the residence halls, both "very positive" as well as "might be improved." Student responses were interesting. Overwhelmingly, they found that living in the dorms was advantageous for the following reasons: accessibility to campus, academic programs provided in the residence hall, academic advice available, opportunity to make friends, security, prepared meals, maid service, and predictability of expenses. They also found the residence hall staff to be helpful. Questioned how often they witnessed or experienced acts of discrimination by sex, race, handicap, ethnicity, or religion, they encouragingly responded rarely or never. Counterintuitively, noise was a problem only occasionally, but, as might be expected, use of alcohol and drugs in the residence halls was common if not flagrant. On the other hand, they also overwhelmingly responded that visitation policies were violated, as were overnight visits by members of the opposite sex. Students also felt safe in the residence halls, although the vast majority of them were concerned about the theft of their possessions at least to some degree. Following this positive feedback, it is somewhat surprising that 86.1 percent of students did not intend to live in a University residence hall the following year. West Virginia residents made up 56.3 percent and non-West Virginians 43.7 percent of the respondents.[58]

President Bucklew's administration brought a new emphasis on international education, and the Board of Regents was highly supportive of this thrust. The University's Honors Program in particular took steps to promote a stronger international exchange program as a method for attracting students who wanted the opportunity to expand their horizons by spending a year abroad. The Honors Program expected 340 students to be enrolled in the fall of 1987, twice the number as in 1982. To qualify for the program, entering freshmen needed a combined ACT score of 27 to 29 and a 3.8 minimum grade-point average.[59]

The University also attempted to attract foreign students, and the number of foreign faculty and graduate assistants teaching introductory courses in the classroom increased. So did the problems. WVU student government informed a meeting of the Board of Regents in the fall of 1986 that "some students cannot understand foreign-born teachers, and requested that unintelligible instructors be removed from the classroom." The student government representative proposed that "if 90 percent of the students in a class can't understand the teacher's English, the instructor would be removed." The proposal called for a panel of students and faculty to hear complaints from students and to sit in on the particular classes to determine the legitimacy of the complaints. If warranted, the instructor could be removed. The issue, not unique to WVU, focused on foreign graduate assistants in the sciences, who hailed from India, China, Taiwan, Iran, Malaysia, South Korea, Spain, and Venezuela. The Board of Regents did not approve the proposal, opting instead for an overall faculty development plan "rather than singling out a particular population," which seemed like a "punitive approach" to solving the problem.[60] Of course many of these students could not afford to attend WVU without teaching assistantships. Many were also talented budding scientists and engineers who were needed by research faculty in order to maintain a critical mass of researchers in their respective fields.

Student newspapers play an important educational role on campuses, but they can cause problems for administrators. Explaining to the student affairs staff how the student newspaper, the *Daily Athenaeum*, was operated, Managing Editor Ken Ward Jr. declared that "the *Athenaeum* does not want to offend readers. But much of what is news everyday offends someone." Some who took offense were clearly fringe elements, but some were not. Chief Judge Larry V. Starcher of the Seventeenth Circuit Court complained to President Bucklew in September 1986 about an advertisement that he personally did not think belonged in "our State University school paper," and he was certain "many other state citizens and parents of WVU students (as I am) might feel the same way." His objection was to the advertisement for "JB Gold Cigarette Paper," which he argued was "drug paraphernalia in a 1986 college setting." He suggested that "those in charge" of the paper should review its advertising policy. In a postscript, the judge added: "Personally, I would allow neither tobacco [n]or alcoholic beverages advertising, let alone 'drug paraphernalia.'" President Bucklew replied that the Student Publication Committee was the appropriate body to consider the matter and informed Judge Starcher that he had brought it to the attention of the committee chairman.[61]

A few months later Judge Starcher wrote again about a few more advertisements that he considered "in bad taste." Assuring the president that he did not want to be a "pest," Starcher nevertheless suggested that these advertisements also be forwarded to the Student Publication Committee for review. "While I admittedly have extremely conservative personal values," the judge wrote, "I also have a daughter who is a student at WVU and from time to time have to deal with students in my official capacity. It is my contention that we should strive to create and maintain a student environment to which parents want to send their children." He added a postscript: "Is this good journalism training? My daughter is in pre-journalism." President Bucklew responded that he too found the advertisements to be "in bad taste" and wished he had "a simple way of resolving this issue. Obviously, there are limitations on my imposing my will and judgment on that of a newspaper." He pointed out that university administrations had little control over student newspapers even though they do try to influence students to exercise "good judgment and to practice good journalism." Even if a faculty adviser tried to guide the students, "the students are not always totally receptive to the advice and suggestions made. Many people assume the University can control and should control the content of the newspaper. The courts have made it clear that that is not to be the case."[62]

On occasion the *Daily Athenaeum* seemed to threaten the city's paper, the *Dominion Post*. The publisher of the *Dominion Post*, David A. Raese, contacted Bucklew in February 1989 because he had "become increasingly concerned about the expanded distribution" of the student paper and requested a private meeting to discuss the issue.[63] Following their March meeting, Bucklew wrote to Raese that he had reviewed the publisher's concerns with the *Daily Athenaeum*'s staff and regarded their response as positive. The *DA* served the University community primarily and "does not view itself as a competitor of the *Dominion Post* even though many people read both papers," Bucklew wrote. The *DA* provided a learning experience for students, and "we believe that can be done without pursuing an unfair competitive attitude." Distribution of the *DA* was Raese's obvious concern. The *DA*'s current distribution was about 14,500 copies, but fewer than one thousand copies were being distributed to sites outside the University or its affiliated units. In the thirty or so non-University locations, "the site is an advertiser or place where students congregate. That appears a reasonable approach."[64]

The recruitment and retention of qualified students was essential for the University in order to maintain the size of the student body, which determined the level of state funding. The enrollment of approximately 23,000 students in 1994 was a relatively small number to support the 176 degree programs offered by WVU. Although some suggested paring back these programs to save money, these programs, located as they were at the state's comprehensive, land-grant institution, were vital for West Virginia's development. This pivotal role was also expressed in a study prepared by the Regional Research Institute:

The people of West Virginia lag far behind the nation in educational attainment. A generation ago, West Virginia's children found well-paying jobs in manufacturing and mining. Those jobs required little formal education, and West Virginians responded by having the nation's lowest percentage of adults with college degrees, only 10 percent as of the 1980 census. Since then the economic situation has changed. Between 1979 and 1990, the state lost almost two-fifths of its manufacturing and mining jobs. West Virginia University is playing an important role in the upward mobility of the region's children.

Seventy percent of the mothers and sixty percent of the fathers of WVU students did not graduate from college; more than half the undergraduates are the first generation in their family to attend college. In that respect, many West Virginia University students are in the same situation as many minority students.[65]

Therefore, WVU's position was to make a strong commitment to providing access to higher education for West Virginians and to recruit quality students. The University's entering freshmen consistently exceeded the national averages on standardized tests. In 1991, for example, entering freshmen had an average ACT score of 22.1 compared with the 20.6 national average, and an SAT average of 911 compared with the national average of 896. WVU's 1993 retention rate of 66 percent was the highest among state institutions, and its graduation rate was competitive with the Southern Regional Education Board peers. Reaffirming what had been known for some time, one of the main reasons WVU attracted quality students was that "in this rural state with no strong tradition of higher education, the best students tend to enroll at the large, comprehensive university. Moreover, in keeping with its mission to 'seek out, challenge, educate, and help create opportunities for those West Virginia citizens who can benefit from its programs,' the University actively recruits those students." The Scholars Program, established in 1987, provided more than 1,800 scholarships each year, 90 percent of which went to in-state students. In addition to University awards, the colleges actively solicited funds for scholarships. The Eberly College of Arts and Sciences, for example, provided awards to twenty-seven students in 1993 through seventeen endowed scholarships. The Department of Intercollegiate Athletics also provided scholarships for athletes. For graduate education the range of scholarships, fellowships, and assistantships was deep and diverse. The University Honors Program also provided an enriching environment for motivated undergraduates through special courses and residence in the honors dormitory, Stalnaker Hall (the former Women's Hall), which was remodeled for the purpose in 1993. The University also promoted numerous educational development opportunities for African American and economically disadvantaged students.[66]

Internal and external reviews of degree programs ensured instructional quality. Sixty-nine programs were accredited by the appropriate professional agency, and all 176 degree programs participated in the periodic Board of Trustees program-reviews, which included the on-going process of student learning assessment. Student evaluation of instruction was a standard feature at the end of the semester. Even though WVU did not mandate such a policy, these evaluations were part of the documentation used in annual faculty evaluations, which determined promotion and tenure. That they were widely used is demonstrated by the fact that the faculty secretary's office reported in 1994 that two thousand requests for the forms were received each semester. Among those responding to WVU's graduating student questionnaire in 1994, 84.3 percent believed that preparation in their major was as good or better than was available at any other public institution, 88.8 percent were satisfied with the curriculum, and 81.8 percent were either "pleased" or "highly pleased" that they had attended WVU and would choose to enroll again if they could do so.[67]

In their conviction that they had made the right decision in selecting WVU, the students of "Generation X" were much like the Baby Boomers. The Boomers of the sixties had changed student life in profound ways by challenging authority and demanding more individual freedoms and recognition of the rights of minority populations. The students who replaced them were much more career-oriented, but the generational process itself remained intact: the world the Boomers fought for, Generation Xers took as a birthright.

THE GAME CHANGES:
INTERCOLLEGIATE ATHLETICS

PRESIDENT JAMES HARLOW demonstrated little interest in athletics, but, as WVU historians William Doherty and Festus Summers observed, "he presided over the greatest expansion of athletic facilities in WVU history." However, he exerted neither influence nor control over the decisions to build new major facilities, especially the Coliseum and Mountaineer Field. Harlow encountered the hard reality that intercollegiate athletics at state universities has a life of its own beyond the control of presidents and governing boards. His request that the Board of Governors reconsider the new Coliseum plan to make it more versatile than a single-purpose basketball court was not heeded; his request that the Board of Regents approve the construction of the Evansdale Library before the Natatorium was also ignored; and his suggestion that the old Mountaineer Field be renovated was brushed aside by the legislature and governor in favor of a new $20 million stadium and a $4.5 million shell building.[1] The fans had spoken through their public servants, and the state's priorities for WVU came into sharp focus for President Harlow.

INTEGRATING BASKETBALL

Harlow had just occupied the president's chair in 1967 when the question of constructing a new basketball facility came across his desk. Multiple competing opinions on its merits made this project a contentious issue. The Board of Governors had awarded an $8.86 million contract to a Charlotte, North Carolina firm to construct a round, mushroom-shaped concrete building. The price tag soon rose to $10 million, and many questioned spending one-half of the construction funds allocated to the University on a single facility. Many argued that a greater need existed for classroom facilities, noting that English Department faculty taught classes in six different buildings, and that biology classes as large as seven hundred met in a downtown theater. Questioning who held decision-making authority, Dean of Law Paul Selby claimed that the ultimate decision rested with the faculty, and the Faculty Senate recommended that construction on the new arena should be delayed. The Morgantown paper editorialized in September 1967 that everybody's voice had been heard except those who would pay for the project: students and parents. The *Dominion Post*, however, sympathized with Athletic Director Robert N. Brown's defense of the project. Brown understood that classrooms were crowded, but his department had outgrown its facilities too, and an arena was "urgently needed." Meanwhile, the *Post* declared that, "throughout the state, thousands of basketball fans are shouting, 'Build that Arena.'"[2]

President Harlow and the Board of Governors understood the wisdom of acquiescing to the wishes of Brown and the fans. The old field house was forty years old, and the interest in WVU basketball had grown so much that a 14,000-seat single-purpose arena, which would double the seating capacity of the old arena and be devoted strictly to basketball, was now a necessity. When the president supported the plan, the hometown paper applauded the recommendation as a "courageous and progressive decision that will serve this state well." On December 1, 1970, WVU met Colgate on the floor of the new 14,000-seat Coliseum in the first game played in the new home of Mountaineer hoops.[3] There was a certain kind of logic to building the Coliseum at the beginning of the University's second century and following its decision to leave the Southern Conference in order to play at a higher level of competition.

When Fred Schaus resigned as WVU's basketball coach to become the general manager of the Los Angeles Lakers in 1960, his trusted assistant George King took up the reins. He left the program in good hands. During the late forties King played college basketball at Morris Harvey College in Charleston, where he was the nation's leading scorer among small-college players. He continued his starring role with the Syracuse Nationals of the National Basketball Association, and led his team to the championship in 1955. Schaus hired King as WVU's first full-time assistant basketball coach, and King was elevated to the position of head coach following Schaus's departure, continuing what had become a tradition of hiring coaches with a tie to the state. Schaus and King had recruited another sensational West Virginia player in Rod Thorn, whom fans expected to replace Jerry West. This was a heavy burden for a young man to bear, and he unwittingly increased that pressure by wearing the same jersey number as West, "44." But Rod Thorn was also very bright, and he planned to become a medical doctor. Duke University, with its major medical school and offer of a basketball scholarship, tried to lure him away, but the state legislature passed a resolution declaring Thorn a "natural resource" and urged him to play at WVU. The University had just launched its own medical school, and Thorn decided that attending WVU would help him establish a practice in his home state.[4]

Thorn did in fact join the ranks of WVU basketball legends, becoming one of the star guards who led the team during the second golden era. Over the course of his three varsity years, Thorn averaged 21.8 points and 11 rebounds per game. In 1962 and 1963, Thorn was named an All-American and was picked third overall in the 1963 NBA draft by the Baltimore Bullets. He went on to play professionally for eight seasons, followed by coaching assignments in the old American Basketball Association and the NBA, before taking the position of general manager of the Chicago Bulls. Thorn then moved into NBA management to become a senior vice president. George King brought other talented players to WVU as well. For example, two other guards, Lee Patrone and Jim McCormick, were star guards in their own right, and both played professionally. King's five seasons as head coach at WVU, 1960–1965, were highly successful; his record of 102-43 was second only to Schaus's record of 146-37. He won three Southern Conference championships and three NCAA tournament games, but, after losing four key players, 1964 and 1965 were rebuilding years. His win-loss record had the die-hard fans calling for his job, and a few went so far as to burn him in effigy on Woodburn Circle. King realized his time was up, and he

Chapter Twelve

quickly accepted a job offer from Purdue. If Thorn felt the pressure of filling the shoes of Jerry West, King must have faced equally high fan expectations in following Fred Schaus.[5]

The extension of the "golden era" of basketball and construction of the Coliseum were historic landmarks in the athletics program, but the most significant long-term change was the integration of intercollegiate sports. The implications reached far beyond athletics to the University and to the entire state of West Virginia. When King left for Purdue, he did not leave the "cupboard bare." In fact, his replacement, Bucky Waters, found one of the greatest players in the country, Ron "Fritz" Williams, coming up from the 1965 freshman team, which had compiled a win-loss record of 20–1. King had successfully recruited the high school All-American from Weirton, another high profile home-state guard in the Hundley/West/Thorn mold. But it had not been easy. Williams's mother was concerned that WVU basketball was still not integrated as it was at the other institutions he was considering, among them Ohio State and Michigan, and she was reluctant for her son to accept the scholarship. King took Athletic Director Red Brown with him to visit the family, and both assured them that Ron would encounter no problems in Morgantown because of his race. King finally resolved this concern by recruiting three other African Americans to enter the program with Williams: Jim Lewis of Washington, DC, ex-Marine Norman Holmes, and Williams's teammate at Weir High, Ed Harvard. Holmes, the former Marine, reportedly took on the role of "looking after" Ron. These four players made history by being the first to integrate a WVU basketball team and by making their team the first in the Southern Conference to be integrated. In 2004, King told a reporter that he was unaware of both historical markers. The coach said that he "never sat in on any plan to integrate our program. I don't remember there being any expressed idea from anyone that we were integrating the Southern Conference. It was a situation where we were simply looking for the best players we could recruit."[6]

Williams encountered few problems while attending WVU. West Virginians liked him because, like Thorn and West, he was a great player, a native, and an unassuming star. Norman Julian, an avid basketball fan and writer who attended WVU at the same time as Williams, claimed that "if a poll had been taken, 'Fritz,' I believe, would have been voted most popular student." He was the right person to integrate WVU basketball, with the right mixture of dignity, even-tempered maturity, and a ready smile. The fact that he was the Southern Conference Player of the Year in 1968 speaks volumes about Williams's talent and character, especially considering the massive resistance to integration in the region where WVU's competition was located.[7]

The African American population in Morgantown during the mid-sixties was very small, and social opportunities for young black men were limited. Basic services catering to blacks, like barber shops, radio stations, and nightclubs were marginal to non-existent. Moreover, they found even fewer black students at WVU, and the institution had not yet made any special provisions to ease their transition to life on an overwhelmingly white campus. The transition was, therefore, difficult even though Williams told Julian: "I never had anyone say anything bad to me." When he and his black teammates did encounter racial hostility, it was when they played on the road. Williams related an episode at an away game when fans sitting behind the WVU bench expressed their prejudice too vigorously, and trainer Whitey Gwynne squirted them with his water bottle. Years later, Jim Lewis recalled encountering blatant racism only when they were playing away, and Richmond, Virginia, seems to have been the worst Southern venue. According to Lewis, at the University of Richmond the team ran onto the floor over the emblem of a confederate soldier while the band played "I Wish I Was in Dixie." "We were beating them pretty badly and we began hearing the racial epithets," he recalled. Teammate Ed Harvard added, "Richmond was the worst experience. Those people were outright calling us every name in the book. We had to have a police escort and have the cops take us in because those people were vicious back then."[8]

George King recruited Williams, but had moved on to Purdue before his young player moved up to the varsity squad. King's game, like Fred Schaus's emphasized the skill of his playmakers, but Bucky Waters preferred set plays, making his style less suited to an explosive scorer like Williams. Raymond "Bucky" Waters played basketball at North Carolina State, and then became a freshman coach after his graduation in 1958. He was serving as number one assistant coach at Duke University when he accepted the position at WVU, making him the youngest major college basketball coach in the nation. The rising sophomore team was rated one of the top five freshman teams in the country. Bucky Waters played an instrumental role in convincing the administration to build the Coliseum. Norman Julian says he "typified a new breed of coach that has since become the standard. He was articulate and stressed public relations." He encouraged students to support the team, appeared on statewide weekly television shows, instituted a dress code for the team, and took other novel steps. The nation and WVU were changing rapidly in the sixties, and "Waters was suited to lead WVU into a less parochial future," Julian wrote.[9]

It was a notable moment in the history of athletics when, on April 5, 1968, WVU announced its departure from the Southern Conference. The University had joined the conference in 1950 as a "marriage of convenience" for facilitating the scheduling of all sports and to provide a mechanism for qualifying for the NCAA playoffs in basketball and baseball, as well as lucrative television contracts for football. However, the conference changed dramatically in 1953 when North Carolina, North Carolina State, Duke, Wake Forest, South Carolina, Clemson, and Maryland withdrew to form the Atlantic Coast Conference, leaving WVU as the only large public university remaining in the Southern Conference. With these major institutions gone, and disappointed that the new conference chose to invite Virginia rather than WVU, the University chose to become an independent. WVU publicists noted that since World War II and the presidency of Irwin Stewart, the University's identification was more "Eastern" than "Southern," and its ties were much closer to long-standing rivals Pitt, Penn State, and Syracuse than to the Southern schools.[10]

The basketball program took a quantum leap in scheduling when WVU became independent. It now faced big-time programs like Kentucky, Ohio State, Florida, and St. John's and could no longer improve its record by feasting on the weaker teams in the Southern Conference. Bucky Waters amassed consecutive 19–9 records in each of his first three seasons at WVU, but the 1969 squad lacked experience. Following the disappointing 1969 season, Waters accepted an offer to coach at Duke. Waters's controlled style of play diminished the unique individual skills of Ron "Fritz" Williams, but he cooperated by playing within the system for the good of the team. Nevertheless, professional team scouts recognized his talent, and he went on to a successful career in professional basketball with the San Francisco Warriors and Milwaukee Bucks. In 1993 he was elected to the WVU Hall of Fame. Wil Robinson, another highly sought after player recruited by Waters, became the next All-American to fill the large gap left by the graduation of Williams.[11] Bucky Waters regretted not having the opportunity to coach in the Coliseum, but he left an enduring legacy by overseeing the smooth racial integration of WVU basketball.

Waters was immediately replaced as head coach by Garland E. "Sonny" Moran whom Bucky Waters had hired as his number one assistant coach in 1965. He was a teammate of George King at Morris Harvey College and had a very successful career as head coach at his alma mater, where he emphasized individual talent in the style of Schaus and King. When Moran took over in 1969, the Mountaineers were no longer playing in a conference they could dominate, but opening the Coliseum, it was presumed, would help to recruit the kind of players who could compete at the highest level, and, WVU would regain its former place among the nation's elite programs. Moran inherited a talented group of young players, particularly sensational sophomore guard Wil Robinson of Laurel Highlands High School in Pennsylvania. Robinson told a reporter that he chose to play at WVU because of his close friendship with Ron "Fritz" Williams and because the coaches recruiting him were "straight" and did not offer anything "under the table" as other schools did.[12]

Like Williams, Robinson was a well-liked big-man-on-campus, but that did not mean everybody knew who he was. A humorous episode reported by WVU sports historian John Antonik illustrates how blissfully unaware some people were:

One morning on his way to work, [President] Harlow noticed Robinson and some of his teammates thumbing along University Avenue, so he pulled over to give them a lift. When Robinson got into the front seat of the car, Harlow asked him if he was a student.

'No, sir,' Robinson answered, 'I'm a basketball player. Who are you?'

'I'm the president,' Harlow answered.

'Oh.'

"That is the story (likely embellished)," Antonik concludes, "of how the two best-known men on campus met." [13]

Robinson performed according to expectations. He joined Rod Hundley as the only sophomores to average more than twenty points per game. In the inaugural game at the Coliseum against Colgate on December 1, 1970, Robinson lit up the scoreboard with 39 points, and the Mountaineers won 113–92. By the time he graduated, his 29.4 career points per game average edged ahead of Jerry West's career average of 29.3. Robinson was ranked fourth in the nation in scoring, earned first-team All-American honors, and was selected by the Houston Rockets in the second round of the NBA draft. [14]

The late sixties and early seventies were a period of dramatic social change in the nation, and the cultural collisions occurring elsewhere in society also affected Morgantown and WVU. Bucky Waters remembered it as "a sensitive time," with demands for civil rights, riots, the war in Vietnam, campus unrest, the Kent State shootings, and long hair and other perceived violations of the dress code, all of which created an adversarial relationship between generations. "It really got into the culture that if you were a coach or a college president or anything of a traditional authority figure," then students dismissed you, Waters informed sports historian John Antonik years later. "It was the reason I left coaching." [15]

Sonny Moran tried to deal with the cultural changes. "We had the problems with the Afro haircuts and the facial hair and the whole bit because we were trying our best to present a good image," Moran informed Antonik. "I told the kids when we had a team meeting, 'I have to go out and beg money for your scholarships and all I'm asking for you to do is clean up your act and not let your peer groups get to you." [16] Levi Phillips, a Charleston native, came to play at WVU because two of his former high school teammates, Curtis Price and Larry Harris, were already on the team. The most vivid memory of his first varsity season, Phillips told a reporter, was Moran's benching him because of his hairstyle. Not surprisingly, his perspective on hairstyles differed from Moran's. "You have to understand that times were different back then, especially with race," he offered. Like most young African American males of the time, he sported an "Afro" style, which many of the politically radical Black Panthers had adopted. "Coach Moran took one look at me and left me at the end of the bench. After the game, he asked what I was doing, and I told him it wasn't anything," just that some girl said she thought he would look cute with his hair parted in the middle. "Well I don't, and I don't ever want to see it again," Moran told him. Phillips complied. He knew where the coach was "coming from," but emphasized, "like I said, times were definitely different."[17]

Moran's hopes for leading the Mountaineers were unfortunately dashed by tragedy rather than Afro hairstyles. The Mountaineers began the season by reeling off six straight wins and a return to a top-twenty ranking. But in January 1973 the wheels came off. Starters Larry Harris and Levi Phillips were declared academically ineligible for the remainder of the season. Twelve days later a tragic car accident took the life of Harris and left Sam Oglesby a paraplegic. No sooner had Moran gone to the bench to replace the two starters when one substitute broke his leg and the other suffered a collapsed lung. Moran lost five of his best seven players. Wil Robinson regarded the tragedy as the worst thing that ever happened to him.[18]

In 1974 Moran recruited some exceptional players, such as Warren Baker from Greenbrier County. For the first time, freshmen were allowed to play on the varsity team, and the following year Moran suited up one of the youngest teams in college basketball. They played hard and would eventually excel, but finished the first season at 10–15. As usual, the fans counted only wins and losses, and Moran was embarrassed when the student section booed him. He resigned his position to become athletic director at Morehead State.[19]

Another turn of the coaching carousel brought in WVU alumnus Joedy Gardner who played guard for Fred Schaus from 1955 through 1957, when the team of Jerry West, Don Vincent, Lloyd Sharrar, and Bobby Joe Smith was ranked first in the nation. Gardner inherited two excellent players in Warren Baker and Jerome Anderson, and Bob Huggins transferred in from Ohio University. Gardner's recruiting expertise brought in several talented players and contributed to his rebuilding effort. In fact, five of them were subsequently drafted by the NBA: Maurice Robinson, Stan Boskovich, Tony Robertson, Lowes Moore, and Greg Nance. (Junius Lewis played professionally in Europe.) But Gardner's career was cut short after four seasons when he was informed that his contract would not be renewed. Gardner landed on his feet by becoming head coach at Northern Arizona University, at twice the pay, he liked to add.[20]

Ten years after the first African American players joined the Mountaineer cagers, the world had been transformed. In 1965, black players were at a minimum a curiosity and often a threat to the racial status quo, depending on one's point of view. By 1975, however, it was hard to imagine the game of basketball without African Americans on the court, or the game of football without them on the field.

INTEGRATING FOOTBALL

Toward the end of James Harlow's term as president, the man who personally cared little about athletics remarked to a reporter that the WVU football team had won more games during his ten years at the helm than during any previous administration. He believed that if the University was going to play sports, it should field winning teams. There was, however, a pronounced gap between his notion of "winning" and that held by Mountaineer fans, and their lack of patience for coaches to make a positive mark on the program characterized the twenty-year transition period between Art "Pappy" Lewis and Don Nehlen.

For football, as with basketball, the real story during the sixties was the integration of the teams, which might have come earlier had WVU and Morgantown been more hospitable places for young black athletes. The leading authority on WVU sports history states that Pappy Lewis tried for years, without success, to lure the state's best black football players to WVU. His successor, Earl Eugene Corum, would finally break the ice. A native of Huntington, Corum played at WVU and then coached high school football for a few years in Marion County. He came to WVU in 1950 as an assistant to Lewis and stayed on as head coach for another six years from 1960 through the 1965 seasons. The Mountaineers were up and down under Corum, and in 1960 he presided over the Mountaineers' only winless season in school history.[21]

At first Gene Corum could not attract black players to WVU. Talented players did not want to risk sacrificing their careers by participating in WVU's desegregation experiment. Then, in 1962, Corum won a major recruiting victory by signing Dick Leftridge, a highly sought-after running back from Hinton High School. Even Governor Wally Barron helped to persuade the young man to stay in state and attend WVU. At the same time, Corum succeeded in recruiting Roger Alford from Wintersville, Ohio. Both played on the freshman team, and in 1963 they became the first African Americans to play varsity football at WVU. They were not the first African American athletes to compete for WVU; that honor belongs to Phil Edwards of Morgantown, who enrolled in 1961 and participated in track, although without a scholarship. Corum expected a hue and cry, especially since Leftridge and Alford were the first black athletes to compete in the Southern Conference, but only two irate calls came into the athletic director's office. Both players posted successful careers at WVU. Leftridge was drafted by the Pittsburgh Steelers in the first round of the 1966 NFL draft, while Alford became a dentist.[22]

Gene Corum will always be known as the man who integrated WVU football, but in retrospect he, along with basketball coaches Waters and Moran, presided over the virtual cultural transformation not only of WVU athletics but the entire University. The presence of Leftridge and Alford opened the doors for others. In 1963, the "second wave" of black recruits arrived on campus, including Garrett Ford from Washington DC, who was drafted by the Denver Broncos after an exceptional collegiate career. He became WVU's first black assistant coach in 1970 and then associate athletic director. Another African American recruit, John Mallory of Summitt, New Jersey, played with Ford from 1965–1967, and both were inducted into the WVU Hall of Fame. In an interview with a Morgantown reporter, Mallory noted that Corum "helped change the culture at the university to bring in black athletes. That is a monumental legacy." Moreover, "he did it so professionally, and in his gentlemanly manner," in a way that did not attract attention to the players or distract the team. They were talented players, and race never came up; they were "just teammates." In fact, the players did not realize the significance of the moment until long afterward. Mallory perceptively acknowledged the risks Corum took in integrating the team: "With athletics comes more socialization, friend-ships born in the fire, things like that. All the things people didn't like." Corum might have shielded his black players from potential problems, but he never raised the issue with them. "The only thing we ever talked about was football."[23]

When "Gentleman Gene" Corum's contract was not renewed after the 1965 season, he remained at WVU as a professor and assistant dean in the School of Physical Education, and briefly as acting athletic director during the search that resulted in the hiring of Fred Schaus. He also served on the Morgantown City Council for six years and in 1967 chaired the com-mittee that oversaw the building of the city's first public swimming pool, located in Marilla Park. The pool was open to all, even though there was some resistance to a racially integrated pool, a resistance that was thwarted by Corum's committee.[24]

Jim Carlen was a thirty-year-old assistant at Georgia Tech when he was hired to replace Corum in 1969, and he brought the vigor of youth and a willingness to do anything to improve the program. With integration no longer an issue, Carlen simply continued what was already the established practice by recruiting the best talent available, including African American players like Jim Braxton, Bob Gresham, and Eddie Williams. John Mallory recalled that Carlen sought advice from this team's black players about how to attract more African Americans to WVU. Acting on their response that the University should encourage more black females to enroll, Carlen urged the administration to develop a plan for increasing the minority student population on campus. Carlen's four-year tenure was capped by a win over South Carolina in the Peach Bowl, followed the next day by his announce-ment that he had accepted a head coaching position at Texas Tech. Im-mediately afterward WVU announced that assistant coach Bobby Bowden would become the new head coach.[25]

Bowden extended the Mountaineers' winning record, compiling an 8–3 record his first year, followed by 7–4 in the 1971 season, and 8–3 in the 1972 season, including a return to the Peach Bowl, where they lost to North Carolina State. In 1973, WVU slipped to 6–5, and in 1974 Bowden experienced his first losing season at WVU. Fan expectations had been rising rapidly, and his earlier successes were forgotten as students booed him and hung him in effigy. In 1975, however, an 8–3 season culminated in the 13–10 defeat of North Carolina State in the Peach Bowl. Perhaps most importantly, Bowden's team defeated archrival Pitt 17–14 by a last-second field goal. Crowds of students reached new heights of exultation when they built a fire in the middle of a Sunnyside neighborhood street next to the stadium, resulting in the arrest of scores of people. With national exposure and a team nationally ranked by the United Press International as seventeenth in the nation, the fans now congratulated Coach Bowden. The praise was too late, for Florida State University offered him a contract he could not refuse. He left WVU with a 42–26 record, and the rest is history.[26]

NEW MOUNTAINEER FIELD

In his annual address to the Faculty Assembly in April 1976, President Harlow proclaimed that the football program at WVU had experienced greater success during the past decade than it had at any other time during the past half-century. Therefore, Harlow announced that improvements were required in physical facilities. With the old Mountaineer Field seating capacity set at 34,000, prominent teams found little financial incentive to play in Morgantown. An upgraded stadium and a shell building used for indoor football practices during inclement weather would allow the University to compete at the highest levels. To finance these improvements, Harlow suggested that taxes on coal production could do for WVU what oil tax revenues did for the University of Oklahoma.[27] Nothing came of his proposal.

Gordon Thorn, a career administrator who served on the planning committee, observed that the atmosphere of football games in the old stadium reflected the student culture of an earlier day, when WVU was small and athletes were closer to the student body. In the fifties and sixties, he recalled, "we had our ups and downs. . . . We didn't have enough of a program to keep us at the peak all the time." It was hoped that new facilities would achieve that "peak" status.[28]

Before the wind of rising expectations, the Harlow administration requested an appropriation of $10 million from the legislature to renovate Mountaineer Field and expand by ten thousand seats. Harlow was stunned when an independent proposal from the Morgantown Elks Club to build a new stadium found traction in the legislature. He was even more surprised during the last week of the session when Senate President William Brotherton (D-Kanawha) successfully offered an amendment calling for the new stadium. On the last day of the 1977 session, the legislature approved a $60.3 million construction bill for higher education which included $20 million for a football stadium and $4.5 million for a shell building at WVU.[29]

In response, Governor Rockefeller met with Harlow to determine what action the University wanted him to take with the bill. President Harlow, now a lame duck, and Athletic Director Leland Byrd both urged the governor to sign the measure, although both of them preferred the less costly enlargement of the old facility over building a new one. One of the "prime movers" of the bill, Senator Robert Nelson (D-Cabell) now criticized it. Initially, a Marshall University request of $18 million for a new basketball arena was the only item formally recommended by the Board of Regents, and Nelson worried that the WVU stadium add-on jeopardized Marshall's new, sorely needed field house. Even the legislators from Monongalia County were ambivalent in voting for the bill. They wanted to approve measures that benefitted WVU but believed that the new stadium would cause "impossible traffic congestion." A feasibility study was completed prior to approval of the Coliseum construction, but none had been undertaken for the new stadium because it was appended to an appropriation bill in the legislature. As the hour approached for Governor Rockefeller's signature, the Morgantown City Council adopted a resolution asking the governor to veto the bill and revise the original concept of renovating the old stadium.[30]

Many who feared the new stadium would adversely affect their interests, therefore, hoped that the governor would veto the bill and then ask the legislature to recast it into a more acceptable form. But

Rockefeller signed the bill, arguing that "the choice was whether we were going to defeat the bill and stop progress or sign the bill and create an atmosphere of progress in higher education." Perhaps anticipating criticism from academics, he also announced receipt of a $4 million dollar letter of commitment from the Board of Regents confirming that the Evansdale Library at WVU would be built. Moreover, he had toured the old Mountaineer Field and decided that the fifty-year-old stadium was not worth renovating. Of the four sites suggested, he ruled out the Mileground entirely because of the higher real estate values and possibility of mine subsidence. He preferred a site near the Coliseum that would be accessible to the interstate highway and the PRT and yet remain part of the campus, but he did not want to choose the site himself. Rockefeller acknowledged that the stadium was very likely to exceed the $20 million, but "if it costs more, so be it; we'll raise more. . . . I think it's good progress for the state of West Virginia." He urged WVU and the Board of Regents to get on with the planning.[31]

The editor of the Morgantown newspaper took issue with the governor's attitude. WVU would get a new football stadium whether or not it wanted one, he lamented, and also warned of the probability of higher taxes as a result. "Pouring untold millions of dollars into the construction of bigger and better sports facilities" was not his idea of progress in higher education.[32] President Harlow offered his own disclaimer: "We never considered a new stadium when we decided to ask the Legislature to upgrade the football facilities. We believe it more practical to renovate than build a new stadium in a place not as easily accessible to students." Harlow also expressed disappointment that the legislature and the Board of Regents had not worked more closely with the University in approving the new stadium. Chancellor Ben Morton "never told me prior to Legislative approval that he favored the new stadium project. He never asked me my opinion."[33] Political interference in the University's internal affairs sometimes came in fancy wrap.

Indecision on where to locate the new stadium heightened the anxieties of local residents who would be affected. Several possible locations were identified, but each of them presented serious drawbacks. The Mileground seemed too far removed from campus and the students, and the Coliseum area was not large enough to support a stadium unless more adjacent land was purchased. There was insufficient space for any new construction downtown. After studying stadiums built near hospitals on several other campuses, WVU decided to locate the stadium on the University's golf course property between the medical center and the law school. Immediately the Morgantown City Council, the Morgantown Planning Commission, the Monongalia County Planning Commission, and the Monongalia County Medical Society all stated their opposition to the chosen location. Demonstrating the statewide importance of the University and its athletics programs, the *Charleston Daily-Mail* countered that Morgantown "began to make noises as though they owned the university, an affliction that has stayed with Morgantown residents through the generations that followed its founding more than 100 years ago." Some in Morgantown entertained the notion that the stadium should be planned as a Morgantown asset; that was "getting rather parochial," the *Daily-Mail* jabbed. With the architectural plan in hand and the location decided, bids were opened in January 1979, with the stadium opening projected for September 1980. Demonstrating that he had fulfilled his promise to build the Evansdale Library, Governor Rockefeller came to Morgantown on July 13, 1978, to participate in the ground-breaking ceremony for the new structure.[34]

TITLE IX TRANSFORMS WOMEN'S ATHLETICS

Title IX was part of the Education Amendments Act of 1972, the first comprehensive federal law to make sex discrimination illegal in educational programs or activities that received federal funds, from elementary schools through universities. The act fundamentally changed the course of life for women in higher education. The most dramatic impact of Title IX was on women's athletics because the act demanded that women be given an equal opportunity to participate in intercollegiate sports. Athletic Director Leland Byrd requested permission in August 1972 to organize women's teams and also presented a plan for the integration of women's teams, which President Harlow formally approved in April 1973.[35]

Basketball (coached by Kittie Blakemore), tennis (coached by Martha Thorn), and gymnastics (coached during the first year by Nanette Schnaible and thereafter by Linda Burdette), were the pioneer women's sports at WVU, and their coaches became the figureheads of women's sports for the next thirty years. The University had to scramble to launch the teams to avoid losing federal funding. According to Coach Blakemore, WVU was the last state school in West Virginia to introduce women's athletic teams. Red Brown, who served as athletic director from 1954–1972, informed Blakemore that "we had money for the women, but he just didn't want to fool with us. . . . He didn't start the women's program until Title IX." But things changed quickly when Leland Byrd replaced Brown as athletic director in 1972. Even though he only held that position until 1978, Byrd oversaw the transition to compliance with Title IX directives. While in his previous position at Miami Dade South Junior College in Florida, Byrd had supervised a women's varsity sports program. Other states, such as Florida, Oklahoma, and Texas, had implemented women's sports a decade earlier.[36]

As pioneers, coaches Blakemore, Thorn, and Burdette confronted and overcame multiple obstacles. Recruiting players was the first priority, but they also needed to provide their teams with uniforms and negotiate practice time on the courts. Blakemore's basketball team played the first season without uniforms. By the time she knew what sizes to order, the season was over, so her team played in WVU physical education uniforms and practice jerseys with numbers on them. When Coach Thorn spoke to Leland Byrd about uniforms for her tennis team, the athletic director responded, "Oh Martha, girls don't want to dress alike." Byrd eventually relented and the tennis team received their uniforms the following season. All three coaches agreed that, in the final analysis, Byrd was supportive, although the coaches of the men's teams were not always as cooperative.[37]

All three coaches had their conflicts with coaches of the men's revenue-generating sports. Thorn was forced to cancel a scheduled tennis match with Pitt when she was informed that the football team wanted to use the shell building for practice. She was informed of this one hour before the match. Thorn took the matter to the new athletic director, Fred Schaus, who, according to Thorn, "stands up and he slams his hand down and he

says, 'so long as they make the money,' they get to do what they want.'"
Burdette also ran afoul of the football program, which used the basketball court in Stansbury Hall before the team got its own indoor practice
facility in the late 1990s. The problem was that gymnastics practiced in
the loft overlooking the Stansbury court, and, when Burdette played the
floor music, the football coaches would tell her to turn it off so the team
could practice. Kittie Blakemore's basketball practices also depended on
the men's basketball coach's plans for using the Coliseum court. When Gale
Catlett became head coach of the men's basketball program, however, they
resolved their differences respectfully because both Catlett and his wife had
been students of Blakemore. If the two teams were to play in the Coliseum
on the same day, it was scheduled as a doubleheader. Still, she constantly
worried that the game would run over because "they would just stop the
game, and that was the score, whatever the stoppage was."[38]

The first three women's varsity sports began their initial seasons
in 1973–1974, but others sports soon followed. In 1974–1975, swimming
(coached by part-time instructor Donna Henderson) and volleyball (first
coached by graduate assistant Judy Sisson and then Veronica Hammersmith) were added; by the spring of 1976 softball was underway (coached by
Veronica Hammersmith). In 1977 Linda King launched the track program,
organized a cross country team in 1978, and an indoor team in 1979. About
one hundred women participated in the new programs in 1975, which subsequently grew in scale. Athletic Director Byrd declared in one WVU publication that "we're trying to give the girls the type of program they want
and need." The women had progressed, their records were improving, the
spectators were coming out to support them, and the women's teams were
becoming "an important aspect of our total program." He pointed out that
women were provided the same travel, facilities, equipment, publicity, and
funding as the men's "non-income-producing" sports. While he noted that
the women had full access to the training facilities and equipment rooms,
Byrd apparently decided not to acknowledge the complications that arose
when their needs were in conflict with the revenue-generating sports.[39]

Looking back on the early years, Kittie Blakemore observed in 1981
that progress came faster than she thought it would. Not only had the num-

ber of teams increased, but "we've gone from no scholarships, to partials, to full scholarships, and increased budgets for travel and recruiting also." The programs improved along with player talent, Burdette observed. "There was a time when I prayed no one would come," she commented about her own gymnastics meets. Many of the first athletes had not competed in high school because the programs were so few at that level. Recruiting was a significant problem. Although her first tennis team compiled an impressive 15–0 record, Thorn recruited its first members by running an advertisement in the *Daily Athenaeum*. The earliest teams played against smaller schools initially, but they were soon competing against teams of national caliber. With improved funding, facilities, and competition, the women's teams became more successful in recruiting as well.[40]

An amendment to Title IX proposed during the 1978–1979 school year prompted WVU to join 320 colleges and universities to form an alliance in opposition. The change proposed by the Department of Health, Education, and Welfare would require that an equal amount of money be spent per athlete on men and women in intercollegiate athletics; institutions that did not comply would be excluded from federal funding. First year Athletic Director Dick Martin explained that the new measure, if implemented as written, would be "almost an impossible financial strain on us." While in agreement with the overall objective of Title IX, Martin expressed the University's position that the revenue-producing sports, football and basketball, should be excluded from the "per-capita aspect of the law." According to the amendment, Martin explained, if the University spent $300,000 on 120 men's scholarships for an average of $2,500 per male athlete, then the same amount must be spent for each women's scholarship. That men's average included basketball and football, but, if those two revenue-generating sports were not exempted, "it's hard to realize where we will come up with the extra money we will need" to cover the difference. He suggested that WVU would have to "cut back" on sponsored teams. Martin believed that women's sports should be treated like all other non-revenue sports, but that basketball and football should be exempt because they provided the funding to operate all the other non-revenue sports. "If Title IX is implemented as written," Athletic Director Martin warned, "then college athletics as we know them may be changed drastically. Some minor sports may have to be dropped." Consequently, WVU had joined the network of schools at opposing Title IX, which hired a Washington firm to lobby against the amendment. The effort failed, and the amendment was enacted.[41]

A "LARGE-SCALE ENTERPRISE"

President Budig "brought with him a great affinity for intercollegiate athletics," according to one of his assistants. While upgrading athletics might not have been his first priority for the University, "he was realistic about the role athletics played in getting the attention of alumni and friends." Out of personal and professional interest, therefore, Budig maintained a direct relationship with athletic administrators and coaches.[42] The commitment to build the new Mountaineer stadium had already been made by Governor Rockefeller and the legislature when Budig arrived in Morgantown in the summer of 1977. Undoubtedly he was in complete agreement with the governor's statement that construction of a new stadium symbolized "the state's growing commitment to both academic excellence and excellence in the field of athletics," that it elevated WVU's "mystique," and that, by association, it elevated the academic status of the University.[43]

When the new Mountaineer Field opened on September 6, 1980, fifty thousand excited fans joined Governor Rockefeller and other state dignitaries crowded in to enjoy the festivities, highlighted by John Denver's rendition of his own song, "Country Roads." When the governor was introduced, however, he was roundly booed, especially by the student section. Although Mountaineer fans are known to boo even their own team when they disapprove of their performance, it seemed shockingly inappropriate for fans to boo the governor, who had been instrumental in building the new stadium they were now enjoying. More likely, the fans were demonstrating their disapproval of the governor's shift in policy toward strip mining. Prior to his first election in 1976 Rockefeller had called for the abolition of the practice. During the nation's energy crisis of the late seventies, however, the governor pulled back from abolition to support regulation rather than an end to that method of extracting coal.[44]

President Budig facilitated the development of intercollegiate athletics in important ways. He realized that intercollegiate sports, particularly football and basketball, were already big businesses. Unlike his predecessor, Budig cared if coaches won and was willing to fire them if they did not. He also sought help from the WVU Foundation to provide funds for multi-year contracts in order to retain the best head football and basketball coaches. President Budig was actively involved in athletics, therefore, and his four-year tenure featured some high-profile personnel changes, including terminating the contracts of head basketball coach Joedy Gardner and head football coach Frank Cignetti, the resignation of Athletic Director Leland Byrd in 1979 to become Executive Director of the Eastern Eight Basketball Conference, and the appointment of Richard Martin as Byrd's replacement.[45]

These personnel changes stirred considerable public controversy and reflected unfavorably on the University during Budig's tenure. They were emblematic of what the public had come to associate with the University's inability to manage big-time athletics. When Bobby Bowden resigned as head football coach in 1975 to take over at Florida State, assistant coach Frank Cignetti was tapped to replace him. After four unsuccessful seasons, however, fans became highly vocal in their demands that he be replaced. In 1980 Leland Byrd resigned, and a selection committee was established to search for a new athletic director. Budig decided that the new athletic director should come from outside the University. Among the many candidates, Fred Schaus, the assistant director of athletics at Purdue University, was the unanimous candidate for the position, but when contacted Schaus expressed some reservation and later withdrew his name as a candidate. Assistant Commissioner of the Big Eight Conference Richard Martin was the only remaining candidate, and he was appointed to the post. Much to everybody's chagrin, Fred Schaus notified the committee a few days later that he would accept the position if it were still open. Had that call been made a few days sooner, WVU might have been spared the series of embarrassing episodes that weakened Martin's ability to carry out the duties of athletic director.[46]

Frank Cignetti's ability to continue coaching while he underwent treatment for cancer was called into question; Martin and Budig received contradictory prognoses from the doctors. A backup coach quietly agreed to fill in temporarily if Cignetti became incapacitated, but the rumor that Martin was secretly negotiating for Cignetti's replacement spread like wildfire among football fans. The growing group of those who opposed Martin, some of whom boosted Cignetti to replace him, kept the rumor alive in their effort to depose the athletic director. The issue died down as Cignetti's health improved. [47]

Martin was saddled with a serious problem when he was forced to cancel a football game for financial reasons. The Mountaineers were scheduled to play San Jose State University in October 1981 for a guaranteed payout of $40,000. But the energy crisis of the late seventies, which forced drivers to wait in line for gasoline at exorbitant prices, meant that the cost of travel to California alone would exceed the guaranteed payout. On the advice of legal counsel, Martin cancelled the contract and was promptly threatened with a lawsuit by the San Jose State athletic director. Unfortunately, his legal advice was not in writing, so Martin assumed full responsibility for his decision. Complicating matters even more, Martin's business manager erroneously included the anticipated revenue of $650,000 from a nationally televised game which never materialized into the following year's budget. The error was detected only after Martin had allocated and spent the money, causing a major overrun in the department's account. Meanwhile, the business manager resigned and accepted a position at another university, leaving Martin once again to bear full responsibility for the deficit. The press had a field day with this revelation as did Martin's detractors, whose campaign to oust him hit full stride.[48]

As a temporary measure the university comptroller became business manager for the Department of Athletics, and as might be expected his first action was to make dramatic cuts in expenditures to balance the budget. When those cuts included the football and basketball budgets, both coaches and fans expressed their displeasure. Martin ordered the basketball team to travel by bus rather than airplane, which prompted Coach Gale Catlett to charge Martin with interference in the basketball program, contrary to the promises given to him when he took the position.[49]

In 1979 Cignetti posted another losing season, and Martin did not renew the coach's contract. Instead, Cignetti became Martin's administrative assistant, and a search committee hired Don Nehlen, an assistant at the University of Michigan, as his replacement. Martin's opponents now clamored for Cignetti's elevation to athletic director, and readers who confined their interest only to the sports pages were treated to the spectacle of a University in disarray. Finally, after a legislative investigation and an official audit of the books, Martin resigned as of June 30, 1981, ending what must have been a two-year nightmare for him.[50]

February 5, 1991, was another momentous day in the history of intercollegiate athletics at WVU. On that day it was announced that WVU would become a football member of the Big East Conference. Although it was not the culminating event in the creation of the conference, it was a major step. WVU had been seeking an appropriate all-sports conference affiliation since leaving the Southern Conference in 1966. In 1991 WVU was a participating member of the Atlantic 10 Conference in sports other than football. Originally, the Big East was a powerful basketball conference but its members did not play Division I football. They continued to compete in the reconfigured Big East Conference in basketball after the conference was expanded to incorporate eight additional institutions that played Division I football as well as basketball: Boston College, University of Miami, Pittsburgh, Rutgers, Syracuse, Temple, Virginia Tech, and WVU.[51] Athletic Director Ed Pastilong and WVU President Neil Bucklew exerted considerable time and energy toward the creation of the Big East football conference. University officials had long desired an all-sports conference made up of the major eastern athletic powers. Initially, the basketball-only schools resisted, but finally they relented, and the Big East expanded to include schools that played football as well as basketball and eventually evolved into an all-sports conference. WVU had explored alignment with the ten-school Southeastern Conference, which was thinking of expanding at the time, but that did not happen. WVU also explored its chances with the Big Ten, but was spurned in favor of expanding either westward or eastward. In the end Penn State was chosen. The Atlantic Coast Conference responded to queries by stating that it had no plans for expansion at the time.[52]

With the growing influence of television in collegiate sports, independent teams such as WVU could no longer avoid belonging to a conference. Attracted by the revenues television generated, conference commissioners were scrambling to sign contracts for their teams. Thus began the "facilities arms race," with the more successful conferences appearing on television and garnering ever more money that was then spent on state-of-the-art facilities, coaches' salaries, and the perks of big-time athletics, which attracted the best recruits and thus produced even better teams. Except for Notre Dame, which had negotiated its own network contract, independents could not compete on a level playing field in this new environment. Seven teams in the new league were already on the schedule for the fall of 1991. Financial security was a high priority, and, since pre-season ticket sales provided the foundation, scheduling team matchups that fans enjoyed watching, especially rivalry games, was important. Big East football also operated in a region of high population density, with more than 20 percent of the television viewing audience in the Northeast, and another 10 percent in the Miami area. Therefore, major television packages for the conference were likely, along with revenue sharing, bowl alignments, and a group of officials. Because it enhanced the image and reputation of each university member, conference affiliation was the key to advancement.[53]

In announcing plans for his retirement in 2010, Ed Pastilong observed that what pleased him most about his nineteen years as director of intercollegiate athletics were the successful establishment of the Big East football conference in 1991 and then full membership for WVU in the Big East Conference for basketball and other sports in 1995–96. "That was the most monumental thing ever to happen for us," Pastilong declared. Of course it was the culmination of a much longer process. He recognized the efforts of his predecessor, Fred Schaus, and President E. Gordon Gee in pursuing policies that led to Big East membership, especially their declining an invitation for WVU to join the Metro Conference out of a conviction that WVU would eventually find a stronger conference affiliation.[54] Basketball Coach Gail Catlett agreed: "The Big East is going to be the best thing to happen to the basketball program in the history of this school. It's something we've needed. By having patience, the best of all worlds has happened. It will give us equal footing with the rest of the schools to recruit. As far as TV exposure, playing the great teams, a financially rewarding situation, we're where we want to be."[55]

The *Alumni Magazine* heralded 1991 as "one of the most significant seasons in West Virginia's football history." Not only had WVU joined the Big East Football Conference; it also marked its centennial year for football, as well as Don Nehlen's twelfth year as head coach, an anniversary that none of his predecessors had reached. A further cause for celebration was the fact that the opening home game against Pitt would be nationally televised on ESPN. Looking back on that team, one is struck by how many of those names are still familiar to WVU fans today. Tailback Adrian Murrell, split end James Jett, right guard Dale Wolfley, center Mike Compton, tackle Rich Braham, defensive lineman Steve Grant, defensive back Darrell Whitmore, and kickers Todd Sauerbrun and Mike Vanderjagt, to mention a few, all went on to play in the NFL. Moreover, that team faced what Nehlen described as the toughest schedule since his arrival.[56]

When WVU was invited to join the Big East Conference as a full member in 1994, Ed Pastilong enthusiastically welcomed the all-sports league that alumni and fans had been envisioning for a very long time. The Big East conducted conference championships in nineteen varsity sports. The teams included Boston College, Connecticut, Georgetown, Miami, Pitt, Providence, St. John's, Seton Hall, Syracuse, and Villanova. Temple and Virginia Tech were football-only at first but subsequently became full members. WVU and Nebraska both went 11-0 during the previous regular season, so it was doubly exciting when WVU was invited to play against Nebraska in Kickoff Classic XII, college football's first game. The honor that came with being invited to play one of the nation's best teams boosted the confidence of supporters who wanted WVU to join the ranks of national powers. Not even a driving rain during the nationally televised game could dampen the fans' excitement.[57]

The wisdom of Catlett's observations about the impact of Big East membership become apparent in WVU's elevated ability to attract recruits, gain television exposure, play excellent competition, and establish financial security for University intercollegiate athletics. As Norman Julian points out, "Four of WVU's final five [basketball] games in the 1996–97 season were on national TV, a first for the program, and ten games went national in 1997–1998." Also, the ability to recruit quality athletes was revealed in the strength of the teams.[58] The Coliseum was sold out for the December 2, 1995 Big East opening game with sixth-ranked Georgetown, cramming 15,183 fans into the stands, the sixth-largest crowd ever. Popular ESPN personality Dick Vitale whipped up enthusiasm, if that was necessary, with a pre-game Dick Vitale sound-alike contest over the public address system. Vitale went on to please the crowd with a shooting demonstration, sinking nine out of ten free throws, and swishing one-for-one from behind the three-point circle. Contradicting some negative comments about the typical unruliness of WVU basketball crowds, Vitale later wrote that the atmosphere of that opening-game night was the best he experienced all year.[59]

If admission to the Big East Conference was one of the best things to occur for WVU athletics, then one of the worst came in the fall of 1989, when President Bucklew withdrew two hundred scholarship waivers for student-athletes. During a period of shrinking state support for a growing university, every department was expected to be self-supporting. Tuition and fee waivers for athletes exempted them from tuition increases, causing the cost per credit hour to grow without a corresponding increase in revenue. The situation was untenable. Why, many asked, should a university value performance on the athletic field more than on the concert stage? Nevertheless, tuition waivers for athletes were common in most major collegiate sports programs. "Taking away those waivers was hard for us to overcome," Pastilong commented, "We had to be resourceful." As of 2010, they had not been reinstated by the University's administration. On the other hand, the necessity to provide athletic scholarships, which were vital to be competitive in recruiting top athletes, led to the creation of a scholarship fund. The fund began with a modest, $1 million gift from Milan Puskar, a founder of Mylan Pharmaceuticals and a major supporter of athletics at the University over many years, but grew to more than $38 million by 2008.[60]

In January 1989, President Bucklew accepted the resignation of Athletic Director Fred Schaus, who entered retirement after a long and distinguished career in athletics. "No other West Virginia alumnus of the last half-century has contributed as much to West Virginia basketball as has Fred Schaus in his roles as All-American, coach and athletic director," one authority observed. Schaus arrived at WVU as a student in 1946 and quickly asserted himself as a leader. He was a standout basketball player, captain of the team for two years from 1947–1949, and earned All-American honors. He was an honors student and also served as student body president. He earned a master's degree in 1953. After several years playing professional basketball, Schaus became head coach of the Mountaineers, posting a 146–37 record in six years and winning the Southern Conference championship all six years with All-Americans Rod Hunley, Lloyd Sharrar, Jerry West, and Lee Patrone (also in that group was the memorable Rod Thorn). His legendary 1959 team, led by Jerry West, played for the NCAA national championship game, losing by one point (71–70) to California. Schaus then moved on to coach the Los Angeles Lakers for seven successful seasons, assisted by his former players Jerry West and "Hot Rod" Hunley, and then spent the next five years as the Lakers' vice president and general manager. Schaus returned to college coaching at Purdue University for the next six years, and then as associate athletic director for three years before returning to WVU as athletic director in September 1981.[61]

STUDENT BEHAVIOR AND STUDENT ATHLETES

Inappropriate behavior at football games has long been detrimental to the good image of the University and an ongoing problem for administrators, who must field the complaints and occasional lawsuits stemming from obnoxious fan behavior. A Wheeling attorney wrote to President Bucklew in October 1989 to complain of student behavior at the Pitt game. He insisted that it was not "in the best interest of the University that adults be seated between students in the upper deck and below." The aisles were full of students where he was seated (Section 109), standing and blocking the view of everyone behind them. The police finally cleared them out, but the experience was harrowing. He thought that the University had "lost control of that portion of the stadium and I truly fear a young person will die there." When a young man climbed on the rail, those around him chanted "jump."

This kind of "emotional contagion" was bound to result in a tragedy sooner or later. The prevalence of young people chanting foul language also disturbed him. "Back in the old days," wrote the attorney, "before students ran universities and athletics eclipsed education, there was a fence that separated the student body from the rest of the fans." He recommended that the University consider restoring that fence. If President Bucklew, Athletic Director Pastilong, and the director of security, along with their wives, occupied the same seats during the next game, he wrote, they would know firsthand why this behavior is a "disgrace to the University which I love so much."[62]

In responding to this concerned alumnus, the University's general counsel, Jon A. Reed, observed that the Pitt-WVU game seemed "to bring out the worst in behavior for a higher than normal number of fans," and that the issue of student seating had become a very difficult problem for the athletic department.[63] The sentiment expressed by the alumnus was undoubtedly sincere, but the problem of fan behavior was one of culture, not control, and called for much more than a fence.

Another football fan forwarded to President Bucklew a copy of his letter to the editor of the *Dominion-Post*. A newcomer to Morgantown, he described himself as an avid fan of college football who had "thoroughly enjoyed the WVU games this season." He claimed that, even though he had read all the complaining articles about WVU student game behavior, he did not find it much different from student behavior at other colleges. He recommended combining the student body and band members in side-by-side sections in the lower portion of the stadium nearer to the football team, thus alleviating the problem of "throwing things from the upper deck onto the heads below."[64] This solution had one major problem: students would occupy the prime seating close to the field that fetched high ticket prices. Therefore, it was an unlikely solution for an athletic department charged with generating its own revenues to stay solvent, and it also demonstrated the difficulty of solving the issue of disruptive fan behavior by seating location alone.

Even misguided moments of exuberant partisanship by the Mountaineer mascot might become a public image issue in the era of big-time media-dominated sports. In a tight football game against Rutgers University in November 1989, for example, with just under two minutes remaining, Rutgers attempted a forty-yard field goal to notch the victory. Just as the ball was spotted by the holder, however, the Mountaineer fired his musket, and the kicker missed the field goal. Whether or not firing the musket distracted him, WVU's athletic director and the *Dominion Post* received letters of complaint from two "ardent supporters" of Rutgers football blaming the University for the Mountaineer's unsportsmanlike behavior, which was "beyond the limits of acceptable behavior under the circumstances."[65] Taking the complaint under serious consideration, Athletic Director Ed Pastilong requested that his marketing and event director investigate the "unfortunate incident." For his part, the Mountaineer claimed that there was no intent to disrupt the game, but the investigator expressed difficulty "believing this since the evidence is so irrefutable." The mascot was aware that firing the musket during the final two minutes of the game was prohibited, and the videotape of the game was unmistakable. The marketing director wrote: "Based upon this incident and the many incidents which we have experienced in the past in relation to the Mountaineer and his gun, I would recommend we take an even closer look at the rules regarding the Mountaineer and his behavior."[66]

Athletics Director Pastilong found himself in the unenviable position of writing a formal apology to the Director of Athletics at Rutgers University: "Unfortunately, our Mascot tarnished this highly competitive and very close, hard fought game, by his firing the musket as your place kicker attempted a field goal in the closing minute and fifty seconds of play. We are extremely embarrassed by his actions." Pastilong further expressed his hope that this episode would not affect the good relations between the two universities.[67]

In the sixties the NCAA used a formula to determine a prospective college athlete's eligibility based on the prospect's high school ranking, high school grade-point average, and SAT or ACT score. The formula changed in 1973, when the NCAA established a 2.0 high school grade point average as the minimum for determining eligibility. During the next ten years, NCAA members came to believe that more stringent minimum standards were essential to maintain the academic integrity of higher education. In 1983, therefore, Bylaw 5–1–(j), generally known as Proposition 48, was approved at the NCAA convention. The new eligibility rule, which went into effect in 1986, required that incoming freshmen athletes complete a high school core curriculum of eleven courses and earn a 2.0 grade-point average over all courses. In addition, the prospective athlete was expected to have a combined SAT score of 700, or a composite ACT score of 15. Students who maintained a 2.0 high school grade-point average but did not achieve the minimum standardized test scores could take the option of sitting out their freshman year. Those who accepted that option would only have three years of eligibility remaining, but they could receive athletic grants-in-aid.[68]

Because of the high-visibility of big-time athletics, every apparently good omen seems to generate a countersign. Quarterback Major Harris, who led the team to the national championship game with Notre Dame in 1989, was selected as a preseason All-American by *Playboy Magazine*. Even before the issue appeared, however, head coach Don Nehlen received a letter from a Catholic priest urging him to persuade Major Harris to decline the recognition. Acceptance, according to the priest, would be the equivalent of condoning the magazine and would only encourage people to buy it.[69] Nehlen acknowledged similar expressions of concern from less altruistic quarters. Nevertheless, he countered that selection to the *Playboy* All-American Team constituted one of the most "prestigious preseason selections in college football, and to snub such an honor would be a disservice to our program and the outstanding accomplishments of our young men."[70]

Poor graduation rates for athletes were decidedly less sensational but had been a perennial concern. Not surprisingly, the problem was concentrated in the "revenue sports" of football and basketball. Collegiate ranks function somewhat like farm clubs for the NFL and NBA teams, and the need for institutions at the top level to compete with equally talented peers, as well as the potential for celebrity, resulted in student athletes who often demonstrated more talent on the field or court than in the classroom. President Bucklew initiated some major changes to address poor classroom performance. Waivers were withdrawn, and $500,000 of the proceeds from a major bowl game, the maximum amount allowed by law, was directed to the University library. The remainder was to be used to improve the academic success of student athletes, such as building a facility to house academic counselors, as well as computer and study rooms. Reports on this use of the funds prompted a West Virginia circuit court judge to write to President Bucklew. The judge claimed to be a lifelong football fan but objected to building a study hall for student athletes because he was disturbed by the "non-graduating athlete dichotomy" among football players. "The free-ride 'student' should have it no better than all others who pay their way but do not play and who will not have farm club status for salaried professional sports. It seems that the highest academic achievement is who has the most players in the NFL or NBA draft." The judge asserted that he could not remain silent before such "fiscal football folly."[71]

Bucklew responded that he shared the judge's concern with the academic progress, or lack of it, among athletes. "However, there must be some recognition of the time demands intercollegiate athletics places on student-athletes and the willingness on the part of the institution to provide academic counseling and support. . . . It is not enough to just decry the problem. We have to be willing to invest in the solution."[72] The idea of an academic facility was indeed permissible, NCAA officials advised, and they were impressed by the concept. The University's general counsel informed President Bucklew that "it was the first time such a question had ever been raised."[73] The athletic director would need to explore the idea before going forward, but eventually an academic facility was created for athletes.

Apparently, few universities had considered an academic facility for athletes, but low graduation rates in high-profile sports like football made it seem like a reasonable solution. A College Football Association report, based on the organization's annual survey, distributed in May 1989, revealed that a total of fifty-three member schools (including WVU) representing the programs with the largest commitment to football had supplied information on the members of the freshman class of 1983 who had received "athletically related financial aid from the institution." The overall graduation rate was 49.8 percent, and the median was 47.8 percent. At WVU the percentage for football athletes seemed to be on the decline: In 1984, the graduation rate for football players was 61.5 percent; in 1985, 46.7

percent; 1986, 53.1 percent; 1987, 47.1 percent; 1988, 58.3 percent; 1989, 44.4 percent. When compared with the graduation rate of 54 percent for all students at WVU, the percentage for football athletes was less alarming. Moreover, the same data showed that the graduation rate of 62 percent for all athletes was much better than it was both for all students and for all football players.[74]

Complaints about low graduation rates for athletes, real and imagined, have resurfaced periodically with the rise of big-time athletics. Generally these concerns are used to illustrate how universities care less about the athletes themselves and more about winning and the revenues the games generate. Closely paralleling this issue is whether student athletes should share in the riches and recognition their services create. The issue received considerable attention during President Bucklew's tenure, and he was forthright in his opposition to paying college athletes. In fact, he addressed his views at a general meeting with student athletes in August 1989: "It would be a mistake for intercollegiate athletics to pay student-athletes for their athletic contributions," not because of the potential for corruption and abuse but because the "fundamental nature" of the student athlete's role is one of "student first and athlete second." Universities, he said, were responsible for preparing all students to participate in a changing world. "Intercollegiate athletics is supplemental to that fundamental mission, and must be understood in that light." The amateur status of student athletes must be guarded and "must affirm the similarities between student-athletes and other students rather than emphasize the distinctions." While athletes may have financial needs beyond what grants-in-aid funds cover, so do many other students. While this calls for creative thinking about how to resolve this problem, it would only harm universities "if we accept the facile solution of paying them." Intercollegiate athletics has become "a large-scale enterprise" and generates a large amount of spectator interest through the televising of regular-season and bowl games, making it difficult to maintain an appropriate perspective. Even in this new environment, however, it is essential to recognize students who participate in intercollegiate completion as student-athletes rather than athlete-students who receive pay for the performances. Scholarships are designed to allow the development of talents, Bucklew insisted, "whether academic, athletic, musical, or something else." Developing talent is time-consuming for all of these students, and the scholarship support they receive "is not meant to pay them for the time they choose to invest, but to provide support for the cost of going to college." Therefore, the level of support should reflect the cost of education and should be managed within the context of student financial aid, not as a payment for services. When universities cross the line toward professionalization of college athletics, Bucklew told the athletes, "such a program would no longer have an appropriate place in our colleges and universities."[75]

Director of Athletics Ed Pastilong wrote to thank President Bucklew for spending the evening talking with the athletes. "We sincerely want them to realize our interest in their lives off the courts and playing fields. This cannot be accomplished overnight and will take a serious effort on our part." Continually emphasizing education and acceptable social and personal behavior, Pastilong agreed, was essential to the growth and development of all young adults. "Many times their assumption is that our primary interest is the number of 'wins' they accumulate. . . . We must convey to these young people our sincerity for their well being."[76]

PART III

THE CORPORATE UNIVERSITY: COMMERCIALIZATION, 1990–

BEGINNING WITH THE PRESIDENCY of David Hardesty, who took office in 1995, a series of state-mandated reforms stripped what legislators regarded as waste and inefficiencies out of the University. By the time this torturous process was completed six years later, WVU had gained more independence in governing its own internal affairs than it had at any time since control over higher education was centralized in the Board of Regents in 1969. Independence came at a price, however; the University now faced the responsibility of generating more of its own operating revenues, as the state's proportion of its operating budget continued to contract. If WVU were to take advantage of its newfound administrative freedom, it must become much more entrepreneurial—a growing national trend after 1980.

"Commercialization," therefore, became the preeminent shaping force at West Virginia University during the era examined in Part III. There is a large and growing literature on the commercialization of research universities. The term itself is used to convey a variety of university behaviors and practices: the general influence of economic forces; the influence of corporate culture, evidenced in the use of business language; student demand for career-track curricula, or vocationalism; the adoption of business methods, or efforts to operate more economically; attempts to quantify all matters, even those best left to qualitative judgment, such as teaching; and the more straightforward definition of efforts by a university to generate revenues from teaching, research, athletics, and other activities on campus.[1] All of these behaviors and reciprocal activities have become commonplace at WVU.

There is nothing new in universities engaging in commercial practices. The Morrill Act of 1862 established the land-grant universities, and the Hatch Act of 1887 established agricultural experiment stations at those institutions to stimulate the discovery of solutions to society's problems through applied science and technology. By the mid-twenties, industrial firms were establishing their own research departments, which formed links with science and engineering faculty to channel their discoveries to those laboratories. The mobilization of scientists and engineers during World War II demonstrated the value of government-funded research for achieving specific goals. The role of federally sponsored research continued during the Cold War, and former links between university researchers and industrial laboratories all but disappeared. In the seventies this government-university relationship began to change as direct federal support for basic research dried up. Government funding became dependent on independent, peer-reviewed proposals, and federal agencies procured the applied research they required as part of their mission. Intercollegiate athletics is the most public example of commercial engagement by universities, but it certainly is not new. Sports historians agree that the first intercollegiate athletic event in American history was a Harvard versus Yale boat race in 1852 that was sponsored by a developer who wanted to publicize a lake as a summer resort. Football replaced crew as America's most popular college sport by the early twentieth century, and the American Tobacco Company became the leading sponsor. With the prevalence of television after World War II, college football and basketball emerged as the "revenue sports."[2] Similarly, naming buildings, professorships, and chairs for major donors has been a common practice at universities for a long time.

Commercialization, therefore, is not new on university campuses; it is the size and scale of these activities, rather, that is unprecedented. Derek Bok, a former president of Harvard, has cited some of the more significant explanations for why commercial activity accelerated in recent times. One is the growing influence of the market in society generally. Commercialism has taken root in many areas that traditionally were outside of the business realm and did not share its values, such as education, the arts, and religion. Some writers point to the presumed loss of a clear mission in higher education as a factor encouraging the intrusion of commercialism. As Bok demonstrates, however, scientists have a very clear sense of mission, and it is the sciences where commercialism is most pervasive. There are critics who charge that the growth of commercial activities at universities is still another manifestation of business interests seeking to "commodify" education and research so that universities will conform to their monetary vision of the world. These critics compare posh schools of business to the shabby schools of education, arts, or social work, and suggest that the composition of university boards of trustees, where wealthy and influential businessmen and corporate lawyers predominate, explains the disparity.[3] Although it is doubtful that a "conspiracy" is afoot to replace traditional university values with those of the marketplace, there are certainly latent fears that the dominance of the business classes in government and higher education might well create the "hegemony" of the business perspective.

Another explanation for the acceleration of commercialization is that, with the slowing economy and declining federal support for higher education in the seventies, state legislatures responded by trimming education appropriations in order to balance their budgets, especially in the eighties and nineties. Universities were forced to look elsewhere to make up the deficit, usually, as at WVU, through cutting expenses and generating new revenue streams. One authority claims that what made the scale of commercialization so much greater after 1980 was "the rapid growth of opportunities to supply education, expert advice, and scientific knowledge in return for handsome sums of money." Before World War II, the opportunities to profit from commercial activities were much less available than they were during and after the war, when the federal government invested heavily in science for national defense.[4]

By the late seventies, the Cold War was winding down, and the federal government shifted its science policy from national defense to maintaining America's supremacy in international trade. During the late seventies and early eighties, the Japanese electronics and automobile industries made deep incursions into U.S. markets, prompting the federal government to refocus its investment in science and technology in order to improve the nation's competitive position and drive economic development. How to manage patents and other intellectual property created by federally funded research and how to facilitate technology transfer from laboratories to the marketplace were major concerns. Previously, intellectual property discovered by government-funded research either became federal property, or was placed into the public domain through publication. It was assumed that the public interest would be served if research results were made available for private industry. Unfortunately, private industry would not invest in developing new discoveries that were in the public domain because another firm might produce the same product without the investment. The costs of developing a concept into a viable product might be significant, and recovering those costs at an acceptable profit stretched a firm's tolerance for risk.[5]

The Bayh-Dole University and Small Business Patent Act of 1980 was a major step toward linking university research to the needs of business. The act reversed the previous policy by assigning intellectual property rights to the universities where the discoveries occurred. Consequently, universities could now patent discoveries and license businesses to develop them into products. Universities might even establish their own start-up companies to develop and market products created from their intellectual property. The act also clarified the point that intellectual property rights did not belong to faculty researchers, but rather to the universities that employed them. However, universities were required to reinvest all revenues generated from this activity back into the university's educational mission. Further encouragement came through federal and state legislation offering subsidies for university and business joint ventures, and tax breaks for industry investments in university-based research.[6]

Research universities were now in the technology-transfer business. By 1990, some two hundred universities had established research offices to patent commercially promising research discoveries and license them to companies. A decade later, the volume of university patents had increased ten times and annually earned more than $1 billion in royalties and license fees. Many institutions had created centers to provide technical assistance to small businesses, invested in start-up companies founded by their professors, and developed business incubators and research-industrial parks to help individuals launch private firms to create products based on university discoveries. One scholar inelegantly described the Bayh-Dole Act as "the Viagra for campus innovation," reporting that campus intellectual property had created 280,000 jobs and generated approximately $33.5 billion in economic activity during 1998 alone.[7] Advances in genetics and biotechnology created new opportunities for medical school faculty to patent new discoveries and start new businesses. "Within a few short decades, therefore, a brave new world had emerged filled with attractive possibilities for turning specialized knowledge into money. University presidents, enterprising professors, and even administrative staff were all busy exploiting these opportunities," Derek Bok observed.[8]

Commercialization has intensified the competition for resources among research universities, and state governments have joined the effort, now that they are much better informed about the economic stimulus that university research can generate. New start-up businesses, as well as the "vibrant economic clusters that have grown up around university communities," have captured the imagination of state governments. Silicon Valley, Cambridge, Massachusetts, and Research Triangle Park are the sirens calling out to enchanted state officials.[9] Certainly West Virginia would like to follow suit by utilizing the I-79 High-Tech Corridor between Clarksburg and Morgantown, which has direct linkages with the faculty at WVU and has received massive support from the state's federal delegation and state officials. State legislators were sending a clear signal to their public research universities, according to one scholar: "It's time to begin commercializing your discoveries to promote local economic development. Nearly a third of the nation's governors have called on legislatures to pump money into public universities' research and technology-transfer programs." States are also eliminating barriers to collaboration between public-university faculty members and private companies in a bid to incentivize public-university employees to bring their discoveries to market.[10]

Despite the emphasis on commercialization in recent decades, relatively few universities have profited from these activities, while most have not received enough revenues from technology transfer to cover the cost of their investment. Only a few institutions have succeeded in discovering a scientific or technological breakthrough that significantly enriched the university since passage of the Bayh-Dole Act in 1980. Nevertheless, there have been substantial benefits to society from commercial activities. Big-time college sports programs have entertained countless millions, and university-industry collaborations have facilitated the process by which scientific discoveries have been turned into products that enhance the health and well-being of society. Moreover, the lure of money has stimulated administrators to pioneer distance learning through web-based courses and closed-circuit television, extending education to those who cannot attend classes on campus.[11]

In the sixties and seventies the federal government provided two-thirds of the funding for research. By 2004, the amount of money spent by industry for research and development, approximately $200 billion, accounted for two-thirds of the nation's total investment in research and development. However, less than $1 billion of that $200 billion was directed to university research. Industry provided only 6.5 percent of university research in 2004; the federal government and the universities were underwriting nearly the entire cost. And yet universities were required to transfer technology to the private sector as soon as possible. It has been aptly noted that Vannevar Bush's famous 1945 report, *Science—The Endless Frontier*, turned science into a "vast publically owned enterprise," while the Bayh-Dole Act drove publically funded university research into the hands of private concerns.[12] While "profits create incentives that can induce universities to behave in ways that benefit the public," Bok insists that one must be cautious in counting these as advantages because commercial competition only produces what the market wants, rather than beneficial academic outcomes. The trap for universities is that the financial benefits seem immediate and tangible, whereas the costs are in the abstract form of values.[13]

Conflicts of interest present an important problem for research universities that shift from their traditional culture of basic, curiosity-driven research to research driven by commercial potential. The biomedical and biotechnological fields highlight the likelihood for conflicts of interest and the corruption of traditional university values. As of 2004, 60 percent of federal funding for university research went to biomedical research. The National Institutes of Health was budgeted $27 billion by Congress in

2003, more than five times the $5 billion allocated to the National Science Foundation. Medical-device manufacturers have paid surgeons to use their products, such as hip-replacement joints, and there are numerous reports of pharmaceutical firms paying physicians in exchange for prescribing their medicines to patients. Pharmaceutical companies pay medical researchers large sums of money to conduct clinical trials to test new drugs. Collegiality and public interest suffer when scientists do not share new knowledge with their colleagues because of the financial implications. In fact, contracts with firms often prevent faculty researchers from doing so. Extraordinary abuses of core values and outright fraud are, fortunately, rare because they are eventually exposed and the violator's reputation is destroyed. More commonly, research results are biased, intentionally or not, by investigators to confirm preconceived outcomes in favor of the company funding the study. Wise university administrations construct mechanisms and procedures to control at least the flagrant conflicts of interest.[14]

Other commercial activities entail conflicts that might more appropriately be called "conflicts of commitment." It has long been a fact of life for university faculty that they must "publish or perish," but increasingly scientists are expected to "publish, patent, or perish." Universities prefer to obtain federal contracts because they generate 40 to 60 percent of the grant total in indirect income for the university, a charge which industry will not pay. Since the nineties, however, the pressures for scientists have shifted from seeking external funding to negotiating contracts with private firms to support research that has commercial potential. In return, companies receive the right to anything developed by the research project. Scientists at research universities are often recruited with the contractual requirement that they generate external funding for their research and new revenue streams for their institutions. This is a pervasive practice in the health sciences and to a lesser degree in the basic sciences. In effect, faculty are expected to raise all or a portion of their own salaries through external funding. Many "buy" their time away from teaching, while star research scientists may never teach at all. High-profile researchers bring prestige and revenue to the university, but they have no particular commitment to the university that employs them.[15]

Critics of commercialization (and they probably outnumber the supporters) point to other potentially insidious effects. The pressure to generate revenues leaves faculty with little time for students or for preparation for classroom teaching. Also, there is a question as to whether the research in question will be judged by its success in attracting external funding and potential commercial value or by its contribution to scientific knowledge. The potential effects on the curriculum might be detrimental as well. Less popular courses, philosophy or the classics for example, may be dropped in favor of business courses that students believe will make them more marketable in the job search after graduation. In the worst cases, undergraduate teaching might become so undervalued that graduate students or part-time adjuncts are called in to pick up the slack. For those who are primarily interested in commercial outcomes, the resulting changes to traditional academic culture might be desirable, but the shift in the university from academic values to vocational values presents a clear and present danger to the traditional idea of a university and to what is in the public interest.[16]

One university scientist testifying at a congressional hearing raised this very issue. "What is ultimately most striking about today's academic industrial complex is not that large amounts of private capital are flowing into universities. It is that universities themselves are beginning to look and behave like for-profit companies. If we value unfettered basic research as the prime function of the academic setting, then it is fair to ask if the extent of current commercial interactions distorts that mission and promotes the public interest."[17]

Commercialization is usually associated with business, and, like other research universities, WVU is beginning to resemble a business. The University has struggled under a poor state economy for most of the half-century following World War II. Dramatic shifts in the national economy produced a decades-long recession in West Virginia. Economic changes in some of West Virginia's basic industries, particularly steel, glass, chemicals, and coal, led to consolidations in those industries that diminished their footprint in the state. Foreign oil took market share from coal, and foreign competitors entered American markets with cheaper products. WVU's financial problems were aggravated in the eighties after the Baby-Boom generation completed its passage through higher education, and enrollments slumped after the anticipated drop in the number of state high school graduates. A smaller pool of students signaled the likelihood of less income from tuition.

The immediate solution was to make WVU more attractive to in-state students, recruit more out-of-state students, and require them to pay higher tuition and fees. The declining pool of high school graduates was a national phenomenon, however, and the University would enter a very competitive market in which most institutions of higher learning were forced to be proactive in recruiting potential students. This strategy required investment in upgrading student amenities. Campus beautification projects and efforts to improve classroom facilities, dormitories, food service, and entertainment options became essential to success in the recruiting wars. Construction projects like the University's state-of-the-art Recreation Center became part of the University's plan to buttress its finances. WVU's "student-centered" emphasis benefited the students and was probably overdue, but it was also a business decision expressed in commercial terms, as students became "customers" and education the "service" that they "purchased."

"Efficiency" was a mantra of the legislatively mandated reforms passed in 1995 (Senate Bill 547) and in 2000 (Senate Bill 653). One way WVU responded to the reforms was to initiate "Integration 2000," which merged academic units and integrated its affiliated institutions, WVU Institute of Technology, WVU at Parkersburg, and Potomac State College, fully into the University system. University units and auxiliaries were transformed into "independent cost centers" and required to stand on their own financial bottoms. Students living in dormitories bore the cost of operating the dorms, and academic units like English and history, which generated no external funding, bore the cost of their operation through increased teaching loads.

If WVU were to thrive rather than merely survive, becoming more commercialized seemed to offer better odds than continuing on the old path of overdependence on state appropriations. The mandated higher education reforms initiated by the legislature were products of the business ethos. What business expected of WVU, the subject of a President Hardesty speech, brimmed with the language of commerce. Business expected WVU to be "customer oriented," in recognition of the importance of its customers (students), to better serve them. Financial "accountability" and operating within budget demonstrated that the University "respected the taxpayer." Rational decision-making, free of politics, and delivery of a "quality product" for a "reasonable cost" were some of the business values the president expressed. He was articulating ideas even more directly stated in the legislation itself. Senate Bill 547 explicitly stated that WVU was expected to play a leading role in developing the state's economy. Faculty objected to the language as being more appropriate for a vocational school, but the bill also stipulated: "It is essential that higher education prepare people for a successful lifetime of work."[18]

After five years of wringing out institutional inefficiencies as dictated by Senate Bill 547, each of the state's institutions of higher education was required to develop a written set of goals for broader community engagement. *The Compact for the Future of West Virginia*, mandated by Senate Bill 653, was a "covenant" between the institutions and the people of West Virginia that was intended to guide the schools from 2001 through 2007. Each institution set its own goals, and WVU's goals included research that served the state's "new economy" by enhancing the state's educational, economic, and social revitalization, and by providing greater access to technical education and workforce development. When the legislature accepted the University's *Compact for the Future* in 2001, self-governance was once again returned to the University's Board of Governors.

Neither the public nor its elected representatives generally thought of WVU as an "economic engine," but the commandment to become one prompted the University to report the magnitude of its economic impact annually. The multi-billion-dollar economic activity it generated became a major defense against further cuts in state appropriations. External funding research alone expanded from $13 million in the eighties to $175 million dollars in 2011, and this kind of activity resulted in a cluster of federal laboratories and high-tech start-up businesses, which was the hallmark of modern university-led economic development.

Intercollegiate athletics at WVU also became a major business by generating tens of millions of dollars in licensing apparel, the University's flying WV logo being one of the most popular in that category; in ticket sales and television revenues from football; and in private donations. Sports represent the "front porch" of the University, so the public was generally aware that athletics was becoming a big business. The greatest culture shift, however, was the University's aspiration to become a major research university and its confidence that this goal was achievable. To do this, WVU would have to become less dependent on "earmark" grants (those written into a piece of legislation) and to seek more aggressively competitive grants. The Kellogg Commission on the Future of Land-Grant Universities, in its 1999 report on "The Engaged Institution," laid out a blueprint for land-grants to recommit themselves to their original mission of solving society's problems. Universities needed to become more "productively involved with their communities" through reciprocal partnerships between the university, government, business, and non-profits in order to jointly solve problems.[19]

The Hardesty administration charted a course for WVU in line with the philosophy of the engaged institution offered in this report. To achieve this goal, WVU re-conceptualized and reorganized the diverse array of individual research projects at the University into a model that elevated research to a university-managed enterprise. University research, thus re-envisioned, became a service operating in the marketplace, applying "the same principles of quality and customer satisfaction that we are applying to student services," President Hardesty declared. The new strategy was to relentlessly pursue external funding, concentrate research on important niches where the University had strategic advantages, and deliver "high-quality research at a competitive price."[20] For example, biotechnology was identified as an area where a large amount of research funding was available from federal agencies, and interdisciplinary research teams were organized to take advantage of the opportunity.

Another major culture shift was signified by the University's effort to work with faculty investigators to patent and commercialize their discoveries. WVU's *Strategic Plan for Research for 2000–2005* was "to increase the portfolio of intellectual property from faculty research and proactively transfer the technologies to the private sector," and that commitment was stated even more forcefully in the *2004–2010 Strategic Plan for Economic Development*.[21] WVU's Economic Development Council identified areas of need where the University could play a role and then coordinated these activities, sought funding, and assessed research programs. The WVU Research Corporation was empowered to run the University's research enterprise. Its mission was "to provide evaluation, development, patenting, management, and marketing services" to faculty researchers. It also served as a fiscal agent for sponsored programs, assisted faculty with developing proposals, and provided resources and assistance to researchers. The Research Corporation established the Office of Technology Transfer in 1999 "to protect, promote, and commercialize" research and intellectual property. To facilitate this mission, the WVU Business Incubator was created and located in the University Research Park to support start-up businesses using WVU research discoveries. With the infrastructure in place, the Research Corporation also established the Office for Congressional and Federal Relations in Washington, DC in 2009 to bolster the University's effort to become a major research partner with federal funding agencies.

Critics of commercialization would find like-minded colleagues in the larger WVU community who shared Derek Bok's concern that "even those who support the university's efforts to aid economic growth worry about the side effects of profit-seeking, and the unseemliness of institutions of learning hawking everything from sweatshirts to adult education." These fears, he writes, "persist as a mute reminder that something of irreplaceable value may get lost in the relentless growth of commercialization."[22] Those fears persist at WVU as well, but viable alternatives remain elusive. In the meantime, the undeniable truth is that West Virginia University has charted a course to a more promising future than it could have hoped for in the past.

THIRTEEN

POLITICS OF GOVERNANCE SINCE THE BOARD OF REGENTS

WEST VIRGINIA'S SEARCH for an appropriate model of higher education governance following World War II was shaped by the interplay of circumstances unique to the state. The mountains created a beautiful landscape, but they also divided the state into distinctive regions and spawned an intense sectionalism that only began to break down with postwar improvements in transportation and communications. Competition among institutions for limited resources, reinforced by sectional interests, also played a significant role in the search for orderly governance. Moreover, the tradition in West Virginia of centralized oversight in education, such as the state Board of Education's supervision of the county boards, served as a model demonstrating how legislators could impose centralized controls on higher education as well. The desire of institutional leaders to chart their own courses worked at cross-purposes with state leaders' insistence on centralized control, thereby generating a constant supply of friction in higher education. Some governors contributed to the conflict by regarding higher educational institutions as state agencies that should be subject to executive control in the same way as, for example, the highway department. The reflexive search for outside "expertise" and the use of consultants to provide guidance has further complicated the process by prompting West Virginia legislators to impose systems designed for other states rather than creating one suited to their own state's political culture. As a consequence, WVU presidents have been forced to expend time and energy defending the University from sectional politics that would have been more productively utilized advancing their institution.

Despite this complicated political environment, expectations were very high following the passage of Senate Bill 420, which created the new University of West Virginia System. "Consider the breadth of what we have accomplished," Board of Trustees Chairman David Hardesty reported in June 1991 at the end of the board's first year of operation. The first order of business was to select board members, set up the office of the chancellor, and develop new philosophies of governance and mission statements for each of the institutions created under the new system. Even before the wide-ranging debates over the myriad of issues facing higher education could be taken up, however, a working relationship with the state government had to be established.[1] Indeed, much had been accomplished in very short order since the long ordeal of political wrangling that led up to the legislature's enacting Senate Bill 420 on April 8, 1989.

HIGHER EDUCATION REFORM CONTINUES

Governor Gaston Caperton III had a vision for higher education, but it took the rare convergence of higher education officials in a common purpose to succeed in reorganizing the system as called for by Senate Bill 420. Two separate boards replaced the Board of Regents: the University of West Virginia Board of Trustees to oversee WVU and its affiliates, Marshall, West Virginia Graduate College, and the West Virginia School of Osteopathic Medicine; and a second Board of Directors to oversee the eight four-year colleges in the state. Both boards fell under the jurisdiction of the state Department of Education and the Arts, headed by then-Secretary Stephen Haid, followed by Barbara Shamberger, both graduates of WVU. The secretary coordinated policies established by the two boards to ensure their compliance with state directives. The Board of Trustees was composed of seventeen members, including the chancellor, who served as the board's chief administrative officer, and twelve other members appointed by the governor. Also, one voting member from each of the three advisory councils of faculty, students, and classified staff occupied three seats. Two nonvoting members were also appointed to the Board of Trustees, the Chancellor of the State College System, and the State Superintendent of Schools.

Among the Board of Trustees' charges were developing a "master plan" for the system, preventing duplication in graduate and professional studies, and monitoring institutional policies. The Board of Trustees also appointed the presidents of WVU and the other institutions under its oversight.[2]

Senate Bill 420 also retained the WVU Board of Advisors. The eleven-member board consisted of four institutional representatives, one each from administration, faculty, staff, and students, and seven lay members (two alumni and no more than four from the same political party). It was the responsibility of the Board of Advisors to review all WVU proposals involving academic programs, the budget, and capital facilities. The Board of Advisors also served as both the search and the screening committees for new University presidents. WVU President Neil Bucklew regarded the reorganization as a vast improvement over the Board of Regents, calling Senate Bill 420 "landmark legislation" that offered the opportunity to improve quality and efficiency at the University. Because the Board of Trustees was responsible only for the two universities, there was bound to be greater recognition of the special needs of doctoral degree-granting institutions, and fewer schools to supervise meant less bureaucracy than under the Board of Regents.[3]

Another result of the reorganization of 1989 was the formal affiliation of both Potomac State College in Keyser and Parkersburg Community College with WVU. Potomac State had been associated with WVU since its establishment in 1909 as a "feeder school," but Senate Bill 420 made the relationship official. Parkersburg Community College, on the other hand, had been autonomous for two decades. After some initial skepticism among its faculty and staff regarding the benefits of affiliation, however, both Parkersburg Community College and Potomac State College became "regional campuses" under the reorganization. Subsequently, both institutions became full WVU branches.[4]

While WVU officials met the reorganization of higher education with guarded optimism, others could not shake their concern that the end result for the new system would mirror the old: "micromanagement" and the continued "politicization of higher education." These concerns proved legitimate when several attempts to ensure accountability prompted by the governor, legislature, and board of trustees were initiated. In 1991, the legislature mandated that each institution produce a "Report Card" that required a massive amount of data presented in formats that would be comprehensive and yet easy to read. The report card was not yet completed when in March 1992 the Board of Trustees initiated a streamlining and cost-cutting process that involved an intensive review of all academic programs and administrative units and a progress report delivered to the Board of Trustees by September 1, 1992. Almost at the same time, the governor established the Higher Education Advocacy Team (HEAT) to identify goals and plans for institutions of higher education. The HEAT process called for meetings throughout the state to consult with all constituencies, including faculty, staff, and the public. WVU hosted a HEAT meeting on September 22, 1992, at the Creative Arts Center which attracted 1,700 people. A summary of the major issues emerging from the process centered around institutional and employee accountability, meeting the financial needs of higher education, institutional autonomy and flexibility, open access to higher education, and economic and workforce development.[5]

The resulting legislation, Senate Bill 377, passed on April 21, 1993, created a "higher and other post-secondary education" coordinating group known as the HOPE council. The specificity of Senate Bill 377 in directing the HOPE council caused many higher education professionals to regard it as another effort to micromanage rather than promote education in the state. SB 377 set goals but provided no state funding, thus requiring those goals to be addressed with institutional resources. Also, such directives as developing policies to minimize textbook changes and utilizing textbooks systemwide and statewide demonstrated to professionals that a limited notion of what goes on in higher education prevailed among those who crafted the bill. University administrators believed that Senate Bill 377's provisions limited their ability to provide "creative leadership" and created a level of tension and distrust that was counterproductive. One administrator described them as "policies, procedures, and processes based on the assumption that we are crooks and/or incompetent."[6]

Nevertheless, WVU officials regarded the provisions of Senate Bill 377 with cautious optimism. If the HEAT legislation proved to be the harbinger of a new awareness of the importance of higher education in the future of West Virginia, then WVU should be able to build a better working relationship with the state, as well as access to much needed resources. Ultimately, WVU administrators believed that the financial difficulties confronting the University were rooted in a political culture that did not perceive education as an agent of change. The HEAT legislation, Senate Bill 377, provided some evidence that this attitude might be changing. The bill presented an ambitious agenda for education in West Virginia: to encourage students to pursue higher education by improving their preparation for college, to encourage partnerships between higher education and business, to improve efficiency and productivity in institutions of higher education, and to enhance compensation for faculty and staff.[7]

In the 1995 session, state legislators continued their pursuit of higher education reform by passing Senate Bill 547, which required all state colleges and universities to reallocate substantial portions of their budgets to meet specified salary targets for faculty and classified staff. But, once again, the unfunded mandate forced the institutions to come up with the money for pay raises out of their own resources.[8]

During the years of Senate Bill 547, 1995–2000, state colleges and universities were asked to slash weak programs and focus on developing programs of strength, particularly those with the potential to contribute directly to the economic development of the state. The Board of Trustees approved WVU's five-year plan to enhance the University as a comprehensive research, doctoral degree-granting, land-grant institution. In addition to the mandated salary increases, WVU redirected its reallocated resources toward enhancing the libraries, technology, student-centered learning and experiences, and an expansion of those services with a direct impact on the state's economic development.[9]

When President Neil Bucklew passed the baton to his successor, David Hardesty, he informed him that he considered Senate Bill 547 to be "the most important public policy guidance" for higher education that had been established in a long time. The measure required that each institution undertake substantial strategic planning, and the first report was due on November 1, 1995, less than five months after Hardesty's tenure began.

The campus plans were to be consolidated by the Board of Trustees into a system-wide plan to be presented to the secretary of education and the arts. The final plan was expected to provide "a road map for campus actions that will create a more streamlined and consolidated institution" and a financial piece documenting how the University would generate the funds to cover the salary increases over the next five years. Unfortunately, President Bucklew noted, "there is nothing in the bill that unravels the complicated policies and statues currently in place regarding personnel changes." The statutes regarding furloughing employees made it "difficult if not nearly impossible" to bring about the desired change.[10]

Bucklew believed that the politicians always considered WVU as "a little fat" and could be "squeezed" to become more efficient. Hardesty thought that Senate Bill 547 resulted from faculty and staff pressure to increase salaries, that the bill was intended to raise salaries over a five-year period, and that it would be paid for in part by increased efficiencies. The bill's author, state Senator Lloyd Jackson, viewed the legislation as an "opportunity to achieve efficiencies," Hardesty observed, and the only way to gain campus cooperation was to promise more money. The bill had already been passed when Hardesty took the helm, but it was his responsibility to find the efficiencies that would generate the needed funds for the mandated pay raises.[11]

REORGANIZATION UNDER SENATE BILL 653

The reforms, which were intended to encourage cooperation rather than competition among the state's institutions of higher education, did not achieve their intended result. A heated debate in 1997 between the university and college boards over state appropriations prompted one legislator to comment that the two state boards "spend so much time arguing that we can't address any education issues." The secretary of education and the arts also informed the press of a "growing concern" among legislators that higher education was a "trouble spot" because of the wrangling over state appropriations.[12] The House of Delegates passed a bill to combine the two boards into one to bring an end to the constant conflict, but the Senate chose instead to create a committee to study the matter. President Hardesty, testifying before the legislative panel, said that creating a single state board was not the solution; rather the solution was to delegate more power to the school-based boards while allowing the state boards to concentrate on statewide matters. Doing so would provide each institution with its own focused mission and would eliminate competition among them. "The changes we face now are the greatest changes since World War II," he told them.[13]

Senate Bill 547, therefore, was only the beginning of the legislative reforms. The National Center for Higher Education Management Systems (NCHEMS) was contracted to provide legislators with an organizational and financial plan. In October 1999 the Special Committee to Study Higher Education in West Virginia was presented with a proposal that outlined what life would be like after Senate Bill 547 ended in 2000. The following month, the NCHEMS consultants announced the results of their eight-month study, which called for a major overhaul of the higher education system. Among the study's recommendations were abandoning the student enrollment method of finance, freezing or decreasing undergraduate tuition, increasing the level of funding invested in higher education, and creating a new oversight committee to monitor the state boards.[14]

Legislators considered the NECHEMS proposals seriously, and the Senate Committee on Education reported out a new plan for higher education in February 2000. Senate Bill 653 proposed that colleges would receive money based on how they compared with their peer institutions and according to their performance. It called for an eight-member higher education policy commission to replace the two state boards and chancellors, and for establishing self-governing boards at each institution. Independent community colleges would also be established statewide.[15]

A revised Senate Bill 653 was passed in March 2000 and went into effect the following June. Governor Underwood appointed seven new members of the Higher Education Policy Commission (HEPC) a few days later. Four were Republicans, two were Democrats, and one was an Independent. The bill also mandated two members from each of the three congressional districts, with no more than four members affiliated with the same political party. There was no provision for faculty, staff, or student representation, as had been the case with the previous governing boards. Under the reorganization, the University of West Virginia System Board of Trustees, established in 1990, was to be replaced in July 2002 by the HEPC. The HEPC assumed the responsibility of developing policy for the state's public colleges and universities. Members consisted of the secretary of education and the arts, the state superintendent of schools, and seven members appointed by the governor.[16]

Senate Bill 653 also declared that on July 1, 2001, the West Virginia University Board of Governors would become the governing body of the University. It would consist of eighteen members, including one faculty member, one classified staff member, and one student member, each elected by their peers; one representative each from the Community and Technical College at the West Virginia University Institute of Technology, West Virginia University at Parkersburg, and the West Virginia University Institute of Technology. Completing the Board of Governors were twelve lay members appointed by the governor with the advice and consent of the state senate, no more than seven of whom were to be of the same political party, and at least eight of whom must be residents of the state. The University president was chosen by the Board of Governors with the approval of the HEPC. The Board of Governors oversees the academic and administrative operations of the University. The president is the chief executive officer and chairman of the board and, as such, was the primary spokesperson for the Board of Governors. Vaughn Kiger, an active WVU alumnus and prominent Morgantown businessman, was chosen as the first president of the new Board of Governors. The advantages of self government were obvious, Kiger told the press, because now we have "people who are just concentrating on WVU. . . . We have a personal stake. It's not just coming out of Charleston."[17] Finally, WVU's long-awaited opportunity to manage its own affairs once again seemed to have been largely realized—but at a price.

The lack of financial resources would continue to plague efforts to reform higher education. The NCHEMS plan called for 6 percent increases to the higher education budget, or about $22 million per year, while at the same time the system was operating under a budget freeze. Higher education officials convinced Governor Cecil Underwood that it would be impossible to implement the reforms while the budget reduction was in place. NCHEMS's recommendation that allocation of funding be linked to a group of peer institutions created an even bigger problem because West Virginia faculty salaries were among the lowest in the nation. NCHEMS helped to select the appropriate peers for WVU; the list included the University of Arizona, University of Cincinnati, University of Florida, University of Kentucky, Michigan State University, University of Missouri, University of New Mexico, Ohio State University, Texas A&M University, and Virginia Commonwealth University. Like WVU, they were either "flagship," land-grant, Research I, and/or health sciences center universities.[18]

Predictably, it was immediately apparent that WVU would not meet the salary goals set by the peer group anytime soon. The classified staff salary schedule that came into effect in 1994 was fully funded as a result of Senate Bill 547 on July 1, 2000. WVU faculty salaries, however, were alternately either unfunded or increasing at an anemic rate, while salaries at peer institutions continued to improve consistently. In October 2000, a NCHEMS consultant provided the HEPC with an estimated cost of $176 million for funding West Virginia's colleges and universities on a roughly equivalent basis to their peers. These numbers were in another league entirely from the paltry $1 million HEPC requested from legislators that year to address the disparity. The budget for WVU's peer institutions averaged about $18,000 per student compared with WVU's $15,000 per student. If the gap was ever to be closed, who could accomplish it, especially since all of the state's colleges rested firmly at the bottom of their peer groups in terms of general revenues per full-time student (the standard gauge)? The consultant informed the HEPC that West Virginia's practice of dedicating 20 percent of tuition revenues to capital funding was "highly undesirable." The state "simply cannot continue to maintain assets by taking the funding out of tuition revenues. It makes West Virginia worse off than it already is which is bad." The challenge for the HEPC was to devise a better way to distribute resources and simultaneously establish a workable tuition policy.[19]

Unfortunately, a week later, when the state legislators met in interim monthly meetings, they received revenue projections of an estimated annual growth rate of 2 percent, or about $102 million over six years, down from the $151 million that legislators had discussed earlier in 2000. There were many reasons for the decline, but all of them stemmed from a slowdown in the economy and a reduction in tax revenues. WVU President David Hardesty observed that, as a former tax commissioner, he knew the state could not spend money it did not have, "but in times of a sluggish economy, there's no better investment than higher education. . . . I hope our lawmakers take a hard look at our true priorities."[20] Unfortunately, by the end of 2000 the estimated cost of funding West Virginia's colleges at the level of their peers in other states had grown to $218 million, amounting to a $146 million gap between the revenues available and the amount needed to meet peer averages. Forced to face the facts, the president of the HEPC informed the press that the peer benchmark, which amounted to a 22 percent salary increase, was a target rather than a mandate. That benchmark, he declared, was "just a pie in the sky to shoot for."[21]

In February 2001, the consultants' and legislators' efforts to devise a reform package that would increase funding for West Virginia's public colleges seemed doomed when newly elected Governor Bob Wise intentionally left the package out of his budget proposal. The higher education package was intended to overhaul the state's system of higher education at a cost of $150 million over six years. Funding colleges on the basis of student enrollment alone was eliminated, substituting instead the financing levels provided to peer institutions in order to make the state's institutions roughly comparable. The reason given by the governor was that the higher education bill would have "required more cuts or taxes in other departments to come up with that money." Legislators were furious. "The most important piece of legislation the Legislature passed last year," complained one delegate, and Governor Wise unilaterally decided to leave it out of his budget just thirty minutes before his State of the State Address.[22] Governor Wise was quick to reassure higher education leaders of his commitment to Senate Bill 653. However, legislators noted that, even though the governor was unable to find the money to fund the first year of the reform, he nevertheless advanced his own Promise Scholarship program, which paid the state college tuition, or the equivalent amount to a private school, for all graduating high school seniors with a 3.0 grade average who attended college in West Virginia.[23]

Shortly thereafter, in an interview with HEPC Chancellor J. Michael Mullen, *Charleston Gazette* Editor James A. Haught asserted that "all these administrative reorganizations seem like wasted motion. . . . The Board of Regents was hatched to take higher education out of politics, and to streamline the university system and reduce the number of colleges and simplify everything." It was all just a lot of "bureaucratic flapdoodle," Haught asserted. "The first time they tried to close a college, an explosion of protest shook the political establishment. Legislators wet their pants and quickly overrode the Board of Regents." Then legislators created two boards instead, and now they were back to one board again. "Do all these boards actually do anything?" Haught challenged. Chancellor Mullen pointed out that Senate Bill 653 created a "new culture" because, beginning on July 1, 2001, the institutional boards of governors would have legitimate authority and responsibility to run their respective institutions. The HEPC only set policy, evaluated performance, and required accountability. "The litmus test for me is going to be the Policy Commission's reaction to the institution master plans and compacts. Senate Bill 653 gave the Commission authority to say, if you don't have an acceptable compact, you don't get any of the new money."[24]

Another newspaper editor suggested that a "powerful incentive" now existed for colleges to consolidate. Just as public school enrollments continued on a thirty-year slide, enrollment of West Virginians at the state's colleges was expected to drop by 11,000 students over the next five years, "the equivalent of five empty Glenville State Colleges." Consolidation would require closing some colleges, and if Governor Wise intended to proceed, the editor opined, he should be reminded that "closing a state college is unheard of in West Virginia," even though it has the lowest rate of college attendance in the nation. The reason for not closing the least viable institutions was simple: some of them were "fluffed-up teacher colleges whose continued existence serves more of a political than an educational purpose." According to the editor, local opponents of closures generally cited non-academic reasons for keeping them open, such as the college's economic impact on the community. Times had changed since the colleges were founded. Modern students were highly mobile and could easily attend any college they chose.[25]

Governor Wise did not declare consolidating the colleges or eliminating redundancies in higher education as his reason for not funding the reforms, but consolidation was not a new concept in policy discussions. The elimination of institutional redundancies was incorporated within the provisions of Senate Bill 653. WVU President Hardesty sent a letter to the state's college presidents inviting them to join him in exploring mutually beneficial opportunities for collaboration, such as teacher education and continuing graduate programs. Hardesty and Glenville State College President Thomas H. Powell were already engaged in discussions regarding the feasibility of converting Glenville State into a regional campus of WVU. State politics never lies far beneath the surface on such occasions, so it was no surprise to learn that plans were also afoot for Marshall University President Dan Angel and President Powell to discuss "many educational issues of mutual concern." Historically, Marshall had fought to extend its influence at the expense of WVU, and both were always prepared to expand their own spheres of influence. WVU had recently acquired West Virginia Tech in Montgomery as a regional campus, and Marshall had taken over the College of Graduate Studies based in Institute, establishing a base of operations for both schools in the Kanawha Valley.[26]

On February 7, 2001, President Hardesty led an entourage of WVU administrators to Glenville State for an on-site visit of the campus. Those who expected WVU to play the part of a "white knight" were disappointed, however, when the delegates from WVU expressed their concern about Glenville State's budget deficit. Any Glenville officials who expected President Hardesty to provide the school with financial assistance were particularly disappointed. One Glenville State advisory board member urged the board to proceed cautiously, reminding them that supporters of West Virginia Tech were "ecstatic" about the merger at first, but "not a penny of WVU money has gone to Tech; they got no enrollment help, either. People in Montgomery are now upset with that merger, so people in Glenville ought to move cautiously." By March, time for a "sober second thought" prevailed on both ends, as Glenville State and WVU decided to wait for the HEPC to develop a policy on mergers before deciding on any proposed collaboration.[27] Undoubtedly many college administrators envied WVU's prominence in the state, but they were not aware that the flagship institution suffered in similar financial straits, only on a larger scale.

House of Delegates Education Committee Chairman Jerry Mezzatesta echoed House Speaker Bob Kiss's public statement in January 2003 that the savings from restructuring higher education would be used to start paying off the $2.4 billion deficit in the state Workmen's Compensation Fund. Mezzatesta put higher education officials on notice that "we're not going to do business as usual," and that education budgets would be "lean, mean and not so green."[28] Mezzatesta also promised to make another attempt to address the "Legislature's perennial gripe" that eleven public four-year colleges were too many. In 2000 he had promoted a reform bill that would have nearly severed the community colleges from Fairmont State, West Virginia State, WVU Tech, and Shepherd colleges; the presidents complained that this action would shut down their institutions.[29] The House bill that eventually emerged called for at least two institutions to be merged, closed, or privatized by June 2007. Greater efficiency was of vital concern, Mezzatesta declared, because "there's nothing left to tax in West Virginia." In Chancellor Mullen's testimony before the Education Committee, he acknowledged that higher education could "do more with less" but emphasized the need for flexibility in how the money was to be spent.[30]

THE ONGOING FINANCIAL CRISIS

On January 8, Governor Wise unveiled a budget proposal that plummeted the college system into the red by $47.6 million, exacerbated by another $7 million earmarked for the Promise Scholarship program. State appropriations to higher education adjusted to 15 percent including inflation now represented a 13 percent reduction. The governor also ordered a 15 percent reduction in the fleet of state cars on campuses by public auction. Of the 519 state vehicles at WVU, four hundred of them were passenger cars, and the cut forced some employees to use their own cars for state business.[31]

President Hardesty reported in April 2003 that the University faced a projected $28 million deficit. On the bright side, offsetting revenues were expected from enrollment growth in 2003–2004, and the legislature had authorized WVU to raise in-state undergraduate tuition by 9.5 percent. However, total state appropriations to WVU were now expected to be reduced by $22 million, and the University also would now bear the costs for providing employees with Public Employees Insurance Agency health insurance benefits, Board of Risk Insurance Management coverage for WVU employees traveling on business, and other mandated costs of $6 million. In the final accounting, WVU would still need to find additional revenues or cost reductions totaling about $15 million in order to balance the budget. And yet, in order to attract the number of students necessary to balance the budget, investments were required in health sciences, athletics, student housing, and new programs. Postponing these investments until the state's economy improved was not an option because a major turnaround in the economy was not likely in the foreseeable future.[32]

Far from the cooperation and collaboration that legislators had anticipated, cutting higher education so close to the financial bone rekindled the competition between the state colleges and universities for state funds. There were too many institutions and too little money to fund them. One point of contention was the state's formula for appropriating bonded debt arising from requiring student tuition to subsidize campus construction. The pool of funds from this source was then distributed from Charleston for construction projects with no consideration for the origin of the funds. WVU students and administrators complained that the formula was unfair because not every institution carried the same burden. WVU annually paid $2.4 million, or $100 per student, to finance construction on other campuses. The grievance was escalated when state legislators entered the conflict to protect the interests of institutions in their districts. West Virginia was one of the few states to rely on tuition revenue to finance campus construction, the primary reason being a twenty-year, $243.8 million bond issued by the state in 1992. Service on the bond had required a transfer of wealth from some colleges to pay for construction at other colleges. Under the two board system, it was not known how the money was redistributed.

With the reorganization of higher education governance initiated in 2001, however, governing boards at each institution now managed their own financial affairs. Students and parents could now see how their tuition was being used. When WVU students and administrators lobbied state legislators and the HEPC for a change in the formula for the distribution of funds, the HEPC devised a new plan that based each college's debt-service payments on the share of money that had gone toward construction on other campuses. Using this formula, WVU's remaining payments would be reduced by $19.4 million, or about 29 percent. Other colleges, however, would see their payments increase substantially, particularly Marshall University, whose debt-service payments would increase by 67 percent to about $15.4 million. Marshall and the other affected colleges lobbied state lawmakers to kill the proposal, naturally, resulting in the HEPC's decision to set aside the plan for further discussion.[33]

In the spring of 2003, the mood among WVU officials was somber. Having already taken draconian measures to comply with state reforms and mandates, they still saw their institution being systematically gutted. Students were paying a tuition increase of 9.5 percent, and the University had been hit with a 3.4 percent budget reduction in midyear, followed by another 10 percent reduction for 2003–2004, all in addition to five consecutive years of budget reallocations to support mandated, unfunded pay raises, and mandated cost increases for employee health care and risk insurance. Moreover, the University had eliminated some academic units, offered a voluntary severance package to employees, standardized purchasing and contracts, and consolidated other services. At the same time, enrollments increased, necessitating investments in capital projects.[34]

And yet no relief from the financial pain was in sight. In May, Chancellor Mullen warned of another two or three years of "belt-tightening" for higher education. Responding to that dire prediction, President Hardesty urged lawmakers to exercise caution. "We're approaching the point at which harm can be done, not only to West Virginia University, but to all of higher education." If the WVU budget did not bounce back with an improving economy, cuts in degree programs could result. "Someone is going to get hurt, and I hope it's not the next generation. There are simply limits to how far we can push this thing." Go too far and students will look for a better deal elsewhere.[35]

Editorials also questioned the wisdom of another large reduction for higher education. As might be expected, the Morgantown paper's position reflected WVU's: "Education is to development what grass is to cows." While the governor talked about economic development, "we are starting to wonder if his commitment to development overshadows his common sense. . . . This is simply not fair, never mind reasonable."[36] The *Charleston Gazette* pronounced it "unwise to slash higher learning as if it were just another bloated bureaucracy," when in fact it was the "very heart of economic progress."[37] Another editorial supported higher education officials who believed the colleges were being penalized for their success. "It seems hypocritical to talk about economic development and then order cuts in higher education."[38]

WVU's mantra that it provided the cutting edge for economic development was more than a public relations campaign. For decades the University had been a major engine in direct economic development as well as indirect economic activity stimulated by University operations. Not until the presidency of Neil Bucklew, however, was this case so systematically articulated. The Bureau of Economic and Business Research at WVU began annual economic impact studies in 1990, and they became important weapons in defense of the University's budget during the Hardesty years.[39]

In the fall of 2003, President Hardesty advanced the argument that WVU was an engine of growth by demonstrating that one thousand students injected $18 million into the economy and generated $1 million in additional tax revenue. Moreover, every dollar the state invested in WVU equaled approximately $10 to the economy through monies WVU leveraged and spent. And since 1994, University-sponsored research projects had brought in $820 million to further stimulate the economy. At the same time, the state's subsidy to WVU had been declining. In fiscal year 2004 state appropriations accounted for 26 percent of the University's general revenues, and "for the first time in recent history" tuition, at about 31 percent, comprised a larger share of revenues than the state subsidy. State appropriations to WVU between 1996 and 2002 grew at a slower rate than

Chapter Thirteen

for any other West Virginia college, 3.7 percent versus nearly double that (6.6 percent) for other schools. In total, WVU's state appropriations grew 19.7 percent during that period, while appropriations to the state's other institutions grew 30.2 percent. This was not a negligible number. Hardesty pointed out that the difference in what the University would have received if allocations had been pro rata amounted to $94 million. Moreover, it was estimated that WVU had lost another $25 million as a result of the inequitable debt-service burden it carried (as mentioned above) over the ten years since 1992, when the higher education system refinanced its construction bonds. If the inequitable assessment method was not corrected, WVU would lose an estimated $50 million over the life of the bonds, which were due to be paid off in 2012. In conclusion, President Hardesty asserted, if every state dollar invested in WVU translated to $10 in the economy, then it followed that, for every dollar not invested in WVU, approximately $10 would be lost to the state's economy. By "cutting off investment before it had a chance to take root, West Virginia lost more than a billion dollars from the economy." Therefore, it was obvious that the state was only hurting itself by imposing further reductions on higher education.[40]

Apparently Governor Wise was not listening, for in August he asked the HEPC to submit a 2004–2005 budget request of $34 million for higher education, or 9 percent less than the current one, to help fill a projected void of $120 million in the next annual budget. The immediate reaction from leaders and the public alike was less than supportive. One lawmaker asserted that it was unfair to force higher education to make up 28 percent of the deficit when it received only 12 percent of the general revenue budget.[41] This time around, instead of accepting the slashed budgets like good soldiers, the two university presidents, David Hardesty of WVU and Dan Angel of Marshall, took their case for restoring the $34 million cut from 2004–2005 budget to the public. Addressing assembled members of WVU visiting boards in September 2003, President Hardesty declared that "public education is at a crossroad," and he urged them to "use your influence to protect the flagship institution of this state" as well as higher education in West Virginia. WVU was being punished for its success, the president complained. As evidence, he pointed out that state funding for higher education had dropped 8.5 percent, while WVU's share had been cut by 17.8 percent.[42] The University would shoulder about $20 million of the $41 million reduction mandated in Governor Wise's budget. Local public officials also feared the economic consequences if Wise's proposed budget were approved. Morgantown City Manager Dan Boroff declared that, "under accepted economic formulas," a $20 million cut at WVU would have a $100 million-dollar impact on the local economy. This same loss would bring even larger consequences for the north-central region, where the impact would measure between $200 and $300 million.[43]

The editorial response from around the state was largely supportive of the presidents. The WVU Student Government Association organized the Students for Higher Education to oppose the budget cuts through a letter-writing campaign and a rally in Charleston. The group worried that further cuts would undermine WVU's ascent as a major university.[44] "Academic types like Hardesty and Angel are hardly people you would expect to rock the boat. But that was before they began watching their schools start sinking like a ship," chimed in an editorial in the Morgantown newspaper. "Whatever happened to being nice when someone asks you to cannibalize yourself?" But the *Dominion Post* went even further by inviting area legislators and others to a roundtable discussion with its editorial board to discuss the funding of higher education. President Hardesty, the featured discussant at the roundtable, expressed his oft repeated complaint that WVU was bearing a disproportionate share of recent appropriation reductions. The University had reached a "tipping point," where further cuts could threaten its mission. When lawmakers vowed that they would not support further cuts, Hardesty declared, "this is music to my ears."[45]

The financial dangers confronting WVU were serious, as graphically illustrated in a *Dominion Post* guest commentary by state Senator Roman W. Prezioso Jr. On the Morgantown campus alone, he asserted, the budget cuts for 2004 and the proposed cuts for 2005, along with other mandated fixed costs, amounted to a $47 million. Cumulatively, since 1995, WVU had watched $118 million melt away from its bottom line, and more than five hundred staff and faculty positions had been eliminated. "You cut liabilities and protect assets," he observed, and WVU was a state asset that produced "a return on investment much richer than any other agency of state government. It is time to set priorities. WVU is part of the solution."[46]

Perhaps the presidents and sympathetic lawmakers were emboldened by Wise's announcement in August that he would not seek a second term after admitting in May that he had engaged in an extramarital affair. The whirlwind of negative public reaction to the exposé, which was prominently dissected and analyzed in the press, certainly weakened his chances for re-election and destroyed most of the political leverage he might have used to bring the presidents into line. As one editorial stated, "with the legislature's current regard for the governor, Hardesty and Angel's efforts to persuade the finance committees may not be in vain."[47]

Governor Wise was, nonetheless, very unhappy with the two university presidents for waging such a public campaign against his proposed funding cut. "I don't need folks that know better drawing lines in the sand," he complained. "They should show us where we could do better." Wise pointed out that the universities had increased funding from the Promise Scholarships as well as tuition and fee increases. Moreover, he was unable to reduce funding for K-12 education because of legal mandates, which represented half of the budget, so reductions had to come from other state agencies.[48] The final budget turned out to be much less punitive than originally anticipated. Instead of a 10 percent cut of $34 million, higher education took a modest hit of 1.4 percent, or $4.8 million. Yet a major watershed in the evolution of higher education in West Virginia had been forded. The consequences of restructuring of higher education governance between 1995 and 2003 were caustically characterized by Marshall President Dan Angel: "In the beginning, there were state universities. Then as money started to decrease, they became state-supported. Now they're becoming state-assisted, and we're heading toward state-located."[49]

HEPC data demonstrate the hard realities behind the sentiment expressed by President Angel. For the decade ending in 2003, the state colleges and universities received smaller and smaller portion of the state's "budget pie," even though state appropriations actually increased steadily from $291,294,000 in 1994 to $432,373,000 in 2003. Revenue from other sources, such as gifts, grants, and government contracts, far exceeded state appropriations. In 1994 state institutions reported attracting more than $429 million dollars from other sources; in 2003 that figure jumped to more than $654 million. WVU attracted by far the largest proportion of this external funding.[50]

Like those presidents who preceded him, David Hardesty believed that colleges and universities should possess more decision-making authority and control over tuition to achieve greater efficiency and create more value. More flexibility would empower the institutions to become more entrepreneurial while maintaining accountability. The *State Journal* thought that, with ever-increasing new sources of revenue and operational flexibility, West Virginia's public colleges were looking more like private schools. President Hardesty seemed to agree: "In effect, we're seeing the privatization of public universities," to a limited degree. "We're going to look more toward large endowments and innovative management practices." Nevertheless, since West Virginia had not garnered the large endowments and research funding found at state universities such as Michigan or Virginia, WVU and other state schools, according to former Governor Caperton, "always will remain far from private."[51]

Even after a decade of reforms following the demise of the Board of Regents, the tendency still existed to treat all state institutions of higher education the same, to homogenize statewide planning, and to fund them all using the same formula. In 2004, WVU's state funding increased 10.5 percent over the previous five-year period compared with a 19.4 percent increase for the state's other public colleges. The struggle to differentiate a research institution from a baccalaureate institution remained a challenge in "a state driven by expenses rather than revenue." Without a capital allocation formula to guide West Virginia lawmakers, operating dollars continued to be dispersed according to the power of individual legislators.[52]

GROWTH IN PRIVATE GIVING

Until the state's political culture changed and legislators began to understand that West Virginia's major research institution was an investment rather than an expense, WVU would become ever more reliant on private giving. David Hardesty elevated fundraising to an entirely new level. When the president publicly announced the Building Greatness Campaign in November 2000, more than $116.5 million of the $250 million goal had already been raised during the "silent phase" of the five-year campaign. Raymond J. Lane, former president and chief operating officer of Oracle Corporation and partner in a Silicon Valley venture capital firm, served as the national chairman. A 1968 WVU graduate, Lane initiated the campaign with a $5 million gift to the Department of Computer Science and Electrical Engineering; the other twenty-seven members of the national campaign board were also prominent in their fields, and all made substantial pledges to the drive.[53]

The decline in state funding for higher education is a long-term trend across the country, and WVU was not immune to its deleterious effects. Like their counterparts nationwide, WVU presidents were expected to raise an increasing percentage of the institution's operating revenues as the state's share declined. President Hardesty estimated that he spent one-third of his time on fundraising activities. During the Building Greatness Campaign, the president, his wife Susan, and the alumni director crisscrossed the nation, visiting forty cities in a tour he described as "friend-raising and fund-raising." They also visited ten West Virginia cities for campaign events and attended hundreds of celebratory events honoring donors on campus. Campaign activities intensified a schedule that was already laden with the continuous effort to secure research grants from federal agencies and private foundations.[54]

The Building Greatness Campaign succeeded beyond all expectations by raising $336.2 million dollars before it came to a close in December 2003. The most ambitious effort to raise private funds in the University's history demonstrated that the reservoir of support for the University among alumni and friends was broader and deeper than anticipated. As WVU Foundation President and CEO F. Duke Perry observed, the campaign "achieved a level of success many thought impossible, especially during these difficult economic times." Among the 50,988 donors, fifty-six contributed $1 million or more. Nine gifts exceeded $5 million.[55]

The campaign aroused a reservoir of goodwill and generated some noteworthy individual gifts. None matched the size of Morgantown businessman and philanthropist Milan Puskar's gift of $20 million dollars for the Department of Intercollegiate Athletics, the largest sum ever donated to the University. Puskar stated simply that it was "my pleasure, my honor, my privilege" to show his support for the University.[56] Few life stories that emerged during the campaign were more stirring than that of the "two farm girls who loved animals," as the press described sisters Gladys Gwendolyn Davis and Vivian Davis Michael, who donated $16.2 million to the College of Agriculture, Forestry, and Consumer Sciences. Since the state of West Virginia had no veterinary schools, some of the money was designated to fund scholarships for WVU students to train in other states.[57] One story, however, stood out as a human-interest story above all others. Regina Jennings, a seventy-five-year-old University employee, donated $93,000 to the WVU law school. During her fifteen years as a University custodian, she earned approximately $10,000 per year and yet contributed nine times that amount in appreciation of the people she worked with at the law school. The money was used to renovate a room to house a sophisticated teleconferencing system for distance education. Some two hundred newspapers featured stories about her generosity, including the *New York Times*, the *Washington Post*, and *USA Today*. *People* magazine and NBC's Today show also recognized her charitable act.[58]

Campaign funds devoted to student scholarships and other support exceeded $68 million, and more than $160 million was generated for research, technology, and investment in strategic opportunities. It would take this much and more to meet the challenges imposed by the decline in state and federal government revenues. Campaign Chairman Raymond Lane announced that, in this economic environment, the University would continue to seek private support: "In the midst of global financial uncertainty and fiscal pressures, one reality remains crystal clear—private support has been and will continue to be critical" to WVU's future. Fundraising became more important than ever during the Hardesty administration, and the WVU Foundation's total assets rose from $183 million at the beginning of his term in 1995 to $991 million at the end of his tenure in 2007. During that same period, the WVU Foundation endowment grew from $140.2 million to $430 million.[59] Private gifts for the University have, therefore, helped to protect and advance its core teaching and research missions in the face of declining government commitment. Nevertheless, donations are one-time-only gifts, and while they improved the quality of University programs, they did not increase the basic operating budget.

FOURTEEN

SELF-GOVERNANCE
RESTORED

APPOINTMENT OF DAVID HARDESTY

THE MAN WHO BECAME the twenty-first president of WVU on July 1, 1995, did not take the conventional academic escalator through the ranks of academe. The selection process that year generated more heat than light. However, it did reveal the cultural chasm between the academy and the worlds of business and politics, and it stood as a metaphor for the transformation of public universities nationwide from quasi-ecclesiastical orders into modern corporate organizations.

David C. Hardesty Jr. had been associated with WVU since his student days. He grew up thirty miles from Morgantown in Shinnston, graduated from Shinnston High School in 1963, and enrolled at WVU. His stellar undergraduate career included serving as student body president, and he is credited with initiating the Festival of Ideas, which brought prominent speakers to campus to discuss major topics of the time, such as the Vietnam War, civil rights, the sexual revolution, and other social issues that roiled America in the sixties. At WVU he also met and married classmate Susan Brown, the daughter of a WVU music professor, who became an active partner in his presidency. Graduating in 1967 with a degree in political science, Hardesty became a Rhodes Scholar at Oxford University, where he received the MA degree. Returning to the United States, he attended Harvard Law School and received the JD degree in 1973. Moving back to his home state, Hardesty became a partner in the Charleston law firm of Bowles, Rice, McDavid, Graff & Love. From 1977 until 1980 he served as the state tax commissioner in Governor Jay Rockefeller's administration, and for more than five years he was a member of the University System Board of Trustees, serving as its first chairman in 1990–1991. His memberships also included the WVU Board of Advisors, the WVU Foundation Board of Directors, and the College of Law Development Council. When Neil Bucklew's tenure at WVU came to an end in 1995, therefore, Hardesty found another opportunity to serve the state and University with which he was so closely associated.[1]

Neil S. Bucklew announced that he would resign effective July 1, 1995, and a seventeen-member search committee was appointed by the University System of West Virginia Board of Trustees to search for a replacement. From the pool of 137 candidates, the committee narrowed its list to three: Elisabeth Zinser, president of the University of Idaho; G. Jay Gogue, acting vice president and vice provost for agricultural and natural resources at Clemson University; and David C. Hardesty Jr., who resigned from the Board of Trustees when he was nominated for the position.[2]

Following his campus visit in April, Gogue withdrew as a candidate, citing his disappointing performance in response to questions about social justice. Although neither the Faculty Assembly nor the Staff Council endorsed either of the remaining candidates, Elisabeth Zinser seemed to be the front-runner among faculty and staff because of her experience as a university president for the past six years. During his campus visit of April 24 and 25, Hardesty avowed that he was not interested in becoming "a university president, I want to be president of *this* University" [his emphasis]. He declared that his skills as a lawyer, chairman of the University of West Virginia Board of Trustees, and tax commissioner would be valuable to the University. He stressed the importance of building a sense of community at WVU. Articulating a rationale for increasing the number of out-of-state students, he declared that, if WVU drew only in-state students, other state institutions would suffer and might be forced to close their doors. Because of Senate Bill 547, discussed below, the University needed to look for new revenues and to consider generating them by attracting additional students with new course offerings. He also argued for maintaining Research I status for the University, even with the budget cuts mandated by Senate Bill 547.[3]

The *Daily Athenaeum* reported that a number of faculty members expressed concern about Hardesty's lack of experience administering a university and about his ability to communicate the research mission of the institution. A Staff Council member characterized Zinser as "more a college-minded person," whereas Hardesty was "more business minded." Another expressed the fear that "cronyism" was once again intruding into University affairs and that Hardesty might be "just an extension of the governor."[4] Even before the candidates visited the campus, Professor Joe Simoni, a member of the Faculty Senate and a former faculty representative on the Board of Trustees, told the faculty that their time would be better spent with their families than listening to the candidates for the University presidency. "If anyone doubts that David Hardesty is not going to be the next president, then you have a lack of understanding about West Virginia," he informed a meeting of the Faculty Senate.[5]

Influential voices beyond the University concurred with this assessment. Don Marsh, retired editor of the *Charleston Gazette*, claimed that neither Hardesty's selection as a Rhodes Scholar nor his service as tax commissioner "is qualification to lead a major university." Agreeing with those who smelled good-old-boy politics in his candidacy, Marsh declared that Hardesty's "principal asset is that he has powerful connections." To make his point, Marsh pointed to the fact that the Board of Trustees would select the next president, and Hardesty had been a member of the board since its inception. Moreover, "he is a Jackson County neighbor of Gov. Gaston Caperton and the Goodwin brothers. Caperton appoints the Board of Trustees. Tom Goodwin was Jay Rockefeller's administrative assistant. Joe Bob Goodwin, a former Democratic state chairman, has been named a federal judge. Joe Bob's wife, Kay Goodwin, is a member of the Board of Trustees." And would Hardesty have put himself in the position of being turned down so publicly if he was not confident of the final decision? He had written no books, nor had he published any scholarship, Marsh opined. "He is a conservative tax lawyer with no discernible signs of leadership and no demonstrated administrative ability. The presidency of West Virginia University is not a place for on-the-job training. . . . better people are available." The Board of Trustees had a duty, Marsh wrote, "to go for the best person for the job, not for the best-connected one."[6]

Marsh summarized the position of those who believed that a major university should hire a chief executive with experience in higher education administration, a stance in opposition to the business interests who thought business leaders would bring a much needed management perspective to the state's leading educational institution. To University people this perspective demonstrated anti-intellectual disdain for the unique assemblage of people required to operate a successful university. Merely acquiring a university education did not prepare one to be its president. Hardesty's home-county paper suggested this very point in its response to Marsh's editorial by declaring, "He is a West Virginian. He is a WVU graduate. He had been a member of the University Board of Trustees from its inception. . . . For goodness sake, the man was a Rhodes Scholar."[7]

Opposition to Hardesty's appointment might have been expressed in terms of his qualifications, but the deeper issue was whether the meritocratic culture that had finally taken root at the University was being circumvented by politics. Academics and other West Virginians, conditioned by past politics to suspect that "cronyism" was at work, found confirmation for their anxieties when Elisabeth Zinser accepted the chancellorship at the University of Kentucky even before the Board of Trustees interviewed her. When Zinser withdrew, leaving only David Hardesty, a *Dominion Post* editorial suggested that the search committee start over: "You don't pick the person to lead a major university by default." As a well-known West Virginian, Hardesty prompted a great deal of sympathy, the editorial continued, but with Zinser's departure there was "no mark to measure his commitment to higher education. We're much in need of scholarship and vision. Reopen the search."[8]

The Board of Trustees refused to restart the search. State law required that the search committee recommend three candidates, and they had complied with that mandate. Because David Hardesty was the only candidate left standing, critics of the process seemed all the more convinced the process was rigged to the advantage of a political insider. Nevertheless, on

May 17, 1995, the Board of Trustees interviewed Hardesty for more than three hours and then announced his appointment as the twenty-first president of WVU, a position which Board of Trustees Chairman John Hoblitzell described as a public position second only in importance to the governor. He characterized Hardesty as possessing "the right skills to lead the important changes that are under way in higher education."[9] Clearly, the board believed it had the right person to undertake the reforms it had in mind.

Whether by accident or contrivance, the selection process cast an unfortunate, and probably unfair, shadow over what was in fact a ringing accomplishment. To faculty and staff, who were conditioned to expect political meddling in the affairs of the state's leading institution, it was not so much the man as the process. Undoubtedly, a silent majority on campus saw the positives in hiring a native son who was highly respected at the state capital, especially when major changes were anticipated as a result of Senate Bill 547. Also, supporters noted that the new president was obviously a quick learner, and WVU students expressed enthusiasm for Hardesty's vision of a "student-centered" University. The student paper called Hardesty "a visionary" who understood the social, political, and economic roles of higher education in transforming society, as well as a "politically astute" leader who understood how West Virginia worked.[10]

Professor of Sociology Joe Simoni, who was resolute in his opposition even after Hardesty occupied the president's office, filed a lawsuit on June 13, 1995, challenging the appointment. On June 30 Kanawha County Circuit Judge Lyne Ranson dismissed the case with prejudice, meaning that it could not be filed again. Simoni appealed the ruling to the West Virginia Supreme Court of Appeals, claiming that Hardesty should not be president because several of those who served on the search committee were also members of WVU visiting committees, most notably the College of Law Visiting Committee. This fact, said Simoni, represented a conflict of interest because the president of WVU appointed members of the visiting committees. The Supreme Court of Appeals disagreed with Professor Simoni's assertions and refused to hear the appeal by a vote of four to none. President Hardesty was clearly relieved by the court's decision. "This litigation has been very wasteful for all concerned and has needlessly and frivolously called into question the reputation of lots of honest people who generously volunteer their time and service to the University," Hardesty told the press. "I've obviously been hired to be president of WVU. Dr. Simoni has been hired to teach. It's time for all of us to get on with doing the jobs we were hired to do."[11] Hardesty regarded becoming president of his alma mater as an act of service, and no doubt a significant financial sacrifice.

As West Virginia's flagship university, WVU attracts the attention of the state's newspapers like no other academic institution. Few editors or reporters actually understood the workings of a university, but they had opinions and a medium in which to express them. Notwithstanding the disapproval of Don Marsh, statewide editorial opinion was almost uniformly favorable toward Hardesty's appointment, and often as not it was contemptuous of what it thought of as academic culture. The *Parkersburg Sentinel* thought supporters who said the new president would help WVU in Charleston were giving him faint praise, for he was "much more capable than their assessment would indicate." The paper pointed out that Hardesty was familiar with the problems facing higher education in West Virginia, since he had served on the Board of Trustees for the past five years, and he was also familiar with the vital role the University played in the state's economic development. The Charleston papers were also supportive. The *Daily Mail* editorialized that "higher education needs people with good management backgrounds." The editor ridiculed the faculty concern that Hardesty had no experience with academic administration. "Not been in academia! This is a plus, not a minus. Too many higher education officials in West Virginia have been unwilling to manage their institutions." The result was low quality, high cost programs. Hardesty had "real-world management experience," and WVU needed that. "Too often, presidents chosen from the ranks of academia have failed to provide it."[12] The *Charleston Gazette* agreed and suggested that "maybe an outsider might bring fresh air into the incestuous realm of professordom." In fact, "an outsider might be an improvement over an insider like Bucklew."[13]

The Beckley newspaper was even more dismissive of faculty concerns. Its derisive editorial, "Faculty Comments not so 'Academic,'" sub-titled "ivy-covered minds," asserted that "universities like to portray themselves as a bastion of free thinking and open mindedness," but the faculty's opposition to Hardesty's candidacy, just because he did not come up through the faculty ranks, was "not much different than you would find in any other bureaucracy." The reason for their opposition might be "a reason for Hardesty to be hired," the editor opined. "Gee, if they weren't the guardians of free thought and open mindedness, we might suspect Hardesty's critics are bigots."[14] After Hardesty's appointment, *Charleston Daily Mail* launched another volley, claiming that "the faculty is laboring under a misunderstanding here—that the president of the university is supposed to serve *them*. He isn't. Hardesty is responsible to the board of trustees . . . faculty members report to Hardesty. It will never be the other way around. That faculty members do not seem to grasp this makes one grateful that Hardesty did not meet their standards. The standards need review [editor's emphasis]."[15]

Other newspapers were supportive of the new president even as they demonstrated how little they knew of university organization and faculty culture. "Certain voices coming from the smoke-free lounges at WVU" lament that Hardesty "has not spent his life passing through the chairs of a half-dozen academic bureaucracies," said the *Huntington Herald-Dispatch*. "In fact, by the only two personal tests that are relevant, I think that the WVU presidency should be Hardesty's by acclamation. First, he was born in West Virginia. . . . Secondly, he has played in the academic big leagues," a reference to Hardesty's education at Oxford University and at Harvard University.[16]

EX-PRESIDENT BUCKLEW'S FACULTY APPOINTMENT

A long line of well-wishers and supporters waited to shake hands with Neil Bucklew and his wife Iona during his farewell reception at the Erickson Alumni Center on May 21, 1995. Many people representing the University's multiple constituencies were there to praise his successes as president. Incoming president David Hardesty praised Bucklew's administration and its ability to find solutions to conflicts that proved satisfactory to all sides. Describing Bucklew as a "major resource for the University," Hardesty announced that the former president would continue to serve WVU as a professor in the College of Business and Economics after he stepped down on July 1. Bucklew agreed to a twelve-month contract to teach and carry out administrative duties as assigned to him by the new president, such as fundraising.[17] In addition to directing a mediation program to train faculty in conflict resolution, Bucklew was assigned to teach one class each semester. This made him a "part-time faculty member," according to the student paper, and yet "he is also the University's highest-paid professor, earning $115,000 a year. The average professor takes home $54,000 a year."[18] Press reports seemed unaware that top administrators who became faculty received a salary based on a percentage of their administrative salary. A salary double that of the full-time faculty salary seemed excessive to the many faculty in the University community who had suffered with chronically low salaries, and it certainly seemed high to most West Virginians, whose per capita incomes were among the lowest in the nation.

Another controversy further clouded an already complicated transition. A piece of Neil Bucklew's social justice agenda at WVU was to provide a same-sex benefits plan for employees. As news of the plan filtered beyond the University, public hackles were ruffled. The response was predictable. The Morgantown newspaper summed up the opposition view in an editorial suggesting that Bucklew conspired to sneak the measure through: "You can almost hear him saying, 'I'll go for it, and let Dave Hardesty take the phone calls.'" Health care benefits for same-sex domestic partners would cost a huge amount of money when the state university system was "crying broke," it argued, and it would create "a campus bureaucracy steeped in secrecy to run the program, for there's no way the public can check these relationships as it can those of legally married couples." The former president was handing the new one "a live grenade, and it's ticking." In the end, Hardesty handed the "grenade" to the Board of Trustees, which promptly rescinded the order. Because the West Virginia Code prohibited same-sex marriages, the University could not initiate such a policy until the law was changed.[19]

Yet another issue roiled the waters of campus politics that first semester of Hardesty's administration, and that was whether he should receive tenure. It was not uncommon to tenure university presidents in the department of their discipline, since most presidents are academics who have risen through the administrative hierarchy after achieving tenure. Hardesty's appointment, therefore, presented a deviation from the norm. Interestingly, the question first arose in the student newspaper regarding a popular professor who was denied tenure by the provost for inadequate research even though his department and college dean supported him. The *Daily Athenaeum* raised the rhetorical question of how the University could justify awarding tenure to President Hardesty, whose otherwise impressive credentials were limited in both research and teaching experience, but deny tenure to an associate professor who had taught at the university level for seventeen years. There were guidelines governing promotion and tenure in the University's *Policies and Procedures for Faculty Evaluations.* On November 13, 1995, the Faculty Senate debated the question of tenure at its monthly meeting and concluded that the decision to award tenure to a president rested with the Board of Trustees. The College of Law had already given its nod of approval for the president's tenure. He began offering a seminar on bill drafting, an advanced form of legal writing, at the law school in 1998. Finally, in December 1999, the Board of Trustees extended tenure in the law school to President Hardesty. "I think the board of trustees probably wanted to watch and wait and see how I did," he said. "I thought there was some uncertainty in their minds about awarding tenure to presidents."[20]

On the eve of Hardesty's takeover, the *Daily Athenaeum* summed up the general disquiet on campus in an editorial titled "A Lack of Trust." The editorial described a climate of mistrust engendered by a series of misjudgments by the Board of Trustees, beginning with the $63,000 search for a new president. Then, in an "unedifying sight," the Board of Trustees interviewed just one of the 137 candidates, who happened to be the former chair of the board, then simply brushed aside Professor Simoni's lawsuit as "frivolous," and hired their man anyway. At the same time, outgoing president Neil Bucklew was given a $9,000 increase in salary when he joined the faculty even though he had not taught in years. Moreover, this came at a time when everybody else was being asked to sacrifice because money was tight. By ignoring these concerns, the Board of Trustees created the impression that it was "insensitive to outside concerns." Finally, the board "further enhanced its reputation for insensitivity" by its decision to suspend the University's domestic partnership policy. In a final act before leaving office Bucklew had tried to bring the University into line with practices at other state universities, but the board killed the policy. The *Daily Athenaeum* concluded that public trust in the board would improve with Kay Goodwin's accession to chair if she "put an end to the cronyism that fuels BOT's work."[21] The students and their newspaper, the *Daily Athenaeum*, were strongly supportive of David Hardesty's candidacy and the student-centered vision he outlined during his interviews, so these editorial opinions were expressions of disaffection with the system itself rather than the person chosen. In fact, the vast majority of the campus community was willing to give the new president a chance to prove himself. They did not have to wait long.

On his first day in office, David Hardesty announced the creation of a task force on student affairs to examine ways to enhance student learning and to improve support for instruction. The revival of Freshman Convocation was the first public event heralding the beginning of the new "student affairs initiative," which became the hallmark of the Hardesty administration. Intended to provide freshmen with the feeling that they were members of a class, the last Freshman Convocation had taken place in 1967, when James Harlow was president. On August 20, the class of 1999 and parents attended the restored convocation in the Coliseum, as faculty paraded into gym to the tune of "Pomp and Circumstance." Speakers urged the class of 1999 to pursue excellence and a commitment to community and service.[22]

President Hardesty was inaugurated on September 9, 1995, during a ceremony intended to reestablish a dignified and formal tradition. In Woodburn Circle approximately 1,800 students, politicians, friends, and family looked on as some three hundred faculty processed in regalia for the occasion, with the chiming bell of the U.S.S. *West Virginia* providing further solemnity to the occasion. The audience heard from Governor Gaston Caperton, MIT President Charles Vest (a Morgantown native), and WVU Alumni Association President Robert Mead. President Hardesty's inaugural address reemphasized his promise to "put students first." Touching on the University's three primary missions, he urged West Virginians "to ponder with great care the interrelated nature of the teaching, research, and service elements of the mission of universities like ours." Higher education should promote leadership; therefore, he promised to foster those values which promote leadership: excellence and continuous improvement; stewardship and accountability; a close-knit University community; new ways to perform "ageless tasks" through technology and innovative approaches; and, finally, effective communication of ideas.[23]

SENATE BILL 547 AND RESTRUCTURING THE UNIVERSITY

If David Hardesty was not shaped by the traditional academic culture, neither was he bound by it. In Hardesty the Board of Trustees found a president who understood the reforms they wanted to implement. He reflected their values and business perspective, but he embraced the academy and was also strongly committed to his alma mater. As a successful business lawyer, he was seen as someone who could bridge the sometimes yawning chasm between the business and higher education communities, and he also possessed the organizational skills to implement the broad reforms mandated in Senate Bill 547 and later Senate Bill 653.

President Hardesty's style of leadership empowered an experienced administrative team. Once he established the goals, the provost and vice president for academic affairs saw them through to completion. Gerald Lang, dean of the Eberly College of Arts and Sciences, was chosen for that position on an interim basis until a national search could be conducted. He came to the University in 1970 as a faculty member and had served as assistant dean and then dean. He was a strong advocate for effective teaching, had a firm grasp of the university's research mission, and understood the importance of university service to the state. Hardesty planned to refocus the vision, mission, and function of the University's Extension Service toward a greater emphasis on West Virginia, and this kind of internal reorganization required a provost with thorough knowledge of the institution. "Dean Lang has the qualities and characteristics to get us through this challenging period," the president's chief of staff told the press.[24]

Hardesty had expressed his views on adapting best business practices to higher education even before he became president. In 1994, he gave a speech to the West Virginia Roundtable, a business trade association, entitled "Can Public Education Be 'Run like a Business'?" This sounded "overly simplistic," Hardesty observed, and it overlooked the simple fact that the decision-making process in business was different from that of education and government. "Nevertheless, I think it is fair to observe that there are important expectations that the business community has for the education community."[25] One of these expectations was "customer orientation." Like business, education needed to recognize the importance of its customers in order to serve them better. Also, financial and program accountability was necessary to ensure that public institutions lived within their budgets. Like business, no educational institution should ignore planning with clear established goals and objectives. Business people expected public education to "respect the taxpayer" by making efficient and prudent spending decisions, and they also expected sound decision-making processes. While they know that politics and government go hand in glove, they expect educational bureaucracies to remain as free of politics as possible. Good leadership is at the heart of every effective organization, and the long-run success of business and education alike is demonstrated by delivering a quality product. "There is significant concern about this issue in the business community," Hardesty emphasized. And good leadership entailed good communication and the ability to share goals and aspirations with the customers. "To the extent that these expectations seem to be recognized and acted on by the education community, the business community of this state is likely to be even more supportive of public education" in the future than it had been in the past.[26] These ideas pervaded Senate Bill 547 and President Hardesty's administrative reforms.

No previous WVU administration confronted such a dramatic restructuring as that imposed by Senate Bill 547 during the Hardesty years between 1995 and 2000. The new law mandated that state institutions meet specified salary targets for faculty and classified staff, and that salary increases must be financed from internally reallocated money within existing budgets. In response, WVU developed a five-year plan that required an internal reallocation of $32 million on the main campus, and another $8 million on regional campuses during the same period. Enhancements were directed to University libraries and to technology infrastructure to improve administrative and programmatic efficiencies. Resources were also redirected to maximize student-centeredness, and also to expand statewide University services that contributed more to economic development and the needs of West Virginians.[27]

The Senate Bill 547 mandates were met only after considerable sacrifice and wrenching decisions. The University was permitted to raise tuition 3.25 percent annually, the same rate of increased state funding as during the five-year plan, which brought total revenue increases to 6.5 percent annually. The faculty were to be paid 10 percent less than their peers but also required to be 10 percent more productive, a calculus many found perplexing. Faculty quipped that they would have to talk 10 percent faster, but instead their workloads were rebalanced with larger classes. The budget was never cut and continued to grow, but there were fewer, better paid employees. There was a redistribution of workload; some programs received higher priority than others, but faculty received raises. At this time, the University also transitioned from across-the-board raises to merit-based raises, and by 2008 all raises were 100 percent merit-based.[28]

According to President Hardesty, Lloyd Jackson, chairman of the West Virginia Senate Committee on Education and author of Senate Bill 547, saw the measure as an opportunity for the University to achieve efficiencies. "The genius of it," Hardesty commented, was the "trade off." WVU would receive more money for higher salaries, but only if efficiencies were realized. As a business lawyer, Hardesty understood this perspective. "I thought a lot of the silos [administrative units] were way too small, that they could be consolidated." A lot of the savings "came out of middle management; a lot came out of putting more things out to bid and using technologies, like doing things on line instead of paperwork. These investments reaped pretty big benefits."[29] Asked by reporters if the University was in a "crisis situation," President Hardesty replied, "I don't think it is. . . . I think there are so many things shifting fundamentally that we will have to redefine ourselves, re-engineer ourselves and recommit ourselves to being an excellent institution and a focused institution in light of a whole new set of circumstances." The intention behind Senate Bill 547 was "to make the institution more competitive and effective in meeting the needs of students, faculty, staff and residents of the state."[30]

Another of the several task forces that Hardesty established when he became president was the twenty-person Administrative Organization Task Force. The role of central administration was to empower the university community. "Operational functions should be at the lowest effective administrative levels, and administration at WVU should be adaptive and flexible to ensure rapid response to the changing environment," Hardesty said. Each administrative unit should provide leadership in support of faculty, staff, and students.[31] The Administrative Organization Task Force report, released in February 1996, advocated that WVU "cut through the bureaucracy and let its faculty and other workers make more decisions." It recommended that five university vice presidents should report to Hardesty: academic affairs; health sciences; student affairs and enrollment; administration, finance, and human resources; and a new position of vice president for university relations, which would manage the University's public image. As one member of the task force observed, WVU needed to become more flexible and accommodating to students and much more like a service organization.[32]

By the end of the spring semester of 1996, it was becoming evident that a period of hardship lay ahead. To cut costs, a severance plan was offered to qualifying WVU faculty and staff, and by May, 325 of them had accepted. Under the plan, some faculty could begin phased retirement over three years, taking half pay for a reduced teaching load. Downsizing the faculty would cut costs directly, but the savings were compounded if better-paid senior faculty were replaced by junior faculty hired at a lower salary. At the same time, college and university presidents received no raises.[33]

By the end of the 1995–1996 academic year, it became clear to WVU administrators where most of the reductions and increased revenues to cover the $32.6 million required to meet the mandates would come from: $9 million would be realized by not replacing retiring faculty and staff; $6.5 million would be generated by increasing student enrollment and retention; another $5.5 million would be saved by investing in technology to improve operational efficiency; $8.3 million would come from expanding competitive research; and $3 million would result from improved financial management.[34]

Since time immemorial, or so it seemed, faculty and staff had received salaries substantially below those of their peers at other universities, and on the eve of the Senate Bill 547 era many were convinced that the University and the state were sliding even further down the scale. Morale at the University was at an all-time low. From their perspective, faculty and staff could not envision the optimistic managerial vista presented by system Chancellor Charles W. Manning in an op-ed piece in the *Charleston Gazette*, where he declared that "the governor and legislature . . . created an excellent five-year strategy for simultaneously empowering institutions with the ability to make themselves more efficient and productive."[35] The faculty's view of the future was embedded in the depressing assessment that they were to become counter clerks in the new educational emporium.

To ensure that the presidents would feel secure in carrying out these draconian reforms, in March 1996 the Board of Trustees guaranteed their job security by giving them five-year contracts. Also, to ensure continuity of leadership, President Hardesty decided to forego a national search for the office of provost and vice president for academic affairs by appointing interim provost Gerald Lang to the position permanently. Hardesty wanted stability in that vital office, which had seen three different occupants in the past four years. According to President Hardesty's chief-of-staff, Lang gave the University "an immediate sense of knowledge, experience and familiarity with the institution. I'd be hard-pressed to believe we could find a better candidate." Stability in the provost's office made the lives of other University leaders much easier.[36]

In the early stages of developing a strategic plan, an apparent lack of enthusiasm emerged with the philosophy and approach for implementing the Board of Trustees initiatives. A few months before Hardesty assumed the presidency, the College of Engineering and the College of Mineral and Energy Resources had merged in response to Senate Bill 547, creating resentment among many employees, who objected to being "left out of the negotiating process" and treated like "we don't count." As one faculty senator summarized this discontent, "the tradition at the University is that they make the decision with the input of the faculty, staff and students. In this process, people feel left out."[37] One member of the Faculty Senate representing the new College of Engineering and Mineral Resources approved of the initiatives, but "everything else is extremely offensive to me. . . . To state that the purpose of the University is to promote the economy of the state is disgusting to me. We must first of all be an institution which is dedicated to the education of students." One of the principal initiatives inserted into the plan by the legislators and the Board of Trustees to meet the standards of Senate Bill 547 stated that "it is essential that higher education prepare people for a successful lifetime of work," an initiative one faculty senator characterized as "just scary." Many of his fellow senators apparently embraced this view, and the Faculty Senate agreed that this sentiment should be presented to the Board of Trustees.[38]

In 1997, WVU also initiated Integration 2000, a plan which merged academic units and integrated affiliated institutions into the University by the year 2000. Even though the plan was to coordinate curriculum, pool research, and streamline services, all of which affected the traditional provinces of faculty, nobody seems to have informed the Faculty Senate until the process was well underway. Although none opposed the goal, faculty senators complained that they had not been consulted, had little input into the process, and would have little time to consider the recommended changes before being asked to approve them. For the administration the proposed integration was about adapting to the legislative dictates imposed on them; one faculty senator expressed the faculty's position on the issue best: "Unless we're let in on things like Integration 2000 and given some kind of role, there's not much need for a Faculty Senate." President Hardesty defended the administration, pointing out that he dealt with the Faculty Senate Executive Committee, and that it was that body's responsibility to relay information to its constituents.[39] While this made business sense in cases where there was a clear chain of command, faculty were accustomed to thinking of the president as one of their own who was entrusted with high administrative duties. In fact, it was not always clear how to draw a distinction between who was a faculty member and who was an academic administrator.

The WVU Faculty Constitution, first passed by the faculty in 1965, was intended to guide members in the conduct of their academic and scholarly responsibilities. Although the president and Board of Governors were ultimately responsible for the operation of the University, the Faculty Constitution outlines procedures for communicating faculty recommendations and codifies faculty governance at the University. Over the years modifications rendered governance more representative. In 1983, the university president was removed as chair of the Faculty Senate, but this did not resolve the issue of the need to draw a distinct line between administrators, most of whom were faculty members serving in administrative positions, and rank-and-file faculty. The faculty seemed to lose interest in the Faculty Senate, as the state's politicians paid little heed to its interests or recommendations. The issue came to a head with the election of Assistant Dean of the Medical School Dr. James Shumway as chair-elect of the Faculty Senate in 1997. Shumway was, according to the constitution, a member of the faculty because he also taught medicine. The Faculty Senate Welfare Committee formed a Constitutional Review Committee to determine who constituted a faculty member and who an administrator. Between 1999 and 2002 the document underwent major revisions, and the faculty approved the new constitution, which became effective on July 1, 2003. It clearly defined faculty members along academic lines and excluded administrators. Faculty Senate meetings remained open to the public, however, and the administration continued to send representatives.[40]

Other mergers occurred on the main campus. Members attending the Faculty Senate meeting a few months later again accused the administration of "going behind their backs" to merge units without consultation or acknowledgement of the faculty's academic responsibilities. Once again, few faculty opposed mergers in general, but they objected to their lack of involvement in the process. One particular merger that stirred controversy involved the Department of Public Administration and the School of Social Work. "Our biggest issue is a faculty issue—we have not been consulted," said one of the affected faculty. Moreover, department chairs were informed of the merger only two days prior to a public announcement. There was a general fear of consolidation among faculty, Provost Lang declared, but the University was streamlining to meet the requirements of Senate Bill 547, and he had not heard any suggestions from the faculty on how to proceed.[41]

Senate Bill 547 mandated that institutions find ways to save money in order to fund faculty pay raises. The goal was to achieve something like parity with the national average, yet three years into the plan WVU's average full professor still earned nearly 20 percent less than his or her counterparts at peer institutions, and even less when compared with many public research institutions in the surrounding region. The *Charleston Daily Mail* probably came close to reflecting public opinion on the subject in an editorial: "Higher education runs on vapors . . . because West Virginia persists in running too many colleges. It's like running a whole fleet of Yugos when you can have a half-dozen Camrys instead. Higher education can have higher salaries—and offer better education—when it manages its resources better. When will higher education figure this out?"[42] The editor was, like most people, a little confused when he suggested that the problem was not the lack but rather the distribution of resources. However, he failed to appreciate that the legislature held the reins, not "higher education." Moreover, regional interests dictated that the "obvious" solution was not politically feasible. That, too, was beyond the control of "higher education."

Nevertheless, Senate Bill 547 brought major changes to WVU, and both President Neil Bucklew and his successor David Hardesty regarded the reform measure as the most important legislation to impact WVU during their tenures in office. In his report to the HEPC, President Hardesty claimed that WVU had successfully met the statutory goals of the bill. Faculty and staff salaries increased each year, technology enhancements had contributed to administrative and programmatic efficiency, resources had been redirected to maximize the student-centered learning experience, and WVU had expanded its services to contribute to the state's economic development.[43]

SENATE BILL 653 AND A COMPACT FOR THE FUTURE OF WEST VIRGINIA

During the first five years of President Hardesty's tenure, WVU experienced a transformation that would have ensured his legacy even if no further accomplishments had followed. In addition to complying with the restructuring mandated by Senate Bill 547, a Facilities Master Plan yielded a new Libraries Book Depository, White Hall Computer Lab, a soon-to-be completed Student Recreation Center, the renovation and expansion of the main library building, and a new Life Sciences Building. A new administrative offices building located at One Waterfront Place marked what would become a transformation of Morgantown's decaying old wharf district. Major investments in computer and communications technology had hard-wired the University to the World Wide Web. The Building Greatness Campaign had generated $339 million from private donors, the University had successfully leveraged state money to bring in ever greater externally funded research projects, and economic development and technology transfer became top priorities for WVU.

The University emerged from Senate Bill 547 a very different institution. With all the changes during those five years, a breather might have been in order. Building on these reforms, however, the legislature proceeded to pass Senate Bill 653, which required each institution of higher education to develop a written set of goals for broader engagement, a "covenant" between the institution and the people it served. The *Compact for the Future of West Virginia*, as it was called, was intended to guide each institution for the next six-year period from July 2001 through June 2007. Each institution set goals to suit its own mission. WVU's *Compact* consisted of the following: develop the capacity to conduct research that would serve the state's "new economy"; provide citizens with opportunities for graduate studies in every region of the state; focus the institution's mission in ways that would enhance the state's educational, economic, and social revitalization; provide greater access to technical education, workforce development, and other educational services through outreach and extension; and help to create independently accredited community and technical colleges in every region to meet local needs.[44]

WVU's *Compact* did not change the mission or the direction of the University, but it did provide some broad-based goals to guide the University's development during the next six years: first, improve academic standards and expectations of success by providing services such as the Center of Writing Excellence and the Institute for Math Learning; second, maintain the commitment to broad access to higher education by means of programs like the Summer Transition Entry Program and the Health Sciences Technology Academy in order to help economically disadvantaged students attend and succeed in college; third, maintain the University's commitment to becoming a student-centered institution with programs like Operation Jump Start, WVUp All Night, and the Recreation Center; fourth, manage enrollments strategically in order to bolster University finances, and improve recruitment and retention; fifth, enhance graduate education to maintain WVU's status as a doctoral/research university-extensive institution; sixth, improve access to WVU libraries through enhanced technology; seventh, enhance the University's research capacity in order to deliver high-quality doctoral education and growing research programs, which are critical to economic development; eighth, continue to deliver high-quality health care to the people of West Virginia through improvements like the Blanchette Rockefeller Neurosciences Institute, the Cancer Center, and the Eye Institute; ninth, upgrade West Virginia's workforce through efforts such as the WVU Center for Entrepreneurial Studies and Development; tenth, "education is the passport to prosperity," so the University should continue provide the means for West Virginians to succeed in the world.[45]

On September 10, 2001, President Hardesty presented his State of the University Address entitled "The New West Virginia University," with the emphasis on "new." Since he began his tenure in 1995, Hardesty had witnessed the University experience radical change, and he allowed himself to muse on the institution's future. Noting that tuition and fees at the nation's public four-year colleges had risen 53 percent over the past ten years, he could foresee a time when students questioned whether college was worth the financial sacrifice. State appropriations and tuition accounted for about half of WVU's revenues, and, despite the fact that state money represented an ever diminishing percentage of the University's operating budget, the state would demand a growing emphasis on efficiency and accountability. The University must adopt the best business practices to meet these expectations, Hardesty asserted. Also, the University should increasingly seek investment in more nationally recognized research. In fact, he foresaw the trendline that would make WVU research and technology transfer a major economic engine for West Virginia. Not only would WVU become a "diversified educational center" that provided traditional student experiences; it would also share knowledge by offering many customized technological advancements. The virtual classroom would enroll students from around the globe in online courses, making WVU not just a geographical place but also a "community of interested persons" connected across time and space. And while the means would evolve, WVU's core mission, vision, and values would remain the same.[46] Six years into his presidency, David Hardesty had become an experienced University leader. More importantly, he had become a leader with a vision.

President Hardesty's was an essentially optimistic view of the future, but he could not have anticipated on September 10, 2001, that the next day terrorists would commandeer four passenger planes and kill thousands when they crashed two into New York's World Trade Center, one into the Pentagon, and another into a Pennsylvania field after its passengers attempted to regain control. It was a day that would live in America's collective memory forever. On September 14, 2001, seven thousand people gathered in convocation in Woodburn Circle to pay tribute to the victims, one of whom was a WVU alumnus.[47]

The events of 9/11 only magnified the atmosphere of caution and foreboding that would later be stirred up by America's wars in Iraq and Afghanistan. But most immediately, WVU's future and ability to meet its goals were directly affected by an economy that collapsed along with the World Trade Center towers. According to Provost Gerald Lang, "all the money the University had gained we started to lose" as the economy slumped into a recession. Beginning in 2001, WVU was forced to increase tuition and fees by

9.5 percent for three consecutive years. By 2006, WVU received the same amount in absolute state appropriations that it had received in 1995.[48]

On learning in 2003 that the era of austerity would continue, WVU administrators initiated measures to cope with further cuts. The inevitable result of reduced state appropriations, tuition increases, prompted a public relations strategy: "They want good degrees, not cheap degrees." This mantra was pronounced in various forms in all of Hardesty's public comments. To everyone who would listen, he stated the belief that the key to dealing with the financial shortfall was to maintain the "highest quality programs, faculty, and facilities." The economic downturn made higher education more important than ever, but parents and students expected the highest-quality educational experience for the increased cost. Increasingly, the national trend was to view higher education as a private good to be paid for by its consumers rather than as a public good to be subsidized by taxpayers. West Virginia did not buck that trend.[49]

President Hardesty's strategy for dealing with significant new reductions announced by the governor was straightforward. The first step was to increase the number of students admitted to WVU, a challenge when the number of in-state high school graduates was in a long-term decline. The second step was to increase tuition. Also, the president sought greater administrative flexibility in order to achieve operational efficiencies through consolidation and standardization. Finally, WVU hoped to gain special funding from the legislature for research projects already underway, for its health science programs, and to resolve the problem of medical malpractice insurance for health sciences staff.[50]

Wise's proposed reductions, a staggering 15 percent for WVU, resurrected an awareness of the University's leading role in West Virginia's economic development. Concurring with this analysis, the state's business newspaper said that the amount of the reduction was "causing some people to wonder: Is West Virginia cutting away at the very economic engine that could pull it forward to prosperity?" With the state undergoing a long-term transition from an older manufacturing economy to one driven by technology, WVU's role as a research institution would have to become preeminent. According to a WVU Bureau of Business and Economic Research study completed in 1999, the University and its affiliated organizations directly and indirectly produced 23,640 jobs, added more than $1.3 billion to the economy, and generated economic activity that garnered $37.2 million for the state in direct and indirect taxes (including sales, personal income, net income, and business taxes). Moreover, WVU was committed to increasing its externally funded research, which had grown to $135 million by 2002; the salaries of more than six hundred people at the University were derived from these grants and contracts for research. Nevertheless, most citizens did not view higher education as an economic engine because they either were not aware or did not understand the significance of the projects underway in University laboratories. Speaking to the Washington, DC chapter of the WVU Alumni Association, President Hardesty described most of the sponsored research at the University as directed toward biometrics, cancer and neurological research, and forensics. Augmented by the ability of the congressional delegation to transfer major operations of the FBI, NASA, and other federal agencies to the state, a "New West Virginia" was being forged.[51]

Predictably, the cost-saving measure that produced the loudest uproar was the decision to eliminate five non-revenue varsity sports during the 2003–2004 school year: rifle; men's indoor and outdoor track; men's cross country; and men's tennis. These five sports were chosen by Athletic Director Ed Pastilong, who estimated that their elimination would save about $600,000 per year. The cuts were not arbitrary but were made with Title IX in mind, the federal law that sought to bring some gender equality to college sports. Cutting the five programs rebalanced the ratio of male to female scholarship athletes from about 60 percent men to 51 percent, and it increased the proportion of the budget going to women's sports as well.[52]

President Hardesty took the heat for approving the program cuts, even though they were determined by the athletic department. All units, or "auxiliaries," were to be operated as "independent cost centers" and were required to stand on their own financially. "People who live in residence halls do not want to subsidize people who live in an apartment, and people who pay tuition do not want to pay for an athletic program," he asserted. Therefore, the administration determined that auxiliaries were to be treated as separate cost centers and that "the people who support those auxiliaries need to pay the cost, no more, no less." To make up for lost state revenues, the University needed to invest in other areas. "We cannot stop giving raises at the university forever to balance our budget in a retrenchment. The people that are here are going to have to get raises. We can't stop fixing buildings and building [new] buildings," Hardesty explained.[53] West Virginians were beginning to discover how the University was funded, or not funded, and Hardesty embraced the task of educating them on the importance of WVU in the life of the state.

Joe Manchin replaced Governor Bob Wise in 2004, and he was more inclined to give institutions the flexibility to manage their own affairs. In the governor's State of the State Address, Manchin announced that he wanted "to remove the shackles from higher education." All of the colleges needed "some flexibility to be able to compete in the marketplace, because we're throwing them in the marketplace," the governor declared. "If they don't compete and show value, we can't support them." The new governor's attitude was music to the ears of WVU administrators. President Hardesty, like his predecessors, argued for more administrative flexibility and relief from "the burden of multiple layers of regulations." Shortly after taking office, Governor Manchin and the legislature demonstrated their confidence in WVU's ability to manage its own affairs by passage of Senate Bill 603, which vested authority in the WVU Board of Governors to oversee the University's own resources and reduced the multiple administrative layers.[54]

West Virginia thus joined a national trend in the funding of higher education. According to David Breneman, the dean of the Curry School of Education at the University of Virginia, the relationship between higher education and state government was undergoing a major shift. "The general pattern is one of reduced state support followed by sharply rising tuition and arguments for less state regulation." In Virginia, state institutions were undergoing this very transition with much less state support but sharp rises in tuition to offset those revenue losses. In exchange the schools received greater autonomy in building projects, purchasing, and personnel matters. West Virginia legislators were following how these changes unwound in Virginia, but key leaders thought some West Virginia institutions might not possess the staff to operate in this fashion. The state's two universities, it was cautiously conceded, probably could undertake many of these operational duties.[55]

Caution was part of the political culture in West Virginia. Because the state was fragmented by regionalism, an excessive amount of distrust prevailed between local and state government leaders. Whether the state or local government should control the institutional purse strings was a question hiding behind every bill. According to Provost Gerald Lang, the University gained much more independence in controlling its own operations, but "we are still hampered by a common state policy on Human Resources. It is the one thing that is really damaging to us. . . . You have the smallest community and technical college having the same classified staff policies as WVU."[56]

Nationally, public colleges and universities were weathering a long period of budget cuts from state legislatures. They responded by raising tuition, often beyond the ability of poor and working-class families to pay. They had also "begun to cannibalize themselves," according to one commentator, by increasing the size of classes and cutting course offerings. Some of the nation's most prestigious public universities were unable to provide students with the classes they needed to graduate. Cutting back funding for research assistants and other research support services threatened some of these schools with not only the loss of professors but also millions of dollars in research grants. In some cases, such losses rendered departments insolvent. This budget-cutting trend began in the 1980s, when legislatures began to scale back their commitments to public higher education and federal and state financial aid failed to keep pace. Pundits predicted that tuition increases would keep poorer students away, and devalued degrees at public universities would cause students who could afford it to go elsewhere. "The states will then learn that important institutions are easy to destroy and devilishly difficult to rebuild."[57]

EMERGENCE OF A "SIGNIFICANT NATIONAL UNIVERSITY"

In October 2005, after a decade of service at WVU, President Hardesty asserted that the University had made impressive strides. "I also think it is fair to say that we have begun to emerge as a very significant national university, recruiting quality students from all 50 states and 90 countries." No one could argue with his assessment. Former President Neil Bucklew had laid the groundwork for the University's emergence on the national scene; David Hardesty and Provost Gerald Lang guided it to new heights. In his 2004 State of the University Address in Washington, DC, President Hardesty compared the WVU of the present with its beginnings nearly 137 years earlier. When its first president, Alexander Martin, delivered the University's very first inauguration speech, WVU housed three departments and five faculty members in a much smaller Woodburn Hall, and six college-level students were enrolled. President Martin dreamed of the day when the student body would number a few hundred. WVU exceeded those expectations beyond anything he could have imagined. Today, President Hardesty observed, WVU consisted of six campuses, six distance learning centers, an extension office in every county, and hundreds of online classes available around the world. In 2005, the University attracted a record-high statewide enrollment of 32,000 undergraduate, graduate, and professional students from every county, forty-nine states, and one hundred foreign countries. The Morgantown campus alone offered 170 degree programs. Carnegie Doctoral/Research University-Extensive WVU ranked among the top 3 percent of universities in the nation, and pulled in $150 million in research. The Robert C. Byrd Health Sciences Center had just celebrated its semicentennial, and the University's economic impact on the state's economy ranged well more than $1 billion.[58]

A comparison of the faculty profile in 1974 versus that in 2004 provides a means of measuring change during those intervening years. In 1974, the 17,000 students enrolled at WVU were taught by 1,350 full-time and 250 part-time faculty, comprising 1,600 total. By 1994, the number of faculty had risen to 1,515 full-time instructional members. The state-imposed budget reductions over the next decade, however, were responsible for a decline by the fall of 2003 to 1,289 full-time faculty teaching 24,260 students. During that same decade, the student/faculty ratio increased from 17:1 to 21:1. Reflecting the increasing reliance on part-time, non-tenure-track, non-benefits-eligible instructors, the number of full-time tenure-track instructional faculty declined from 78 percent in the fall of 1995 to 68 percent in the fall of 2003.[59]

When Hardesty became president in 1995, WVU, like higher education nationally, confronted a number of daunting issues. Globalization and the internationalization of markets challenged America's economic dominance, and West Virginia's basic industries, coal, steel, and glass. The information technology revolution would facilitate globalization and eventually link everybody in the world in real-time, requiring major investments in infrastructure. Also, demands for "accountability" from universities were imposed at a time when public resources were limited even as parents and students were demanding better academic programs, campus services, and amenities. Competition for a declining number of students and federal funds for research only magnified the economic pressure. Alumni, donors, businesses, and government agencies increasingly demanded that higher education become more "business-like" in its operation. Because public funds were shrinking and tuition increases had their limits, the University was forced to raise private money through a major capital campaign led by the WVU Foundation.[60] Because these challenges faced all of higher education, the success with which they were not only met, but superseded, during a single decade at WVU was an impressive achievement, particularly in the aftermath of the unexpected tragedy of September 11, 2001, and the subsequent collapse of the financial markets.

HARDESTY RESIGNS

On September 20, 2007, David Hardesty and his wife, Susan, stepped down as president and first lady. Their partnership was characterized by teamwork, and Susan was more fully engaged in service to the University than any preceding president's wife. Just as many had considered Hardesty's appointment to the presidency the result of political intervention into the University's business, so too many now saw the interfering hand of politicians involved in selecting his replacement. Hardesty clearly wanted to continue in office because he had stated on more than one occasion that he and Susan had "pretty much decided we want to spend our lives doing what we're doing now." He believed that WVU "deserves our commitment."[61] The reasons for his resignation and the appointment of Michael Garrison as his replacement were not revealed to the public. Some governors have demonstrated that they are not bound by any academic tradition of the university being beyond ordinary political machinations, and academicians and laymen alike were convinced that the popular president had been forced out for political reasons. Years later, Hardesty spoke against this assumption. His comment that he and Susan had decided they wanted to spend the rest of their lives at WVU was true in 2003. Three years later, however, they were both "very tired, mentally and physically," due to the "constant stress" of entertaining, politics, and executive work. Although the board had approved an extension of Hardesty's contract to 2010, the couple decided that it was in the best interest of all parties if they stepped down. Twelve years at the helm was twice as long as the average tenure for a president.[62]

Not long after relinquishing the president's office, Hardesty reflected on the political relationship between the state and the University. "The University is such a gem it's hard for a governor or the legislature to let it go. That's going to hold it back in the end. As long as the state's tentacles are very, very strong, you will have new governors come in to manage it their way," Hardesty mused. To every governor, WVU is a state agency, he continued, and the governor "determines what the culture of the University is, whether it is political, citizen friendly, or future oriented. . . . There is a constant tension of how we should conceive of the University. Is it quasi-independent because it has its own board of governors or is it a state agency directly responsible to the governor?" This is the reason governors participate in the selection of presidential candidates. For WVU faculty and administrators, who were generally educated elsewhere, West Virginia presents a confusing, novel system. At Penn State, for example, the state constitution vests decision-making powers with the university, and in California a strong Board of Regents is intended to buffer the institutions from raw politics. The issue facing WVU, and higher education generally in West Virginia, is whether the University is a state agency or a bipartisan institution created to serve the people rather than public officials.[63]

David Hardesty has told the story of attending a seminar for new university presidents at Harvard University and asking the question, "Who owns the university?" The leader of the seminar replied, "Oh my, never ask that question, let alone try to answer it, because the university has so many owners. And each of these owners has an image."[64] The question of ownership becomes most problematic when a president resigns and a new one is selected. Unlike the corporate world, presidents of academic institutions generally are not involved in the selection of their replacements. Because so many people "own" the university, and the university's vision changes with the times, policies, and decision-makers, replacing presidents is always a political process.

Outgoing President Hardesty and his wife shared their views on how WVU had changed during his tenure as president. The greatest change, according to Susan, was that the University became "much more customer-oriented." David Hardesty believed that his most important contribution may have been "fostering a broad-based understanding on campus that the University is enrollment-driven and that it must be a student-centered enterprise to compete in the global marketplace."[65] Beginning in the eighties, the prevailing perception that a college education was a public good and therefore should be subsidized by the taxpayers slowly shifted to the view that it was more of a private benefit. Consequently, students should bear the larger measure of its cost. The "days of heavy subsidy are over at universities like ours," the former president observed, and the "vast majority of revenues that drive this institution are customer revenues" generated from students, patients, or clients.[66]

Above all, Hardesty believed, WVU was now "clearly a national university," a theme to which he returned time and again. "We should think of ourselves as a national university, a major national university located in the state of West Virginia."[67] Asked how he would like his administration to be remembered, Hardesty replied, "Everyone associated with the leadership team, including my wife Susan, worked hard every day to advance the University, its national reputation, and its impact on West Virginia."[68]

David Hardesty left office in 2007, much admired for the accomplishments of his administration. In this case, matching the president to the task of remaking the University into a modern institution had been a success. As a student of leadership, he did not make all of the important decisions, nor did he micromanage. Instead, he appointed an experienced leadership team headed by Provost Gerald Lang, who led the University toward his larger vision of what the institution should become. Across the state the press and key political leaders acknowledged the role Hardesty played in the University's transformation. The titles of editorials referring to his retirement tell the story: "Hardesty Gets High Marks at WVU"; "WVU Must Build on Hardesty Legacy"; "Hardesty Has Strengthened WVU"; "Hardesty's Decision to Step Down at WVU Exemplifies Leadership Skill"; "He'll Be Missed"; "Hardestys Will Be Difficult to Replace"; "Hardesty Leaves Us in Good Shape." Perhaps the greatest compliment came from the state's largest newspaper, the *Charleston Gazette*, which declared David Hardesty "West Virginian of the Year."[69]

FIFTEEN

RISE OF THE UNIVERSITY AS A RESEARCH ENTERPRISE

DAVID HARDESTY'S ADMINISTRATION is most widely remembered for reforming undergraduate education by aligning the University with the national movement among large public research institutions to become more "student-centered." Much less appreciated is his effort to join the nation's land-grant institutions in shifting from "outreach" to "engagement." The philosophy behind the new approach reflected trends articulated in the third report of the Kellogg Commission on the Future of State and Land-Grant Universities, "Returning to Our Roots: The Engaged Institution."[1]

The Kellogg commissioners, all current or former university presidents, claimed that universities faced a "growing public frustration with what is seen to be our unresponsiveness. At the root of the criticism is a perception that we are out of touch and out of date. Another part of the issue is that, although society has problems, our institutions have 'disciplines.'" In short, even though universities possessed resources and expertise, they were not organized to focus on society's problems. At the same time, financial constraints and demands for affordability and accountability imposed by public officials ran directly counter to the demand to find solutions to major societal problems. The commissioners concluded that the time had arrived to move beyond traditional outreach and service to a new policy of "engagement." Institutions should redesign their teaching, research, and service functions to become "even more sympathetically and productively involved with their communities." Traditionally, outreach emphasized a one-way process in which the university transferred its expertise to its constituents. The engagement ideal called for a commitment to reciprocity. The commission envisioned partnerships: "two-way streets defined by mutual respect among the partners for what each brings to the table. An institution that responds to these imperatives can properly be called what the Kellogg Commission has come to think of as an 'engaged institution.'"[2]

The commissioners offered several guiding principles that characterized the "engaged institution." First, it must be attentive to the demands coming from the outside, deliver services in the right time and format, and maintain open and clear lines of communication. Second, the purpose of engagement is not to channel the university's expertise to the community but "to encourage joint academic-community definitions of problems, solutions, and definitions of success." Therefore, the university must respect the skills of its partners and learn from its collaboration. Third, some research activities will inevitably involve contentious issues that have a profound impact on society. Consequently, maintaining the university's role of "neutral facilitator" is vitally important when public policy issues are at stake. Fourth, universities are complicated structures for "potential partners" to understand and navigate, so they need to become more accessible. Universities are decentralized "ivory towers" composed of disciplines governed by academic principles that seem arcane to outsiders. Fifth, universities should integrate their service, research, and teaching missions; engagement provides the opportunity to do this. The commissioners believed a commitment to interdisciplinary research to be indispensable in an integrated approach. There must be incentives and encouragement for faculty and students to participate. Sixth, so many moving parts make up the engaged approach that someone must be responsible for actively coordinating the effort. Finally, engagement carries costs, most obviously, in the time and effort of faculty, in curriculum, and in limitations on institutional choices, but "the most successful engagement efforts appear to be those associated with strong and healthy relationships with partners in government, business, and the non-profit world."[3] The engaged institution would not create itself, the commissioners asserted. Universities needed to "transform their thinking about service so that engagement becomes a priority" on campus and an integral part of the institution's mission.[4] This model provided

President Hardesty with the concepts in which his initiatives were rooted. Conceptualizing and organizing the multitude of individual research projects underway at WVU as a centralized "research enterprise" arguably transformed the institution. Under the new university model, research was elevated to an entirely new level, from individual creative inquiry to a university-managed enterprise.

In 1996, President Hardesty articulated his vision of the University as a service operating in the marketplace. "As we focus on research," he said, "we will want to apply many of the same principles of quality and customer satisfaction that we are applying to student services." The partnership between government, business, and research universities that had prevailed for a half-century following World War II was being pared back as business and government sought to economize. Significant cuts in research funding were expected to continue into the foreseeable future. "We must be relentless in seeking funding for our important work. We must develop a strategy that recognizes where the research dollars are, focuses our research, carves out some niches to concentrate on, and delivers high-quality research at a competitive price."[5]

THE RESEARCH TASK FORCE

In his 1996 State of the University address, President Hardesty announced that he had created a research task force to help formulate a university-wide research strategy. WVU research activities played a major role in the economic development of the state at a time when state-mandated reductions from 1995 to 2000 cut state appropriations significantly. In 1994, WVU expended $48 million in externally funded research and development projects in science and engineering. That year, more than 30 percent of the University's operating resources derived from externally funded research and educational service agreements. This was second only to state appropriations, which were 37 percent, and larger than the 20 percent generated by tuition and fees. No wonder WVU's new president quickly initiated a review of the University's research enterprise with a view to expanding its role. Six months later, in January 1996, President Hardesty commissioned a research task force to investigate how the University could maintain its growing research program.[6]

The Research Task Force was charged with identifying quantifiable measures for evaluating the significance of research and scholarly productivity at the University. Of course, no single set of criteria applies to the diverse array of research and scholarly activities that occur at a research university, but the "over-riding expectations for individual performance" were that every faculty member would participate in quality research or scholarly creative activity, that the outcome would be published or presented in the appropriate peer-reviewed venues for the discipline, and that research would "positively influence" the teaching mission. The great diversity of disciplines rendered it difficult to judge scholarship. Funding was the primary measure in the sciences because the costs associated with research, such as laboratories, equipment, and supplies, largely determined its scope and extent. In the humanities, research generally required the use of library resources and an individual's time; therefore, peer-reviewed publication was the standard measure of performance.[7]

Externally funded activity is vital to WVU's primary missions, the task force reported, a point emphasized by the fact that 30 percent of total University revenues came from these sources. In 1996 WVU ranked 110th in external research funding among the top five hundred research institutions in the United States according to the National Science Foundation. Since 90 percent of all federal research support to colleges and universities is directed toward the top one hundred research universities, one might expect WVU to receive 1 percent of the funding; in fact, it receives considerably less than 1 percent. Another method for measuring WVU's research funding status compared the University with its Southern Regional Education Board (SREB) peer institutions. By this measure, WVU was last among its peer group with WVU faculty bringing in nearly $68 million in fiscal year 1994, well below average funding of slightly more than $117 million for the SREB schools. WVU's major goal was to break into the top one hundred research universities within two years, the task force argued. This required a 22 percent increase in funding over fiscal year 1994 and a significant increase in faculty participation in externally funded research, as well as in attracting more funding from federal agencies.[8]

A significant problem identified by the task force was the University's failure to recapture true indirect costs for research. Direct costs, those clearly identified with a specific project, were easily determined, but indirect costs, those supportive of research but not specifically identified with a project, were another matter. WVU's negotiated indirect cost rate for on-campus research was 43 percent of direct costs, but the University was recovering only one-fifth of the negotiated rate. The University's recovery rate compared very unfavorably with its peers and with other major research institutions, which recovered 60–90 percent of the negotiated rate.[9]

Although it was vital to encourage a "research culture," more than fifty "major impediments" inhibited the efforts of the University to achieve this overarching goal. They fell into three main categories: conflicting objectives, such as encouraging interdisciplinary research without providing incentives or credit for this kind of work; internal issues related to administrative support and physical facilities, such as inadequate laboratories and budgetary assistance; and external developments associated with a declining trend in the availability of federal funding.[10]

The report also noted that WVU's approach toward research had been "ad hoc and opportunistic," rather than strategically focused on areas of expertise. Also, the percentage of faculty who had developed active research agendas varied by college or school from a high of 88 percent in pharmacy to a low of 5 percent in physical education during the period from 1993 through 1995. Most funded efforts were concentrated in a few federal and state agencies, and a significant amount of recent federal research funding had been obtained from 'earmarked' projects, which are discussed below. Anticipating a future without Senator Robert C. Byrd in Congress, the report warned that federal earmark opportunities would be limited. Furthermore, the task force concluded, WVU had lacked success in either attracting or cultivating senior faculty who could serve as leaders. In fact, in some disciplines junior faculty carried a larger research load than senior faculty. Finally, it must be recognized that WVU had not developed "a comprehensive strategy for presenting itself as a research university."[11]

The task force advanced several recommendations for enhancing research productivity. WVU must establish research as a clear priority. The barriers to research must be removed, the University should invest in it, and all faculty should be expected to pursue some form of scholarship or creative activity. Moreover, WVU should foster collaborative research relationships internally, as well as with other institutions, businesses, and government, to bolster research that would enhance its national and international reputation. Since a decline in federal funding was expected into the foreseeable future, WVU researchers were encouraged to refocus their energies on winning competitive grants. The task force also recommended that special attention be given to those areas of research important to West Virginia's economic development. Finally, a core of senior faculty researchers should be developed to mentor younger faculty. The promotion and tenure process should establish an expectation for faculty to demonstrate excellence in teaching, research, and service, while faculty who emphasized research should be supported by equitable workload assignments. For humanities scholars, the Research Task Force recommended developing a "viable and competitive University Press."[12]

RESEARCH AND ECONOMIC DEVELOPMENT

The economic malaise that held a tight grip on West Virginia during the half-century following World War II resulted from dramatic shifts in the national economy. Company consolidations prompted the removal of headquarters from the state. Globalization prompted industrial enterprises to look for cheaper labor in other countries such as Mexico and China. Foreign oil took market share from coal, and the basic industries, such as coal, steel, and chemicals all confronted foreign competitors who flooded the U.S. market with cheaper products. Modernization, the substitution of capital for labor, the technology and communications revolution, and the out-migration of the workforce in search of employment opportunities imperiled West Virginia's economic health.[13]

Placing WVU research into the forefront of state and national economic development was a prominent theme of David Hardesty's agenda, one to which he returned repeatedly in speeches throughout the twelve years of his presidency. Higher education was expected to lead the state's economic development and therefore was a strategic investment by the public, government, donors, and businesses rather than a financial burden. An insight into Hardesty's thinking about economic development is found in a 1998 op-ed in which he asserted that nearly every study of West Virginia's path to improving the economy identified creating more and better jobs as the top priority. The long-term solution was an "integrated statewide system of work force developers," with WVU providing workforce development through its statewide system of schools, colleges, campuses, extension offices, and distance learning sites. The integrated approach envisioned WVU researchers working hand-in-hand with businesses and government to provide solutions to current problems and inventions for the businesses of tomorrow. He cautioned, however, that West Virginia was part of a global economy, to which higher education was a doorway. Higher education's responsibility was to broaden horizons in the state rather than to erect "state-imposed roadblocks." If the demand existed for teachers in the global economy, why should WVU not train students who want to enter the profession even though there is no current need for their services in West Virginia? West Virginians needed to see their children's futures in the context of a larger world of opportunities. "Limiting their options is obviously not in their interest and not a good plan for the state. An integrated, cooperative approach to workforce development with a global outlook is a strategy that will serve us well today and tomorrow."[14]

At the dawn of the new millennium, state political leaders finally accepted the idea that research universities were central to the creation of new jobs through the development of technology and economic opportunities. In 2002, Governor Bob Wise proposed, and the legislature subsequently approved, a plan to encourage scientific development by creating a $25 million pool for venture capital firms and a package of tax credits intended to stimulate investment in research and development. He also proposed $9 million in state matching funds for the West Virginia Experimental Program to Stimulate Competitive Research (EPSCoR), which promotes collaboration in research and technology development among universities, state government, and state businesses. WVU boasted more than thirty specialized research centers and institutes devoted to such activity in 2002, and all held great potential for economic development. Among the best known were the Concurrent Engineering Research Center, the National Research Center for Coal and Energy, the Regional Research Institute, the Center for Chinese Business, the Mary Babb Randolph Cancer Center, and the Center for Rural Emergency Medicine.[15]

In 2000, the Carnegie Foundation for the Advancement of Teaching reclassified WVU from Research I to Doctoral/Research University-Extensive based on its commitment to graduate education, the conferral of fifty or more doctorates per year in at least fifteen disciplines, and the amount of federal funding that the University received for research. Only 3.8 percent of the 3,856 institutions of higher education in the United States held that classification, and WVU was the only one in West Virginia. The Carnegie classifications are revised annually, and by 2006–2007 WVU had been further elevated to the designation of Research University—High Research Activity.[16]

ECONOMIC IMPACT OF WVU

The policy of investing in research that began during the presidency of Neil Bucklew was continued and amplified at an unprecedented level by his successor. The wisdom of this decision can be measured by the economic impact on the local and state economy of externally sponsored projects directed by the University and its affiliates. Total sponsored funding grew from $88.7 million in fiscal year 2000–2001 to a new peak of $150.6 million in fiscal year 2005–2006, and, after a brief dip, it climbed to a new all-time high of $175 million in fiscal year 2009–2010.[17]

The WVU Bureau of Business and Economic Research has undertaken detailed studies of the University's economic impact annually since 1997–1998. These studies demonstrate the powerful impact of WVU research and sponsored programs, and why it is important for state policymakers to support the institution. The studies analyze both WVU's main campus in Morgantown as well as its affiliated institutions: the WVU Institute of Technology, Potomac State College, the WVU Alumni Association, WVU Foundation, and the WVU Research Corporation. The latter group includes West Virginia United Health System (WVU Hospitals, WVU Hospitals East, and United Hospital Center), WVU Physicians of Charleston, and WVU United Health Associates (WVU Medical Corporation and WVU Dental Corporation).[18]

The growth in the economic impact of WVU in Morgantown and the total economic impact of WVU and its affiliates are revealing. The total (direct and indirect) economic impact of WVU grew more than five times during the decade between 1998 and 2009, from $948 million to $4.9 billion dollars. Even more dramatically, the total economic impact of WVU and its affiliate organizations grew nearly sixfold, from $1.4 billion to $8.3 billion during the same period. Impressively, this economic impact came at a time (1998–2009) when direct employment was reduced by 40 percent, from 11,360 to 6,856. The indirect employment generated by WVU business activity was also an obvious benefit, since it doubled from 6,368 to 13,700 during the period. Moreover, total job creation for WVU expanded from 17,728 to 20,556, an expansion which clearly benefitted the private sector. Total job creation by WVU and its affiliates grew even more dramatically, from 23,640 in 1998 to 45,000 in 2009. Total direct and indirect employment compensation also indicates the massive impact of growth at WVU. Total compensation for WVU more than doubled from $430 million to $1 billion in 2009, with direct compensation to WVU employees totaling nearly $600 million. Total compensation for WVU and its affiliated organizations also more than doubled from $636 million to a little more than $1.8

billion in 2009. In short, every dollar the state spent on WVU became $23 in the state economy, and every dollar in appropriations spent on WVU and its affiliated organizations returned $40 to the state's economy.[19]

"EARMARKS" TO COMPETITIVE GRANTS

When Vice President of Research and Economic Development John Weete first came to WVU in September 1998, competitively funded research was relatively low. Instead, there was "a high dependence on earmarks as a first choice for seeking funds to support major projects."[20] His observation was validated by the publicity surrounding WVU during the late 1990s and early 2000s as the champion of "academic pork-barrel" projects. A *Chronicle of Higher Education* survey in 1999 identified "pork" projects funded by congressional "earmarks," that is projects funded without competitive reviews by the agencies that provide federal money. Good government advocates charge that this is an unfair and wasteful way to distribute federal money. But many politicians disagreed, including West Virginia's powerful Senator Byrd and Representative Alan Mollohan, who sat on their respective appropriations committees, and junior Senator John D. Rockefeller III, a major advocate for state development through science and technology. They viewed directing federal dollars to their state as a major part of their jobs. Academic research universities nationwide argued that spending on science and technology was essential for economic development, and their representatives listened. The evidence seemed compelling since economic development had in fact occurred where high concentrations of research facilities existed. As one authority observed, "everyone wants another Silicon Valley."[21]

According to the *Chronicle of Higher Education*, Congress earmarked $797 million dollars for universities and colleges in 1999. WVU ranked second with $15.1 million dollars. The following year Congress funded more than $1 billion in research for the very first time. Two of the state's universities were ranked in the top ten for pork-barrel funding that year. WVU was sixth with $17.3 million, and Wheeling Jesuit University was ninth with

$14.5 million. Statewide, West Virginia ranked fifth in earmarked projects, receiving $38.86 million.[22]

Critics opposed "pork" spending that did not require scientific peer review, but supporters countered that earmarks often were "a lifeline for worthy projects" that otherwise might not get off the ground. At WVU, recent examples were the WVU Eye Center, National Small Flows Clearinghouse, and the Institute for Software Research, which included a research as well as a service mission.[23] Far from being repentant, President Hardesty was proud of his university's ranking in "pork" funding. In 2002, WVU was ranked second by the *Chronicle of Higher Education*, receiving $31.6 million. "There are a lot of good things that happen with earmarks," the president declared. "In this list you will see 50 institutions, some of them very prestigious. I think it's a good list to be on, I'm glad to be No. 2." For perspective, Hardesty also emphasized that WVU received $134 million in total funded support the previous year; only 24 percent, or $31.4 million, was derived from congressional earmarks.[24]

Congressional spending on university research continued, and in 2003 the *Chronicle of Higher Education* reported that congressional earmarks for higher education totaled more than $2 billion. Again West Virginia schools were major recipients. At nineteenth, WVU garnered $22.8 million, Marshall University, in twenty-first place, received $17.2 million, and Wheeling Jesuit University, in thirty-fourth, got $13.7 million.[25] The state's business newspaper registered its approval: "If higher education funding is pork, bring more." For too long "West Virginians sat back and watched all the federal money go to other states," but now, with strong leaders in Washington like Senator Byrd and local Congressman Mollohan, "the shoe is on the other foot." In seeking to answer the needs of higher education, the editor opined, Congress was doing "much better than the state government is doing."[26]

With most of his student-centered programs in place, President Hardesty proclaimed that 2000 was the year when the University would emphasize research. West Virginia arguably had suffered from the shift to a global economy, with the state's mainstay industries of coal, steel, glass, and chemicals dramatically affected by the loss of traditional jobs and an increase in high-technology jobs. Discovering new products and services that would energize the state's restructuring economy, therefore, was part of the University's mission as a land-grant institution.[27] One of the primary goals of the University's Strategic Plan for Research for 2000–2005 was "to increase the portfolio of intellectual properties from faculty research and proactively transfer the technologies to the private sector." The University declared an even stronger commitment to research in its 2004–2010 Strategic Plan for Economic Development, asserting that research at land-grant universities represented economic development "magnets" for high technology businesses and the invention and commercialization of intellectual properties. The Bayh-Dole Act of 1980, which permitted universities to fully participate in economic development through technology transfer and in the commercialization of innovations, was the seminal federal legislation. "For the first time, universities could own, protect, transfer, license, and commercialize innovations supported with federal funds and developed by their faculties." Before the Bayh-Dole Act, universities produced about 250 patents a year, and most of them were not commercialized. In 2000 alone, however, American universities filed for 8,534 patents and created 386 companies.[28]

The need for WVU to respond to the challenge was evident by the fact that, in 2004, according to the Progressive Policy Institute, West Virginia was ranked forty-eighth in the nation in adapting to the "new economy" and was described as "still deeply embedded in the tenets of the old economy." John D. Weete, who came to WVU from Auburn University in 1998 to serve as president of the WVU Research Corporation, highlighted several compelling reasons why the University should pursue external funding for research. First, research would be the driving force in economic development into the foreseeable future, resulting in a significant diversification of the West Virginia economy ten or fifteen years down the road. Also, the greater the external funding for the University's research, the greater the improvement in the University's reputation. Since major universities actively seek those research dollars, WVU must follow suit in order to reap future benefits. "The greater our reputation," Weete observed, "the more we can help diversify the economy, and the more people will want to stay here." Moreover, "with a greater reputation, you don't have to go after [the funds] so much as they start coming to you."[29] Creating a new research culture at WVU was necessary, however, before that lofty status could be achieved.

John Weete encountered "a lot of skepticism" from the outside in his efforts to match faculty researchers with external funding opportunities. The University administration fell short in its responsibility to monitor external grants and ensure that the funds were used as intended. Therefore, funding agencies complained that all too frequently faculty accepted grant money but failed to report the final results of their research. According to Weete, this left a "negative legacy" with Senator Byrd and Congressman Mollohan who were embarrassed by the lack of performance after they secured large federal grants for WVU projects during the eighties and early nineties.[30]

Another obstacle to be surmounted before WVU could hope to achieve its goal of doubling the University's research funding was bringing together specialized interdisciplinary faculty research teams to lead the effort. Only about 20 percent of the faculty were nationally competitive researchers, according to Weete. For that reason the University's long-term plan was to invest in recruiting researchers and redeploying current faculty into fields that would help the University become more competitive. The shift in commitment to research and economic development, begun in earnest under David Hardesty, actually originated earlier during President Bucklew's administration. However, it is misleading to assume that the University had no reputation for research prior to this change in emphasis. In 1977–1978, WVU was ranked ninetieth out of the top one hundred universities that received federal funding. The difference was that in 1977–1978, prior to the 1980 Bayh-Dole Act, which unleashed a torrent of research dollars flowing into universities, the amount of federal funding directed toward WVU research was only $13 million. WVU lagged behind its peer institutions in taking advantage of the new opportunities presented by Baye-Dole. Whereas sponsored research grew only modestly at WVU, research funding at peer institutions grew dramatically. Research at WVU was still cast in the single-investigator mold, whereby individual faculty members received research grants that, along with a few graduate students, kept them going. With research grants and contracts shifting to big science and technology projects, most federal funding agencies began to look for interdisciplinary research to solve problems that were far too complex for a single individual or discipline to resolve. Presidents Bucklew and Hardesty attempted to reset this model of faculty research culture.[31]

The reorientation from individual researchers to interdisciplinary teams raised the larger question of just how a University could change the faculty research culture. "With a lot of difficulty," was Weete's terse assessment. Change called upon faculty to embrace a more entrepreneurial way of thinking that linked research projects to the likelihood of receiving external funding. Individual researchers needed to connect their work with that of other researchers engaged in solving complex problems that funding agencies chose to support. Significant disincentives also had to be overcome for younger, untenured faculty, who needed to be rewarded for interdisciplinary research with salary, promotion, and tenure.[32]

Another culture shift encouraged faculty inventors to work with the University to patent and commercialize their inventions. The traditional faculty reward system emphasized publishing rather than patents but disconnected the process from the world of external funding agencies. If upper-level administrators demanded that faculty make this shift, ever greater resistance might be encountered down the chain of command as core disciplinary identities were challenged. To prevent the initiative from coming to a grinding halt, the supporting infrastructure needed to be put into place. "Before, we had a few faculty that were inventors, but we did not have the support system to help them and they would go out and get a patent on their own, which was technically University-owned property," Weete observed. Even though technical support was in place by 2007, Weete claimed that faculty still had to develop confidence in the system.[33]

Inadequate state support for research also posed an obstacle to the plan to transform the research enterprise effort at WVU. Senate Bill 547 created a significant financial challenge. The loss of some $35 million in state funding and about five hundred positions, one hundred of which were faculty, impeded the entire University, deteriorating its ability to support research at exactly the time when the state demanded more externally funded research. Moreover, the capacity and structure of research support infrastructure, such as accounting, sponsored programs, procurement, and facilities, were insufficient to support growth of the research enterprise.[34]

To make matters worse, the state was slow to realize that research would drive economic development. The state of West Virginia provided $10 million, split equally between Marshall and WVU, for hiring specialized research faculty, but the two universities were required to match the grant with funds from private sources. Entering the competition for major funding with such a thin reserve was an unrealistic expectation imposed on the University. Until there was a dramatic improvement in its financial resources, WVU did not possess the funds to hire prominent research faculty and bring instant success. Promising young faculty were hired instead, with the hope that they would become established researchers and stay long enough to lift the research enterprise.[35]

While the state's investments were taken as a hopeful sign, they did not reach the level required to make a significant difference and were well below the level of recent investments by other states in their research universities. For example, California approved $3.5 billion over ten years to finance stem-cell research at state universities. The University of Texas planned to launch a $2.5 billion program to expand research in the sciences, medicine, and technology. The state of Texas and the city of Dallas committed $300 million over five years to advance the University of Texas at Dallas as a research institution, hiring two Nobel laureates to jumpstart the effort. Arizona State University invested $150 million on a new Biodesign Center. Kentucky committed $350 million to higher education to build competitiveness. Oklahoma established a billion-dollar endowment to support scientific research. Even Wyoming established a $500 million higher education endowment, which would generate approximately $23 million per year to attract the best graduate students and faculty.[36] This was the kind of competition WVU confronted in seeking major external funding.

Faculty who can compete for federal funding from agencies such as the National Science Foundation (NSF) and the National Institutes of Health (NIH) are essential to a successful research enterprise. In 2006, an estimated 20 to 25 percent of the tenure-track faculty were actively engaged in funded research, and a "much smaller proportion" of them brought in most of the research funding. The nationally competitive faculty were essentially doing all that could be "reasonably expected of them" to bring in federal funds to support their research. Nevertheless, funding from the NSF and NIH continued to be far below what was expected of a research university with a comprehensive health sciences center and a "high research activity" classification. Continued advancement toward the goal of becoming one of the top research universities, therefore, depended largely on the further development of nationally competitive faculty. Most likely, moving ahead was contingent on the one hundred new faculty the University expected to hire between 2004 and 2010, nearly all of them in the science, technology, engineering, and medical fields. Filling those positions required high laboratory start-up costs averaging between $250,000 and $450,000 in 2006, as well as salary and fringe benefits for each assistant professor over six years, which would reach almost $620,000. The investment for each new faculty member over the first six years of employment, therefore, totaled about $1.1 million.[37] If all were successful, however, they could generate about three times their cost in new research funding. Thus, while the University's investment was substantial, the potential rewards were even greater.

The University could accelerate this long-term strategy by hiring some "rising stars" with established funding records who would bring their funded projects with them to WVU. It might even hire some "superstars" who had already established research programs and multi-million- dollar grants to elevate performance standards and motivate junior faculty to become competitive. The vice president for research recommended that the University create a core of non-tenure-track research professors who would be responsible for generating their own salaries and research support through external grants. Another option was to hire more full-time postdoctoral researchers who typically stayed two to three years working with lead faculty members and had their salaries paid from external research grants. Both research faculty and post-docs would augment the number of researchers at the University without the long-term commitment. Finally, an increase in graduate students from the current three thousand to at least four thousand primarily doctoral students was necessary to bolster the ranks of assistants. To recruit superior doctoral students, however, required competitive stipends.[38]

Economic development, therefore, had become a major, fully articulated WVU mission by 2004. In its broadest sense, as implemented by the academic institutions, economic development involved a diverse array of activities requiring the University to emphasize coordination and control. Consequently, the WVU Economic Development Council took the lead in coordinating economic development activities by identifying areas of need, seeking funding sources, facilitating the delivery of services, and assessing research programs.

WVU RESEARCH CORPORATION

The WVU Research Corporation was created as a not-for-profit entity in 1987 to foster and support research at WVU. Its stated mission is "to provide evaluation, development, patenting, management, and marketing services for inventions of the faculty, staff and students of the University." The corporation also serves as the fiscal agent for sponsored programs on behalf of the University. It was intended to provide resources and assistance to develop faculty research into products for the market and, thereby, to foster economic development. It provides the flexibility in hiring researchers and purchasing supplies and equipment. WVU, as a state agency, lacks the ability to make some equipment purchases because state regulations require competitive bids, and scientific equipment is often produced by only one company, thus eliminating the possibility of finding a competing bid. Also, the University does not have the flexibility to hire temporary employees as researchers to work for the duration of funded research projects. The Research Corporation employs some 175 people in various offices to support researchers with services and oversight to ensure their compliance with official guidelines, facilitate grant applications, and manage grant money received. A portion of the money awarded to faculty through grants and contracts is retrieved by the Research Corporation to support its services.[39]

The Office of Technology Transfer was established in 1999 "to protect, promote, and commercialize research generated by faculty, staff and students of the University, and is responsible for the protection and commercialization of intellectual property for all WVU organizations." Faculty researchers are the primary generators of intellectual property through the invention of new products or processes, or through expertise. Their research or inventions are protected through patents, copyrights, trademarks, or trade secrets, and is commercialized primarily through the licensing of patents or knowledge to existing companies, or through the creation of a joint venture. The Office of Technology Transfer is staffed by these specialists in the language of science, business, and the law who manage the commercialization of discoveries.[40]

Technology transfer was a relatively new venture for WVU in 2001 and was approached with caution. "Some believe that state educational institutions should refrain from becoming involved in what would appear to be private-sector endeavors," President Hardesty observed in a press release, but the research conducted at WVU should offer "the most direct benefits possible for the people we serve." As technology transfer was ramped up, West Virginia would reap rewards in economic development. Previously, technology transfer simply resulted in the publication of research in scientific journals, "but it also allowed ideas that could lead to economic development to walk right out of the state," he said. Now, scientists could develop the product of their research into new businesses in West Virginia. Some claimed that the attention given to technology transfer diverted higher education from its primary missions of teaching, research, and service. But West Virginia's transition from extractive industries to a "new economy" required the introduction of new ideas into the marketplace for the future of the state's economy. "We've got a lot to do in West Virginia to get this state on firm economic ground, and if the state's research land-grant institution can help . . . then our course is clear."[41]

Another link in the scaffolding connecting research to economic development was created in 2004 with the opening of the WVU Business Incubator. Operated by the WVU Research Corporation's Office of Technology Transfer, the Business Incubator was located in the Chestnut Ridge Research Building and charged with accommodating and nurturing start-up businesses launched with WVU intellectual properties. Tenants received office space, wireless and broadband access, and common office equipment, along with other types of business support, such as accounting, advertising, graphic design, information technology, finance, corporate services, professional staff, and skilled student interns. Created in 2001 by the College of Business and Economics, the Entrepreneurship Center works closely with the Business Incubator. The Entrepreneurship Center has been an active partner in creating a "culture of entrepreneurship" in West Virginia through its West Virginia Entrepreneurs Forum and helps to teach students and arrange their internships with new businesses. By 2006, the Business Incubator already operated at capacity in the Chestnut Ridge Research Building location and was scheduled to move into the first building constructed at the new WVU Research Park.[42]

The stated mission of the WVU Research Park is "to advance innovation, commercialization, and economic competitiveness by forging collaborations among WVU, industry, and government while supporting the University's strategic plan." The park was expected to attract high-tech business, serve as a center for innovation, and furnish a home for the WVU Business Incubator for start-up companies that would benefit from close proximity to a research university. The Research Park is the final component in WVU's economic development infrastructure and a critical piece in the plan for commercializing WVU intellectual properties and attracting high technology businesses to the area. Acquired by the Research Corporation, the Research Park was established on eighty-eight acres, at the former site of the WVU Poultry Farm along Highway 705. Planned in two phases, the Research Park will eventually include 650,000 square feet of laboratory and office space encompassing a dozen buildings, and will employ more than 2,600 people. Site preparation for the first phase, which includes the construction of roads and infrastructure, was completed in 2007, and the first 65,000 square foot building to be constructed in phase two would provide space for the WVU Business Incubator and an additional 40,000 square feet of leasable space for businesses and government agencies, creating a synergy for high-technology development.[43]

WVU's adoption of the "integration model," in which the institution's programs are integrated with those of the research park, produced a value-added dimension to tenancy. In other words, a synergy created by the intellectual discoveries and innovations would result when WVU faculty and students worked closely with external researchers on enhanced technology transfer. Weete, who served as WVU's vice president for research and economic development and president of the WVU Research Corp. from 1998 to 2007, was the key architect of the University's research enterprise during these years, and he spearheaded the Research Park's development. "This park is not just about WVU, and it's not just about Morgantown," Weete told a reporter. "It's about the state economy and keeping bright, talented people in the state. Our planned research park would act as an economic engine for the state." The disciplines involved in biotechnology, biometrics, environmental studies, energy and information technology would lead the state into the "new economy," and encouraging this development was the University's role.[44]

Progress on the University Research Park quickly bogged down over financing, as some University administrators, state politicians, and some of the original business investors became cautious. Weete resigned in 2007 to take a similar position at Auburn University and was replaced by his protégé, Curt Peterson. Slowly, the project began to move forward again. Peterson was hopeful that the funding would materialize for construction of the first WVU-occupied research building in the Park by mid-2009. "There hasn't been enough creativity invested in how to get the funding for that first building. That's been the issue," Peterson informed a reporter. Construction on a building for the U.S. Department of Energy's Office of Legacy Management was underway in 2008, and the University had constructed a depository for WVU Libraries, which did not contribute to research in the park but was a significant addition for the University. As part of WVU's research enterprise, the Research Corporation also established the Office for

Congressional and Federal Relations in the nation's capital in March 2009. A few blocks from the U.S. Capitol, the office would be used to bolster the University's efforts to work with the state's congressional delegation in order to make the University a major research partner with federal funding agencies.[45]

BENEFITS OF RESEARCH

Prior to the Bucklew and Hardesty administrations, WVU evolved toward a research university model without much institutional planning. The wisdom of developing such a plan was borne out in 2010 with the death of Senator Robert Byrd and Congressman Alan Mollohan's failure to be reelected. Both men held powerful positions on their respective Senate and House appropriations committees. Together they were responsible for directing more than $30 million per year in federal earmarks to West Virginia. Anticipating the inevitable day when its politicians could no longer deliver so much federal largesse, and recognizing the declining commitment to federally sponsored research, the University increasingly emphasized competitive funding. It was necessary for the University to increase non-governmental funding to remain competitive with its peers, which called for a much more strategic approach toward research.[46]

Basic and applied research is part of WVU's mission as a land-grant institution, as it is for the institutions with which WVU compares itself. Expanding the research enterprise not only generates more money; it also helps the institution to maintain its status among its peers and enhances its academic reputation. The intellectual property and products that flow from faculty research often generate revenues, and the University takes 40– 60 percent of that money as its share, depending on the costs associated with a particular project. These revenues represent a significant portion of the University's operating budget. For example, in 2008 WVU research generated more than $72 million from which the institution benefitted significantly for the use of its space and facilities. Faculty researchers also filed twenty-nine U.S. patent applications and thirty-eight invention disclosures.

Three U.S. patents and seven license agreements were also issued to WVU faculty, and the University will share in any income realized from these. Four high-tech companies reportedly grew out of WVU research projects in 2008, and fourteen have done so since 2002.[47]

WVU reported spending about $133.5 million for research and development during fiscal year 2007, and the National Science Foundation ranked the University 112th among the top two hundred universities and colleges in total research and development expenditures. Yet, among its twenty peer institutions, WVU's eighteenth position in research and development expenditures for the period 2004–2007 kept it far from the top. Even though WVU trailed in its peer group, its newfound commitment to research was demonstrated by the fact that only two of those institutions outpaced of WVU's growth in research investment during the period 1999–2006 when its expenditures nearly doubled from $63.3 million to $112.1.[48]

Research funding originates not only from the University itself but also from federal and state government, industry, and private organizations. Most of the money spent for research is sponsored funding, that is, external money received for a specific purpose. Because neither the state nor the University could ever provide the entire level of support necessary, the Office of Research and Economic Development and the Research Corporation offer assistance to faculty in developing proposals for competitive grants. Apparently practice brings improvement, for faculty researchers have become increasingly successful. In 2008 faculty garnered funding for 409 out of 819 submitted proposals. The University measure of "total sponsored funding" exceeded $140.7 million in fiscal year 2008, $83 million of which was dedicated to research and the remainder for non-research projects such as educational services. By far the largest amounts of sponsored funding came from federal agencies. For example the National Institutes of Health provided about $17.4 million in grants for 2008, but the National Science Foundation, Department of Energy, Environmental Protection Agency, and National Aeronautical and Space Administration also made significant funding commitments. Nearly all of this money was for research in science, engineering, and medicine.[49]

Governor Bob Wise unveiled in 2004 a plan to provide seed money for university research projects, but it stipulated matching funds from the institution and was never large enough to create an economic impact. Governor Joe Manchin signaled a dramatic new direction in 2008 when he convinced the state legislature to fund the "Bucks for Brains" program, which would match dollar for dollar up to $35 million to either Marshall University or to WVU for research in four strategic areas: nanotechnology; material science; biological, biotechnological, and biomedical sciences; and biometrics, security, sensing, and related identification technologies.[50] The intention was to stimulate development of "new economy" industries in order to diversify the state's economy. The state was late to the game, however, for WVU had shifted its strategic research focus in this direction years earlier.

With its close ties to industry, the College of Engineering and Mineral Resources has always been a major center for research at WVU, and the University had no intention of abandoning its comparative advantage in this "old economy" research. Instead, new technologies were brought to bear on old problems associated with the coal industry, most specifically "clean coal" technologies and electric power generation. Coal and electric power have been integral to West Virginia's economy for more than a century, and nearly all of the state's coal production is used to fire power-generating plants. With a long tradition of providing the industry with engineers, managers, and advanced production and distribution know-how, WVU's College of Engineering is strategically positioned to continue to play a leading role in energy research.

WVU is also home to the National Research Center for Coal and Energy (NRCCE), which was established in 1978 by the federal government to increase the utilization of fossil fuels through basic and applied research, to sponsor technology transfer, and to disseminate knowledge generated by NRCCE research projects. The center also facilitates sponsored programs with external partners and research units within WVU. Over the years, the NRCCE has expanded its scope by focusing on the development of a secure and inexpensive energy supply for electric power generation, and

Dr. Perley Issac Reed, shown here in front of Martin Hall, founded WVU's School of Journalism in 1939.

B1

Opposite: Coliseum construction (ca. 1969); Below (top): The Black Unity
Organization (1969); Below (bottom): The women's tennis team started in
1973, along with the women's gymnastics and basketball programs. They
were the pioneers of women's sports at WVU.

Below: Vietnam War protester; Opposite (top): In May 1970, police in riot gear clashed with anti-Vietnam War demonstrators in front of the Mountainlair; Opposite (bottom): Student protesters of the Vietnam War attend a lecture by the activist-attorney William Kunstler in the Mountainlair (1970).

Below: The men's basketball team's final game in the old Field House (Stansbury Hall) against Pitt in March 1970. Opposite: Homecoming Queen and her court, 1975.

B7

B8

Opposite (top): WVU President Gene Budig (1977-1981) with then-Governor Rockefeller and Senator Byrd at the dedication ceremony for the Robert C. Byrd Room in Colson Hall (1980).

Opposite (bottom): Current and Past WVU presidents celebrate West Virginia's birthday (1992). From left to right: Diane Reinhard, Harry Heflin, Paul Miller, Elvis Stahr, Neil Bucklew.

Above: Ellie Mannette, director of the University Tuning Project, a wide-scale steel drum initiative at WVU. He is a National Heritage Fellow and started WVU's Steel Drum Band in the 1990s.

Left: Phil Faini, who retired as dean of the College of Creative Arts in 2000, served WVU for 40 years as an educator and administrator. He headed the percussion program, directed the Percussion Ensemble, and founded WVU's World Music Center.

The WVU Marching Band performing at Mountaineer Field. The Band was formed in 1901 as an all male ROTC Band.

Aerial view of the Medical Center and Mountaineer Stadium (1979).

Mountaineer Field opened on September 6, 1980, a day highlighted by John Denver performing "Country Roads" with backup singers Bill Danoff and Taffy Nivert.

B13

Don Nehlen was the first coach to improve on Pappy Lewis's winning record, and led the team to national prominence as head football coach (1980 to 2000).

MILAN PUSKAR STADIUM

Above: Linda Burdette-Good served as gymnastics coach from 1975 until her retirement in 2011. Burdette-Good, along with Kittie Blakemore, Martha Thorn, and Nanette Schnaible, was one of the forces behind the integration of women into WVU sports in the 1970s; Opposite (bottom): Ed Pastilong, WVU Athletic Director (1989-2010), and Milan Puskar outside Milan Puskar Stadium. In 2004, the stadium was named for the founder of Mylan Pharmaceuticals, and major WVU benefactor.

Opposite (top): The National Research Center for Coal and Energy was established in 1978. Over the years it expanded its focus to include the development of a secure and inexpensive energy supply for electric power generation, and to promote technology exchange through cooperative programs.

Opposite (bottom): Construction of the Student Recreation Center was completed in 2001.

Left (top): Diane L. Reinhard was appointed interim president in 1985 while also serving as dean of the College of Human Resources and Education. She was the first and only woman to occupy the president's office at WVU.

Left (middle): E. Gordon Gee served as Dean of the College of Law and then WVU President (1981-1985).

Left (bottom): Morgantown native Neil Bucklew served as WVU's twentieth president (1986-1995).

B17

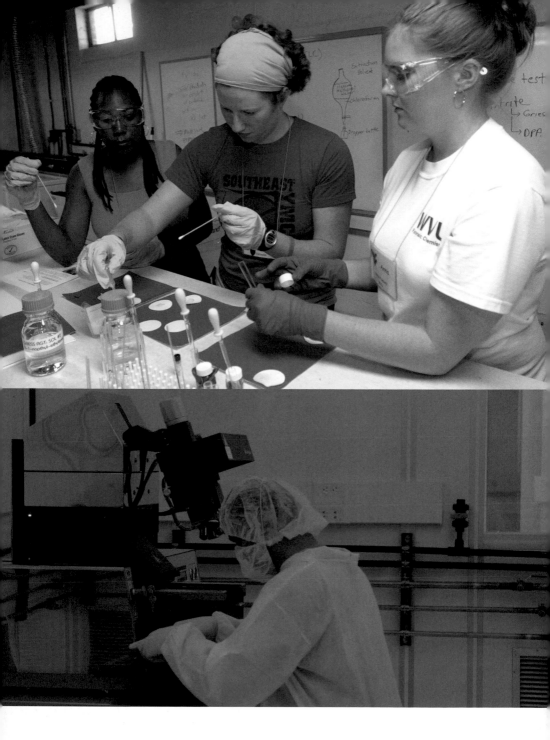

Top: Forensic crime scene house. WVU began working in cooperation
with the FBI's Clarksburg, WV Fingerprint Identification Facility in 1993.
Bottom: Nanofabrication Clean Room. In 2004 WVU established the
interdisciplinary WVU Nanoscale Science, Engineering, and Education
Initiative.

Above: Michael Garrison, a 1992 WVU graduate, was named WVU President in April 2007. He is joined by Governor Joe Manchin on his left, and then Chairman of the BOG Stephen Goodwin on the right.

Right: C. Peter Magrath, a senior presidential adviser to the College Board and president emeritus of the National Association of State Universities and Land-Grant Colleges, was selected as interim president to replace Michael Garrison in 2008.

Left: In March 2009, a search committee chaired by former president Gene Budig announced James P. Clements as WVU's twenty-third president.

Below: John D. Weete, President of the WVU Research Corporation and Vice President of Research and Economic Development (1998-2007), was the architect of WVU as a research enterprise.

Opposite (top): WVU Tech, located in Montgomery, WV, has been a regional campus of WVU since 1996.

Opposite (bottom): WVU Dairy Farm.

Left: The WVU Women's Basketball team and head coach Mike Carey (2004).

Below: The WVU Rifle Team (2002). By 2013, the team had won its fourth straight Great American Rifle Conference title—the first team ever to do so—and won fifteen NCAA national championships.

The early 21st century is a time of great upheaval in college sports, with conference realignments and escalating costs posing major challenges to WVU's student athletic programs. Clockwise from top: Randy Mazey, head baseball coach; Oliver Luck, Athletic Director; Dana Holgorsen, head football coach; Bob Huggins, men's basketball head coach. All three men's coaches were employed by institutions in WVU's current conference, the Big 12, before coming to Morgantown.

international initiatives such as the promotion and exchange of technology through cooperative programs involving the U.S. Department of Energy and the governments of India and China.[51]

Morgantown is also home to the National Energy Technology Laboratory (NETL), one of five Department of Energy laboratory systems focusing on fossil fuel. Two of the five NETL facilities are located in Morgantown and Pittsburgh. In cooperation with the NETL and NRCCE, College of Engineering researchers continue to search for environmentally responsible methods for using coal. Much progress has been achieved in reducing carbon and sulfur dioxide emissions in coal-fired power plants, improving power plant efficiency, and creating the technology for producing efficient fuels from coal. Carbon by-products extracted from coal can fetch as much as $300 per pound, which would make coal too expensive to burn, so technologies such as gasification, hydrogen production, and carbon sequestration have become the focus of new research to revitalize an old industry and help it meet twenty-first century standards.[52]

Coal remains the primary fuel for power generation and therefore still has the potential to attract major funding. In 2008, NETL partnered with researchers at WVU, the University of Pittsburgh, and Carnegie-Mellon University to acquire a $26 million grant from the Department of Energy. The three partners plan to develop new technologies that would reduce the problems of greenhouse gasses and other negative environmental impacts brought about from using fossil fuel energy. Several months later, WVU launched the Advanced Energy Initiative, an interdisciplinary science and engineering program to form research partnerships in the areas of fossil energy, sustainable energy, and energy policy. From 2004 through 2008, WVU raised $98.4 million for energy research, and the AEI planned to bring in an additional $52 million by 2012.[53]

With Senators Byrd and Jay Rockefeller leading the effort, the emphasis on clean-coal technology was carried over into the administration of President Barack Obama. In September 2010, U.S. Secretary of Energy Steven Chu came to Morgantown to announce that the NETL would serve as lead agency on a $40 million federal project to develop computer simulations that would greatly accelerate the development of clean-coal technology. Secretary Chu also announced that WVU would receive $12.5 million over five years through the U.S.-China Clean Energy Research Center. WVU would lead a consortium that included a number of other prominent scientific institutions in the effort to test new technologies for carbon capture and storage.[54]

Even though the study of energy continued as a major focus for WVU researchers, the most excitement now surrounds the "new economy" fields of forensics, biometrics, and nanotechnology. WVU began working with the Federal Bureau of Investigation in 1993 to find housing and other services for FBI employees who had begun to move from their former locations in Washington, DC, to the Morgantown area, where the new FBI Fingerprint Identification Facility would soon open in April 1995. This facility employed more than three thousand people and supported more than $1 billion in high technology criminal justice projects. In 1997 WVU signed an agreement with the FBI to develop the first degree-granting program in forensic identification to create the kinds of expertise required at the FBI complex.[55] Forensic science is the application of natural sciences to the analysis of evidence discovered at crime scenes. "The perpetrator is typically unknown at the time of the crime and, therefore, must be identified through fingerprints, dental records, DNA, or some other forensic method."[56]

The new forensics program was widely applauded by the FBI and other law enforcement leaders, who saw the need for professional rather than on-the-job training. About twenty students were accepted into the first freshman class from a pool of about 650 applicants, but forensics quickly became one of the University's most popular undergraduate majors, growing to two hundred students in 2002, and six hundred by 2005. A master's program was soon added. At the time of its creation, the forensic identification program was the only one of its kind in the nation.[57]

The Forensic Science Initiative, a part of the forensic identification program, was launched to help state and local forensic science laboratories improve their skills and the quality of their work by providing research and academic resources. By 2010 the forensics identification program at WVU had become one of the top three departments in the nation, producing sixty graduates per year.[58]

By its very nature, forensic science is a multidisciplinary field, and a growing number of WVU engineers and scientists (particularly in physics, biology, and medicine) are engaged in biometrics and related fields. The Lane Department of Computer Science and Engineering offers degrees in biometrics, one of its principal areas of research. Like forensics, biometrics is an identification science, but with an important difference. Whereas forensics is applied to "post-event situations," biometrics is applied to "pre-event situations," such as controlling access to secure areas, surveillance, and identity verification. Biometrics is a field of technology "devoted to automated methods for authentication of individuals using physiological and behavioral traits, such as retinal or iris scans, fingerprints, hand geometry, face recognition, handwriting, and gait." The technology increasingly is being used for government and corporate IDs, secure electronic banking, retail sales, law enforcement, health and social services, and homeland security. Biometrics experts seek to prevent crime; forensic experts look for resolution.[59]

The potential uses of biometrics for economic development became readily apparent to both University and state political leaders, and they lost little time in designating north central West Virginia along I-79 between Clarksburg and Morgantown as a "biometrics corridor." Anchoring the corridor is the West Virginia High-Tech Consortium near Fairmont. Of its 227 member-businesses in 2001, several dozen were either directly or indirectly involved in biometrics. At the southern end of the corridor, near Clarksburg, sits the FBI's Criminal Justice Information Services Division which stores fingerprints from more than forty-million criminal records. The Department of Defense Biometric Fusion Center, also located near Clarksburg, tests standard commercial biometric products for use in military information systems. A national leader in biometrics research and educational programs, WVU stands at the northern end of the corridor in Morgantown. This rapidly growing scientific complex prompted the director of the International Biometrics Industry Association, a trade group based in Washington, DC, to compare the I-79 corridor to Silicon Valley.[60]

In 2002 the *Wall Street Journal* published one of those sneering stories that West Virginians have come to expect from time to time, in which the reporter's arrogance reveals his ignorance. West Virginia leaders were "betting the farm" that the war on terrorism following the tragedy of 9/11 would cut a path to a twenty-first-century economy by spurring the biometrics industry, the story began. The state got its start in biometrics through old-fashioned pork-barrel politics, but state leaders hoped West Virginia would "rise above its backwoods reputation" and lure out-of-state entrepreneurs with the "Silicon Holler." Interviewed for the article, Professor Michael T. Yura, then director of the forensic identification program, acknowledged that the state had an "image problem" but puzzled the reporter by actually suggesting that image represented only a minor obstacle to be overcome. Unconvinced, the reporter asserted that "the obstacles to West Virginia's success are as easy to spot as the mobile homes just over the hill from its nascent technology park near Fairmont." Among them, he pointed out that most of the industry had chosen more appealing locations such as California; that the state was burdened with old economy smokestack industries; and that only 15 percent of the workforce had college degrees.[61]

Just as predictably, the state's leaders took exception to the article. They were supported by John Siedlarz, chairman of the International Biometric Industry Association, who informed the *State Journal* that the article was "condescending" and wrote a letter of complaint to the *Wall Street Journal*. Siedlaraz reportedly informed the author of the *Journal* article that, "while some elitists may be amazed by how a bunch of backward mountaineers and children of coal miners could have such vision and energy in creating a new economy in what they see as an unlikely place, they need to spend more time speaking to and working with such folks before they assume that they don't have the 'right stuff.'"[62]

Senator Byrd initiated the biometric initiative by relocating the FBI fingerprint facility to Clarksburg. Then he and Senator Jay Rockefeller nursed the young industry by ensuring that it received the government funding it needed to sustain itself. Paul Collier, the executive director of the Biometric Foundation in Washington, DC, who had been involved with developments in West Virginia since 1997, believed that "WVU was way ahead of the pack" in the field of biometrics and was "the hub of our industry." The first degree in biometrics was established at WVU in 1998 to dovetail with its degree in forensics. The undisputed leader in the biometrics field at WVU was Professor Lawrence Hornak of the Lane Department of Computer Science and Electrical Engineering. He coordinated the program and served as director of the Center for Identification Technology Research (CITeR), the only NSF center focused on biometrics. In 2010, Hornak received a prestigious appointment as program director in the NSF's Division of Industrial Innovation and Partnerships of the Engineering Directorate.[63]

WVU also plays a strategically significant role in the development of this industry through its academic degree programs and research. The Biometric Knowledge Center (BKnC) conducts multidisciplinary research related to biometrics, including "detection, diagnosis, and treatment of disease and injury, as well as the enhancement of the human-computer interface," such as workforce development. The BKnC also "maintains information exchange networks with other academic and research institutions, the biometric industry, the federal government, and the West Virginia biometric enterprise." BKnC also collaborates with CITeR. Their activities are complementary in supporting biometric research, education, and enterprise at the national level.[64]

In February 2008, an agreement was signed recognizing WVU as the FBI's lead academic partner in biometrics research and its liaison with the academic biometrics research community nationwide. The University also became affiliated with the FBI's proposed Biometrics Center of Excellence, which, when built, would "focus on biometrics research and identity management services used to combat terrorism." The FBI realized that WVU was becoming a "national hub for biometrics research in the United States," and that data collected by WVU could be made available to researchers, something that the federal government could not do. Several months later, the National Security Agency and the Department of Homeland Security designated WVU as a National Center of Academic Excellence in Information Assurance Education, making it one of ten universities nationally to be awarded such a distinction.[65]

Nanotechnology refers to the manipulation of matter to build useful devices one atom at a time, from the molecular scale up to the macro-scale. The nanoscale ranges from one to one hundred nanometers, or about one one-thousandth the width of a human hair.[66] Related to, and supportive of, forensics and biometrics in focusing on the microscopically small world, nanotechnology brings together biologists, chemists, physicists, engineers, and health scientists. "When you start looking at things on the scale of nanotechnology, all those traditional concepts of physics, biology, and chemistry begin to break down. The traditional walls between the disciplines just dissolve," according to physicist Edwin Rood, who coordinates this research at WVU's Research Office.[67] In 2004, the University established the interdisciplinary WVU Nanoscale Science, Engineering, and Education Initiative (WVNano). The primary objective of this initiative is to advance the research enterprise, specifically interdisciplinary research, and to diversify West Virginia's economic base through cultivation and growth of vigorous research in targeted areas of nanoscale science and engineering."[68] Rood claimed that specific applications are limitless. "We can mimic biology at the molecular level. . . . If you had to repair the nervous system, you could go in without surgery. . . . Organically built nanobot cancer-fighters infused with life-saving proteins could be ingested or injected to disassemble wayward cells on their way to mutating into tumors."[69]

The largest NSF Experimental Program to Stimulate Competitive Research grant ever awarded to the state of West Virginia was announced on June 7, 2006. The $9 million science and technology grant, "Next Generation Biometrics: Achieving Strength in Molecular Recognition and Transport," was designated for the West Virginia EPSCoR, with the research to be led by WVU. The state contributed an additional $4.5 million through EPSCoR, bringing the total program size to $13.5 million for nanoscale research. The EPSCoR award was an infrastructure and improvement grant intended to elevate the University's research competitiveness and stimulate the innovation needed for the technology-based economic development that is so important to the knowledge-based "new economy."[70]

DAVIS COLLEGE OF AGRICULTURE, NATURAL RESOURCES, AND DESIGN

The Davis College evolved from the Hatch Act of 1887, federal legislation which established agricultural experiment stations in each state. The West Virginia Agricultural Experiment Station was established as a separate unit within the University the following year. In 1895, the experiment station became part of the agriculture college, and the Division of Extension was established in the College of Agriculture in 1911. Ninety years later, in September 2001, the college was renamed the Davis College of Agriculture, Forestry, and Consumer Sciences in recognition of two sisters, Gladys and Vivian Davis, and their mother, Estelle Davis, who bequeathed their large estate as an endowment to help fund the college's operation.[71]

Approximately one-half of the operating revenue for the Davis College comes directly from the state and federal governments to support applied research and the distribution of new knowledge to farmers, but the relative funding proportions vary. For example, total annual revenues and expenditures between 1988 and 2004 rose from $7 million to $11.9 million. The most significant funding pattern during this period was that of grants and contracts, primarily for research. This category grew from $1.3 million to $3.9 million. The relatively flat state appropriations and outright decline in federal appropriations during this period were offset by the growth in external funding for research and reflect the larger pattern of funding at the University as a whole. At the same time, this increase in research funding was accompanied by a large reduction in total numbers of faculty, research scientists, and other professional personnel.[72]

While the Davis College researchers have continued their efforts in the traditional areas of applied agriculture and forestry, they have also periodically refocused research priorities to suit the changing times. In 1990, for example, the Experiment Station Committee on Organization and Policy recommended that five research areas receive the highest priority: consumer food safety, water quality protection, nutrition, safe and effective pest management, and international markets and trade. Since then, new emphases like environmentally related research have emerged. Traditional problems were also cast in a new light. Thus, research related to the proper disposal of poultry manure in the eastern panhandle was concentrated on protecting the Potomac River Basin and the Chesapeake Bay from the runoff. Mine-land reclamation became a massive problem in the context of modern mountaintop-removal mining and the need to protect streams and waterways many miles downstream from such mining sites.[73]

Another new dimension impacting research in the Davis College was the emergence of multidisciplinary and collaborative research, as well as advances in computers and other technology, including genetic engineering, spatial analysis, and remote sensing. Because a single discipline cannot address problems in these fields, they must be attacked from multiple perspectives. The Genetics and Development Biology Program exemplifies the multidisciplinary approach to modern scientific research, given its numerous research collaborations with other universities and federal laboratories.[74]

Similarly, the Aquaculture Food and Marketing Development Project used federal funding, multidisciplinary researchers, and an outreach goal to develop programs in West Virginia. This project, initiated by Senator Robert C. Byrd, involved Davis College researchers from the fields of animal and veterinary sciences, fisheries and wildlife, agricultural and resource rconomics, as well as researchers from the College of Business and Economics, the College of Engineering, and the Extension Service. Aquaculture is one of the most rapidly developing segments of agriculture and represents a major opportunity for economic development in West Virginia. The Aquaculture Food and Marketing Development Project was engaged in uncovering the genetic bases of reproduction, nutrition, growth, and other qualities in trout in order to enhance the quality and quantity of their production for the market. Genetic "mapping" of the trout was essential so that the best genes could be brought together to make a superior fish. Because of the excellent fresh-water resources found in West Virginia, local and out-of-state fishermen would take advantage of the fee-fishing enterprises, as well as the motels, resorts, and state parks. Also, cold-water trout species presented an opportunity to develop commercial trout farming for human consumption.[75]

Thus by keeping abreast of modern approaches even in an era of declining state resources, the Davis College of Agriculture, Natural Resources, and Design increased its national profile in research. In 2007, WVU was conducting about $17 million in agricultural research funded from competitive grants and state and federal sources. Agricultural research undertaken by the Davis College was ranked by the National Science Foundation in 2006 as forty-first in the country. By 2007, it had reached thirty-ninth in the nation and fifth among colleges and universities in the northeastern United States.[76]

WEST VIRGINIA UNIVERSITY PRESS

State-imposed reforms forced the University to become increasingly responsible for raising its own operating revenues, which, in turn, necessitated the concentration of research funds in areas where they would generate the greatest reward. Invariably, these funds were directed to the STEM disciplines: science, technology, engineering, and mathematics. These disciplines required an entrepreneurial approach from their researchers, who were compelled to search out sponsors in industry, private foundations, and government agencies to fund their work. Scholars in the humanities and some social sciences, on the other hand, generally worked alone; time and access to archival resources were their primary requirements. Funding was welcomed, but these scholars were judged chiefly by the quantity and quality of their publications. To foster research in these fields, WVU decided to resurrect its moribund press. The move was an acknowledgment of the time-worn tradition that saw universities as institutions engaged in the production of knowledge for its own sake.

WVU's publishing program dated to the early sixties. A number of scholarly books and bibliographies had been published under a WVU Libraries imprint established by Dean of Libraries Robert F. Munn. His untimely death in the mid-eighties left the University's publishing program in the hands of his replacement as dean of libraries, Ruth M. Jackson. During Dean Jackson's tenure, the University's libraries, like libraries everywhere, experienced a dramatic transformation initiated by computer technology. With the shift in focus, library administrators had little time and less inclination to invest in an activity that seemed peripheral to the modern library's mission. Because there was no serious effort to market scholarly books under the WVU Libraries imprint, other regional university presses stepped in to fill the void. One notable example was a college textbook in West Virginia history, published by the University Press of Kentucky in 1993.[77] Other publishing projects of importance to West Virginians were often ignored entirely by out-of-state publishers.

University faculty had initiated some tentative gestures to create a WVU Press after Munn's death, but they instilled no urgency in their efforts. The issue of establishing a university press in West Virginia was brought before the West Virginia Universities Board of Trustees Progress Council of Presidents in 1989 by Interim Chancellor James W. Rowley.[78] The proposal spurred some progress toward creating the WVU Press, but not enough concrete results to still the agitation of those in Charleston who argued for an "academic press" under the auspices of West Virginia's "higher education authority." Governor Gaston Caperton's wife, Rachael Worby, and Gordon Simmons of Trans Allegheny Books sponsored another proposal five years later. They incorrectly claimed that West Virginia was "virtually alone in this nation in never having had a university press conforming to the guidelines of the Association of American University Presses." However, they were essentially right in concluding that, as a result, "our best academic work" was published outside the state.[79]

By 1998 a WVU Press administrative board had been established, and in July of that year Malcolm M. MacDonald, director emeritus of the University of Alabama Press, was retained as a consultant. He visited campus for several days and then reported his recommendations for establishing a press to University administrators. MacDonald suggested that the first step for the administrative board was to draw up a mission statement and establish goals. A director should then be hired to manage the press. However, control of the press's imprint must rest with a faculty committee or board consisting of a rotating membership appointed by the president or provost. The faculty advisory board, as it came to be called, would establish qualitative standards for manuscripts. At least two unmasked, positive evaluations of each manuscript by senior scholars should be required for publication. Also, specialists were required to manage the four functional areas of book publishing: editorial, production and design, marketing, and business. Because it was "unrealistic to think that the Press will become self-supporting," the University must be willing to make a financial commitment to ensure success. Employees' salaries should be paid by the University, but, as the publication list grows, the press should increasingly assume more responsibility for its operating expenses. No academic press publishes in all disciplines; therefore, MacDonald recommended that the WVU Press concentrate on the University's areas of strength. Because the critical mass of scholars and resources were already in place, African studies, literary studies, the economics of coal, West Virginia, and Appalachia were logical areas of focus for pursuing manuscripts.[80]

Nearly all of the consultant's recommendations were followed in reestablishing the WVU Press. Instead of placing the press under the administrative aegis of the president or provost, however, it became a unit within the College of Arts and Sciences with a director appointed by and reporting to the dean. In 1999, Patrick Conner, a professor of English, became the new director. A faculty advisory board was then established, and the first two series were initiated: Medieval European Studies and West Virginia and Appalachia. By 2012 the series offerings had expanded to include Regeneration: African American Literature and Culture, Rural Studies, and West Virginia Classics. The mission of the press had evolved as well. As the press proclaimed in 2012, "A university press is an extension of its parent institution, charged with serving the public good by publishing works of scholarly, intellectual, and creative merit for a diverse range of readers. West Virginia University Press's primary goal is to find, develop, select, and publish scholarship and creative works of highest quality and enduring value. Through the publication of all such works, WVU Press helps to fulfill West Virginia University's land-grant mission."[81]

The success of the press since 2000 can be seen in the high quality of the books it publishes each year, some of which have won national recognition. For example, Robert J. Kapsch's *Potomac Canal: George Washington and the Waterway West* (2007) was awarded a Book of the Year silver medal in history by *Foreword Magazine*, an American Institute of Graphic Arts award, and a Washington Book Publishers Design and Effectiveness award. Chosen from more than three thousand entries, Davitt McAteer's *Monongah: The Tragic Story of the 1907 Monongah Mine Disaster, the Worst Industrial Accident in US History* (2007) received an Independent Publishers Book Award bronze medal. The press also reprints West Virginia classics, such as Charles Henry Ambler's path-breaking study *Sectionalism in Virginia from 1776 to 1861*. The WVU Press Sound Archive makes available Appalachian music from outdated aluminum disc collections and field recordings, which are valuable sources in the fields of folklore and ethnomusicology, as well as items of great interest to lay enthusiasts.[82]

Five peer-reviewed scholarly journals, which are an integral component of many academic presses, are also published by the WVU Press. *West Virginia History: A Journal of Regional Studies* has been a major outlet for historical scholarship on West Virginia and Appalachia since 1939. Founded in 1962, *Victorian Poetry* publishes scholarly articles on British poets and poetry of the period 1830–1914. *Essays in Medieval Studies* is an online-only journal publishing interdisciplinary scholarship. *Education and the Treatment of Children* offers an important source for professionals involved in improving the teaching, training, treatment, and development of children. Scholarly and critical commentary on the voluminous fiction of J. R. R. Tolkien can be found in *Tolkien Studies: An Annual Scholarly Review*. Vandalia Press, an imprint of WVU Press, publishes creative works by Appalachian writers, including West Virginia poet laureates Louise McNeill and Irene McKinney, as well as Lee Maynard and Meredith Sue Willis, among others. M. Glenn Taylor's *The Ballad of Trenchmouth Taggart* was a fiction finalist for the 2008 National Book Critics Circle Award, and a Barnes & Noble Great New Writers selection.[83]

Upon Patrick Conner's retirement in 2008, Carrie Mullen became the new director and has continued to build a press with a flourishing list of books and journals in the social sciences and humanities. The reconstituted

WVU Press has met the goal it set for itself in 1999 by publishing quality books of fiction and nonfiction, particularly those of interest and value to the state of West Virginia, and has enhanced the University's reputation as a center for scholarship. It also has fulfilled its first measure of success by becoming a member in the Association of American University Presses, a goal that seemed a very distant aspiration in 1999.[84]

It might reasonably be debated whether West Virginia University has yet become a national university as measured by the scale and complexity of the research conducted by its faculty. However, there is little question that research has grown into a major enterprise that, if continued, might indeed become the path leading WVU to that lofty aspiration.

SIXTEEN

THE ROBERT C. BYRD
HEALTH SCIENCES CENTER

Construction on the new hospital had already begun when Neil Buck-lew became president of WVU in 1986. The University had by this time already decided to divest West Virginia University Hospitals, and this deci-sion was second in importance only to the building of the new facility itself. Many factors influenced the divestiture decision, nearly all of them involv-ing state regulations treating WVU Hospitals like any other state agency (when indeed it was not like any other state agency). Under those regula-tions, hospital employees could work only 37.5 hours per week, the facility had to observe eighteen holidays a year, and the state treasury had to issue all checks. "It was just strangled. It couldn't compete in the field," Bucklew recalled. Because of a need for repairs and a lack of state investments, the surgery unit was closed. For lack of bathroom facilities, hospital patients were forced to trek down the hall to a "gang shower," which they used only as a last resort. The University and hospital lobbied the state to make its own personnel policies, construct its own buildings, and set its own fees. Fi-nally, the legislature passed the divestiture bill, approving an independent University hospital governed by a board, the majority of whose members were associated with the Health Sciences Center, and chaired by the presi-dent of WVU.[1]

WVU was only the second state university in the nation to divest its hospital, entering relatively uncharted waters out of necessity. It was clear to Bucklew, however, that the hospital must be divested not only from the state, but also from the University. "Everywhere we could, we tried to al-low them to be independent," he recalled. Under the new setup, the Health

Sciences Center was the division approved and funded by the state consisting of the academic degree-granting units, namely the Schools of Medicine, Dentistry, Nursing, and Pharmacy. The University Health Associates, which is the private practice system for physicians, and the West Virginia University Hospital are both legally independent entities. The three divisions function together, and the new arrangement has succeeded beyond expectations due in large part to the capable leadership of Vice President John Jones and his successor, Vice President Robert D'Alessandri. Although the University president retained ultimate control and power to approve University Health Associates policy, that authority was generally delegated to the vice president of health sciences. None of the three divisions could operate separately or without University compliance, and policy was controlled by a board whose members constituted an interlocking directorate.[2]

Although not a foregone conclusion at the time, all of these reforms assumed that the new Health Sciences Center would simply replace the old one. "The most critical event" in this story, Bucklew recalled, was "the attempt to take the Health Sciences Center away from WVU and our . . . successful defense against that initiative." That effort came from Governor Gaston Caperton and some legislative leaders who were concerned that the center was not as responsive as it should be to the state's needs. They wanted more involvement in rural health, in the form of training for health care professionals to work in rural West Virginia, and they thought that the Health Sciences Center overemphasized training specialists. Marshall University had previously used this ploy to win political approval for launching its medical school, claiming that, unlike WVU, Marshall's medical school would focus on rural practice. These political leaders decided that WVU's Health Sciences Center, the osteopathic school in Lewisburg, and Marshall University's Joan C. Edwards School of Medicine would all be centralized in Charleston and governed from there. Unlike WVU, Marshall had little invested in the school, so it accepted the plan, while WVU strenuously objected. Despite WVU's objections, the governor and legislative leaders announced that they would introduce legislation to create the new model. "A horrible fight" ensued, which unfortunately cost Vice President John Jones his job. "They couldn't fire me, but they would have liked to," said Bucklew. He was informed by the Board of Regents that they had decided to relocate the medical school, and that he should be prepared to acquiesce when the Board of Regents met in five days. The phone call came on Thursday, and the meeting was to be on the following Tuesday. Immediately upon learning of the fate planned for the Health Sciences Center, the WVU School of Medicine Advisory Board met and prepared to oppose the move. These influential members of the medical profession contacted colleagues throughout West Virginia, most of whom were WVU alumni, and a barrage of physicians' phone calls flooded the Board of Regents' and governor's offices to register opposition. Their efforts succeeded: on Monday Bucklew received a call from Governor Caperton to inform him that the meeting was cancelled and the plan abandoned.[3] David Hardesty, who was a member of the Board of Regents at the time, recalled receiving "an enormous amount" of mail and phone calls about the issue. Confronted by strong opposition, and by the likely result that WVU would lose its status as a Research I university if the Health Sciences Center were split away, Governor Caperton aborted the effort.[4]

Although some players in this high-stakes drama were motivated by a political agenda, Bucklew believed that Caperton simply wanted the WVU School of Medicine to be more involved in solving the state's health problems. The president informed the governor that a plan was already underway to establish clinics in most of the counties in the state and to place medical students in those clinics. Caperton was satisfied and backed away from the reorganization plan. Some of the regents preferred to have the medical school in Charleston, believing that its Morgantown location was too far from the state's population center, an attitude reminiscent of the struggle nearly a half-century earlier over where the new medical school should be constructed. At the time, Governor Okey Patteson decided that it should be located in close proximity to the main campus (see chapter 2), but the idea resurfaces periodically in one form or another in southern West Virginia. Once convinced of WVU's commitment, Governor Caperton took the lead in obtaining a $6 million grant from the Kellogg Foundation to invest in his rural health initiatives. The governor matched that amount in state money to assist WVU in the creation of its rural health clinics.[5]

Chapter Sixteen

The political struggle over merging the three medical schools was one of the most painful, but also one of the most successful, battles in the state's legislative history, Senate Education Committee Chairman Lloyd Jackson declared, because "ultimately, everyone got the message." In February 1991, a Legislative Task Force on Medical Education set the goal of increasing the retention rate for medical school graduates at 45 percent. By 1998 the retention rate had increased modestly to 40 percent but still fell short of the goal. Legislators questioned whether the taxpayers were receiving an adequate return on their investment. Senate Health and Human Resources Chairwoman Martha Walker asserted that either a larger percentage of physicians must be retained or tuition should be increased. In 1998 WVU in-state tuition was $8,672, roughly one-third of the actual costs of a medical education, and out-of-state tuition was $21,748.[6]

Prior to the merging issue, WVU had initiated a Kellogg Community Partnership grant proposal, and with Caperton's assistance $12 million was secured to create the Rural Health Education Partnership. This initiative set up a mechanism for training all health sciences students, not just medical students, at 187 different sites throughout West Virginia. To boost retention, each student was required to complete a three-month rotation in one of these rural locations before graduation. The University's new emphasis on retention and primary care (family, internal, pediatric, and ob/gyn) dramatically altered the retention rate for WVU graduates. The 1988–1993 Higher Education Report Card showed retention rocketed from 15 to 40 percent, prompting Senator Jackson's observation that finally West Virginia was gaining some benefit from financing medical education.[7]

The percentage of WVU medical school graduates practicing in the state for the years 1996–2001 was 42.3 percent, with nearly a quarter of them in primary care, but only 7.7 percent practiced in non-urban places. The retention rate for graduates in dentistry, pharmacy, and nursing was greater for those practicing in West Virginia from 2002–2006 as well, reaching 60 percent, 70 percent, and 85 percent respectively. The number of health professionals grew, therefore, with the new emphasis, but the cost of tuition increased nonetheless. By 2005–2006, annual in-state tuition for

WVU medical school students had more than doubled to $17,002, and for non-resident medical students tuition vaulted to $38,000.[8]

The WVU School of Medicine was ranked ninth among the nation's medical schools for rural health by 2008, according to the *U.S. News & World Report*; this marked the first time WVU had cracked the top ten in this area. Almost half of WVU's graduates became primary care physicians, and the Rural Health Education Partnerships helps explain this turnaround. West Virginia was the first state to require all medical school students to do a rotation in a rural health clinic. This positively affected the distribution of doctors and other health care providers to rural areas because 60 percent of them established their practices where they received this learning experience. The following year the American Academy of Family Physicians named WVU School of Medicine as one of the top ten medical schools for graduates choosing family medicine. WVU tied for third with two other institutions, one of them being Marshall University, for guiding an average of 16.8 percent of its graduates into family medicine residencies each year. Again, the Rural Health Education Partnerships program was credited with placing students with family physicians for training.[9]

Improving medical service to rural areas of the state is of critical importance because West Virginia is the second most rural state in the nation and in 2000 had the second-oldest median-age population (38.6 years). Ranking fourth in the country in residents over 65 years of age (15.3 percent) in 2000, it is estimated that West Virginia's over-65 percentage will reach nearly 25 percent by 2025. The specific medical problems facing this large slice of the population, therefore, required special attention.[10]

RESTRUCTURING AND EXPANDING TO SERVE A RURAL STATE

The rapidly expanding Health Sciences Center and the University Hospital became increasingly complicated, and the public commonly referred to the entire complex as the Health Sciences Center. The confusion was understandable but, following several major reorganizations, the WVU Health Sciences Center was composed of distinct educational components that incorporated the schools of medicine, dentistry, pharmacy, and nursing. The Health Sciences Center has four missions: education, clinical service, outreach service, and research. In 2002, the twenty-nine degree programs offered by the Health Sciences Center provided West Virginia with a strong group of professionals prepared to meet the varied health care needs of the state. The more than ten thousand alumni of WVU Health Sciences Center programs include about one-third of the state's practicing physicians, two-thirds of its dentists, three-quarters of its pharmacists, and hundreds of nurses, medical and dental technologists, physical therapists, and other health professionals.[11]

The clinical enterprise was organized under WVU Healthcare, which includes WVU Hospitals and University Health Associates (UHA). UHA was founded in 1971 as a private, non-profit corporate entity. Its role was to support the clinical practice of some one thousand WVU medical and dental school faculty. The Health Sciences Center also operated rural clinics strategically located throughout the state and two teaching-clinical facilities, the Eastern Medical Division in Martinsburg, and the Charleston Division. West Virginia United Health System was organized in 1996 to help hospitals and health care professionals provide quality services. Since then it has grown into the largest state-based health care network covering all of north central West Virginia. West Virginia United Health System operated in partnership with WVU Hospitals, which includes Ruby Memorial, Chestnut Ridge, and the Children's Hospitals. Also included are the John Michael Moore Trauma Center in Morgantown; West Virginia University Hospitals-East, which includes City Hospital in Martinsburg and Jefferson Memorial Hospital in Ranson; and United Hospital Center located in Clarksburg. WVU Cheat Lake Physicians, a multispecialty ambulatory center near Morgantown, and United Physicians Care, a network of privately-owned practices at sixteen sites in West Virginia, also belong to the West Virginia University Hospital System.[12]

The state's tendency to expect more from the University while providing less of its operating expenses carried over to the health sciences. Cutting services was neither socially responsible nor politically feasible. As with the rest of the University, the Health Sciences Center shifted away from over-dependence on state financing or waiting around for the next federal earmark to a more entrepreneurial approach that required each unit to contribute financially to the operation of the entire institution. The health sciences were in a position to take advantage of federal grants in targeted areas of research. The NIH was a particularly important source of the very large amounts of money required to undertake medical research. Under the growing necessity to become more competitive in seeking these research funds, the Health Sciences Center joined the University in pursuing the strategic goals of providing greater service to the state and leading the way in economic development. If these goals were to be realized, WVU would have to become a nationally recognized research institution.

The Strategic Plan for the Health Sciences Center for 2004–2010 emphasized interdisciplinary research in areas of strength, with the goal of doubling NIH funding, and targeted the recruitment and retention of faculty researchers in those critical areas. Elevating the national reputation and visibility of the PhD research programs and providing high quality research facilities were deemed critical to the new focus on elevating the research profile of the Health Sciences Center. The center had grown by leaps and bounds since the early eighties, and under the Bucklew and Hardesty administrations the Health Sciences Center became an expansive healthcare complex. A large rehabilitation center offering physical therapy and rehabilitation services was constructed in the late nineties as a partnership between WVU Hospitals and the Monongalia General Hospital. In June 2001, Senator Byrd delivered the keynote address at the dedication of the new WVU Eye Institute at the Robert C. Byrd Health Sciences Center. The Department of Ophthalmology's new Eye Institute offered comprehensive vision diagnosis and treatment, faculty offices, research labs, and teaching space for its faculty. With the full range of specialists, patients would no longer need to leave West Virginia for care.[13]

The Ronald McDonald House celebrated its tenth anniversary in 2000–2001 as a valued addition to the Health Sciences Center complex. During its first ten years the house welcomed more than nine thousand families whose severely sick or injured children required long-term hospital treatment. The house not only provided food and lodging, but also communication with other families in the same situation and a sympathetic, experienced staff who anticipated their daily needs. The WVU Rosenbaum Family House, founded in 1999 by a generous gift from Hilda Rosenbaum, was another "home away from home" for families whose loved ones were patients at Ruby Memorial Hospital. Like the Ronald McDonald House, families who stayed at the Rosenbaum House were asked to contribute only what they could afford.[14]

A major milestone was attained when the American College of Surgeons Committee on Trauma verified the Jon Michael Moore Center at WVU Hospitals as a Level I trauma center in January 2001. Founded in 1985 with federal support garnered by Senator Byrd, the center was named for the senator's grandson, who died from injuries received in an automobile crash. The only West Virginia hospital among the 150 recognized nationally as level I, its recognition was based on the institution's commitment to trauma care. Level I trauma centers are comprehensive regional providers of care for injuries in every aspect, from prevention through rehabilitation. They are staffed twenty-four hours a day by surgeons and technical specialists and are involved in injury prevention, public and continuing education, and research. Few Level I trauma centers in the nation serve mostly rural populations. By agreement with other regional hospitals in thirteen north central West Virginia counties, Ruby Memorial Hospital is the command center for the system and is connected within the region by the HealthNet helicopter network. Because ambulance service in rural West Virginia is a formidable challenge, HealthNet helicopters provide vital and immediate service to patients. The Ruby emergency room, it was reported in 2001, received 30,000 patients per year, and 13,000 of those were trauma cases, two thousand of which were life-threatening.[15]

The multiple risks to health presented by natural disasters and acts of terrorism placed even more pressure on the Trauma Center to upgrade in order to mobilize more health care services even more rapidly. No national, comprehensive control center for orchestrating this response existed in the United States or in other countries in 2001; responsibility and resources were scattered among hundreds of private and public organizations. This situation made it nearly impossible for responders to access medical information during major emergencies. WVU formed a partnership called the International Telemedicine Collaboratory with a number of health organizations and the U.S. National Guard Bureau in order to use technology to provide information during public health emergencies. Their first initiative was a Virtual Medical Campus, which used the University's technology for telemedicine and distance learning to provide quick diagnoses when time was of the essence. The importance of this rapid response to natural and man-made health emergencies was underscored by the terrorist attacks on the World Trade Center towers and Pentagon on September 11, 2001. The Virtual Medical Campus became even more significant in preparing doctors and emergency specialists to respond to terrorist attacks on American soil.[16]

In 2002 the University announced plans for a major expansion of the health sciences complex over the next five years. The original building was constructed in the early sixties as a top-notch facility of one million square feet under four acres of roof. But after four decades it was outdated and badly in need of renovations. The new expansion provided an additional eighty-one beds for the hospital, six more operating rooms, a parking garage, and an administrative office building. Ruby Memorial took in sixty-five more patients a day than it did three years previously, and on average 85 percent of its beds were full, compared with 50–60 percent at other West Virginia hospitals.[17]

The justification for this major expansion was that many state residents who required highly specialized medical care were forced to travel to Pittsburgh or Cleveland. Out-of-state health care siphoned approximately $250 million out of the state each year. When Medicaid and PEIA funds were added, that figure came to about $500 million and five thousand patients each year. It was expected that the investment in expanding the facilities would be recouped quickly and many times over as more than five hundred new jobs were generated in Morgantown.[18]

From the mid-eighties on, the Health Sciences Center complex seemed to be a perennial construction site. A $17 million Learning Center, a $3 million Simulation Training in Education and Patient Safety Center, and the $40 million Erma Byrd Biomedical Research Center, among other facilities, were in the new construction pipeline. Much of the explosion in growth at the hospital and the center was the result of federal dollars directed through the offices of West Virginia's congressional delegation, most notably Senators Byrd and Rockefeller. Ever larger private donations also played an important role, as was the case with the Center for Neuroscience, a large portion of the funding for which came through the Rockefeller trust, and the new Pediatric Research Institute, funded largely by a $12 million bequest from former WVU physician James H. Walker.[19]

WVU also expanded its outreach to the eastern panhandle during this period with a Community Based Clinical Campus of the WVU School of Medicine, centered in the Martinsburg area. The Eastern Panhandle Health and Human Services Collaborative, as the cooperative venture was called, consolidated ongoing medical education partnerships with health care providers in the nine-county eastern panhandle, Martinsburg City Hospital, Jefferson Memorial, Shenandoah Valley Medical Systems, and the Veterans Affairs Medical Center. Many residents in the panhandle were driving out of state for their health care, a relatively small number of physicians were struggling to care for a growing population of patients, and local hospitals found it difficult to retain staff physicians. In West Virginia as a whole, 16.8 doctors served every ten thousand people, compared with twenty doctors per ten thousand nationally, while in the eastern panhandle only 9.3 doctors served every ten thousand. The initiative was intended to address these problems by enlisting doctors and medical centers in the University's effort to establish residency programs in the panhandle counties.[20]

Not surprisingly, there were those in the southern part of the state who suspected that the new clinical campus was more than just a low-cost method for addressing the need for physicians in the panhandle. An editorial in the *Charleston Gazette* suggested that the new venture was yet another round in the "empire-building" struggle between the state's two universities, and that Marshall would soon follow suit with its own training network in the southern counties. One widely read Huntington reporter opined that the new medical campus was nothing but a new medical school in a state that "already has more medical schools than it can afford." Some people even thought that the state had "a fourth medical school in Charleston," a reference to the WVU Health Sciences Center Charleston Division. This prompted WVU's Robert D'Alessandri, vice president for health sciences and dean of the School of Medicine, to respond with a guest newspaper commentary in which he rejected the notion of a "stealth" medical school as "sheer fantasy." In fact, the new initiative would function in the same way as the Charleston Division, with medical students receiving their third and final year of clinical training at the site. The initiative actually ensured that a new medical school would not be necessary, he observed, by supplying health care providers in a region where they were increasingly needed. WVU's mission was to serve all the state's residents, including those in the eastern panhandle as well as those in southern West Virginia.[21]

Serving all the residents of West Virginia is an inherent obligation of WVU's status as a land-grant university. Therefore, expansion of facilities to extend better health care throughout the state became a central tenet of the University's mission. More specifically, the School of Medicine's mission was to improve the health of all West Virginians by "educating professionals; providing excellent state of the art patient care; conducting basic science, clinical, translational and rural public health research; and offering a variety of supportive health services to our residents." Its primary goal was to be "nationally recognized as a leader among academic health care organizations by cultivating a tradition of excellence and innovation in education, patient care, research, and service to the state." The top priority for the School of Medicine, therefore, was to become "a top 25 School of Medicine and Top 100 hospital," and the second priority, to institutionalize an "achievement culture," was directly related to the first. It called for the recruitment and retention of an outstanding faculty and staff, and the creation of a strong academic, clinical, and research center to provide high-quality health-care services. Strengthening the School of Medicine's financial position was imperative, and all of these goals were to be leveraged by modern technology. The third priority was to expand and promote multidisciplinary collaborations within the school rather than concentrating on individual and separate projects "in our traditional silos."[22]

The medical school was committed to building a stronger research program as part of its modernization plan. Six new interdisciplinary research centers were created at the Health Sciences Center: neuroscience, cancer cell biology, cardiovascular sciences, respiratory biology and lung diseases, immunopathology and microbial pathogenesis, and diabetes and obesity. Each center was closely related to common health concerns in West Virginia. The school identified strong researchers who were already members of the faculty and began to "aggressively recruit top scientists from around the country" to lead the new centers. One key measure of success was the level of financial support garnered from the NIH. Therefore, Health Sciences Center research was reorganized specifically to increase NIH funding by promoting multi-disciplinary collaboration among research teams.[23]

The strategic plan adopted by the Health Sciences Center in 2005 set a goal of recruiting forty-two new faculty researchers by 2010. This was an expensive goal because start-up costs to equip a single research laboratory could easily surpass $400,000. New faculty were recruited for their research specialties and for the role they could play within the strategic interdisciplinary biomedical research centers. The NIH practice of directing research funding to scientific projects undertaken by teams of interdisciplinary researchers effectively mandated reorganization of research enterprises that hoped to be competitive. Each NIH grant created jobs in the labs or in community services so these grants had an ancillary economic development effect as well. Vice President for Health Sciences Robert D'Allessandri estimated that, once the plan was fully implemented, the expanded research capacity could generate $200 million for the local economy. The effort to enhance the research profile of the Health Sciences Center succeeded. NIH grants topped $20 million in 2007, double the amount of a few years earlier. Grants from all sources garnered by the four Health Sciences Center schools during the academic year 2000–2001 totaled $32.46 million, and that total reached $55.34 million by 2005–2006.[24]

Administrators viewed these increases as clear evidence that the strategic plan was working. The scientists in the interdisciplinary neuroscience group had boosted the reputation of the Department of Otolaryngology into the ranks of the top ten research departments in the nation, a fact which further confirmed the plan's success. The University was on track to its goal of developing a critical mass of researchers in strategic areas that would lift the Health Sciences Center to national competitiveness. By 2006 the next step for the center's administration was to expand clinical-translational research closer to application in patient care, and the center moved to improve this phase of its operation. "If we are successful at that, we will have a top 25 medical school," vowed the dean of the medical school.[25]

One of the strategic centers of excellence at the Health Sciences Center devoted to translational research is the Mary Babb Randolph Cancer Center, named for West Virginia Senator Jennings Randolph's wife, who died of colon cancer in 1981. An example of how the traditional doctor-centered culture has been modernized through interdisciplinary research and a patient-centered approach to health care, the cancer center has been a leader in cancer prevention, diagnosis, and treatment, especially in rural areas. Higher rates of chronic illness and poorer health in general exist in rural areas than urban areas, and, as the land-grant university located in the second-most rural state in the union, WVU responded. Since 1988, the Mary Babb Randolph Cancer Center has endeavored to link theory and practice, and along the way has created a nationally recognized system of administrators, researchers, public and private partnerships, health care providers, and community groups all working together to overcome cancer.[26]

A very important milepost was passed in 2002 when the cancer center received an $11 million grant from the NIH to study the molecular activity of cancer cells and to develop appropriate therapies. At the time it was the largest grant ever received by the Health Sciences Center, and among the largest in the University's history. The grant established a Center of Biomedical Research Excellence, one of only seven nationwide. The NIH funding was also used to recruit five researchers to join the molecular biology team studying changes in cells in cancer patients, and to fund laboratory facilities. The necessity for new cancer research was demonstrated by the fact that in 2001 11,000 West Virginians were diagnosed with some form of cancer, and 4,800 died from the disease, giving the state the unenviable ranking of sixth in the nation for cancer deaths.[27]

Major strides continued in subsequent years. WVU and the University of Kentucky led a national effort, funded by the Centers for Disease Control and Prevention (CDC), to create a network, in collaboration with four other universities (Harvard, South Carolina, Texas, and Washington), to develop and promote culturally appropriate programs in cancer prevention and research. With CDC funds, WVU and the University of Kentucky also set up the Appalachian Cancer Research Consortium and charged it with developing community-based research on cancer prevention and control to facilitate effective diagnosis and intervention. The Comprehensive Breast Cancer Program exemplifies how research is translated into practice. The most comprehensive program in the state, it, too, is patient-centered. In one morning, a patient is seen by all of his or her specialists, and in the afternoon those specialists meet as a team to discuss and finalize a treatment plan, which is provided to the patient that same day. The Cervical Cancer Screening Program was also funded by the CDC in collaboration with other Health Sciences Center units. The cervical cancer rate and mortality rate is higher than the national average among Appalachia women. West Virginia led the nation in cervical cancer mortality from 1950 to 1970, and in spite of the fact that the rate dropped significantly over the next twenty years, it was still nearly 50 percent higher than the national rate. In 2006 it was third-highest in the nation. In cooperation with other state organizations, WVU has become a leader in providing free education and guidance as well as low-cost screening and related diagnostic services.[28]

The impressive quality and growth of the Mary Babb Randolph Cancer Center testifies to the wisdom of funneling resources into areas of excellence. Originally constructed in 1988, the cancer center received a $22 million renovation and expansion in 2009, which doubled the Health Sciences Center space for patient care and research and created one of the finest cancer treatment facilities in the nation.[29]

The Blanchette Rockefeller Neurosciences Institute was launched in 2000 with commitments of $10 million from WVU and $20 million from

Neurologic, a pharmaceutical company. This would become the largest scientific research venture in the University's history, and stands as a witness of what can be achieved with the right level of resources. Initially, the institute was housed in the old hospital building, the remodeled Health Sciences Center South, but the plan was to construct a separate building within five years. The institute was named for Senator Jay Rockefeller's mother, who died of Alzheimer's disease in 1992. He established the institute in 1999 in her memory.[30]

The neuroscience institute attracted major grants almost immediately. In October 2000, an $8 million grant from the NIH was announced, followed a few months later by a federal appropriation of $20 million, courtesy of Senator Robert Byrd. Aspirations soared as planning for the construction of the new neuroscience research center commenced and the vice president of the Health Sciences Center declared that WVU expected to be "a world leader in the study of human memory and the diseases which cause memory disorders."[31] Rockefeller's long-term relationship with Toyota Motor Company, which had invested more than $900 million in a Putnam County engine and transmission plant that employed eight hundred people, prompted the company to donate $1 million in June 2001, the largest single private donation to the institute to date. By December 2001, that donation was topped many times over with a $15 million gift from Senator Rockefeller and other members of his family.[32]

From the beginning the Blanchette Rockefeller Neuroscience Institute was unique in focusing on the study of human memory. Its primary emphasis was Alzheimer's disease, which affected 25 million people worldwide and four million Americans, but it also explored Parkinson's Disease, schizophrenia, and epilepsy, as well as depression and anxiety disorders. Although based at WVU, the institute developed a strong partnership with Johns Hopkins University in order to attract the best researchers in the world. The vision was lofty from the beginning: "to develop a world-class basic science and clinical research program for the purpose of preventing, diagnosing, treating and curing neurological, psychiatric and other cognitive disorders affecting the human brain."[33] The scientific board was "nothing short of stunning," according to one writer. The board included two

Nobel Prize winners, one of whom had isolated the first Alzheimer's gene and the other who had helped to decipher the genetic code.[34]

Another distinctive feature, and probably a glimpse of the future, was the way the neuroscience institute's researchers shared technology. Scientists had their own labs, but the interdisciplinary approach among researchers meant that they shared technology and equipment as well. The goals and project determined the allocation of people and resources. Other centers conducting related research were interconnected with the institute. For example, the WVU Sensory Neuroscience Research Center, founded in 2001, and the Erma Byrd Biomedical Research Center, both located on the Health Sciences Center campus, focus their research on different aspects within the larger field of neuroscience.[35] The Center for Advanced Imaging is also part of this working relationship. The Positron Emission Tomography Center was founded in 1996 when the Health Sciences Center received $10 million in federal funds to purchase the most advanced positron emission tomography (PET) scanner available. The center placed WVU in the forefront of universities in the United States. Only a few of the very advanced machines were in use among the sixty PET centers around the country. It continues to advance the diagnosis of cancer and neurological and heart diseases, and it allows physicians to examine other organs as well. Researchers at the Blanchette Rockefeller Neuroscience Institute also joined the international "global alliance network" composed of neuroscience research scientists and other research centers around the world.[36]

Like research generally in the new paradigm embraced by the science and technology disciplines at WVU, the neuroscience institute was also viewed as an investment in economic development. On the occasion of the Toyota donation, WVU President David Hardesty declared that "our ambitions in the neurosciences are global and humanitarian, scientific and even philosophical, but we also aim to benefit West Virginia economically." The enterprise was expected to stimulate further biotechnology investment and become "an engine for economic and technological growth." The new 78,000 square-foot building housing the institute was completed in the fall of 2008 at a cost of $30 million. Along with the increased potential for the developing a high-technology sector in the region and the economic stimulus from construction and the purchase of new equipment and supplies, the new institute anticipated hiring one hundred scientists who would spend their high-income salaries on housing, food, and other consumer goods.[37]

GROWTH AND POLITICS CREATE PROBLEMS

On May 16, 2008, the Pittsburgh consulting firm R&V Associates provided WVU President Michael Garrison with an outline of its interim report. The company had been hired to conduct a study of the Health Sciences Center to determine how best to improve its organizational structure and administrative efficiency. After several months of investigation, the issued report outraged the center's leadership by claiming that the health sciences division and the affiliated hospitals had "serious deficiencies." Some of those deficiencies allegedly put patients' lives at risk, particularly the shortages of anesthesiologists, general surgeons, and heart surgeons. WVU initially refused to release the interim report, declaring it a work-in-progress, but the University soon reversed course and released the unflattering report on June 13, 2008. At the same time, it was announced that President Garrison considered the report unfinished and had directed the consultants to "revise and verify" the accuracy of some of its information. R&V Associates disputed the president's characterization of the report, asserted that it was indeed finished, stood by its conclusions, and refused to consider any changes. Interim Vice President for Health Sciences Fred R. Butcher stepped into the fray by issuing a seven-page summary of the problems with the report and informed R&V Associates that its contract was concluded. Butcher claimed that the consultants had not provided constructive advice, nor had they identified ways to resolve problems within the Health Sciences Center as requested.[38]

The center's faculty and staff attended a "town hall" meeting on the same day that the report and Butcher's response were released. They expressed outrage at the consultants' report, but they also posed some tough questions and comments of their own about the Health Sciences Center. One complaint addressed the admittedly troubled anesthesiology department and the fact that there had been no visible movement toward a solution. Paraphrased in the local newspaper, one faculty member's description of a recent case in which more than thirty hours had elapsed before a woman in "grave neurological danger" could be treated, had prompted him to wonder "how much longer I should continue to wait for these solutions so that I can provide a level of care that I'm comfortable with." A number of the questions raised at the meeting concerned the administration of the Health Sciences Center, which was searching at the time for a new vice president and a new dean of the medical school. Another commentator claimed that the medical school and University Health Associates, the physicians' practice plan, were at the mercy of WVU Hospitals' inadequate funding for faculty recruitment and retention measures. "I think this is a critical issue for a lot of the faculty, especially clinical faculty," he asserted, and asked how this situation would be addressed.[39]

Pent-up frustrations about the administration of Health Sciences Center engulfed the meeting, the most pointed criticisms relating to the political environment in West Virginia. The root of most problems at WVU was "increasing politicization of an institution that really should be free of politics," one person asserted. People should be committed to "changing the ability of Charleston's political structure to govern and determine what happens at the flagship university of this state. WVU should take positive action to implement a system that serves the University rather than making the university a slave to the system." Another complained that it was "a damn shame that we get more reliable information from a blog site than we get from the spinmeisters at Stewart Hall." Others agreed that "politicization" had become a major issue. The governor was receiving the wrong advice, one person claimed, and for this reason the center's faculty and staff should be "in his ear" on a routine basis. Still another commented: "If the governor cared as much about us as the football team, we'd be in great shape."[40]

Revealing the deep undercurrent of discontent, one faculty member observed that the center had suffered an identity crisis. A reporter's characterization of this comment reveals the deep undercurrent of discontent: "I feel like, as a member of this institution, we've really lost our identity. I think what really worries me a lot is how, over the last few years, there's been almost a corporate takeover of the Health Sciences Center. The university used to be more focused on research and academics, and many faculty members still are, but the administration has lost its way. . . . I think we're really off track and becoming more of a corporate entity rather than a true academic institution."[41]

During the public discussion that followed the release of R&V Associates' interim report, a consensus seemed to emerge among Health Sciences Center faculty and staff that administrative problems could be amended internally. However, the political questions were far more problematic. An editorial in the *Charleston Gazette* demonstrated how the consultants' report shifted the focus from a medical to a political issue. WVU President Mike Garrison's chief of staff, Craig Walker, had negotiated a contract with R&V Associates worth $450,000 to evaluate the Health Sciences Center. R&V Associates also managed Wheeling Hospital, and the hospital's executives were known by Governor Manchin and other state political leaders. Huron Consulting Group of Chicago believed it had won the center's consulting contract with a lower bid of $355,000 but was surprised when WVU President Garrison announced that R&V Associates was the winner. Another unidentified WVU official reportedly claimed that Huron's price tag was significantly higher when, in fact, the reverse was true.[42]

When Garrison and his chief-of-staff defended their decision to hire R&V Associates over the Huron's lower bid, they had argued that they made their choice because R&V Associates' regional perspective would be valuable in restructuring the Health Sciences Center. The day after mounting their defense, however, WVU fired R&V Associates, but only after the company had collected $321,789 from West Virginia taxpayers. "What's going on in the WVU medical conglomerate?" asked the *Charleston Gazette* editor. "Why were high-bid analysts hired—while a WVU official said they were low-bid? Why did the University praise the decision to hire them—then dismiss them the following day? Were the analysts correct about dangerous problems—or were they blunders, as the university now says?" The editorial called for the Higher Education Policy Commission, or the appropriate legislative committees, to look further into these puzzling questions.[43]

The local Morgantown newspaper joined in: "If ever anyone needed a clear diagnosis of what ails WVU, no one need look beyond the recent dismissal of R&V Associates." In dismissing R&V Associates without consulting Health Sciences Center administrators, President Garrison once again "overstepped his bounds and did not defer to the people who have expertise in the matter at hand," the editor declared. This was just "another case of politics being exerted on an institution that should be free of politics." Favoring a high bidder over the low bidder of equal or better qualifications raises the perception of a conflict of interest and "confirms our suspicions that the politicization of WVU was being extended to Health Sciences. . . . With any luck, those who make such calamitous decisions or influence them will soon be cleaning out their desks."[44]

Three days later, another *Dominion Post* editorial declared: "The more we find out, the worse it gets." Within a month after signing the R&V Associates contract in February 2008, the consulting firm "handpicked" by the Garrison administration had "stretched the ethics line by trying to enlist HSC's support in a complaint filed by another R&V client—Wheeling Hospital—against MedExpress" in an effort to block MedExpress from opening a facility in Wheeling, the editorial charged. Although the president's office did not respond to the Wheeling Hospital's request for assistance in this political fight, the administration, nevertheless, failed to see an "obvious conflict of interest as reason to can the firm for its lack of integrity and unprofessional conduct." The editorial declared that this failure represented "another instance involving integrity issues" associated with the Garrison administration. Citing the Bresch scandal and the Rodriguez affair, which are discussed elsewhere, the editorial concluded that "the integrity track record of the [current] WVU administration hasn't been a winner."[45]

Undoubtedly, Interim Vice President for Health Sciences Fred Butcher was at least partially correct when he informed the press that the problems at the Health Sciences Center were the result of "unprecedented growth." The inability to maintain a high level of service during a period of very rapid growth was a phenomenon experienced by academic health centers nationally. To illustrate, Butcher pointed out that, since the fall of 2001, enrollment in courses had grown from 1,728 full-time students to

2,751 students projected for fall 2008. More than 1,500 jobs had been created at the Health Sciences Center in Morgantown. Patient visits to WVU medical offices and clinics increased by 14 percent from 2005 to 2007, to about 607,000. Also, research funding from the NIH increased from $13.7 to $18.9 million between 2004 and 2007. In the final analysis, the Health Sciences Center had failed to adapt to these changes. "We grew and we grew and we grew, but we didn't change anything fundamentally about what we do," Butcher declared. The issues related to staffing and organization were being sorted out internally by a Joint Planning Group composed of leaders from Health Sciences, WVU Hospitals, University Health Associates, and the West Virginia United Health System. Together they drafted "Charting Our Path," which outlined problems and recommended better ways to make joint decisions.[46]

A new vision for the future organization of the Health Sciences Center was outlined by Steven Wartman, president of the Association of Academic Health Centers, a national expert who made a presentation to the center's faculty and staff in August 2008. According to a reporter, Wartman favored "a corporate approach to [the center's] restructuring efforts, in order to improve efficiency." He observed that academic health centers had been transformed over the past twenty years from academic institutions to "complex business enterprises." Health care had become the nation's leading industry, employing 11 percent of the American workforce. The problem was that "we have missions that must continue regardless of profitability," a challenge unique to academic medical centers. Wartman advocated using clinical revenue, or patient-care dollars, to support research initiatives, and argued that the public would support research intended for the improvement of health care.[47]

The Joint Planning Group, including WVU Interim President C. Peter Magrath, who assumed the office temporarily when Garrison resigned in July 2008, and Fred Butcher, interim chancellor of West Virginia United Health System, who assumed the post after Robert D'Allessandri resigned in June 2007, worked with a health care consulting firm to develop a new organizational plan for the Health Sciences Center. Under the new plan, effective July 1, 2009, WVU Hospitals and University Health Associates would continue as separate entities but would function jointly under WVU Healthcare, whose chief executive officer would report to the chancellor of the West Virginia United Health System. The chancellor, in turn, would report to the WVU president. The change was expected to streamline decision-making and give faculty in the School of Medicine more control over patient care. It was hoped that poor communication and the confusion in the chain of command would be eliminated, thus improving patient service. The restructuring was also expected to bolster the financial position of the Health Sciences Center by reallocating money from the "clinical enterprise" to the "research enterprise." No internal opposition surfaced because "everyone wanted change," Butcher declared. Christopher Colenda assumed the permanent post of chancellor in November 2009.[48]

One of the most pressing problems facing the center was the retention of physicians, largely the result of inadequate compensation. In 2007, WVU increased salaries by $60,000 per doctor to help retain physicians and recruit new ones. The problem became acute in certain specialties, particularly the aforementioned anesthesiology department. A national shortage of anesthesiologists drove up their salaries and drew specialists away from academic programs. The Anesthesiology Department at the Health Sciences Center had lost twenty-two physicians between July 2005 and April 2008, even though twenty-three anesthesiologists had been hired during that same period. At its low point, only seventeen anesthesiologists, less than half the number actually needed, were on staff. By the end of 2008, their numbers had reached thirty-two, which was considered fully staffed given the current volume of surgery.[49]

A serious shortage of cardiothoracic surgeons at WVU reflected a similar national trend that had not only created problems at WVU Hospitals but also at Monongalia General, Morgantown's community hospital. Since a 1985 agreement between the two hospitals, surgeons at WVU Hospitals had performed open heart surgeries for Monongalia General patients. When the number of cardiothoracic surgeons dropped from four to two in 2007–2008 (a shortage compounded by the desperate need for anesthesiologists), Monongalia General placed a moratorium on referring nonemergency open heart surgery patients to WVU Hospitals, citing concern for patient safety and quality of care. Naturally, the idea that patients were at risk was rejected by administrators at WVU. The agreement signed two decades earlier between the two hospitals virtually down the street from one another had prevented the two from competing for heart surgery. The moratorium would cause patients, in all probability, to be transferred to other institutions outside the state.[50]

After several months of fuming between the two hospitals, serious discussion began in November 2008, and a new agreement was signed in February 2009. Each hospital would recruit its own cardiothoracic surgeons. However, they would be engaged at both hospitals, would be appointed as adjunct faculty at the WVU School of Medicine, and would agree to be on call at both hospitals for emergency surgery. The surgeons would be based at WVU Hospitals, but could go to perform open heart surgery at Monongalia General when needed.[51]

The dynamic growth of the WVU medical school and the University hospital in both scale and organizational complexity over the half-century since its founding undoubtedly would have astounded the founders. That growth was not a straight-line trajectory upward, however, and by the seventies a lack of investment resulted in deteriorating and outdated physical facilities and equipment. Also, professionals became difficult to recruit and retain because of uncompetitive compensation. From the eighties on, however, the health sciences complex began a long-term modernization that propelled its educational and clinical services, as well as vital fields of research, to a level of national leadership by the first decade of the twenty-first century.

SEVENTEEN

BECOMING A STUDENT-CENTERED UNIVERSITY

WHEN DAVID HARDESTY assumed his duties as WVU's new president in 1995, he recalled former President Paul Miller's comments at Freshman Convocation: "The purpose of an education is to bring change amid order and order amid change." Orderly change became a major theme of Hardesty's twelve-year administration and the stabilizing force behind his intention to transform the University into a "student-centered" institution.[1]

Hardesty had been involved in higher education since 1979 as a member of the WVU Board of Advisors and also as a member of the University of West Virginia Board of Trustees. Having served in leadership roles on both boards, he was familiar with the issues confronting the University and higher education generally. Experience had taught him that "letting students grow up on their own without guidance was taking the abandonment of *in loco parentis* too far." University leadership seemed to lack a focus on undergraduate students even though their education was what distinguished the university from a think tank, private research enterprise, or social service agency. He believed that students desired more structure, and this conviction led to the major changes embedded in the notion of a "student-centered" institution. *In loco parentis* became *in loco amici*. The University did not intend to act in the place of a parent, but instead would develop a friendship with students, helping them to grow into responsible adults. WVU was a relatively safe campus, but Hardesty hoped to create a more structured and caring environment that would satisfy both students and their parents.[2]

Hardesty was not alone in this assessment. In fact, his plans to transform student culture at WVU were part of a national discussion among higher education leaders, particularly the National Commission on Educating Undergraduates in the Research University. Created in the summer of 1995 under the auspices of the Carnegie Foundation for the Advancement of Teaching, the commission was headed by Ernest L. Boyer and produced what is generally referred to as the *Boyer Report*. The commission's findings represented not so much a critique of higher education as an assessment of the challenges research universities commonly faced in educating undergraduate students.[3]

Research universities are defined by their commonalities. In 1994, they were divided into two groups. Eighty-eight were classified as Research I, those offering a full range of undergraduate programs but committed to graduate education through the doctorate, with a high-priority focus on research. They awarded fifty or more doctoral degrees each year, and also received $40 million or more in federal funding annually. Another thirty-seven institutions were classified as Research II universities only because they received lesser amounts, $15.5 and $40 million in federal support each year. All 125 Research I and II universities considered research capability a primary qualification for the appointment, promotion, and tenure of faculty because the creation of new knowledge was regarded as a primary mission.[4]

Even though the 125 research universities represented only 3 percent of the total number of institutions in higher education in the United States, they conferred 32 percent of the baccalaureate degrees. Nevertheless, the commission concluded, "the research universities have too often failed, and continue to fail, their undergraduate populations. Tuition income from undergraduates is one of the major sources of university income, helping to support research programs and graduate education, but the students paying the tuition get, in all too many cases, less than their money's worth." Undergraduates receive degrees "without knowing how to think logically, write clearly, or speak coherently." Even though improving undergraduate education is a matter of perennial discussion among these institutions, "for the most part fundamental change has been shunned; universities have opted for cosmetic surgery, . . . when radical reconstruction is called for."[5]

Research productivity was consistently given higher priority in decisions about promotion and tenure than was teaching effectiveness, and the teaching and research missions of research universities were regarded as separate activities. The university's standing was measured by the research of its faculty, and prominent scholars were lauded for the number of books, articles, and papers they published, and research grants they procured. Because research was so highly valued, graduate students who assisted faculty with their projects were also held in higher esteem than undergraduates, who were not involved in the production of research. The *Boyer Report* posed the central issue: "Why, then, should baccalaureate students give their loyalty and their money to research universities?" The answer lay in the potential for "acquiring a virtually matchless education." The research universities possessed an "unparalleled wealth in intellectual power and resources," but they faced the challenge of how to share this wealth with baccalaureate students. Realizing their potential demanded an entirely "new model of under graduate education at research universities that makes the baccalaureate experience an inseparable part of an integrated whole."[6]

The Boyer commission proposed an "Academic Bill of Rights" to provide the ideal opportunity for intellectual and creative development. The bill included: inquiry-based learning rather than simple transmission of knowledge; the skills necessary for effective oral and written communication; appreciation of the arts, humanities, sciences, and social sciences; and comprehensive preparation for life beyond college. Undergraduate students at a research university should be granted additional rights: the opportunity to study with senior researchers; access to first-class facilities to pursue their studies; a variety of options among fields of study; and opportunities to interact with people of diverse backgrounds, interests, and cultures.[7]

The Boyer commission was soon joined by the Kellogg Commission on the Future of State and Land-Grant Universities in reporting on the issues of improving undergraduate education. The state and land-grant universities were research institutions, but with a special emphasis on the "public" aspects of education, research, and service. Like the Boyer commission, the Kellogg commission was composed of educational leaders from that particular circle. The annual reports issued by the Kellogg commission became the intellectual and administrative formula guiding the reforms President Hardesty initiated at WVU. In fact, they became a template for reform and provided the language and rationale for the initiatives that transformed student life at WVU. The Kellogg commission acknowledged that public higher education was beset by challenges presented by a world in which economic, environmental, educational, technological, and demographic changes preoccupied the American people. The public believed that state and land-grant universities held the key to the resolving these thorny problems.[8]

Other challenges confronted public universities. Enrollment pressures would mushroom during the next decade as the children of the Baby Boomers arrived on college campuses. The student body was becoming increasingly diverse as a result of more minorities, mature students, and life-long learners enrolling for classes. New for-profit and non-profit competitors would emerge to compete with the traditional universities. Funding for state and land-grant universities would continue to contract at the same time that institutions struggled to maintain access and services by streamlining programs and operations while increasing student tuition and fees to recover the deficit. Universities also faced eroding public trust from a fragmenting public consensus on the direction and purpose of higher education, aggravated by the rapidly rising cost of attending college. Moreover, some influential university critics seemed to cling to tradition rather than confront the need to modernize. The Kellogg commission concluded that universities were not organized to deal with the issues posed by the modern world. "As the nature of knowledge changes, our departmental structure has difficulty responding. As the challenges facing our communities multiply, we find it hard to break out of the silos our disciplines create. The world has problems; universities have departments."[9]

The Kellogg commission sought to commit the universities to several goals and ideals. It encouraged them to become "learning communities" that provided students, staff, and faculty with learning as a common enterprise. Learning was not reserved for the classroom or laboratory, but for wherever teaching, scholarship, and service were available to students and families, to the region's schools, and to those constituencies with important stakes in the university (graduates, taxpayers, business, governments, and the public). Secondly, the commission asserted that the learning community should be "student-centered." That is, it should give all students the opportunity to "develop essential life skills and values: critical thinking; knowing how to learn; effective oral and written communication; a multicultural and global perspective; respect for individuals and the sources of their individuality; civic and individual responsibility; self-esteem, self-confidence, and a sense of one's own competence; and leadership and the ability to work well with others, either as a leader or member of a team."[10]

Thirdly, the Kellogg commission called for "healthy learning environments," which referred to "the atmosphere on campus and the intellectual, physical, and technical conditions supporting it," or in other words, the aspects of campus life that graduates would remember long after they forgot who taught what courses. These included extracurricular activities, "bull sessions," food service, and the excitement of game days. "Every office, every service, every program, and every employee must help students to understand that the academic community exists for them. Its purpose is to help them grow and develop." To do this, institutions needed to develop residential environments that encouraged learning, fostered "solid values and sound character," created an environment that encouraged and respected the diversity of cultures and opinions, provided quality facilities and technical services, and encouraged healthy lifestyles. According to the commission, "If there is a more unhealthy factor on campus today than excessive consumption of alcohol, we cannot identify it."[11]

These were the reforms circulating among higher education leaders during President Hardesty's initial years in office, and his own reform program mirrored the recommendations of the Boyer and the Kellogg reports.[12] Many faculty regarded these proposed reforms as old wine in new bottles, and few would take issue with the content. Because WVU had always been primarily an undergraduate teaching institution with less emphasis on its graduate school, very few faculty, including researchers, were far removed from undergraduate students. Refocusing on the importance of the undergraduate experience was significant on multiple levels, however, and anticipated the University's emergence as a fully engaged research institution.

ELEVATING THE LEARNING ENVIRONMENT

Elevating the student academic environment at WVU was Hardesty's top priority, and rapid reforms did indeed transform the University both inside and outside the classroom and elicited favorable responses from students, faculty, staff, and state leaders. President Hardesty pointed to several challenges converging on the University at the beginning of his tenure. Administrators expected federal and state funding for higher education, health care, and other programs to continue to decline while government demanded greater accountability from the University. Also, mandated salary increases from current University resources shifted more of the costs to students even as the number graduating from West Virginia high schools was expected to decline 20 percent over the next decade. More profoundly, mega-trends, such as globalization, the technology revolution, and the constant pursuit of lower costs and higher quality were reshaping the American economy and directly affecting the University. The current leadership in higher education had been raised and educated in an era when rising expectations were justified by a growing student population, as well as increasing tuition and federal support for research and student aid. The emerging landscape education leaders now had to navigate was one of declining government support, declining enrollments, and rising costs. The University had to adapt or be left behind, "We have no choice but to change ourselves," Hardesty observed, "and we are charting a new course."[13]

In the future WVU need to focus on students' needs, expectations, and quality of experience. Considering the ever-rising cost of tuition, parents and students increasingly selected colleges based on the institution's reputation and the perceived value of its products. Parents expected a safe environment, comfortable residence halls conducive to study, availability of required courses, helpful advising, and respectful treatment of their children. If the University failed to provide these basic expectations, students would choose to go elsewhere. Parents and students also expected high-quality instruction, assistance in job placement, preparation for admission to graduate school, a pleasant campus, and all for a reasonable cost. A Student Affairs Task Force was organized to develop a student-centered vision for WVU, to improve student recruitment, retention, and the learning environment, and to harness support services aimed at facilitating student success. The new approach would, in the president's words, "make WVU an accessible, helpful, responsive, and less confusing institution to our students and their parents."[14]

One of the first problems Hardesty grappled with in improving the quality of the academic environment was the seemingly endless lines to register for courses as burgeoning enrollment overwhelmed the system. The source of the long registration lines was the inability of two departments, student affairs and administration and finance, to agree on a way to improve the system and to pay for the changes. To demonstrate students' frustration, in the fall of 1995 Hardesty sent representatives from both departments to stand in the financial-aid line with students and parents for four hours. By the next spring, the line was shortened to thirty minutes. The press observed that Hardesty was a problem solver, and even previous critics were now praising his efforts. To demonstrate that student-centeredness was to become the institution's focus in his administration, Hardesty established the position of vice president for student affairs, who would report directly to the president. Chosen for the position was Kenneth D. Gray, a retired two-star general and the Army's second-ranking attorney, who assumed the post in May 1997. A native of Excelsior, West Virginia, Gray received his bachelor's degree from West Virginia State University in 1966 and a law degree from WVU in 1969, followed by a long and distinguished career in the Army. He was not a student-affairs professional, but he was an effective organizer who could take charge. During his interview, Hardesty posed the question: "Are you going to do all right with 22,000 adolescents on a Friday afternoon?" Gray's response: "I've got a million around the globe right now . . . and I know exactly what the issue is here."[15] Gray would play a significant role in moving the University in its new student-centered direction.

As charted by Hardesty, this new direction was manifested in a range of initiatives and programs to enhance the undergraduate experience. Operation Jump Start helped to define how the change in institutional culture would be implemented by integrating academic and student affairs initiatives. Its goals included the recruitment and retention of quality students and faculty, ensuring academic success, personalizing the freshman year experience, creating a more positive environment in residence halls and on campus, providing opportunities for student and faculty interaction, encouraging healthy lifestyles, raising students' expectations of themselves, and turning the dormitories into residential learning communities. In other words, the institution's culture would undergo a thorough reengineering.[16]

Noteworthy among a suite of programs designed to help freshmen get off on the right foot was the Jump Start Academy, a two-day series of activities created for new students that emphasized academic expectations, alcohol and health education, and "survival tips" for freshmen. The University also resurrected Freshman Convocation to welcome students to the "community of scholars" and address what was expected of them. In order to incorporate parents into the transition to college life, a Parent Advocate Office with a toll-free help line was established, and its success was demonstrated by the receipt of about three hundred inquiries each month. Beginning in 2000, each class was assigned a class advocate, a faculty member who would interact with the students and gather feedback regarding their WVU experiences. A Career Success Academy, another innovation, assisted students in exploring career opportunities.[17]

Alcohol abatement was central to several initiatives. WVUp All Night became a highly visible and nationally recognized program that kept the student union open on Thursday, Friday, and Saturday nights and provided free food and entertainment. Intended as an alternative social venue to the downtown bar scene, it was instantly popular and attracted an average of four thousand students each weekend. As a welcome back to school, FallFest replaced the notorious, and dangerous, Sunnyside block party at the beginning of the fall semester by providing a University-sponsored event featuring headliner bands, hit movies, dancing, comedians, snacks, and much more. The University and the fraternities reached an agreement that by 2000 they would be alcohol-free. The Pit, an open area near the stadium where students gathered before football games to drink, was first regulated and eventually eliminated by new construction. Alcohol-education programs were intensified, and a new full-time alcohol and drug therapist, as well as two new alcohol educators, were added to the University Health Service. A new comprehensive outreach program served about 14,000 students per year in various University organizations with individual counseling, and academic classes for student athletes, student leaders, residential assistants, and peer educators. The Carruth Counseling Center sponsored an Alcoholics Anonymous group, a 24-hour crisis hotline, life skills classes for all freshmen, and other on-campus programs.[18]

Another major initiative placed faculty in residence halls. Influenced by his experience at Oxford, Hardesty thought that Oxford's residential college concept had value for undergraduate students. Based on this model, faculty couples were chosen from volunteers and housed in WVU residence halls in new living quarters. Special funding was also available for hall-sponsored activities, and additional living/learning floors were created. In order to bring the residential-college concept to fruition, a new Evansdale Residential Complex was constructed, and in the fall of 1998 the first resident faculty leaders moved in.[19]

Special emphasis was placed on strengthening academic advising in order to encourage student success, and programs for academically at-risk students were also implemented. The Structured Transitional Entry Program (STEP) brought students to a residential summer tutoring program prior to their freshman year. The Structured Academic Year (STAY) program gave students who would otherwise have been suspended for academic deficiencies a second chance by assigning them mentors and more structured living accommodations. Student-centered technology became a major investment. An online class registration and records system shrank or eliminated beginning-of-semester lines. Further communications enhancements included student e-mail accounts, computer labs, laptop computer checkouts, electronic classrooms, and the complete wiring of residence halls for online access in every room. Design and site preparation for a student recreation center had begun, and other facilities were in the works as part of phase one in a $225 million master plan, which included a new library and a life sciences building in addition to the recreation center.[20]

A few of the new programs to enhance the student experience attracted national attention. The Festival of Ideas was originally conceived in 1966 by David Hardesty when he was president of the WVU Student Government Association. Its initial purpose was to demonstrate that student government was still relevant at a time when campuses were in turmoil over issues such as the Vietnam war, civil rights, and women's rights. Instead of undertaking acts of civil disobedience, Hardesty recalled, students wanted to sponsor a public forum where new and controversial ideas could be presented in a display of free speech. "Our idea was that campus is a place where ideas are discussed," Hardesty recalled; hence the name of the forum implied a celebration of ideas. The original Festival of Ideas series came to a close following Hardesty's graduation, the decline of campus unrest, and President James Harlow's disinterest in maintaining the series. Convinced that "a great university has to be a cauldron of ideas in the making, that controversial speakers have to come to campus, and that debates have to take place," David Hardesty, as the new president of WVU, brought the festival back to life in 1996.[21]

Perhaps the most notable program among initiatives undertaken during Hardesty's administration was the decision to organize the Mountaineer Parents Club. Susan Hardesty, the founder and permanent volunteer chairperson during her husband's tenure as president, was clearly the driving force behind the establishment of the club when she recognized that no vehicle existed for families to share their children's university experiences. Only fifteen such parent organizations existed in the nation when she launched the club in 1995; a decade later there were more than three hundred. This dramatic growth took place within the national context of an evolving relationship between parents, their students, and colleges and universities. A seismic shift that began in the eighties brought a new generation of parents born after World War II, the so-called Baby Boomers. Thirty years earlier, the previous generation, the so-called silent generation, was much less directly involved in the education of their children. This earlier generation had generally entrusted the institutions to provide a semi-protective environment in which their children could grow up, and experts to turn them into educated adults. Boomer parents, however, had been directly involved in their children's education throughout their school years, and by the nineties their engagement in higher education required a strategic response from college administrators. The Boomers had much higher expectations than their predecessors. They saw themselves as equal partners in their children's education, and this attitude placed universities in the awkward position of trying to balance the dictates of federal privacy laws, the institution's own philosophy of student development, and increasing parental expectations. Families were having fewer children, and they spent more time and money on their upbringing to ensure the best for them. Parents now were involved in the student's selection of a college, paid increasingly large sums of money to those institutions, and sometimes terminated the student's career at the college if they were dissatisfied. Student and parents alike have been shaped by the modern "consumer society" to expect colleges to provide them with the convenience, cost, quality, and service. Colleges and universities confronted the challenges of finding an appropriate relationship with these new "customers," and parents clubs offered the opportunity to engage this involvement in a constructive way.[22]

The Hardestys chose to engage parents rather than keep them at arm's length, and the dramatic success of the Mountaineer Parents Club at WVU is undoubtedly the result of Susan Hardesty's enthusiastic direction. The club was conceived as a way to develop a "community of support and engagement" among students and their families. Membership was open and free, and recruitment began with new student orientation in the fall of 1995 when about eight hundred parents joined. By 2005, the Mountaineer Parents Club boasted sixty-three local clubs, with thirty-eight of them in West Virginia, twenty-three in states across the nation, and two in foreign countries (Canada and Germany).[23]

ACADEMIC STANDARDS AND EXPECTATIONS

Following the first round of initiatives to restructure the student experience, the Commission on Academic Standards and Expectations was established in May 1998 to review the University's goals and expectations for undergraduate education. Membership of the twenty-eight member commission was broad and representative of the entire University community and campuses. The commission was initiated subsequent to the *Boyer Report*, which, as outlined previously, set forth the elements of a quality education in an "Academic Bill of Rights" that every university should guarantee to undergraduate students. The concepts articulated in the *Boyer Report* exerted a major influence on both President Hardesty's initiatives to revamp undergraduate education at WVU and the recommendations generated by the Commission on Academic Standards and Expectations.[24]

Among the most important proposals of the commission implemented by the University, those intended to enhance the academic environment stand out. Revamping the first-year experience was accomplished by providing a set of academic supports to assist new students in making a successful transition to college life. Entering students were required to enroll in a one-credit orientation course to enhance academic skills, critical thinking, time management, test taking, and computer skills, and to help students make important life choices relating to alcohol, drugs, sex, and safety. The course was subsequently shown to have a positive impact on student retention and completion. WVU also developed "learning communities" for first-year students, which brought them together in the residence hall and placed them in courses as a group. As of 2004, there were three "freshman interest group" floors in the residence halls for first-year students in engineering, forensic science, and creative arts.[25]

As the changes recommended by the commission were being implemented, the Department of English was establishing a Center for Writing Excellence, which was designed to help freshmen and sophomores to improve their writing skills. Simultaneously, the Department of Mathematics initiated the Institute for Math Learning to provide assistance to all University students taking mathematics courses below the level of calculus. Both initiatives supported the University's goal of enhancing the first-year experience and raising academic expectations among the student body.

The commission also recommended, and the Faculty Senate approved, that each academic program require a capstone experience for its students beginning in the fall of 2002. The capstone served as a culminating experience that required students to demonstrate their ability to integrate the knowledge they had accumulated, independently gather new knowledge, and demonstrate skills utilized in their chosen disciplines.[26]

Another initiative to enhance the quality of undergraduate learning resulted in a thorough overhaul of the general education requirements. The Liberal Studies Program (LSP), implemented in 1988, required all undergraduates to take a total of fifty-one credit hours from a core curriculum chosen from course clusters, such as sciences and humanities, to provide a broad general education. Assessing student learning outcomes, however, was difficult under the LSP. Consequently, following a thorough review of the LSP system, along with information gathered from peer institutions, in 2002 the Ad Hoc General Education Review Committee developed a new General Education Curriculum (GEC). The purpose of the GEC was "to provide students with a foundation of skills and knowledge necessary to reason clearly, communicate effectively, and contribute to society." Therefore, students were required to distribute the courses they selected from approved groupings to teach them effective communication in English and basic mathematical skills; to expose them to methods of scientific inquiry, the past and its traditions, contemporary society, artistic expression, and the individual in society; and to provide them with an understanding of American, Western, and non-Western cultures. The Faculty Senate approved the GEC in 2004, and it was instituted in the fall of 2005.[27]

Even though most professors approved of the student-centered reforms, a few skeptics worried that the University was coddling students. At a year-end faculty forum in May 1998, several expressed concern that the University was becoming too "student-friendly," by "giving good grades and being nice to people" in order to increase enrollment and tuition dollars. Another professor complained that WVU was in danger becoming a "summer camp."[28]

The University's image as a "party school" presented a significant obstacle to President Hardesty's plan to increase the number and quality of student enrollment, and particularly to recruit out-of-state students. The student-centered initiatives involved a change in culture, and by hiring Carolyn Curry, former communications director for Governor Gaston Caperton, the president hoped to create a "unified," positive image of WVU. In doing so, Curry worked closely with the president's office and the vice presidents. On her tentative list of "communications goals" were promoting the faculty's academic reputation, attracting more research grants, improving internal communication, and integrating the regional campuses with the main campus. To improve the University's "brand," more evidence of the corporatism of the era, slogans such as "Success, Expect It," and "Where Greatness Is Learned," appeared in WVU's communications with the public. Although the slogans were often regarded as hollow nods to public relations, they were in fact chosen by students rather than Curry. Because she was hired without a search, and because her substantial salary raised eyebrows, the editor of the *Charleston Gazette* opined: "It's sad that the University values a PR flack more highly than professors."[29]

The "party school" image, however, posed the most significant public-relations problem confronting Hardesty's efforts to recast the University's image. The president had taken dramatic steps toward improving student culture at WVU, but a dark cloud was cast over those improvements in 1997 when the *Princeton Review's Best 311 Colleges* guidebook crowned WVU the nation's number one party school. It was an honor few friends of the University welcomed. Thereafter, alcohol abuse and related behaviors became the center of attention in the campaign for change, even though this negative image was not of recent vintage.

In 1985, some legislators were alarmed by reports that "cohabitation and drinking" had reached "deplorable" levels at WVU, and a legislative subcommittee was established to investigate student behavior on the Morgantown campus. "The Legislature is very concerned about WVU's image," Senator Gino Colombo was quoted as exclaiming. "The situation up there has gotten totally out of hand. There is absolutely no leadership, no direction." WVU complained about the lack of legislative support, he asserted, but "if they'd clean up their act, we might be more prone to financing them."[30] Rebuttals of University administrators that the image was unjust seemingly were ignored.

Some of the state's newspaper editors were not sympathetic to such an investigation, especially at a time when the University was searching for a new president. Just when the Board of Regents should be "beating the ivy-covered towers" to find an educational leader, "some self-appointed standard bearers of integrity drag out their clown suits and grease paint and play to the crowd," said one editor. Every generation of youth, past, present, and future, is interested in parties, drinking beer, and the opposite sex, and that is "a tradition in Morgantown that students have endured for decades. Big deal." Present and former students complained to local newspapers, one accusing Senator Colombo of trying to divert attention from the fact that the legislature did not provide adequate financial support to the state's flagship institution.[31]

The *Weston Democrat* offered the most acerbic editorial on the legislative subcommittee's investigation by claiming that WVU's reputation as a party school went back at least to the thirties. At a time when the University was suffering a $3.3 million budget reduction, the legislature was worried about students drinking beer, "sleeping over," and throwing parties. "Where have our legislators been? Or more precisely, where did they go to school? Not the university, evidently" for WVU "has always had a reputation as a party school." The editor, Robert S. Earle, found the legislators' newfound concerns amusing. "We will have our readers know, that in our time WVU not only acquired a national reputation as a party school, it had an international one." According to Earle, it began with a theme for the Phi Sigma Kappa informal dance during homecoming weekend in 1938. The fraternity chose to mock Adolph Hitler, whose armies had recently occupied Austria and were poised to enter Czechoslovakia. All of the fraternity brothers put on brown shirts, and Hitler-like mustaches, and otherwise mocked the "little dictator." Presumably, they also drank a lot of beer. A *Life* magazine photographer documented the event, and the article appeared in that popular national magazine. The editors of a Nazi weekly (*Das Schwarze Korps*), which circulated among Hitler's elite SS guard, were not pleased and castigated the WVU students as "playboys" and "guttersnipes," which the students must have found amusing. Of course this incident occurred before Hitler had unleashed total war on the world, and the students thought he was merely "crazy." In keeping with this view of the dictator, the editors of the *Daily Athenaeum* took up a collection and sent a cablegram to *Das Schwarze Korps* severing relations between WVU and Germany. Shifting his focus to the seventies, the newspaper editor cited former president James Harlow's appropriate response when asked by concerned parents what he planned to do about all the partying: "Nothing. I am not running a kindergarten." The editor concluded that, if the legislature would fund the University appropriately, "some real partying" would be in order.[32]

While students continued to find plenty of opportunity to drink in Morgantown, the ad hoc Grant Avenue block party in the student ghetto of Sunnyside drew the most concerted attention from both town and gown. As a way to kick off the new school year, students gathered in growing masses on Grant Street. Over the years the crowd grew to thousands, and young people came to the event from two hundred miles away. Police and University officials became increasingly uneasy, and their fears were realized on the night of August 22, 1994, when an estimated ten thousand people congregated on Grant Avenue. A young man with a long police record but no connection to the University fired a .38 handgun into the crowd, wounding two undergraduate students.[33]

The incident prompted the Morgantown police chief to call a halt to any further Grant Avenue block parties. If students persisted, he threatened to bring in the National Guard and arrest all violators of the city's noise, loitering, and open-container laws. Ninety police officers would be placed on duty, and steel-mesh fencing erected in the city parking garage would serve as a make-shift holding pen for those arrested. According to the West Virginia Civil Liberties Union (WVCLU), the city was overreacting when it declared that three or more students on Grant Avenue would constitute a party because such individuals would be private citizens on private property. The WVCLU acknowledged that the block party had gotten out of control and had no objection to enforcing laws on underage drinking and open containers, but it petitioned the court to prohibit the police from making mass arrests and punishing private citizens for engaging in private acts, and to prohibit WVU from punishing students for off-campus activities.[34]

If the Morgantown Police Department's policy of "zero tolerance" for block parties was the stick, FallFest was the carrot extended to students by the University. In 1995 the inaugural FallFest brought in top entertainers, the food court remained open for patrons, and shuttle buses ran until two a.m. between the Lair and the Evansdale Residential Complex. The idea for FallFest originated with students, President Hardesty supported it, and by all estimations it was an enormous success. Five different bands performed on the Lair Plaza and only thirty people were arrested that night (twenty-six of them on Grant Avenue and mostly for alcohol-related offenses). The University's counter-party drew approximately ten thousand people to the Mountainlair for live music, beer, and food. Hardesty issued a prepared press statement that "WVU and the Morgantown community confronted a tough problem and worked together to solve it." Students who attempted to continue the block-party tradition instead of embracing FallFest encountered a resolute police detachment determined to bring an end to the infamous event. The Grant Avenue block party was on its way into history.[35]

FallFest was a single initiative in the campaign to change the drinking culture at WVU by providing an alternative to the block party. On the other hand, WVUp All Night was an ongoing initiative to provide a desirable alternative to the downtown bar scene. This program, initiated in the spring of 1998, kept the Mountainlair open all night Thursday through Saturday. Because some four thousand students passed through the Lair each night, administrators considered the $8,000 per weekend cost to be a good investment. Two corporate sponsors also pledged support of about $25,000. Movies, comedians, concerts, food, and beer, were offered by the University free of charge. Students seemed genuinely appreciative as survey comments indicated: "it keeps me out of trouble," "it keeps me out of the bars," "it keeps students from driving home drunk," and "I can't believe all the money I'm saving."[36]

ABC's *Good Morning America* featured WVUp All Night and President Hardesty's efforts to curb binge drinking at WVU. ABC-TV correspondent Beth Nissen was on campus September 4–5, 1998, during the Ohio State football game weekend. Taped for national airing, President Hardesty claimed that every college president was concerned about alcohol abuse among students. He estimated that least 25 percent of the student body were availing themselves of the WVUp All Night programming, and as a result student arrests and injuries were down significantly. Nissen announced that she was "proud to have done a segment on a program so promising to tackling a national college problem." Shortly after the segment aired, WVU officials began receiving calls from college administrators and politicians from across the nation. One newspaper editorial proclaimed, "What a splendid testament to Hardesty's and WVU's clearheaded thinking about how to attack the long-standing problem of drinking on college campuses."[37]

Hardesty's efforts brought favorable national attention to WVU, offsetting to a degree its negative party school image. Several years later, *The Templeton Guide* listed WVU as a leader among universities because of its program to give students options other than the weekend party scene. Programs such as WVUp All Night, which attracted thousands every weekend, a new Recreation Center, which attracted a half-million visits in the first nine months of its existence, and FallFest, which drew 14,000 annually, substantively demonstrated the University's commitment to creating a safe learning environment. Improved rankings of WVU were also to be found in *America's 100 Best College Buys*; in *U.S. News & World Report,* for outstanding academic programs; and in the *Chronicle of Higher Education,* for WVU's "proud tradition" of producing Rhodes, Goldwater, and Truman Scholars.[38]

"Welcome to Touchdown City" was another cooperative effort between WVU and Morgantown's *Dominion Post* to present a safe way of celebrating the beginning of football season and welcoming fans to Morgantown. A concert and pep rally on Mountainlair Plaza drew five thousand to seven thousand people to the inaugural event in 1997. Other pieces of the program to curtail alcohol abuse were designed to address other problems associated with drinking on game days. Rowdiness and the use of obscene language at the games sometimes turned dangerous, as when students, carried away with alcohol-fueled excitement, threw objects onto the field and onto other spectators sitting below them in the stands. The University's decision to sponsor a tailgating event in the area once appropriately known as the Pit was one which emanated directly out of the massive amount of alcohol consumed by the large crowd of students who gathered at this impromptu pre-game event outside the stadium. One of the worst and most publicized incidents associated with the Pit occurred on a fall football Saturday in 1996 when a nineteen-year-old-freshman woman became so inebriated that she nearly died from alcohol poisoning.[39]

The initiatives taken to curb drinking did indeed have some effect. WVU sat on the top ten list of party schools for some time, ranking number one in 1997, dropping to eleventh in 1998, and falling off the list entirely for a time. Many students regarded the ranking, or lack thereof, as humorous. One reportedly observed that the *Princeton Review* got it wrong: "We are the top party school. They just don't know how to rank professionals."[40] Discounting that possibility, the measures taken by University and city officials probably did account for a modest decline in alcohol-related crime. The WVU Department of Public Safety reported a drop in arrests for public intoxication from thirty-six in 1996 to twenty-five in 1997, and the Morgantown Police Department measured a dip from forty-three to twenty-nine student arrests. The number of WVU students involved in drunken driving also declined 14 percent during that period from ninety-five to eighty-two. While these were snapshots, officials believed that they indicated some progress, and they were right. By the end of Hardesty's tenure in 2007, the most outlandish and dangerous behavior among students had been tamed. WVU had always been considered a relatively safe university community, and the March 2008 issue of *Reader's Digest* ranked WVU eighteenth in a survey of 135 U.S. colleges and universities, earning it an "A" for its strong commitment to safety.[41]

Closely associated with the Grant Avenue block party in Sunnyside was couch burning, another undesirable practice that brought negative national publicity to WVU. When the first couch fire was set is unknown, but from the eighties on it became an increasingly common form of student celebration after a football game, usually accompanied by drinking parties. Needless to say, to an administration dedicated to elevating student culture and the learning environment, and a city increasingly concerned with the dangers that escalated with a burgeoning student population, setting fire to furniture in the streets was a practice that needed to end. In 1998, the Morgantown City Council began discussing an ordinance that would prohibit indoor furniture from being placed on outside porches, where students dragged their couches during Sunnyside block parties, and that would make it illegal to set them ablaze in the streets. Indoor couches on front porches were an "aesthetic problem" that had turned into a "safety problem," one councilman observed.[42]

Although torching couches was originally part of celebrating or protesting the outcome of a big game, by the late nineties it had become a commonplace occurrence with no reasonable explanation beyond the exuberance and poor judgment of youth. The unsightly housing in Sunnyside was also a problem for recruiting new students, so WVU and the city cooperated in efforts to make the area more attractive. One member of student government told a reporter that he initially planned to attend another institution because, in his estimation as a prospective student, Sunnyside was a "slum." He came to regard his first impression as unfortunate because WVU was "such a wonderful university." Nevertheless, "a lot of the best don't come here" because dilapidated housing and old furniture on porches were eyesores that put off prospective students. Now those couches had become a safety issue.[43]

These issues would require a long-term effort to resolve, however, and by 2003 the couch fires had escalated rather than diminished. In October, the rival Virginia Tech "Hokies," ranked third in the national football polls, came to Morgantown. When WVU won the game in an upset, students, overcome by excitement, poured out of their stadium seats and rushed the goalposts. A long legacy of riotous behavior prepared the police to expect the worst, however, and the goalposts were heavily guarded. Police repulsed the students with clouds of pepper spray in a scene carried nationally on ESPN television. It was not a good scene for a school trying to elevate its public image, but the worst was yet to come outside the stadium gates. Couch fires lit up the night sky in Sunnyside with students whooping it up around them. Just before midnight police were summoned to a fire that had attracted five thousand students.[44]

The post-football ritual of couch burning soon expanded to include basketball, given the team's resurgence to national prominence. In March 2005, Coach John Beilein's team reached the NCAA elite eight, and ESPN game announcers predicted on air, "Oh boy, couches are going to burn tonight in Morgantown." They were right, although their remarks only added encouragement. Students took to the streets, setting fires to whatever would light, including dumpsters and even a car. The following month WVU expelled eleven students for setting fires and other antisocial behavior. That same month, *Gentlemen's Quarterly* rated WVU fans second-worst in the nation, citing as evidence the fact that 1,129 street fires had been intentionally set between 1997 and 2003.[45]

Campus fraternities were not immune to alcohol-related episodes, as demonstrated by the serious injury of a nineteen-year-old freshman pledge who fell from the roof of the Pi Kappa Alpha house on February 20, 1998. A University hearing was scheduled for late March to investigate the episode, and, apparently in rebellion, fraternity members dragged couches into the street and set them on fire. Burning clothes and other material were thrown from the windows. Nearly every window in the three-story house was broken, and glass was scattered throughout the building. Large holes were punched in the walls and ceilings, electrical wires were pulled from the ceilings, and toilets were smashed. On March 20, the University condemned the Pi Kappa Alpha house, the chapter surrendered its charter, the national fraternity suspended the local chapter indefinitely, and the Morgantown building inspector condemned the building. The vice president for student affairs surmised that members decided to close the fraternity rather than go through with the hearing.[46]

The corporation that managed the building filed a lawsuit in Monongalia County Circuit Court on May 1 against the twenty-nine Pi Kappa Alpha members responsible for the night of destruction. The damages amounted to more than $40,000. The national chapter's attorney said that Pi Kappa

Alpha officials were "stunned" by the students' behavior and asserted that as adults they should be held responsible and pursued in the courts until they had paid for the damages and court costs.[47]

As an outgrowth of this shabby affair, WVU struck another blow against student party culture by drafting a new alcohol policy that would make fraternity houses virtually dry. Closely following the version suggested by Select 2010, a national program in collaboration with thirty-two different national fraternities that required their houses to be alcohol-free zones, WVU's new policy permitted alcoholic beverages to be consumed only in the rooms of members who were twenty-one or older. Alcohol would not be permitted anywhere else in fraternity houses. Social functions where alcohol was consumed were required to be held off campus. The new policy went one step further by prohibiting fraternities from serving alcohol in tailgate areas at football games.[48]

The student newspaper challenged the University's right to stretch the limits of its authority in the matter. Fraternities were private organizations and the houses were owned by private corporations that worked with the national organizations. While it was recognized that universities nationwide faced political pressure to control alcohol problems on campus, the extent of their authority was open to question. WVU's position was clear; its goal was to change the campus culture, and Greek life was a significant part of that campaign. On the other hand, an editorial in the *Daily Athenaeum* stated the student perspective clearly: "It is not the responsibility of the University administration to 'promote changes in campus culture,' much less single out one student organization as a cultural engineering guinea pig. . . . Simply put, the fraternity houses are neither on campus nor University property. . . . The administration is overstepping its bounds." The administration was responding to more powerful pressures than what the students could muster, however, and the decision was made that the campus fraternity houses would in fact be dry starting in the fall of 1998.[49]

"The Greeks" were not a homogeneous lot, of course, and members of fraternities and sororities could engage in both constructive and destructive behaviors without a second thought. In 1999 a distinct drop in reports on Greek activities in the press took place, and some of the change must be credited to the efforts of the University administration. In some ways it was easier to deal with the Greek organizations because they were in fact organizations, and additional governing structures were found in the Intrafraternity Council and the Panhellenic Council. University officials persuaded the leaderships of these organizations to participate, and thereafter progress was swift. Greeks were soon making news for their service activities rather than their drinking parties. In the fall of 1999, the local newspaper complimented the Greeks for helping to clean up litter along the Monongahela River, sponsoring a blood drive for the Red Cross, and collecting items for the Toys for Tots Christmas campaign.[50] Clearly some refocusing of Greek culture on campus had taken place.

ENROLLMENT STRATEGIES

If judged by the recruitment and retention data, WVU's efforts to create a student-centered university were impressively successful. In 1998, President Hardesty informed alumni that their university offered "the most comprehensive student-life programs anywhere in the United States." As a result of the student-centered programs, total campus enrollments grew steadily each year from 21,743 in 1996 to 25,255 in 2004. The retention rate, the percentage of students who returned the following year, also improved from 76.45 percent in 1995 to 80.77 percent in 2003.[51]

Even though freshman enrollment continued to grow, the increases did not come at the expense of lowered academic standards. In fact, the standardized test scores of incoming students were increasing at the same time that enrollments were expanding. President Hardesty claimed that expanding enrollments demonstrated that the University offered "a student experience that rivals small private institutions," while at the same time providing "the academic opportunities and quality that can only come from a major comprehensive research institution." Enrollment in the fall of 2005 reached 26,051 marking the fifth consecutive year of growth, the retention rate held at nearly 81 percent, and the average freshman ACT composite score was slightly over 23, well above the national average. When Hardesty left the presidency in 2007, total enrollment on the Morgantown campus had reached 27,825, just shy of the 28,500 goal for 2008.[52]

With the financial burdens placed on WVU by Senate Bill 547, the University was forced to rely even more on student tuition for operating revenues and less on state appropriations. As a result, enrollment increases were part of a strategic plan to keep the University healthy. Aggressively recruiting students both inside and outside the state was a major component of that plan, and by the fall of 2007 a major shift had occurred in the freshman demographic. For the first time, out-of-state freshmen slightly outnumbered in-state freshmen, 2,426 to 2,358. In overall enrollment, however, residents still surpassed out-of-state students, 15,910 to 11,915. The following year, 2008, out-of-state students again outnumbered resident West Virginians in the largest-ever freshman class of 5,180, although residents still made up 56 percent of the total student body. Most of the non-residents came from Pennsylvania, although Maryland, Virginia, and New Jersey contributed substantial numbers. Nearly every state in the union was represented in the student body, as was every county in the state of West Virginia. One of the main reasons for this influx of out-of-state students was the cost: residents paid $5,100 a year for tuition, but nonresidents paid $15,770. Nevertheless, tuition for many nonresidents at WVU was still cheaper than tuition in their home states. With the improving academic quality, student-centered environment, and investments in facilities and technology, it became a real bargain.[53]

WVU's Enrollment Strategic Plan 2005–2010 set a target of thirty thousand students at the main campus and Potomac State by 2010, and a goal of achieving equal numbers of first-year nonresident and resident students. No qualified in-state applicants were to be denied admission, but the declining pool of students graduating from high school in West Virginia necessitated attracting nonresident students. The rationale behind the decision to expand enrollments was sound and had evolved over many years of parsimonious state appropriations. President E. Gordon Gee (1981–1985) chose the financially disastrous strategy of shrinking enrollments in order to meet the level of appropriations from the state. President Neil S. Bucklew (1986–1995) reversed this policy by increasing enrollment to cover the shortfall in state appropriations. Bucklew oversaw the first major effort to recruit nonresident students as enrollment peaked at about 23,000 and then began to slip as the trend of declining West Virginia high school graduates set in. Under President Hardesty (1996–2007), a plan was designed to arrest declining enrollments and to attract both residents and nonresidents. Recruitment and retention were stressed as two sides of the same issue. The pool of first-year students who were West Virginia high school graduates was expected to decline by three thousand between 2000 and 2013; consequently, nearly every institution of higher education in the state was actively recruiting nonresident students. Because applications to WVU continue to increase each year, a higher quality nonresident student was being admitted while at the same time no qualified West Virginia resident was turned away.[54]

Many in the University community raised questions about increasing the enrollment, but the answer was simple. "We had two options, but really only one choice," Provost Gerald Lang explained. One option called for imposing significant budget cuts beyond those that were initiated under Senate Bill 547. These cuts would have effectively diminished the University's research and instructional capacity. The other option, the only real choice if WVU were to continue as a viable Research I university, was "to grow strategically to our capacity," recognizing that the institution could not cut spending to achieve prosperity. Growth would generate increased revenues from student tuition and fees and provide the opportunity to resolve the "looming deficits" from Senate Bill 547, pay the mandated salary increases, utilize the physical plant efficiently, and invest in information technology, the libraries, and campus upgrades.[55]

Increasingly, a higher percentage of costs were transferred to individual students as higher education became perceived more as a private benefit than as a public good. Across the nation, state funds declined as tuition and fees increased. Financial aid officers were forced to remind students that college graduates earn a million dollars more over their careers than do high school graduates. The increasing difficulty of financing that education was the problem that many, if not most, students and their parents faced. WVU adhered to a policy that held tuition increases to a minimum of what was required to protect quality of education. Still, tuition increases generally exceeded the rise in the family cost of living because the institution required far greater support to pay fixed costs, such as libraries, security, energy, employee health care, investment in technology, and the recruitment and retention of high-achieving faculty.[56]

Consequently, growing numbers of students became dependent on financial aid to pay for their education. Students in West Virginia were paying 30 percent more for their public college education in 2000 than they did a decade earlier, even after adjusting for inflation. During the nineties, the percentage of West Virginia students who depended on aid grew to 37 percent, compared with the national figure of 49.7 percent. Financial aid in the form of loans, rather than grants and scholarships, became the rule. This trend made it more difficult for the state to retain students after graduation because those with substantial loans to repay had little choice but to leave West Virginia's sluggish economy for greater opportunities elsewhere.[57]

The Higher Education Policy Commission released data it had compiled for the average education and related spending per (full-time equivalent) student at WVU in 2003 and compared it to spending in 2008. Net tuition was $6,683, and the average state subsidy was $5,822 per student in 2003; in 2008 those figures were $8,620 net tuition, and $3,599 average state subsidy per student. Statewide, the net tuition share of education and related costs per student by 2008 was 71 percent in West Virginia; nationally, that same figure was 50 percent. These figures revealed a national trend. The Delta Cost Project, a national study, found that students were paying more but getting less for higher education. College tuition and fees at public colleges rose about 87 percent between 1984 and 2008, more than twice the rate of inflation. Not surprisingly the public began to question whether the rising costs translated into expanded access and improved quality. As a consequence, the calls for financial transparency in higher education grew louder, reflecting growing insistence for higher education reforms from state legislatures.[58]

WVU administrators have carefully maintained a cost position below competing institutions in nearby states. With WVU forced to operate more like a business, the rising cost of education prompted concerns that the quality and affordability of education would suffer. The National Center for Public Policy and Higher Education gave West Virginia an "F" in affordability for 2008 because, according its criteria, "poor and working-class families must devote 34 percent of their income, even after aid, to pay for costs at public four-year colleges."[59]

Governor Bob Wise delivered on a campaign promise when the legislature passed a bill in 2001 authorizing the Promise Scholarship program for qualified residents. These state-funded scholarships paid the cost of tuition and fees at a West Virginia state college or university, or the equivalent at one of the state's private colleges, for students who earned a 3.0 grade-point average or better in high school and scored a minimum of 21 on the ACT or 1000 on the SAT. The first scholarships were awarded in the fall of 2002 to 3,862 of the 5,800 applicants. Based on Georgia's HOPE (Helping Outstanding Pupils Educationally) Scholarship, the first state-sponsored scholarship program of its kind, Promise Scholarship rules allowed students two semesters and thirty credit hours to maintain a 2.75 grade-point average during the first year and a 3.0 thereafter in order to keep the award. Nearly half of those receiving the scholarships for the fall of 2002 were bound for WVU.[60] The following academic year, one-third of WVU's first-year class of 4,300 qualified for Promise scholarships, and by 2006–2007 that number tripled to 9,500. The rising numbers of West Virginia students who qualified posed the question of whether Promise would be strangled by its own success. Significantly, the costs had not escalated as they had in Georgia but were contained by elevating the standards. Between 2004 and 2009, Promise Scholarship standards were elevated three times until the minimum ACT had risen to 23, thus denying access to 42 percent of previously eligible high school graduates. Furthermore, a $4,750 cap was imposed. Reducing eligibility gave some cause to wonder whether the state might be undermining its own goal of increasing the number of West Virginia college graduates.[61]

Educating the workforce in West Virginia was a large part of the rationale for passage of the Promise Scholarships. Whether students, once educated, would chose to remain in the state and join the workforce, therefore, became an important policy question. The WVU Bureau of Business and Economic Research attempted to answer the question by examining workforce participation rates for college graduates in West Virginia. Its report released in 2008 was not encouraging. Examining the academic years 1995–1996 through 2004–2005, the study found that 56.2 percent of health care graduates and 56.3 percent of education graduates worked in the state. Science and technology related fields were seriously underrepresented, with only 28.5 percent of engineering graduates and 33.7 percent of biomedical and physical science graduates remaining in the state during the decade. The period examined was too short to provide a definitive answer to the question of how many Promise Scholars remained in West Virginia after graduation. As of 2009, the jury was still out.[62]

INTERNATIONAL STUDENTS

Senate Bill 547 called on institutions to prepare students to compete in the global economy. To do so effectively, students needed to be prepared for the challenge both culturally and academically. The year that Hardesty became president approximately 4 percent of the University's total enrollment was international, with three-quarters of them being graduate/professional students and one-quarter undergraduates. To convey the University's serious commitment to international engagement, international exchange and cultural diversity in the University's educational mission took on a whole new level of significance.[63] In the fall of 2002, the Office of International Programs reported increases in international student enrollment from 849 to 1,315 over the period 1996– 2002. Nearly one hundred countries were represented in the student body. In 2002, India provided the most students (365); the People's Republic of China was second (230); and countries of the Middle East represented a distant third. The vast majority of international students that year were enrolled in the colleges of engineering and mineral resources, arts and sciences, and business and economics.[64]

The new focus on educating students for a globalized world spurred the University to become proactive by creating programs for sending students abroad as part of their education, primarily through study-abroad programs administered by the Office of International Programs. The Study

Abroad Fair became an annual event acquainting WVU students with the various opportunities to study in another country through exchange programs with sister institutions at the same tuition cost. The reverse exchange was available to students from those sister institutions at WVU. In 2000, cooperative exchange programs sent students to institutions in a number of countries, including Australia, Austria, Denmark, England, France, Germany, Japan, Mexico, Morocco, Northern Ireland, and South Africa. Many faculty-led courses that included travel abroad were also available. Destinations included Ghana, Cuba, China, England, Mexico, Germany, Spain, France, and Nepal.[65]

In 1994 the University established a Center for Chinese Business in the College of Business and Economics to provide a two-way conduit for educational and business community members who desired to do business in China. Twelve Chinese government employees spent five months in 2001 at the WVU Center for Chinese Business to learn how to prepare for China's rapidly emerging market-based economy. The center also held workshops in China for those who wanted to learn about business in America, and for Americans who wanted to explore opportunities to market or manufacture their products in China. The relationship opened doors for business, but also for students who were preparing to enter the global marketplace.[66]

Temporary hiccups associated with global political events sometimes interfered with forging greater ties with other world cultures. As might be expected, the terrorist attacks on September 11, 2001, created great anxiety among Arab students in the United States. Twenty of the twenty-one Kuwaiti students at WVU left the campus, mainly because their parents feared a backlash. There were no official reports of anti-Arab harassment filed at WVU during the weeks following the tragedy, and the Kuwaiti students returned for the spring semester. A doctoral student in engineering and his wife, a graduate student in journalism, returned to complete their degrees. Asked about how they were treated, the young man informed a reporter: "Everybody is nice. It's just outside [the University]. You know, though, for every dirty look [we encounter many more] nice people. The people I'm associated with—at school, at work—they're really nice. They know me. They know my family. They're happy that I'm back."[67]

EIGHTEEN

INTERCOLLEGIATE SPORTS AND THE MARKETPLACE

INTERCOLLEGIATE ATHLETICS experienced a major transformation beginning in the final decades of the twentieth century with the emergence of big revenue sports, especially football and basketball, which fans were willing to pay a significant price to watch. The communications revolution brought multiple ways to experience sports beyond attending the events, particularly through television and, eventually, the plethora of cable channels providing sports programming. Regional conferences, which had been forged for the convenience of travel for games among similar schools, evolved into media-driven organizations of teams that could be packaged for television in the most lucrative markets. Geography ceased to play the dominant role, as advances in communications technology made games played anywhere accessible for viewing everywhere. A dramatic growth in revenues resulted along with the division of colleges and universities based on the ability of their athletic programs to attract the largest number of viewers. Consequently, powerhouse conferences located in major media areas, such as the Big Ten, SEC, Big 12, and Pac 10, became the nation's elites of college football and basketball. It was to this status WVU aspired and always believed it belonged.

COMMERCIALIZATION OF THE REVENUE SPORTS

The state-instituted reforms requiring the University to become more financially self-sufficient, which began during President Bucklew's administration and reached their apogee under President Hardesty, made it painfully clear that WVU football and basketball must generate a superabundance of revenue if the University's aspirations were to be achieved. Football usually accounted for a little more than one-half of the athletic department's revenues, and basketball was the second-highest-grossing sport. In short, college football and basketball had become businesses, and a rationale for the University-operated sports businesses reached its fullest development.[1]

The commercialization of intercollegiate athletics precipitated significant changes in the administration of college sports. The involvement of college presidents in the business of maintaining a top athletic department was imperative in order to ensure that the institution's academic integrity was not sacrificed for a winning record, and also because so much money was at stake. President Hardesty believed his involvement was necessary to keep "athletics within appropriate limits compared to our budget as a whole," he told one reporter. He pointed out that WVU could hardly be considered a "farm" for professional teams because five hundred to six hundred WVU students competed in twenty-one intercollegiate sports at any one time, and very few of them became professional athletes.[2]

Hundreds of television channels made intercollegiate sports a main feature of television programming. In the seventies a WVU football or basketball game on television was a major event for fans; thirty years later all of the games were broadcast and most of them telecast as well. WVU, like other major universities, now received money from commercial television networks for providing programming, and the revenues from football and basketball appearances supported the University as a whole. According to President Hardesty, revenue from sports programming was "one reason the presidents have to be involved. They have to balance the commercial aspects of athletics with the educational realities." While some decried the commercialization of college sports, Hardesty pointed out that "the challenges of the large university and its relationship with business extend beyond athletics." For example, private companies sponsor research, pay for clinical drug trials, and give internships to students, so athletics presented no greater challenge than this relationship with business. As for coaches' salaries, commercialization is the "canary in the mine." The president again believed that they could get out of hand, but he drew a comparison to the payment of exorbitant salaries for rare specialists in medicine, engineering, or other fields. Winning could be overemphasized, but Hardesty did not foresee that likelihood at WVU. "We do not win at all cost here," he said. "I'm happy we are competitive and keeping it in perspective."[3]

One of the most often expressed criticisms of the commercialization of college athletics was that universities benefited from the performance of their student athletes, who received no compensation in return, and that standards were sacrificed to keep athletes in school while they filled the universities' coffers. President Hardesty expressed "serious reservations" about student athletes entering into any kind of financial relationship with the University on the basis of their athletic skills. Even part-time employment during the school year was bound to create problems because the rules could be skirted so easily. Scholarship athletes already received considerable compensation in the form of tuition, room and board, fees, books, and other expenses. During the fiscal year ending July 2002, WVU athletes received $3.6 million in athletic-related aid.[4]

The practice of sacrificing academics to keep athletes in school is an issue that continues to attract attention nationwide. Generally discussed in terms of graduation rates for athletes, the popular notion was that athletes took courses like "basket weaving," received grades they had not earned, or remained in school even though there was little likelihood that they would graduate. This was not a problem at WVU. In 2002 more than one-third of all WVU student athletes earned a grade-point average of 3.0, and the graduation rate for athletes (66 percent) was higher than for the student body as a whole. There was some variation by sport, but even in football (traditionally carrying the lowest academic ranking) eighty-three of the 103 players carried a grade-point average of 2.5 or better, while forty-nine carried a 3.0 or better. The overall GPA for the 2001 football squad was 2.8. The most serious criticism of basketball coach Bob Huggins's record before his arrival at WVU centered on the low graduation rate of his players. During his sixteen seasons at the University of Cincinnati only twenty-seven of his ninety-five players graduated, a graduation rate of only 28 percent. Of course, extenuating factors played a role, such as a number of players who left school early for the NBA. However, his graduation record at WVU has been excellent. In fact, all of his players during the first three seasons graduated except Joe Alexander and Devin Ebanks, both of whom were drafted early by professional teams.[5]

In no small part, the better than average graduation rate can be attributed to Garrett Ford, associate athletic director for student services. A former WVU football player (1965–1967), Ford was one of the pioneers who integrated football at the University. In 1977, Ford became an academic counselor for student athletes, and for three decades he provided thousands of athletes with career and personal counseling, tenaciously tracked class attendance, and monitored eligibility issues.[6]

Even though a university could never purchase the kind of favorable national publicity it receives when its sports teams play on national television, especially in bowl or championship games, a major college athletic program carries a significant financial burden. In 2003, Ohio State reportedly spent $78 million to run its intercollegiate athletic program in thirty-six sports, three times what it cost WVU to compete in twenty-one sports. Five years later, Ohio State's annual athletics budget was about $110 million, the nation's largest. President of Ohio State and former WVU President E. Gordon Gee put this cost in context by pointing out that Ohio State's overall budget was $4 billion. As a percentage of the total, therefore, the athletics budget was relatively insignificant. It should be noted that the athletic department at Ohio State is a self-supporting unit within the institution, as is also true at WVU, although on a much smaller scale. In Gee's view, ensuring that the athletic programs and their athletes were fully integrated into the life of the university was made more difficult by the escalation in spending on big-time sports, the so-called "arms race." Intercollegiate athletics was "increasingly becoming separated and segregated, both in structure and function, and even values, from the rest of the institution. And it's bringing that back into focus which I think is important," Gee declared.[7]

Sporting-goods companies also extend business into college sports through licensing agreements. In 2010, for example, the sportswear company Nike held contracts with twenty-one college football teams that were ranked in the preseason Associated Press top twenty-five. WVU was one of these institutions, with a contract with Nike worth more than $1 million per year in exchange for all teams using Nike uniforms and accessories. The University also earned significant revenue from Nike sales of apparel with the WVU logo in retail stores. WVU had climbed rapidly in the rankings to reach eleventh among leading sellers of college-licensed apparel in 2010. By comparison, however, WVU's contract with Nike paled alongside that of the University of North Carolina, which received $33.7 million over ten years. Adidas, Nike's competitor, led the licensing contract race with its ten-year, $66.5 million deal with the University of Michigan. Adidas's ten-year arrangement with Notre Dame came in second at $60 million.[8]

The large amounts of money coming into university athletic departments from television appearances and licensing agreements have triggered alarms among the wary. The revenues present a mixed blessing. They allow the University to provide the kind of sports programs that bring national attention and swell the pride of West Virginians, but they also reveal how the decline in state support has made it necessary for the University to join the "arms race." A knowledgeable Morgantown sportswriter expressed his fear that college basketball was becoming "more business than a sport," and he concluded that it was in "a downright, scandalized, win-at-all-cost mess" from which it was not likely to be saved. He was not referring to the scandals involving college players who accepted money from boosters. Nor was he referring to fudged SAT or ACT test scores, recruiting violations, or players who joined the pros after only one year in college. He was referring instead to infractions by some of the best coaches in the game that forced teams to vacate their NCAA tournament appearances. Because coaches earned millions in annual compensation, losing games meant losing jobs. During the three seasons ending in 2009, for example, there were 125 basketball coaching changes. "This is no longer just a game," said the sportswriter. "It's become more of a business than a game, and in today's economic times, there's a certain understanding to that. Colleges and universities have to survive and college basketball plays a big part in that survival. Still, we are all left wondering what is going to happen next?"[9] The same rhetorical question could be asked about football.

MOUNTAINEER ATHLETIC CLUB AND THE FACILITIES "ARMS RACE"

As the fund-raising arm for athletics within the WVU Foundation, the Mountaineer Athletic Club has a primary mission to provide the money to pay for more than 350 scholarships awarded annually to student athletes. Since the athletic department became a self-sustaining unit within the University, the Mountaineer Athletic Club has raised money from private donors to cover this expense, which amounted to more than $7 million in 2010. Donors have been generous even when the economy suffered through serious downturns. Club donations grew exponentially from $3.76 million for the 1999–2000 fiscal year to $6.2 million for 2003–2004. By 2006–2007, the amount had grown to $13.8 million, reached $15.5 million in 2008–2009, and set another record of $18.7 million in 2009–2010. Since the athletic department's budget was $56 million in 2009–2010, the $18.7 million provided by the club was a significant portion of the total.[10]

The Mountaineer Athletic Club also raises money for building construction and maintenance. The new basketball practice facility, the Dick Dlesk Soccer Stadium, and the Cary Gym have all benefited from its efforts. Club funds also support a number of smaller programs such as the 1100 Club, which covers football recruiting expenses, and the Legacy Fund, its counterpart for basketball recruiting. Smaller funding amounts are made available to the other intercollegiate athletic teams. Because money is the lifeblood of intercollegiate athletics, the Mountaineer Athletic Club was forced to adapt its fundraising methods to increase the level of giving from generous fans. It decided to build skyboxes at Milan Puskar Stadium, and long-term discussions began regarding the feasibility of constructing luxury boxes in the Coliseum. The club also doubled its staff and adopted the strategy of meeting potential donors face-to-face rather than simply sending impersonal solicitation letters. There is the danger that, as the athletic department (and the University) becomes ever more dependent on private donors, large donors will demand greater influence over how their contributions are used.[11]

The "arms race" also created pressure for athletic departments to construct the best facilities in order to attract the very best high school athletes and impress donors and fans, particularly important with ever rising ticket prices. The most significant improvement in the WVU football program after the construction of the new stadium was completion of the indoor practice facility, consisting of a ninety-yard field topped with artificial turf, and many additional features such as men's and women's locker rooms and training rooms. The $6.3 million Caperton Indoor Facility was named for former West Virginia governor Gaston Caperton, who played a major role in financing the facility. Any question as to why he supported its construction was laid to rest at the dedication. "The football program is a money-maker for the university," he declared and added that, when Mountaineer games are broadcast on national television, "it's great free advertising for the school. This is a good financial investment." Further upgrades came in 2000 with the addition to Mountaineer Field of a new scoreboard, and the construction of skyboxes, which were so popular that all were leased even before completion. Suite donors gave the University five years of rent in advance to launch the addition.[12]

Closing the Coliseum for asbestos abatement and upgrading the offices was a major event in the life of that facility. When the facility was completed in 1969, asbestos was still commonly used in construction. Upon the discovery in the seventies that the material could cause cancer, it ceased to be used, and eventually facilities everywhere began the removal process. The work at the Coliseum was completed in fourteen months at a cost of $7.8 million, and it reopened in October 2000. During the period it was closed, all employees were moved elsewhere, and the basketball team was forced to play "home" games sometimes as far away as Charleston and Wheeling.[13]

In June 2002, WVU Athletic Director Ed Pastilong revealed that further improvements were in store for the Coliseum. Improving the fan experience would generate more money. More revenue equaled better recruiting opportunities, coaching salaries, and renovations, all of which would make the teams more competitive. "It's clear to all of us we need to invest to win," he informed reporters, and while "dollars aren't everything, they're very important." With a 2002 budget of $24 million, ticket sales and donations were crucial to the financial stability of WVU athletics. WVU's spending was on a par with the Big East average of $24.2 million for all sports, but it varied widely, among individual schools ranging from $10.4 million to $38.6 million. Within the Big East average comparison, however, there were also significant differences in spending on the two major revenue sports. WVU men's basketball spent $1.4 million per year compared with the Big East average of $2.6 million, and WVU football spent $6.2 million annually compared with the Big East average of $8.9 million. Within the athletic program were 162 employees and 539 student athletes, and Pastilong announced that, in order to pay the bills, another $20 million must be invested in capital improvements, such as special cushioned-seating sections on the Coliseum floor, to bring in more revenues. Again, WVU was one of only a few Division 1 schools that did not include athletic funding in its overall budget.[14]

When basketball head coach Bob Huggins returned to his hometown to lead the Mountaineers, WVU was already committed to a long-term plan unanimously approved by the WVU Board of Governors in December 2008 to build a separate basketball practice facility. At a projected cost of $26 million, the new facility would be located behind the Coliseum and would house two separate practice courts for the men's and women's teams, locker rooms, a training room, theater-style meeting spaces for each team, and a Basketball Hall of Traditions. Because the Coliseum was used by so many groups for different kinds of functions, the new basketball-only facility would improve flexibility in scheduling, significantly impact recruiting, and help to keep WVU teams in the "upper echelon" of college basketball. Groundbreaking took place in spring 2010 with an expected completion date of May 2011.[15]

As one of the fastest growing sports in America, soccer has begun to play a greater role at WVU. Both the men's and women's soccer teams have improved significantly. The women finished the 2003 season ranked tenth in the nation and advanced to the Sweet Sixteen of the NCAA tournament for the first time ever. Although the men were less successful, they finished with higher expectations for the future. With the elevation in the programs came improvements in the facilities. Both teams played in a new purpose-built venue, the Dick Dlesk Soccer Stadium. Built next to the baseball field near the Coliseum complex, the facility was named in honor of S. J. Dick Dlesk of Wheeling, who committed more than $1 million to WVU intercollegiate athletics. The stadium, which can seat up to 1,600 people and includes an adjacent practice field for women, cost an estimated $2 million.[16]

BIG EAST DEFECTIONS AND ADDITIONS

In May 2003 the Atlantic Coast Conference announced its intention to raid the Big East of three of its strongest athletic programs (Boston College, Syracuse University, and the University of Miami), causing a panic among the remaining members. The plan was designed to make the Atlantic Coast Conference the dominant eastern athletic conference. The move was bold, revealing the new geopolitics of college sports, and how an athletic conference can supply an identity, and a brand, for its members in the game of marketing. Until the late eighties, most colleges belonged to "bus leagues," conferences composed of regional rivals within geographic proximity. That changed by the early nineties when colleges began to view sports as a way to market the institution's "brand." Conference affiliation in this environment became crucial for cultivating donations, enrollment management, and corporate sponsorships. The simultaneous emergence of cable television stations looking for cheap programming found that college football and basketball filled this need perfectly. In 1984, the U.S. Supreme Court ruled against the NCAA in an antitrust case, effectively killing its monopoly on televising football games and giving conferences the power to negotiate their own television contracts. The result was a proliferation of bowl games that provided greater access to postseason play—and the money the bowl games generated. In the basketball arena, the NCAA expanded its tournament to sixty-four teams. The practice had been that each conference sent only one team to the tournament. Now stronger conferences could send a number of teams, increasing the revenues for those teams who progressed through the tournament.[17]

As the sports landscape changed, colleges and universities invested more and more capital in intercollegiate athletics to keep abreast of the competition. Schools frantically sought appropriate conference affiliations, along with the heightened visibility and increased revenue garnered from conference championships and television contracts. The "arms race" continued. The Big East mounted a football conference in 1991, alongside its established basketball conference. As the realignments went forward, the Atlantic Coast Conference, Big East, Big Ten, Big 12, SEC, and Pac 10 emerged as the elite conferences in college sports, and they controlled the terms of bowl bids and television appearances. The NCAA reorganized them into the Bowl Championship Series (BCS), which resulted in large cash awards and the crowning of a national champion. The other 261 Division 1 institutions and their conferences formed the Football Championship Subdivision, but they found no automatic path to a national championship open to them. Instead, they were forced to scramble for the lesser gold and glory unclaimed by the BCS teams.[18]

In an attempt to forestall what seemed at the time to be the imminent destruction of the Big East Conference in 2003, the remaining five presidents filed a lawsuit to prevent its breakup. WVU President David Har-desty, a corporate lawyer by training and experience, played a leading role in the defensive moves employed by the Big East. Early in the process he explained to the press why the situation was so dire for the University: "We have built up enrollment patterns around whom we play in the Big East. We have developed revenue streams based on participation in the Big East. From the Bowl Championship Series, from television, from seat sales, premium seating, donations, and so forth," he informed the press. All of these revenue streams would be diminished by a reconfiguration of the Big East. In addition, Hardesty asserted, "we've made commitments which were made in part on the understanding that the Big East was solid for a number of years. To one extent or another, all the Big East schools are in the same situation. . . . For us, though, it's millions of dollars a year."[19] One very significant aspect of the raid on the Big East that is not well documented was the behind-the-scenes effort to retain Big East membership in the Bowl Championship Series. President Hardesty was the Big East representative to the BCS, and, with the assistance of the conference commissioner and a consultant, he succeeded in convincing the BCS members to give the Big East an opportunity to prove that they belonged.[20]

Unfortunately, the presidents were perceived as fighting over intercollegiate athletics to the detriment of their institutions' reputations. According to Hardesty, the lawsuit was neither a nuisance nor a stall tactic as some claimed; it was "first and foremost a means of protecting our interests. It is a means of saying that we will be damaged and we intend to recover. It was not filed frivolously." The three institutions that were invited to join the Atlantic Coast Conference had months to prepare for the move while the remaining schools had little advance notice and very little time to respond. His major fear, however, was that "West Virginia University, my alma mater, is going to be hurt badly by all of this. That's guiding me."[21]

Mourning the demise of the Big East was premature. Working with the league's commissioner, Mike Tranghese, the five Big East presidents and athletic directors went to work on the only option available if the conference was to remain intact as a major presence. The new geopolitics of conference realignment forced the Big East to respond in kind by a raid of its own. In the fall of 2003, the Big East invited Conference USA members Cincinnati, Louisville, and South Florida to join in 2005. Because the Big East could offer access to an automatic BCS bowl bid for winning the league championship, which Conference USA lacked, the schools readily accepted. By adding three more football teams, the conference retained its Division I status. The additions also proved attractive enough to maintain the league's automatic berth in the Bowl Championship Series, which was vitally important because the bid was worth $12 million to $14 million annually to the Big East. In basketball, the conference grew into a powerhouse of sixteen teams, some of which had long been perennial national powers.[22]

Although the teams joining the Big East were not as prominent as the defecting teams, there was confidence that the three new teams would become nationally competitive within five years. Moreover, with the addition of South Florida, which was considered to have the best chance of making an impact in football, the league gained the Tampa and south Florida media market, as well as access to a large pool of potential players. In its new incarnation, the Big East covered a wide geographic expanse and major media markets from Chicago to Connecticut to Tampa, an area that represented 25 percent of the nation's population and 27 percent of the television market. With the three new members in football, and sixteen members for basketball, the Big East had regained stability. The penalties for leaving the league were strengthened, however, including a $5 million exit fee and a requirement for twenty-seven months' notice.[23]

FIVE NON-REVENUE SPORTS ELIMINATED

State-mandated budget cuts imposed by Senate Bill 547 applied to all departments, including athletics. What form that sacrifice would take in athletics was revealed in April 2003, when the athletic director announced the elimination of five non-revenue sports beginning with the 2003–2004 school year. Eliminating rifle, men's tennis, men's indoor track, and men's cross country would cut nearly $600,000 from the athletic department's annual budget of $24 million, and the fifty-six athletes who participated in those sports. The savings did not seem proportional to such drastic action, but it was taken as a hedge against future budget cuts and the anticipated substantial increases in tuition paid to the University for scholarships by the athletics department. That amount was calculated to increase by as much as $300,000 the next year and $2 million over the next five years. Reducing the number of teams to sixteen meant that those remaining would be financially stronger and, therefore, competitive.[24]

WVU faced a $22 million cut in state appropriations in 2003 in addition to an expected $6 million increase in expenses, and another reduction of $30 million in 2004. It was not possible to meet these legislative mandates, President Hardesty informed the press, without making some drastic changes. Hardesty backed the move to eliminate five sports, but emphasized that the decision was the athletic director's. Yet it seemed an unfortunate piece of timing to be diminishing the number of sports while granting hefty raises to football coaches, building a soccer stadium, and investing millions in luxury suites at the football stadium. But the athletics department was an auxiliary unit, like the University hospital and residence halls, which were required to operate on their own without drawing on the University's academic funds. Like other auxiliaries, those who used or supported them were also expected to pay for services provided. Hardesty refused to reconsider the University's 1990 decision to make the athletics department absorb the cost of tuition waivers for athletes because otherwise that amount would have to come from scholarships available elsewhere in the University. The spending on facilities should be regarded as investments in order to increase future revenue, the president said, and the University could not balance the budget by denying salary increases, or it would lose its personnel.[25]

As the Department of Intercollegiate Athletics explained the situation it faced in 2003, it was charged with developing a strategic plan to "ensure it remain self-supporting, reduce expenditures, build a cash reserve, invest in facilities and sports, continue to be competitive, and comply with Title IX requirements." Financial challenges of serious magnitude lay ahead: increases in the dollar value of athletic scholarships, the expense of required maintenance on facilities, increases in employee and student-athlete health insurance, and skyrocketing salaries for coaches. In addition to reducing costs, the strategic directive required that new revenue streams must be created, such as from increased ticket sales, providing suites at the stadium, premium seating at the Coliseum, and private donations. In order to generate more revenue and remain competitive, "athletics determined the best direction was to focus on fewer sports, reducing the number from 21 to 16."[26]

Although the main consideration in cutting the five sports was reducing costs, Title IX, which mandated gender equality, also played a role in the decision of where those cuts would be made. Without these sports the proportion of male to female scholarship athletes was reconfigured from 60 percent to about 51 percent men, or close to the fifty-fifty parity required by Title IX. Moreover, funding for women's sports increased as well, but still fell far short of spending on the revenue-producing men's sports. In addition to Title IX, other considerations that determined which sports to eliminate included the financial benefit, the impact on student athletes, and the competitiveness and viability of each sport regionally and

Chapter Eighteen

nationally. According to President Hardesty, NCAA Division I teams were required to compete in a minimum of sixteen sports, so they selected six major sports and some minor sports and cut the rest.[27]

Predictably, the editorial response was negative, describing the action as a "Wednesday afternoon massacre." Commentators worried that, if WVU was willing to cut non-revenue sports, art classes might not be far behind. The hometown paper opined that, "in a world where not even the rifle team is sacred, what's a class in sculpting or modern dance?"[28] Since fifty-four of the fifty-six athletes who participated in the five sports were male, many criticized the athletic department for cutting just to meet Title IX requirements. In an interview with the *Daily Athenaeum*, the associate athletic director admitted that "we got a lot of flak," but that Title IX was only one factor in the decision. Whatever decision was made, "we couldn't drop women's sports and worsen the University's position regarding Title IX mandates. Fans, student-athletes, and alumni protested in the Mountainlair Plaza the day after the announcement. Although none of the affected athletes lost their scholarships, they either switched to another sport or transferred to other schools so they could continue competing in their chosen sports. The passage of Title IX forced many schools around the country into difficult decisions in order to comply with its mandates, but, according to gymnastics coach Linda Burdette, the right thing to do was to raise enough money to fund Title IX.[29]

Eliminating rifle caused the greatest public consternation because the team had compiled an impressive record of thirteen national titles (more than any other institution) since the NCAA began competition in 1980. In fact, its 1999 third-place finish was the team's worst showing in the history of the sport at WVU. Although there is some uncertainty on the exact date the WVU rifle team entered its first competition, it dated back at least to 1951, nearly thirty years prior to the NCAA tournament, when the National Rifle Association (NRA) sponsored the college championships. By 1960 the team's national reputation was solidified when WVU Rifle won its first NRA title. With such a pedigree, it is little wonder that a hue and cry arose from around the state when the rifle team was eliminated. To justify its decision, the Department of Intercollegiate Athletics issued a summary sheet stating that the prognosis for rifle as an NCAA sport was not good, with the number of teams in decline and forty schools electing not to field teams since 1980. In fact, only forty members out of the 1,025 NCAA institutions sponsored the sport, and only fourteen in Division I. WVU Rifle became a club level sport at the University, while a major effort was launched by people outside the University to raise the money to support its continuation. By 2005, rifle had returned as an NCAA sport after the state legislature earmarked $100,000 annually to help cover the team's expenses. Subsequently, fundraising became a way of life for WVU Rifle.[30]

THE COACHING CAROUSEL

Just how much the world of intercollegiate athletics had changed is amplified in the coaching profession, particularly in the revenue sports of basketball and football. Nowhere is there greater evidence of the transformation than in the role of the coach. Beginning as a Spartan father figure who was compensated at a rate befitting a warrior's life of sacrifice, the coach has evolved to the role of star CEO of an athletic enterprise, the highest paid university employee, as befits his celebrity status.

The skyrocketing salaries commanded by successful head coaches in this new environment presented a serious challenge to WVU athletics. How could a cash-strapped institution like WVU compete at the highest level? The question forced itself on WVU administrators during President Hardesty's tenure, when in February 2002 Gale Catlett retired after twenty-four years as head coach of men's basketball. Catlett had earned $300,000 during his final year. Dan Dakish, the initial replacement for Catlett who was on campus only eight days, apparently was offered and declined a similar contract. Shortly thereafter, John Beilein accepted the position at a salary of $550,000 per year year, $150,000 of which was base state salary, and $400,000 from guaranteed promotional income for Mountaineer Athletic Club appearances, radio, television, Internet, and endorsements. He had the opportunity to earn an additional $175,000 a year in incentives and income from summer camps. Beilein was bound by a payback clause of $2.5 million should he leave without fulfilling the terms of his contract. In 2007,

Chapter Eighteen

after only one year into his five-year contract extension, Beilein did indeed depart for the University of Michigan. He was immediately replaced by Bob Huggins, one of the most prominent college coaches in the nation. After his initial salary of $800,000 plus incentives, his contract was rewritten the following year to extend the mutual commitment for eleven years to age sixty-five (he was then fifty-four). Huggins was now to be paid $1.5 million annually ($250,000 in state salary, the remainder from private sources, such as the Mountaineer Athletic Club, and the Mountaineer Sports Network) plus performance incentives. Huggins's buyout for early departure was $4 million.[31]

Nehlen retired as head football coach in 2000, having served the University for twenty-one years. He elevated the program to a new level, even playing for the national championship in 1989. At the end of this remarkable career, Nehlen's salary of about $300,000 had been compressed by a lack of pay raises that reduced his salary well below his true market value. WVU was not only forced to pay a current-market salary to his successor, Rich Rodriguez; it also was forced to pay a premium for the new head coach's celebrity factor. Rodriguez's initial 2000 contract paid him $402,600 plus $100,000 in incentives. At the end of the 2002 season, he was awarded a new seven-year contract, to begin in 2003, worth $700,000 per year, with additional money from incentives, such as a Big East championship, postseason bowl games, revenue from summer camps, and increased season ticket sales. In 2006, Rodriguez renegotiated a modified contract that included a new salary reportedly in the neighborhood of $1.5 million, including incentives. Increasing through the life of the contract ending in 2013, the package was worth a total of $13.6 million dollars. In August 2007, a second contract extension to 2014 increased the figure again to an average salary of $1.9 million, although it was still not sufficient enticement to keep the coach in Morgantown. Four months later, Rodriguez announced that he had been hired as the head coach at the University of Michigan.[32]

Bill Stewart replaced Rodriguez, signing a six-year contract from September 2008 to January 2014, providing him with a salary of $800,000, plus $200,000 in incentives. When Stewart was given a modified contract marking the beginning of the process to replace him, an editorial writer observed that "college football is a big-money business, and Bill Stewart didn't generate enough profit. That partly explains why the popular, winning, head coach is being bounced at West Virginia University."[33]

Sticker shock for WVU football was only beginning. Stewart's package seemed like merely a respite before a resumption of the climb to new heights. Dana Holgorsen was hired in the spring of 2011 as offensive coordinator with a salary of $750,000, twice that of his predecessor. Although he had never held a head coaching position, his annual salary was set at $1.4 million when he replaced Bill Stewart a year sooner than expected. That figure would rise for each of the next four years until it reached $2.4 million in 2016. Holgorsen could also earn up to $600,000 in incentives for each year of his contract as head coach, with the potential to earn $3 million in the final year of his contract.[34]

Former athletic director Ed Pastilong, not to mention former coaches Don Nehlen and Gale Catlett, must have had plenty of occasions to wonder about the wisdom of remaining at their posts rather than selling their services in the marketplace. The salary compression experienced by WVU faculty and administrators was also apparent in the athletic director's office. When Pastilong retired in 2010, his base salary was $225,000, and with incentives his take home pay that year was $280,181. He was replaced by Oliver Luck, whose previous career was on the business side of professional sports; he had never held such a position before. Luck's five-year contract contained a base salary of $390,000 and the potential to earn up to an additional $130,000 in incentives, which was guaranteed to be 75 percent of what WVU coaches earned in their incentive clauses. He also received a retention incentive of $25,000 for each year he remained at WVU as athletic director, as well as other perks, including two courtesy automobiles.[35] During the two decades of the seventies and eighties, when big-time college sports was changing from a Spartan culture to a celebrity culture, WVU benefitted from stability in its head coaching and athletic director positions. When the University was forced into the marketplace, however, the sticker price was all the more jarring.

NINETEEN

PLAYING ON THE NATIONAL STAGE: CORPORATISM COMES TO INTERCOLLEGIATE ATHLETICS

MEN'S BASKETBALL: THE GALE CATLETT ERA

HEAD BASKETBALL COACH Gale Catlett was a coach for all seasons. He took the post in 1979 and retired in 2002 after twenty-four years at the helm. He set the standard that the University came to regard as the norm, a winning coach whose team competed at a high level, who ran a clean program, and who was respected as a man of character. Quality and stability became the standards forged by Catlett during his long tenure. He was a West Virginia native who came to WVU as a freshman in 1958, and lettered for three seasons (1961–1963). Catlett participated in one of the greatest eras of WVU basketball. During his three varsity seasons, the basketball team won seventy of eighty-eight games. Between 1957 and 1961, WVU teams ranked in the national top twenty for sixty-one straight weeks, and from 1951 to 1961 they had a 78 percent winning percentage, second only to the University of Kentucky. Legends Willie Akers and Rod Thorn were among Catlett's teammates.[1]

Immediately following graduation in 1963, Catlett began a string of assistant coaching jobs at the University of Richmond, Davidson College, the University of Kansas, and the University of Kentucky. At this point, Gale Catlett had worked under some of the best coaches in America, including Lefty Driesell, Ted Owens, and the legendary Adoph Rupp at Kentucky. This kind of experience prepared him to become head coach at the University of Cincinnati in 1972 at the age of thirty-one. Catlett's Bearcats made three NCAA tournament appearances during his six years at Cincinnati and in 1976 ranked as high as second in the nation. In 1979, Catlett had nearly universal support when he replaced Joedy Gardner as head coach of the Mountaineers. At the time of his hiring, WVU had not been invited to the NCAA tournament in eleven years and had just concluded a losing season in 1978. Catlett rebuilt the program swiftly, and by 1982 the Mountaineers were in the national ratings for the first time since 1962, ranking as high as sixth. Over the next twenty-four seasons, WVU played in sixteen postseason national tournaments, made eight appearances at the National Invitational Tournament, and went to the NCAA tournament eight times. Catlett compiled a winning percentage of .638 for his career, and .614 (439–278) at his alma mater.[2]

There were many moments that endeared Catlett to loyal Mountaineers. In 1983, WVU defeated the first-ranked University of Nevada-Las Vegas at the Coliseum, which was establishing a reputation as a very difficult venue for opposing teams. Public support for his teams was broad and deep, and in the 1982 game against Pitt a single-game attendance record was broken with a packed house of 16,704. That same year, the Coliseum's average attendance for basketball games was 11,384 fans.[3]

Perhaps the most memorable year of the Catlett era was the exciting 1997–1998 season, when he became the all-time leader in the number of victories among WVU basketball coaches, and the forty-fifth Division I coach to reach five hundred wins. In the NCAA tournament, WVU defeated Temple in the first round and then met the Cincinnati Bearcats, led by WVU alumnus Bob Huggins in the second round. In the closing seconds of the game Cincinnati held a two-point edge. With only seven seconds on the clock, guard Jerrod West raced down the court and launched a desperate three-point shot that found the net and gave the Mountaineers a 75–74 victory. "The shot," as it came to be called, advanced WVU to the Sweet Sixteen round in Anaheim, California, for the first time since 1959, when the team was led by another West, named Jerry. The team's good fortune did not follow the Mountaineers in the Sweet Sixteen game, as a last-second three-point shot by Jerrod West to tie the game did not fall in the basket and the team lost to the University of Utah by a 65–62 score. Although the Mountaineers lost, the entire state beamed with pride in their play.[4]

It was Utah that went on to the Final Four that year, but fresh off his sensational season Gale Catlett banished any thoughts he might have had about retiring. Even though he was only 57, he had thirty-five years of coaching under his belt. With the outpouring of support from fans and the administration, Catlett decided to return the following season and stayed on for another four years. They were disappointing years, however, and the team posted only one winning season. On February 14, 2002, following a loss to Virginia Tech and with five games remaining in the regular season, Gale Catlett resigned. Although he had compiled 439 victories, more than any other coach in the history of WVU basketball, it was "becoming unbearable to digest the difficult losses," which were "weighing heavily on him," Athletic Director Ed Pastilong recalled.[5]

Upon retirement it became clear just how much influence Catlett had over his players. They came out by the scores to praise Catlett for shaping them as men of substance and character. Former player Vic Herbert noted that Catlett "talked as much or more about life than he did about basketball." He was an ethical man who cared about his players as people, said President Hardesty, who declared Catlett's retirement to be the "end of an era at West Virginia University."[6]

More than two decades had elapsed since WVU had needed to hire a new basketball coach, and the marketplace was far different. The first foray into this new landscape led Athletic Director Pastilong to University of Cincinnati coach Bob Huggins, but negotiations with the WVU alumnus were unsuccessful. Although these negotiations were never made public, it was believed that "sticker shock" got in the way. In other words, WVU was not yet prepared to meet the salary expectations of a high-profile coach. Following the exit of eight-day coach Dan Dakich, WVU appeared to have clumsily botched both efforts, seemingly confirming the suspicion held by many that WVU was too poor to play in the new arena of big-time athletics.[7]

WVU appeared much more agile in landing the next coach, John Beilein, just six days after Dakich resigned. Beilein was a twenty-four-year veteran who ranked in the top thirty in victories among active Division I head coaches. At forty-nine, he had compiled a record of 447 wins against

257 losses (a .635 percentage) and had posted winning seasons in all but two years as a head coach. He graduated from Wheeling Jesuit College in 1975, where he played basketball, and then embarked upon a coaching career. Prior to moving to Morgantown, Beilein was head coach at the University of Richmond from 1997 to 2002 and was the only current college coach to record twenty-win seasons at all four levels of college competition: junior college, the National Association of Intercollegiate Athletics, NCAA Division II, and NCAA Division I.[8]

MEN'S BASKETBALL: THE JOHN BEILEIN YEARS

Beilein developed his own version of the Princeton offense that incorporated the three-point shot because it gave smaller teams a major weapon, and he embraced the little-understood 1-3-1 defense. Both became hallmarks of John Beilein teams. His first few seasons at WVU were up and down, with flashes of brilliance that kept fan hopes alive and earned the team an invitation to the 2004 National Invitation Tournament. In his second season, the Mountaineers attained ranking for the first time in seven years and played their way into the Big East tournament championship, where they fell to Syracuse. By then the media had embraced WVU as the Cinderella team of the 2006 NCAA tournament. To astonished Mountaineer fans everywhere, the team became "media darlings" behind the play of an unheralded group of players who, like their coach, had previously received little national attention. Kevin Pittsnogle, a unique 6' 10" center with an accurate three-point shot, became something of a sports celebrity, and the media turned his name into a verb. "You've just been Pittsnogled" signified that a player had just been scored on by a Pittsnogle three-point jump shot. When the Mountaineers defeated fifth-ranked Wake Forest in a tough double-overtime battle to move into the Sweet Sixteen, obscurity was left behind. Defeating Texas Tech, coached by Bob Knight, the Mountaineers moved on to the Elite Eight, achieving the deepest run into the NCAA tournament since the 1959 team led by Jerry West.[9]

Unfortunately, the fairy-tale season came to an end in a loss to the Louisville Cardinals on a missed shot at the buzzer. The team's spirits were lifted, however, when the buses pulled into the Coliseum parking lot, where they were greeted by some six thousand fans. The 2006–2007 Mountaineers began the following season nationally ranked, and for the second consecutive year they advanced to the Sweet Sixteen. The University of Texas Longhorns were ranked ninth nationally, but the Mountaineers battled them down to the wire, only to lose the nail-biter by a score of 76–75 on a Longhorn three-point shot at the final buzzer.[10]

John Beilein's spectacular career at WVU was not over. Even after losing four of his five starters from the 2006–2007 team, Beilein's cagers produced another miracle season for Mountaineer fans. However, the Mountaineers lost some critical games and were denied another NCAA bid. Instead, they were invited to the National Invitation Tournament and were determined to prove that they belonged in the "big dance." They made quick work of several teams before advancing to the championship game. In a 78–73 win over the Clemson Tigers, the Mountaineers became the 2007 tournament champions, the first WVU team to bring home the trophy since Dyke Raese's team accomplished that feat back in 1942.[11]

The euphoria among WVU supporters over another history-making season was brief. Three days after the victory over Clemson, John Beilein announced that he would be turning in his Mountaineer gear to coach the University of Michigan Wolverines. With his resignation, five years still remained on his renegotiated 2005 contract, which also contained a $2.5 million buyout clause. He eventually settled with the University and agreed to pay $1.5 million in five yearly installments.[12] Beilein had not only been a successful competitor who returned WVU basketball to national prominence; he was also an honorable person who met the standards University leaders expected from their head coaches. There was a deep sense of disappointment, even abandonment, therefore, with the Beilein's departure.

MEN'S BASKETBALL: THE BOB HUGGINS ERA BEGINS

Learning from the two false starts before John Beilein's hiring, WVU was better prepared this time around to enter the hunt for a new coach. But two days after Beilein's resignation, Athletic Director Ed Pastilong announced that Beilein's replacement would be none other than Bob Huggins. Attempts to lure him back when Catlett retired had failed, and many surmised that the quick hiring had been informally negotiated long before Beilein's resignation. Huggins's acceptance was heralded as a "coming home" event. Huggins was born in Morgantown to parents who had grown up in the town, but his father, Charlie Huggins, moved to Ohio to coach basketball when Bob was nine years old. Bob starred as a player for his father at Indian Valley South High School in Midvale, Ohio, and was highly sought after by college recruiters. He chose Ohio University (over Ohio State) but was dissatisfied with his choice and decided to transfer to WVU. (All four of his grandparents still lived in Morgantown.) After sitting out his first year as a transfer, Huggins was a starter for coach Joedy Gardner. He became a graduate assistant at WVU in 1978, and two years later joined Eldon Miller's staff at Ohio State, which led to his first head-coaching post in 1980 at Walsh College in Canton, Ohio. Four years later he was appointed head coach at the University of Akron, and in 1989 he became head coach at the University of Cincinnati. There he remained for the next sixteen years, compiling a spectacular record of 399–127. Along the way, he led his teams to ten regular-season conference titles and eight tournament championships. In 1992, the Bearcats reached the NCAA Final Four. Having been named Conference USA Coach of the Year three times, he was unanimously chosen as the conference's Coach of the Decade. Huggins left Cincinnati after the 2004 season and, after a one year hiatus, became head coach at Kansas State, where he won twenty-three games in 2006–2007. The following year brought him to WVU. By that time he had compiled a career record of 590–211 in twenty-five years as a head coach, and he was ranked sixth in total victories and eighth in winning percentage among active Division 1 head coaches. Thirteen of his players had become NBA draft picks. According to one knowledgeable observer, "never before had West Virginia University managed to hire a basketball coach with a national pedigree quite like that of Bob Huggins." No less an authority than Jerry West declared that "there are good coaches and there are great coaches. Bob is one of the greats."[13]

Huggins inherited a team that had been recruited specifically for John Beilein's system, and Huggins wisely adapted to his players' strengths. In

December 2007, on the road at Canisius College, Huggins won his six hundredth career victory to little fanfare. The Mountaineers' winning season against strong opponents earned them a bid for the 2008 NCAA tournament, where they defeated the University of Arizona and perennial power Duke to advance to the Sweet Sixteen for the third time in four years but then lost in an upset to Xavier University. Huggins became the first coach to lead the Mountaineers to the Sweet Sixteen round in his first year. The team ended the season in the national rankings, and junior forward Joe Alexander, who emerged as an impact player under Huggins, was taken as the eighth overall pick of the 2008 NBA draft by the Milwaukee Bucks, becoming the University's first player chosen in the first round since Ron Williams in 1968. Just after the end of the season Coach Bob Huggins signed a new contract that extended his WVU commitment to his sixty-fifth birthday.[14]

Even though the Mountaineers suffered a disappointing upset in the 2008 NCAA tournament, greater things were in store for the following year. The 'Eers began the season nationally ranked in the top ten, and one popular ESPN analyst predicted that WVU would be a Final Four team in March 2010. Bob Huggins did his best to prepare his team to meet the expectations by organizing the most difficult non-conference schedule in WVU history. During halftime of the Ohio State game in the Coliseum, January 23, 2010, Hot Rod Hundley's jersey number 33 joined Jerry West's number 44 as the only two Mountaineer numbers ever retired.[15]

What was developing into a sensational season was marred, however, by fan behavior during the Pitt game on February 3 at the Coliseum. The night did not begin well, as students chanted profane slogans during the playing of the national anthem. Following a call by an official, fans registered their disapproval by throwing items onto the court from the student section. Huggins took to the floor with a microphone to berate this kind of behavior, calling it "stupid." Later, someone from a general admission section threw a coin that struck a Pitt assistant coach on the face near his eye. An official statement was released by the University declaring that it was "appalled and embarrassed by the fan behavior" during the game, but the damage had been done, as the unruly episode was featured in the national media, including ESPN's popular television show Sports Center.[16]

A more positive public image resulted when the Mountaineers won the 2010 Big East tournament in Madison Square Garden by pulling out a narrow 60–58 victory against Georgetown on a shot from Da'Sean Butler with four seconds left on the clock. For the sixth time that season, the Mountaineers won because of the last-second heroics of Butler, and he was named the tournament's Most Valuable Player. He also joined the legendary Jerry West and Hot Rod Hundley as one of only three players in WVU history to score more than two thousand career points. The faithful might be forgiven if they believed that another Golden Era of WVU basketball had begun with this team's winning the first Big East championship in school history. All of the starters hailed from the New York metro area, so defeating five Big East powers in Madison Square Garden and claiming the championship trophy with John Denver's rendition of "Country Roads" blaring from the Garden's public address system all seemed a bit surreal to them.[17] Winning the championship of the toughest league in the nation was a major event in the school's history, and the entire Mountaineer nation drew pride from the accomplishment. The student paper, the *Daily Athenaeum*, spoke for the many West Virginians who had long hungered for respect when it declared that winning the Big East championship "proved to the basketball world that this program is one of the nation's best. What John Beilein started, Bob Huggins has taken to an entirely different level. Recruits are taking notice. With that has come respect and notoriety like rarely before. Not since the days of Jerry West has this program experienced such success and national recognition."[18]

The Big East championship ensured a high seed in the 2010 NCAA tournament. With victories in the first two rounds, the Mountaineers once again advanced to the Sweet Sixteen and then on to the Elite Eight for a regional showdown with the Kentucky Wildcats. Kentucky was ranked first in the country and was an intimidating, talent-laden team. In fact, the first six men on this team were first-round picks in the 2010 NBA draft. WVU had beaten Kentucky only once before in school history. It was all the more remarkable, therefore, when WVU stunned the Wildcats 73–66 behind brilliant three-point shooting and a ferocious defense. During the postgame ceremony, Huggins thanked West Virginians. "I talked to these guys about being special—two more [wins] and we're going to be really special," the coach declared.[19]

In the Final Four game in Indianapolis, however, WVU cagers confronted another basketball power in Duke University and were overpowered. Any hope for a comeback in the second half was crushed when Da'Sean Butler collided with Duke's seven-foot center and lay on the floor writhing in pain for several minutes. The tragedy produced one of those indelible moments when Huggins knelt on the floor and held the injured Butler in his arms, trying to console him.[20]

Aside from losing the game and the injury to Butler, the season was a memorable one, marked by a number of "firsts." The Mountaineers finished in the top ten for the first time in almost fifty years, won a school-record thirty-one games, and captured their very first Big East championship. Butler also became part of WVU basketball history: he was chosen first-team All-American by John Wooden and *Basketball Times*, and second-team All-American by the Associated Press; he received the Lowe's Senior CLASS Award, presented at the Final Four to the most outstanding senior student-athlete in NCAA Division I men's basketball. Without the injured knee, Da'Sean Butler would almost certainly have been a first-round selection in the NBA draft; nevertheless, he was chosen in the second round by the Miami Heat. Teammate Devin Ebanks, who opted for the draft at the end of his sophomore year, was also selected in the second round by the Los Angeles Lakers.[21]

WVU did not neglect the marketing opportunity that was presented by all of the national attention and recognition. A multimedia campaign promoting WVU was launched using mobile, Internet, and television. Because of the high national rankings enjoyed by the team, University public relations staff prepared a thirty-second video promoting WVU that was presented on the CBS Spectacular board in Times Square and Macy's Vision Big East board at the corner of 34th Street and 7th Avenue, New York.[22] The promotional impact of performing and especially winning, in nationally televised tournaments provided the kind of exposure for the University that it simply could not buy. Since WVU's finances were now driven by student tuition, and since increasing the student body was essential to its financial health, the 22 percent increase in visits to the WVU admissions' homepage and the 18 percent increase in visits to the WVU homepage during and after these high-profile events were hopeful signs for healthy future enrollments and private giving. Across the United States and in foreign countries, alumni were proud to be watching representatives of their alma mater on network television. Once considered for the role of "David," they were now described as a "Goliath." One website chirped: "WVU has turned the corner . . . the Mountaineers are a top dog." WVU President James P. Clements agreed, observing: "The national attention of the NCAA Final Four appearance has been unbelievable in terms of building relationships [with supporters] of our University."[23]

WOMEN'S BASKETBALL: SUCCESS UNDER MIKE CAREY

The women's basketball team has undergone major changes as well since Kitty Blakemore organized the first team in 1973 and served as head coach until her retirement in 1992. Assistant Coach Scott Harrelson took over for Blakemore but resigned in 1995. Susan Walvius was then hired and had begun to develop a respectable program in her second year, when she was lured away by a more lucrative salary with the University of South Carolina. Former WVU player and Assistant Coach Alexis Basil replaced her, but in four years as head coach she failed to post a winning season. In 2001, Basil resigned, and WVU hired Mike Carey, who brought immediate improvement to the struggling program.[24]

A Clarksburg native and graduate of Liberty High, Mike Carey excelled in basketball at Salem College, where he scored more than two thousand points in his collegiate career. Girls' high school basketball was a fall sport in those days, and Carey coached the Flemington High School girls' team between 1976 and 1983, and then at Liberty High from 1983 to 1987. In 1987 he became an assistant coach at Salem College and was promoted to head coach in 1989. Carey's accolades at Salem included NCAA East Region Coach of the Year in 1997 and 1999. His teams won twenty games in each of the six seasons prior to his arrival at WVU. He led the Tigers to four straight NCAA Division II Regional Tournaments, advanced to the Division II Final Four in 1997, the Elite Eight in 1999, and the Sweet Sixteen round six times. His record of 288–102 included five West Virginia Conference regular-season titles and three league tournament championships.[25]

Under Carey's direction, the women Mountaineers advanced to the 2004 Big East semifinals, their best performance in the history of the program. The women, led by Kate Bulger, a WNBA draft pick, received a bid for the NCAA tournament and concluded their season with a 21–11 record. Carey was voted Big East Coach of the Year. Over the next several years, Carey's teams became a formidable presence in the Big East. The 2009–2010 campaign was a record-breaker. For the second time in school history, they finished their home season undefeated at 17–0, and their twenty-nine wins was the best-ever. During the season the Mountaineers climbed as high as seventh in the national rankings, but unfortunately fell in the second round of the NCAA tournament. Honors accumulated for the players, culminating when Liz Repella was named to the all-Big East first team and to the *ESPN The Magazine* first team for Academic All-American Women's Basketball Division I. Mike Carey recorded his 450th career win during the season and was named 2009–2010 Big East Conference Co-Coach of the Year.[26] Women's basketball has not been an intercollegiate sport long enough to achieve the storied past of the men's basketball program, but Carey's career and his teams' accomplishments encourage the higher expectations for the future that come with being a nationally recognized program.

FOOTBALL: THE DON NEHLEN ERA

Only three times since WVU first fielded a football team in 1891 has "Golden Era" been used to characterize the program. The first came in 1921–1924 under Clarence Spears, who led the team to a 30–6–3 record, including a 10–0 undefeated season in 1922. The second "Golden Era" arrived in the fifties, when Art "Pappy" Lewis led the Mountaineers to a 58–38–2 record over a ten-year stretch, earning him the distinction of winning more games than any previous football coach. Lewis's team defeated Penn State in three consecutive encounters, a first for the program, and played Georgia Tech in the 1953 Sugar Bowl, its first major postseason bowl. Lewis set another record by serving ten years as head coach; the average for head coaches prior to Lewis was 2.4 years. The third "Golden Era" of WVU football bracketed the two decades from 1980 to 2000 under the leadership of Don Nehlen.[27]

College football in the United States changed profoundly during Nehlen's tenure, and so did football at WVU. The editor of WVU *Alumni Magazine*, Tony Cook, characterized it this way: "In a very real sense, Coach Nehlen is a father to West Virginia University football. You might say that, before he arrived in Morgantown, WVU football had enjoyed a long adolescence. Under Nehlen's steady hand it grew strong and entered the world mature and confident."[28] When Nehlen signed on as head coach in December 1979, the football program had suffered through four straight losing seasons. The new coach reversed that trend immediately.

Nehlen was a graduate of Bowling Green State University who went on to become a successful coach at Canton (Ohio) South High School, before returning to Bowling Green as head coach. At the end of the 1976 season, Nehlen resigned to take an assistant coaching position under Bo Schembechler at the University of Michigan. When WVU released Frank Cignetti, Nehlen was chosen to replace him. Schembechler provided WVU officials with a glowing recommendation for Nehlen as both a person and a coach, but he told his protégé that he did not consider the WVU job as a real opportunity. Referring to the schedule, which included teams like Oklahoma, Pitt, and Penn State, Nehlen recalled Schembechler's words: "You've got about four, five or six losses on here right away. Every coach that's ever coached there, if they win they leave, and if they lose they get fired. You're making good money; we go to the Rose Bowl every year. In two or three years I'll get you a good job." Fortunately, Nehlen did not take his advice, although he did recognize the challenges. Before the interstate system was built, WVU was more isolated and less accessible, making it difficult to recruit players from beyond the state or the border areas of nearby states. The completion of I-79 running north-south and later I-68, running east-west and intersecting at Morgantown facilitated travel to and from the

Chapter Nineteen

city. With a new stadium also slated to open in the near future, Nehlen envisioned an opportunity to build a major program and signed on as the Mountaineers' thirtieth head football coach on December 7, 1979.[29]

Reconstructing the Mountaineer football program began immediately. In Nehlen's first season, 1980, his team broke even with a record of 6–6, a great relief for fans. In the following season the Mountaineers compiled an 8–3 record, accepted a bid to play Florida in the Peach Bowl, and surprised everybody by defeating the University of Florida 26–6. The Peach Bowl win caught the attention of several athletic directors who were searching for head coaches, including South Carolina's athletic director, who offered him the job. Nehlen was inclined to accept the offer but, by his own recollection, two things changed his mind. The first was that South Carolina's president insisted that he come immediately and became more insistent when Nehlen said he could not leave without talking to his team (he did not want them to read about it in the newspaper). Also, Nehlen recalled, Governor Jay Rockefeller asked him to stay and help to build a national program. Echoing Shembechler's words, Rockefeller said that in the past coaches had quit for better jobs after compiling some wins, and if they didn't win enough they had been relieved of their duties. "If you leave West Virginia now, I don't think we'll ever be able to build a program," Rockefeller said.[30] Nehlen decided to remain at WVU, and Mountaineer football changed forever.

Nehlen's success with the football program was measured not only by winning percentage but by other qualitative factors as well. Certainly, memorable games against powerful opponents were measuring rods along the way. Nehlen's third season as head coach, 1982, began with a remarkable statement victory over ninth-ranked Oklahoma in Norman, by a score of 41–27. Quarterback Jeff Hostetler, a transfer from Penn State, passed for more than three hundred yards and four touchdowns,and was named Offensive Player of the Week by *Sports Illustrated*. The amazing coming out of "Hoss," as he was nicknamed, inspired a song, "Ole Hoss: The Ballad of West Virginia's Jeff Hostetler." The Mountaineers accepted a bid to the Gator Bowl and closed the season ranked in the top twenty. The following year, 1983, thrilled fans watched as the Mountaineers defeat Pitt, ending a drought of seven straight losses to their arch-rivals. Another long losing streak, this one stretching back to the early fifties, was snapped the following week when WVU upset Penn State at Mountaineer Field. When the final gun sounded, the fans poured onto the field, and down came the goalposts. The season ended with the Mountaineers defeating Texas Christian University in the Sunbonnet Bowl.[31]

The Mountaineers slumped the following three seasons, 1985–1987, but in that third season freshman quarterback Major Harris donned the Gold and Blue, bound for glory and the WVU record books. Indeed, the young quarterback from Pittsburgh took the Mountaineers to heights never visited before. By the fall of 1988 he was ready to show the nation how exciting college football could be. Harris outgained the entire Penn State team, 301 yards to 292, as he led the Mountaineers to a 51–30 victory. WVU won the first-ever Lambert Trophy that year as the best team in the east, "the Beast of the East," setting up the third-ranked Mountaineers to play first-ranked Notre Dame in the 1989 Sunkist Fiesta Bowl for the national championship. Both teams were undefeated. Don Nehlen recollected that Michigan "Coach Bo Schembechler called, and he said, 'Hey boy, what are you doing down there? How in the world did you get in the national championship game? You're not cheating there, are you?'" Nehlen replied, 'Bo, they don't pay me anything, let alone pay the players.'"[32] Nineteen years later, in WVU's first return to the Fiesta Bowl since 1989, defensive coach Bill Kirelawich remembered that earlier trip as if it were yesterday. On the third play of the game Major Harris took a hard hit and suffered a shoulder separation. He tried to play through it, but it affected his ability to run and pass the ball. Because WVU's offensive game plan was built around Harris, the Mountaineers were unable to recover. "There's no doubt in my mind. If Maj doesn't get hurt we beat Notre Dame that day," Kirelawich declared.[33]

Major Harris was a two-time Heisman Trophy finalist, in 1989 and again in 1990. The Mountaineers defeated Clemson in the Gator Bowl, and many of the players were graduating. Harris decided that he had accomplished all he could at the college level, and chose to enter the 1990 NFL draft and forego his senior season. Reggie Rembert, Renaldo Turnbull, and Mike Fox were all drafted in the first two rounds. Harris was picked up by the Oakland Raiders but never given the opportunity to play in the NFL. Recognition of his special talents came much later when, in 2010, he was inducted into the College Football Hall of Fame.[34]

Don Nehlen and Major Harris established the Mountaineers as national competitors and proved that they belonged there. Not only could they climb the ladder, but they could stay on top. By 1993 WVU was back in the race for the national championship with a record of 11–0, its second-ever undefeated season. Ranked second in the coaches' poll and third in the AP poll, WVU fans expressed outrage when the 'Eers were not selected to play for the national championship. Instead, WVU accepted a bid to play the Florida Gators in the Sugar Bowl, where the Mountaineers suffered an embarrassing 41–7 loss.[35]

The last several seasons of the Don Nehlen era, 1994–2000, presented unrealistically high fan expectations, when even winning seasons and post-season bowl bids were regarded as disappointments. The 1998 team was probably Nehlen's most talent-laden team, led by Marc Bulger, Amos Zereoue, Anthony Becht, Gary Stills, Barrett Green, John Thornton, and Jerry Porter, all of whom played in the NFL and several of whom attained All-Pro status. The WVU marching band added sparkle to some otherwise disappointing seasons. Known as "The Pride of West Virginia," it had grown from eighty-eight members in 1971 to well more than three hundred in 1997, when the band was selected to receive the John Philip Sousa Foundation's Sudler Trophy as the outstanding collegiate marching band in the nation.[36]

Nehlen led the Mountaineers to a 7–5 record in his final season, culminating in a 49–38 victory over the University of Mississippi in the December 2000 Music City Bowl, breaking an eight-bowl-game losing streak. Before the bowl game, he had announced that it would be his last. As the clock ran out, WVU fans in the stands began chanting, "Nehlen, Nehlen." One hometown sportswriter noted that "the world will look at him [Nehlen] as a coach who was 149–93–4 at WVU, 202–128–8 for a 30-year head coaching career. But he will mean more. Much more because he was a coach who cared more about his players than even about winning and losing."[37]

Nehlen's record at WVU underscores the claim espoused by many that he took the football program to national prominence. His 202 career wins ranked him at the time as one of only seventeen college football coaches ever to break the 200-game threshold in Division I. Seventy-eight of his players became professionals, and fifteen were selected as first-team all Americans. He was chosen National Coach of the Year in 1988 and Big East Coach of the Year in 1993. Most notably, his peers elected him president of the American Football Coaches Association in 1997. Sportswriters called Mountaineer Field "the house that Nehlen built." The new indoor football practice facility, the facilities building with its weight room, and the $2 million video scoreboard were built during his tenure. WVU President David Hardesty summed up the veteran coach's legacy: He had "forever changed the way people look at West Virginia University" by focusing "the spotlight on us through his leadership of the American Football Coaches Association and other national positions."[38] Nehlen further endeared himself to West Virginians by choosing to remain in the state after his retirement. He had not been kidding after all; he actually had turned down other job offers over the years because he liked his job at WVU. Measured against the Nehlen standard, the behavior of the next coach would produce as much outrage about his departure as there was excitement in his arrival.

FOOTBALL: THE RICH RODRIGUEZ SAGA

WVU officially announced on November 26, 2000, that Rich Rodriguez would become the next head football coach at WVU. A native of Grant Town in Marion County, West Virginia, Rodriguez was a star athlete in high school who went on to letter three times as a defensive back at WVU from 1982–1984. After two seasons as a student assistant, he earned a master's degree and began his college coaching career at West Virginia's Salem College. A promotion to head coach of the Salem College squad made him, at twenty-four, the youngest head coach in college football. When Salem dropped its football program, Rodriguez returned to WVU to work on Nehlen's staff. Soon another opportunity arose, this time at Glenville State College where he served as head coach from 1990–1996. During his tenure Glenville won four West Virginia Intercollegiate Athletic Conference championships and played in the 1993 National Association of Intercollegiate Athletics (NAIA) national championship game. Rodriguez was named NAIA National Coach of the Year for 1993. Still moving onward and upward, he became Tommy Bowden's offensive coordinator at Tulane in 1998, and then followed Bowden to Clemson the next year when he became head coach.[39]

"What a first-class story this is!" chirped Rodriguez's hometown paper when news of his hiring by WVU became known. Here was a young man from Marion County who led his North Marion High School football team to the state championship in 1980, had excelled at his home-state university, and was now a successful coach in the major college ranks. At only thirty-seven, Rodriguez was now returning home to become the head coach at his alma mater. Accompanying him was his wife, Rita Setliff Rodriguez, a native of Jane Lew in Lewis County and a 1986 WVU graduate. This was "the most popular choice ever made by the university in selecting a head coach," a newspaper editor noted. "He's been the people's choice for several years."[40]

Rodriguez promised major changes in the program, even though his first season ended with a disappointing 3–8 record. But the Mountaineers surprised everybody the following year by hard-nosed victories over some quality teams to finish the regular season with a 9–3 record and a bid to play in the Continental Tire Bowl. At the end of his second season, Rodriguez had his team ranked twenty-fifth, the highest ranking in nine years.[41]

At the end of the 2002 season, Rodriguez's original contract was discarded and a new one negotiated. Prompted by the 9–3 record, a bowl-game bid, and contacts from other universities interested in hiring a new football coach, the new contract contained a substantial increase in salary and incentives. Chaos reigned in 2003 when the Atlantic Coast Conference raided the Big East of three of its strongest teams. In the midst of the upheaval, the Mountaineers closed the season with an 8–4 record and a share of the Big East championship but suffered an embarrassing loss to Maryland in the Gator Bowl. The 2004 season followed a similar pattern, with an 8–4 finish, the Big East championship, and another Gator Bowl loss, this time to seventeenth-ranked Florida State.[42]

The Big East Conference once again became an eight-team conference in 2005 with the addition of Cincinnati, South Florida, and Louisville to replace the three purloined by the Atlantic Coast Conference. That year was also noteworthy for the emergence of four very talented players who would reshape Mountaineer football: defensive back Darius Reynaud and offensive stars Steve Slaton, Owen Schmitt, and Pat White. Quarterback Pat White was unquestionably the key to making this squad one of the most impressive in Mountaineer football history. The breakout game for the offensive three came against nineteenth-ranked Louisville. White led a fourth-quarter comeback from a 24–7 deficit to tie the game, and the Mountaineers then outlasted the Cardinals through three overtimes. Freshman Steve Slaton rushed for six touchdowns. WVU went on to finish with only the third eleven-win season in school history and the Big East championship.[43]

Following its powerful 2005 performance, the eleventh-ranked Mountaineers were invited to their first-ever BCS bowl to meet the eighth-ranked Georgia Bulldogs in the Nokia Sugar Bowl on January 2, 2006. It was a contest between the champions of the Big East Conference and the Southeastern Conference, and most fans and sportswriters expected WVU to struggle against the more powerful Southeastern Conference foe. Hurricane Katrina had decimated the city of New Orleans, home to the Sugar Bowl, necessitating a move to the alternative site in Atlanta's Georgia Dome, essentially granting home-field advantage to the Bulldogs. Fans in the dome and those watching on national television were shocked to see the Mountaineers jump out to a 28–0 lead by the second quarter, lead 31–21 at halftime, and then hold off a furious Bulldog comeback to win the game, 38–35. It was a signature game for WVU and the Big East Conference. Final rankings placed WVU at fifth place in the Associated Press poll and sixth in the *USA Today* coaches' poll. An especially striking statistic was that this game marked the Mountaineers' first January win since a 1948 Sun Bowl victory over Texas Western. Some believed that the Sugar Bowl victory over the Southeastern Conference champion saved the Big East Conference as a BCS participant because knowledgeable football analysts regarded the Southeastern Conference as the strongest in the nation.[44]

WVU fan expectations now soared to astronomical levels because all of the stars in WVU's newest firmament were to return the following season. The 2006 season began with the Mountaineers still nationally ranked at fifth, and they climbed to the third spot before losing two games. No longer contenders to repeat as Big East champions, they did receive a bid to play in the Gator Bowl, where they defeated Georgia Tech. At the end of the season, WVU was ranked tenth, marking the first time in school history that it finished in the top ten in two consecutive seasons. Running-back Steve Slaton and center Dan Mozes were named consensus All-Americans. Mozes became WVU's first player to capture a major national award when he received the Remington Trophy, given to the most outstanding center in Division I.[45] A little tension erupted just prior to the Gator Bowl, however, when Rodriguez interviewed for the head-coaching position at the University of Alabama. The Mountaineer faithful exhaled a sigh of relief when, after a few days of suspense, the coach announced that he was staying at WVU. His contract was extended to 2014, but a $4 million buyout clause was inserted as a safety precaution.

For the first time ever, the Mountaineers attained second place in the Associated Press poll and first in the coaches' poll during the 2007 season. Confidence was at a fever pitch in Morgantown going into the final game of the season at home against Pitt. The Panthers had endured a losing season and were 28-point underdogs, but tradition prevailed in the "backyard brawl" when Pitt upset the Mountaineers, 13–9. The "what might have beens," had quarterback Pat White not been injured and reliable kicker Pat McAfee not missed two field goals, could never change the outcome. It was a defeat of historic proportions in that century-old series because the loss eliminated WVU as a contender for the national championship.[46]

Sixteen days later, as the team was preparing for its January confrontation with third-ranked Oklahoma in the Fiesta Bowl, the Mountaineers and their fans were stunned to learn that Rich Rodriguez had accepted an offer to become head coach at the University of Michigan. Associate Head Coach Bill Stewart immediately took the helm, directing the team to forget what they could not control and head for the practice field because the next game on the calendar was the Fiesta Bowl.[47]

Three days later, Stewart was named interim coach until a replacement could be found. WVU supporters feared the worst, but Stewart kept the team focused, with their eyes on the prize. When the Mountaineers met the Sooners in Glendale, Arizona, they jumped out to a commanding lead and never looked back until the final gun sounded a lopsided 48–28 victory. Quarterback Pat White was named MVP of the 2008 Fiesta Bowl and became a household name in the sports world. "Historic" is a term overly used in sports, but it truly defined the impact of this victory for the Mountaineer program. Given what seemed an impossible task, Bill Stewart had succeeded in holding together a team that felt betrayed and abandoned. The following morning, the new WVU President Michael Garrison removed the interim title and named Bill Stewart as the new head coach.[48]

The manner of Rich Rodriguez's departure for Michigan was unparalleled in school history and unusual even in the wider world of sports. After interviewing at Alabama in December 2006 and renewing his vows to WVU, and after a major revision in his contract, Rodriguez had declared: "Nothing is going to pry me away from my home state." Just a year later, in December 2007, Rodriguez renounced his vow and headed for Ann Arbor. The team was not informed of his decision until 1:30 p.m. on Sunday, December 16. Adding insult to injury, the coach had chosen to contact his top recruits earlier that day to inform them of his departure for Michigan, even before addressing the team. His critics cited this incident as evidence that he was giving them the opportunity to switch their commitments to Michigan. After the team meeting Rodriguez handed his letter of resignation to a graduate assistant and slipped out a side door to avoid reporters. A few hours later, the man who had compiled a WVU record of 60–26 and had led the Mountaineers to four Big East championships and six straight bowl appearances boarded a plane with his family and left the state.[49] Mountaineer fans everywhere believed that Rodriguez had "stabbed them in the back."

The coach's actions clearly represented more than just another turn of the coaching carousel. After all of the renegotiated contracts and extensions, not to mention pledges of loyalty, West Virginians determined that Rodriguez simply shopped himself to the highest bidder. One fan exclaimed that "I just felt really disappointed by the fact that a WVU grad and native son would leave. I understand the need to improve yourself, but I feel betrayed that he would leave a position of such esteem as the head coach of WVU. It kind of perpetuates the erroneous stereotype that we suffer in West Virginia of being backwoods, Podunk or whatever." Another fan complained: "Basically, . . . what he did is what's wrong with people today. No integrity. You sign a contract. You work out the contract. You just don't leave. We've been pretty great to him . . . [only] to leave just for the money. What does that teach my 8-year old boy? Money beats integrity. That's it."[50]

Governor Joe Manchin, an old friend of the former coach, called Rodriguez "a victim of a college coaching system driven by high-priced agents." If so, he seemed a willing victim, and no doubt most West Virginians found it difficult to consider a coach receiving a $2 million annual salary as a victim. However, in former WVU coach Don Nehlen's opinion, "Michigan is a very prestigious job and it's a great football program and I can understand why he would leave. And yet, a lot of people in West Virginia don't understand."[51] There were also some major donors who blamed the University for not doing whatever it took to keep the acclaimed coach in Morgantown.

A local sportswriter probably came as close to discerning the real reasons for Rodriguez's departure as will ever be known. While Rodriguez proclaimed love for his home state and alma mater, said the writer, he was driven more by professional ambitions, "fame and fortune," than local loyalties. Rodriguez wanted to win a national championship, which he could accomplish more easily in the Big Ten Conference. He constantly complained about the facilities and how hard it was to recruit to Morgantown. Finally, "he whined so much that the WVU athletic department likely couldn't stand it anymore. They could stand the whining when he was winning. But losing to Pitt, and then making a run at his second national job in as many years was just too much to stomach for an athletic department that Rodriguez, frankly, thought he was running." Tellingly, the writer also noted that even though WVU was supposed to be Rodriguez's "dream job," he "treated it more like a business."[52]

The ugly side of the commercialization of big-time college sports, and WVU's delayed, bumpy entry into that national marketplace after twenty-one years of stability under Nehlen, were all too clearly exposed, to the chagrin of fans and the curiosity of observers nationwide. Irrespective of the blame game, the wrangling became a public-relations nightmare for WVU at a time when it was trying to project its most favorable image. WVU's Board of Governors filed a civil action against Rodriguez to claim the $4 million buyout. President Garrison considered himself a friend of Rodriguez, and he felt they had developed a good working relationship. "At the same time, I think we've got to get back to a point in college athletics where your word means something. . . . If you choose another option, we'll respect that. There's a reason these contracts are written the way they are; to avoid the loss of business opportunity that you're premising your contract upon," Garrison told the press. When basketball coach John Beilein left WVU, President Hardesty settled the disputed $2.5 million buyout by lowering it to $1.5 million. Under President Garrison and very different circumstances, there was no sympathy for renegotiating Rodriguez's buyout clause. The president dug in his heals because, unlike Beilein, Rodriguez had told potential recruits about his new coaching assignment even before notifying his WVU team or the University. At least two top recruits withdrew their commitments to WVU afterward.[53]

Rodriguez expressed "disappointment" when WVU filed its lawsuit and surprise at the hostility created by his departure from West Virginia. He claimed that he was treated unfairly by the administration, which had "fraudulently" induced him to sign a less than satisfactory contract by offering him verbal promises. Seven months later, on July 10, 2008, after much legal wrangling that was widely reported in the national media, WVU's Board of Governors approved a settlement in the lawsuit against the former coach. The terms of the settlement required Rodriguez to pay the full $4 million stipulated by the buyout clause: $2.5 million by the end of July 2008 and $1.5 million in three annual installments of $500,000 from January 2010 through January 2012.[54]

Many asked what prompted Rodriguez to decide to pay the full amount WVU demanded. It was reported that Rodriquez wanted to settle the dispute so he could concentrate on preparing for his first season at Michigan. However, the University of Michigan was also instrumental in the settlement, because it agreed to pay $2.5 million in addition to the coach's legal fees. According to one experienced observer, when the court ordered that all communications between the University of Michigan and Rodriguez should be disclosed, Michigan decided it must bring the lawsuit to a close. "As long as this was WVU v. Rodriguez, Michigan could stand to be an observer. But WVU was now trying to compel Michigan president Mary Sue Coleman and athletic director Bill Martin to testify in the case" and a hearing was set in a Michigan state court on WVU's motion to issue subpoenas. "Michigan finally realized that this thing was hitting too close to home." A Detroit newspaper reporter who covered University of Michigan football drew a similar conclusion, claiming that President Mary Sue Coleman was ordered to provide a deposition in the WVU v. Rodriguez case, and she chose not "to be dragged into it."[55]

During the course of the lawsuit, other issues pertaining to University governance came to light. Rodriguez's letter of resignation was published in the Morgantown newspaper. He claimed that he had spoken to both Garrison and Pastilong in August 2007 prior to signing the new contract and had received verbal and handshake agreements promising to reduce or eliminate the $4 million buyout clause, and that Governor Joe Manchin and several members of the Board of Governors pressured him to sign the contract. The coach concluded that those verbal and handshake agreements represented breaches of contract and bad faith.[56]

These and other claims advanced by Rodriguez were refuted by Athletic Director Ed Pastilong and the governor. In an August 1, 2007 email from Rodriguez's agent, Mike Brown, to WVU President Mike Garrison's chief of staff, Rodriguez alleged, "I am sure you have figured it out that there is a chain of command issue at WVU. Pastilong is talking directly to the governor and probably to the [Board of Governors] members." Queried by a reporter about this kind of personal contact between a coach and a governor, Todd Bell of the American Football Coaches Association replied that this was not something he had ever come across before and assumed that "it is outside of the normal chain of command. I think this situation would be unusual in any state government." Ed Pastilong, however, admitted that he spoke to Governor Manchin regularly, but because they were "very good friends" and WVU teammates. He emphasized that the governor "has never intervened in our athletic department." Governor Manchin's press secretary concurred: "Let me make it clear, that the Governor has never been involved with the running of the athletic department, nor given direction on how that department should be run."[57]

Despite their denials, the local Morgantown paper was prompted to publish an editorial urging Governor Manchin "to make less time for his friendships and Mountaineer football, and more time for the affairs of state. Manchin was too involved in WVU's athletic department last year. There's visible and tangible evidence he was too involved—including e-mails, phone calls, visits, videotape—which has opened the door to all kinds of speculation" regarding his motives. Although the governor claimed his involvement was out of friendship with Pastilong and Rodriguez, and that "his friendships come above all else," the commentator observed, "that apparently includes his sense of propriety and his priorities." When he became governor his primary obligation was "doing the state's business. . . . Manchin is the state's chief executive, and as such must refrain from self-interest and work for the state's best interest, not what's in the best interest of friendship or WVU football." There might well be a problem with the chain of command at WVU, the editorial continued, "but the governor's place is certainly not in retaining or ousting a football coach. All public officials and many other people, by virtue of their position, walk a fine line in their professional and private lives to maintain their integrity and credibility. It appears Gov. Manchin might have crossed that line."[58]

In addition to the nature of the governor's involvement in the athletic department, another chain-of-command issue surfaced during the Rodriguez affair. According to reports released during the court proceedings, President Garrison and his chief-of-staff Craig Walker told Rodriguez to contact Walker if the athletic director did not respond promptly to his requests or if disagreements arose between them. In other words, even though the chain-of-command required Rodriguez to go through Pastilong, the president gave the coach permission to bypass the athletic director if he felt it was necessary. It was also revealed that Garrison had made the suggestion at a meeting on August 24, 2007 that did not include Pastilong—a week before he was installed as president. One local reporter characterized this incident as evidence of a "rift opening amongst the main players" in charge of the football program, and noted agent Mike Brown's charge that "Pastilong and the governor were working together, against the alliance of Garrison and Rodriguez."[59]

Brown also was the agent for Calvin Magee, Rodriguez's offensive co-ordinator at WVU. During the legal wrangling Brown accused the University of violating its Equal Employment Opportunity and Affirmative Action policies in searching for Rodriguez's replacement. He claimed that Governor Manchin not only inserted himself into the chain-of-command and athletic department operations but also was involved in the hiring process. Although Manchin denied involvement, Brown insisted that "the governor was an integral part of the search process. . . . When the governor is on the phone interviewing candidates, receiving calls from Coach Bobby Bowden, calling donors in the middle of the process asking for advice and recommendations, and acting on their advice, . . . then he is part of the search committee and process."[60]

This accusation fell on receptive ears because the belief was already widespread among many faculty and the public that the governor was responsible for Mike Garrison's becoming president of WVU. Many assumed that Garrison, a former top aide to Manchin, could provide a back door to interfere in University operations. Correct or not, this was an issue that angered a WVU community, which had historically opposed the politicization of the University. These claims appeared alongside a potentially more embarrassing charge from Brown that, on the weekend Rodriguez decided to accept the Michigan post, Calvin Magee had asked an unnamed administrator his opinion on whether he might have a chance to become head coach at WVU. According to Brown, the administrator told Magee that his skin color would deny him that opportunity, and for that reason Magee joined Rodriguez on the plane bound for Michigan. On December 17, 2007, Rodriguez, during a press conference at the University of Michigan, publically accepted the position as head coach and introduced Magee and Tony Gibson as assistants from WVU who would be joining his Michigan staff. Although Rodriguez and Gibson resigned effective December 19, Magee did not resign until after the Fiesta Bowl.[61]

Magee and Pastilong presented two strikingly different versions of the sequence of events that followed. According to Magee's agent, the executive director of Black Coaches and Administrators, Floyd Keith, called the athletic director on December 20 to inquire if he had interviewed any African American candidates for the position of head football coach. Pastilong then came to Magee's office the next day to ask if Magee was interested in being a candidate, prompting Magee to ask if Keith's call was the only reason for Pastilong's visit. Pastilong replied that Magee could go through the process, but "it wouldn't mean much." Magee was insulted, Brown claimed, because he realized that the action was taken just to appease the Black Coaches and Administrators. Pastilong's version of what transpired differed considerably. Pastilong contended that he initiated the call to the Black Coaches and Administrators representative, who then faxed him a list of potential candidates. He then met with Magee in a team meeting room, not in the coach's office, and asked if he was positively going to Michigan. Magee replied in the affirmative but said he wanted to coach in the Fiesta Bowl and also declared his interest in being considered for the head-coaching position. According to Pastilong, he replied that it would be awkward for Magee to be considered for the position, since he had already accepted a position at Michigan. Magee's application would have been seriously considered had he not already taken a new job as Michigan's offensive coordinator. Reporters' attempts to confirm the correct version of these events with the Black Coaches and Administrators representative proved unsuccessful, although Brown claimed that the University did not interview any minority candidates, while Pastilong denied the agent's assertion.[62]

Executive Director Jennifer McIntosh of the Office of Social Justice was charged by WVU President Michael Garrison with leading an investigation into whether University policy on racial discrimination had been violated as Calvin Magee alleged. She declined to discuss the candidates who were considered for the head-coaching position but observed that she had participated in the process, and that, to the best of her knowledge, social justice policies were followed. Nevertheless, even the allegation of discrimination tarnished WVU's image as an institution. It had always been a difficult task to recruit African Americans, both players and coaches, to WVU because Morgantown and the state were overwhelmingly white.[63]

Magee did not reveal the administrator on whose comments the serious allegations were based, but the social justice office's investigation was intended to discover the person's identity. About three months later (in mid-April), the mysterious source of the comment that sparked the allegation of racial discrimination was revealed as Larry Ashebrook, former executive director of the Mountaineer Athletic Club, who had resigned around this time to take a similar position at Arizona State. Ashebrook signed an affidavit "categorically denying" Magee's allegations and asserting that Ashebrook had called Rodriguez to complain about the misuse of his name.[64] The story immediately disappeared from the media but left a negative impression of WVU as a place that did not foster racial diversity.

FOOTBALL: BILL STEWART'S TENURE

At a news conference on January 2, 2008, less than twenty-four hours after winning the Fiesta Bowl, Bill Stewart was introduced by the athletic director as the University's thirty-second head football coach. Players and fans rejoiced, and Stewart became the man of the hour. Responding to a reporter, Stewart declared: "I want to tell you as calmly and rationally and as passionately as I can—I cherish the opportunity to be the head football coach at the state flagship university—the finest institution in the country—West Virginia University." It was music to the ears of the faithful at a magic moment in time. It was the old-school sense of loyalty, rather than the new-school mercenary values, that seemed reinforced by Stewart's approach to his contract. There were no negotiations, no agents, and no lawyers. He was appointed and the deal sealed by a handshake between Athletic Director Pastilong and Stewart, who had known each other for forty years. Agreeing on the terms took about five minutes, according to Pastilong. Stewart's contract provided $800,000 per year plus incentives.[65]

An editorial summed up public opinion: "The decision to hire Stewart appears to have been made for the right reason. Not because he's a native

West Virginian, not because of his years as an assistant coach, not because his word is his bond, not even because he deserved it. No, the best reason to make Bill Stewart the coach was because he earned it." Following "the most disastrous months in the football program's history," Stewart kept hope alive and the players' belief in themselves strong. In an obvious reference to Rodriguez, the editorial emphasized that, "unlike some coaches, he accomplished it all by earning his players' respect, not their fear, and his agent is his handshake."[66] Stewart's ascension was a feel-good story covered sympathetically by local and national media, and it helped to counterbalance the negative image created by the Rodriguez affair. Clearly the two coaches represented opposite poles in the transition to the new school of coaching and big-time athletics.

A noticeably different atmosphere settled over Stewart's football program. While Rodriguez's style was intense and busy, allowing little time for horseplay, Stewart's was characterized as "a lot lighter." Stewart and his staff spent more time with the players and wanted them to be comfortable in the complex where they spent so much of their waking lives. At least part of the reason for the increased comfort level was the older and experienced coaching staff, which was committed to athletics as a way of life rather than a path to fame and fortune. Coaching was a teaching profession, not an entertainment industry. Most were also old friends. Rodriguez took a number of coaches with him, and Stewart replaced them with coaches who had worked together for years during the Don Nehlen era. These were people driven to win, but win in the right way. Stewart brought back Steve Dunlap from Marshall and Doc Holliday from the University of Florida, both of whom had been released when Rodriguez was hired. Along with David Lockwood and Bill Kirelawich, they formed the core of the "old guard" reconstituted under Stewart. According to Kirelawich, "these guys were special" not just because they were good coaches, but because "they bleed blue and gold, they want to be here. This isn't just a job to them. This is *the* [his emphasis] job to them, and you can't buy that kind of 'esprit de corps.' That's gotta come from the inside."[67]

A native of New Martinsville, and a Magnolia High School graduate, Bill Stewart attended WVU where he was a member of the 1970 football team before transferring to Fairmont State, where he played from 1971–1973. After a short stint as a high-school coach, Stewart began his long college coaching career as an assistant at Salem College, followed in succession by stops as an assistant at North Carolina, Marshall, William and Mary, North Carolina again, Arizona State, and the U.S. Air Force Academy. After three years as head coach at Virginia Military Institute, he spent some time with the Montreal Alouettes, and Winnipeg Blue Bombers of the Canadian Football League. Finally, he returned to his home state as assistant coach under Don Nehlen in 2000 and was one of the few coaches after Nehlen's retirement retained by Rodriguez, who elevated him to associate head coach.[68]

Bill Stewart confronted a challenge of enormous proportions in his first year as head coach, highlighted by unrealistic expectations from all quarters. Even the national preseason eighth-place ranking indicated that the pundits expected the first-year coach to perform miracles in the 2008 season. The Mountaineers returned star quarterback Pat White, running back sensation Noel Devine, and the entire offensive line, and all signs pointed toward a dream season. Hopes were dashed, however, when the squad lost its first game to East Carolina, lost again to Colorado in overtime, endured a defeat against Cincinnati, and fell to Pitt. Instead of winning another Big East championship and heading for a BCS bowl, WVU played North Carolina in the Meineke Car Care Bowl. Even though the Mountaineers won and Pat White ended his career as the bowl MVP, expectations that the team would continue its heroics of the previous season left fans disappointed. Following another disappointing season in 2009, the Mountaineers landed in the Gator Bowl against Florida State's Bobby Bowden, who was coaching his last game. The Mountaineers lost the game in a lackluster performance, and fan disenchantment grew deeper. The 2010 campaign ended with a regular-season record of 9–3 and a share of the Big East title. WVU then faced North Carolina State in the Champs Bowl and was defeated.[69] In years past, an overall 28–11 record, a 718 winning percentage, three nine-win seasons, and three postseason bowl games would have been applauded. But WVU had been to the mountaintop, and in that context existed only lofty expectations.

In the midst of one of the most tumultuous periods in the history of athletics at WVU, still more profound changes were on the way. The next transformational event began to unfold when Athletic Director Ed Pastilong announced in March 2010 that he would retire on June 30, 2010, and that a national search for his replacement would begin. He was the longest-serving athletic director in the University's history. Pastilong graduated from high school in Moundsville, West Virginia, and came to WVU on a football scholarship in 1961. In 1966 he graduated in physical education, and after more than a decade of coaching in high school and college, WVU hired him in 1976 as the football recruiting coordinator. He was promoted in 1979 to assistant athletic director, the same year Don Nehlen became head football coach, was promoted to associate director in 1987, and two years later was named the University's tenth athletic director.[70]

Stability ruled the athletic department for the more than twenty years that Pastilong, Nehlen, and Catlett all occupied their respective leadership positions. Pastilong learned the necessity for conservative money management, and the department survived some extremely lean financial years. Improvements in facilities and revenues arrived slowly but surely, although not as quickly as coaches would have liked. When Pastilong became athletic director in 1989, revenues for the self-supporting department totaled $12 million, and by 2008–2009 they reached an all-time high of $60 million. Everybody who knew and worked with Pastilong regarded him as a very knowledgeable professional, and his unflappability earned him the sobriquet "Steady Eddie."[71] Now a new regime would take over the athletics department and redirect its development.

ATHLETIC DIRECTOR OLIVER LUCK CHARTS A NEW DIRECTION FOR FOOTBALL

Oliver Luck was introduced as the eleventh director of intercollegiate athletics at WVU, his duties to officially begin on June 30, 2010. From Cleveland, Ohio, Luck came to WVU to play quarterback for the Mountaineers from 1978–1981. He was an outstanding football player, leading the Mountaineers to a victory in the 1981 Peach Bowl. He was also an academic All-American, a finalist in the Rhodes Scholar competition, and a 1997 inductee into the WVU Sports Hall of Fame. Luck was selected in the second round of the NFL draft by the Houston Oilers in 1982, where he played quarterback until his retirement from professional football at the end of the 1986 season. While playing for the Oilers he earned a law degree from the University of Texas. Subsequently, Luck was appointed vice president of business development for the NFL and president and CEO of NFL Europe. Back home in Houston, the Houston Dynamo of Major League Soccer hired him as president in 2005. Luck's career circled back to WVU in 2008, when he was appointed to the WVU Board of Governors, a post he resigned when he became athletic director.[72]

The new athletic director inherited an old problem. An investigation of Rich Rodriguez's football program at the University of Michigan revealed a pattern of violations that reached back to WVU. On August 4, 2010, the NCAA submitted an official Notice of Allegations to WVU that claimed that five major violations had occurred between 2005–2006 and 2009–2010, beginning during Rodriguez's tenure and continuing into Bill Stewart's. Following a nine-month investigation, the NCAA determined that both Rodriguez and Stewart "failed to promote an atmosphere of compliance within the football program and failed to adequately monitor the duties and activities of graduate assistant coaches and the non-coaching sport-specific staff members." Five major violations involved non-coaching staff functioning in the capacity of coaches both on and off the field.[73]

Showing a good-faith willingness to comply, and probably hoping to diminish the eventual penalties, the football program implemented significant changes to bring an end to the illegal practices. An effort to educate staff regarding compliance was also initiated. Asked for some insight into these violations, former coach Don Nehlen maintained that "to be honest, I don't know that anything like this has ever happened" at WVU. "Nothing like this ever happened when I was coaching—people were always getting in trouble for recruiting violations back then. But when I retired, it seemed like all these coaching staffs increased so big that you never knew who was coaching."[74]

Oliver Luck inherited a program which also confronted some serious grumbling among major donors who reportedly wanted Stewart to be replaced, and Luck apparently agreed. Replacing a coach who owned three nine-win seasons in his first three years seemed a strange way to reward success, but other factors were also instrumental in the decision. Flagging interest in the football program among the Mountaineer faithful, resulting in shrinking attendance at home games and declining revenues, not to mention the NCAA allegations, convinced Luck that Bill Stewart was not the man to lead the Mountaineers to a national championship.[75]

At a press conference on December 16, 2010, Luck ended the speculation by announcing Dana Holgorsen as the Mountaineer's new offensive coordinator and head coach-in-waiting until the 2011 season. Stewart signed a modified contract with the University on November 17, 2010, which allowed him to finish the 2010 season as head coach and continue in that capacity for the 2011 season and then be appointed to an unspecified position within the athletic department. Dana Holgorsen was the other participant in this transitional process. Regarded as one of the bright offensive minds in football, Holgorsen, at only thirty-eight, had already received numerous honors, was a finalist for the 2010 Broyles Award, which was given to the nation's top assistant football coach, and was also a finalist for the Rivals.com Offensive Coordinator of the Year Award based on his outstanding performance at Oklahoma State.[76] Having never held a head-coaching position before, Holgorsen's year as offensive coordinator with Stewart still at the helm would allow him time to prepare for that greater responsibility.

Publicly, Stewart and Holgorsen shook hands, and both said the right things, but many expressed doubt about the practicality of such an arrangement. The editor of the local newspaper questioned the hiring process itself. Apparently, WVU had not learned, he said, that "a quiet, focused search for the best candidate is a more sound approach than a knee-jerk decision. . . . WVU has been criticized before for not having an actual search for a football coach. Now, it's done it again with someone who has no collegiate head coach experience. Excuse us for lacking confidence."[77]

Another reporter offered a succinct analysis of events: "Bill Stewart became WVU's head football coach during one of the most tumultuous periods in the history of the program. He exited the same way."[78] Speculation and rumors swirled around the University and in the national media in yet another public-relations nightmare.Some thought Stewart was trying to undermine Holgorsen, and Luck launched an investigation to determine if that rumor had emanated from within the athletics department. The suspicions were never substantiated, but according to a reporter, who cited sources within the WVU coaching staff, "Stewart never got over the snub of last December."[79] Under pressure, therefore, Stewart submitted his resignation, and Holgorsen was appointed head football coach a year sooner than anticipated.

One further sign that the "old guard" was being replaced came with the retirement of Garrett Ford on June 30, 2011, after forty-four years of service in the athletic department. He came to WVU in 1965 as one of the first African American football players to integrate the football program and held the honor of being the first running back in WVU history to rush for more than two thousand yards. After two seasons with the Denver Broncos, he returned to his alma mater to become associate athletic director for student services. In that role, he monitored the academic progress, ensured that students attended class, and shared a large portion of the credit for WVU's graduation rate for student-athletes. Ford influenced the lives of countless student-athletes on his way to becoming a WVU legend.[80]

College sports have always carried some aspects of commerce, but with the flood of revenues generated by television programming came the danger that market values would supplant the traditional values that were the very heart of institutions of higher learning. WVU has always aspired to offer athletic competition at a national level, and the new revenues were essential in offering the salaries required by winning coaches and in maintaining the kind of facilities that would attract star recruits and convince fans to pay ever higher costs to attend events. The potential for damage to the University's reputation and its public image by market values pushing aside core mission were on full display as WVU entered the modern sports marketplace during the first decade of the twenty-first century.

AFTERWORD

THE ADMINISTRATIONS of Irvin Stewart and David Hardesty provide the bookends for this history of West Virginia University. Both were transformative leaders. Stewart guided WVU during its dramatic expansion in the post-World War II era (1946–1958) from a small state institution of a few thousand to one three times that size. More importantly, Stewart convinced the University community that its aspiration to become a major university was a worthy and achievable goal. In effect, he taught WVU "to think like a university," as one long-serving administrator declared. During the fifties and sixties, the vision of higher education as a public good reflected the values society regarded as important: egalitarianism, meritocracy, and education that prepared a knowledgeable citizenry for majority rule in a democratic society. Public universities were structured to conform to these social values by providing access and equality, and by promoting teaching, research, and service that benefited society.[1]

Nearly four decades later, David Hardesty assumed the presidency of a mature university of 21,500 students which grew to nearly thirty thousand when he retired twelve years later. By then, American higher education had undergone a dramatic transformation that has fueled a scholarly industry to analyze the cultural shifts behind these changes and their implications for society. These shifts began in the seventies, when a different vision of higher education began to emerge in which the university was no longer the seedbed of democracy that produced good citizens but, in the words of critics, a "privatizable knowledge factory" that would produce "flexible, adaptable, innovative workers."[2] The rise of neoliberalism during the last quarter of the twentieth century provided the energy and vision that transformed higher education. The modern conservative movement penetrated higher education through ideas that lauded the efficiency of private enterprise, elevated the value of professional university management, and promoted managerial oversight to ensure institutional accountability. The role of the private sector in determining the state's political and economic priorities was fundamental to controlling the desired restructuring of the relationship between public universities, the state, and the private sector. Consequently, the university became something quite different as the emphasis shifted from higher education as a public good that emphasized civic participation to a private good that emphasized values attuned to consumer culture.[3]

Consumer society emerged slowly at first after World War II, bringing with it a desire for a house in the suburbs, and dreams of sending the children to college. At the time a public college education was still readily affordable. By the seventies the triumph of consumerism had ensured the permanence of the idea that higher education was a private good. Previously, college attendance had emphasized the benefits of exposing young people to new ideas and critical thinking, meeting different people, and intellectual breadth as preparation for a successful life. Now consumer society viewed higher education in vocational terms. College graduates obtained better jobs and earned more than high school graduates. College students gained a heightened awareness that some majors were more likely than others to lead to lucrative careers. "A Mind is a Terrible Thing to Waste" was a fundraising slogan that resonated with the public and required no explanation. The consumer society expected to get as much for its tax dollars as possible. Students wanted to go to a college that offered all the comforts of home. To compete for these students, public universities were forced to engage in the "amenities race," providing dormitory suites with kitchens, food courts, fitness centers, and libraries well-equipped with computer terminals and coffee shops.[4]

There was nothing inherently wrong in the new university environment, but it was very different from the one that it replaced. It was also much more expensive. Public funding declined as the idea that education was a private good took root. The public university's only recourse was to raise more of its own resources, either by increased private giving, external research grants, marketing commercial goods and services like athletics, and increasing student tuition and fees. The cost of public higher education rose so dramatically during this period, one scholar argues, because the "amenities race" and commercialization was accompanied by an increase in administrators and staffers to provide "student services." Between 1975 and 2005, the number of administrators expanded at twice the rate of faculty, and administrative staffs have surged five times faster than the ranks of faculty. Administrators tend to regard management as an end in itself, not as a way to improve research and scholarship. Meanwhile the number of part-time adjuncts teaching undergraduate courses continues to grow.[5] The increase in administrative personnel can be justified to some extent by the need for appointment in new, complex areas of expertise, such as information technology, enrollment management, and professional advising. Nevertheless, it is a staggering statistic for the parents and students who pay the price that the cost of attending college has climbed every year, approximately 300 percent nationally, between 1990 and 2010.

By the time David Hardesty became president in 1995, American society had changed dramatically. WVU lagged behind in the trend toward creating student-centered environments because its system of governance concentrated power in the Board of Regents, which perpetuated a relationship of dependency of the University to the state. Under the new power relationships and their associated values, a new system of governance was called for that would allow the state to retain managerial oversight while at the same time shifting more of its financial obligations to the University itself. President Hardesty understood what was required and between 1995 and 2001 he oversaw the University's transition from less state-dependency to more of a business model. Between 1990 and 2010, tuition increased nearly 150 percent. Every unit became "accountable" for the costs of its own operation, and goods and services provided by the University were paid for by the user.

West Virginia University's delayed adoption of this new paradigm made the change all the more difficult. Those who were suspicious of the commercial values implemented under Hardesty were now convinced beyond all doubt by what they regarded as the unethical selection process that tapped Michael Garrison as Hardesty's replacement. A 1992 WVU graduate, Michael Garrison was named president of his alma mater on April 13, 2007. Following brief employment in Senator Robert C. Byrd's office and a year spent abroad as a Rotary Scholar at the University of Oxford, Garrison received a law degree from WVU in 1996. He practiced law until 2001, when Governor Bob Wise appointed him to the position of secretary of the West Virginia Department of Tax and Revenue and then elevated him to chief of staff later that year. In 2003 he left state government to become a managing partner in the firm of Spilman, Thomas & Battle's Morgantown office where his specialty was state and federal government relations and legislative initiatives, economic development, and crisis management. That same year he was appointed to the West Virginia Higher Education Policy Board, one of his numerous public service commitments prior to his appointment as president of WVU in 2007.[6]

More than one hundred candidates expressed interest in the position, and the search committee received sixty applications. Three finalists were interviewed on campus, and two of them were known to the Board of Governors: former Dean of the Eberly College of Arts and Sciences at WVU M. Duane Nellis, who was at the time of his application provost at Kansas State University, and Michael Garrison. The third candidate withdrew his name from consideration two days before Garrison was introduced as the new president. Even before his selection, the Faculty Senate had taken the unusual step of voting "no confidence" in Garrison. A vocal segment of the faculty favored the more experienced Nellis for the position, and claimed that Garrison's selection was "predetermined" by well-placed political friends, a claim Board of Governors Chairman Stephen Goodwin denied. One prominent faculty member voiced the faculty's objection to the search process: "Garrison wasn't selected by higher-education professionals, he was selected by developers, bankers, lawyers, realtors, and other members of the business community." The public forums were "packed" by Garrison supporters who "stuffed the evaluation sheet box with glowing evaluations," he charged. "As far as I can tell, no other university anywhere close to the size of WVU has picked someone with zero experience in academic administration and virtually no experience teaching or doing research," he continued. "WVU now has had two in a row forced upon it."[7]

Change produces anxiety, and WVU's increasingly commercial relationship with its constituencies, combined with a long history of political interference from the state level, elicited serious concern from friends of the University. Although President Hardesty successfully calmed the sea of anxiety during his own presidency, it was still a potent force when Michael Garrison filled his seat in the president's office. The problem confronting Garrison was that his appointment was widely viewed as a political imposition, and he was seen as an agent of those who intended to replace traditional university values with those imported from the business world.

Students were generally supportive of Garrison during the selection process, but they also worried that academic culture was becoming more like private business. Shortly after Garrison took office, an editorial in the student newspaper cogently noted that WVU was increasingly dependent on private funding as state support declined. Citing the new president's inaugural address, the editorial observed that WVU was no longer "an obligation of state government, but rather an engine of economic growth." The challenge for Garrison's presidency, it continued, "is to figure out how to operate in a world that has become increasingly driven by economics, where liberal arts are being pushed to the back burner, and where universities around the country function more like businesses than a public service, with their own intense demeaning efforts to meet bottom lines. We know he knows the challenge, but it's hard to tell yet what he will do." Students were wary of where the transformation was leading the University. "The danger of becoming a corporate University is that we throw all our eggs into the basket of industry and do not stand by the liberal arts like philosophy, English or puppetry, or that we ignore the ability of people with a rounded education (one not so centered on merely getting one certain kind of job) to fend for themselves in the flotsam and jetsam of globalization." Hopefully, the editorial continued, the new president must find a way for WVU to avoid "the pitfalls of other public institutions that, at the insistence of fickle

Afterword

cost cutters, have rolled back the nation's commitment to fine and liberal arts and driven the country into the hands of an industrial-complex that seems to see nothing without thinking of how much money can be made." The editor hoped that the new president would stand up to "the corporate mentality that might seem to let us stand on our own but then will take our feet out from under us."[8]

President Garrison laid out an ambitious plan for his administration that included significant pay raises for faculty and staff, paid for by an 8 percent hike in tuition, and the initiation of "Bucks for Brains," which offered state matching funds for research grants.[9] But only a few months after his inauguration, the new president encountered the perfect storm that would sink his administration. It all began with the appointment of Heather Bresch, a WVU graduate and daughter of Governor Joe Manchin, as chief operating officer at Mylan Pharmaceuticals. In response to a routine call to WVU's Office of Admissions and Records from a *Pittsburgh Post-Gazette* reporter seeking confirmation that Bresch had received the bachelor's degree in business and executive master's in business administration listed on her resume, a records officer replied that Bresch had not completed the requirements for the MBA. When the reporter informed Bresch that WVU had no record of granting her the MBA degree, she reportedly replied that the WVU president's office "was working on it." Subsequent calls from the president's office informed the reporter that, on closer examination, Bresch had indeed received the degree. A few days later, on October 12, 2007, Craig Walker, the president's chief of staff, met with Provost Gerald Lang to discuss the matter, followed three days later by a top-level administration meeting on the issue. On October 17, Walker directed dean of the College of Business and Economics R. Stephen Sears to write a letter confirming that Bresch had in fact been awarded the degree in December 1999 as she had indicated on her resume. However, it was subsequently revealed that six classes, including grades, were added to Bresch's transcript, and that marks for two courses were changed from "incomplete" to letter grades. The revisions totaled the twenty-two missing credits required to complete the forty-eight credit-hour program, even though no evidence existed that Bresch had ever registered for those courses. An assistant in the president's office then informed the *Post-Gazette* reporters (two were now covering the story) that all forty-eight hours had been completed, and that WVU had "all the records and all the transcripts."[10]

The two reporters sensed something amiss and continued their investigation. An editorial in the *Post-Gazette* observed that Heather Bresch's name did not appear on the class rosters for the five classes that were added to her record, and that her record at the business school no longer existed. "This mysterious episode raises questions of integrity not only for Ms. Bresch as a high-ranking executive . . . but also WVU."[11] During the inquiry, Steven Crow, president of the Higher Learning Commission of the North Central Association of Colleges and Schools, WVU's accrediting agency, was asked whether a fraudulently granted degree would jeopardize WVU's accreditation. Although equivocal in his response, Crow asserted that "higher education in West Virginia is and always has been marked by state politics," but it was "no different than a lot of my states that I work with where the line between higher education and politics at times gets blurred."[12]

The integrity of WVU degrees became the focus of a major discussion in all parts of the University and took front and center stage in Faculty Senate meetings. Provost Gerald Lang initially appointed an investigative panel composed of two faculty and Bruce Flack, an official from the West Virginia Higher Education Policy Commission, in January 2008, but the Faculty Senate found Flack's association with the Manchin administration unacceptable and requested a new panel with a new charge. The senate wanted three people "independent of any governmental agency or interested party," and Provost Lang agreed to the alternative plan, further stating that the panel's integrity was his primary concern. In addition to the two WVU faculty members already appointed, the Faculty Senate chose three external members to serve on the investigative panel: a retired dean at Pace University, a former provost at the University of Missouri-Columbia, and a law professor at the University of Pittsburgh.[13]

Investigating such a case was difficult in West Virginia because a close web of personal relationships linked many of the state's political, public sector, and campus higher-education leaders. Garrison was a longtime friend of the Manchin family, a classmate of Heather Bresch, served as former

Governor Bob Wise's chief of staff, and served on Governor Joe Manchin's transition team. Bresch worked for Milan Puskar, one of the founders of Mylan Pharmaceuticals, a major political supporter of Governor Manchin, and also the University's most generous benefactor. Board of Governors' chairman Stephen Goodwin was a political ally of Governor Manchin, and his son was the governor's chief lawyer. Even if no unethical behavior ever took place, appearances inevitably lead to the suspicion of impropriety. The *New York Times* quoted a retired Charleston lobbyist: "In West Virginia there is a proverb that says that everything is political except politics, and that is personal." With only 1.8 million people, she observed, West Virginia is a "tiny state, with just two major universities, just one major law school and where many of us grow up in the same small towns or counties, so there ends up being just one degree of separation between people involved in business and politics and whatever else."[14]

On April 23, 2008, the Special Investigative Panel for Review of Executive MBA Program Records released its report. The panel determined that the executive MBA degree retroactively awarded to Heather Bresch was "inappropriately granted," and that the College of Business and Economics created records and grades to support its decision despite insufficient supporting evidence. Although it discovered that no "political or external pressure" had been applied to render that decision, it did surmise that "unvoiced" pressure was felt by some decision-makers. The panel did not recommend censure or any other steps regarding the administrators involved, but the panelists unanimously concluded that their actions in changing Bresch's transcript in order to award the degree were "seriously flawed and reflected poor judgment." The report also contained a number of recommendations for improving the record-keeping process. The report also asserted that the administrators were "driven primarily and inappropriately by concerns about public relations and by Ms. Bresch's high profile. She was, in fact, treated in an unusual and unique manner. Mistake was compounded by mistake. An unnecessary rush to judgment, spurred in some measure by an understandable desire to protect a valued alumna and to respond to media pressure, produced a flawed and erroneous result. It didn't have to happen this way." WVU officials "should have done just what they said they were doing," the panelists declared; "they should have treated Ms. Bresch like they would or should have treated any other student who was raising such a complaint about the accuracy of his or her attendance and/or graduation records."[15]

That same day, the WVU Board of Governors voted to accept the final report, recommended that President Garrison take responsibility for the "errors in judgment and procedures" and that Ms. Bresch be informed of the panel's decision, and directed that Garrison develop a plan and policies to ensure that such a situation never happened again. Finally, the Board of Governors directed the president to present the plan for implementing the new corrective policies and procedures to the board at its next regular meeting in June 2008. The board recommended no action against the administrators involved.[16]

The question surfaced immediately as to why the Board of Governors would leave implementation of the panel's and board's recommendations in the hands of those who had participated in the sequence of events. President Garrison's acceptance of responsibility stopped short of taking the blame for the actions of his administrators, however, which prompted the normally WVU-friendly local newspaper to call for "a clean sweep" of the top administrators, beginning with Garrison and including all of the administrators involved. The paper also scolded the board: "Who are these people? Why do they act as though business as usual is acceptable and that this matter is secondary? How can they function as though no more need be shared about this matter at this time? WVU is not a private club."[17] Editorial pages in the state's newspapers, particularly the Morgantown paper, were expanded to accommodate all of the letters they had received, written mostly by people expressing their outrage over the episode. Students held large open meetings to express their displeasure, and the *Daily Athenaeum* bristled with negative articles, editorials, and letters to the editor. The fallout spread to wealthy donors. One supporter, who had donated more than $1 million dollars to the University, asserted: "It's hard to conclude that anything but significant wrongdoing has occurred." Another exclaimed that he was "disgusted by this humiliating experience. . . . The politicization of the University and the abject absence of standards reflected in this episode

Afterword

cheapens all of our degrees." He called for the resignation of President Garrison, Provost Lang, and Board of Governors Chairman Stephen Goodwin along with other members involved in the presidential search. "My ability to support the University, until these circumstances are appropriately resolved, has been compromised," he concluded.[18]

The Special Investigative Panel placed much of the blame on Provost Gerald Lang and business school Dean R. Stephen Sears. On April 28, Lang, a member of the faculty since 1976, submitted his letter of resignation as provost and vice president of academic affairs, effective June 30. In a memorandum to the campus community, Lang said that the panel's findings had convinced him to step down: "I am very sorry that my one action in ratifying a Dean's decision in a single situation has had a negative impact on the institution. I love this place and would never intentionally take an action that would reflect negatively upon it." Lang continued: "Even though the panel looking into the Bresch case did not find any willful misconduct, their conclusion that the result was flawed and erroneous has convinced me to resign. I hope this decision will begin the healing process and focus attention onto the future." The second administrator to resign was Dean Sears, whose responsibility it was to validate that Bresch had completed requirements for the MBA. Upon resignation of their administrative positions, both Lang and Sears returned to the faculty.[19]

President Garrison accepted his administrators' resignations but continued to reject the growing chorus of calls for his own resignation. While accepting responsibility, Garrison insisted that the academic officers bore the blame for the decision to award Bresch the degree. The Board of Governors released a statement of support for the increasingly beleaguered president in late April, expressing confidence in his ability to implement the changes recommended by the board. In his own statement, Garrison reiterated that he had not asked anyone, either directly or indirectly, to award credits, grades, or a degree. He restated his agreement with the panel's assessment, but he refused to resign. He also refused to release his phone records, prompting a lawsuit from the press under the Freedom of Information Act.[20]

Meanwhile, the tide of discontent continued to swell over the way WVU administrators were handling what had now become a public-relations disaster. Even the *State Journal*, the voice of business in West Virginia, joined in the cacophony by charging that, for at least "one sad and disturbing moment," WVU had become "more of a bastion of political expediency than academic excellence or accountability." Referring to the October 15, 2007 administrators' meeting convened to determine how to proceed with Bresch's claim, the editor and publisher of the *State Journal* declared: "It appears that no one there said what he really wanted to say—not in real words anyway. But the nodding and winking—the language used to cut backroom political deals in a state that knows all about such destructive leadership—seems to have set the stage for a calamitously bad decision." As a result, the editor continued: "WVU appears to have slid into the cesspool of politics. The WVU Board of Governors—a politically appointed body—had embraced political leadership to manage WVU." Instead of appointing an experienced academic leader to replace David Hardesty, the board's decision "to hire attorney and lobbyist Michael Garrison as WVU's president set the stage for the politicization of the WVU culture." He expressed his belief that the state had had enough of this kind of leadership.[21]

As the calls grew louder for resignations at the top, WVU men's basketball coach Bob Huggins publically supported Garrison, as did football coach Bill Stewart, who declared his "unwavering loyalty" to the president.[22] Others within the University also came to his defense. Dr. Julian E. Bailes, chairman of the medical school's neurosurgery department, circulated a letter of support that garnered twenty-three signatures from the six hundred faculty members at the medical school. Some said they felt they were being coerced. According to one faculty member, "there's a lot of paranoia and discomfort at the health sciences center over this whole thing," and another said "it's become unbelievably political."[23] The chairman of the Faculty Senate and faculty representative on the Board of Governors, Steven Kite, believed that the Special Investigative Panel's report exonerated President Garrison from charges that he had maneuvered to award Bresch the MBA degree retroactively. "I don't see where you can really find President Garrison particularly culpable on this," he told a talk-show host, and he rejected faculty demands for the president's resignation.[24] An op-ed piece in the *Sunday Gazette-Mail* regarded the clamor for more resignations as an example of "mob mentality." In fact, it reminded the writer of the French Revolution's call for "off with their heads!"[25] Meanwhile, a petition circulating the state had gathered 1,800 signatures in support of Garrison.[26]

A complete vote of either the 1,418 full-time faculty or the 1,925 full- and part-time instructors on campus never took place, but it was obvious that a large percentage of them opposed Garrison's continuation in office. The results of two faculty meetings lend support to this conclusion. The first was a special meeting of the Faculty Senate to vote on three motions intended to express the will of the faculty. One called for the faculty and administration to work together toward improving record keeping in order to prevent the recurrence of problems exposed by the degree scandal. A second called for censuring the president. The third and most stringent motion stated: "The Faculty Senate of West Virginia University votes no confidence in President Mike Garrison. For the good of the institution and for the benefit of our students, he must resign or the Board of Governors must require his resignation."[27]

It is a gauge of faculty sentiment that, of the 114 representatives of the Faculty Senate, those present voted for the harshest of the three motions: 77–19 with one abstention. Of the twenty-five members who spoke at the meeting, twenty argued in favor of Garrison's resignation, pointing out that, even though the president may not have been directly involved in the degree-granting process, he nevertheless influenced the outcome. They especially cited the actions of Craig Walker, his chief of staff, who admitted to "pushing" the process to quick resolution. Many faculty also objected to Board of Governors Chairman Stephen Goodwin's comments, in an interview a week earlier, that the board was legally charged with choosing the president of WVU and faculty would have to change the law if they wanted that responsibility. He also restated that the investigative panel had not incriminated Garrison, and that the board remained "solidly behind" the president. The Faculty Senate had voted "no confidence" in Garrison when he was a candidate, and its vote this time around represented more of a referendum on the president's appointment than on his handling of the degree scandal. Therefore, Goodwin asserted, "it would be irresponsible at this point in time for us to simply remove the president because people were unsatisfied we picked him last year. We have nothing before us which shows he is guilty of any misconduct."[28] President Garrison's comments regarding the "no confidence" vote did nothing to reassure the critics. The Board of Governors had asked him to implement the changes recommended by the independent panel: "It is the work I love to do. It is the work I intend to do."[29]

On May 8, an editorial in the *Charleston Gazette* queried "why Gov. Manchin asked a special 2007 summer session of the Legislature to change State Code 18B-2A1, which enabled political insider Stephen Goodwin to remain chairman of the WVU Board of Governors for four years instead of two." Two days later Goodwin announced that he wanted to end speculation that he would be seeking a third term as chairman of the board by declaring that he would not, but further declaring his intention of serving out his term on the board, which ended in 2010.[30] Goodwin insisted that the board still supported the president, and, since the Faculty Senate vote was non-binding, the contending parties faced a standoff until something or someone changed the dynamic. Contributing to that change was the Mountaineers for Integrity and Responsibility, a group established by faculty, students, and staff following the Faculty Senate's "no confidence" vote to maintain the pressure on Garrison to resign. Its goals went further, however, toward restoring the integrity and academic values of the University community, and the group played an important role in initiating a rare meeting of the Faculty Assembly.[31]

Traditionally, the faculty were invited to a general annual meeting to provide an audience for the president's State of the University address. However, the Faculty Constitution permitted a special meeting to be called upon a request by 5 percent of the faculty. Not since the Faculty Senate was created in 1977 had all full-time faculty at WVU found an issue so important that a special meeting of the Faculty Assembly was necessary. Now, the requisite number had spoken, and a special meeting was set for May 14, 2008, to allow full-time faculty the opportunity to express their opinion directly rather than through Faculty Senate representatives. Decisions of the Faculty Assembly were no more legally binding than those of the Faculty Senate in determining whether or not Garrison would stay, but the organizers believed that the full voice of the faculty would be more difficult to ignore. At the appointed hour, 615 faculty convened. Because the number was insufficient for a quorum of the 1,415 full-time faculty, the proceedings continued unofficially as a "mass meeting of faculty." Eight motions sparked considerable discussion, most of which denounced the politicization of the University, which had usurped traditional academic values and treated the University as "a political playground rather than an academic institution." By a vote of 565 for, thirty-nine against, and eleven abstentions, the "mass meeting" finally reaffirmed the "no confidence" motion previously passed by the Faculty Senate.[32]

Another motion, unanimously approved, demanded a reexamination of the composition of the WVU Board of Governors, "with the aim of increasing its transparency, representativeness and accountability."[33] This issue stemmed from the faculty's belief that the WVU administration had been "politicized." Governor Manchin, who attempted to remain aloof from the turmoil, calling it a "witch hunt," felt compelled to point out that the power of the governor to control the WVU Board of Governors was misunderstood. "I have seen it stated many times by individuals and the press that because I appointed certain members of the Board of Governors they must be following my orders as to what to think and say regarding President Garrison and the independent panel's report. This simply is not true," he declared. In addition to the fact that board members were "extremely capable" individuals, the rules of appointment were written to insure their independence from the governor. "While many members are appointed by a governor, they do not serve at the will and pleasure of a governor. They may act as they wish during their four-year terms as long as it is within legal and ethical reason." Therefore, he continued, members of the WVU Board of Governors "are not under my control and remain free, as they always have been, to make their own individual and collective decisions. . . . I am not in a position to make a recommendation to them in this instance even if I wanted to because . . . it would not be viewed as being made objectively—I absolutely understand and accept that." Consequently, Governor Manchin refused to interfere and stated that he would allow the board to determine the final outcome.[34]

On June 6, 2008, President Garrison was scheduled to report to the Board of Governors concerning progress toward implementing the reforms called for by the Special Investigative Panel. On May 20 an emergency meeting of the board was convened to discuss "personnel matters," but the chairman announced the board's intention to defer making any decisions on "personnel issues" until Garrison presented his report on June 6. Representatives from Mountaineers for Integrity and Responsibility were also scheduled to make a presentation at the June 6 board meeting. Professor Boyd Edwards, one of the leaders of the organization, told a reporter that Garrison's resignation was inevitable. "The faculty takes these matters very seriously. Many people view the faculty as just employees, but they are much more than that. The faculty are part of the shared governance of the university. The faculty senate and the administration work hand-in-hand to make important decisions." Edwards said that further pressure must be applied because "the administration has effectively ignored the no-confidence vote of the faculty senate and faculty assembly."[35]

How much influence an outraged faculty exerted on the board's decision regarding Garrison's presidency is difficult to gauge, but there is little question that the revolt among some of the University's most important benefactors riveted their attention like few others could. A Charleston philanthropist revoked a gift valued at $2 million as a result of the scandal, and he was joined by others. A letter dated June 3, 2008, was sent to the board from five members of the Academy of Distinguished Alumni, described as WVU graduates "who have attained national or international distinction in their profession or discipline." The letter "deplored recent events" at the University and asserted that "all right-thinking people know that universities should be citadels of independence and integrity." The board's decision to maintain its support for "a disgraced and increasingly isolated" president had focused their attention on the actions of the board itself. The solutions to WVU's problems were unambiguous, they wrote: the president must resign or be removed from office. "Most importantly, the Board of Governors must undertake a thorough self-assessment beginning with its flawed and politicized search to select David Hardesty's successor—to determine how WVU was allowed to get to this sorry state under its stewardship."[36]

Furthermore, R. Wayne King, director of the WVU Foundation, said he had received 130 letters, emails, and phone calls regarding the situation prior to Garrison's resignation. Only six of those letters expressed support for the president. A number of correspondents pledged large amounts of money which they would honor only after the president resigned.[37]

By the time the Board of Governors met on June 6, the tide had turned against President Garrison. The content of the personnel matters discussed by the board are always confidential, but at the end of the day, Garrison resigned the presidency. His contract was in effect through June 30, 2008; however, he offered to stay on through August to assist the interim president with the transition. Before the end of June, all three Garrison assistants most directly involved in the affair, Chief of Staff Craig Walker, Communications Director Bill Case, and Vice President for Legal Affairs Alex Macia, had stepped down. Walker and Macia left the University, and Case was reassigned to the Health Sciences Center. Three departing Board of Governors members were replaced by new members Charles Vest, Ray Lane, and Oliver Luck.[38] By August 30, former provost Gerald Lang was reassigned to managing the "Bucks for Brains" program in the WVU Research Office, and Michael Garrison had rejoined his former law firm. By the end of December two board members had resigned. The proposal by the Mountaineers for Integrity and Responsibility to change the state code in order to increase faculty representation on the Board of Governors was approved by the Faculty Senate and presented to the governor by members of the Mountaineers for Integrity. On May 19, 2009, Governor Manchin signed a bill that added a second faculty representative to the Board of Governors.[39]

In the wake of the degree scandal, a WVU faculty member posed the question facing WVU and the state in an op-ed: "Ultimately, the question is, where will WVU be in 20 years? Will WVU be a regionally-focused institution, mired in political controversies and lacking the courage to seek national or even international status? Or will WVU be a forward-looking world-class institution at the forefront of research and education—an engine for growth in West Virginia?" If WVU was to realize its full potential, leadership had to begin with the Board of Governors.[40] This was not a new question confronting WVU, but rather a variation of the same one it had grappled with since World War II.

Selection of an interim president to replace Michael Garrison was swift, and the choice met with universal approval. The Board of Governors picked C. Peter Magrath, a vigorous seventy-five year old higher education professional who possessed all of the credentials demanded by critics. A senior presidential adviser to the College Board and president emeritus of the National Association of State Universities and Land-Grant Colleges, Magrath had also served as president of three public universities: the University of Missouri system, the University of Minnesota, and the State University of New York at Binghamton, as well as interim president at the University of Nebraska. Magrath assumed his interim post effective July 15, 2008, and Garrison assisted in the transition until August 1. Former WVU president Gene Budig had initially suggested his old friend Magrath to the Board of Governors, and former WVU President E. Gordon Gee also spoke highly of him. He had also worked closely with former Governor Gaston Caperton, now president of the College Board, and shared a friendship with former WVU president David Hardesty and his wife, Susan. Magrath's chief of staff was John "Jay" Cole, a 1994 WVU graduate who served under Caperton as director of federal policy for the College Board. He had extensive experience in West Virginia higher education as an adviser to Governor Manchin on educational policy, as deputy secretary of education and the arts, and as senior policy adviser for former Governor Bob Wise prior to joining Caperton at the College Board.[41]

The demoralizing fog that had blanketed the WVU campus began to lift almost immediately after Magrath's arrival. While he acknowledged the "recent problems," he insisted that WVU had not suffered irreparable damage from the degree scandal. "This is not a ship that's even remotely sinking." Formerly vocal opponents of Garrison were effusive in their praise of Magrath's selection. Mountaineers for Integrity and Responsibility lauded his experience and leadership in higher education and thought it healthy that he brought an outside professional's perspective to the University. Faculty, staff, and student leaders all met with Magrath and reached a consensus that he was "the right man for the job." The faculty senator who had drafted the "no confidence" motion asserted that Magrath was "the kind of person we needed—someone with a national reputation that can show that WVU may be serious about the future development of the university."[42] Others agreed, and emphasized that the interim president was the right person because he was "an outsider—someone without links to West Virginia or its politics. . . . What he does know about academics and doesn't know about political cronyism, alone, recommends him." He was just the man to heal the University's wounds, and restore its self-assurance.[43]

One of the interim president's primary duties was to supervise the search for his replacement, and the process had begun by early September 2008. Selected to chair the search was former WVU President Gene Budig. In addition the committee included two Board of Governors representatives, two classified staff, two students, two administrators, three faculty members, and one representative each from the WVU Foundation, WVU Alumni Association, and the WVU Parents Club. Characteristics desired in the next president included experience in academic affairs, strong leadership skills, management of complex organizations, a balance of national and state experience, an appreciation of West Virginia ideals, experience in fundraising, a total understanding of land-grant universities, a student-centered focus, and a clear understanding of diversity.[44]

In October 2008, Magrath delivered the State of the Campus address, a speech emphasizing the importance of an "engaged university," a constant theme of David Hardesty. Perhaps it was only symbolic, the local paper editorialized, but in the audience was former President Hardesty, "who was also responsible for a virtual sea change at the university. It was a delight to see Hardesty and others rallying around Magrath's message of engagement. . . . One member of the Faculty Senate commented after Magrath's rallying cry, 'it's amazing how the demeanor of the whole university seems to be changing. We're all working together rather than against each other.'"[45] In the short time he was on campus, Magrath led an amazing turnaround in the confidence of the University community and its supporters. "Universities are so much more than something bad that happened," he told a student reporter. "I know enough about universities that when they have a really bad period, a scandal, it's not the end of the world."[46]

The search for a new president attracted about sixty individuals with an "active interest" in the position, and the committee hoped to announce its selection on or before a scheduled board meeting in April 2009. Ahead of schedule in early March, James P. Clements, the unanimous choice of the Board of Governors, was presented to the public as the University's twenty-third president. He officially stepped into his new position on June 30, 2009. Clements was educated at the University of Maryland, Baltimore County, and Johns Hopkins University, where he received advanced degrees in computer science. He became a faculty member at Towson State University in 1989, then served as chair of the Department of Computer and Information Sciences, the executive director of the Towson University Center for Applied Information Technology, and vice president of economic and community outreach. He was also appointed to the position of provost in 2007.[47]

Clements brought with him to WVU considerable expertise in the STEM fields of science, technology, engineering, and mathematics, all of which were disciplines the University depended on to elevate its national stature. Under Clements, the University returned to the Strategic Plan of 2010, which had been instituted under President Hardesty in 2005, by reinstating these goals in a new 2020 Strategic Plan. As a statement of its aspirations for the future, the most striking feature of that plan was its emphasis on improving WVU's research stature both nationally and internationally, supported by improvements in research facilities, increasing the number of international and graduate students, and investing in outstanding faculty committed to "research success in targeted areas in the institution," that is, the STEM fields. To achieve this goal, WVU would "transparently select programs, units, research areas and ventures that offer fertile ground for a high return on investment." To measure progress toward realizing these goals, the University would "monitor national visibility of programs and promote programs with high success metrics."[48]

One of President Clements's initiatives to bolster the University's research capacity was to continue to build new and renovate old research facilities. Examples were the $33 million renovation of White Hall, the new home of the physics department, and the $150 million construction and renovation plan for upgrading the Evansdale campus. Another was the plan to hire one hundred new faculty and make strategic appointments in the STEM disciplines. In effect, there was a seamless transition from Hardesty to Clements in positioning the University to become more entrepreneurial in research that would generate external funding and foster economic growth. WVU Hospitals announced a $280 million expansion project to construct a new ten-story tower to accommodate the growing number of patients. WVU Healthcare recorded 156,302 inpatient days in 2011, up about 50 percent from 1998.[49]

More change appeared on the horizon for intercollegiate athletics, as well, when WVU announced that it would leave the Big East Conference to join the Big 12 Conference on July 1, 2012. Premature withdrawal would cost WVU in the vicinity of $11 million in penalties, but those costs would quickly be recovered in increased income received from the Big 12, primarily from shared television revenues. The Big East payout to each team for 2010 was around $8 million; in comparison, the Big 12 distributed approximately $18 million to each team. More money made the move possible, but WVU supporters were most excited by the prospect of joining a conference that included schools such as Oklahoma, Texas, and Kansas. The invitation was seen as a confirmation that in sports WVU had arrived as a national university.[50]

Private giving was another area of growth highlighted on January 13, 2012, when Benjamin M. Statler and his wife Jo were honored at a ceremony to name the Benjamin M. Statler College of Engineering and Mineral Resources. Both were natives of Monongalia County, and Ben had received a WVU degree in mining engineering in 1973. The couple had given generously to the University over the years, but on this day they were heralded for contributing $34 million to the engineering college, the largest single gift ever received by WVU. The Statlers' extraordinary giving over time totaled approximately $60 million.[51]

One of the great fears about the commercialization of higher education was that so much emphasis would be placed on the disciplines with the potential to generate revenue that the liberal arts would suffer. This fear has not been realized at WVU. In fact, it might reasonably be argued that through the administration of David Hardesty the liberal arts disciplines were stronger than ever. Another commitment under serious stress is providing the most affordable education possible in an environment where students increasingly are expected to absorb more and the state less of the expenses for public higher education. Nationally, tuition rose approximately 300 percent from 1990 to 2010.[52] At WVU that increase was in the range of 150 percent, but without close monitoring the rising cost of a WVU education could tip the balance the University has meticulously maintained with its competitors in neighboring states. Skyrocketing student debt is a corollary concern. At some point the cost and threat of starting a career burdened by massive debt will be perceived to outweigh the benefits of a college degree, especially for students in the liberal arts.

Within a few years, Magrath's observation had proven to be true, the degree scandal was largely a thing of the past if not totally forgotten, and WVU had regained its footing on the road to the national stature to which it has aspired since World War II.

NOTES

PART I

1. Louis Menand, *The Marketplace of Ideas* (New York: W. W. Norton & Co., 2010), 64–65 (quotation); Roger L. Geiger, "The Ten Generations of American Higher Education," in *American Higher Education in the Twenty-first Century: Social, Political, and Economic Challenges*, ed. Philip G. Altbach, Robert O. Berdahl, and Patricia J. Gumport, 6–7 (Baltimore: Johns Hopkins University Press, 1999); Jonathan R. Cole, *The Great American University: Its Rise to Preeminence, Its Indispensable National Role, Why It Must Be Protected* (New York: Public Affairs, 2009), 139, 145; "Enrollment by Gender at WVU," *Morgantown Dominion Post*, March 31, 2008.
2. Cole, *Great American University*, 139. For a summary of the impact of the G.I. Bill, see Roger L. Geiger, *Research and Relevant Knowledge: American Research Universities since World War II* (New York: Oxford University Press, 1993).
3. Cole, *Great American University*, 85–87. See also Vannevar Bush's report, U.S. Office of Scientific Research and Development, *Science—The Endless Frontier* (Washington, DC: U.S. Government Printing Office, 1945).
4. Cole, *Great American University*, 88–96; Geiger, *Research and Relevant Knowledge*, 5–6.
5. Cole, *Great American University*, 96–99; Robert Franklin Maddox, *The Senatorial Career of Harley Martin Kilgore* (East Rockaway, NY: Cummings & Hathaway Publishers, 1997), 162–74, 232–34.
6. Cole, *Great American University*, 33–34.
7. Roul Tunley, "The Strange Case of West Virginia," *Saturday Evening Post*, February 6, 1960, 19–21, 64–66.
8. For recent works on the War on Poverty in Appalachia, see Michael Bradshaw, *The Appalachian Regional Commission: Twenty-five Years of Government Policy* (Lexington: University Press of Kentucky, 1992); Thomas Kiffmeyer, *Reformers to Radicals: The Appalachian Volunteers and the War on Poverty* (Lexington: University Press of Kentucky, 2008); Jerry Bruce Thomas, *An Appalachian Reawakening: West Virginia and the Perils of the New Machine Age, 1945–1972* (Morgantown: West Virginia University Press, 2010); Ronald D Eller, *Uneven Ground:*

Appalachia since 1945 (Lexington: University Press of Kentucky, 2008); Huey Perry, *They'll Cut Off Your Project: A Mingo County Chronicle* (Morgantown: West Virginia University Press, 2011, orig. 1972).

9. Menand, *Marketplace of Ideas*, 67–68 (quoting the act). See also Gary S. Becker, *Human Capital: A Theoretical and Empirical Analysis, with Special Reference to Education* (New York: National Bureau of Economic Research, 1964), and Theodore William Schultz, *The Economic Value of Education* (New York: Columbia University Press, 1963).

10. Menand, *Marketplace of Ideas*, 68; Elizabeth A. Duffy and Idana Goldberg, *Crafting a Class: College Admissions and Financial Aid, 1955–1994* (Princeton, NJ: Princeton University Press, 1998), 4, 22, 170.

11. Cole, *Great American University*, 134–38. For an explanation of the "multiversity," see Clark Kerr, *The Uses of the University*, 3rd ed. (Cambridge, MA: Harvard University Press, 1982, orig. 1963), 1–45.

12. Kerr, *Uses of the University*, 41–45 (quotation on 41), 46, 48.

13. Kerr, *Uses of the University*, 20 (both quotations).

CHAPTER ONE

1. William T. Doherty Jr. and Festus P. Summers, *West Virginia University: Symbol of Unity in a Sectionalized State* (Morgantown: West Virginia University Press, 1982), 89–90 (hereafter cited as Doherty and Summers, *WVU*); Charles C. Wise Jr., "Development of Policy for Higher Education in West Virginia," 94, in *West Virginia Policy Issues: Perspectives on the Past and Future of Coal, Water Resources, Higher Edcation, Welfare, Human Rights and Public Employee Bargaining*, ed. Allan S. Hammock and Sophia Peterson (Morgantown: West Virginia University Library, 1979), 91–101; Charles H. Ambler, *A History of Education in West Virginia: From Early Colonial Times to 1949* (Huntington, WV: Standard Printing and Publishing Co., 1951), 501–2.

2. Ambler, *History of Education*, 506–7; Wise, "Higher Education in West Virginia," 93.

3. Ambler, *History of Education*, 509–10; Doherty and Summers, *WVU*, 90.

4. Quotations from cited papers as reprinted in the *Morgantown Post Chronicle*, July 25, 1914 .

5. Doherty and Summers, *WVU*, 108–9; Ambler, *History of Education*, 512; quotations from cited papers as reprinted in the *Morgantown Post Chronicle*, December 31, 1913. See also,*Athenaeum*, February 20, 27, 1915.

6. *Morgantown Post Chronicle*, February 18, 1915; *Charleston Gazette*, February 20, 1915; William T. Doherty, "West Virginia's University: Symbol of Unity in a Sectionalized State," Morgantown, WV, 1980, typescript, vol. 1, 275 (hereafter cited as Doherty, "Symbol of Unity").

7. Quotations from cited papers as reprinted in *Morgantown Post Chronicle*, February 22, 1915; Doherty, "Symbol of Unity," 275.

8. *Charleston Mail*, October 4, 1916; Ambler, *History of Education*, 512–13; Doherty, "Symbol of Unity," 276–77.

9. *Charleston Mail*, December 28, 1916; Doherty and Summers, *WVU*, 112; Ambler, *History of Education*, 512, 514.

10. Ambler, *History of Education*, 515.

11. Ambler, *History of Education*, 515, 516; Marshall Buckalew, *The Life of Morris Purdy Shawkey* (Charleston: West Virginia Publishing Co., 1914), 94–95.

12. Ambler, *History of Education*, 517; Buckalew, *Life of Shawkey*, 74, 86–89. See also Charles Hill Moffatt, *Marshall University: An Institution Comes of Age, 1837–1980* (Huntington, WV: Marshall University Alumni Assoc., 1981).

13. Ambler, *History of Education*, 517–18 (quotation on 517); Buckalew, *Life of Shawkey*, 86.

14. Buckalew, *Life of Shawkey*, 87, quoting undated issues of the *Morgantown Dominion* and *Wheeling Intelligencer*.

15. Buckalew, *Life of Shawkey*, 90, reprints the *letter*. See also Ambler, *History of Education*, 519, and Wise, "Higher Education in West Virginia," 94.

16. Buckalew, *Life of Shawkey*, 91–92, quoting undated issues of the newspapers.

17. Ambler, *History of Education*, 555–57, quoting (on 556) State Board of Education, Minutes, January 18–19, 1923.

18. Ambler, *History of Education*, 502–3; Doherty, "Symbol of Unity," 312–13; Wise, "Higher Education in West Virginia," 94.

19. Ambler, *History of Education*, 519; Doherty and Summers, *WVU*, 136–37 (quotation on 136).

20. Ambler, *History of Education*, 600.

21. Ambler, *History of Education*, 843.

22. Ambler, *History of Education*, 850–51.

23. *Charleston Gazette*, December 17, 1920.

24. *Morgantown Post*, September 25, 1930.

25. Doherty and Summers, *WVU*, 148–49; *Charleston Gazette*, January 12, 1931 (quotation).

26. Doherty and Summers, *WVU*, 154–55.

27. Doherty and Summers, *WVU*, 156–57; Ambler, *History of Education*, 896; *Athenaeum*, October 17, 18, 1934.

28. *Morgantown Post*, May 17, 1934 (quotation); Ambler, *History of Education*, 843.

29. Ambler, *History of Education*, 843–44; Doherty, "Symbol of Unity," 417–19.

30. Ambler, *History of Education*, 844; Minutes of a Special Meeting of the Board of Governors, May 10, 1935, Order No. 207, 5–6. See *Who's Who* volumes after 1945 where Sly claimed he was "acting president."

31. Ambler, *History of Education*, 844–45 (quotation on 845); Wise, "Higher Education in West Virginia," 95; Doherty, "Symbol of Unity," 417–23.

32. Matthew M. Neely, "Inaugural Address," January 1941, *State Papers and Public Addresses* (Charleston: Mathews Printing Co., 1945), 48 (quotation); *Morgantown Post*, October 17, 1942.

33. Board of Governors of West Virginia University, Minutes, June 16, 1944, and June 20, 1944; *Morgantown Post*, June 20, 1944; Ambler, *History of Education*, 845–46.

34. Board of Governors of West Virginia University, Minutes, August 8, 1944, June 20, 1944, and June 24, 1944; Doherty, "Symbol of Unity," 451, 453.

35. *Morgantown Post*, June 20, 1944.

36. *Acts of the West Virginia Legislature*, Regular Session, 1921 (Charleston, WV: Tribune Co., 1921), 231; Matthew M. Neely, "The West Virginia University," an address broadcast over the West Virginia Network, July 6, 1944, *State Papers and Public Addresses* (Charleston, WV: Mathews Printing Co., 1945), 309–22.

37. *Morgantown Post*, July 8, 14 (quotation), 1944.

38. *Morgantown Post*, June 30, July 8, August 24 (quotation), 1944; Doherty, "Symbol of Unity," 460–61.

39. *Morgantown Post*, August 24, September 22, 30, 1944; Wise, "Higher Education in West Virginia," 95.

40 George D. Strayer, *A Digest of a Report of a Survey of Public Education in the State of West Virginia*, State of West Virginia, Legislative Interim Committee, 1945, 117 (hereafter cited as *Strayer Report*).

41. *Strayer Report*, 118–19.

42. *Strayer Report*, 120.

43. *Strayer Report*, 123–34, 136 (quotation).

44. *Morgantown Post*, October 30, 1946.

45. *Morgantown Post*, October 7 (quotation), November 7, 1946; Ambler, *History of Education*, 847.

46. Clarence W. Meadows, "Message to the Legislature," Regular Session, January 8, 1947, *State Papers and Public Addresses* (Charleston [stet]: Jarrett Printing Co., 1950), 179 (quotation); *Morgantown Post*, January 9, 1947.

47. *Morgantown Post*, June 28, 1947; Ambler, *History of Education*, 847; Doherty and Summers, *WVU*, 182; *Acts of the West Virginia Legislature*, Regular Session, 1921 (CharlestonV:[stet] Tribune Co., 1921), 231.

48. Doherty and Summers, *WVU*, 187–88.

CHAPTER TWO

1. Charles H. Ambler, *A History of Education in West Virginia: From Early Colonial Times to 1949* (Huntington, WV: Standard Printing and Publishing Co., 1951), 114–15. William T. Doherty Jr. and Festus P. Summers, *West Virginia University: Symbol of Unity in a Sectionalized State* (Morgantown: West Virginia University Press, 1982), 185–86 (hereafter cited as Doherty and Summers, *WVU*). See also Irvin Stewart, *Organizing Scientific Research for War* (Boston: Little, Brown and Co., 1948) for Stewart's wartime service. He was awarded the President's Medal for Merit by President Truman in 1948.

2. Ambler, *History of Education*, 915, 920. See also Inaugural Address of President Irvin Stewart, April 26, 1947; Address of President James Bryant Conant of

Harvard University, April 26, 1947; and Address of Dr. Vannevar Bush of the Carnegie Institution, April 25, 1947, all in Stewart Display, Non-Correspondence, Box 331, A&M 690.

3. "Ike's visit to W.V.U.," *West Virginia University Alumni News*, 34 (Spring 1969): 1, 21.

4. Irvin Stewart, *West Virginia University, 1946-1958: A Report Covering the Administration of Irvin Stewart as President of the University, July 1, 1946–June 30, 1958*, West Virginia University *Bulletin*, Series 58, No. 12–2, June 1958, 4.

5. Speech before the Faculty Dinner for the President, July 19, 1946, Irvin Stewart Speeches, Notebook 1, Box 355, A&M 690.

6. West Virginia University Day Speech, February 1952; and "The Impending Tide: W.V.U. Birthday Speech," February 1955, Irvin Stewart Speeches, Notebook 5, Box 354, A&M 690.

7. Inaugural Address of President Irvin Stewart, April 26, 1947, Stewart Display, Non-Correspondence, Box 331, A&M 690.

8. Inaugural Address of Irvin Stewart, April 26, 1947, Stewart Display, Non-Correspondence, Box 331, A&M 690.

9. Address of Irvin Stewart before the Mount Hope Lions Club, November 20, 1952, Irvin Stewart Speeches, Notebook 4, Box 354, A&M 690.

10. "The Impending Tide: W.V.U. Birthday Speech," February 1955, Irvin Stewart Speeches, Notebook 5, Box 354, A&M 690.

11. Stewart, *Report on WVU*, 5–7. See also Ambler, *History of Education*, 915; Becky Byrd Lofstead, "A Little Luck for No. 13," *West Virginia University Alumni Magazine* 13 (Summer 1990): 4.

12. Speech before the Faculty Dinner for the President, July 19, 1946, Irvin Stewart Speeches, Notebook 1, Box 355, A&M 690.

13. *Morgantown Post*, August 3, 1946.

14. *Morgantown Post*, July 31, 1946.

15. William T. Doherty, "West Virginia's University: Symbol of Unity in a Sectionalized State," vol. 1, 492–93, Morgantown, WV, 1980, typescript (hereafter Doherty, "Symbol of Unity"); Stewart, *Report on WVU*, 5.

16. Stewart, *Report on WVU*, 6–7; West Virginia University Day Speech, February 1952, Irvin Stewart Speeches, Notebook 4, Box 354, A&M 690.

17. Quoted in J. William Douglas, *School of Physical Education at West Virginia University: An Historical Perspective 1891-1999* (Morgantown: WVU School of Physical Education, 2000), 37–38.

18. Stewart, *Report on WVU*, 5–6, 9, 11; Doherty and Summers, *WVU*, 199; Ambler, *History of Education*, 915.

19. Stewart, *Report on WVU*, 9–11; Doherty and Summers, *WVU*, 200–1. See also multiple mentions of physical facilities in Irvin Stewart Speeches, Notebooks 1, 2, and 4, Box 354, A&M 690.

20. Statement by Irvin Stewart before Subcommittee of Committee on Education and Labor, on House Resolution 73, 82nd Cong., 1st Sess., 89–93 of hearings for October 16–19, 1951, Irvin Stewart Speeches, Notebook 4, Box 354, A&M 690.

21. Stewart, *Report on WVU*, 7–8; Doherty, "Symbol of Unity," vol. 2, 513–18; Ambler, *History of Education*, 972; Douglas, *School of Physical Education*, 40.

22. Doherty, "Symbol of Unity," vol. 2, 520–22.

23. Charles Ciotti, District Supervisor, War Assets Administration, to Irvin Stewart, February 28, 1949, Stewart Display, Correspondence, Box 329, A&M 690; Stewart, *Report on WVU*, 8.

24. C. F. Neff Jr. (Vice President) to Irvin Stewart, attachment, "Attested True Copy of the Offer of the Monongalia County Court for the Proposed Medical, Dental and Nursing School," February 20, 1951 (renewing the offer of June 18, 1951), President's Office, Box 329, A&M 690; Stewart, *Report on WVU*, 8.

25. Address to the West Virginia Coal Mining Institute, August 1, 1947, Irvin Stewart Speeches, Notebook 1, Box 355, A&M 690; Doherty and Summers, *WVU*, 194; Lofstead, "A Little Luck," 4; *Morgantown Post*, August 1, 1947.

26. *Morgantown Post*, October 4, 24, 1949, June 5, 1950; deed, June 5, 1950, in Stewart Display, Non-Correspondence, Misc., Box 329, A&M 690; Doherty, "Symbol of Unity," vol. 2, 498.

27. WVU Foundation, History, *http://www.wvuf.org/?q=node/23&cat=4*; Doherty and Summers, *WVU*, 195.

28. "Certificate of Incorporation, West Virginia University Foundation, Inc.," October 23, 1962, vol. 18, 539, Stewart Display, Non-Correspondence, Box 329, A&M 690; Stewart, *Report on WVU*, 31–32 (quotation); J. C. Atkins, "Private Support Fuels Foundation," WVU *Alumni Magazine* 13 (Summer 1990): 10.

29. Doherty and Summers, *WVU*, 195.

30. Stewart, *Report on WVU*, 23, 43.

31. Stewart, *Report on WVU*, 38.

32. Stewart, *Report on WVU*, 38.

33. Stewart, *Report on WVU*, 38–39.

34. See West Virginia Supreme Court, June 1939, *Glover v. Sims*; and *Morgantown Post*, April 26, 1950.

35. Minutes of a Special Meeting of the Board of Governors, January 27, 1951, and Minutes of the Twenty-fifth Annual Meeting of the Board of Governors, June 23, 24, 1951, Res. No. 678; Minutes of the Board of Regents, January 27, 1951, and June 2, 1951, Res. No. 678; *Morgantown Post*, October 5, 1949, April 10, 1950, October 24, 1951, and January 29, 1952; Stewart, *Report on WVU*, 39–40.

36. John Brewton, *Public Higher Education in West Virginia: A Survey Report*, Joint Committee on Government and Finance, West Virginia Legislature, Charleston, WV, 1956, 48–50 (quotations on 50) (Hereafter cited as *Brewton Report*).

37. *Brewton Report*, 51–52.

38. John Douglas Machesney, "The Development of Higher Education Governance and Coordination in West Virginia," (PhD diss. West Virginia University, 1971), 83, 86–87; *Brewton Report*, quotation on 49.

39. *Brewton Report*, 47.

40. *Brewton Report*, 54.

41. *Brewton Report*, 4.
42. *Brewton Report*, 5.
43. *Brewton Report*, 64. See also Machesney, "Higher Education," 87–90.
44. *Morgantown Post*, June 1, 1957; Doherty and Summers, *WVU*, 213; Lofstead, "A Little Luck for No. 13," 2–5.
45. *Morgantown Post*, June 3, 1957; Harold J. Shamberger, "A Score and More Years at West Virginia University, 15, typescript.
46. *Morgantown Post*, June 1, 1957; Doherty, "Symbol of Unity," vol. 2, 542–43; Lofstead, "A Little Luck for No. 13," 2–5.
47. *Morgantown Post*, October 3, Aug. 4, 1959.
48. *Morgantown Post*, August 4, Oct. 3, 1959; WVU *Alumni Magazine* 22 (Spring 1999): 4; Doherty, "Symbol of Unity," vol. 2, 626. Stahr died at his home in Greenwich, CN, age 82, on November 11, 1998. See his obituary in the *Dominion Post*, November 14, 1998.
49. Max Fullerton, "We Will Be 'Increasingly Proud': A Visit with Elvis Stahr," WVU *Alumni Magazine* 24 (Fall 1958): 6.
50. "After 92 Years—Which Way WVU in a Rapidly Changing World," University Day Banquet of the Kanawha County Alumni Association, Charleston, February 13, 1959, Speeches of the President, Elvis Stahr, Folder 1, Box 357, A&M 690.
51. "After 92 Years," University Day Banquet, February 13, 1959. See also the same speech at University Day Banquet, Ohio County Alumni Assoc., Wheeling, February 7, 1959, Speeches of Elvis Stahr, Notebook 1, Box 354, A&M 690.
52. Presentation to Governor Underwood, Members of the Board of Public Works, Members of the Council of Finance and Administration, Charleston, December 8, 1958, Speeches of Elvis Stahr, Notebook 1, Box 354, A&M 690.
53. Presentation to Governor Underwood et al., December 8, 1958.
54. Presentation to Senate Finance Committee, February 19, 1959, and Presentation to House of Delegates Finance Committee, March 4, 1959, Speeches of Elvis Stahr, Folder 1, Box 357, A&M 690.
55. Remarks before the Greater Fairmont Development Association, April 8, 1959, Speeches of Elvis Stahr, Folder 1, Box 357, A&M 690.
56. Remarks at the Annual Banquet of the Morgantown Chamber of Commerce, April 29, 1959, Speeches of Elvis Stahr, Folder 1, Box 357, A&M 690.
57. Golay and Stahr shared similar backgrounds. Both were Rhodes Scholars, flight lieutenants in World War II, and professors (Doherty, "Symbol of Unity," vol. 2, 700).
58. Minutes of the Board of Governors Meeting, April 13, 1960, Order No. 3116; Elvis Stahr, interview by Barbara Howe, July 1, 1992; Shamberger, "A Score and More," 1–4; "Your University Enters the Sixties," Address at the University Day Banquet, New York Chapter of the Alumni Assoc., February 11, 1960, Speeches of Elvis Stahr, Folder 1, Box 357, A&M 690.
59. "Your University Enters the Sixties," Speeches of Elvis Stahr, Folder 1, Box 357, A&M 690; Atkins, "Private Support Fuels Foundation," 10; "The Greater University Drive," WVU *Alumni News* 30 (Winter 1960): 3–4, 19.

60. Stahr interview; *Charleston Gazette*, January 14, 16, 1961; *Morgantown Post*, January 14, May 16, 1961(quotation); Doherty and Summers, *WVU*, 246–47.

61. Report of the Comptroller to the President of West Virginia University, 1961–1962, and Report of the President to the Members of the Board of Governors, July 1, 1960 to June 30, 1962, Speeches of Elvis Stahr, Box 357, A&M 690; *Daily Athenaeum*, January 17, 1961; *Morgantown Post*, February 9, 1961.

62. *Morgantown Post*, February 25, 1961.

63. *Morgantown Post*, February 27, 1961 (quotation); Doherty, "Symbol of Unity," vol. 2, 657–59.

64. *Morgantown Post*, March 2, 1961; Doherty and Summers, *WVU*, 248.

65. Dolores A. Fleming, Jeanne Grimm, and Patricia Schumann, *Generation of Growth: A Contemporary View of the West Virginia University School of Medicine* (Morgantown: WVU Publication Services, 1990), 1–2; Arthur C. Prichard, "Phoebia G. Moore, MD: First Woman to Study Medicine at West Virginia University," *Goldenseal: West Virginia Traditional Life* 5 (October-December 1979): 36.

66. Fleming, Grimm, and Schumann, *Generation of Growth*, 2–3.

67. Irvin Stewart, "Four Year School of Medicine for West Virginia, a 10-point program adopted by the West Virginia State Medical Assoc.," July 11, 1948; Doherty, "Symbol of Unity," vol. 2, 562.

68. Irvin Stewart, Speech before the West Virginia Medical Assoc., July 1948, Notebook 3, Box 355, A&M 690; Ambler, *History of Education*, 973; Doherty, "Symbol of Unity," vol. 2, 565.

69. Minutes of a Special Meeting of the Board of Governors, October 29 and 30, 1948, Res. No. 621, and Minutes of a Special Meeting of the Board of Governors, December 15, 1948 (quotation), Stewart Display, Non-Correspondence, Box 331, A&M 690; Ambler, *History of Education*, 973.

70. *Morgantown Post*, October 15, 22, 1948, countered arguments of the cities cited. See also Doherty, "Symbol of Unity," vol. 2, 568–69.

71. *Morgantown Post*, January 28, 1949; Doherty, "Symbol of Unity," II, 570.

72. *Morgantown Post*, February 8, 1949.

73. Report by Governor Okey L. Patteson Concerning the Location of the Medical School for Doctors, Dentists and Nurses in the State of West Virginia, June 30, 1951, 13 (hereafter cited as "Report of Governor Patteson"); *Morgantown Post*, February 18, 1949.

74. Irvin Stewart, Memorandum to Members of the West Virginia Legislature, February 6, 1957, Stewart Display, Non-Correspondence, Box 331, A&M 690; Fleming, Grimm, and Schumann, *Generation of Growth*, 4; Doherty, "Symbol of Unity," vol. 2, 585.

75. *Dr. Gregg Comments on Dean Davison's Report, The Case for Keeping the School of Medicine on University Campus* (Morgantown: Morgantown Printing and Binding Co., n.d.), 6; Doherty, "Symbol of Unity," vol. 2, 586–87.

76. *Morgantown Post*, March 8, 1951; Report by Governor Patteson, 1; Fleming, Grimm, and Schumann, *Generation of Growth*, 4.

77. Report by Governor Patteson, 2.

78. Report by Governor Patteson, 26–33.
79. Stewart, *Report on WVU*, 16; Kenneth A. Penrod, "A Modern Medical Center is Born," Journal of Medical Education, 36 (May 1961): 393–97; *Morgantown Post*, July 2, 1951, reported reaction of other state newspapers.
80. Stewart, *Report on WVU*, 16–17; Doherty and Summers, *WVU*, 228–29, 238.
81. Address of Irvin Stewart before the Mount Hope Lions Club, November 20, 1952, Irvin Stewart Speeches, Notebook 4, Box 354, A&M 690.
82. West Virginia University Day Speech, February 1952, Irvin Stewart Speeches, Notebook 4, Box 354, A&M 690 (quotation); Doherty and Summers, *WVU*, 230.
83. Fleming, Grimm, and Schumann, *Generation of Growth*, 5.
84. Fleming, Grimm, and Schumann, *Generation of Growth*, 5–6 (quotation on 6).
85. Fleming, Grimm, and Schumann, *Generation of Growth*, 5.
86. Remarks to the West Virginia State Medical Association, August 22, 1963, Speeches of Paul A. Miller, Box 357, A&M 690.
87. Remarks to the West Virginia State Medical Association, August 22, 1963, and Remarks to Special Meeting of Faculty and Officers of Administrative Staff, October 22, 1963 (quotation), Speeches of Paul A. Miller, Box 357, A&M 690.
88. Stewart, *Report on WVU*, 14.
89. "Eighty-Three Years Later," Address of Irvin Stewart before the Kanawha County Alumni, February 7, 1950, Irvin Stewart Speeches, Notebook 3, Box 355, A&M 690.
90. Stewart, *Report on WVU*, 14.
91. Irvin Stewart, "Coal and the University," Address before the West Virginia Coal Mining Institute, November 15, 1946, Huntington, WV, reprinted in *Proceedings of the West Virginia Coal Mining Institute*, 39th Annual Meeting, Bluefield, WV, 128.
92. Stewart, "Coal and the University," 128, 130–31, 133, 136; Inaugural address of Irvin Stewart, April 26, 1947 (quotation), Stewart Display, Non-Correspondence, Box 331, A&M 690.
93. George D. Strayer, *A Digest of a Report of a Survey of Public Education in the State of West Virginia*, State of West Virginia, Legislative Interim Committee, 1945, 657 (hereafter cited as *Strayer Report*).
94. Lofstead, "A Little Luck for No. 13," 5.
95. Irvin Stewart, "Eighty-Three Years Later," Address before the Kanawha County Alumni, February 7, 1950, Irvin Stewart Speeches, Notebook 3, Box 355, A&M 690.
96. "The Impending Tide: W.V.U. Birthday Speech," February 1955, Irvin Stewart Speeches, Notebook 5, Box 354, A&M 690.
97. *Brewton Report*, 204.
98. Doherty and Summers, *WVU*, 204; William C. Marland to Irvin Stewart, Stewart Display, Correspondence, May 7, 1955, Box 331, A&M 690.
99. Walter R. Thurmond to Irvin Stewart, December 12, 1956, Stewart Display, Correspondence, Box 331, A&M 690.
100. Irvin Stewart to Deans, July 29, 1948, Stewart Display, Non-Correspondence, Box 331, A&M 690; Stewart, *Report on WVU*, 19.
101. Stewart, *Report on WVU*, 20.

1. Paul Miller, interview by Barbara Howe, June 18, 1992; William T. Doherty, "West Virginia University: Symbol of Unity in a Sectionalized State," vol. 2, 671–72, typescript.

2. Miller, interview by Howe. See also, Harold J. Shamberger, "A Score and More Years at West Virginia University," 1999, 14, typescript.

3. *Daily Athenaeum*, November 21, 1961 (quotation); Harold J. Shamberger, interview by Ronald L. Lewis, March 6, 2008.

4. *Sunday Gazette-Mail*, November 19, 1961 (quotation); Doherty, "Symbol of Unity," vol. 2, 673.

5. *Wheeling Intelligencer*, November 8, 1961.

6. Miller, interview by Howe.

7. Shamberger, "A Score and More," 15.

8. Paul Miller to Irvin Stewart, August 3, 1966, Presidents' Papers, F-8, Box 4, A&M 5017.

9. Miller, interview by Howe.

10. *Morgantown Post*, April 11, 1961; "Inauguration of Miller," WVU *Alumni Magazine*, 27 (Spring 1962): 5–7; William T. Doherty Jr. and Festus P. Summers, *West Virginia University: Symbol of Unity in a Sectionalized State* (Morgantown: West Virginia University Press, 1982), 252.

11. Address before Presbyterian Men's Panel of Morgantown First Presbyterian Church, October 9, 1963, Speeches of Paul A. Miller, Box 357, A&M 690.

12. Miller to Professor John S. Zawacki, May 12, 1964, Presidents' Papers, F-8, Box 4, A&M 5017; Shamberger, "A Score and More," 14–15; Doherty, "Symbol of Unity," vol. 2, 680.

13. Remarks to Special Meeting of Faculty and Officers of Administrative Staff, October 22, 1963, Speeches of Paul A. Miller, Box 357, A&M 690.

14. Remarks, Council of Administrative Retreat, April 13, 1964, Speeches of Paul A. Miller, Box 357, A&M 690.

15. Remarks to Special Meeting of Faculty and Officers of Administrative Staff, October 5, 1964, Speeches of Paul A. Miller, Box 357, A&M 690.

16. Remarks to Special Meeting of Faculty and Officers of Administrative Staff, October 22, 1963, Speeches of Paul A. Miller, Box 357, A&M 690.

17. Remarks, Council of Administration Retreat, April 13, 1964, Speeches of Paul A. Miller, Box 357, A&M 690.

18. Remarks, Council of Administration Retreat, April 13, 1964, Speeches of Paul A. Miller, Box 357, A&M 690.

19. West Virginia University, "Self Study Reports Prepared for the North Central Association Review Visit," March 27, 1964, E-II, 1 and E-III, 3 (hereafter cited as "Self Study 1964").

20. Remarks before the Board of Public Works, December 9, 1963, and Remarks before the Senate Committee on Education, January 21, 1964, Speeches of Paul A. Miller, Box 357, A&M 690; Miller, interview by Howe.

21. Address before the XX Club of Morgantown, February 21, 1967, Speeches of Harry Heflin, Box 357, A&M 690.

22. "Self Study 1964," C-IV, 2.

23. Remarks before the Board of Public Works, 1964–65 Budget Request, December 9, 1963, Speeches of Paul A. Miller, Box 357, A&M 690.

24. Remarks before the Board of Public Works, 1964–1965 Budget Request, December 9, 1963, Speeches of Paul A. Miller, Box 357, A&M 690.

25. Remarks before the Board of Public Works, 1965–1966 Budget Request, December 7, 1964, Speeches of Paul A. Miller, Box 357, A&M 690.

26. Remarks: Special Convocation of the Faculty, September 21, 1962, Speeches of Paul A. Miller, Box 357, A&M 690.

27. Remarks to Special Meeting of Faculty and Officers of Administrative Staff, October 5, 1964, Speeches of Paul A. Miller, Box 357, A&M 690.

28. Remarks, Council of Administration Retreat, April 13, 1964, Speeches of Paul A. Miller, Box 357, A&M 690.

29. Doherty and Summers, *WVU*, 272.

30. Miller, interview by Howe.

31. Shamberger, "A Score and More," 17–18.

32. "Self-Study 1964," 157–58.

33. President Paul Miller to Members of the Board of Governors, "The West Virginia Center for Appalachian Studies and Development as Approved on February 5, 1963," 1–3, President's Office, Folder 6, Box 4, A&M 5017.

34. Miller to Members of the Board, "Center for Appalachian Studies," 4–5.

35. "Self-Study 1964," 158; Miller to Members of the Board, "Center for Appalachian Studies," 6–7. See also "Research Proposal on West Virginia Center for Appalachian Studies and Development, Presented to Area Development Administration," July 1962, President's Office, Folder 6, Box 4, A&M 5017.

36. Miller, interview by Howe (quotations); Edward Steel, interview by Ronald L. Lewis, May 19, 2009; Doherty and Summers, *WVU*, 256–57.

37. Miller interview; Doherty and Summers, *WVU*, 258.

38. "New and Current," WVU *Alumni Magazine* 27 (Winter 1962): 3.

39. Earnest Nesius, interview by Barbara Howe, August 24, 30, 1989; Barbara J. Howe, "Center for Appalachian Studies and Development, 1963–1974," 24–25, typescript.

40. Quoted in Howe, "Center for Appalachian Studies and Development," 25; Nesius, interview by Howe, August 24, 1989.

41. Howe, "Center for Appalachian Studies and Development," 25; Nesius, interview by Howe, August 30, 1989.

42. Howe, "Center for Appalachian Studies and Development," 13–14. See also Louis Alfred Trosch, "A Case Study of the West Virginia Center for Appalachian Studies and Development" (MA thesis, George Washington University, 1966), 89, and *Appalachian Center Report*, passim.; Nesius interview, September 14, 1989. For the legal issues entailed in financing the new college see the "Parkersburg Center File," President's Office, Box 338, A&M 690, and Billy Coffindaffer, interview by Barbara Howe, September 29, 1993.

43. Howe, "Center for Appalachian Studies and Development," 15; Nesius, interview by Howe, September 14, 1989; "Self Study 1964," B-IV-1.

44. Howe, "Center for Appalachian Studies and Development," 15–16; Report of the Study Made on the Feasibility of Expanding the Graduate-Research Center in the Kanawha Valley, March 8, 1965, President's Office, Box 357, A&M 690; Address, University for the State, Living Resources Forum, Morgantown, January 28, 1964, Speeches of Paul Miller, Box 357, A&M 690.

45. Progress Report, Study of the Proposal for the Establishment of a Law and Public Affairs Center of West Virginia University, Speeches of Paul A. Miller, Box 357, A&M 690.

46. *West Virginia University Bulletin*, Series 67, No. 4:2, October 1966, 16 (quotation); Office of the President, Working Paper with reference to the establishment of a Law and Public Affairs Center, May 11, 1966, and Progress Report, Study of the Proposal for the Establishment of a Law and Public Affairs Center of West Virginia University, Speeches of Paul A. Miller, Box 357, A&M 690.

47. The *Morgantown Post* called on all supporters of the University to mobilize to defend the "integrity and unity" of WVU in Morgantown (May 9, 1966).

48. Quotation from the Faculty of the College of Law to the President and Board of Governors of West Virginia University, May 25, 1966, F6–8, Box 4, A&M 5017.

49. Willard D. Lorensen, Professor of Law, to the Board of Governors, n.d., F 6-8, Box 4, A&M 5017; Doherty and Summers, *WVU*, 260.

50. Jerome S. Sloan, Professor of Law, quoted in the *Daily Athenaeum*, May 12, 1966.

51. Richard E. Ford, President, Herschel Rose, retiring president, WVU Law School Assoc. to the Board of Governors, June 16, 1966, President's Papers, F 6-8, Box 4, A&M 5017; Minutes of a Special Meeting of the Board of Governors held in Morgantown, March 10-11, 1967, and April 14-15, 1967; *Morgantown Dominion News*, May 13, 17, 1966.

52. Miller interview; Shamberger, "A Score and More," 32 (quotation).

53. Miller interview.

54. Doherty, "Symbol of Unity," vol. 2, 701.

55. Doherty and Summers, *WVU*, 262.

56. "The Future Direction of the University—A White Paper," April 11, 1967.

57. Miller interview.

58. "Appalachian Development," WVU *Alumni News* 28 (Summer 1962): 4; Billy Coffindaffer interview, and Howe, "Center for Appalachian Studies and Development"; "Research Proposal on West Virginia Center for Appalachian Studies and Development," presented to U.S. Area Redevelopment Administration, July 1962, President's Office, Folder 6, Box 4, A&M 5017.

59. Coffindaffer interview.

60. *Charleston Gazette*, June 29, 1966; Shamberger, "A Score and More," 36; quote from Miller interview; Edward Steel interview.

61. Statement of the Board of Governors, July 8, 1966, Misc. file, Box 357, A&M 690; *West Virginia University Bulletin*, Series 67, No. 4:2 (October 1966), 8; *Charleston Gazette*, July 6, 1966.

62. Statement on New Appointment, July 8, 1966, Speeches of Paul A. Miller, Box 357, A&M 690.

63. Minutes of a Special Meeting of the Board of Governors, July 7–9, 1966, 1–4; Doherty and Summers, *WVU*, 271.

64. *Morgantown Post*, July 11, 1966; Stanley Lawson, Superior Court of the State of California to the Board of Governors, August 16, 1966 (quotation), Minutes, Board of Governors, Aug. 15-16, 1966; Doherty, "Symbol of Unity," vol. 2, 420–21.

65. "Campus Scene: 18th President," WVU *Alumni Magazine* 4 (Fall 1981): 22–23; David C. Hardesty Jr., "Character Matters: Remarks at the Funeral of a Former President," October 3, 2006, *Leading the Public University: Essays, Speeches, and Commentary*, by David C. Hardesty Jr. with Susan B. Hardesty (Morgantown: West Virginia University Press, 2007), 222-28.

66. Harry Heflin, Supporting Remarks before the Senate Finance Committee, the 1967–1968 Budget Request, February 3, 1967, Speeches of Harry Heflin, Box 357, A&M 690; *Morgantown Post*, December 30, 1966, March 15, 1967; Minutes, Board of Governors, April 14–15, 1967.

67. Doherty and Summers, *WVU*, 274-75.

68. Harry B. Heflin, Address before the American Right of Way Association, December 8, 1966, Speeches of Harry Heflin, Box 357, A&M 690.

69. Harry Heflin, Address before the XX Club of Morgantown, February 21, 1967, Speeches of Harry Heflin, Box 357, A&M 690.

70. "Self Study 1964," B–II, 9–10.

71. Remarks, Special Convocation of the Faculty, Speeches of Paul A. Miller, Box 357, A&M 690.

72. Miller interview; Max Fullerton, "I Call on President Miller," WVU *Alumni Magazine* 28 (Winter 1963): 5; "Self Study 1964," B–II, 9–10.

73. *Charleston Gazette*, July 15, 1966; *Morgantown Post*, December 6, 1966; Doherty and Summers, *WVU*, 272-74.

74. "Festivity Ahead," WVU *Alumni News* 32 (Winter 1967): 3.

75. Address before the Ohio County Chapter, WVU Alumni Association, February 11, 1967, Speeches of Harry Heflin, Box 357, A&M 690.

76. Address before the Ohio County Chapter, February 11, 1967.

77. Address before Faculty Honors Convocation, March 7, 1967, quoted in Doherty and Summers, *WVU*, 280-81.

78. Doherty and Summers, *WVU*, 280.

CHAPTER FOUR

1. Elvis Stahr, interview by Barbara Howe, July 1, 1992 (quotation); News Release, Admission of Out-of-State Students to the Medical School, August 31, 1960, Misc. File, Box 357, A&M 690; *Morgantown Post*, May 10, 1960.

2. West Virginia University, "Self Study Reports Prepared for the North Central Association Review Visit," 1964, A–I, 1–11, F–II, 2.

3. "Self Study 1964," A–I, 12, A–II, 3, and G–I, 4–5.

4. *Bluefield Telegraph*, November 22, 1947.

5. *Clarksburg Exponent Telegram*, October 26, 1947.

6. Address of Irvin Stewart before the Mount Hope Lions Club, November 20, 1952, Irvin Stewart Speeches, Notebook 4, Box 354, A&M 690.

7. Charles H. Ambler, *A History of Education in West Virginia from Colonial Times to 1949* (Huntington, WV: Standard Printing and Publishing Co., 1951), 937–38.

8. *Daily Athenaeum*, October 3, 1947 (quotation); *Morgantown Post*, April 17, 1950.

9. Ambler, *History of Education*, 942–43 (quotation on 943).

10. *Morgantown Post*, January 18, 1950.

11. *Morgantown Post*, February 6, 1950; Ambler, *History of Education*, 942.

12. *Insight*, Oct. 29, 1979.

13. *Morgantown Post*, May 5, 1949; Becky Byrd Lofstead, "A Little Luck for Number 13," WVU *Alumni Magazine* 13 (Summer 1990): 4 (quotation).

14. Lofstead, "A Little Luck," 4. The Mountaineers were led to the National Invitational Tournament by Leland Byrd in 1947, and again in 1948.

15. Gordon R. Thorn and Scott B. Rubin, *The Mountaineer Statue* (Morgantown: WVU Printing Services, n.d.); *Morgantown Post*, November 17, 1950.

16. Roger Tompkins, Student Body President, to President Irvin Stewart, May 15, 1957, and Ruth E. Robinson, Manager, WVU Book Store to Irvin Stewart, May 28, 1957, Stewart Display, Correspondence, Box 331, A&M 690.

17. "New & Current," 27 (Winter 1962): 2; *Morgantown Post*, March 18, December 7, 1961.

18. Ambler, *History of Education*, 944–47.

19. "Self Study 1964," F–II, 6.

20. Irvin Stewart, *West Virginia University, 1946–1958: A Report Covering the Administration of Irvin Stewart as President of the University, July 1, 1946–June 30, 1958*, West Virginia University *Bulletin*, Series 58, No. 12–2, June 1958, 24 (hereafter cited as Stewart, *Report on WVU*).

21. Rose Yaromy (Cassville) to Irvin Stewart, February 9, 1949, (quotation), Andrew Thomas (St. Francis High School) to Irvin Stewart, February 19, 1949, and Irvin Stewart to Andrew Thomas, February 21, 1949, all in Stewart Display, Correspondence, Box 331, A&M 690.

22. Irvin Stewart to Edward P. Bartkus, February 21, 1949, Stewart Display, Correspondence, Box 331, A&M 690.

23. Patrick W. Gainer to Joseph Gluck, November 10, 1951, Stewart Display, Correspondence, Box 331, A&M 690. Without a faculty sponsor, *Moonshine* disappeared.

24. Marian B. Ingram to Irvin Stewart, May 19, 1953, Stewart Display, Correspondence, Box 331, A&M 690.

25. Joseph C. Gluck to Irvin Stewart, May 26, 1953, Stewart Display, Correspondence, Box 331, A&M 690.

26. C. T. Neff Jr. to Irvin Stewart, May 22, 1952, Stewart Display, Correspondence, Box 331, A&M 690.

27. Irvin Stewart, Press Release, May 22, 1952, and Irvin Stewart, Report to the Board of Governors, May 22, 1952, Stewart Display, Correspondence, Box 331, A&M 690.

28. Irvin Stewart to Board of Governors, November 11, 1955, Stewart Display, Correspondence, Box 331, A&M 690.

29. William T. Doherty and Festus P. Summers, *West Virginia University: Symbol of Unity in a Sectionalized State* (Morgantown: West Virginia University Press, 1982), 243.

30. *Daily Athenaeum*, April 28, 29 (quotations), 1960. See also, Elvis Stahr, interview.

31. "Self Study 1964," F–II, 1, 3.

32. Remarks to Special Meeting of Faculty and Officers of Administrative Staff, Oct. 22, 1963, Speeches of Paul A. Miller, Box 357, A&M 690. See also Harold J. Shamberger, "A Score and More Years at West Virginia University," 1999, typescript, 16.

33. Paul Miller, interview by Barbara Howe, June 18, 1992 (quotation); *Daily Athenaeum*, May 10, 1962.

34. Miller interview.

35. The literature on the civil rights struggle is immense. For a standard, see Richard Kluger, *Simple Justice: The History of Brown v. Board of Education and Black America's Struggle for Equality* (New York: Alfred A. Knopf, 1976); Ambler, *History of Education*, 819 (quotation).

36. Connie Park Rice, *Our Monongalia: A History of African Americans in Monongalia County, West Virginia* (Terra Alta, WV: Headline Books, Inc., for the Community Race Relations Forum Association, 1999), 130; *Dominion Post*, March 31, 2008; "Mountaineer Miscellany," WVU *Alumni Quarterly* 1 (Summer 1978): 27.

37. Kathy Daweese, "Living Through History: *Brown v. Board of Education* and WVU," WVU *Alumni Magazine* 28 (Fall 2004): 33–37; Horace Belmear quoted in J. William Douglas, *The School of Physical Education at West Virginia University: An Historical Perspective, 1891–1999* (Morgantown: WVU School of Physical Education, 2000), 39.

38. *Morgantown Post*, November 19, 1943 (quotation); Deweese, "Living Through History," 33–37 ; Rice, *Our Monongalia*, 131; Geraldine Harrison, interview by Barbara Howe, June 21, 1992.

39. Personal letter, Arthur Garrison Phillips (WVU '51) to Ronald L. Lewis, July 15, 2008, Ronald L. Lewis Papers.

40. Jack L. Hodge, "A Proud Day," *West Virginia University Magazine* 7 (Summer 1975): 12.

41. Hodge, "Proud Day," 14–15.

42. Kluger, *Simple Justice*, passim. For a short treatment of desegregation in West Virginia, see Jerry Bruce Thomas, *An Appalachian Reawakening: West Virginia and the Perils of the New Machine Age, 1945–1972* (Morgantown: West Virginia University Press, 2010), 105–8.

43. William P. Jackameit, "A Short History of Negro Public Higher Education in West Virginia, 1890–1965," *West Virginia History* 37 (1976): 319; Irvin Stewart to Attorney General John G. Fox, May 21, 1954, Attorney General Fox to Irvin Stewart, June 1, 1954, Stewart Display, Correspondence, Box 331, A&M 690.

44. Quotation from Irvin Stewart to Board of Governors, June 2, 1954, Stewart Display, Correspondence, Box 331, A&M 690; *Charleston Gazette*, November 11, 1955; Stewart, *Report on WVU*, 25.

45. For McCarthy's speech, see the *Wheeling Intelligencer*, February 10, 1950, reprinted in *West Virginia: Documents in the History of a Rural-Industrial State*, 2nd ed., ed. Ronald L. Lewis and John C. Hennen Jr. (Dubuque, IA: Kendall/Hunt Publishing Co., 1991), 288–89.

46. Irvin Stewart to Board of Governors, November 3, 1947, Stewart Display, Correspondence, Box 331, A&M 690.

47. Speeches of Irvin Stewart, Notebooks 1-5, Boxes 354-355, A&M 690; Stewart to Edward L. Blake, Ranson, WV, January 12, 1948, Stewart Display, Correspondence, Box 331, A&M 690.

48. Address before the West Virginia Association of School Superintendents, Charleston, WV, April 9, 1948, Irvin Stewart Speeches, Notebook 2, Box 355, A&M 690.

49. Rush Holt to Irvin Stewart, May 22, 1951, and Irvin Stewart to Board of Governors, May 23, 1951, Stewart Display, Correspondence, Box 338, A&M 690.

50. Stewart to "budget officers," September 30, 1950, and Loyalty Oath file, Box 338, A&M 690.

51. Stewart to Board of Governors, June 20, 1949; Doherty and Summers, *WVU*, 209.

52. William R. Ross to Irvin Stewart, January 28, 1952, and Stewart to William R. Ross, January 30, 1952; Stewart to Board of Governors, January 30, 1952 (quotations); Stewart to Governor Patteson, September 15, 1952; and Stewart memo to faculty, September 17, 1952, all in Stewart Display, Correspondence, Box 338, A&M 690.

53. Remarks to a Special Meeting of Faculty and Officers of Administrative Staff, October 22, 1963, Speeches of Paul A. Miller, Box 357, A&M 690; Doherty and Summers, *WVU*, 266.

54. Minutes, University Senate, February 9, 1965; *Daily Athenaeum*, May 10, 1962, October 21, 1963, November 11, 1964, February 9, 1965, April 6, 1965.

55. *Daily Athenaeum*, November 23, December 2, 1965; Douglas, *School of Physical Education*, 39.

56. *Daily Athenaeum*, January 27, 1967; *Charleston Gazette*, November 23, 1967; *Morgantown Post*, April 30, 1969; Doherty and Summers, *WVU*, 268–69.

57. *Morgantown Post*, December 20, 26, 1946, March 8, 1947; West Virginia University *Bulletin*, Series 58, No. 12-2 (June 1958): 35; Ambler, *History of Education*, 904–9, 916–18.

58. Irvin Stewart, "A Note on Higher Education in West Virginia," May 1, 1953, Stewart Display, Non-Correspondence, Box 331, A&M 690.

59. Stewart, *Report on WVU*, 35 (quotation).

60. John Antonik, *West Virginia University Football Vault: The History of the Mountaineers* (Atlanta: Whitman Pub., LLC, 2009), 20–29, 38.

61. Antonik, *Football Vault*, 53–56, quoting the *Charleston Gazette* on 56.

62. *Morgantown Post*, January 5, 1949, January 28, 1950; Antonik, *Football Vault*, 59 (quotations).

63. *Morgantown Post*, February 17, March 7, 1950; Antonik, *Football Vault*, 59–65.

64. Quoted in Antonik, *Football Vault*, 65–66.
65. Mickey Furfari, *Mickey's Mountaineer Memories* (Beckley, WV: Beckley News-papers, Inc., 2008), 47–50, 8–10; Antonik, *Football Vault*, 67–69, 72; *Dominion Post*, November 29, 2007; Douglas, *School of Physical Education*, 46.
66. Statement of Elvis Stahr regarding West Virginia University Football Program, Jan-uary 17, 1960, Speeches of Elvis Stahr, Box 357, A&M 690; Antonik, *Football Vault*, 74–75; Doherty and Summers, *WVU*, 245.
67. Antonik, *Football Vault*, 76.
68. Douglas, *School of Physical Education*, 47; John Antonik, *Roll Out the Carpet: 101 Seasons of West Virginia University Basketball* (Morgantown: West Virginia University Press, 2010), 46–53; Norman Julian, *Legends* (Morgantown, WV: Tril-lium Publishing, 1998), 69–76; Doherty and Summers, *WVU*, 141, 198.
69. Douglas, *School of Physical Education*, 47; Doherty and Summers, *WVU*, 198.
70. Antonik, *Roll Out the Carpet*, 68–69; Julian, *Legends*, 31–34, 80–89; Douglas, *School of Physical Education*, 47–48.
71. Julian, *Legends*, 84–89; Antonik, *Roll Out the Carpet*, 63–85; Douglas, *School of Physical Education*, 48; Furfari, *Mickey's Memories*, 40–42. See Hundley's auto-biography, Rod Hundley and Tom McEachin, *Hot Rod Hundley: "You Gotta Love It Baby"* (Champaign, IL: Sports Publishing Inc., 1998).
72. Antonik, *Roll Out the Carpet*, 85–91; Douglas, *School of Physical Education*, 48; Mark Scharf, "Where Are They Now?" (Joe Smith and Willie Akers), *Dominion Post*, April 3, 2010, 11–12.
73. Antonik, *Roll Out the Carpet*, 85–101; Douglas, *School of Physical Education*, 48–49.
74. *Dominion Post*, November 27, 2005, and January 24, 2010. There are a number of books about West. Most noteworthy is his autobiography, Jerry West and Jonathan Coleman, *West By West: My Charmed, Tormented Life* (New York: Little, Brown and Co., 2011).
75. *Morgantown Post*, July 7, 1959; Doherty and Summers, *WVU*, 244–46

PART II

1. Louis Menand, *The Marketplace of Ideas* (New York: W. W. Norton & Co., 2010), 68. See also Elizabeth A. Duffy and Idana Goldberg, *Crafting a Class: College Ad-missions and Financial Aid, 1955–1994* (Princeton, NJ: Princeton University Press), and United States, Bureau of the Census, *Statistical Abstract of the United States* (Washington, DC: U.S. Government Printing Office, 1996).
2. Menand, *Marketplace of Ideas*, 68–69; Duffy and Goldberg, *Crafting a Class*, 22.
3. Menand, *Marketplace of Ideas*, 69–70 (quotation on 70); Martin J. Finkelstein, Robert K. Seal, and Jack H. Schuster, *The New Academic Generation: A Profes-sion in Transformation* (Baltimore: Johns Hopkins University Press, 1998), 26–32.
4. "Enrollment by Gender at WVU," *Morgantown Dominion Post*, March 31, 2008. This article recapitulates WVU enrollment data from 1912–1913 to 2007–2008.

5. Menand, *Marketplace of Ideas*, 73–75; Thomas Bender, "Politics, Intellect, and the American University, 1945–1995," in *American Academic Culture in Transformation: Fifty Years, Four Disciplines*, ed. Bender and Carl E. Schorske, 17–55 (Princeton, NJ: Princeton University Press, 1998); Daniel Bell, *The End of Ideology: On the Exhaustion of Political Ideas in the Fifties* (New York: The Free Press, 1962), 17–54.

6. Jonathan R. Cole, *The Great American University: Its Rise to Preeminence, Its Indispensable National Role, Why It Must Be Protected* (New York: Public Affairs, 2009), 154.

7. Cole, *Great American University*, 152–53; Menand, *Marketplace of Ideas*, 77–79.

8. Menand, *Marketplace of Ideas*, 79–80; Earnest L. Boyer, *Scholarship Reconsidered: Priorities of the Professoriate* (San Francisco: Carnegie Foundation for the Advancement of Teaching, 1990).

9. Lionel Trilling, *Beyond Culture: Essays on Literature and Learning* (New York: Viking Press, 1965), vii–viii (quotation); Cole, *Great American University*, 153–54. See also Daniel Bell, *The Coming of Post-Industrial Society* (New York: Basic Books, 1973), 477–78; and Alvin Kernan, ed., *What's Happening to the Humanities?* (Princeton, NJ: Princeton University Press), 1997, 3–4.

10. Menand, *Marketplace of Ideas*, 91.

11. *The Strategic Plan for Achieving Social Justice at West Virginia University*, David Hardesty Papers, Box 5, A&M 5114.

12. David C. Hardesty Jr., "Diversity: Tomorrow's Source of Organizational Strength," and "A Preliminary Look at the Evolution of Social Justice at WVU," prepared by Barbara Howe, director of women's studies, April 1999, both documents in David Hardesty Papers, Box 5, A&M 5114.

13. Cole, *Great American University*, 156. In this regard, WVU is not exceptional.

CHAPTER FIVE

1. William T. Doherty Jr. and Festus P. Summers, *West Virginia University: Symbol of Unity in a Sectionalized State* (Morgantown: West Virginia University Press, 1982), 242–44, 270–71; Charles C. Wise Jr., "Development of Policy for Higher Education in West Virginia," 94, in *West Virginia Policy Issues: Perspectives on the Past and Future of Coal, Water Resources, Higher Education, Welfare, Human Rights and Public Employee Bargaining*, ed. Allan S. Hammock and Sophia Peterson (Morgantown: West Virginia University Library, 1979), 96–97.

2. John D. Machesney, "Development of Higher Education Governance and Coordination in West Virginia" (EdD diss., West Virginia University, 1971), 99–100; *Acts of West Virginia Legislature, 1964* (Charleston: Jarrett Printing Company, 1964), Chap. 13, 1357–59; House Concurrent Resolution No. 51, adopted March 13, 1965, *Acts of West Virginia Legislature, 1965* (Charleston: Jarrett Printing Company, 1965), 640–41.

3. Machesny, "Higher Education Governance," 101–3; West Virginia Committee on Higher Education, *Report to the Honorable Hulett C. Smith, Governor of West*

Virginia, and the Legislature of the State of West Virginia: Vol. 1, Summary of Major Conclusions and Recommendations, and *Vol. 2, Higher Education in West Virginia: A Self Assessment* (Charleston: October 31, 1966).

4. Doherty and Summers, *WVU*, 270–71.

5. Machesney, "Higher Education Governance," 104–5; *Journal of the West Virginia Senate, Regular Session 1967* (Charleston: Jarrett Printing Company, 1967), 294–95, 1470, 1702, 1719–22, 1529–30, 1580–97, 1685–88, 1701–25; *Charleston Gazette*, December 24, 1967 (quotation).

6. Machesney, "Higher Education Governance," 106–107; *Charleston Daily-Mail*, September 5, 1967 (quotation).

7. "Governor's Message," communicated January 10, 1968, *Journal of the West Virginia House of Delegates, 1968* (Charleston: Rose City Press, 1968), 16–17 (quotation); Machesney, "Higher Education Governance," 107–8.

8. *Morgantown Post*, January 25, 1963.

9. Machesney, "Higher Education Governance,"108–9; *Fairmont Times*, January 26, 1968, editorial quoting Stewart.

10. Machesney, "Higher Education Governance," 110–15; *Charleston Gazette*, February 5, 1969 (quotation).

11. William D. Evans Jr., "W.V.U. and the 59th: An Eye (& Ear) Witness Account of What Happened in the Legislature," WVU *Alumni News* 33 (Spring 1969): 6.

12. *Morgantown Post*, February 7, 1969; WVU *Alumni News*, 33 (Spring 1969): 7 (quotation); "Casualty I: The Board of Governors," WVU *Alumni Magazine* 33 (Spring 1969): 7; Doherty and Summers, *WVU*, 293.

13. Joseph Wayne Corder Jr., "A History of the West Virginia Board of Regents as the Governing Board of Higher Education, 1969–1989" (EdD diss., West Virginia University, 1992), 42; Machesney, "Higher Education Governance," 114–16; *Acts of West Virginia Legislature, Regular Session,1969* (Charleston: Jarrett Printing Company, 1969), Chap. 130, 144–53.

14. *Charleston Gazette*, October 17, 1969.

15. Doherty and Summers, *WVU*, 293–94.

16. Doherty and Summers, *WVU*, 294; West Virginia University, "Self Study 1973," prepared for the North Central Assoc. of the Colleges and Secondary Schools, III-3.

17. Jay Barton to Professor I. D. Peters re: "July 18 Draft on Academic Freedom and Responsibility, Appointment, Promotion, Tenure and Termination of Employment of Professional Personnel," August 9, 1973, quoted in William T. Doherty, "West Virginia's University: Symbol of Unity in a Sectionalized State," Morgantown, WV, 1980, typescript, vol. 2, 795; West Virginia University Annual Report, 1971–72, and 1972–73.

18. Doherty and Summers, *WVU*, 295, citing Harlow's semiannual state of the University address to the Faculty Assembly in 1973.

19. A Report of the University Governance Committee to the University Senate, June 12, 1973, quoted in Doherty, "Symbol of Unity," vol. 2, 799–800.

20. A Report of the University Governance Committee to the University Senate, June 12, 1973, quoted in Doherty and Summers, *WVU*, 297–98.

21. *Dominion Post*, August 31, 1979.
22. *Dominion Post*, October 4, December 7, 1979.
23. *Dominion Post*, September 5, 1980.
24. *Dominion Post*, May 17, 1979.
25. *Dominion Post*, April 4, 1979.
26. Corder, "West Virginia Board of Regents," 217–18.
27. *Dominion Post*, August 29, 1979 (quotations). For a full account, see Academy of Educational Development, Inc., "Support, Performance, and Protection of Higher Education in West Virginia: A Final Report to the Joint Committee on Finance and the Joint Committee on Higher Education," West Virginia Legislature, 1979, 170–71.
28. *Dominion Post*, August 30, 1979 (for editorial); September 12, 24, 1979.
29. *Dominion Post*, August 30, and December 24, 1979 (quotations); Corder, "West Virginia Board of Regents," 220–22.
30. West Virginia Board of Regents, *Profile of Progress: Higher Education in West Virginia* (Charleston: By the Author, 1979), iii. See also West Virginia Board of Regents, *A Plan for Progress: West Virginia Higher Education in the Seventies* (Charleston: By the Author, 1972).
31. *Dominion Post*, September 12, 25 (quotations), and October 2, 1979.
32. *Dominion Post*, October 4, 1979.
33. Corder, "West Virginia Board of Regents," 243–44; *Dominion Post*, January 9, 1980 (quotation).
34. Corder, "West Virginia Board of Regents," 244–45; *Dominion Post*, June 1, 1980 (quotations).
35. Academy for Educational Development, *Revitalization and Renewal: Report of the Benedum Study Project at West Virginia University* (New York: AED, 1984), vii–viii, 13–14 (hereafter cited as *Benedum Report*). See also, "Benedum Consultants," President's Office, Folder 15, Box 6, A&M 5012.
36. *Benedum Report*, 3–5.
37. *Benedum Report*, 9–10.
38. *Benedum Report*, 124 (quotation), 238.
39. *Benedum Report*, 3.
40. Robert L. Jacobson, "The Dream vs. the Reality at West Virginia U.," *Chronicle of Higher Education*, February 27, 1985, photocopy (n.p.), President's Office, Folder 25, Box 3, A&M 5012.
41. *Wheeling News-Register*, January 9, 1985.
42. Jacobson, "Dream vs. Reality."
43. Jacobson, "Dream vs. Reality."
44. Dale Nitzschke to Gordon Gee, January 23, 1985, letter and attachment, President's Office, Folder 12, Box 6, A&M 5012.
45. Corder, "West Virginia Board of Regents," 294–95; Jacobson, "Dream vs. Reality," (quotation).
46. *Charleston Daily-Mail*, February 7, 1985.
47. Memorandum, John W. Fisher, Executive Officer to President's Cabinet, February 5,

1985, and Leon H. Ginsberg to Alvin C. Eurich, January 9, 1985, and attachment "Errors in the AED Report," Folder 15, Box 6, A&M 5012. AED was the consulting firm for the review funded by the Benedum Foundation; I have not used "AED Report" to avoid confusion with its 1979 report.

48. Alvin C. Eurich to Leon H. Ginsberg, January 31, 1985, President's Office, Folder 15, Box 6, A&M 5012.

49. Leon H. Ginsberg to Alvin C. Eurich, February 21, 1985, Folder 15, Box 6, A&M 5012.

50. Alvin C. Eurich to Leon H. Ginsberg, February 15, 1985, Folder 15, Box 6, A&M 5012.

51. Julian W. Nash to Leon Ginsberg, February 4, 1985, Folder 15, Box 6, A&M 5012 (quotation); *Dominion Post*, February 1, 1985.

52. *Charleston Gazette*, February 5, 1985 (quotations); *Welch Daily News*, February 8, 1985.

53. AP reporter Jill Wilson in *Dominion Post*, February 9, 1985, quoting the bill; *Charleston Daily-Mail*, February 4, 1986; Corder, "West Virginia Board of Regents," 308–9.

54. *Dominion Post*, October 25, 28 (quotations), 1985.

55. *Dominion Post*, April 10, May 4, 1987.

56. *Dominion Post*, April 10, 1987.

57. *Dominion Post*, October 7, 1987.

58. *Dominion Post*, April 14, 1987.

59. *Dominion Post*, May 4, 1987.

60. *Dominion Post*, Aug.16, 1983.

61. *Dominion Post*, August 3, 1986.

62. Corder, "West Virginia Board of Regents," 309; *Charleston Daily-Mail*, February 4, 1986; *Dominion Post*, February 5 (quotation), 9, 1986.

63. *Dominion Post*, July 6, 1986.

64. *Dominion Post*, August 3, 1986.

65. *Dominion Post*, June 19, 1987.

66. *Dominion Post*, June 30, 1985. Extended interview by reporter Jeff Morris with E. Gordon Gee, and the discussion and quotes come from that piece. See also *Dominion Post*, June 28, 1985.

67. *Dominion Post*, June 30, 1985.

68. *Dominion Post*, June 30, 1985.

69. *Dominion Post*, June 30, 1985.

70. *Acts of the Legislature of West Virginia, Third Extraordinary Session, 1988* (Beckley, WV: BJW Printers, 1988), Chap. 6, 1124--27; *Dominion Post*, January 5, 6 (quotation), 1989.

71. *Dominion Post*, September 1, 1988.

72. Report by the Carnegie Foundation for the Advancement of Teaching, *Building for a New Century: Higher Education in West Virginia* (1987), 37–39 (quotation on 37) (hereafter cited as *Carnegie Report*).

73. *Carnegie Report*, 16.

74. *Carnegie Report*, 21–22.
75. *Carnegie Report*, 25.
76. *Carnegie Report*, 27–29 (quotation on 28).
77. *Carnegie Report*, 33–34.
78. *Dominion Post*, March 3, 9, 14, 15, 1989.
79. *Dominion Post*, April 16, 1989.
80. *Dominion Post*, June 6, 23, 1989; WVU *Alumni Magazine* 12 (Summer 1989): 13.

CHAPTER SIX

1. William T. Doherty Jr. and Festus P. Summers, *West Virginia University: Symbol of Unity in a Sectionalized State* (Morgantown: West Virginia University Press, 1982), 282–83; *Charleston Gazette*, October 15, 1967 (quotation).
2. *Martinsburg Journal*, September 15, 1968; *Morgantown Post*, September 15, 1968; *Charleston Gazette-Mail*, October 15, 1967; Doherty and Summers, *WVU*, 283.
3. *Charleston Gazette-Mail*, October 15, 1967.
4. *Charleston Gazette-Mail*, October 15, 1967.
5. *Charleston Gazette*, August 27, 1967.
6. *Charleston Gazette*, August 27, 1967.
7. "President Harlow's Inaugural Address," WVU *Alumni News* 33 (Fall 1968): 4–9, 25.
8. *Daily Athenaeum*, June 22, 1967; "Report of a Visit to West Virginia University, Morgantown, West Virginia, April 8–10, 1974, for the Commission on Institutions of Higher Education of the North Central Assoc. of Colleges and Secondary Schools," 14 (hereafter "NCACSS Report 1974").
9. Doherty and Summers, *WVU*, 284, citing Harlow's speech to faculty, Fall 1969, and WVU Annual Reports.
10. Doherty and Summers, *WVU*, 285, citing Harlow's report to Morton, member of the Board of Regents, November 4, 1974; "NCACSS Report 1974," 14.
11. West Virginia University, "Self-Study, 1973," [for North Central Assoc. of the Colleges and Secondary Schools] IV–5–7 (hereafter "Self-Study 1973"); WVU *Alumni News* 37 (Fall 1971): 1–2.
12. "NCACSS Report 1974," 3.
13. Doherty and Summers, *WVU*, 300; *New York Times*, April 13, 1974.
14. Doherty and Summers, *WVU*, 301, citing *Railway Age* (September 8, 1975), and *Aviation Week and Space Technology* (November 8, 1971).
15. Doherty and Summers, *WVU*, 302; *New York Times*, April 13, 1974; *Washington Post*, June 2, 1974.
16. Doherty and Summers, *WVU*, 303; *New York Times*, April 13, 1974; *Washington Post*, June 2, 1974.
17. Doherty and Summers, *WVU*, 304, quoting *Engineering News-Record*, November 29, 1973; *New York Times*, April 13, 1974; *Washington Post*, June 2, 1974.

18. Doherty and Summers, *WVU*, 305; *New York Times*, April 13, 1974; *Washington Post*, June 2, 1974.

19. Harry W. Ernst Memorandum, September, 1976, Box 4, A&M 5020.

20. "Self-Study 1973," V–2–4.

21. Doherty and Summers, *WVU*, 338; Doherty, "Symbol of Unity," vol. 2, 933–34.

22. *Daily Athenaeum*, April 6, 10, 1979; Doherty, "Symbol of Unity," vol. 2, 934–37 (quoting Collins on 937).

23. "Self-Study 1973," V–16–18.

24. "Self-Study 1973," V–18–19.

25. "Self-Study 1973," V–21–26.

26. WVU *Alumni News* 37 (Winter 1972): 21; James G. Harlow, "A Very Fragile Thing," *West Virginia University Magazine* 6 (Winter 1975): 8–12 (quotation on 10); Harry W. Ernst, Memorandum, n.d., Box 4, A&M 5020.

27. Barron's Educational Services, *Barron's Profiles of American Colleges: An In-Depth Study of West Virginia University*, 1973, 34; J. William Douglas, *History of Physical Education at West Virginia University: An Historical Perspective, 1891–1999* (Morgantown: West Virginia University Printing Services, 2000), 57–58.

28. Harlow, "A Very Fragile Thing," 10.

29. Gordon Thorn, interview by Charles Dusch, December 18, 2007.

30. Frank Scafella, interview by Ronald L. Lewis, September 3, 2008.

31. Gordon Thorn interview.

32. Harold J. Shamberger, "A Score and More Years at West Virginia University," 77–78, typescript.

33. Shamberger, "A Score and More," 78–80; Harold J. Shamberger, interview by Ronald L. Lewis, March 6, 2008; WVU *Alumni News* 42 (Spring 1977): 1, 5.

34. "Budig Named New WVU President," WVU *Alumni News* 42 (Winter 1977): 2; Doherty and Summers, *WVU*, 334.

35. "Budig Named New WVU President," WVU *Alumni News* 42 (Winter 1977): 2, 19; *Daily Athenaeum*, Jan. 1, 1977; Shamberger, "A Score and More," 91; *Huntington Herald-Dispatch*, October 12, 1977; C. T. Marshall to Gene A. Budig, October 14, 1977, Folder 11, Box 7, A&M 5012.

36. David Nilsson, "University Considered the State's Principal Asset by New President," WVU *Alumni News* 43 (Fall 1977): 8–9 (quotations); WVU *Alumni Magazine* 2 (Fall 1979): 20.

37. *Dominion Post*, July 13, 1977; Doherty and Summers, *WVU*, 335; Shamberger, "A Score and More," 90.

38. Joel M. Hannah to Gene A. Budig, March 17, 1977, Folder 16, Box 1, A&M 5016.

39. Joel M. Hannah to Budig, March 17, 1977, and Gene A. Budig to Joel M. Hanna, March 22, 1977 (quotation), Folder 16, Box 1, A&M 5016. A note in the margin documents their meeting on June 9, 1977.

40. Doherty and Summers, *WVU*, 336–37, 340–41; Gene A. Budig, "Challenges of the Eighties," WVU *Alumni Magazine* 3 (Winter/Spring 1980): 8–10.

41. Susan W. Breslin, "Threshold to Greatness: The West Virginia University Campaign,"

WVU *Alumni Quarterly* 2 (Winter–Spring 1979): 20-24; "Campaign Exceeds Goal," WVU *Alumni Magazine* 8 (Summer 1984): 27.

42. Shamberger, "A Score and More," 100, 102.

43. *Daily Athenaeum,* August 24, 1981; *Dominion Post,* December 15, 1981; WVU *Alumni Magazine* 4 (Fall 1981): 23; David C. Hardesty Jr., "Character Matters: Remarks at the Funeral of a Former President [Harry B. Heflin]," in David C. Hardesty Jr. with Susan B. Hardesty, *Leading the Public University: Essays, Speeches, and Commentary* (Morgantown: West Virginia University Press, 2007), 222–28.

44. *Dominion Post,* March 21, April 23, 1981; *Daily Athenaeum,* April 23, 1981; *Charleston Daily-Mail,* May 6, 1981; *Huntington Herald-Dispatch,* June 5, 1981 (quotations).

45. *Charleston Gazette,* May 16, 1981.

46. *Dominion Post,* May 24, 1981.

47. *Charleston Daily-Mail,* July 8, 16, 31, and August 28, 1981; *Dominion Post,* July 9, 29, August 28, 1981; *Charleston Gazette,* August 14, 29, 1981; *Huntington Herald-Dispatch,* August 29, 1981 (quotation).

CHAPTER SEVEN

1. WVU *Alumni Magazine* 5 (Winter/Spring 1982): 29; *Huntington Herald-Dispatch,* August 29, 1981; Harold J. Shamberger, "A Score and More Years at West Virginia University," 106, typescript.

2. E. Gordon Gee, "Administrative Reorganization of West Virginia University: A Report to the Board of Regents," June 30, 1982, 1–3 (quotations on 3), 5–15 and appended flow charts, Folder 12, Box 1, A&M 5009; "West Virginia University Self-Study Report, January 1984," prepared for the Commission on Institutions of Higher Education of the North Central Association of Colleges and Schools, 140 (hereafter cited as "Self Study 1984").

3. Charles H. Ambler, *A History of Education in West Virginia from Early Colonial Times to 1949* (Huntington, WV: Standard Printing and Publishing Co., 1951), 603; William T. Doherty Jr. and Festus P. Summers, *West Virginia University: Symbol of Unity in a Sectionalized State* (Morgantown: West Virginia University Press, 1982), 342.

4. *Dominion Post,* December 9, 1983 (quotations), January 11, 1984.

5. WVU Press Release, September 10, 1984, Folder 11, Box 1, A&M 5009.

6. Memorandum, John Fisher to President E. Gordon Gee and Vice President for Institutional Advancement Edward Flowers, November 5, 1984, Folder 11, Box 1, A&M 5009.

7. Memorandum, John Fisher to E. Gordon Gee and Edward Flowers, November 5, 1984, Folder 11, Box 1, A&M 5009.

8. *Dominion Post,* May 7 (quotations), July 10, 1984.

9. *Dominion Post,* July 11, July 13 (quotation), 1984.

10. West Virginia University, *Annual Report,* 1984–1985, 14, Folder 13, Box 3, A&M 5000.

11. WVU, *Annual Report*, 1984–1985, 15, Folder 13, Box 3, A&M 5000.

12. WVU Annual Report, 1983–1984, 14–15, Folder 13, Box 3, A&M 5000.

13. "Self Study 1984," 119–20.

14. "Self Study 1984," 120–21.

15. "Self Study 1984," 122.

16. "Self Study 1984," 123.

17. "Self Study 1984," 135–36.

18. "Self Study 1984," 135–36.

19. "Self Study 1984," 136–37.

20. WVU, *Annual Report*, 1983–1984, 20–24, F13, Box 3, A&M 5000.

21. "Self Study 1984," 59–60.

22. "Self Study 1984," 60.

23. "Self Study 1984," 40–41, 65–67; WVU, *Annual Report*, 1983–1984, 10. See also, Geraldine Kessel, "From the Ohio to the Potomac," WVU *Alumni Magazine* 3 (Summer 1980): 11–12.

24. WVU, *Annual Report*, 1983–1984, 11–13.

25. Paul D. Stewart to Stanley Wearden, November 9, 1976 (quotations), Folder 11, Box 7, A&M 5012; Pamphlet, "A Cooperative EdD in Educational Administration for Southern West Virginia, Folder 10, Box 7, A&M 5012.

26. Robert B. Hayes to Gene A. Budig, January 16, 1980, and Budig to Hayes, February 12, 1980, Folder 11, Box 7, A&M 5012.

27. Dick Meckley, Coordinator EdD Program, to Stanley Wearden, Dean of the WVU Graduate School, October 12, 1981, Folder 10, Box 7, A&M 5012.

28. Robert B. Hayes to E. Gordon Gee, March 5, 1982, Folder 10, Box 7, A&M 5012.

29. Stanley Wearden to James A. Martin, May 13, 1982, Folder 10, Box 7, A&M 5012.

30. Jim (James A.) Martin to Stanley Wearden, May 26, 1982 (quotation), Folder 10, Box 7, A&M 5012. See also Memorandum, "Past and Projected Coop. EdD WVU Doctoral-Level Course Offerings," May 24, 1982, Folder 10, Box 7, A&M 5012; "Status of Cooperative Ed.D. Students," May 1982, Folder 10, Box 7, A&M 5012. Regarding Board of Regents support, see Olen E. Jones (Marshall's provost) to David R. Powers, vice chancellor of the Board of Regents, Oct. 1, 1982, and attached "Guidelines for Cooperative Doctoral Programs," Folder 10, Box 7, A&M 5012.

31. Robert B. Hayes to E. Gordon Gee, May 24, 1982, and Gee to Hayes, May 28, 1982, Folder 10, Box 7, A&M 5012.

32. William E. Collins to E. Gordon Gee, June 3, 1982, Folder 10, Box 7, A&M 5012.

33. William E. Collins to E. Gordon Gee, April 7, 1983, Folder 10, Box 7, A&M 5012.

34. Robert E. Swartwout to William E. Collins and E. Gordon Gee, and attached note, October 13, 1982, Folder 10, Box 7, A&M 5012.

35. E. Gordon Gee to Robert Swartwout, October 18, 1982, quotation, Folder 10, Box 7, A&M 5012; Comments, "Conferral of Doctor of Education Degrees," May 11, 1985, Folder 10, Box 5, A&M 5017.

36. *Dominion Post*, June 12, 1985.

CHAPTER EIGHT

1. *Dominion Post*, June 12, 1985, and March 30, 2008 (quotation).
2. *Dominion Post*, December 29, 1985.
3. *Dominion Post*, January 7, 1986; Robert Fullerton, "Our Twentieth President," WVU *Alumni Magazine* 9 (Winter/Spring 1986): 2–4; Neil Bucklew Interviewed by Ronald Lewis, August 30, 2007; "A Beautiful Day," WVU *Alumni Magazine* 9 (Fall 1986): 21.
4. West Virginia University, "Annual Report to the Higher Education Central Office, 1988–89" August 25, 1989, 27, Folder 13, Box 3, A&M 5000.
5. "Annual Report 1988–89," 27.
6. "Annual Report 1988–89," 28.
7. "Annual Report 1988–89," 29–30
8. Tim Terman, "President Bucklew Discusses University Finances," WVU *Alumni Magazine* 12 (Winter 1988–89): 2–4 (quotation on 4).
9. Terman, "President Bucklew Discusses," 5.
10. *Dominion Post*, October 5, 1987.
11. *Dominion Post*, June 2, 1988.
12. *Dominion Post*, June 22, 25 (quotation), 1988.
13. *Dominion Post*, March 14, 1989.
14. Dale F. Nitzschke to Neil S. Bucklew, March 23, 1988, Folder 21, Box 2, A&M 5012.
15. *Dominion Post*, April 6, 1988.
16. Nitzschke to Bucklew, April 15, 1988, Folder 9, Box 5, A&M 5017.
17. Neil Bucklew to Stephen Haid, February 22, 1990, Folder 17, Box 3, A&M 5003. See also, "Governor's Hiring Freeze, Discussion Outline," Folder 17, and "Impact of Hiring Freeze on West Virginia University," Folder 18, Box 3, A&M 5003.
18. Neil Bucklew to Stephen Haid, February 22, 1990, Folder 17, Box 3, A&M 5003.
19. Neil Bucklew to Stephen Haid, February 22, 1990, Folder 17, Box 3, A&M 5003.
20. David Greenstreet and Tom S. Witt, "Economic Impact of WVU and Affiliated Organizations on the West Virginia Economy," September 1990, Bureau of Business Research, College of Business and Economics, WVU.
21. West Virginia University Foundation, "The Campaign for West Virginia University," Final Report, 1994; Marcella Williamson, "Campaign Nets $130 Million," WVU *Alumni Magazine* 17 (Summer 1994): 2–3; Marcella Williamson, "Eberly College of Arts and Sciences Named," WVU *Alumni Magazine* 16 (Fall 1993): 2–4.
22. Bucklew Interview by Lewis; WVU *Alumni Magazine* 14 (Winter 1991): 23.
23. *Dominion Post*, Jan. 7, February 4, 1987.
24. Frank A. Franz, Office of the Provost, "Size and Vitality of West Virginia University: Contributions of Non-Resident Students," January, 1990, Folder 18, Box 3, A&M 5003.
25. Franz, "Size and Vitality of WVU," Folder 18, Box 3, A&M 5003.
26. Franz, "Size and Vitality of WVU," Folder 18, Box 3, A&M 5003.
27. Buckler Interview by Lewis.

28. West Virginia University, "Institutional Self-Study Report Prepared for the North Central Association of Colleges and Schools, 1994," 78–80 (hereafter "Self Study 1994").

29. "Annual Report 1988–89," 30, Folder 13, Box 3, A&M 5000.

30. "Self Study 1994," 80–81.

31. "Self Study 1994," 83.

32. Bucklew Interview by Lewis.

33. J. Richard Toren, "WVU High Tech Scores Twice," WVU *Alumni Magazine* 10 (Winter/Spring 1987): 16.

34. "West Virginia University Campus Networking Study Draft," May 7, 1990, 12 (quotation),18, Folder 8, Box 1, A&M 5003 (hereafter "WVU Networking Study").

35. "WVU Networking Study," 5.

36. WVU Networking Study," 1, quoting Caroline Arms, Campus Strategies for Libraries and Electronic Information, EDUCOM Strategies Series on Information Technology (Digital Press, 1990).

37. "WVU Networking Study," 1, quoting Daniel A. Updegrove; John A. Dunn Jr., "Electronic Mail and Networks: New Tools for University Administrators," *CAUSE/EFFECT* 12:1 (Spring 1990).

38. "Self Study 1994," 12, 19–20, Appendix D.

39. Becky Byrd Lofstead, "East Africa Tour Strengthens International Ties," WVU *Alumni Magazine* 12 (Summer 1989): 10–12.

40. Becky Byrd Lofstead, "Ten Years of Fostering International Education," WVU *Alumni Magazine* 14 (Winter 1991): 6–8.

41. Tim Terman, "Creating a World Music Center, WVU *Alumni Magazine* 16 (Summer 1993): 8–9 (quotation on 8).

42. Neil S. Bucklew to David C. Hardesty, "Transition Report," June 13, 1995, 1. Copy in possession of the author.

43. "Transition Report," 2.

44. "Transition Report," 3.

45. "Transition Report," 4

46. "Transition Report," 5.

47. "Transition Report," 6.

48. "Transition Report," 10.

CHAPTER NINE

1. James G. Harlow, "A Very Fragile Thing," WVU *Magazine* 6 (Winter 1975): 10, 12.

2. Harlow, "A Very Fragile Thing," 10–11; "West Virginia University Self-Study Report, 1973," prepared for the North Central Association of Colleges and Schools, V-12-16 (hereafter "Self Study 1973").

3. Robert F. Munn, Report to the Graduate Faculty, July 1966, Binder, Box 338, A&M 690.

4. Munn, Report to the Graduate Faculty, July 1966, Binder, Box 338, A&M 690.

5. Munn, Report to the Graduate Faculty, July 1966, Binder, Box 338, A&M 690.

6. Dean Stanley Wearden, Report to the Graduate Faculty, Binder, Box 338, A&M 690.

7. Robert F. Munn, "Library Development at West Virginia University, 1970–1980," Box 338, A&M 690.

8. Munn, "Library Development at West Virginia University," Box 338, A&M 690.

9. Munn, "Library Development at West Virginia University."

10. West Virginia University, "Self-Study Report,1984," prepared for the North Central Association of Colleges and Schools, 38 (hereafter "Self Study 1984").

11. Academic Planning Committee, Supplementary Observations and Recommendations, May 1983, and "Report of the Academic Planning Committee, Position Paper 6," November 1982, Folder 33, Box 7, A&M 5017.

12. Academic Planning Committee, Final Report, May 1983, Folder 33, Box 7, A&M 5017.

13. "Self Study 1973," IV–10–12.

14. "Self Study 1973," VI–2.

15. "Self Study 1973," VI–3–4.

16. "Self Study 1973," VI–5–8.

17. "Self Study 1973," VI–9–10.

18. "Self Study 1973," VI–11.

19. "Self Study 1973," VI–12–13; West Virginia University, "Annual Report, 1983–1984," 20 (quotation), Folder 13, Box 3, A&M 5000.

20. "Self Study 1984," 72–74.

21. "Self Study 1984," 74–77, 82–84.

22. "Self Study 1984," 98, 90 (quotation).

23. "Self Study 1984," 91, 92–93 (quotation on 92).

24. "Self Study 1984," 93–95 (quotation on 95).

25. "Self Study 1984," 95–97.

26. West Virginia University, "Institutional Self-Study Report, 1994," prepared for the North Central Association of Colleges and Schools, 51–52 (hereafter "Self Study 1994").

27. "Self Study 1994," 52–54.

28. "Self Study 1994," 55–56.

29. Shirley Dowdy to Frank Franz, December 7, 1990, and appended, "Impressions of Recently Hired Faculty," College of Arts and Sciences, October 8, 1990, Folder 14, Box 3, A&M 5000.

30. Dowdy to Franz, December 7, 1990, and "Impressions."

31. "Self Study 1984," 46.

32. "Self Study 1984," 56–58.

33. "Self Study 1984," 39–40, 46, 58.

34. WVU, "Annual Report, 1983–1984," 3–4.

35. "Self Study 1994," 105–7, 109.

36. "Report on the Use of Temporary Faculty," Advisory Council of Faculty to the Board of Regents, August 1988, and Kathleen K. Bissonnette, WVU Office of Institutional

Analysis and Planning, to Mark Stotler, Board of Regents, August 16, 1988, Folder 10, Box 2, A&M 5003.

37. Alecia Sirk, "Quasquicentennial Celebration," WVU *Alumni Magazine* 16 (Winter 1993): 8–9 (quotation on 9).

38. W. Vernon Smith to Neil Bucklew, June 6, 1988, Folder 21, Box 2, A&M 5012.

39. *Wheeling News-Register*, June 7, 1988.

40. WVU Economic Development Council, "Strategic Plan for Economic Development at West Virginia University, 1990," 1–3, Folder 1, Box 2, A&M 5003.

41. WVU, "Economic Development Plan 1990," 4.

42. WVU, "Economic Development Plan 1990," 5–7 (quotation on 7).

43. Barbara Burke Ankrom, "Alternative Transportation Fuels," WVU *Alumni Magazine* 13 (Winter 1989/1990): 6–7.

44. Bill Case, "The World Comes to Kearneysville," WVU *Alumni Magazine* 12 (Summer 1989): 14–16.

45. WVU *Alumni Magazine* 11 (Spring 1988): 21.

CHAPTER TEN

1. "West Virginia University Equal Employment Opportunity Report and Affirmative Action Program, Morgantown, West Virginia, 1970," Folder: Affirmative Action, Box 347, A&M 690; West Virginia University, "Self-Study, 1973," prepared for the North Central Association of Colleges and Schools, IV-1.

2. "Equal Employment Opportunity Report 1970," 5–6.

3. "Equal Employment Opportunity Report 1970," 7–15.

4. "Equal Employment Opportunity Report 1970," 17–22.

5. "Equal Employment Opportunity Report 1970," 23–28 (last quotation on 28).

6. "Equal Employment Opportunity Report 1970," 34.

7. West Virginia Human Rights Commission, Complaint of Michael Woodson v. West Virginia University, December 12, 1967, Docket No. E 14–67, and Complaint of Charles C. Blue Jr. v. West Virginia University, December 12, 1967, Docket No. 13–67, both documents in Folder 5, Box 3, A&M 5016.

8. Affidavit of H. D. Jones, Feb. [n.d.] 1968, Affidavit of Robert F. McWhorter, Feb. [n.d.] 1968, and Affidavit of James G. Harlow, Feb. [n.d.] 1968, Folder 5, Box 3, A&M 5016.

9. Robert F. McWhorter to Joseph C. Gluck, February 8, 1968; Londo H. Brown to James G. Harlow, February 16, 1968; James G. Harlow to West Virginia Human Rights Commission, February 27, 1968, all in Folder 5, Box 3, A&M 5016.

10. H. D. Jones to Robert F. McWhorter, April 25, 1968, and James G. Harlow to Mr. [Carl W.] Glatt, May 8, 1968, Folder 5, Box 3, A&M 5016.

11. "Statements of Discrimination Charges in Student Handbill," presented to Office of Personnel, April 18, 1968, in "An Investigative Report on Alleged Employment Discrimination Charges against West Virginia University," Prepared for James G. Harlow by S. Thomas Serpento, June 21, 1968, 2, Box 3, A&M 690.

12. *Daily Athenaeum*, April 19, 1968 (quotation); *Dominion News*, April 19, 1968.

13. S. Thomas Serpento, Director of Personnel, "An Investigative Report on Alleged Employment Discrimination Charges against West Virginia University," June 21, 1968, 1, 6, Box 3, A&M 690.

14. Serpento, "Investigative Report on Alleged Employment Discrimination," 7–14.

15. "Summary of Investigation," and "Suggested Measures to Help Improve Communications and Better Insure Nondiscrimination within the University," in Serpento, "Investigative Report on Alleged Employment Discrimination," 35–38, Box 3, A&M 690.

16. David Nilsson, "University Considered the State's Principal Asset by New President," WVU *Alumni News* 43 (Fall 1977): 8–9; WVU *Alumni Magazine* 2 (Fall 1979): 2; Minutes, Affirmative Action Committee, July 6, 1977, Folder 5, Box 1, A&M 5009.

17. Franklin Parker, "Liberating the Labor Force," WVU *Alumni Quarterly* 1 (Spring 1978): 2–7 (quotation on 6).

18. "1978–79 Annual Report," Special Assistant to the President and Coordinator of Affirmative Action-Equal Employment Opportunity, Folder 5, Box 1, A&M 5009.

19. "1979–1980 Annual Report," Folder 5, Box 1, A&M 5009.

20. Irene N. Mee, Assistant Regional Administrator to President Harry Heflin, September 30, 1981, "Conciliation Agreement between U.S. Department of Labor, Office of Federal Contract Compliance Programs," Folder 4, Box 1, A&M 5009.

21. Mee, "Conciliation Agreement."

22. Mee, "Conciliation Agreement."

23. West Virginia University, "Institutional Self-Study Report, 1994," prepared for the North Central Association of Colleges and Schools, 1–2 (hereafter "Self Study 1994"); "Dial-a-Bus," WVU *Alumni Magazine* 8 (Winter/Spring 1985): 15–16.

24. Judith DeStefano to Marion F. Dearnley, "Title VI: Black Community Concerns Interim Report," January 5, 1982, Black Community Concerns Committee Folder, Box 338, A&M 690.

25. WVU, "Annual Report, 1984–1985," 17, Folder 13, Box 3, A&M 5000.

26. "Self Study 1994," 2.

27. Neil Bucklew, interview by Ronald L. Lewis, August 30, 2007.

28. "Self Study 1994," 30–31 (quotation on 31).

29. "Self Study 1994," 2–3, 5–9.

30. Quoted in WVU Women's Centenary Project, *WVU Women: The First Century, An Historical Digest* (Morgantown: Women's Centenary Project, 1989), 87.

31. Proposal, Black Cultural Center, May 1, 1985, and "Report of the President's Task Force on the Center for Black Culture," July 9, 1986, both in Folder 14, Box 3, A&M 5003.

32. Karen Zeller, "New Home for Black Culture Center," WVU *Alumni Magazine*, 13 (Summer 1990): 14–15 (quotation on 14).

33. Tim Terman, "Center for Black Culture," WVU *Alumni Magazine* 12 (Winter 1988–1989): 6–7 (quotation on 6); Zeller, "New Home," 15. For the many initiatives undertaken by the University to improve social justice for minorities, see President's Office for Social Justice, "West Virginia University Minority

Report, Sept. 1989," Folder 2, Box 8, A&M 5003, and Stephanie Bock, "Minorities, Financially Disadvantaged Encouraged to Enter Health Sciences Careers," WVU *Alumni Magazine* 17 (Fall 1994): 8–9.

34. Horace E. Belmear, "Annual Report: Minority Recruitment/Retention (Enrollment Services), 1989–1990," 4–6, 8, Folder 4, Box 3, A&M 5000.

35. "Self Study 1994," 110; Belmear, "Annual Report, 1989–1990," 16, 27.

36. Report, "University-Wide Issues Related to Black Student Retention," July 12, 1990, Folder 2, Box 8, A&M 5003.

37. *Dominion Post*, April 1, 2008.

38. "Title IX Report," WVU *Alumni News* 42(Fall 1976): 4–5.

39. *WVU Women: First Century*, 69; *Morgantown Post*, April 23, 1969.

40. Jenny Parsons, "It Was Curtains for the Women's Curfew in 1969," *Dominion Post*, March 30, 2008 (quotations). See also Evelyn Ryan, "The Times They Were A-Chan-gin' at WVU in 1960s," *Dominion Post*, March 30, 2008; *WVU Women: First Century*, 35–36. See also, "Betty Boyd's 35 Years at WVU Spent 'helping students grow,'" *Dominion Post*, May 28, 1983.

41. Gordon Thorn, interview by Charles Dusch, Dec. 5, 2007.

42. *Dominion Post*, March 30, 2008 (quotation); *WVU Women: First Century*, 70; William T. Doherty Jr. and Festus P. Summers, *West Virginia University: Symbol of Unity in a Sectionalized State* (Morgantown: West Virginia University Press, 1982), 321.

43. *Dominion Post*, March 30, 2008; Thomas J. Birdsong, "Liberating the Student Body Presidency," WVU *Magazine* 7 (Summer 1975): 8.

44. Birdsong, "Liberating the Student Body Presidency," 8, 10.

45. "Timeline of Women at WVU," *Dominion Post*, March 30, 2008; WVU *Alumni News* 42 (Summer 1976): 2; WVU *Alumni News* 43 (Summer 1977): 7; *Alumni Magazine* 3 (Summer 1980): 24–25; "The Mountaineer," WVU *Alumni Magazine* 14 (Winter 1991): 23; "Tennant Still the Sole Female Mountaineer," *Dominion Post*, March 30, 2008.

46. *Dominion Post*, March 31, 2008.

47. *Dominion Post*, April 1, 2008.

48. Judith Stitzel, interview by Barbara Howe, April 13, 1999.

49. Lillian J. Waugh, "100 Years of Women's Education," WVU *Alumni Magazine* 10 (Summer 1987): 6.

50. Becky Byrd Lofstead, "The Celebration Begins," WVU *Alumni Magazine* 13 (Winter 1989–1990): 8–11, and "The First Hundred Years," WVU *Alumni Magazine* 12 (Summer 1989): 18–19.

51. *WVU Women: The First Century*, 85.

52. *WVU Women: The First Century*, 85–86; WVU *Alumni Magazine* 14 (Fall 1991): 12; Karen Zeller, "New Law School Dean," WVU *Alumni Magazine* 17 (Summer 1994): 24–25

1. "To Be a Friend to Students," WVU *Alumni Magazine* 3 (Winter/Spring, 1980): 12–13.
2. William T. Doherty Jr. and Festus P. Summers, *West Virginia University: Symbol of Unity in a Sectionalized State* (Morgantown: West Virginia University Press, 1982), 307 (hereafter Doherty and Summers, *WVU*); *Morgantown Post*, November 6, 1967.
3. WVU *Alumni News* 33 (Fall 1968): 3.
4. Gordon Thorn, interviewed by Charles D. Dusch Jr., December 5, 2007.
5. Jeffrey A. Drobney, "A Generation in Revolt: Student Dissent and Political Repression at West Virginia University," *West Virginia History* 54 (1995): 107 (quoting Joseph Gluck).
6. John C. Hennen Jr., *Caught Up In Time: Oral History Narratives of Appalachian Vietnam Veterans* (Huntington, WV: Aegina Press, 1988), 11.
7. *Daily Athenaeum*, September 28 (quotation), October 14, 1969; Doherty and Summers, *WVU*, 313–14. See also Thorn interview.
8. *Morgantown Post*, October 1, 1969; FBI file on Scott Bills, Scott Bills Papers, A&M 2828.
9. *Morgantown Post*, October 1, 1969.
10. *Morgantown Post*, October 16, 1969.
11. *Washington Post*, October 17, 1969.
12. Statement of President James G. Harlow, January 26, 1970, "Campus Unrest, 1968–1971," Microfilm 403, President's Archives.
13. David L. Geary, "When the Powder Ignited," WVU *Alumni Magazine* 18 (Summer 1995): 6.
14. Drobney, "Generation in Revolt," 105–6; Doherty and Summers, *WVU*, 316. For a recent study of the Kent State events from an insider's perspective, see William H. Hildebrand, *"A Most Notable Enterprise": The Story of Kent State University, 1910–2010* (Kent, OH: Kent State University Press, 2009), especially 132–56.
15. *Morgantown Dominion News*, May 9, 1970; Joseph Gluck to James Harlow, May 29, 1970, Report on Student Demonstrations, and WVU Press Release, June 8, 1970, both in Incident Week May 8, 1970 File, Microfilm # 420, President's Archives.
16. *Dominion News*, May 6, 1970; Drobney, "Generation in Revolt," 108.
17. *Daily Athenaeum*, May 7, 1970; *Dominion News*, May 7, 1970; Drobney, "Generation in Revolt," 109.
18. Joseph Gluck to James Harlow, Report on Student Demonstrations, Incident Week File; Doherty and Summers, *WVU*, 316; Harold J. Shamberger, interview by Ronald L. Lewis, March 6, 2008; Harold J. Shamberger, "A Score and More Years at West Virginia University," 51, typescript; *Dominion News*, May 7, 1970; *Daily Athenaeum*, May 7, 1970; *Charleston Gazette*, May 8, 1970; Drobney, "Generation in Revolt," 109.

Notes

19. *Daily Athenaeum*, May 7, 1970; *Dominion News*, May 7, 1970 (quotation); Drobney, "Generation in Revolt," 109–10.

20. Joseph Gluck to James Harlow, Official Report on Demonstration Damage, May 11, 1970, Incident Week File; *Dominion News*, May 8, 1970; *Daily Athenaeum*, May 8, 1970; Drobney, "Generation in Revolt," 111. See numerous reports and correspondence in the Incident Week File between President Harlow and Governor Moore, in which Harlow explained punitive actions the administration was taking against some of the students after the demonstrations ended.

21. *Dominion News*, May 8, 1970.

22. *Dominion News*, May 8, 1970; WVU Press Release, June 8, 1970, Incident Week File; David L. Geary, "When the Powder Ignited," WVU *Alumni Magazine* 18 (Summer 1995): 8 (quotation); Thorn interview.

23. Joseph Gluck to James Harlow, Official Report on Demonstration Damage, Incident Week File; WVU Press Release, May 8, 1970, Incident Week File (quotation). See also Shamberger, "A Score and More Years," 51–52.

24. Doherty and Summers, *WVU*, 318–19.

25. James G. Harlow to Governor Arch Moore, July 7, 1970, and Harold A. Gibbard to James Harlow, May 20, 1970 (quotation), Incident Week File.

26. Don P. Mudock to James Harlow, May 8, 1970; James G. Harlow to L. H. Harris, June 12, 1970; Harlow to Moore, July 7, 1970; James Harlow to William Haymond, May 22, 1970 (quotation), all in Incident Week File; *Dominion News*, May 21, 1970.

27. Drobney, "Generation in Revolt," 114; Londo H. Brown to James Harlow, May 18, 1970, and Gluck to Harlow, May 29, Report on Student Demonstrations, both in Incident Week File.

28. WVU, Press Release, June 8, 1970, "Motion for Continuance," June 24, 1970; James Harlow to Joseph Laurita (county prosecutor), July 2, 1970; Laurita to James Harlow, July 17, 1970; and Paul C. Camilletti (U.S. Attorney) to James Harlow, July 8, 1970, all in Incident Week File; *Daily Athenaeum*, June 25, 1970; *Dominion News*, June 25, 1970; Drobney, "Generation in Revolt," 115–16.

29. Drobney, "Generation in Revolt," 116–17; Memorandum, June 9, 1970; Joseph Gluck to Stanley R. Harris (university registrar), June 13, 1970; Joseph Gluck to Thomas Scott King, July 22, 1970; and Joseph Gluck to John Brisbane, August 13, 1970, all in Incident Week File.

30. Scott Bills to Harry Heflin, August 18, 1970, Incident Week File; Harry Heflin to Stephen Stepto and Scott Bills, August 19, 1970, and Graduate School Admission Appeals Committee to President James Harlow, October 6, 1970, Scott Bills, Student Activist Records, A&M 2828; *Morgantown Post*, October 2, 1970; *Charleston Gazette*, October 7, 1970; WVU, *Alumni News* 36 (Winter 1971): 1; Drobney, "Generation in Revolt," 117–18.

31. *Daily Athenaeum*, April 19, 1973; Doherty and Summers, *WVU*, 320, 324.

32. James G. Harlow, "A Very Fragile Thing," WVU *Magazine* 6 (Winter 1975): 8–12. See also Harry W. Ernst, Memorandum, n.d., Box 4, A&M 5020.

33. Doherty and Summers, *WVU*, 325.

34. Shamberger, "A Score and More Years," 50.

35. Doherty and Summers, *WVU*, 332 (quoting without attribution).

36. WVU *Alumni News* 41 (Winter 1976): 4.

37. WVU *Alumni News* 42 (Spring 1977): 1, 5.

38. Both quoted in WVU *Alumni Quarterly* 1 (Spring 1978): 19.

39. Harry Ernst, *A Pictorial History: 1867-1979* (Morgantown: West Virginia University Press, 1980), 98.

40. West Virginia University, "Self Study 1973," prepared for the North Central Association of Colleges and Schools, VII, 1-2.

41. *Barron's Profiles of American Colleges: An In-Depth Study of West Virginia University* (Woodbury, NY: Barron's Educational Series, 1973), 2, 7, 10.

42. *Barron's Profiles*, 10-11.

43. *Barron's Profiles*, 1973, 28.

44. *Barron's Profiles*, 10-11, 28 (quotation).

45. West Virginia University, "Self-Study Report, 1984," prepared for the North Central Association of Colleges and Schools, 99 (hereafter "Self Study 1984").

46. "Self Study 1984," 100-101.

47. "Happy Seniors," WVU *Alumni Magazine* 8 (Winter/Spring 1985): 21.

48. "Self Study 1984," 104-7.

49. "Self Study 1984," 111-12, 113-14 (quotation).

50. "Self Study 1984," 116-18.

51. James F. Dent, "Changing of the Bars," WVU *Alumni Magazine* 6 (Winter/Spring 1983): 1, 3.

52. Dent, "Changing Bars," 5.

53. "Alcohol Alert," WVU *Alumni Magazine* 8 (Winter/Spring 1984): 16-17.

54. "Marketing Alcoholic Beverages on Campus," draft, September 17, 1984, folder 17, Box 9, A&M 5006.

55. *Dominion Post*, August 30, 1979.

56. Proposal for Additional Security at the Mountainlair," November 1980, no folder, Box 1, A&M 5001.

57. Carl Hadsell, "Student Neighbors," WVU *Alumni Magazine* 7 (Fall 1983): 2-3.

58. Nancy Lohmann to Neil S. Bucklew, "Survey of Task Force on Residence Halls," July 16, 1986, cover memo with questionnaire and results appended, Folder 22, Box 10, A&M 5003.

59. "Honors Program," WVU *Alumni Magazine* 10 (Summer 1987): 23. For emphasis being placed on international education, see *Dominion Post*, November 7, 1986, and, for the exchange program started with University of Guanajuato, Mexico, see *Dominion Post*, March 11, 1989.

60. *Dominion Post*, September, 27, 1986.

61. Larry V. Starcher to Neil Bucklew, September 23, 1986, and Bucklew to Starcher, November 5, 1986, Folder 14, Box 1, A&M 5003.

62. Starcher to Bucklew, November 13, 1986, and Bucklew to Starcher, November 19, 1986, Folder 14, Box 1, A&M 5003.

63. David A. Raese to Bucklew, February 27, 1989, and Bucklew to Raese, March 7, 1989, Folder 14, Box 1, A&M 5003.

64. Bucklew to Raese, April 27, 1989, Folder 14, Box 1, A&M 5003.

65. West Virginia University, "Self-Study Report, 1994," prepared for the North Central Assoc. of Colleges and Schools, 62 (hereafter "Self Study 1994").

66. "Self Study 1994," 88, 63–65 (quotation on 63).

67. "Self Study 1994," 87–88..

CHAPTER TWELVE

1. William T. Doherty Jr. and Festus P. Summers, *West Virginia University: Symbol of Unity in a Sectionalized State* (Morgantown: West Virginia University Press, 1982), 325 (hereafter Doherty and Summers, *WVU*).

2. *Morgantown Post*, September 22, 1967.

3. J. William Douglas, *The School of Physical Education at West Virginia University: An Historical Perspective, 1891–1999* (Morgantown: WVU Printing Services for the School of Physical Education, 2000), 53; *Morgantown Post*, September 25, 1967 (quotation); Doherty and Summers, *WVU*, 287; WVU *Alumni News* 36 (Fall 1970): 7.

4. John Antonik, *Roll Out the Carpet: 101 Seasons of West Virginia University Basketball* (Morgantown: West Virginia University Press, 2010), 104–7; Norman Julian, *Legends: Profiles in West Virginia University Basketball, 1938–1998* (Morgantown, WV: Trillium Publishing, 1998), 104–5.

5. Antonik, *Roll Out the Carpet*, 117–18; Julian, *Legends*, 37–38, 108.

6. Antonik, *Roll Out the Carpet*, 119 (quotation); John Antonik, "Breaking Barriers," WVU *Alumni Magazine* 27 (Summer 2004): 36–37; Julian, *Legends*, 110–11.

7. Julian, *Legends*, 110–11.

8. Quotes from Antonik, "Breaking Barriers," 36–37; Julian, *Legends*, 111.

9. Antonik, *Roll Out the Carpet*, 126–28; Julian, *Legends*, 41 (quotation).

10. WVU *Alumni News* 32 (Spring 1968): 7.

11. Antonik, *Roll Out the Carpet*, 138–43; Julian, *Legends*, 112–13.

12. Antonik, *Roll Out the Carpet*, 146–47.

13. Quoted in Antonik, *Roll Out the Carpet*, 149.

14. Julian, *Legends*, 115; Antonik, *Roll Out the Carpet*, 157.

15. Antonik, *Roll Out the Carpet*, 143.

16. Antonik, *Roll Out the Carpet*, 151.

17. *Dominion Post*, February 12, 2011.

18. Antonik, *Roll Out the Carpet*, 154–56; Julian, *Legends*, 115; *Dominion Post*, February 12, 2011.

19. Antonik, *Roll Out the Carpet*, 158–59.

20. Julian, *Legends*, 48–51; Antonik, *Roll Out the Carpet*, 160–69.

21. "Coach Corum Responsible for Integrating WVU Football," *Morgantown Times*, January 23, 2010.

22. John Antonik, *West Virginia University Football Vault: The History of the Mountaineers* (Atlanta: Whitman Publishing, 2009), 84; *Morgantown Times*, January 23, 2010.

23. *Dominion Post*, January 5, 2010 (quotations); WVU Sports Hall of Fame, www.msnsportsnet.com/halloffame.cfm.

24. *Dominion Post*, January 11, 2010.

25. Antonik, *Football Vault*, 86–89; Doherty and Summers, *WVU*, 327; Douglas, *School of Physical Education*, 71.

26. Doherty and Summers, *WVU*, 327–28; Douglas, *School of Physical Education*, 71; *Dominion Post*, August 2, 2009.

27. Annual Report to Faculty Assembly, April 23, 1976, cited in Doherty and Summers, *WVU*, 288.

28. Gordon Thorn, interview by Charles D. Dusch Jr., December 5, 2007.

29. *Morgantown Post*, April 22, 27, 1977; Doherty and Summers, *WVU*, 328

30. *Morgantown Post*, April 26 (quotation), 27, 1977.

31. *Morgantown Post*, April 27, 1977.

32. *Dominion Post*, April 28, 1977.

33. Report to the Faculty Assembly, quoted in Doherty and Summers, *WVU*, 329.

34. Thorn interview; *Charleston Daily-Mail*, December 4, 1977 (quotation); *Charleston Gazette*, May 23, 1978; *Dominion Post*, July 14, 1978; Doherty and Summers, *WVU*, 330–31.

35. Memorandum, Leland Byrd to President James Harlow, August 9, 1972, and Memorandum, Harlow to Byrd (and others), April 10, 1973, cited in *WVU Women: First Century: An Historical Digest* (Morgantown: WVU Women's Centenary Project, 1989), 48.

36. *Dominion Post*, April 1, 2008 (quotations); *WVU Women: First Century*, xiii, 48.

37. *Dominion Post*, April 1, 2008.

38. *Dominion Post*, April 1, 2008.

39. "Sugar and Spice," WVU *Alumni News* 40 (Spring 1975): 4–5, 21.

40. Tammy Taylor, "Liberating the Mountaineers," WVU *Alumni Magazine* 4 (Winter/Spring 1981): 10–12.

41. *Charleston Daily-Mail*, February 10, 1979.

42. Harold J. Shamberger, "A Score and More Years at West Virginia University," 91, typescript.

43. *Dominion Post*, May 4, 1979 (quotation); Doherty and Summers, *WVU*, 336.

44. Douglas, *School of Physical Education*, 78; Otis K. Rice and Stephen W. Brown, *West Virginia: A History*, 2nd ed. (Lexington: University Press of Kentucky, 1993), 286.

45. Doherty and Summers, *WVU*, 336; Douglas, *School of Physical Education*, 74–75.

46. Shamberger, "A Score and More," 95.

47. Shamberger, "A Score and More," 97–98; *Dominion Post*, January 13, 1980; Mark Scharf, "Cignetti Thankful for Time at WVU," *Dominion Post*, November 13, 2010, WVU Goal Post section, 17.

48. Shamberger, "A Score and More," 98.

49. Shamberger, "A Score and More," 99; *Dominion Post*, March 25, 1981.

50. Shamberger, "A Score and More," 99; Doherty and Summers, *WVU*, 341.

51. Becky Byrd Lofstead, "Big East Brawl," WVU *Alumni Magazine* 14 (Summer 1991): 8–9.

52. Neil S. Bucklew, interview by Ronald L. Lewis, August 30, 2007.

53. Lofstead, "Big East Brawl," 9–10.

54. Mickey Furfari, *Mickey's Mountaineer Memories* (Beckley, WV: Beckley Newspapers Inc., 2008), 278.

55. Quoted in Julian, *Legends*, 56–57.

56. Mickey Furfari, "The 100th-Year Team," WVU *Alumni Magazine* 14 (Fall 1991): 6–10 (quotation on 6); "Join the Celebration," WVU *Alumni Magazine* 14 (Summer 1991): 10.

57. "Great News!" WVU *Alumni Magazine* 17 (Summer 1994): 7.

58. Julian, *Legends*, 57.

59. "Welcome to the Big East," *Alumni Magazine* 19 (Winter 1996): 21; Julian, *Legends*, 175 on Dick Vitale.

60. Quoted in Furfari, *Mountaineer Memories*, 28–29.

61. Julian, *Legends*, 31; WVU News Service Media Advisory, "Fred Schaus to Step Down as WVU AD," Jan. 6, 1989, Folder 13, Box 3, A&M 5003; Furfari, *Mountaineer Memories*, 19–21; Julian, *Legends*, 31–34.

62. James E. Seibert to Neil S. Bucklew, October 5, 1989, Folder 12, Box 3, A&M 5003.

63. Jon A. Reed to Seibert, Oct. 31, 1989, Folder 12, Box 3, A&M 5003.

64. T. L. Price to the editor, copied to President Bucklew, n.d. [October 1989], Folder 12, Box 3, A&M 5003.

65. Dr. and Mrs. Leonard Weissburg to WVU Athletic Director, November 13. 1989, Folder 12, Box 3, A&M 5003.

66. Jay Redmond to Ed Pastilong, November 15, 1989, Folder 12, Box 3, A&M 5003.

67. Ed Pastilong to Frederick E. Gruninger, November 22, 1989, Folder 12, Box 3, A&M 5003.

68. Susan Hiller, "The Debate Over Proposition 42," College Football Association, *Sidelines* (March 1989): 6–7, clipping, Folder 13, Box 3, A&M 5003.

69. Rev. Jude J. Mili to Don Nehlen, May 4, 1989, Folder 12, Box 3, A&M 5003.

70. Don Nehlen to George Nedeff, Director of Facilities, May 2, 1989, Folder 12, Box 3, A&M 5003.

71. Honorable John C. Ashworth to Neil S. Bucklew, June 19, 1989, Folder 13, Box 3, A&M 5003.

72. Bucklew to Ashworth, July 5, 1989, Folder 13, Box 3, A&M 5003.

73. Jon A. Reed to Bucklew, June 30, 1989, Folder 13, Box 3, A&M 5003.

74. Memorandum, Charles M. Neinas, Executive Director, College Football Association, to Athletic Directors and Head Football Coaches, May 5, 1989, Folder 13, Box 3, A&M 5003; Memorandum, Paula Jones to Neil Bucklew, May 17, 1989, attachment, "Graduation Rate Nine Year Compilation, 1981 through 1989, compiled by Garrett Ford, Folder 13, Box 3, A&M 5003; Freshmen entering in 1985–1986 receiving a bachelor's degree within six years, as reported in *USA Today*, June 3,

1993; West Virginia University, "Institutional Self-Study Report, 1994," prepared for the North Central Association of Colleges and Schools, Appendix L.

75. Neil S. Bucklew, "Should Student-Athletes Be Paid? A Counterpoint," August 24, 1989, Folder 12, Box 3, A&M 5003.

76. Ed Pasitlong to Neil S. Bucklew, August 24, 1989, Folder 12, Box 3, A&M 5003.

PART III

1. Derek Bok, *Universities in the Marketplace: The Commercialization of Higher Education* (Princeton, NJ: Princeton University Press, 2003), 2–3.

2. Mary L. Good, "Increased Commercialization of the Academy Following the Bayh-Dole Act of 1980," 48–50, and Murray Sperber, "College Sports, Inc.: How Big-Time Athletic Departments Run Interference for College, Inc., 17–19, in *Buying In or Selling Out? The Commercialization of the American Research University*, ed. Donald G. Stein (New Brunswick, NJ: Rutgers University Press, 2004).

3. Bok, *Universities in the Marketplace*, 4–7. See, for example, Robert Kuttner, *Everything for Sale: The Virtues and Limits of Markets* (New York: Alfred A. Knopf, 1997); Stanley Aronowitz, *The Knowledge Factory: Dismantling the Corporate University and Creating True Higher Learning* (Boston: Beacon Press, 2000); Allan Bloom, *The Closing of the American Mind* (New York: Simon and Schuster, 1987); Wesley Shumar, *College for Sale: A Critique of the Commodification of Higher Education* (Washington, DC: Falmer Press, 1997).

4. Bok, *Universities in the Marketplace*, 8–11 (quotation on 10). See also Sheila Slaughter and Larry L. Leslie, *Academic Capitalism: Politics, Policies, and the Entrepreneurial University* (Baltimore, MD: Johns Hopkins University Press, 1997).

5. Good, "Increased Commercialization of the Academy," 50–51.

6. Cole, *Great American University*, 163; Bok, *Universities in the Marketplace*, 11–12.

7. Rebecca Zacks, quoted in Good, "Increased Commercialization of the Academy," 52.

8. Bok, *Universities in the Marketplace*, 13–14.

9. Good, "Increased Commercialization of the Academy," 52–54.

10. Peter Schmidt, "States Push Public Universities to Commercialize Research," *Chronicle of Higher Education*, March 29, 2002, A26; James J. Duderstadt, "Delicate Balance: Market Forces Versus the Public Interest," in Stein, *Buying In or Selling Out?* 58.

11. Derek Bok, "The Benefits and Costs of Commercialization of the Academy," in Stein, *Buying In or Selling Out?* 33–34.

12. Duderstadt, "Delicate Balance," 62, 68 (quoting Donald Kennedy).

13. Bok, "Benefits and Costs," 34–36 (quotation on 34).

14. Cole, *Great American University*, 173–74; Donald G. Stein, "A Personal Perspective on the Selling of Academia," in Stein, *Buying In or Selling Out?* 6.

15. Stein, "A Personal Perspective," 2–3.

16. Stein, "A Personal Perspective," 5–10.

17. Testimony of Paul Berg, quoted in Duderstadt, "Delicate Balance," 63.
18. "Can Public Education Be Run like a Business?" March 17, 1994, in David C. Hardesty Jr., *Leading the Public University: Essays, Speeches, and Commentary* (Morgantown: West Virginia University Press, 2007), 71–77.
19. Kellogg Commission on the Future of State and Land-Grant Universities, *Returning to Our Roots: The Engaged Institution* (Washington, DC: National Association of State Universities and Land-Grant Colleges, February 1999).
20. Hardesty, *Leading the Public University*, 118–19.
21. Both strategic plans are in the David C. Hardesty Papers, Box 5, A&M 5114.
22. Bok, *Universities in the Marketplace*, 17.

CHAPTER THIRTEEN

1. David C. Hardesty Jr., "Report of the Chairman to the Board of Trustees, University of West Virginia System," June 21, 1991, Box 4, A&M 5114, David Hardesty Papers.
2. West Virginia University, "Institutional Self-Study Report, 1994," prepared for the North Central Association of Colleges and Schools, 43-44 (hereafter "Self Study 1994"). See also Bob Brunner, ed., *The Caperton Years, 1989–1993. Official Papers of the Honorable Gaston Caperton, 31st Governor of West Virginia* (Beckley, WV: BWJ Printing and Office Supply, 1993), 74–75.
3. "Self Study 1994," 45.
4. "Self Study 1994," 46.
5. "Self Study 1994," 50; "Speak Out For Higher Education: Reports from the Regional HEAT Forum held in Morgantown, September 22, 1992."
6. "Self Study 1994," 50–51.
7. "Self Study 1994," 133–34.
8. West Virginia University, "Self-Study Submitted to the Higher Learning Commission of the North Central Association of Colleges and Schools, Site Visit of April 19-21, 2004," 123 (hereafter "Self Study 2004"). See Senate Bill 547, *Acts of the Legislature of West Virginia*, Regular Session, 1995, vol. 1, chap. 99 (Beckley, WV: BJW Printing and Office Supply, 1995), 608–87.
9. "Self Study 2004," 6. See also "A Final Report of the Accomplishments in Response to Senate Bill 547, December 1, 2000, Box 5, A&M 5114, David Hardesty Papers.
10. Neil Bucklew to David Hardesty, "Transition Report," June 13, 1995, copy in Ronald L. Lewis Papers.
11. David Hardesty, interview by Ronald L. Lewis, August 22, 2007.
12. *Charleston Gazette*, March 25, 1998.
13. *Dominion Post*, September 15, 1998. See Senate Bill 653, *Acts of the Legislature of West Virginia*, First Extraordinary Session, 2000, vol. 1, chap. 100 (Charleston, WV: Printing Press Ltd., 2000), 600–771.
14. *Daily Athenaeum*, October 22, 1999; *Dominion Post*, November 16, 1999.
15. *Times West Virginian*, February 25, 2000.
16. *Charleston Gazette*, June 29, 30, 2000; "Self Study 2004," 4–5, 7, 123-24.
17. "West Virginia University Board of Governors, Power and Duties," online at *http://*

bog.wvu.edu/powers, and "West Virginia University Board of Governors' Operating Procedures," Article 1.2, 1.6, and 1.12, online at *http://bog.wvu.edu/procedures*; *Dominion Post*, June 30, September 16 (quotation), 2000. The Board of Governors was initially called the WVU Board of Advisors until the Compact was accepted. Then, on July 1, 2001, it once again became the Board of Governors.

18. *Charleston Gazette*, September 11, 2000; *Daily Athenaeum*, October 4, 2000.
19. *Charleston Gazette*, October 4, 16, 2000; *Daily Athenaeum*, October 9, 4 (quotation), 2000.
20. *Dominion Post*, October 11, 2000.
21. *Charleston Gazette*, December 13, 2000.
22. *Charleston Daily-Mail*, February 16, 2001.
23. *Dominion Post*, March 14, 2001.
24. *Charleston Gazette-Mail*, April 8, 2001.
25. *Times West Virginian*, March 5, 2001.
26. *Daily Athenaeum*, February 13, 2001; *Glenville Democrat-Pathfinder*, February 15, 2001 (quotation).
27. *Glenville Democrat-Pathfinder*, February 15, 2001 (quotation); *Charleston Gazette*, March 9, 2001.
28. *Charleston Gazette*, January 10, 2003.
29. *Charleston Gazette*, January 12, 2003.
30. *Charleston Gazette*, January 15, 2003.
31. *Charleston Gazette-Mail*, January 12, 2003.
32. "Remarks of David C. Hardesty Jr., Delivered to the WVU Board of Governors," April 5, 2003, Speeches, A&M 5114, David Hardesty Papers.
33. Peter Schmidt, "Colleges in West Virginia Debate Who Should Pay for Facilities," *Chronicle of Higher Education*, 48 (July 19, 2002): A20.
34. *Clarksburg Exponent Telegram*, April 13, 2003.
35. *Dominion Post*, May 9, 2003.
36. *Dominion Post*, August 8, 2003.
37. *Charleston Gazette*, August 14, 2003.
38. *Times West Virginian*, August 15, 2003.
39. WVU Bureau of Business and Economic Research, "Economic Impact of WVU and Affiliated Organizations on the West Virginia Economy," September 1990, by David Greenstreet and Tom S. Witt.
40. "Tipping Point: A Case for State Funding for West Virginia University," Report presented to the Board of Governors, September 5, 2003, and WVU Bureau of Business and Economic Research, "Economic Impact of a 1,000 Increased Student Enrollment at West Virginia University on the Monongalia County Economy," August 14, 2002, both in Box 5, A&M 5114, David Hardesty Papers (quotation). See also *Dominion Post*, September 6, 2003, and *Daily Athenaeum*, September 8, 2003.
41. *Charleston Gazette*, August 4, 2003.
42. *Charleston Gazette*, September 13, 2003 (quotation); *Clarksburg Exponent Telegram*, September 13, 2003.

43. *Dominion Post*, October 1 (quotation), 5, 2003; *Clarksburg Exponent Telegram*, October 3, 2003.

44. *Daily Athenaeum*, September 22, October 3, 2003; *Dominion Post*, October 19, 2003.

45. *Dominion Post*, October 17, 2003.

46. *Dominion Post*, November 15, 2003.

47. *Charleston Gazette*, September 17, 2003; *Daily Athenaeum*, September 22

CHAPTER FOURTEEN

1. Hardesty's Resume, August 31, 2007, Office of the President, copy in Ronald L. Lewis Papers; Becky Lofstead, "WVU Lands One of Its Own," WVU *Alumni Magazine* 18 (Fall 1995): 3–5.

2. *Charleston Gazette*, April 6, 1995; *Dominion Post*, April 29, 1995.

3. *Dominion Post*, April 29, May 2, 1995; *Spirit*, April 27, 1995, 5 (quotations).

4. *Daily Athenaeum*, April 28, 1995; *Dominion Post*, May 2, 1995; *Mountaineer Spirit*, May 11, 1995, 6 (quotation).

5. *Dominion Post*, April 11, 1995.

6. *Wheeling Intelligencer*, January 1995, clipping in Box 4, A&M 5114, David Hardesty Papers.

7. *Jackson Herald*, January 18, 1995.

8. *Dominion Post*, May 12, 1995.

9. *Charleston Gazette*, May 12, 1995; *Clarksburg Exponent*, May 18, 1995 (quotation).

10. *Daily Athenaeum*, April 21, 28, 1995. See also, *Spirit*, May 11, 1995, 6.

11. *Charleston Gazette*, August 24, 1995; *Charleston Daily Mail*, August 24, 1995; *Daily Athenaeum*, September 15, and October 2, 10, 1995; *Dominion Post*, September 30, October 7 (quotation), 1995.

12. *Parkersburg Sentinel*, May 10, 1995; *Charleston Daily Mail*, December 31, 1995.

13. *Charleston Gazette*, n.d., Box 4, A&M 5114, David Hardesty Papers.

14. *Beckley Register-Herald*, April 26, 1995.

15. *Charleston Daily Mail*, May 18, 1995.

16. *Huntington Herald-Dispatch*, May 14, 1995.

17. *Dominion Post*, May 22, 1995; *Daily Athenaeum*, June 7, 1995 (quotation).

18. *Daily Athenaeum*, April 10, 1996.

19. *Dominion Post*, June 9 (quotation), August 23, 1995; *Charleston Gazette*, June 9, 1995. See also "1992–1993 Equal Employment Policy and Affirmative Action Plan," 11th ed., WVU President's Office for Social Justice, 1993.

20. *Daily Athenaeum*, September 29, November 14, 1995; *Times West Virginian*, December 13, 1999 (quotations), Box 10, A&M 5114, David Hardesty Papers.

21. *Daily Athenaeum*, June 21, 1995.

22. *Daily Athenaeum*, July 26, 1995; *Dominion Post*, August 21, 1995.

23. *Dominion Post*, September 9, 1995; David C. Hardesty Jr., "Inaugural Address,"

September 8, 1995, in David C. Hardesty Jr., *Leading the Public University* (Morgantown: West Virginia University Press, 2007), 91–104 (quotations).

24. *Dominion Post*, October 30, 1995; *Daily Athenaeum*, October 31, 1995 (quotation).

25. Hardesty, *Leading the Public University*, 73.

26. Hardesty, *Leading the Public University*, 73–77.

27. "Final Report of Accomplishments in Response to SB 547," 1–3, December 1, 2000, Box 5, A&M 5114, David Hardesty Papers; West Virginia University, "Self-Study Submitted to the Higher Learning Commission of the North Central Association of Colleges and Schools Site Visit of April 19–21, 2004," 6, 123 (hereafter "Self Study 2004").

28. Gerald Lang, interview by Ronald L. Lewis, February 14, 2008.

29. David Hardesty, interview by Ronald L. Lewis.

30. *Wheeling Intelligencer*, August 16, 1995.

31. *Wheeling Intelligencer*, August 16, 1995.

32. *Dominion Post*, February 21, 1996.

33. *Charleston Gazette*, May 18, 31, 1996.

34. "Final Report of Accomplishments in Response to SB547," passim; *Charleston Daily Mail*, July 15, 1996; *Charleston Gazette*, July 15, 1996; *Dominion Post*, July 15, 1996.

35. *Charleston Gazette*, May 27, 1996.

36. *Charleston Gazette*, May 31, 1996; *Daily Athenaeum*, April 12, 1996; Dominion Post, May 12, 1996 (quotation).

37. *Daily Athenaeum*, April 19, 1995.

38. *Daily Athenaeum*, November 14, 1995.

39. *Dominion Post*, November 11, Dec. 9 (quotation), 1997.

40. "Self Study 2004," 39; *Dominion Post*, February 8, 1998; Faculty Constitution, online at *http://facultysenate.wvu.edu/faculty_constitution*.

41. *Dominion Post*, February 10, 1998.

42. *Dominion Post*, April 8, 1998; *Charleston Daily Mail*, April 30, 1998 (quotation).

43. WVU, "A Final Report of Accomplishments in Response to Senate Bill 547, December 1, 2000," Box 5, A&M 5114, David Hardesty Papers.

44. West Virginia Higher Education Policy Commission, "Compact for the Future of West Virginia, 2000"; David C. Hardesty Jr., "State of the University Address 2001: The WVU Compacts," February 12, 2001, 5, Box 5, A&M 5114, David Hardesty Papers.

45. Gerald Lang comments following David C. Hardesty Jr., "State of the University Address 2001: The WVU Compacts," February 12, 2001, 5–10, Box 5, A&M 5114, David Hardesty Papers. See also *Times West Virginian*, March 23, 2001, and *Daily Athenaeum*, January 22, 2001.

46. David C. Hardesty Jr., State of the University Address, "The New West Virginia University," September 10, 2001, in Hardesty, *Leading the Public University*, 138–48.

47. Becky Lofstead, "September 11, 2001, America's New Date of Infamy," WVU *Alumni Magazine* 24 (Fall 2001): 12–13.

48. Gerald Lang, interview by Ronald L. Lewis, February 14, 2008.

49. *Daily Athenaeum*, February 11, 2003.

50. Remarks of David C. Hardesty Jr., "WVU Financial Strategies to the Board of Governors," February 7, 2003, Speeches, A&M 5114, David Hardesty Papers.

51. *State Journal*, February 20, 2003; *Dominion Post*, June 11, 2003.

52. *Charleston Gazette*, April 17, 2003.

53. *Dominion Post*, April 29, 2003.

54. *Charleston Daily Mail*, February 11, 2005 (quotations); Amy Quigley, "A Decade of Service, Part II," WVU *Alumni Magazine* 29 (Spring 2006): 28–33.

55. Breneman quoted in the *Charleston Daily Mail*, February 11, 2005.

56. Gerald Lang, interview by Ronald L. Lewis, February 14, 2008.

57. "Universities in Decline," *New York Times*, August 26, 2003.

58. David C. Hardesty Jr., State of the Campus Address, "Quality Matters," October 10, 2005, in Hardesty, *Leading the Public University*, 153–54; David C. Hardesty Jr., State of the University Address on Capitol Hill, Hyatt Regency, Washington, DC, "A University on the Move," June 17, 2004, Speeches, A&M 5114, David Hardesty Papers.

59. West Virginia University, "Self-Study, 1973," VI–2; "Self Study 2004," 41–43.

60. David C. Hardesty Jr., State of the Campus Address, "Quality Matters," October 10, 2005, 149–64.

61. Hardesty quoted in the *Dominion Post*, April 20, 2003.

62. David C. Hardesty Jr. Supplemental Interview by Ronald L. Lewis, March 14, 2012, Ronald L. Lewis Papers.

63. David Hardesty, interview by Ronald L. Lewis.

64. "Hardestys Look Back on a Dozen Years at WVU," *State Journal*, n.d., 2007, Office of the President, copy in Ronald L. Lewis Papers.

65. "Hardestys Look Back on a Dozen Years at WVU"; "Opening the Way for Dreams to Come True: David Hardesty and the Student Experience," WVU *Alumni Magazine* 30 (Spring 2007): 25–29 (quotation on 26).

66. "Hardestys Look Back on a Dozen Years at WVU."

67. "Hardestys Look Back on a Dozen Years at WVU."

68. "Opening the Way for Dreams," 25–29 (quotation on 26).

69. Citations in order: *Clarksburg Exponent Telegram, State Journal, Charleston Daily Mail, Morgantown Dominion Post, Beckley Register-Herald, Wheeling News-Register, Daily Athenaeum, Charleston Gazette*. Taken from Office of the President homepage (dates not provided), *www.wvu.edu/administration/retirement/difficult.html*, URL not functioning, copy in Ronald L. Lewis Papers.

CHAPTER FIFTEEN

1. Kellogg Commission on the Future of State and Land-Grant Universities, "Returning to Our Roots: The Engaged Institution," Third Report (Washington, DC: National Association of State Universities and Land-Grant Colleges, February 1999).

2. Kellogg, "Returning to Our Roots," vii (quotations), 4–5.

3.   Kellogg, "Returning to Our Roots," x, 4–5.

4.   Kellogg, "Returning to Our Roots," xi.

5.   David C. Hardesty Jr., *Leading the Public University: Essays, Speeches, and Commentary* (Morgantown: West Virginia University Press, 2007), 118–19.

6.   Hardesty, *Leading the Public University*, 118–19; "West Virginia University Research Task Force Report," April 30, 1996, 1, 7 (hereafter "WVU Research Report, 1996").

7.   "WVU Research Report, 1996," 12 (quotation), 14–15.

8.   "WVU Research Report, 1996," 20.

9.   "WVU Research Report, 1996," 20–22.

10. "WVU Research Report, 1996," 26–27.

11. "WVU Research Report, 1996," 29–33.

12. "WVU Research Report, 1996," 33, 35.

13. David C. Hardesty Jr., "Economic Development in West Virginia," n.d., 3–11, Speeches, Box 5, A&M 5114, David Hardesty Papers. The themes in this speech appeared in various forms in many of his economic development speeches. See, for example, "Can We Get It Right This Time: Thoughts on Economic and Community Development," 2001, 312–24, and "Leading Economic Change in America's Communities," 2004, 324–33, both reprinted in Hardesty, *Leading the Public University*.

14. David Hardesty Jr., "Workforce Development Needs Integrated, Cooperative Approach," *Huntington Herald-Dispatch*, September 22, 1998, op-ed page. The call for collaboration was frequent in Hardesty's public communications about research. See, for example, "WVU Research: Supporting the Economic Transformation of Our State and Nation" 23 (Winter 2000): online, 1–3, copy in Ronald L. Lewis Papers.

15. David C. Hardesty Jr., "Higher Education Plays Key Role in Spurring Economy," February 5, 2002, guest column, online version, Office of the President, *www.wvu.edu/administration/speeches/feb252002.htm*, URL not functioning, copy in Ronald L. Lewis Papers; John Weete, "Research Dollars Help West Virginia," *Charleston Gazette*, March 8, 2004, op-ed page.

16. *Daily Athenaeum*, August 22, 2000; David C. Hardesty Jr., "WVU Research: Supporting the Economic Transformation of Our State and the Nation," September 11, 2000, online version, President's Office, *www.wvu.edu/administration/speech/feb142000.htm, URL not functioning, copy in Ronald L. Lewis Papers*; "Research and Economic Development, Aug. 4, 2007," *www.research.wvu.edu*.

17. "Measures of Success for Research and Other Sponsored Programs," WVU Research Corporation, factsheet; "A New Era," WVU Office of Sponsored Programs Newsletter, No. 4, July 2010, 2.

18. Amy Higginbotham, Christiadi, Eric Pennington, and Tom S. Witt, "West Virginia University: Expanding West Virginia's Economy, FY 2009," Bureau of Business and Economic Research, West Virginia University, 2010, 3–4. Also available at *www.be.wvu.edu/bber/*. The BBER reports quantify the direct, indirect, induced, and total economic impacts of WVU, focusing on such indicators as employment, business volume, employee compensation, and selected state taxes. Total purchases by

WVU for annual operations and capital expenditures are included, along with pur chases by faculty, staff, and students. These direct and indirect expenditures and employment are magnified by economic multipliers from the additional spending by suppliers and re-spending of wages by employees. At the time, Parkersburg was an independent community college.

19. Extrapolated from Randall A. Childs, David Greenstreet, and Tom S. Witt, "Eco-nomic Impact of West Virginia University, FY 1998," Bureau of Business and Eco-nomic Research, West Virginia University, 1999, 8–10, and Higginbotham et al., "West Virginia University: Expanding West Virginia's Economy, FY 2009," 2010, 1–3, 5–8, 11–12.

20. John D. Weete, interview by Ronald L. Lewis, August 6, 2007.

21. As reported in the *Times West Virginian*, July 18, 1999.

22. The *Chronicle* cited in the *Times West Virginian*, July 18, 1999; *Clarksburg Ex-ponent Telegram*, July 23, 2000.

23. *Wheeling News-Register*, August 3, 2000.

24. *Dominion Post*, September 24, 2002.

25. As reported in the *Charleston Gazette*, September 23, 2003.

26. *Times West Virginian*, September 30, 2003.

27. *Times West Virginian*, March 17, 2000.

28. John D. Weete, "Strategic Plan for Research: A Brief Overview," West Virginia University, Spring 2000; WVU Research Corporation, *West Virginia University Research, 2006*, 12–13, and "2004–2010 Strategic Plan for Research and Eco-nomic Development for West Virginia University," 2004, 3.

29. "2004–2010 Strategic Plan," 4; Weete interview (quotations).

30. Weete interview.

31. Weete interview.

32. Weete interview.

33. Weete interview.

34. Weete interview.

35. Weete interview; WVU Vice President for Research and Economic Development, "Trends and Future Prospects for External Funding for Research at West Virginia University: a Critical Analysis," December 15, 2006, 14–15. The report was prepared by John D. Weete for President David Hardesty, Provost Gerald Lang, and Vice President of Health Sciences Robert D'Alessandri.

36. "Trends and Future Prospects," 14.

37. "Trends and Future Prospects," 16.

38. "Trends and Future Prospects," 17–18.

39. "2004–2010 Strategic Plan," 8–9 (quotation); Cassie Shaner, "Corporation Aims to Move Research into the Marketplace," *Dominion Post*, December 28, 2008, 6-A.

40. WVU Research Corporation, *West Virginia University Research, 2006*, 12–13, and "2004–2010 Strategic Plan for Research and Economic Development for West Virginia University," August 2004, 11.

41. David Hardesty Jr., "WVU's Role in Technology Transfer," Guest Opinion, *Mont-gomery Herald*, May 30, 2001, Box 12, A&M 5114, David Hardesty Papers.

42. WVU Research Corp., "West Virginia University Research, 2006," 15, and "2004–2010 Strategic Plan," 2004, 10–11; "Incubating New Businesses," WVU *Alumni Magazine* 28 (Spring 2005): 6.

43. WVU Research Corporation, "West Virginia University Research, 2006," 14. See also "Research Park Construction Under Way," WVU *Alumni Magazine* 28 (Spring 2005): 6–7 (quotation); "2004–2010 Strategic Plan," 12–13.

44. Quoted in the *Dominion Post*, September 1, 2002; John D. Weete, "Academic Research: A Key to Economic Growth in West Virginia," *Dominion Post*, November 12, 2002.

45. Cassie Shaner, "After Slow Start, Work Speeds up at the WVU Research Park," *Dominion Post*, December 28, 2008, 6-A (quotation); *Dominion Post*, March 15, 2009.

46. Weete interview; Cassie Shaner, "Mission Discovery: WVU Aims to Improve Research Status," *Dominion Post*, December 28, 2008, 5-A.

47. Shaner, "Mission Discovery," *Dominion Post*, Dec. 28, 2008, 5-A.

48. Table, "Total Research and Development Expenditures for WVU and Peer Institutions," *Dominion Post*, December 28, 2008, 6-A; National Science Foundation, "University Ranking Watch," September 17, 2008, Table 27, and "R&D Expenditures at Universities and Colleges, ranked by FY 1999–2006," both at http://rankingwatch.blogspot.com/2008/09/university-research-expenditure.html.

49. Shaner, "Mission Discovery," *Dominion Post*, December 28, 2008, 5-A.

50. *Charleston Gazette*, February 7, 10, 17, September 7, and December 15, 2008.

51. WVU College of Engineering and Mineral Resources, "Revitalizing the Energy Research and Education Agenda at West Virginia University: Strategic Initiative for Energy and Environment, 2006-2010," November 2006, 7–8.

52. "Revitalizing the Energy Research and Education Agenda," 7, 10. See also WVU, Office of Research and Economic Development, *West Virginia University Research*, 2003, 26–27.

53. *Dominion Post*, March 27, August 20, 2008; Gov. Joe Manchin and C. Peter Magrath, "W.Va. Is Best Place to Turn Coal into Fuel," *Dominion Post*, December 17, 2008.

54. *Dominion Post*, September 9, 2010.

55. Becky Lofstead, "New Degree Program Makes a Great Impression," WVU *Alumni Magazine* 21 (Winter 1998): 12–13.

56. WVU Research Office, *Research at West Virginia University*, 2003, 8 (quotation), 9.

57. Vicki Smith, "A Different Approach: Forensic Students Face Unique Challenges," WVU *Alumni Magazine* 22 (Summer 1999): 18–19.

58. WVU Research Office, *Research at West Virginia University*, 2003, 8–9.

59. WVU Research Office, *Research at West Virginia University*, 2003, 8; "Biometrics: High-Tech Crime Prevention," WVU *Alumni Magazine* 22 (Summer 1999): 20–21.

60. Nora Edinger, "Biometrics Capital of the World?" *Clarksburg Exponent Telegram*, December 9, 2001.

61. Michael M. Phillips, "Drawing New Technology to Old Economy: West Virginia Bids to Shed Backwoods Image with Biometrics," *Wall Street Journal*, March 11, 2002.
62. Danny Forinash, "West Virginia Positioning Itself to Be Silicon Valley of Biometrics Industry," *State Journal*, July 8, 2002.
63. Forinash, "West Virginia Positioning Itself"; *Dominion Post*, October 3, 2010.
64. WVU, Research Office, *West Virginia University Research*, 2003, 7.
65. *Dominion Post*, February 7, May 29, 2008.
66. Kassy Kelly, "A Work in Progress," WVU *Alumni Magazine* 27 (Spring 2004): 30–33; WVU Research Office, *West Virginia University Research*, 2006, 5.
67. Jim Bissett, "Dreaming Big by Thinking Small," WVU *Alumni Magazine* 28 (Fall 2004): 4–5.
68. WVU Research Office, *West Virginia University Research*, 2006, 2. See also "2004–2010 Strategic Plan," 10.
69. Bissett, "Dreaming Big by Thinking Small," 4-5.
70. WVU Research Office, *West Virginia University Research*, 2006, 2.
71. Robert A. Dailey, *History of the Davis College of Agriculture, Forestry, and Consumer Sciences at West Virginia University* (Bloomington, IN: AuthorHouse, 2006), 5–11.
72. Dale Colyer, "History of the West Virginia Agricultural and Forestry Experiment Station: 1989–2004," Davis College, typescript, 2005, Table 1, 3–5.
73. Colyer, "History of the Experiment Station," 7, 9.
74. Colyer, "History of the Experiment Station," 7–8.
75. Colyer, "History of the Experiment Station," 7–8; Jill Wilson, "Fulfilling the Mission," WVU *Alumni Magazine* 24 (Summer 2001): 17–21; Research Office, "Comparative Genomics," and "Aquaculture Food and Market Development Project," *West Virginia University Research*, 2002, 18–19.
76. "Ag Research on Rise," *Mountaineer Spirit*, September 6, 2007, 4.
77. *State Journal*, November 27, 2000; Otis K. Rice and Stephen W. Brown, *West Virginia: A History* (Lexington: University Press of Kentucky, 1993).
78. James W. Rowley to Emory L. Kemp, August 28, 1989. See also Ronald L. Lewis to Frank A. Franz, "West Virginia University Press Proposal," April 8, 1986; William E. Vehse to Ronald L. Lewis, September 25, 1989; Gordon Simmons to Ronald L. Lewis, November 9, 1990, all in Ronald L. Lewis Papers.
79. Rachael Worby and Gordon Simmons to Ronald Lewis, December 11, 1995, Ronald L. Lewis Papers.
80. Malcolm M. MacDonald, "Report of Site-Visit to the West Virginia University Press, July 4–7, 1998, Ronald L. Lewis Papers.
81. *http://wvupressonline.com*.
82. *http://wvupressonline.com*.
83. *http://wvupressonline.com*; *Dominion Post*, June 29, 2008.
84. *Dominion Post*, June 29, and July 21, 2008. See also *http://en.wikipedia.org/wiki/West_Virginia_University_Press*.

CHAPTER SIXTEEN

1. Neil S. Bucklew, interview by Ronald L. Lewis, August 30, 2007.
2. Bucklew Interview.
3. Bucklew interview.
4. David C. Hardesty Jr., supplemental interview by Ronald L. Lewis, March 14, 2012.
5. Bucklew interview.
6. *Sunday Gazette-Mail*, September 27, 1998; *Dominion Post*, September 28, 1998.
7. *Sunday Gazette-Mail*, September 27, 1998; *Dominion Post*, September 28, 1998; West Virginia Higher Education Policy Commission, "The 2006 Report Card for Health Sciences and Rural Health" (2006), 8, 17–23.
8. West Virginia Higher Education Policy Commission, "The 2006 Report Card for Health Sciences and Rural Health" (2006), 5, 11, 12.
9. "America's Best Graduate Schools," *U.S. News & World Report*, 2008 edition, 144 (April 7, 2008): 45–70; *Dominion Post*, April 2, 2008; "WVU School of Medicine Again Earns Top 10 Recognition," Byrd HSC, *Health News*, online version, http://www.wvu.edu/newsreleases/news-details.aspx?ID=1196, URL not functioning, copy in Ronald L. Lewis Papers.
10. Bill Case, "The Rural Elderly," WVU *Alumni Magazine* 23 (Fall 2000): 10–11.
11. WVU, "Self-Study Submitted to the Higher Learning Commission of the North Central Association of Colleges and Schools, 2004," 137 (hereafter "Self Study 2004"); David C. Hardesty Jr., "Reaching Out to More People: WVU, 1995–2005," Office of the President, n.d., http://www.wvuh.com/; http://www.wvu.edu/administration/wvuinefive/reaching.htm, URL not functioning, copy in Ronald L. Lewis Papers.
12. "Self Study 2004," 120; Hardesty, "Reaching Out to More People."
13. WVU, "2004–2010 Strategic Plan for Research and Economic Development," August 2004, 9; *Daily Athenaeum*, November 14, 1997; *Dominion Post*, November 14, 1997, April 9, 2000, June 1, 2001; "WVU Eye Institute Opens," WVU *Alumni Magazine* 24 (Fall 2001): 9.
14. *Daily Athenaeum*, September 11, 2000; *Dominion Post*, "Local Facility Celebrates 10 Years," clipping (n.d. 2000), Box 12, A&M 5114, David Hardesty Papers.
15. *Charleston Gazette*, January 26, 2001; *Dominion Post*, January 25, 26, 2001; *Daily Athenaeum*, January 26, 2001; *Clarksburg Exponent Telegram*, March 25, 2001.
16. Tim Terman, "WVU's Virtual Medical Campus," WVU *Alumni Magazine* 23 (Winter 2000): 14; *State Journal*, November 12, 2001.
17. *Charleston Daily Mail*, June 3, 2002, and July 8, 2002.
18. *Dominion Post*, April 23, 27, 2002.
19. *Dominion Post*, July 25, 2010; "WVU Announces Creation of Multimillion-Dollar Pediatric Institute," *Health Sciences News Service*, October 30, 2008, online version, http://www.health.wvu.edu/newsreleases/news-details.aspx?ID=1004, URL not functioning, copy in Ronald L. Lewis Papers.
20. *Martinsburg Journal*, December 24 and 29, 2000, May 31, 2001; *Dominion Post*, May 31, 2001.

21. *Charleston Gazette*, June 26, 2001; Robert D'Alessandri, guest newspaper commentary, "Eastern West Virginia Healthcare Initiative Not a 'Stealth' Medical School," June 25, 2001 (quotation), online version, http://*www.wvu.edu/administration/speeches/dalessandri_june252001.htm*, URL not functioning, copy in Ronald L. Lewis Papers.]

22. R.C. Byrd Health Sciences Center, School of Medicine website, "Mission and Goals," http://*www.hsc.wvu.edu/som/administration/missionAndGoals.asp*, URL not functioning, copy in Ronald L. Lewis Papers.

23. WVU Research Corp., *West Virginia University Research, 2006*, 16.

24. Janet L. Metzner, "Scientists Wanted: University Recruiting New Scientists through 2010," *Dominion Post*, June 24, 2007.

25. *West Virginia University Research, 2006*, 17.

26. *Dominion Post*, August 23, 2001; WVU Research Corporation, *West Virginia University Research, 2003*, 16.

27. *Charleston Gazette*, January 26, 2002.

28. *West Virginia University Research, 2003*, 17.

29. Cassie Shaner, "Expanded Cancer Facility Plans Celebration," *Dominion Post*, April 6, 2009.

30. Susan Case, "Illuminating an Enveloping Darkness," WVU *Alumni Magazine* 25 (Spring 2002): 27–28; Susan Case, "A Family's Loving Memory Inspires," WVU *Alumni Magazine* 25 (Spring 2002): 29; *Dominion Post*, April 9, 2000.

31. *Charleston Gazette*, October 21, December 22, 2000; *Dominion Post*, December 22, 2000 (quotation).

32. *Charleston Gazette*, June 19, 2001; *Charleston Daily Mail*, December 17, 2001; Susan Case, "A Family's Loving Memory Inspires," 29.

33. *Dominion Post*, May 21, 2000; *Charleston Daily Mail*, May 20, 2001 (quotation).

34. Karin Fischer, "Alzheimer's Center Will Look at 'Forest,'" *Charleston Daily Mail*, May 20, 2002.

35. Case, "Illuminating an Enveloping Darkness," 27–28; "Exploring the Frontiers of Neuroscience," Research Office, *West Virginia Research, 2002*, WVU Research Corp., 2002, 12–17; *Dominion Post*, June 24, 2007, August 14, 2008.

36. Bill Case, "Pet Center Advances Study of Body Chemistry," WVU *Alumni Magazine* 19 (Winter 1996): 16–17; Case, "Illuminating an Enveloping Darkness," 27–28.

37. David C. Hardesty Jr., "Toyota's Gift to WVU Will Leave a Lasting Impact," *Charleston Gazette*, June 25, 2001, op-ed (quotation); Cassie Shaner, "Neurosciences Institute Should Be Complete Oct. 1," *Dominion Post*, June 17, 2008.

38. R&V Associates, "Outline of Interim Report," May 16, 2008, 1–9, online version, http://*www.health.wvu.edu/rvrr/responseRV.pdf, URL not functioning, copy in Ronald L. Lewis Papers*; also reproduced in the *Dominion Post*, June 14, 2008, and *Charleston Gazette*, June 3, 2008; Fred R. Butcher to Ron Violi and Vincent C. Deluzio of R&V Associates, June 13, 2008, http://*www.health.wvu.edu/rvrr/rv/rv2.pdf. URL not functioning, copy in Ronald L. Lewis Papers.*Also reproduced in the *Dominion Post*, June 14, 2008.

39. "HSC Faculty Praise Dismissal of R&V," *Dominion Post*, June 14, 2008.

40. "HSC Faculty Praise," *Dominion Post*, June 14, 2008.
41. "HSC Faculty Praise," *Dominion Post*, June 14, 2008.
42. *Charleston Gazette*, June 17, 2008, editorial.
43. *Charleston Gazette*, June 17, 2008, editorial.
44. *Dominion Post*, June 22, 2008, editorial.
45. *Dominion Post*, June 25, 2008, editorial.
46. Cassie Shaner, "Health Sciences Tackles Problems," *Dominion Post*, August 31, 2008.
47. Cassie Shaner, "Corporate Model for WVU, HSC?" *Dominion Post*, August 14, 2008.
48. Cassie Shaner, "BOG Joins WVU Health Care," *Dominion Post*, April 4, 2009. For Colenda's appointment, see *Dominion Post*, November 5, 2009.
49. Cassie Shaner, "WVU Hires New Doctors, *Dominion Post*, July 18, 2008; Cassie Shaner, "WVU Seeking Anesthesia Chairperson," *Dominion Post*, November 12, 2008.
50. J. Miles Layton, "Mon, WVU at Odds Over Heart Care," *Dominion Post*, June 15, 2008.
51. Tracy Eddy, "Cardiac Program Revised," *Dominion Post*, February 5, 2009.

CHAPTER SEVENTEEN

1. WVU *Alumni Magazine* 18 (Fall 1995): frontis.
2. David C. Hardesty Jr., interview by Ronald L. Lewis, August 22, 2007. "In *loco amici*" was coined to indicate this shift by William H. Willimon and Thomas H. Naylor, *The Abandoned Generation: Rethinking Higher Education* (Grand Rapids, MI: William B. Eerdmans Pub. Co., 1995). The authors argued that there was a disconnect among undergraduate students between intellectual content in the classroom and anti-intellectual behavior outside the classroom. The authors attributed this to out-of-control dormitories, alcohol abuse, and vandalism on campus. David Hardesty embraced these ideas.
3. Carnegie Foundation for the Advancement of Teaching, the Boyer Commission on Educating Undergraduates in the Research University, *Reinventing Undergraduate Education: A Blueprint for America's Research Universities* (1995), 1. Ernest L. Boyer, former chancellor of the State University of New York, and a former U.S. commissioner of education, served as president of the Carnegie Foundation for the Advancement of Teaching. In July 1995 he presided over the first meeting of the commission, but died in December 1995. The commission was named in his honor (hereafter cited as *Boyer Report*).
4. *Boyer Report*, 2.
5. *Boyer Report*, 5–6.
6. *Boyer Report*, 7.
7. *Boyer Report*, 12–13.

8. National Association of State Universities and Land-Grant Colleges, Kellogg Commission on the Future of State and Land-Grant Universities, *Returning to Our Roots: The Student Experience* (1997), 3–7.

9. *Returning to Our Roots*, 3–7 (quotation on 7).

10. *Returning to Our Roots*, 9–12 (quotation on 12).

11. *Returning to Our Roots*, 14.

12. See also Kellogg Commission on the Future of State and Land-Grant Universities, Sixth Report, *Renewing the Covenant: Learning, Discovery, and Engagement in a New Age and Different World* (2000).

13. Amy Quigley, "A Decade of Service: David C. Hardesty Jr. Marks His Tenth Year as WVU's President," WVU *Alumni Magazine* 28 (Fall 2005): 28–32; "The Student Experience," Office of the President, WVU: 1995–2005," online version, http://*www.wvu.edu/administration/wvuninefive/experience.htm, URL not functioning, copy in Ronald L. Lewis Papers*; David C. Hardesty Jr., *Leading the Public University* (Morgantown: West Virginia University Press, 2007), 111–13, (quotation on 113). See also David Hardesty, "A Student-Centered Vision," State of the University Address, 1996, 4–5, Speeches, Box 5, A&M 5114, David Hardesty Papers.

14. Hardesty, *Leading the Public University*, 113–15; Hardesty, "Student-Centered Vision," 5–7 (quotation on 7).

15. *Sunday Gazette-Mail*, May 5, 1996; *Dominion Post*, June 12 (quotation), 20, 2003.

16. James A. Troha, "The Mountaineer Parents Club at West Virginia University: A Case Study" (PhD diss., University of Kansas, 2005), 90.

17. "Operation Jump Start," and "WVU Indicators of Success," in Misc. Files, Box 5, A&M 5114, David Hardesty Papers; Troha, "Mountaineer Parents Club," 90–91.

18. "Operation Jump Start," and "WVU Indicators of Success;" Troha, "Mountaineer Parents Club," 90–91.

19. "RFLs Move Into New Houses," WVU *Alumni Magazine* 21 (Fall 1998): 3.

20. "Operation Jump Start," and "WVU Indicators of Success;" Troha, "Mountaineer Parents Club," 90–91.

21. *Dominion Post*, March 5, 1966, January 21, 1997, and January 25, 2009 (quotation).

22. Troha, "Mountaineer Parents Club," 10–13, 92; Quigley, "A Decade of Service," 28–32.

23. Troha, "Mountaineer Parents Club," 17.

24. West Virginia University Commission on Academic Standards and Expectations, "Strengthening Success through Undergraduate Expectations," May 1999, Box 5, A&M 5114, David Hardesty Papers; *Boyer Report*, 12–17; Becky Lofstead, "Reinventing the Undergraduate Experience," WVU *Alumni Magazine* 21 (Fall 1998): 13–14; *Daily Athenaeum*, September 2, 1999.

25. WVU, "Self-Study Submitted to the Higher Learning Commission of the North Central Association of Colleges and Schools Site Visit of April 19–21, 2004," 68–69

(hereafter "Self Study 2004"); WVU, "Academic Standards and Expectations," 10–11, copy in the Ronald L. Lewis Papers.

26. "Self Study 2004," 69; *Daily Athenaeum*, May 31, 2000, January 30, 2001; "Academic Standards and Expectations," 11–12.

27. "Self Study 2004," 72–73, 92–94, and Appendix C-Chapter 4 B, 218–24 (quotation on 218).

28. *Weirton Daily Times*, May 14, 1998 (quotation), clipping, Box 9, A&M 5114, David Hardesty Papers; *Dominion Post*, May 20, 1998.

29. As reported in the *Daily Athenaeum*, January 9, 1996 (quotation), August 18, 2000; David C. Hardesty Jr., supplemental interview by Ronald L. Lewis, March 14, 2012.

30. *Parkersburg Sentinel*, July 12, 1985.

31. *State Journal*, clipping, n.d. (quotation), and *Wheeling News Register*, clipping, July 29, 1986, F24, Box 3, A&M 5012, David Hardesty Papers. Student letters to the *Daily Athenaeum* are found in clipping file, F24, Box 3, A&M 5012, Office of the President.

32. *Weston Democrat*, July 24, 1985. A full treatment of this very interesting story was published by WVU's historian of Nazi Germany, a concentration camp survivor, who stumbled on the reference in the SS newspaper while doing research. See Kurt Rosenbaum, "Every Man a Fuhrer," WVU *Alumni Magazine* 2 (Fall 1979): 2–6.

33. *Dominion Post*, August 15, 1995; *Charleston Gazette*, August 24, 1995, April 1, 1997; *Daily Athenaeum*, April 1, 1997.

34. *Dominion Post*, August 16, 19, 21, 1995.

35. *Dominion Post*, August 29, 1995, and undated clipping, clipping file, Box 4, A&M 5114, David Hardesty Papers; *Daily Athenaeum*, August 29, 1995; *Charleston Gazette*, August 23, 1995 (quotation).

36. Becky Lofstead, "Do Students Have a Right to Party?" WVU *Alumni Magazine* 21 (Fall 1998): 16–19.

37. *Parkersburg News*, October 2, 1998.

38. As reported in the *Dominion Post*, October 5, 2002.

39. Lofstead, "Do Students Have a Right to Party?" 16–19; *Dominion Post*, April 25, 30, 1997.

40. Quoted by the *Dominion Post*, October 5, 2002.

41. *Dominion Post*, May 27, 1999; WVU Intranet News, February 11, 2008.

42. *Daily Athenaeum*, April 30, 1998.

43. Quoted by the *Dominion Post*, April 29, 1998. See also *Bluefield Daily Telegraph*, April 30, 1998.

44. *Dominion Post*, October 23, 2003.

45. As reported in the *Dominion Post*, November 9, 2008.

46. *Charleston Gazette*, March 21, 1998.

47. *Times West Virginian*, May 5, 1998.

48. *Daily Athenaeum*, April 29, 1998.

49. *Daily Athenaeum*, May 1, 1998 (quotation); *Dominion Post*, May 7, 1998.

50. *Dominion Post*, November 8, 1999.

51. "A Letter from President Hardesty," WVU *Alumni Magazine* 21 (Summer 1998): frontis (quotation); Institutional Analysis and Planning, Division of Planning, WVU, Oct. 2004, Box 5, A&M 5114, David Hardesty Papers; "Self Study 2004," 186–87.

52. "Setting Records: A Note from the President," WVU *Alumni Magazine* 25 (Fall 2002): frontis (quotation); "Another Enrollment for the Record Books," WVU *Alumni Magazine* 29 (Spring 2006): 8; "Opening Day Report," Fall 2007, email memorandum, Box 5, A&M 5114, David Hardesty Papers.

53. "First Day of Class Enrollment Report, Fall 2007," Office of Admissions and Records, WVU, email memorandum, Box 5, A&M 5114, David Hardesty Papers; *Daily Athenaeum*, October 30, 2007; *Charleston Gazette*, August 25, 2008; *Dominion Post*, August. 22, 2008.

54. "West Virginia University's 2010 Plan: Building the Foundation for Academic Excellence," 2007, 7; Gerald Lang, "Remarks on Enrollment on the Main Campus," February 11, 2008, presentation to the WVU Faculty Senate, online version, *http://wvu.edu/~facultys/08files/facultysenateenrollmentupdate08.ppt*, URL not functioning, copy in Ronald L. Lewis Papers.

55. Lang, "Remarks on Enrollment."

56. *Daily Athenaeum*, October 30, 2007.

57. *Dominion Post*, September 26, 2000, citing data from the West Virginia Higher Education Policy Commission; West Virginia Higher Education Policy Commission, "2006 Higher Education Report Card," http://*www.wvhepcnew.wvnet.edu*, URL not functioning, copy in Ronald L. Lewis Papers.]

58. "2006 Higher Education Report Card;" Delta Project on Postsecondary Education Costs, Productivity, and Accountability, "Delta Cost Project State Database, 2003–2008: West Virginia," http://*www.deltacostproject.org/analyses/delta_reports.asp*.

59. *Dominion Post*, February 1, 2009 (quotation), and July 4, 2010.

60. *Charleston Daily Mail*, March 1, 2001, March 18, 2002, June 12, 2002, and August 20, 2003; *Charleston Gazette*, August 15, 2002.

61. "2006 Higher Education Report Card;" *Dominion Post*, August 20, 2003, March 15, 27, 2009.

62. WVU Bureau of Business and Economic Research, "West Virginia Work and Wages by Major, Gender, and Race, 2006" (2008), for the Higher Education Policy Commission. For summaries, see *Dominion Post*, August 10, 2008, October 18, 2009, and "2006 Higher Education Report Card."

63. Fact Sheet, "West Virginia University: A Focus on International Students," 1995, Box 5, A&M 5114, David Hardesty Papers.

64. George Lies, "WVU Office of International Programs News," October 14, 2002, Box 5, A&M 5114, David Hardesty Papers.

65. *Daily Athenaeum*, September 7, 2000.

66. *Dominion Post*, August 26, 2001.

67. *Charleston Gazette*, January 17, 2002.

1. *Charleston Gazette*, October 26, 2000, Box 11, A&M 5114, David Hardesty Papers.
2. Mickey Furfari, "Hardesty: College Presidents Involved in Athletics," *Times West Virginian*, August 12, 2001.
3. Furfari, "College Presidents Involved in Athletics."
4. Mickey Furfari, "Hardesty Looks Backward, Forward," *Charleston Daily Mail*, August 1, 1998; David C. Hardesty Jr., "University's High-Quality Athletic Program Benefits School, State," *Charleston Gazette*, January 7, 2003. See also Hardesty's guest commentary, "Sports Make the Grade," *Dominion Post*, December 28, 2002.
5. Furfari, "College Presidents Involved in Athletics;" Furfari, "Hardesty Looks Backward, Forward," and Hardesty, "University's High-Quality Athletic Program Benefits School, State," in Box 14, A&M 5114, David Hardesty Papers; *Times West Virginian*, May 31, 2002; *Daily Athenaeum*, June 2, 2010, 9, 12; *Dominion Post*, August 6, 2010.
6. *Dominion Post*, January 29, 2011.
7. "Buckeyes' Leader Believes Presidents Should Help Contain Spending," *Chronicle of Higher Education* 54 (January 11, 2008): A24.
8. Justin Jackson, "WVU, Nike Have a Million-Dollar Deal," *Dominion Post*, September 2, 3, 2010.
9. Justin Jackson, "College Hoops More Business than a Sport," *Dominion Post*, August 25, 2009.
10. Ed Owens, "Fundraising Group on Record Run," *Dominion Post*, February 13, 2011, 1, 5C.
11. *Dominion Post*, February 13, 2011.
12. Caperton quoted in *Dominion Post*, April 25, 1999; *Charleston Gazette*, August 11, 2000.
13. *Dominion Post*, August 9, 2000; *Wheeling News-Register*, October 16, 2000.
14. "WVU Planning Major Upgrades," *Huntington Herald-Dispatch*, June 8, 2002.
15. *Dominion Post*, December 13, 2008, and July 9, 2009; April Johnston, "From Newton to Naismith," WVU *Alumni Magazine* 33 (Summer 2010): 43.
16. Pam Fronko and Shawn Fluharty, "WVU Soccer Gets New Home: Stadium Named for Wheeling Entrepreneur Dlesk," WVU *Alumni Magazine* 28 (Fall 2004): 13; Stefanie Loh, "Where Major Projects Stand," *Dominion Post*, July 9, 2009.
17. Welch Suggs, "Conference Soap Opera Is Driven by Cash, but Cachet Matters Too," *Chronicle of Higher Education*, May 30, 2003, clipping, Box 14, A&M 5114, David Hardesty Papers.
18. Suggs, "Conference Soap Opera."
19. Hardesty quoted in Mitch Vingle, "Q&A with David Hardesty," *Charleston Gazette*, June 13, 2003.
20. David C. Hardesty Jr., supplemental interview by Ronald L. Lewis, March 14, 2012.
21. Hardesty quoted in Mitch Vingle, "Q&A with David Hardesty," *Charleston Gazette*, June 13, 2003.

22. "Big East Adds Five Teams to Conference," *USA Today*, November 5, 2003, and Ken Wright, "New Big East May Be Hoops Powerhouse," *Washington Times*, November 5, 2003, clippings, Box 14, A&M 5114, David Hardesty Papers.

23. Welch Suggs, "In Bid to Shore Up Its Ranks, Big East Conference Invites 5 Universities to Join," *Chronicle of Higher Education*, November 5, 2003, clipping, Box 14, A&M 5114, David Hardesty Papers; *Dominion Post*, November 5, 2003.

24. Dave Hickman, "WVU Cuts Five Sports," *Charleston Gazette*, April 17, 2003, clipping, Box 14, A&M 5114, David Hardesty Papers.

25. *Dominion Post*, April 29, 2003.

26. Abstract, "Why Did WVU Drop Rifle?" n.d. 2003, Box 5, A&M 5114, David Hardesty Papers.

27. *Charleston Gazette*, April 17, 2003; David C. Hardesty Jr., interview by Ronald L. Lewis, August 22, 2007.

28. *Dominion Post*, April 25, 2003, editorial.

29. Sharp and Burdette quoted in the *Daily Athenaeum*, October 22, 2008.

30. *Charleston Daily Mail*, July 6, 1999; Adriene J. Mullikin, "Olympic Dreams," WVU *Alumni Magazine* 23 (Summer 2000): 31–32; "Why Did WVU Drop Rifle?" *Daily Athenaeum*, October 22, 2008; Hardesty interview.

31. *Dominion Post*, April 19, 2002, May 3, 2008; Bryan Messerly "John Beilein is New Basketball Coach," WVU *Alumni Magazine* 25 (Summer 2002): 38.

32. Gleaned from various accounts: John Antonik, "Rodriguez Is WVU's New Football Coach," WVU *Alumni Magazine* 24 (Spring 2001): 47; *Sunday Gazette-Mail*, December 16, 2007; *Dominion Post*, December 22, 2002, December 17, 2007, and January 25, 2008; *Pittsburgh Post-Gazette*, December 18, 2007.

33. *Dominion Post*, September 23, 2008; *Charleston Gazette*, December 18, 2010 (quotation).

34. *Dominion Post*, January 25, 2011.

35. *Dominion Post*, January 22, 2011, and January 23, 2011.

CHAPTER NINETEEN

1. John Antonik, "Coach Gale Catlett Gave Everything He had to His Alma Mater; West Virginia Loved Him in Return," WVU *Alumni Magazine* 25 (Summer 2002): 22–27.

2. Antonik, "Coach Gale Catlett," 22–27.

3. Antonik, "Coach Gale Catlett," 25.

4. "Catlett Wins 500th Game," WVU *Alumni Magazine* 21 (Winter 1998): 19; *Daily Athenaeum*, March 17, 1998; *Charleston Gazette*, March 17, 1998; *Elkins Inter-Mountain*, March 18, 1998; *Dominion Post*, March 21, 1998.

5. *Dominion Post*, March 24, 1998; Antonik, "Coach Gale Catlett," 27 (quotation).

6. Both are quoted in the *Charleston Gazette*, February 15, 2002.

7. *Dominion Post*, April 19, 2002.

8. Bryan Messerly, "John Beilein Is New Basketball Coach," WVU *Alumni Magazine* 25 (Summer 2002): 38.

9. John Antonik, *Roll Out the Carpet: 101 Seasons of West Virginia University Basketball* (Morgantown: West Virginia University Press, 2010), 211–12, 214–22.

10. Antonik, *Roll Out the Carpet*, 222–26.

11. Antonik, *Roll Out the Carpet*, 226–29.

12. Antonik, *Roll Out the Carpet*, 229.

13. April Johnson, "Bob Huggins: Home Where He Belongs," WVU *Alumni Magazine* 33 (Summer 2010): 34–35; *Dominion Post*, December 23, 2007; Antonik, *Roll Out the Carpet*, 232–34, (quotations on 233, 234).

14. *Dominion Post*, April 13, June 27 and 28, 2008; Antonik, *Roll Out the Carpet*, 239–43. WVU's previous first-round NBA picks were Mark Workman 1952, Rod Hundley 1957, Jerry West 1960, Rod Thorn 1963, and Ron Williams 1968 (*Dominion Post*, June 28, 2008, and Antonik, *Roll Out the Carpet*, 235–39).

15. Antonik, *Roll Out the Carpet*, 246–47; *Dominion Post*, January 24, 2010.

16. Huggins quoted in the *Daily Athenaeum*, February 5, 2010. Sentiments ranging from displeasure to outrage expressed in the state press and by students on campus were cited in the same issue.

17. *Dominion Post*, March 14, 2010; Antonik, *Roll Out the Carpet*, 248–52.

18. *Dominion Post*, January 2, 2011; *Daily Athenaeum*, March 15, 2010 (quotation).

19. *Dominion Post*, March 15, 28 (quotation), April 3, 2010; Antonik, *Roll Out the Carpet*, 254–55.

20. *Dominion Post*, April 3, 2010.

21. Antonik, *Roll Out the Carpet*, 255–57.

22. *Dominion Post*, March 13, 2010.

23. WVUToday, press release, "WVU Basketball Success Increases West Virginia Prominence, Pride on National Stage," April 1, 2010, online version, *http://wvutoday. wvu.edu/n/2020/04/01/let-s-go-mountaineers-wvu-basketball-success-incre*, URL not functioning, copy in Ronald L. Lewis Papers.

24. *Times West Virginian*, March 22, 2001.

25. *Times West Virginian*, March 22, 2001.

26. "Athletic Excellence," WVU *Alumni Magazine* 27 (Summer 2004): 36; Allison Toffle, "Home-Court Perfection," WVU *Alumni Magazine* 33 (Summer 2010): 40.

27. *Times West Virginian*, November 26, 2000.

28. Tony Cook, "Nehlen: Days of Glory, Years of Greatness," WVU *Alumni Magazine* 24 (Spring 2001): 22–27 (quotation on 22).

29. John Antonik, *West Virginia University Football Vault: The History of the Mountaineers* (Atlanta: Whitman Publishing, 2009), 100 (quotation), 103.

30. Nehlen's recollections quoted in Antonik, *Football Vault*, 106.

31. Cook, "Nehlen: Days of Glory," 24 (quotation); Antonik, *Football Vault*, 104–5, and inserts on 107–8.

32. Cook, "Nehlen: Days of Glory," 25; Antonik, *Football Vault*, 108–10; *Dominion Post*, January 2, 2008 (quotation).

33. Quoted in *Dominion Post*, January 2, 2008.

34. Cook, "Nehlen: Days of Glory," 25; Antonik, *Football Vault*, 110–13. The story of Major Harris's football career at WVU and afterward has received extensive

coverage. See, for example, Bob Hertzel, "Harris: Place in Football History," *Morgantown Times*, July 24, 2010, 1–2 A; Stephanie Loh, "A Major Deal," *Dominion Post*, 4–6 C.

35. Cook, "Nehlen: Days of Glory," 25; Antonik, *Football Vault*, 112.

36. Cook, "Nehlen: Days of Glory," 25; Antonik, *Football Vault*, 113–18; *State Journal*, June 5, 2000.

37. "Winning One for Nehlen," *Dominion Post*, December 30, 2000. See also *Dominion Post* December 29, 2000; *Charleston Gazette*, December 29, 2000; *Times West Virginian*, December 29, 2000.

38. Mike Cherry, "The House That Nehlen Built," and David C. Hardesty Jr., "Thank You, Coach," WVU *Alumni Magazine* 24 (Spring 2001): 27. For additional praise of Nehlen on his retirement, see "Nehlen Changed the Shape of WVU Sports," and John Dahlia, "'Gentleman Coach' Nehlen Has Truly Made a Difference," *Times West Virginian*, November 26, 2000, and Jim Bissett, "Saying Goodbye to Nehlen Not Going to Be Easy," *Dominion Post*, November 19, 2000, all in Box 11, A&M 5114, David Hardesty Papers. See also *Charleston Gazette*, November 18, 2000.

39. John Antonik, "Rodriguez Is WVU's Football Coach," WVU *Alumni Magazine* 24 (Spring 2001): 47.

40. *Times West Virginian*, November 29, 2000.

41. *Charleston Gazette*, November 28, 2000; Antonik, *Football Vault*, 123–25; *Dominion Post*, December 29, 2002.

42. *Dominion Post*, December 22, 2002; Antonik, *Football Vault*, 125–28.

43. Antonik, *Football Vault*, 126–29.

44. Antonik, *Football Vault*, 129–31; "Sweet Victory," WVU *Alumni Magazine* 29 (Spring 2006): 39.

45. Antonik, *Football Vault*, 133–34.

46. Antonik, *Football Vault*, 134–35; *Believe: The Story of the 2007 West Virginia Mountaineer Football Team* (n.p.: Piedmont Publishing for the *Dominion Post*, 2008), 109–16.

47. *Believe*, 117; Antonik, *Football Vault*, 136.

48. *Believe*, 121, 139–56; John Antonik, "Let the Healing Begin," January 2, 2008, for MSNsportsNET.com; Antonik, *Football Vault*, 136–38.

49. *Sunday Gazette-Mail*, December 16, 2007 (quotation); *Dominion Post*, December 17, 2007.

50. *Dominion Post*, December 17, 2007 (quotations). The state press was filled with letters from outraged fans. See, for example, the editorial pages of the following issues: *Dominion Post*, December 19, 22, 23, 2007; *Charleston Gazette*, December 19, 2007, and January 17, 2008.

51. Quoted in the *Dominion Post*, December 17, 2007.

52. *Dominion Post*, December 17, 2007.

53. *Dominion Post*, December 17, 29 (quotation), 2007.

54. *Dominion Post*, January 2, July 10, 2008.

55. *Dominion Post*, January 2, 2008; Dave Hickman in the *Charleston Gazette*, July

10, 2008 (quotation); Michael Rosenberg article reprinted from *Detroit Free Press* in the *Charleston Gazette*, July 10, 2008.

56. Rodriguez's letter of resignation to Athletic Director Ed Pastilong, reprinted in *Dominion Post*, January 25, 2008. See also Stefanie Loh's article in the *Dominion Post*, January 25, 2008.

57. As quoted in the *Dominion Post*, January 25, 2008.

58. Editorial, *Dominion Post*, February 1, 2008.

59. *Dominion Post*, January 24, 2008.

60. Quoted in the *Dominion Post*, January 21, 2008.

61. *Dominion Post*, January 21, 2008.

62. *Dominion Post*, January 21, 2008.

63. *Dominion Post*, January 21, 24, 2008.

64. *Dominion Post*, January 23, 2008; *Daily Athenaeum*, April 18, 2008. See also "Accused Worker Says Former WVU Football Coach Rich Rodriguez Offered Job Assistance," an AP story reprinted in the *Daily Athenaeum*, April 18, 2008, 13.

65. *Believe*, 157–60; *Dominion Post*, January 3, 2008; Stewart quoted in John Antonik, "Stewart Named 32nd Grid Coach," January 3, 2008, for *MSNsportsNET*. See also articles by Drew Rubenstein and Todd Murray in the *Dominion Post*, January 4, 2008.

66. *Dominion Post*, January 4, 2008.

67. *Dominion Post*, March 16, June 27, 2008.

68. *Dominion Post*, August 17, 18, 2008.

69. Antonik, *Football Vault*, 139–40; *Dominion Post*, January 2, 2011.

70. *Dominion Post*, June 27, 2010.

71. *Dominion Post*, March 9, 2008 and June 27, 2010.

72. *Morgantown Times*, June 26, 2010; *Times West Virginian*, April 17, 2000.

73. The NCAA Notice of Allegations is reproduced in *Dominion Post*, August 6, 2010.

74. Quoted in *Dominion Post*, August 6, 2010.

75. *Times West Virginian*, January 29, 2011.

76. *Morgantown Times*, December 25, 2010.

77. *Charleston Gazette*, December 19, 2010; *Dominion Post*, December 17, 2010, January 25, 30 (quotation), 2011. For examples of letters for and against replacing Stewart, see those in *Dominion Post*, January 17, 2011.

78. Ed Owens in the *Dominion Post*, June 11, 2011.

79. Mitch Vingle in the *Charleston Gazette*, June 10, 2011.

80. *Dominion Post*, October 9, 2008, December 14, 2009, January 29, 2010.

AFTERWORD

1. Christopher Newfield, *Unmaking the Public University: The Forty-Year Assault on the Middle Class* (Cambridge, MA: Harvard University Press, 2008), 1–3.

2. Newfield, *Unmaking the Public University*, 9.

3. Gaye Tuchman, "Metrics, Business Plans, and the Vanishing Public Good," *Thought and Action*, 27 (Fall 2011): 25.

4. Tuchman, "Metrics, Business Plans, and the Vanishing Public Good," 26–27.
5. Newfield, *Unmaking the Public University*, 10; Benjamin Ginsberg, *The Fall of the Faculty: The Rise of the All-Administrative University and Why It Matters* (New York: Oxford University Press, 2011).
6. Amy Quigley, "Coming Home," WVU *Alumni Magazine* 30 (Fall 2007): 26; "Welcome, President Garrison," *Morgantown Dominion Post*, October 14, 2007.
7. Faculty senator Paul Brown quoted in the *Dominion Post*, June 25, 2007.
8. "What Is the University's Destiny?" *Daily Athenaeum*, October 22, 2007.
9. *Dominion Post*, October 14, 2007; *Charleston Sunday Gazette-Mail*, February 17, 2008.
10. *Pittsburgh Post-Gazette*, December 21, 2007, January 25, 2008.
11. *Post-Gazette*, December 23, 2007.
12. Crow quoted in the *Post-Gazette*, January 3, 2008. See also *Sunday Gazette-Mail*, January 6, 2008.
13. *Daily Athenaeum*, January 15, 2008 (quotation); *Dominion Post*, January 10, 15, 16, 29, 2008.
14. *Charleston Gazette*, May 6, 2008; *New York Times*, January 22, 2008.
15. The Report of the Special Investigative Panel was available on the Faculty Senate's website, http://www.facultysenate.wvu.edu/, and reprinted in the *Dominion Post*, April 25, 2008.
16. Mountaineer E-News (*enews@mail.wvu.edu*), April 23, 2008, copy in Ronald L. Lewis Papers; *Dominion Post*, April 24, 2008.
17. *Dominion Post*, April 25, 27 (quotation), 2008.
18. *Charleston Gazette*, April 27, 2008; *Dominion Post*, April 27, 2008 (quotations), and May 4, 2008.
19. Quoted in the *Dominion Post*, April 28, 2008. See also the *Daily Athenaeum*, April 28, 2008, and *Charleston Gazette*, April 29, 2008.
20. *Dominion Post*, April 29, 2008.
21. *State Journal*, May 1, 2008.
22. *Sunday Gazette-Mail*, May 4, 2008; *Dominion Post*, May 6, 2008 (quotations).
23. *Post-Gazette*, May 2, 2008.
24. "Faculty Senate Chairman Says Garrison Not to Blame," MetroNews Talkline, April 28, 2008, copy in Ronald L. Lewis Papers.
25. *Sunday Gazette-Mail*, May 4, 2008.
26. *Dominion Post*, May 16, 2008.
27. "Motions to Be Offered Today at Special Meeting of Faculty Senate," WVUFaculty @listserv.wvu.edu, handout, May 5, 2008, copy in Ronald L. Lewis Papers.
28. *Charleston Gazette*, May 6, 2008; *Daily Athenaeum*, May 2, 2008; *Dominion Post*, May 6, 2008 (quotation).
29. *Mountaineer E-News*, May 5, 2008, copy in Ronald L. Lewis Papers.
30. *Charleston Gazette*, May 8, 2008 (quotation); *Dominion Post*, May 10, 2008.
31. *Dominion Post*, May 8, 2008.
32. *Dominion Post*, May 9, 2008; *Charleston Gazette*, May 15, 2008 (quotation); "Proposed Motions for May 14th Meeting," copy in Ronald L. Lewis Papers.

33. *Charleston Gazette*, May 15, 2008.
34. *Charleston Gazette*, May 2, 2008; Governor Manchin's statement to the press was reprinted in the *Dominion Post*, May 20, 2008.
35. *Dominion Post*, May 21, 31 (quotation), 2008.
36. *Charleston Gazette*, May 2, 2008.The letter was reprinted in the *Dominion Post*, June 4, 2008.
37. *Dominion Post*, June 7, 2008.
38. *Dominion Post*, June 7, 25, 26, 2008.
39. *Dominion Post*, August 6, 30, Dec. 7, 9, 19, 2008, and May 19, 2009; *Charleston Gazette*, January 1, 2008.
40. Timothy Warner's commentary in the *Dominion Post*, June 1, 2008.
41. *Dominion Post*, July 9, 12, 2008.
42. *Dominion Post*, July 9, 2008.
43. *Dominion Post*, July 10, 2008.
44. *Dominion Post*, September 13, 2008; *Daily Athenaeum*, September 15, 2008.
45. *Dominion Post*, October 14, 15 (quotation), 2008.
46. *Daily Athenaeum*, December 14, 2009.
47. *Dominion Post*, December 16, 2008, March 7, May 25, June 14, 2009.
48. West Virginia University, *2020: Strategic Plan for the Future* (October 2010).
49. *Dominion Post*, January 3, October 29, 2011, and April 29, 2012.
50. *Dominion Post*, January 14, February 15, 2012.
51. *Dominion Post*, January 13, 2012.
52. *Dominion Post*, April 29, 2012.

INDEX

ABOUT
THE AUTHORS

RONALD L. LEWIS received the BA degree from Ohio University in 1966, and from the University of Akron earned the MA (1971) and PhD (1974) in American history. He taught at the University of Delaware for eleven years (1974–1985) prior to becoming professor of history at West Virginia University in 1985. At WVU he offered undergraduate and graduate courses in American labor, West Virginia, and Appalachian history. He served as department chair for six years (1989–1995), was appointed Eberly Family Professor of History (1993–2001), and then Stuart and Joyce Robbins Chair in History (2001–2008), a position he held until his retirement in 2008. He is currently professor emeritus and Historian Laureate of West Virginia.

Dr. Lewis's publishing career includes numerous journal articles, book chapters, and essays, along with fourteen co-edited books that include *Transnational West Virginia: Ethnic Communities and Economic Change, 1840–1940* (WVU Press, 2002). In addition to *Aspiring to Greatness*, he is the author of: *Coal, Iron, and Slaves: Industrial Slavery in Maryland and Virginia, 1715–1865* (1979); *Black Coal Miners in America: Race, Class, and Community Conflict, 1780–1980* (1987); *Transforming the Appalachian Countryside: Railroads, Deforestation, and Social Change in West Virginia, 1880–1920* (1998); and most recently *Welsh Americans: A History of Assimilation in the Coalfields* (2008).

CHARLES M. VEST is President Emeritus and Professor of Mechanical Engineering at the Massachusetts Institute of Technology. A native of Morgantown, Dr. Vest earned a B.S. in mechanical engineering from West

Virginia University in 1963, and M.S.E. and PhD degrees in mechanical engineering from the University of Michigan in 1964 and 1967, respectively. He serves on the boards of several non-profit organizations and foundations devoted to education, science, and technology. Since 2008, he has been a member of the West Virginia University Board of Governors. He has authored a book on holographic interferometry and two books on higher education. He has received honorary doctoral degrees from seventeen universities. He was awarded the 2006 National Medal of Technology by President Bush and received the 2011 Vannevar Bush Award from the National Science Board. He currently serves as the President of the National Academy of Engineering.